AND JOBS

A Book of Readings

Edited by
Louis A. Ferman
Joyce L. Kornbluh
and J. A. Miller

Foreword by
A. Philip Randolph

Ann Arbor
The University of Michigan Press

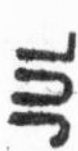

Library of Congress Catalog Card No. 67-25340
Published in the United States of America by
The University of Michigan Press and simultaneously
in Rexdale, Canada, by Ambassador Books Limited
United Kingdom agent: The Cresset Press
Manufactured in the United States of America

Foreword

A. Philip Randolph

The articles in this collection present overwhelming evidence that the Negro is caught today in a severe economic crisis. They document the fact that the mass of black Americans stand today in much the same economic position they occupied in the depths of the great depression—at the bottom of the economic ladder. The destructive forces that have been at work on the American economy over the past decade have hit the Negro especially hard. Two out of three Negro families subsist on less than $4000 a year; the gap between Negro and white median incomes has widened in recent years and the same is true of the gap between Negro and white unemployment rates.

Thus, despite progress towards social and political equality, the Negro worker finds that his relative economic position is deteriorating or stagnating. The desperation and frustration that this paradoxical situation engenders is responsible for much of the militance and impatience of the current civil rights revolution. And this militance will not abate. Long ago, during Reconstruction, the Negro learned the cruel lesson that social and political freedom cannot be sustained in the midst of economic insecurity and exploitation. He learned that freedom requires a material foundation. Recent civil rights gains are based largely on the economic progress the Negro made in the 1940's and early 1950's and these gains could be cancelled out by the economic stagnation that has characterized Negro communities since 1953.

Automation and technological change are destroying tens of thousands of unskilled and semiskilled jobs to which Negroes have traditionally been relegated. Meanwhile, centuries of discrimination and exploitation have deprived Negro workers of the education and training required by the new skilled jobs which are opening up. Thus, we find that approximately 25 percent of the long-term unemployed are black Americans and that as unemployment becomes increasingly structural, the Negro is increasingly rendered economically useless. And this at a time when there is a shortage of highly skilled technical and professional workers. These skilled workers are so much in demand that they work overtime and enjoy high standards of living while millions of other workers are unemployed, underemployed, or unemployable. These millions are creating what the great Swedish economist Gunnar Myrdal has described as a vast "underclass" in

American society. They are the pariahs, the untouchables, the exiles in our economy.

The Negro is trapped in this underclass, trapped in the growing slums and ghettoes of the big cities, while the more prosperous white workers are migrating to the pleasant suburbs. A racial and occupational separation is taking place which dooms our aspirations for integrated housing and schools. In fact, residential and educational segregation is actually increasing in our metropolitan centers. Deprived of decent integrated education, how are Negro youth to acquire the skills demanded by our technically advancing economy?

In the past few years the rumblings from the Negro underclass have exploded into thunderous and wildly destructive violence, from the tenements of Harlem to the slums of Cleveland and Watts. It serves no purpose simply to denounce the riots without understanding their causes. Of this much we can be certain: if those causes are not identified and uprooted, radically and finally, we will be courting disaster in this country.

Much interest has focused on the problem of the Negro family, as articles in this book point out. Under two centuries of slavery, the Negro family was systematically destroyed. The right of Negroes to marry is barely one hundred years old. After slavery, a system of segregation was introduced which denied the Negro family, particularly the Negro male, even the rudiments of economic security. To this very day many of our welfare laws encourage family desertion by Negro males.

I do not need to expand on how family breakups encourage delinquency, crime, school dropouts, and many forms of destructive antisocial behavior. When all of this is said, the question remains: how do we strengthen the Negro family and the fabric of the Negro community? The answer is jobs—decent jobs at decent pay. We know that when the Negro unemployment rate dropped during World War II, so did the Negro rate of divorce, illegitimacy, and other indications of family instability.

I have spent all of my life in the labor and civil rights movements, which is to say that I have spent a lifetime in search of solutions to the problem of race and the problem of jobs. In the early days, the task, so far as I was concerned, was a relatively simple one: I could—had to—concentrate exclusively on helping Negroes to break into the job market from which they were almost totally excluded. The situation today is somewhat different. As the economy has become more sophisticated and complex, both in its methods of production and in its relation to the total American labor force, the problems of securing wider employment opportunities for Negroes has ultimately become connected with the problem of finding wider employment opportunities for all the poor. Therefore, it is no longer possible to make the struggle for jobs exclusively a Negro struggle. As Michael Harrington has remarked in his essay "The Economics of Protest," one of the main responsibilities of the Negro struggle is "a concern with the question of full employment. And this is an 'integrated' task, for it is clearly impossible to provide jobs for Negroes while leaving whites behind. The issue will be resolved on a national basis for all."

The Negro is not alone in the vicious circle in which he finds himself. Many white workers are also caught short by the profound transformations our economy is undergoing. The problem of these workers, black and white, is social as well as economic, since social justice and economic reform are intertwined in our time. If we are to speak for the needs of all these poor Americans, we must understand that the Negro protest is today but the first rumblings of the underclass. As the Negro has taken to the streets, so will the unemployed of all races take to the streets. Thus, to discuss the civil rights revolution is to write the agenda of labor's unfinished revolution in this country.

There have been many sincere criticisms of the Negro's demands for preferential or compensatory treatment. Rather than debate the validity of that demand, let us recognize that it will grow louder as unemployment continues. As the gap between Negro and white unemployment rates widens, the Negro's demand for preferential treatment to close the gap becomes more vociferous. But there is no need to demand preferential treatment in a full-employment economy. To achieve a full-employment economy, in fact, we must be in favor of preferential treatment and not just for the Negro but for all the unemployed, the poor, the aged, and the deprived youth of the nation.

The record of the past ten years shows that we cannot look to the private sector of the economy to achieve the goal of full employment. But we can meet that goal through the expansion of the public sector—through meeting the vast unmet social needs of the country. We can put the unemployed back to work by clearing our slums and rebuilding our cities, by building schools and hospitals, by modernizing and expanding our rapid transit facilities, by investing in flood control and by combating air pollution. We can open new jobs for the poor by expanding our social services. One of the side effects of this progress would not only be the creating of new jobs but also the creation of new careers, particularly a new kind of public service employment in our society for the nonprofessional. Some of these careers have already been created by the antipoverty program: teacher aides, mental health aides, police aides, code enforcement inspectors, and welfare aides. Besides being an antipoverty strategy, the new careers' model contains a new approach to education, training, and manpower development and calls for a revolutionary reorganization of professional practice which has implications far beyond those for the poor. As Frank Riessman, who has done much thinking in this area, suggests: "It is based on certain assumptions about the emerging service economy, the new rights of man in an affluent, automated age, and the limitations of quality of human services as presently organized. Finally, it is rooted in a theory of history which sees a new significant underclass rising which represents a source of progress and new human values."

It is with these concepts in mind that I proposed at the planning session of the 1966 White House Conference on Civil Rights a national Freedom Budget of 100 billion dollars for a ten-year-period, a feasible and realistic proposal if we are indeed serious about building a great society to replace the physical, social, and psychological environment of poverty.

If we can make the necessary social and economic investments in new housing, schools, and hospitals, if as a result we can create full employment for the next generation, then the unity of the black and white working class is possible and perhaps inevitable. There is the task of persuading poor whites and poor blacks that it is in their own interest to submerge their fears and frustrations in the larger interest of common social betterment. There is the task of mobilizing national sentiment behind these objectives and program priorities. Beyond that, there is the task of getting all the institutions of our society—political parties, business, labor, federal, state, and local governments, liberals, churchmen, educators, and civil rights activists to cooperate in effective alliance and effective action. All of these obstacles will deter us at our own peril, for without the unity of effort that is vitally necessary at this moment of our history, the Negro minority will be politically unable to emerge from social frustration and economic degradation; the large segments of the white poor will continue in their fear and in their poverty; progressive social change will have been set back perhaps another generation, and the hearts of our cities will continue to erode in social and economic decay.

An antipoverty strategy as broad and in many respects as bold as the one worked out in the Freedom Budget is bound to come under searching examination and even unfriendly criticism. Already one hears many objections. For instance, it has been said of the argument for a guaranteed annual income that it would destroy the responsibility of the individual and the very nature of work in our society. I think this kind of criticism either misunderstands the problem we are addressing or does not understand the proposal for a guaranteed annual income. We are not suggesting that a guaranteed annual income replace work. What we mean is this: Roughly half the people in the United States, according to the government's figures, are in the labor market. These people, as well as many of the employable who are presently without work, are in a position to be affected by programs providing for full employment.

But millions of poor Americans are not in the labor market at all. Some are either too young or too old to work, or have been automated out of economic usefulness. Moreover, it is one of the tragedies of our knowledge about poverty that nearly half of the American poor are under age eighteen and thus that poverty has an enormous growth potential. For these people, even a job program as broad as the one called for in the Freedom Budget is no solution, because they cannot work. Thus, in short, every citizen who cannot earn an income should be guaranteed an income. That is a fundamental right.

At the White House Conference on Civil Rights, a report was submitted which emphasized one of the most shocking facts about America's treatment of the poor. According to the report, during the entire post-World War II period almost all the subsidies for housing in the United States have gone to the middle class and the rich. The subsidies for low-income housing have been minimal and appear, beyond that, to have gone almost exclusively into building high-rise, segregated projects. Indeed, since most of the subsidies for the rich and middle class have gone into suburban housing and into the highways, expressways, and roads that lead there, the flight to suburbia and its resultants of affluence and de facto segregation have been subsidized by the federal government. All of this, of course, while the central city sleeps among rats and roaches in high-rent, run-down tenements.

We are not proposing a subsidy at all but a social investment. We believe that if we sink a small part of our enormous resources into the rebuilding of cities, if we proceed with the business of structuring a new urban civilization, then we will not only be eliminating poverty but also investing in the improvement of conditions for all the people in the society. We have to realize also that programs to achieve full employment have values beyond the immediate one of solving poverty. For instance, if we had a policy of general full employment, the resultant increase in the gross national product would result in the creation of a social dividend in the course of ten years of more than two trillion dollars. If this is the case, and I must say that I am not an economist and therefore cannot argue numbers, then such a dividend would easily allow us to undertake a program of expenditure that would improve the quality of life for all our citizens.

If there is any *single* step that will raise Negroes out of poverty, it is labor's demand for a national two-dollar minimum wage. In this land of affluence, two out of every three Negro families live below the poverty line. In part, this fact reflects the astronomically high unemployment rates in the Negro community but, in most cases, the head of the Negro family is working—forty hard hours a week. He does not need to be lectured about self-help. Give him a decent wage and he will be able to help himself. He will be able to keep his family together, educate his children, contribute to the wellbeing of the community. And he will be in a stronger position to struggle effectively for the dignity and rights which he has been denied.

A national two-dollar minimum wage, extended to millions not now covered by minimum wage legislation, would redress a shame of this nation. It would mean a revolution in Southern racial and economic relations, since it would weaken the position of runaway plants that locate in the South in order to escape unionism and to exploit a cheap labor market. In many Southern towns such companies become entrenched in the local power structure and fiercely resist civil rights efforts to change the status quo. The impact of a two-dollar minimum wage on ghetto-entrapped Negroes is no less revolutionary. In short, if the civil rights revolution is to have meaning outside of the South—in the teeming slums of the cities, in the industrial centers of the nation—the needs of the dispossessed Negro masses must be hitched to the economic demands of organized labor.

In pressing our campaign to ensure a greater and fuller commitment of the federal government to programs to end poverty, we should not ignore a very important point: that Presidents Kennedy and Johnson did a great service to our society by making the issue of poverty a federal concern and by interpreting the issue of civil rights in a social, political, and economic context. Consequently, we have made significant strides since 1960. Yet, there is a great danger if having publicly recognized, defined, and admitted the problem—if having called upon the nation to make an unconditional attack upon poverty—we then, for whatever reason, abandon our bold beginnings. In times of war or international crisis, there is a tendency to divert attention from crying domestic needs and problems. Now there are those who exploit the situation in Viet Nam for their narrow political purposes, who eagerly call for a cutback in funds for the war on poverty, hoping to push the struggle for racial equality off the stage of history. These tendencies must be vigorously fought. The sacrifices and burdens of our country's citizens must be evenly distributed. We must not place the heaviest loads on those least able to bear them—the poor and dispossessed, white and black.

We cannot excite hope and aspiration in the slums, in the ghettoes, and in the backwoods, and then leave the residents to pant in a vacuum. The consequences of failing to fulfill these social promises are likely to be just as devastating as our refusal to make them. I think, therefore, that if we become specific, if we adopt targeted priorities, if we give concrete promissory notes and move on to pay them, then we will have made, as the Freedom Budget urges, a profound social investment in freedom and human dignity for all of our people.

Contents

Editors' Introduction

The central concern of this book is with Negroes and jobs. What purpose is served by a discussion of Negro employment at a time when there is an increasing tendency to view Negro job problems as dimensions of a much larger context—the American underclass? Are Negro employment patterns a variant of the more general problem of poverty or do they deserve special attention?

A number of important considerations justify a book on Negro employment problems, although fundamentally we agree with A. Philip Randolph and others who argue that many of these problems cannot be understood or solved apart from the broader context of the economics of poverty and the deprivation of the poor in our society. The difference, however, between the employment problems of Negroes and the employment problems of the American underclass is sufficiently large to demand a careful analysis of Negroes and their relationship to the world of work.

Five basic considerations serve as a rationale for our undertaking:

Negroes in the city are not just another urban migrant group with a marked potential for assimilation into the mainstream of society; rather, as a group, they have failed after three generations to gain the rewards and statuses attained by other urban migrant groups (e.g., the Jews, the Irish, the Italians, and the Poles). It is wishful thinking to characterize Negro problems in employment, education, and politics as transitory and capable of resolution with time. Many of these problems have become worse over the years and have been strongly resistant to solution. While the ghettoes of earlier urban migrant groups dissolved as social and economic opportunities increased, the Negro ghettoes have become more isolated and crowded as urban renewal in the city centers and the suburban drift of whites have depressed opportunities in employment, housing, and education. The end result has been the development of ghettoes where tensions are high and explosive riots occur with increasing frequency.

Often, we err in not seeing any differences between the ghettoes of earlier urban migrant groups and the Negro ghettoes of today. The ghettoes of earlier groups were *transitory*, perceived as a first step on the road to affluence, and for this reason, the squalor and the deprivation could be borne. To the Negro, whose parents and perhaps grandparents grew up in deprived economic circumstances, the real or perceived chances of movement may be slight, making it difficult to bear the conditions of deprivation. Many ghettoes of earlier migrant groups were in close proximity to places of work, and in some cases economic opportunities existed within the geographical limits of the ghetto itself. The Negro today faces a far different situation. The decentralization of industry from the city center has erected a bar of physical distance between himself and many job opportunities. Few jobs, other than unskilled service employment, are to be found in his ghetto.

The Negro ghetto of today is characterized by a level of resentment and hostility that has little parallel to earlier types of ghettoes. Numerous factors contribute to this state of affairs: (1) there is a high concentration of the *permanently unemployed*—old and young—who have years of productive life left but see no possibility of jobs; (2) the allocation of municipal and state resources for social services and education is inadequate to deal with the needs generated in ghetto life; (3) the tensions and animosities between ghetto residents and the police have heightened as the relationship between them has deteriorated; (4) the opportunity structure facing Negro youth is perceived as restrictive and controlled by a white power structure unresponsive to change; (5) there is an alienation—both felt and real—from the mechanisms that might produce needed changes (e.g., the political and economic systems); and (6) there are few "success models" and sources of job information from those whose experiences could provide guidelines for social mobility in the larger society, while, frequently, models exist who have used subrosa or illegitimate means to gain status and prestige. Finally, the Negro ghetto usually lacks social and psychological links with the larger society. The Negro may view his situation as one of exploitation by segments of the white community (e.g., the absentee landlord, the storekeeper, the employer) and seek to avoid unnecessary contacts with whites. Furthermore, such links may be discouraged by some Negro leaders and professionals who view their power in the ghetto as being dependent on social distance between Negro and white. More often, the absence of links reflects an absence of meaningful contacts between Negro and white. Like well-worn Indian pathways, these discriminatory situations tend to be perpetuated for reasons that defy rational explanation. The low social power of Negroes in the past—coupled with intentional and unintentional discrimination in society—excluded most of them from participation in the community decision-making process—a basic step for the establishment of meaningful linkages.

Some of these phenomena characterized the ghetto experiences of older migrant groups, but in time, the barriers eroded for them. For the Negro these conditions have shown both a stubborn persistence and no real sign of imminent change.

While Negro employment patterns may have much in common with those of other underclass, minority groups, there is a certain measure of irreducible discrimination against Negroes that reflects their high racial visibility and historical tradition. Insofar as black skin color is used as a criterion for invidious distinctions in employment, there is a dimension of Negro employment patterns that is unique and idiosyncratic. In the South, in particular, the history of Negro-white relations has resulted in distinctions that label certain jobs as white and others as Negro. Skin color and history, then, introduce a measure of uniqueness in Negro employment patterns.

Even were discrimination in employment for Negroes to be ended tomorrow, it is doubtful whether there would be immediate equality in employment. As we indicate, the solution to Negro employment problems lies only partly in equalizing employment opportunities. Employment discrimination is a reflection—indeed an end product—of many other forms of discrimination against the Negro: housing and education, as well as certain political and social processes. There is a "vicious cycle of discrimination," and an understanding of the causes and sustaining conditions of job discrimination against Negroes is necessary background for proposals of realistic solutions. Solutions for the economic problems of the American underclass may prove ineffective for Negroes if simultaneous programs do not eliminate institutional barriers that support job discrimination against Negroes.

Although the Negro shares many economic problems with the American underclass (low income employment, underemployment, and unemployment), his economic plight is being made *more* desperate by the high numbers of unemployed Negro youth and by a high degree of "invisible unemployment" in the Negro ghettoes. Although youth in the American underclass suffer higher rates of unemployment than other groups in the labor market, the unemployment rate for Negro youth is generally double the rate of whites and higher than for any other group of the similarly disadvantaged. "Hidden unemployment"—the retirement from the labor force of able-bodied men who refuse to seek jobs in the regular labor market and exist on social service aid or marginal employment—is a phenomenon that is almost exclusively Negro. Exact figures are difficult to cite because the very nature of hidden unemployment makes it difficult to measure, but various estimates indicate that almost one million Negro youth live this socially ambiguous existence.

The implications of these facts suggest that there are large numbers of Negroes whose attachment to the world of work—and possibly to society—is tenuous. There is certainly much to cause alarm in the high rate of "invisible unemployment" among Negroes. Unemployed workers who are so alienated from the world of work that they have stopped job-hunting are symptoms of a basic flaw in our society and pose certain questions about the viability of our economic system.

Finally, of all minority groups, Negroes have been the most *vocal* and *organized* in protesting discrimination in housing and education as well as in employment. This protest has taken many forms: direct action (demonstration, boycott, and picketing), negotiation between Negro action groups and business organizations, and political action. The Negro Civil Rights Revolution has developed a number of models for protest that are currently being studied and that in time will be emulated by other minority groups. This alone justifies an increasing preoccupation with all aspects of Negro life, since it frequently becomes possible to predict the future behavior of other groups based on an understanding of a model movement and its techniques.

Furthermore, the summer explosions in the large urban cities did not happen in just any ghetto; they happened in Negro ghettoes. These holocausts have shaken Americans as never before. There is a new awareness, *not* of the power of the American underclass but of the American Negro. Such mass behavior becomes possible only when individuals sever their ties with the social order or where individuals are weakly integrated into the society. The explosions themselves are strong indications that, for many Negroes, the American institutions are no longer workable.

In the wake of the ashes and smoke of the Negro ghettoes, questions have been raised about the relationship of employment to forms of civil disturbance. A large segment of the intellectual and policy-making community contends that the riots are closely related to long-term unemployment among Negroes and that the ultimate anti-riot measure would be to provide more and better jobs for the Negro underclass.

The evidence, however, suggests that the relationship between Negro employment patterns and Negro extremism may be more complex than imagined at first. Although our knowledge of the Negro riots is still sketchy, recent findings from Watts in Los Angeles and Twelfth Street in Detroit indicate that participation in the rioting was broad-based, including large numbers of educated and employed Negroes who had objectively bettered their economic situation over the years.

However, although Negro economic progress may have been considerable in absolute terms, it is miniscule relative to the progress of whites in our society. In addition, an improvement in jobs or wages has not necessarily meant a concomitant improvement in housing, recreational facilities, neighborhood services, or educational resources for Negro families.

Jobs cannot be viewed as *the* deterrent to Negro extremism. But this does not mean that comprehensive programs of human resource and manpower development are not necessary as measures of sound social policy to reduce the economic and social problems of a significant number of Americans. To decide that such programs are necessary *merely* on the basis of whether Negro extremism can be reduced is to introduce a criterion that flaunts the American doctrine of equal opportunity for all.

Throughout this book, we present both a socioeconomic portrait of the Negro underclass and discuss the social policies that may lead to a solution of problems that beset disadvantaged Negroes. Social policies for the relief of poverty in this country have tended to be pragmatic rather than utopian, and person-oriented rather than system-oriented. Thus, little has been said about the goals that we should set to eliminate inequality, and much is said about the means. Technical training, education, and income support are viewed as means to eliminate inequality, but little has been said about what exactly the elimination of inequality means. Our preoccupation with the *available means* of our society suggests that goals are largely derived from existing means, rather than setting broad goals and seeking new means compatible with these goals.

In a like manner, we develop social policies that are person-oriented (e.g., train the worker, educate the Negro) as if to suggest that the solution to an individual's problems is to change his attitudes, motives, or skills, rather than the opportunity structure that confronts him. In employment, stress has been placed on improving the Negro's education and skills to bring him up to the demands of the labor market, rather than change or modify employment qualifications to fit the capacities and skills of the worker. All too often, the social cure suggests tailoring the individual to the system, rather than modifying the system to fit existing skills or capacities of the worker.

What is needed to understand the dilemmas of the Negro and his behavior in America is a critical look at his relationship to the major institutions of the society: economic, educational, political, and social.

Such an inquiry must deal with the following questions. In what way(s) do institutional forces cause and/or sustain discrimination against the Negro? What are the principal ways to right the situation? Our undertaking is, then, part of a larger inquiry into one of the major concerns of our time—how to increase the access of a minority group to the institutional memberships, services, and rewards of our society.

The extent to which we answer this last question will determine, in part, our ability to provide a long-run and permanent solution to ghetto rioting. While the problem of Negro access to other institutions (e.g., education or politics) might have been a possible topic for this book, we chose to deal with the problem of Negro access to economic institutions.

The choice was predicated largely on the belief that access to and training for jobs have been primary driving forces behind both Negro agitation and rebellion. Obviously, the Negro "vicious circle of disadvantagement" may be penetrated at a number of points (e.g., access to housing or education), but our belief is that decent employment is a first step to make access to other institutional spheres easier. The development of Negro job opportunities is a key to the *real* integration of the Negro into American national life.

We also hope to shed some light on one of the major intellectual debates of our times, viz., the "causes" of disadvantagement. The controversy surrounding explanations of disadvantagement has risen to fever pitch largely as a result of a U. S. Department of Labor report supervised by the sociologist Daniel P. Moynihan. The "Moynihan Report" pinned the causes of Negro disadvantagement on the erosion and lack of stability of Negro institutions, particularly the family. In contrast, such writers as Bayard Rustin and Hylan Lewis have argued that Negro disadvantagement stems not from institutional instability but from inadequate opportunity that denies Negroes access to good jobs, quality education, and desirable housing.

While the "Moynihan Report" argues that Negro life does not *prepare* the Negro to play a prominent role in the occupational structure, critics of the report claim that the large society, through discrimination and institutional barriers, denies the Negro *access* to adequate opportunity to fulfill his needs. The controversy pits *lack of preparation* of the Negro for work roles against *lack of access to a suitable opportunity structure* as explanations for Negro disadvantagement. The resolution of this controversy will influence the programs of intervention to be proposed, as well as the assignment of responsibility for Negro poverty.

The organization of this book reflects concern with this controversy. The first chapter presents a general review of Negro employment patterns and economic history in American society. The next two chapters are concerned with the causes of Negro job disadvantagement and social conditions that sustain it. Chapter 4 deals with the operation of the labor market for Negro workers and Chapter 5 with an intensive treatment of Negro experiences in the labor market. Our concluding chapter discusses some past as well as some proposed programs to increase the Negro's access to job opportunities.

In preparing this volume our intention was to present a well-rounded account of the Negro's economic position in the contemporary American labor market, to suggest reasons why this position has developed and is sustained, to detail some of the consequences of Negro job inequality, and to review some programs of action—intervention strategies—that might be used to reduce Negro job disadvantagement.

The articles represent a variety of viewpoints and contribute to an understanding of the issues posed. Although we surveyed relevant literature dating back to the 1940's, we have restricted our presentation of articles to those of the 1960's. This contributes a contemporary relevance to the undertaking that would not be possible with earlier data. We hope that the book may be used as an analytic tool to gain perspective on the issue that has become crucial for our democratic society and way of life.

Although "Negro worker" implies a unitary term, we have recognized that there are a number of Negro worker types:

Professionals, technicians, business managers
White-collar workers (sales and clerical)
Blue-collar craft workers
Blue-collar industrial workers
Service workers

We elected to restrict ourselves to intensive treatment of problems faced by a few of these job categories for several reasons. First, with few exceptions, the pertinent literature of the 1960's emphasizes *disadvantaged* Negro workers, usually in blue-collar or service employment. Remarkably little has been written on Negro professionals or white-collar workers. Second, we were concerned with Negro job problems as generators of social unrest, and these were more likely to be found among Negro workers at the lower end of the occupational ladder. Third, the affluence of the 1960's has created an unprecedented demand for trained and skilled workers, and this trend, coupled with the pressures from the civil rights movement, has led to increased opportunities for Negro professional and white-collar workers.

Select groups of trained and educated Negro workers have been the most direct beneficiaries of fair employment practices and equal opportunity legislation. Such workers may have temporary job adjustment problems, but these are hardly of the magnitude of the problems faced by undereducated and underskilled Negroes. Only in a few cases have we dealt with Negroes in higher level jobs.

It was obvious throughout our inquiry that only the barest beginnings exist in the research and literature on Negro job problems. Although interesting and provocative studies are under way, few written reports have been completed. As a result, there are gaps in our presentation. For example, there are no recent definitive articles on the job problems of Negro youth, on the process of job searching, on the integration of Negroes into all-white work forces, on the attitudes of Negroes toward work, etc. However, this book represents a range of ideas which can be examined with considerable intellectual profit. It is our hope that the gaps in our work may be a stimulus for needed research in this very important problem area.

Acknowledgments

It would be impossible to list all those who contributed to this undertaking. We would like, however, to acknowledge the following: Ronald W. Haughton and Charles M. Rehmus, codirectors of the Institute of Labor and Industrial Relations, The University of Michigan–Wayne State University, made available resources and encouraged us. Dr. Ray Marshall of the University of Kentucky and staff personnel of the major federal agencies in Washington were helpful in locating hard-to-find literature. Herbert Hill of the National Association for the Advancement of Colored People and Phyllis Wallace of the Equal Employment Opportunity Commission also made valuable suggestions. We were also helped by the wise counsel of Dr. Sar Levitan of the George Washington University and Dr. Hylan Lewis of Howard University.

Finally, the book would not have been possible without the counsel, encouragement, and patience of Patricia Ferman, Hy Kornbluh, and Nancy Miller.

Chapter 1

The Economic Situation of Negroes in the United States

Introduction

"It takes a lot of running to stand still on the treadmill of this technologically advancing society," as Tom Kahn points out in the first article of this chapter. Although statutory racism has vanished in most areas of the country, the Negro is still victimized by the inadequacies and tokenism of the economic system. Unemployment rates for Negro youth have risen to disaster proportions in recent years, and the Negro-white differential of unemployment rates has increased. Moreover, the income gap between Negroes and whites has not closed in the period following World War II, and the median income of Negro families today is only slightly more than half that of white families.

The majority of Negroes are concentrated in low-skilled, low-paid jobs and are often the last hired and the first fired as technological changes eliminate jobs for poor whites as well as for non-whites. They tend to be out of work for longer periods of time than whites, suffer from underemployment and part-time jobs, and are employed in disproportionate numbers in jobs with substandard pay. Unemployment rates for non-whites are more than double the average for whites. There is evidence that even these high rates have underestimated real unemployment among Negroes.

Negro life during the last fifty years has been characterized by numerous changes, but none so dramatic as the "journey to the city." Moving out of Southern rural areas to cities, North and South, during the past one hundred years Negroes became a predominantly urban population and in doing so raised their levels of living, life expectancy, educational attainment, and job skills.

Moving by the millions, Negroes migrated to regions where they could find work, taking whatever jobs were available, and settling in areas where they were allowed to live. Although over half of all Negroes live in the South, even in that region three out of five live in metropolitan areas. In contrast to three-quarters of the white population in the North and West, almost all Negroes in those regions live in cities. The percentage of non-whites living in cities outside of the South has increased over five times since 1900, from 8 percent at the turn of the century to 39 percent at the beginning of this decade. In 1960 one-fifth of all Negroes in the United States lived in five Northern cities and in Washington, D.C. Over half of the Negroes in most metropolitan areas lived in central cities, racial ghettoes like Harlem, Bedford-Stuyvesant, Chicago South Side, and other neighborhoods where the density of population is 90 percent or more Negro.

The shift of Negroes from a rural to an urban population has meant that Negro employment problems have become a national rather than a regional issue. Heightened competition between Negroes and whites with a diminishing number of unskilled and semiskilled jobs and the high levels of unemployment especially among non-white teenagers have affected all of the institutions of the urban community and have shaped a number of aspects of urban life in contemporary America.

In March 1966 non-white workers constituted about 11 percent of the civilian labor force but accounted for over 21 percent of the unemployed and 25 percent of the long-term unemployed. The gap between whites and non-whites is greatest for heads of households (particularly Negro women), who need jobs to support families, and for the teenage jobseekers, who as a group come from families with a median income of $3,677. In some areas such as Watts in Los Angeles, 40 percent of Negro residents were without work during 1966, and throughout the "long hot summer" of the July-September 1966 quarter, 10 percent of non-white adults and over 50 percent of teenage jobseekers had no employment in Negro neighborhoods in Northern and Southern cities.

In five of the cities with 100,000 or more Negro population in 1960 (New York, Chicago, Baltimore, Newark, and Los Angeles), the total employment gain between 1963 and 1965 fell below the national average of 7 percent. In New York City and Los Angeles, the two cities with the largest Negro in-migration and population, there was no gain whatever in manufacturing employment during those years. In most of the cities with large minority populations, employment gains took place only in the service and trade industries.

An overview of labor market patterns in this country indicates that occupational gains by Negroes have only been made during periods of severe labor shortages and low unemployment, such as the World War I and II periods during which Negroes moved into unskilled and semiskilled occupations vacated by whites who were climbing into higher status occupations. As the article by Ray Marshall in this chapter indicates, most Negroes were farm laborers or household servants during the two centuries of slavery preceding Emancipation. When the Civil War ended they remained, for the most part, as tenant farmers, share croppers, or day laborers on the land of white owners. Those Negroes who had been trained as skilled artisans to service and maintain a self-sufficient plantation system, lost their jobs and eventually their trades after the war as the competition for the traditionally "Negro jobs" increased from Southern white workers.

Resistance against the influx of Negroes into Northern cities in the immediate post-Civil War period stemmed from the fears of native-born and immigrant workers that non-whites would flood the labor market and lower wage rates. Competition for unskilled and semiskilled jobs was especially keen from foreign-born workers who were immigrating to Northern cities by the hundreds of thousands during the late nineteenth and early twentieth centuries. Despite this, three factors combined to push Negroes out of the South during the last decades of the nineteenth century: the enactment of Jim Crow laws during the 1890's depression, the entrance of Southern white women into the factories which rigidified taboos against integrated work forces, and successive crop failures caused by the boll weevil, floods, and droughts.

Northern industry expanded rapidly at the turn of the century. With the draft, the booming armaments industry, and the curtailment of European immigration at the start of World War I, Northern companies faced severe labor shortages. Many companies sent labor agents to the South to recruit Negroes for job openings—as they had done in southern Europe a few decades before—and on some occasions for strikebreaking in coal and iron mines, iron and steel mills, packing houses, and food processing plants.

Approximately 1.4 million Negroes came North from 1910 to 1930 and experienced relative prosperity in contrast to their condition in the South. As the article by Marion Hayes suggests, the labor demand remained brisk during the 1920's, and Negroes entered unskilled manual jobs in the rapidly growing automobile and steel plants, foundries, highway construction, railroad maintenance, and the garment industry—for the most part, taking jobs which the native-born or foreign white workers had vacated as better occupational opportunities opened for them.

Being at the bottom of the occupational ladder, Negroes were especially devastated by the depression of the 1930's. Yet, despite the keen competition from whites for even the most menial jobs, Negroes continued to migrate North in great numbers, leaving depressed

Southern rural communities where the failure of cotton crops and the shrinking demand for that commodity had resulted in total economic havoc. Over 300,000 Negroes moved to Northern cities during the 1930's; despite the mass layoffs, work staggering, and sharpened job discrimination they were saved from starvation by more liberal government relief allowances and jobs on W.P.A. work projects.

The industrial expansion which started with World War II was slow in reabsorbing Negroes into public or private industries. Although the proliferation of defense industries during the early years of the war brought relief to the mass of unemployed white workers, community patterns of job discrimination against Negroes continued despite severe labor shortages. Although barred at the beginning of the war from government training programs, Negroes found new work opportunities in the construction and servicing of military projects and in expanding consumer services.

Executive Order 8802, signed by President Franklin Roosevelt in June 1941, was a turning point in opening job and training opportunities for non-white citizens. The original Fair Employment Practices regulation stipulated that defense contracts after that date must include nondiscrimination clauses, and that Negroes could participate in government-sponsored vocational training programs. For the first time, Negroes entered job fields in which few if any Negroes had ever been employed. Benefitting from the labor shortages, they made advances in many occupational classifications. The period of economic prosperity extended beyond World War II and the industrial demands created by the Korean conflict facilitated further economic gains for Negro workers.

Some Negroes entered craftsman and foreman jobs, mostly in trades such as cement finishing and painting. Few non-whites, however, gained access to higher paying work in the electrical and plumbing crafts and in other building trades occupations. In the 1940's and 1950's a substantial number of non-whites entered the postal service and other federal government jobs, largely because of the official policy of nondiscrimination in government employment. Many Negro women became nurses because of the severe labor shortages in hospitals.

Yet, for all this geographic and occupational mobility, most Negroes only advanced one rung up the occupational ladder, from the largely unskilled jobs as service workers, farm laborers and domestic workers—jobs which they held after they left Southern farms—to the semiskilled job category of operative, the only category in which Negroes attained parity with white workers in the four decades from 1920 to 1960.

In the South, neither wartime labor shortages or other labor market demands made any significant changes in the entrenched patterns of racial segregation in industry during the 1940's and 1950's. The South's greater labor surplus, the migration of rural whites to Southern cities and the greater reserve of agricultural labor, gave Southern employers enough manpower to meet their needs of the war years and continue to resist integration. Although most Northern cities adopted Fair Employment Practice laws during the last few decades, several Southern cities and states passed laws reinforcing racial segregation in industry. Negroes continued to be excluded from "white office work" and retail trade, as well as managerial and professional employment, in many locations of the South.

Throughout the country Negroes have made less progress in gaining entrance to skilled manual work, white collar work, and jobs of professional status. Even within the professional-technical category, Negroes have been concentrated in lower-paying occupations such as clergymen, teachers, and nurses, and until recently, have been dramatically underrepresented in professions such as medicine, accounting, and engineering. In 1960 they constituted less than half of 1 percent of all salaried managers and business officials. In the South Negroes who hold more desirable business and professional jobs usually serve an all-Negro clientele. In the North Negro businesses are but a small percentage of all mercantile establishments and offer no viable source of employment opportunities for the Negro unemployed.

Mechanization and automation have drastically changed the type of manpower needed in this country, and although the demand for professional and technical workers has increased with this country's emphasis on research and development in the space and defense industries, the routine, repetitive, low-paid jobs—those which most Negroes have held in the past—are being ruthlessly eliminated by the machine. During the past twenty years, the proportion of workers in manufacturing, mining, contract construction, and agriculture has decreased. Professor Vivian Henderson has recently noted that the industries with a declining rate of employment are the industries which have absorbed Negroes while the areas of growth in employment, excluding government, are not the areas in which Negroes traditionally find employment.

Previous patterns of job discrimination and current higher skill requirements still combine to limit the number of Negroes in growing occupational areas and to concentrate them in technologically vulnerable industries. A report of a U. S. Department of Labor study suggests that if the experienced non-white civilian labor force had the same occupational distribution as the comparable white group, the difference between white and non-white unemployment rates would be cut in half.

The economic situation of the Negro has continued to fluctuate over the past four years. Increased economic growth spurred by the 1964 tax cut and the rising military spending for the war in Viet Nam accelerated factory production in 1965 for the first time since 1953. Negro adults, especially experienced males with job seniority, experienced a brief improvement in their job situations. By 1965 and the first months of 1966, many unemployed Negroes had been rehired on their old jobs or had found work in most industrial areas. Still jobless, however, were large numbers of unskilled Negroes and teenage Negroes with little if any work experience, vocational training, or higher education.

In the summer of 1966 unemployment rates increased selectively and many Negroes who had temporarily benefited from the quickening of economic activities in the preceding years found themselves jobless. As labor economist Nathaniel Goldfinger wrote in a recent article on Negroes and jobs in *The American Federationist:* "Negro workers hardly needed this additional lesson that the employment and unemployment conditions of the Negro labor force respond quickly and directly to a slowing of economic activities, particularly when it is concentrated in heavy goods industries, home building and related activities. Moreover, it underscored the fact that another full-blown recession could be a calamity for Negroes by displacing experienced adult workers and sharply reducing the pace of new job opportunities for the growing number of youngsters entering the job market."

Even in the best of times, the occupations and industries in which most Negroes have found employment are subject to seasonality and high unemployment. A larger proportion of Negroes are not covered by minimum wage laws, collective bargaining agreements, or social security, and even Negroes who are union members tend to be newer members with less seniority and other forms of security.

As a result, Negro family incomes averaged about 56 percent of white incomes in 1964, and there are dramatic differences in the ratios of Negro to white incomes in different sections of the country, as Alan Batchelder points out in his article. Even for those workers who had year-round, full-time employment, the median yearly earnings for non-white men was a little over $4000 in 1964, and the median income for non-white women was less than $3000. A much larger proportion of non-white than white families—40 percent compared to 12 percent—had incomes under $3000 in 1964, despite the fact that more Negro families include several wage earners. The amount of non-white poverty remains high, especially in families headed by young adults, women, the elderly, and those with many children.

Although in recent years, a number of better-paying, higher status jobs have become available in the fast-growing, higher-paying service occupations, Negroes have been unable to share proportionately with whites in the shift to this occupational category. Many adult Negro members of the labor force in this decade spent part or all of their childhood in Southern schools in which the per pupil expenditure and teachers' salaries fell far below those in other sections of the country and where school segregation, financially and psychologically, worked in favor of the white Southern pupils. Even for workers schooled in the North, discrepancies in the allocation of resources between central city slum schools attended by most Negro students and the suburban schools catering to white populations have accented the sharp differences between the quantity and quality of Negro and white educational preparation, as articles in Chapter 3 detail.

What will the future hold for the Negro worker? As the occupational forecasts by Joe Russell in this chapter predict, the short-term prospects for narrowing the Negro-white occupational gap are not good. Massive public and private job-creating efforts are necessary to plan for large numbers of unskilled, semiskilled, and skilled jobs for white and Negro workers. Large-scale financial commitments must improve and enrich education and vocational training to provide Negroes with the ability to compete fully in the job market, and aggressive efforts must be mustered against the resistance of unions and companies to undertake positive efforts to increase the position of Negroes in the work force. Only with such an environment of full and fair employment can the heritage of discriminatory job practices be overcome.

The Economics of Inequality

Tom Kahn

[*From* The Economics of Equality, *by Tom Kahn (New York, 1964), by permission of the League for Industrial Democracy.*]

The Treadmill

It takes a lot of running to stand still on the treadmill of this technologically advancing society. When you know you're running hard and everyone tells you you're moving at a fast clip, and yet the scenery around you remains the same, the most appropriate word to describe your reactions is . . . frustration.

Running fast to stand still is essentially the position in which the Negro finds himself today. This harsh fact cannot be obscured by dramatic progress in the integration of public accommodations. Lunch-counters, hotels, bus terminals, and the like are the easiest targets of direct action and boycotts. There are enough of these establishments to accommodate everybody; in fact, overcrowding them is profitable. Once the sit-in movement in a city integrates all the lunch-counters, thus securing a given establishment from segregationist competition, lunch-counters enjoy a potentially larger consumer market.

Overcrowding in employment, housing, and schools has vastly different consequences. If the segregated lunch-counter is a hollow relic of the *ancient régime,* one which would inevitably topple at an early stage in the revolution, the more fundamental, institutional forms of discrimination are more securely rooted in our economic system. And current trends in that system imperil the Negro's economic future.

The remaining pages of this chapter are concerned with the decline of the Negro's relative position in terms of jobs and income. But trends in these purely economic categories underlie demographic developments which profoundly affect housing and schools . . . Yet, we should remember that they are intermeshed with the jobs situation and are therefore economic matters as well.

But first things first. What emerges from the statistics on jobs and income are the following trends:

1. There is a widening *dollar gap* between Negroes and whites.

2. The *relative* income gap between Negroes and whites has remained virtually constant over the past decade.

3. The unemployment gap between Negroes and whites has been widening.

4. The industries and occupations where the Negro made his greatest gains have either declined or shown relatively little growth over the past decade.

5. Negroes constitute a growing percentage of all workers in most of the declining job categories.

Widening Dollar Gap

The median Negro family income is $3,233, or 54% of the white family's $5,835. Approximately two out of every three Negro families subsist on less than $4,000 annually—and are therefore poor or de-the Negro worker has remained stuck at about 55% of the white [*N.Y. Times*, Aug. 12, 1963.]

The Negro's *relative* income gains were actually registered between 1940 and 1954, when Negro family median income jumped from 37% to 56% of the white figure.

Behind this gain was World War II (not the New Deal, after eight years of which 25% of the Negro work force was still unemployed as against 13% of the white). War production created a shortage not only of skilled workers, but of semiskilled and unskilled workers as well. Consequently, thousands of Negroes left the rural South and poured into the factories. Protected by a federal FEPC, needed by an expanding economy, and absorbed in large numbers into the CIO, they won higher wages than the farms could offer. Many acquired new skills. The base of the Negro lower middle class was considerably expanded.

After Congress killed FEPC in 1946, job discrimination surged up and many of the newly acquired skills were lost to the Negro community through lack of use. Still, in the relatively prosperous post-war years, the unemployment rate among Negroes was only about 60% higher than the white rate. *Since 1954 it has been at least 200% higher.*

The point to be stressed here is that the Negro's income gains were the result of peculiar employment opportunities that no longer exist. In part, as Michael Harrington has observed, these gains were due to "economic geography rather than the workings of the society." They reflect the shift of rural Negroes to cities and Southern Negroes to the North. In these cases, the people involved increased their income by going into a more prosperous section of the economy as a whole. But within each area—Northern city, Southern city, agriculture—*their relative position remained the same: at the bottom.*

Thus, masses of Negroes entered industrial production but were concentrated in unskilled and semiskilled jobs. And these are precisely the jobs now being destroyed by automation. The "bottom" is falling out of society; it is no longer needed.

"Invisible Army of the Unemployed"

Just as the dollar gap between Negroes and whites has been widening, so has the unemployment gap, as Figure 1 indicates. Whereas the unemployment rate from 1947 to 1953 never exceeded 8.5% for Negroes and 4.6% for whites, now it stands at 12.4% and 5.9% respectively. Not only have there been rising levels of unemployment since 1954, but—and this is of strategic importance—the Negro-white un-

prived—as compared with 27.7% of the white families. Only one ou five Negro families earns $6,000 or more, as compared with one ou two white families. In the whole country there are only 6,000 Ne families that can boast of incomes of $25,000 or more.

These figures tell us where the Negro is today, but they beco more meaningful when compared to the 1945 figures.

Between 1945 and 1961, the percentage ratio of whites w escaped from the below $4,000 category (63.3%) is almost double th for Negroes (33.1%), despite the fact that a larger percentage Negroes were in that category in 1945 (90.1%) as against 75.5% white families. Similarly, whites entered the $6,000-and-over categor at a faster rate than Negroes.

On the other hand, the percentage increase of Negro familie entering the $4,000-$5,999 category seems very impressive when com pared with the figures for whites. But the percentage gain is grea only because the starting figure was so low.

> Fisk economist Vivian Henderson emphasizes that while . . . relative growth in wage and salary income of Negroes since 1940 has been greater than that of whites ... the absolute, or *dollar,* difference has widened considerably. . . . People spend and save dollars. It is this dollar difference that counts. Pronouncements regarding economic progress which are confined to acceleration concepts and percentage change obscure the real predicament—*Negroes are losing ground rapidly in gaining dollar parity with whites.* The "dollar gap" trend ... means very simply that earnings are increasing for whites at a faster pace than for Negroes. [*The Economic Status of Negroes,* Southern Regional Council, pp. 12-13.]

One aspect of the earning gap is particularly astonishing. When we compare the lifetime earnings of Negro and white males by education we find that the Negro who finishes four years of college will earn less than a white with only eight years of elementary school.

Relative Income Gap

Not only is the dollar gap widening, but the *relative* income gap has remained virtually constant for almost a decade. While the figures reported by statisticians vary slightly, they point to the conclusion of Herman P. Miller of the Census Bureau:

> In the last decade ... there has been no change in income differential between [Negroes and whites]. The median pay of

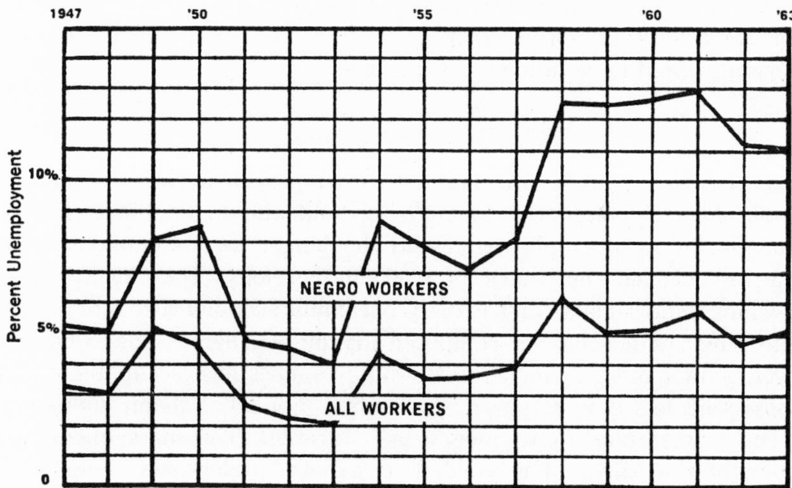

Figure 1: Negro and Over-All Unemployment Rates, 1947–1963

Estimates based on statistics of U.S. Department of Commerce, Bureau of the Census, and other sources.

employment gap has tended to widen in times of high unemployment and narrow in times of low unemployment. Historically the Negro fares better, absolutely and relatively, the closer the economy is to full employment.

Both tendencies–rising unemployment and a widening unemployment gap–come into sharper focus if we replace the official figures with more realistic ones which take into account what Professor Charles C. Killingsworth of Michigan State University has called the "invisible army of unemployed"–"people forced out of the labor market some time ago who are willing and able to work, but have become too discouraged to search for jobs" and are therefore not counted as part of the labor force by the government. Professor Killingsworth carefully calculated the size of this "invisible army" at 1½ million. They would raise the national unemployment rate to 8.8%. Gunnar Myrdal, the eminent Swedish economist, likewise taking into account the number of persons who would re-enter the labor force if jobs opened up, put the figure at 9%.

While Killingsworth has not made a racial breakdown of the "invisible army," he emphasized that its members are educationally disadvantaged. A disproportionate number are undoubtedly Negroes, many of whom support themselves in the ghettos by means they are not likely to report to census takers. Labor economists believe the real

Negro unemployment rate is probably close to 20%. In the words of the *New York Times,* "Unemployment of these proportions, were it general, would be a national catastrophe."

The Under-class

Especially ominous is the long-term unemployment rate among Negroes. For the long-term unemployed tend also to be the most frequently hit by unemployment, and the longer they are unemployed the less chance they have of ever finding jobs. They make up a swelling "under-class" that is daily becoming economically more obsolete. This "under-class" is composed mainly of Negroes, males 65 and over, young men, farm laborers, those in unskilled occupations and those with less than 12 years of schooling. For all of them, unemployment is worsening in frequency and duration. The mass unemployment of the thirties has yielded to a new "under-class" unemployment.

The seriousness of the problem is illustrated in Figure 2, which shows that since 1953 the long-term unemployed have been constituting *an increasing percentage of the total unemployed.* This means that a growing section of the work force is being more or less permanently detached from the economy and sinking into the "under-class."

Within this "under-class," Negro representation is mounting. Vivian Henderson reports that

> In September, 1958, the average duration of unemployment for Negroes was 17.8 weeks and for white workers 13.3 weeks. The average length of unemployment in September, 1962, for Negroes was 18 weeks while that for whites had dropped to 13 weeks. Negroes accounted for about 25% of all the long-term unemployed, but for only about 11% of the labor force. About 29% of the very long term unemployed in September, 1962, were Negroes compared with 21% in September, 1961. Long-term joblessness among Negroes results from discrimination in hiring and inadequate training and inadequate manpower development. [*op. cit.,* p. 16.]

Generally, the long-term unemployed are more likely to be the victims of technological change, while the short-term unemployed may be seasonal lay-offs, retrainees, or seekers of better jobs. What percentage of long-term joblessness among Negroes is attributable to discrimination *per se* and what percentage to inadequate training is difficult to state with precision.

The role of discrimination is clearest in the areas of income and occupational distribution of Negro college graduates. Lack of training certainly cannot explain the figures in Table 2. Nor can it satisfactorily explain why only 5% of Negro college men become proprietors, managers, or officials as compared with 22% of white college men; or why Negroes with some college training are found in service and laborer jobs in numbers five times greater than whites with similar training. It absolutely cannot explain why 10% of Negro women who finish college end up as domestics! Here is an obvious waste of skills that can be ascribed only to blatant discrimination and segregation.

On the other hand, college graduates constitute only 3.5% of the non-white population, and they are not usually to be found in the ranks of the long-term unemployed. In fact, because of skilled manpower shortages, educated Negroes are likely to make the most rapid progress in the period ahead.

For the vast majority of Negroes, however, an economic crisis is in the offing. And overt discrimination seems less a part of it than the weight of centuries of past discrimination combining with portentous economic forces that are themselves color-blind. *It is as if racism, having put the Negro in his economic "place," stepped aside to watch technology destroy that place.*

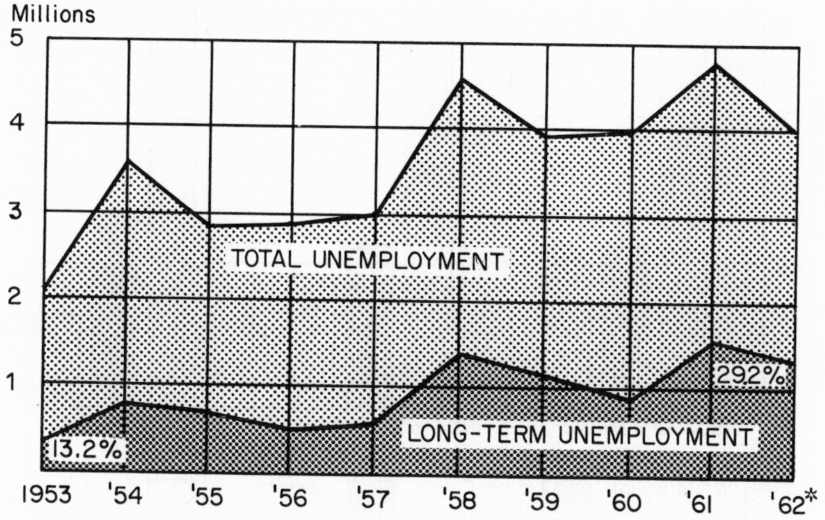

Figure 2: Long-Term Unemployment, 1953–1962 (15 weeks or more)

Source: U.S. Bureau of Labor Statistics *January-June, seasonally adjusted.

Changing Labor Force

As indicated above, most of the Negroes' economic gains in recent years were made in the period 1940-1953 and reflect their movement out of agriculture into mining, manufacturing, and construction, where they took up unskilled and semiskilled jobs. These blue-collar jobs in the goods-producing industries paid better than the unskilled and semiskilled jobs in the service-producing industries. But they were also the jobs most hit by automation and technological change.

The past decade has witnessed a decline of 339,000 jobs in the goods-producing industries and an increase of 7.3 million jobs in the service-producing industries.

But these figures reveal only part of the impact of the technological revolution on the work force. Customarily, goods-producing jobs

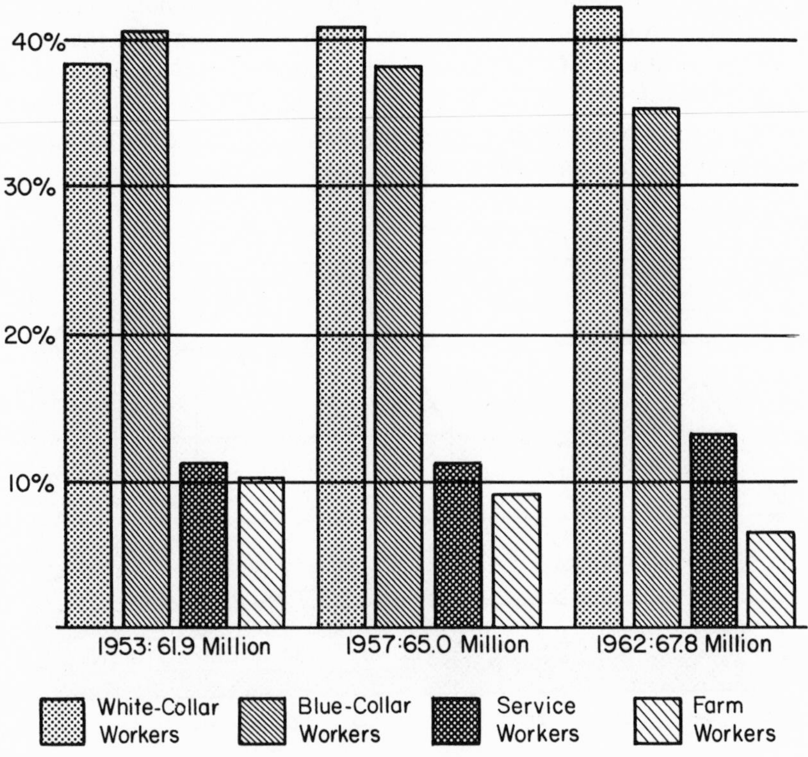

Figure 3: Growth in White-Collar Jobs, 1953–1962

Source: U.S. Bureau of Labor Statistics

are considered blue-collar and service-producing jobs are considered white-collar. The fact is that *within* the goods-producing industries there has been a dramatic increase in the number of white-collar jobs and an even more dramatic loss of blue-collar jobs.

In manufacturing, for example, 1.6 million blue-collar (production and maintenance) jobs have been obliterated in this decade while more than one million white-collar (non-production) jobs have been added. The blue-collar decline is also evident in the service-producing industries. Note that the only service-producing jobs that declined since 1953 were in transportation and utilities (especially in railroading).

Thus the growth in white-collar jobs resulted not only from the expansion of the service industries, but also from the application of technology to the productive process itself. The economic revolution wrought by these developments became fully evident in the mid-1950s when, as Figure 3 shows, the number of white-collar workers exceeded the number of blue-collar workers for the first time in history. This graph also indicates the decrease in the agricultural work force. As a consequence of agricultural mechanization, more than 1.5 million farm jobs have been wiped out since 1953.

It is against this background that the economic position of the Negro must be viewed. Figure 4 shows the percentage of whites and non-whites in each of the occupational categories. Notice the disproportionate concentration of Negroes in blue-collar and service jobs. (These service jobs are not to be confused with white-collar jobs in *service-producing* industries.)

That these jobs are becoming increasingly marginal to the economy becomes clear when we examine Figure 5, which shows the rate of unemployment in each occupation. Note that the occupations in which unemployment is highest—for example, laborers, operatives, and "other service workers"—are precisely the occupations in which Negroes are most heavily concentrated. Conversely, the occupations with the lowest unemployment rates—for example, managers, officials, and proprietors—are those in which Negroes are least concentrated. Taken together, Figures 4 and 5 suggest that if Negroes suddenly changed their skin color but not their occupations, their unemployment rate would still be far above the national average.

Further study reveals that while the national trend is toward a white-collar labor-force, the percentage of Negroes in blue-collar jobs is increasing. Thus, while the percentage of white males in blue-collar jobs *fell* from 53% in 1950 to 50% in 1960, the percentage for Negroes rose from 64% to 67%. And the greater part of this increase was in the "laborer" category. These are the figures for Negro *males*. More shock-

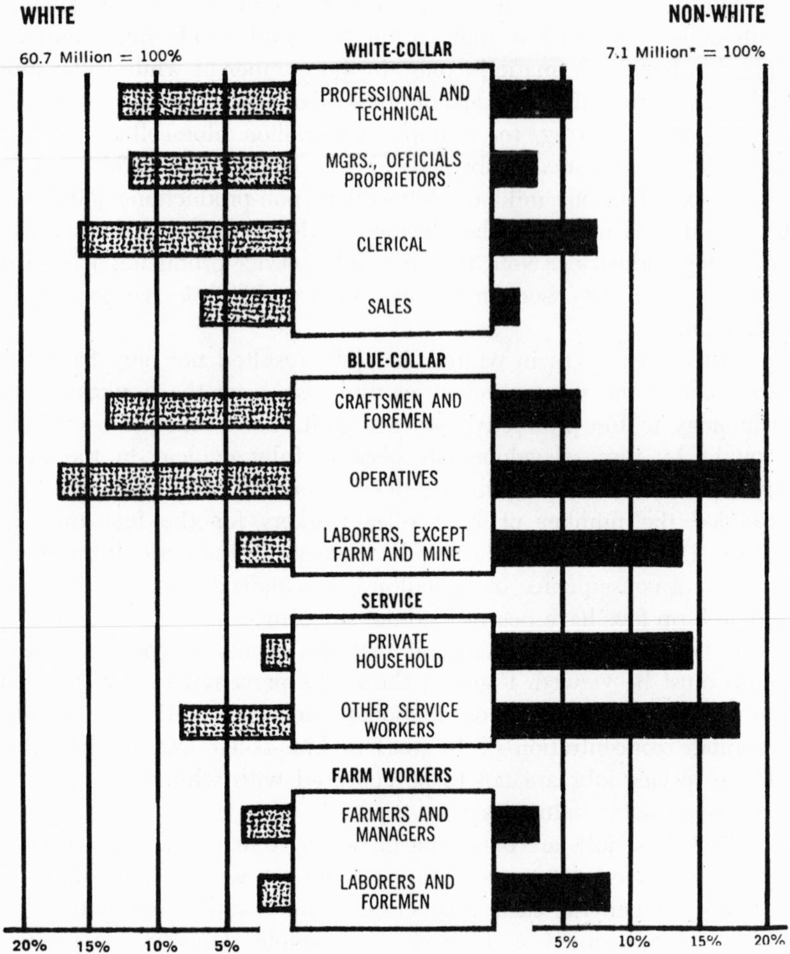

Figure 4: Occupational Breakdown by Race

Source: U.S. Bureau of Labor Statistics

ing are those for Negro females, an increasing percentage of whom are now in *blue-collar jobs* (15% in 1950, 17.2% in 1962; corresponding figures for white women are 22.3% and 17.3%).

The percentage of Negroes in white-collar jobs is also increasing, though in percentage points whites gained more than Negroes in professional and technical jobs. Most of the Negroes' gains were in clerical jobs where wages are generally lower than in manufacturing. It is precisely in the professional and technical field that the job market is expanding most rapidly. Herman Miller concludes, "In most

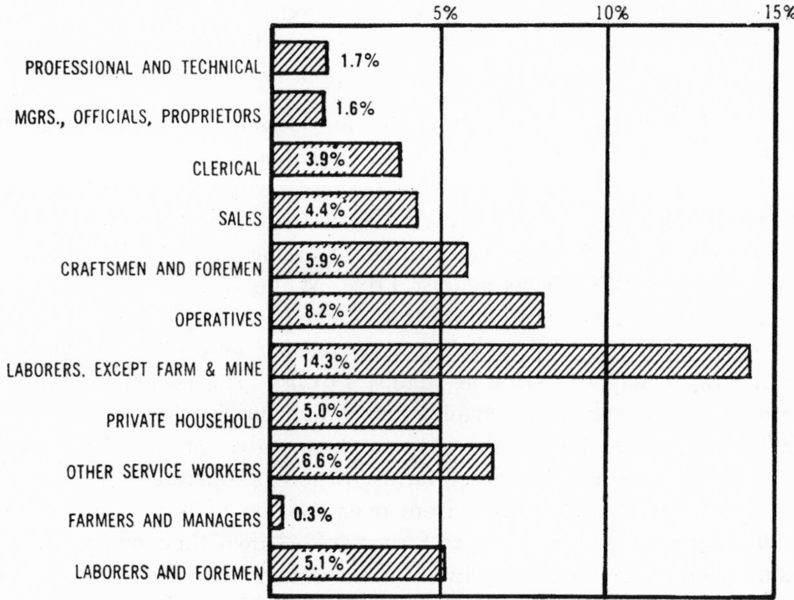

Figure 5: Unemployment by Occupation

Source: U.S. Bureau of Labor Statistics

states, the nonwhite male now has about the same occupational distribution relative to whites that he had in 1940 and 1950."

But unless this occupational distribution is radically altered, disaster looms for the Negro. Not only will the unemployment gap widen because of increasing automation in categories where Negroes are concentrated, but so will the dollar gap. As Henderson summarizes,

> Whites are acquiring the highest paying jobs in the higher occupational classifications. The benefits of general economic expansion and technology, therefore, have only trickled down to the Negroes, putting more of them into wage and salary jobs. These benefits automatically produced high acceleration in income change, but were restricted tightly to lower occupational classifications. Thus, despite the unprecedented growth of income among Negroes and the percentage gains made, the fact remains that *income progress of Negroes has leveled off*. The percentage of Negro families in lower income brackets is twice as high as whites, and *the differential in earnings of whites and Negroes continues to widen,* largely offsetting percentage gains. Ac-

cordingly, it is still difficult for Negroes to purchase health, education and the amenities of life on the same level as other members of the population. [*op. cit.*, pp. 12-13. Italics added.]

Not only are Negroes trapped in declining and stagnant job categories; *they constitute a growing percentage of the total workers in these categories.* Of all laborers (except farm and mine), Negroes were 27.6% in 1960 as against 21.2% in 1940; among operatives and kindred workers, Negroes constituted 11.6% as against 6.1%; among clerical workers, 6.7% as against 1.6%. While Negroes constituted a larger percentage of farm laborers and foremen in 1960 (23.6%) than in 1940 (22.5%), they make up a decreasing percentage of farmers and farm managers (8.6% as against 13.1%). The reason for this, of course, is agricultural mechanization, which has hit Negroes hardest. Between 1940 and 1959, the drop in the number of American farms was 39%, but the number of farms owned or operated by Negroes was cut more than one-half, from over 700,000 to less than 300,000. (Only 23% of Southern Negro farm workers own their own farms as contrasted with 60% of white farm workers. On the other hand, almost half of all tenant farmers and over 65% of all sharecroppers are Negroes.)

The Talk of Progress

To sum up, then, the decline in the relative economic position of the Negro is evident in the widening dollar and unemployment gaps between Negroes and whites, stagnation of the relative income gap, erosion of the job categories in which Negroes are concentrated, and the increasing segregation of Negroes in the declining job categories.

Underlying these trends are basic changes in the structure of the total labor force. The rising productivity caused by technological advances has reduced the number of workers required to produce the goods and services we need. While the effect of automation will become increasingly widespread, the blue-collar production and maintenance jobs are hardest hit. Paralleling the erosion of unskilled and semiskilled jobs is the growth of white-collar jobs and a mounting demand for skilled labor, where manpower shortages already exist. Because of centuries of discrimination and exploitation Negroes have been disproportionately concentrated in the unskilled and semiskilled jobs now being obliterated and lack the training demanded by the new skilled jobs. Even if every racial barrier were immediately torn down, the mass of Negroes would still face a disastrous economic future.

This dangerous situation is neglected in the talk of "progress." Status quo propagandists are desperately trying to serve up a "new Negro"—an upper-middle-class professional type, urbane and bourgeois, an ideal next-door neighbor—to symbolize an allegedly radical improvement in American race relations. Thus *Time* magazine (January 2, 1964) devotes seven pages to lavish color photographs of Negroes who have "made it"—athletes, entertainers, diplomats, bishops, architects, judges, mathematicians, dentists, educators, realtors, and doctors. The section begins with a headline reminiscent of the language of Booker T. Washington: "Every Negro Who Discharges His Duty Faithfully is Making a Real Contribution." It closes with this statement: "The main source of Negro discontent is economic hardship. Fortunately, this is the one area where progress seems most likely—more and better jobs for Negroes are on the way."

The question is: more and better jobs for *which* Negroes—and how many? . . . For now it should be clear that focusing the achievements of individual Negroes obscures the economic forces at work on the Negro community *as a whole*. It is these fundamental forces, reasserting themselves through any veneer of optimism imposed upon them, that shape the patterns of Negro life and the racial attitudes of whites.

Image and Reality

The image of the Negro that *Time* projects is not utterly unreal, and to the extent that it overturns humiliating stereotypes and whets the aspirations of Negro youth, it serves a purpose. But to a larger extent it causes frustrations. For the drive toward achievement which the image might normally inspire is overwhelmed and distorted by the greater social reality it conceals. Frequently that drive, when not extinguished, is channeled into illegal activities which offer material rewards and a status which may be considered disreputable in the white world but commands respect in the ghetto where the only alternative appears to be demoralization.

Between image and reality, between the progress Negroes are alleged to have made and the actual conditions of their daily existence there is, then, an enormous disparity which breeds frustration, disillusionment and anger. These are among the ingredients that make up the militancy which upsets so many whites.

Whites, on their part, are also affected by the disparity. On the one hand, *Time's* image of the successful Negro projects standards of middle-class behavior which shapes white expectations of what Negroes *should* be like. On the other hand, it is the reality of the ghetto, though the white may have only fleeting contact with it, that conditions his emotional attitudes toward Negroes.

For example, the trend toward *de facto* segregation of Negroes in declining low-paying job categories can only reinforce the association between *Negro* and *failure.* Thus most whites perceive no transformation of the Negro as a "social type." Yet a transformation is precisely what they have considered the *sina qua non* of integration—whether as a precondition or as an after-effect. *Since we are integrating the Negro into the mainstream of American life, why isn't he improving himself?*

Meanwhile, poverty and social disorganization continue to take their toll, burdening the Negro with disabilities which many whites construe as evidence that he is not ready for integration. More often acted upon than explicitly verbalized, this attitude is not necessarily rooted in racist dogma, and it seems to be gaining ground in the urban non-South. Instead of the view that Negroes are racially inferior, there arises a vaguer, but no less malevolent, conception of Negroes as somehow socially or morally incompetent to realize their potential.

Industrialization and Race Relations in the Southern United States

Ray Marshall

[*From Chapter IV of* Industrialisation and Race Relations: A Symposium *(Oxford University Press, copyright 1965) under the auspices of the United Nations Educational, Scientific and Cultural Organization.*]

The Formation of the Relationship: Slavery and the Civil War

The economic and social system built upon slavery had important consequences for the South and the nation. In adapting the Negro to his needs, the planter sought to turn him into a machine and to keep him in that status by a system of firmly established controls and customs which conditioned the attitudes and personalities of whites and blacks alike.[1] As Dabbs put it:

[1]For a discussion of the profitability of slavery see Robert Evans, Jr., 'The Economics of American Negro Slavery, 1830–60', in *Aspects of Labour Economics.* New York, National Bureau of Economic Research, 1962.

> When the planter bought the abstract, diagrammatic African, he bought essentially a machine, a stripped-down powerhouse. Into that machine he tried to build certain gadgets. The slave was to be docile, submissive, unreflecting. In general, he was to be inferior, and therefore by various methods he was made inferior.[2]

While the planter was never really able to reduce the slave to this ideal, the mark of inferiority became firmly stamped upon him in the minds of whites, and the Negro was in some degree forced to conform with this image in order to survive in the plantation economy.

The effects of slavery extended far beyond the Negro, however; it produced an economy which made progress extremely difficult at a time when other areas were advancing rapidly and was partly responsible for the Civil War which rent the nation and left its ugly scars for generations. Slavery did very little to improve the productive powers of whites, and while slaves acquired some skills in order to produce the goods and services for the plantation economy, these skills were usually very rudimentary and too crude to permit the freed Negro to compete with more highly skilled white artisans. Since the plantation was largely a self-contained economic unit, few towns grew up to promote non-agricultural pursuits and diversify the economy. Moreover, immigrants generally avoided the South where they would have to compete directly with slaves, so that the region lost the advantages of the economic, intellectual, and social stimulation given to other areas by skilled immigrants. The South was also largely avoided by American capitalists, because the agricultural creed that buttressed slavery and the plantation system was hostile to commercial and industrial undertakings; indeed, men like John C. Calhoun evolved fairly elaborate philosophies to defend slavery and the agricultural system as a means of avoiding the class conflicts which they saw as the inevitable consequences of industrialisation.

The diverging pattern of the South's economy from that of the North produced growing differences of outlook which tended to divide the nation and which had a profound influence on the South. While the economy of the North was industrialising, that of the South was relatively static; as the political and social institutions of the North were responding to this changing economic base, the institutions of the South continued to reflect the relatively static slave system upon which they were founded.[3]

[2]James McBride Dabbs, *The Southern Heritage.* New York, Alfred A. Knopf, 1959, p. 172.

[3]Ibid., pp. 174–5.

Slavery also had profound intellectual effects on Southern whites. While slave owners were a relatively small minority of the total white population in 1860, the values and interests of this class dominated the political life of the South. White supremacy arguments caused common whites increasingly to identify themselves with planters as the conflict between the North and the South over slavery grew. There were many reasons for this white unity in spite of the economic and social differences separating the whites from each other. In the first place, as Cash emphasised, the relatively free and easy life of the common white caused him to be unreflective or unanalytical and therefore blind to his real interests. In addition,

> If he had no worth-while interest at stake in slavery, if his real interest ran the other way about, he did nevertheless have that, to him, dear treasure of his superiority as a white man, which had been conferred on him by slavery; and so was as determined to keep the black man in chains, saw in the offensive of the Yankee as great a danger to himself, as the angriest planter.[4]

We must add to this the sectional pride and patriotism that tends to exist in any group under outside attack. Moreover, the common white's patriotism and identification with the planter was strengthened by his lack of class feeling and the contrast which his leaders painted between the Southern gentlemen (with whom he identified) and the crass, uncouth Yankee:

> For continually, from every stump, platform, and editorial sanctum, they gave him on the one hand the Yankee—as cowardly, avaricious, boorish, half Pantaloon and half Shylock—and on the other the Southerner—as polished, brave, generous, magnificent, wholly the stately aristocrat, fit to cow a dozen Yankees with the power of his eye and a cane—gave him these with the delicate implication that this Southerner was somehow any Southerner at random.[5]

The common whites hated the Negro because, though the latter was a slave, he frequently lived better than free whites, especially if the slave were a personal or stable servant and not a field hand. Moreover, the slaves in these preferred positions scarcely concealed their disdain for the 'po white trash' or 'po buckra'; a disdain which

[4]W. J. Cash, *The Mind of the South*, New York, Alfred A. Knopf, 1941, pp. 68–9.

[5]Ibid., p. 70.

angered the common whites all the more because it was made possible by the protection of powerful white men. The slave-owners' protection extended not only to the status which a few Negroes enjoyed but to the economic position which some of them occupied because of training given them by their masters. White men were thus forced to compete sometimes directly and always indirectly with slaves. Given the Southerner's well-documented tendency to violence during these days, there is little wonder that the Negro stood in great personal and economic jeopardy once he lost the protection of the slave-owner and Federal troops were removed from the region.

Reconstruction and Redemption[6]

The half century following the Civil War had tremendous importance for economic and social relations in the South and in the United States, because it was during this period that the South's economy readjusted itself to the abolition of the slave economy and Southern whites adjusted themselves to living with the Negro as a freedman.

The fundamental economic problem of the South after the Civil War was how to re-establish or reconstruct economic relations in an economy whose capital had been freed by emancipation and depleted by the War, and how to re-establish labour relations on some basis other than slave labour. The freedmen in some instances were so exhilarated by their new freedom that they refused to work. But this situation could not last long, because the freedman's dream that the Yankees would provide him with forty acres and a mule proved unfounded and he was forced to turn to his old masters and the sharecropping system for subsistence. The ambitious Negro's problems were also complicated by the obstacles to land ownership placed in his path; he had to find a white who was willing to sell him land and generally had to be acceptable to whites in the area before he could buy land. Negroes also had great difficulty improving their conditions by moving into urban areas because the rate of growth of non-agricultural industry in the South was very small until after 1880, and even then the Negro was generally excluded from most of the new non-agricultural occupations except for the generally disagreeable or low status jobs which were reserved for Negroes. The Negro's inferior education and low degree of skill also made it difficult for him to

[6]Reconstruction refers to that period of Federal control following the South's defeat in the Civil War (1860–65). Redemption refers to the resurgence of white Southern control after Northern troops were withdrawn from the South in 1877.

acquire good industrial jobs. Moreover, the planters and their political allies took measures to restrict the Negro's movements from agriculture in order to assure a continuous supply of agricultural labour; the so-called 'Black Codes' were ostensibly vagrancy laws, but had as one of their primary objectives the assurance of labour supplies for plantations. Finally, the share-croppers were frequently in debt to the planter and thus not allowed to leave the plantation until this debt was cleared. As we shall see, the disfranchisement of the freedman after 1890 made it virtually impossible for Negroes to improve their conditions through political action.

It would be very misleading, however, to leave the impression that the system established after the Civil War was entirely the fault of the planter. The planters themselves were impoverished by the War, which had also virtually destroyed the region's credit structure. Credit was therefore available to the planter only on very harsh terms from bankers or supply merchants, who sprang up throughout the region during these years. These merchants and financiers frequently had virtual monopolies in their areas, but they were also subject to harsh terms from Northern financiers because of the risks involved in cotton growing. Moreover, the suppliers of credit perpetuated cotton culture by insisting that their debtors restrict themselves to that commodity because it could be readily translated into money. But as cotton growing was extended to new areas of the world during the last quarter of the nineteenth century, and as men in the South tried to get money by growing more cotton, their economic conditions were worsened by falling prices.

The condition of Negroes and poorer whites was even worse than that of the planters. They were unfitted by training and inclination to meet the harsh conditions imposed by the Southern economy after the Civil War. They also had poorer lands, less credit or capital, and higher birth rates. Their rapid multiplication during the last quarter of the nineteenth century gave rise to increasing competition between Negro and white tenants and sharecroppers for declining positions on the land. Though the white croppers were given no better terms than their coloured competitors, there appears to have been little class feeling, since the planters were apparently considered public benefactors, while the white cropper's hatred and frustration was vented on his Negro competitor. Indeed, one motive for the Ku Klux Klan movement of these years was a desire by low-class whites to remove the Negro as a competitor, especially in the renting of land.[7]

The Negro was also restricted to certain kinds of jobs and where

[7]Dabbs, op. cit., p. 107.

unions existed was either excluded from membership or, where coloured workers were too numerous to be excluded (longshoremen, cement finishing, plastering, bricklaying, carpenters), was organised into racially segregated locals. Unions did not create the pattern of occupational segregation in these years, but were used by whites to restrict Negroes to certain kinds of jobs or to remove Negroes from jobs they had formerly held. Railroad unions took positive measures to remove Negroes from jobs like locomotive firemen, building trades unions generally restricted Negroes to work in Negro neighbourhoods, and the few unions in manufacturing plants negotiated contracts which restricted Negroes to certain menial jobs. In almost no case before the 1930s were Negroes and whites organised into the same unions and they almost never shared job opportunities equally, and union social events were apparently even more completely segregated.

It looked for a time during the 1880s and 1890s, however, as if Negroes and whites might forget their racial differences and be welded together politically and economically in the Knights of Labour and the Populist movement. The Knights of Labour were active in the region in the 1880s and emphasised, though they did not always accomplish, racial equality. The Knights' main Southern strength appears to have been among farmers who joined the Populist movement as the Knights declined in the 1890s, but the Knights also organised thousands of Southern workers in a variety of occupations and industries.[8] While Populism was not restricted to the South (it was a national agrarian movement which registered the farmer's dissatisfaction with financial interests, tariffs, and railroads), it profoundly influenced Southern politics. Indeed, for a time it appeared that the racial equalitarianism of the Populist movement would succeed in establishing a class movement. Ultimately, however, the Populists were defeated by the Negro votes controlled by conservative Democrats in the plantation belts. This political chicanery caused the Populists to drop equalitarianism in favour of disfranchising the Negro; they felt that a truly class movement could not be established until the Negro vote was removed from the control of white planters. Of course, other whites favoured disfranchising Negroes because the latter were able to exert considerable political influence as a balance of power when whites divided on purely economic grounds. The upshot was the gradual disfranchisement of the Negro through such devices as the

[8]See Frederic Meyers, 'The Knights of Labor in the South,' *Southern Economic Journal,* April, 1940, and F. Ray Marshall and Lamar B. Jones, 'Agricultural Unions in Louisiana', *Labor History, Fall, 1962.*

white primary, various voter qualifications which the Negro could not meet or which were applied only to him, and the poll tax.

Not only was the Negro disfranchised by the turn of the century, however, but the Democratic Party became the party of the South and Republicanism was equated with 'treason to race, country, God and Southern womanhood'. This one-party tradition elevated the race question to paramount importance in Southern politics; this issue filled the political void left by the absence of political opposition. Politicians realised the importance of the issue and, in an area where politics were a favourite pastime, competed with each other in their invitement of racial fears and prejudices, damaging the democratic fabric of the region's politics. Democracy was replaced by 'whitocracy'. As Cash put it; 'the . . . master class, freed from all chance of challenge or check, could and would go on more and more dealing with the government machinery of the South as their private property and sink deeper into the naïve and complacent assumption of their interest as the common interest.'[9]

Just as disfranchisement of Negroes did not occur immediately after the withdrawal of federal troops, it took some time for a rigid form of legal racial segregation to become the pattern in the South. Whether for fear of the return of Yankee troops or fear of the Negro vote, it was about a decade after the end of military occupation before the first segregation laws were passed. In Mississippi, Wharton found that saloons in Jackson served Negroes and whites at separate tables and the governors of Louisiana and South Carolina went on record in favour of protecting the Negroes' right to vote.[10]

Complete legal segregation became the accepted way of handling the race problem in the South by 1900, however, because of a number of circumstances, one of the most important of which was a general feeling in the South that a majority of Northern whites favoured segregation and second-class citizenship for the Negro and therefore would not send the troops back South. This conviction was supported by the segregation of the Negro in the Federal army and the refusal of many Northern states to enfranchise the Negro, even after they insisted that the South do so; the prevalence of segregation in the North; the acquiescence of Northerners in the political compromise of 1877, which resulted in the withdrawal of Federal troops; the use of race arguments by Northerners to support the adventures of the

[9]Op. cit. p. 33.

[10]Vernon L. Wharton, *The Negro in Mississippi*, 1877–80, Chapel Hill, The University of North Carolina Press, 1947; George B. Tendall, *South Carolina Negroes*, 1877–1900, Chapel Hill, University of North Carolina Press, 1952.

United States in the Pacific and Caribbean areas after 1898, making it difficult for them to counter the same arguments when used by Southerners against Negroes; and finally, a series of U.S. Supreme Court decisions between 1873 and 1898 establishing the legality of 'separate but equal facilities' and denying the Negro Federal protection for acts committed against him by private individuals.

By 1900, therefore, the Negro had become almost completely segregated by law or custom. He rode in separate compartments or in the back of public conveyances, went to segregated public schools, could not marry whites, was buried in segregated cemeteries, and ate in separate restaurants. Employment was also segregated and Negroes generally were frozen out of occupations they had formerly held and relegated to 'Negro' jobs in urban occupations. The jobs set aside for Negroes were usually the most disagreeable ones that whites would not take.

Industrialisation

While we have stressed the predominantly agricultural nature of the antebellum South, that region actually had achieved a significantly high level of industrialisation before cotton culture became the predominant economic characteristic of the region. In 1810, for example, the South produced 20 per cent of the value of manufactures in the United States—a proportion it has not since equalled. After 1810, however, agriculture absorbed the region's economic resources, almost halting the growth of manufacturing until after the Civil War.[11]

The 'New South' is usually defined in terms of the resurgence of manufacturing around 1880. By that time, the economic vicissitudes of cotton culture had convinced many Southerners that the region's economic salvation lay in industrialisation. While there were some who lamented the passing of the 'agrarian way of life', the drive to industrialise the South assumed almost religious proportions by the 1920s. The number of manufacturing wage earners increased by 109 per cent between 1880 and 1890, while the value of manufactured products increased by 111 per cent. Though the numbers of manufacturing workers did not increase so spectacularly in subsequent decades, they increased steadily until the depression of the 1930s, when manufacturing employment in the region was virtually constant. Decades of particularly marked increase in manufacturing employment were 1899–1909 (56 per cent) and 1890–99 (36 per cent). Thus,

[11]Bureau of Labor Statistics, U.S. Department of Labor, *Labor in the South,* Bulletin No. 898, 1946, p. 5.

the period from 1880–1910 was one of very rapid economic growth. Thereafter, the *number* of manufacturing wage earners did not increase so rapidly but there was a great increase in the value of manufactures in the region; the value of manufactures increased by 118 per cent between 1899 and 1909 and by 227 per cent between 1909 and 1919. The South's proportion of the wage earners in the United States was only 7.7 per cent in 1880 and its share of the value of the country's manufactures was only 5.9 per cent; the region's proportion of manufacturing wage earners increased steadily to 17.2 per cent and its value of manufactures to 14.5 per cent in 1939.

The early upsurge in manufacturing industry during the 1880s came mainly in the textile and tobacco industries of the Piedmont, but other important industries included the Birmingham, Alabama, iron and steel complex, forestry products, and cotton seed and its products.

The discovery of oil caused a great economic development in the South-west and the South's petroleum resources and abundant water supplies have greatly expanded the chemical industry in the region. Other industries came South to take advantage of timber and other resources, ports, labour supplies, and markets. Industrialisation was spurred by the establishment of military installations and war plants during World Wars I and II. Moreover, the development of the Tennessee Valley Authority during the 1930s caused a virtual transformation of that area while the installations were being built and because of the abundance of relatively cheap electricity it provided. Growing cities and rising incomes attracted additional industries, which came South to get nearer their markets. Improved economic conditions led to, as well as stimulated, better transportation and communications facilities tying the South closer to the rest of the United States, and tying rural towns closer to metropolitan areas. The growth of electricity and the automobile have been particularly important in the region since the 1930s, while the mechanisation of agriculture and Federal agricultural policies have greatly reduced the need for agricultural labour and virtually transformed many rural areas. In short, while the South's industrialisation cannot be classed as 'revolutionary' at any time, the changes have been steady and even rapid since World War II. Moreover, the economic growth produced rising incomes; the median *per capita* income in the South was only 55 per cent of that of the United States in 1929, but 60 per cent in 1939, 72 per cent in 1950 and 75 per cent in 1960. The median incomes of non-whites in the United States improved from 46.8 per cent of whites in 1949 to 50.9 per cent in 1959. In the South, though, the statistics reveal that non-whites generally lost relative to whites in these years; the Southern statistics are distorted, however, by the migration of more highly skilled Negroes out of the South. Construction was the only skilled craft in which non-whites increased faster than whites in the South, while they increased much faster than whites in every craft in the non-South.

The most striking change has been the decline in farms as a source of total income from 18.1 per cent in 1940, to 8.5 per cent in 1959, and the growing diversification of the region's economy.

Impact of Industrialisation

What has been the influence of all these changes on race relations in the region? They have probably had greater impacts than are clearly manifested on the surface, though it would be difficult to untangle those factors operating within the region from outside pressures. The rigid pattern of school segregation has been broken by U.S. Supreme Court decisions, but rural schools remain almost completely segregated. The Courts have also outlawed the 'white' primary, and the poll tax—which is really not a very important impediment to voting—remains in only five states. The various 'literacy' tests (which operate mainly to bar Negroes) and overt intimidation remain important obstacles in many areas, but are being challenged at this writing by the Federal Government.[12] Negroes are able to register and vote in the major cities of the South with little difficulty; Negro registration will undoubtedly become even more important in view of the U.S. Supreme Court's 1962 ruling that state legislatures can no longer ignore constitutional requirements concerning re-apportion. . . .

There are some other evidences of desegregation in the South: military installations have been desegregated throughout the region, as has Federal employment generally; interstate transportation has been ordered desegregated, though some facilities in fact remain segregated in the deep South; some restaurants and lunch counters in various cities are desegregated, as are some athletic events; and desegregation has been accomplished in some hotels in border areas, and a few churches. While many local unions of skilled craftsmen and railroad workers continue to exclude Negroes from membership, every national union except two on the railroads (the independent Order of Railway Conductors and Brotherhood of Locomotive Engineers) has

[12]For a more detailed summary of these decisions and the current status of discrimination in various areas based on the *Report of The United States Commission on Civil Rights,* see Wallace Mendelson, *Discrimination,* Englewood Cliffs, New Jersey, Prentice-Hall, Inc., 1962.

removed the formal colour bar from its constitution and these unions must remove their colour bars or face prosecution under the Civil Rights Act of 1964. Segregated locals have rarely been formed in the South since World War II and a number of segregated locals have been integrated since World War II; almost all of the unions organised in the South by the Congress of Industrial Organisations (CIO) after 1938 were on an integrated basis wherever Negroes existed in the industries. Only in exceptional cases, like the United Packinghouse Workers, have unions actively promoted job integration, and while integrated union social affairs are still rare, they are by no means non-existent and seem to be held with increasing frequency since World War II. In short, while racial segregation is still the predominant form of race relations in the South, the extent of segregation is now much less than it was in 1900 and there is evidence that change will be even more rapid in the future. The violence accompanying the admission of a Negro to the University of Mississippi in September, 1962, seems to have had a sobering effect on leaders in other states, many of whom have announced that they would integrate peacefully in order to avoid having 'another Mississippi' in their states; the less violent but unruly integration of public schools at Little Rock, Arkansas, had a similar effect. Indeed, Governor Terry Sanford of North Carolina has even come out publicly against racial discrimination in employment.

While we can trace the South's transformation from a relatively rural area to one that is largely urban and 'industrialised' and examine the changes in the race relations in the area during these years, it is much more difficult to establish the precise causal relations between these phenomena. Our discussion of these relations must therefore be based more on speculation than we would like it to be. This is not only because of the difficulties involved in establishing precise causation, but also because of the difficulties involved in isolating the many complex relations changing and perpetuating race relations in the South. The best we can do therefore is to present a general discussion of the various factors that appear to be working to change race relations without attempting to assign relative weights to each factor.

Many writers have emphasized the impact of industrialisation on social relations, especially the incompatibility of a caste or static social system with the dynamism and rationalism of industrial societies. For instance, Kerr, Dunlop, Harbison and Myers, concluded in their recent study that 'The industrial society tends to be an open society, inconsistent with the assignment of workers to occupations or to jobs by traditional caste, racial groups, by sex or by family status'.[13] These writers emphasise that industrialisation introduces rational planning which tends to destroy static societies. Economic efficiency becomes important, and, theoretically, industrialisers tend to value people more for their individual abilities than their race or social status. An industrial society requires an increasingly highly qualified work force, so the role of education changes from the promotion of tradition to preparing for the future, and agriculture becomes simply another industry, not a way of life.

While these tendencies might be at work in the South, they would appear to have produced very gradual changes in occupational race relations. Indeed, the first significant industries in the South (textiles) were designed to give employment mainly to whites, and other industries in the region have placed Negroes in menial occupations regardless of their education and ability. Northern manufacturers, with rare exceptions like the International Harvester Company, have tended to follow local racial employment practices in their Southern branches. And as we have seen, trade unions tended to segregate Negroes in the South, or exclude them from membership entirely.

This is not to argue, however, that these rigid racial employment patterns were entirely impervious to market forces. During labour shortages, such as those of World War II, Negroes moved into some previously all-white jobs, and Negroes have lost 'Negro' jobs when the latter became attractive to whites because of technological improvements or economic recession.

Moreover, job segregation has not been entirely detrimental to Negroes, because in some industries coloured workers have been able to maintain their positions and have had some relatively high-paying jobs reserved for them. The main market forces establishing these patterns seem to have been the supply of labour and the extent to which job technology changed. Negroes were able to maintain their positions in such jobs as longshoring, bricklaying, cement finishing, and plastering because they had sufficient supplies of labour to meet the requirements of employers who were boycotted by whites; construction employers are easily boycotted because of the casual nature of the work, and whites have frequently threatened to strike if manufacturing employers move Negroes into new jobs. Negroes have also been able to perpetuate themselves in these occupations in the South because the techniques have changed relatively little, making it im-

[13]Clark Kerr, Frederick Harbison, John T. Dunlop and Charles Myers, *Industrialism and Industrial Man*, Cambridge, Mass., Harvard University Press, 1960, p. 35.

possible for whites to monopolise the better jobs by denying Negroes access to training in more modern techniques.

While employers seem to prefer whites to Negroes at the same wages, they favour Negroes for certain low status jobs in the South because they cannot depend upon whites to remain in these jobs when alternatives become available; Negroes are more dependable because racial discrimination prevents Negroes from leaving these low status jobs. There was a time when employers preferred Negroes because the latter would not join unions, but this was changed during the social ferment of the 1930s, especially when the formation of the CIO caused the Negro community to assume a more pro-union position. Employers also have certain stereotyped ideas concerning the desirability of Negroes for certain jobs. Thus, some employers prefer Negroes for jobs requiring great strength, subject to intense heat, or requiring other traits which they think Negroes possess. On balance, of course, these stereotypes work against Negroes, restricting them to the more undesirable jobs. And while the pattern of racial employment has changed some in the years since World War II, the *basic* pattern remains virtually unchanged.[14] It should also be made clear, of course, that the Negro's economic position is not due entirely to direct discrimination by unions and employers but also to the Negro's lower education and training; cultural and family factors which limit job knowledge and aspirations; and the relatively slow process of occupational improvement, even in the absence of discrimination.

[14]Vivian W. Henderson concluded, concerning the employment situation for Negroes in Nashville, Tennessee, that when Negroes were employed above the unskilled level it was mainly in the Negro community and that 80 per cent of the Negroes in Nashville were in menial, unskilled occupations. He found, further, that there were very few Negroes in manufacturing jobs, that 80 per cent of the unskilled jobs in Nashville were held by Negroes, that Negroes were not employed as managers, clerks, or supervisors in bus companies though Negroes furnish the most lucrative markets for the companies. He noted, however, that Negroes were hired as bus drivers in Nashville in 1960. Most Nashville Negroes also attended segregated schools and vocational training was available to them only in jobs they customarily held. The white school offered courses in electronics, IBM, refrigeration, air conditioning, drafting, radio, television and electronics. The Negro school offered courses in tailoring, bricklaying, cabinetmaking, and diversified occupations to include cook, maid, maintenance and dietetics. ('Employment Opportunity for Nashville Negroes', Community Conference on Employment Opportunity, Fisk University, 22–23 April 1960.)

Negroes were concentrated disproportionately in the lower job classifications in companies like International Harvester, which has one of the most equalitarian racial positions of any company in the South. In a study of three Harvester plants in the South, John Hope II found that 'Except in one maintenance shop at the Louisville works, the plants have not employed Negro journeymen or journeymen's helpers in the apprenticeable trades, nor have they enrolled Negroes in

Thus, while industrialisation might *tend* to produce relatively 'rational' behaviour, this does not necessarily mean that race or status will become irrelevant in employer decisions or that racial occupation patterns will disappear very rapidly. The Southern experience suggests that employers will use Negroes where this is advantageous to them (lower wages, anti-union, dependable supply), but that the usual situation has been for them to discriminate against Negroes because of racial prejudices, fear of the reaction of white workers or the white community, or an abundance of white labour. The evidence suggests, therefore, that non-market forces are required to break racial occupational barriers.

There are a number of these forces external to the economic decision-making process tending to change race relations. A factor of great significance has been the equalitarian principles upon which the country was founded and which have been imputed to the Constitution by the U.S. Supreme Court.

company-sponsored apprentice programmes'. ('3 Southern Plants of International Harvester Company', in *Selected Studies of Negro Employment in the South*, Washington, National Planning Association, 1955.)

In '4 Studies of Negro Employment in the Upper South' (in ibid.) Donald Dewey found that not only were Negroes restricted largely to unskilled or menial jobs for the most part, but that the pattern had remained fairly constant before and after World War II. (See also Donald Dewey, 'Negro Employment in Southern Industry', *Journal of Political Economy*, August 1952.)

Similarly, in 'Negro Employment in the Birmingham Metropolitan Areas', (in *Selected Studies of Negro Employment in the South*), Langston Hawley found that a great majority of Negroes were located in unskilled and semi-skilled jobs and in personal and building service occupations and that 'For the most part, both the occupations filled by Negroes and the nature of the work required was found to have been remarkably stable since 1939' (p. 247).

William H. Wesson's study of 'Negro Employment Practices in the Chattanooga Area', (in ibid.) found that 18.3 per cent of the 2,376 Negro workers surveyed in that area were in skilled jobs, but that these were mainly in foundry work or in the trowel trades in construction. Wesson found strong regional industry and company biases against using Negroes in higher occupational categories outside these traditional areas.

The '1961 Report of the United States Commission on Civil Rights' concluded that 'Although their occupational levels have risen considerably during the past 20 years, Negro workers continue to be concentrated in the less skilled jobs. And it is largely because of this concentration in the ranks of the unskilled and semi-skilled, the groups most severely affected by both economic layoffs and technological changes, that Negroes are also disproportionately represented among the unemployed' (*Employment* p. 153).

Recent studies by the Southern Regional Council in Chattanooga, Atlanta, Miami, and Houston, confirm the Negro's concentration in low-paying jobs and that discrimination in opportunities for education and training tend to perpetuate this pattern.

Another important factor has undoubtedly been the growing importance of urban and Negro voters. There has been a decline in racial demagoguery in those Southern states and cities where large proportions of Negroes have registered to vote and where industrialisation tends to divide whites along economic lines. Sometimes Negroes form potent political alliances with other minorities, such as Spanish-speaking citizens of the South-west and the trade unions which become more important as the region industrialises.[15] Indeed, the political future of the South (and the United States) could well depend upon what happens to such alliances as the region industrialises and the Negro vote becomes more important.

We have noted the decisions of the U.S. Supreme Court which tend to promote equal opportunities for Negroes, but governmental efforts on the Negro's behalf have not been restricted to the judiciary, since the Federal executive branch has also adopted a number of policies to eliminate segregation and discrimination. In 1948 the United States Army was ordered desegregated, so that Southerners in the armed forces serve with Negroes and sometimes under coloured officers. Moreover, Federal employment in the South has been desegregated and Negroes serve on an equal basis with whites in Federal employment throughout the region. Equal employment policies for private employers contracting with the Federal Government have been adopted by every American President since 1940 and these policies have been implemented with increasing vigour by each succeeding administration. As Federal expenditures become more important in the region, the Government's power to promote equal job opportunities for Negroes will grow. To date, however, the implementation of equal employment opportunities for Federal contracts has had limited success because Congress has refused to give the policy legislative support, requiring the Presidents to create less powerful agencies by executive orders.

In spite of these limitations of the Federal contracts programmes, they have been used by Negro groups—particularly the National Association for the Advancement of Coloured People—to break down job segregation in such Southern industries as petroleum refining, pulp and paper manufacturing, aircraft and automobiles, construction, rubber products, telephones, and food processing. The Committee on Equal Employment Opportunities (PCEEO) created by President Kennedy has created the impression that for the first time contracts

[15]For discussions of this point see Ray Marshall, 'Some Factors Influencing Union Racial Practices', *Proceedings of the Industrial Relations Research Association,* 1961; and idem., 'Union Racial Problems in the South', *Industrial Relations,* May 1962.

might be denied (or lost) because of racial discrimination. The future impact of the programme could well depend upon how much this impression becomes a reality. The PCEEO created considerable excitement among Southern employers in 1962 when it announced that contracts would not be renewed with several specific firms because of their racial policies. This action caused some Southern firms to step up their activities to recruit Negroes, especially in the technical categories.

These Federal policies were themselves less important than the forces which caused them, however; after all, we have always had the equalitarian creed, but after the Civil War the North compromised its position and left the Southern states to disfranchise the Negro. A number of forces intervened, however, to change Federal policies. Of particular importance was the migration of Negroes out of the South and to urban areas North and South.[16] Negroes did not find an end to segregation in Southern cities, but they did find that their political power was greater, because in the cities it became more difficult to keep them from voting by extralegal intimidation. Moreover, in urban areas Negroes made their political power effective through coalitions with other groups. At the national level, Negro concentration in key states made the Negro vote a powerful force in national elections.

A number of other factors in urban environments make it possible for Negroes to improve their economic position. In the first place, a Negro professional class has grown up to serve the Negro communities, and give leadership to Negro movements. A number of significant Negro publications serve this community, making it possible to rally Negro opinion on specific issues. Negro leaders have likewise been strengthened by the importance of the race question in international affairs. Federal officials have sought to avoid embarrassment on this issue in their efforts to gain the support of the emerging non-white nations of Africa and Asia. The speed of communications throughout the world, brought about by industrialisation, makes it possible for Negro leaders to apply such moral pressures to governmental officials because racial incidents in the United States become known immediately over vast areas of the globe.

Industrialisation exerts other influences on racial attitudes in the South. Rising incomes and educational levels tend to reduce racial fears and prejudices. Radio and television facilities are changing the

[16]See Henry Allen Bullock, 'Urbanism and Race Relations', in *The Urban South,* edited by Rupert B. Nance and Nicholas J. Demerath, Chapel Hill, The University of North Carolina Press, 1954, p. 20.

traditional Southern stereotypes of the Negro's inferior status; these communications innovations have penetrated to the remotest rural area, broken the informational monopolies exercised in many of these communities by local media, and brought Southerners in touch with racial sentiments prevailing in the larger American community. Industrialisation has also brought better roads, automobiles, and other transportation improvements, which have dissolved the plantation economy, while mechanisation and federal agricultural policies have reduced the planter's demand for labour, causing migration out of agriculture and out of rural areas.

Industrialisation has also influenced the attitudes of Southern white community leaders. There has been growing awareness by the region's business leaders that the pressures on the Federal Government are such that it will press for integration of employment and public facilities. They also realise that Federal contracts are going to be permanent and important elements in the economic situation. Moreover, the region's motive to improve the economy by 'balancing agriculture with industry' has forced leaders to consider the impact of race relations on industrialisation. It is, for example, becoming increasingly apparent to Southern leaders that racial violence—especially if it appears to be incited by public officials—will repel industry, not only by creating a fear of destruction of physical property or boycotts, but also by producing images of public officials as irrational people; prospective industrialists are likely to feel that such leaders are too radical and that their areas are too risky. Employers who need to attract highly trained technical personnel have been especially concerned about the difficulties involved in getting these skilled workers to go South at a time when there were dangers of racial conflict—or that public schools might be closed if forced to accept Negroes.

The impact of overt violence on industrialisation is difficult to establish with precision, but that racial conflict has in fact impeded industrialisation seems to be generally accepted by the Southern business community. There are, however, more subtle and less obvious incompatibilities between industrialisation and the South's traditional political, economic and social structure, and it is becoming increasingly obvious to Southern leaders that industrialisation will not only change the region's traditional values, but that those values must be changed before its full economic potential can be realised. These relationships have been very convincingly analysed by W. H. Nicholls, Professor of Economics at Vanderbilt University.[17] Nicholls

[17] *Southern Tradition and Regional Progress,* Chapel Hill, The University of North Carolina Press, 1960.

shows that the South's tradition is a barrier to economic development in the following ways: agrarianism has caused a disproportionate amount of the region's resources to be channelled into agriculture and has produced attitudes which are incompatible with the disciplined work required in an industrial society; the South's rigid social structure has made for a 'backward looking, pessimistic, and static outlook', has made the region's upper classes 'accept as normal and inevitable socio-economic arrangements based on a disproportionate number of low-income people, arrangements made tolerable to lower-income rural whites by a social structure which at least clearly supported their claims to superiority over the Negro', and has impaired the development of Southern cities; the South's undemocratic political structure has impeded economic growth by 'embracing a negative and defensive States' Rights doctrine' and a 'blind sectionalism'; has 'kept the masses of Southern people, white and Negro, in relative ignorance in a world in which knowledge and skills are increasingly the key to both personal and social betterment', and has produced 'the intellectually debilitating effects of the Southern tradition of conformity of thought and behaviour'. In short, whether or not the South should have the economic progress to which a majority of its leaders seem committed is a value judgment, but that the region cannot have economic progress *and* its traditional political and social values seems well established.

Union leaders, especially in the state labour councils, have generally adopted equalitarian racial positions; indeed, some of the first integrated meetings attended by Negroes in the South were sponsored by unions. The state federations, despite the continued discrimination by some of their affiliates, especially craft organisations on the railroads and in the building trades, have frequently exerted their influence in favour of equal rights for Negroes.[18]

Southern politicians have taken note of the developments noted above, though many of them still keep the race issue alive as a potent, though weakening, political device, in a one-party area. But the racial demagogue tends to disappear as Negroes register to vote in greater numbers, whites overcome some of their racial fears and prejudices as they improve their economic and education positions, urbanisation grows and legislatures are forced to give urban voters more equal representation, unions become more important and form political alliances with Negroes and other minorities, and the two-party system becomes increasingly important. Moreover, a few Southern politicians

[18]See Ray Marshall, *The Negro and Organized Labor,* New York, London and Sydney, John Wiley and Sons, 1965.

with national political aspirations already exhibit increasing weariness with racial stances which isolate them from the mainstream of American politics.

Summary and Conclusions

In conclusion, we have seen that a pattern of racial segregation became established in the South between the abolition of slavery during the Civil War and 1900, but that industrialisation and other factors have tended slowly to erode this pattern of rigid segregation. Especially important factors include: the migration of Negroes out of rural areas into cities, where they have greater political and economic power; the importance of racial discrimination as an issue in international politics; the growing economic, political and social integration of the country with improved transportation and communications, the extension of Northern firms into the South and the ferment associated with World War II; and the growing importance of the Federal Government (where Negroes have considerable influence) on the Southern economy. While the South remains basically a segregated region, there has been a limited amount of de-segregation and there is evidence that the foregoing factors are accelerating this trend. As might be expected, of course, the Negro's *legal* position has changed much more rapidly than his actual condition, because the latter is determined by a host of economic and social factors which change very slowly.

TABLE I

MEDIAN YEARS OF SCHOOLING, BY RACE,
SOUTH AND SELECTED NON-SOUTHERN STATES
1960

Southern States	Whites	Non-Whites	Selected Non-Southern States	Whites	Non-Whites
Louisiana	10.5	6.0	Massachusetts	11.6	10.3
Alabama	10.2	6.5	Michigan	11.0	9.1
Georgia	10.3	6.1	Minnesota	10.8	9.9
Florida	11.6	7.0	Iowa	11.3	9.5
Arkansas	9.5	6.5	Indiana	10.9	9.0
Mississippi	11.0	6.0	Connecticut	11.1	9.1
Texas	10.8	8.1	Colorado	12.1	11.2
Kentucky	8.7	8.2	Oregon	11.8	9.9
North Carolina	9.8	7.0	S. Dakota	10.5	8.6
Tennessee	9.0	7.5	Rhode Island	10.0	9.5
South Carolina	10.3	5.9	Pennsylvania	10.3	8.9
Oklahoma	10.7	8.6	Utah	12.2	10.1
Virginia	10.8	7.2	Washington	12.1	10.5
			Wisconsin	10.4	9.0
			Wyoming	12.1	9.3

Source: U.S. Census, 1960.

TABLE II

INDUSTRIAL COMPOSITION OF CIVILIAN INCOME RECEIVED FOR PARTICIPATION IN CURRENT PRODUCTION, SOUTH AND UNITED STATES, 1940-1959
(Nos. in Millions)

	Total	Farms	Mining	Contract Construc- tion	Mfg.	Whole- Sale and Retail Trade	Finance Ins. and Real Estate	Trans- portation	Com- munica- tions Pub. Util.	Services	Govern- ment	Other
1940												
South	10,986	1,992	401	490	1,834	2,109	368	738	219	1,240	1,538	57
% of Total	100.0	18.1	3.7	4.5	16.7	19.2	3.3	6.7	2.0	11.3	14.0	0.5
United States	62,851	5,603	1,367	2,444	16,320	12,920	2,892	3,972	1,607	7,706	7,847	173
% of Total	100.0	8.9	2.2	3.9	26.0	20.6	4.6	6.3	2.6	12.3	12.5	0.3
Non-South	51,865	3,611	966	1,954	14,486	10,811	2,524	3,234	1,388	6,466	6,309	116
% of Total	100.0	7.0	1.9	3.8	27.9	20.8	4.9	6.2	2.7	12.5	12.2	0.2
1950												
South	35,337	5,212	1,248	2,311	7,160	7,489	1,177	2,163	826	3,877	3,737	137
% of Total	100.0	14.7	3.5	6.5	20.3	21.2	3.3	6.1	2.3	11.0	10.6	0.4
United States	180,945	16,020	3,567	10,736	52,870	37,926	7,031	10,618	4,459	20,062	16,999	567
% of Total	100.0	8.8	2.0	5.9	29.2	21.0	3.9	5.9	2.5	11.1	9.4	0.3
Non-South	145,608	10,808	2,319	8,425	45,710	30,437	5,854	8,455	3,723	16,185	13,262	430
% of Total	100.0	7.4	1.6	5.8	31.4	21.0	4.0	5.8	2.6	11.1	9.1	0.3

TABLE II (continued)

	Total	Farms	Mining	Contract Construction	Mfg.	Wholesale and Retail Trade	Finance Ins. and Real Estate	Transportation	Communications Pub. Util.	Services	Government	Other
1959												
South	62,322	5,322	1,944	4,484	13,919	12,799	3,003	3,324	1,697	7,386	8,196	248
% of Total	100.0	8.5	3.1	7.2	22.3	20.5	4.8	5.3	2.7	11.9	13.2	0.4
United States	303,798	14,722	4,402	20,197	91,795	59,634	15,204	15,452	8,502	37,771	35,108	1,011
% of Total	100.0	4.8	1.5	6.6	30.2	19.6	5.0	5.1	2.8	12.4	11.6	0.3
Non-South	241,476	9,400	2,458	15,713	77,876	46,835	12,201	12,128	6,805	30,385	26,912	763
% of Total	100.0	3.9	1.0	6.5	32.2	19.5	5.1	5.0	2.8	12.6	11.1	0.3

Sources: 1940, 1950, Personal Income by States since 1929
1959, Survey of Current Business, August 1960

TABLE

NON-WHITE MALE CRAFT EMPLOYMENT[1] -
NON-WHITE SHARE OF TOTAL U.S.[4] NON-WHITE

SOUTH

	Total		*Non-White*		*Percentage Non-White of South*	
	1950	1960	1950	1960	1950	1960
Foremen (n.e.c.)[6]	185,697	277,369	3,544	5,504	1.90	1.98
Mechanics and Repairmen[7]	439,312	617,538	34,660	53,051	7.88	8.59
Metal Craftsmen[8]	157,671	178,465	9,670	8,153	6.13	4.57
Construction Craftsmen[9]	750,027	787,727	76,416	89,552	10.19	11.37
Other Craftsmen[10]	259,639	429,503	18,900	28,352	7.28	6.60
TOTAL	1,752,406	2,290,602	143,190	184,612	8.17	8.06

[1]Figures compiled from: Census of the Population: 1950, U.S. Department of Commerce, Bureau of the Census, Vol. II, Gen. Social and Economic Characteristics, By State Table 77–'Detailed Characteristics–Role and Class of Worker of Employed Persons, by Occupation and Sex, for the [each one individually] State and for Standard Metropolitan Areas of 100,000 or more; 1950 Census of Population; U.S. Department of Commerce Bureau of the Census, Vol. II–General Social and Economic Characteristics, By State, Table 58–'Occupation Group of Employed Persons By Colour and Sex, for the State, Urban and Rural: 1960.'

[2]South is defined as including Alabama, Arkansas, Delaware, District of Columbia, Florida, Georgia, Kentucky, Louisiana, Maryland, Missouri, North Carolina, Oklahoma, South Carolina, Tennessee, Texas, Virginia and West Virginia.

[3]Non-South is defined as including all other states except Alaska and Hawaii.

[4]U.S. is defined as including all states except Alaska and Hawaii.

[5]Non-White includes Negro, Indian, and Oriental.

[6]Same as 1940 census–foremen 'not elsewhere classified' (n.e.c.).

[7]Same as 1940 census.

[8]Includes: blacksmiths, forgemen, hammermen, boilermakers, machinists and job setters, millwrights, moulders, tinsmiths, coppersmiths, sheet metal workers, tool makers, die makers, and setters. 1960 figures

III

SOUTH[2] AND NON-SOUTH[3] AND SOUTHERN EMPLOYMENT[5] - 1950 AND 1960

NON-SOUTH

TOTAL		*Non-White*		*Percentage Non-White of South*		*Total U.S. Non-White*		*Percentage Southern of Total U.S. White*	
1950	1960	1950	1960	1950	1960	1950	1960	1950	1960
548,481	815,177	5,768	12,365	1.05	1.52	9,312	17,869	38.1	30.8
1,180,857	1,568,041	38,194	71,513	3,23	4.56	72,854	124,564	47.6	42.6
798,258	919,087	17,295	28,980	2.17	3.15	26,965	37,133	35.9	22.0
1,553,677	1,600,813	37,331	47,782	2.40	2.98	113,747	137,334	67.2	65.2
836,622	1,254,405	17,030	34,732	2.04	2.77	35,930	63,084	52.6	44.9
4,917,895	6,157,523	115,618	195,372	2.35	3.17	258,808	379,984	55.3	48.6

also include heat treaters, metal rollers and roller hands which were classified in the 1950 'other' category.

[9]Includes: masons, tile setters, carpenters, electricians, painters, paperhangers, plasterers and cement finishers, plumbers and pipefitters and structural metal workers. Cranemen, hoistmen and construction machine operators have been substituted in the 1950 figures for the 1960 classification of excavating, grading, and road machine operators. Glaziers and stone cutters, including under 'construction' in 1950, are found in the category of 'other craftsmen' in 1960.

[10]Includes: bakers, compositors and typesetters, locomotive engineers and firemen, pressmen, bookbinders, cabinet makers, engravers, furriers, goldsmiths, inspectors, jewellers, lens grinders and polishers, log and lumber scalers and graders, millers, motion picture projectionists, opticians, piano and organ tuners and repairmen, shoemakers (except in factories), silversmiths, tailors, telegraph and telephone linemen and servicemen, upholsterers, watchmakers, and window dressers. The 1950 figures also include heat treaters, annealers and temperers, metal rollers and roll hands, roofers and slaters, craftsmen and kindred workers (not elsewhere classified), and members of the armed forces whereas the 1960 figures contain cranemen, derrickmen, electrotypes, glaziers, lithographers, loom fixers, plate printers, stereotypes, stone carvers, and stone cutters.

TABLE IV

NEGRO VOTER REGISTRATION IN THE SOUTH
1952-1962

States	Negroes Registered To Vote		Negroes as a Percentage of Total Voters Registration		Negroes as a Percentage of Population
	1952	1962	1952	1962	1960
Alabama	25,000	90,000	4	9	30
Arkansas	61,000	75,000	11	13	22
Florida	121,000	195,000	10	11	18
Georgia	145,000	185,000	11	14	29
Louisiana	120,000	152,000	12	14	25
Mississippi	20,000	24,000	5	6	42
North Carolina	100,000	211,000	6	11	25
South Carolina	80,000	91,000	13	19	35
Tennessee	85,000	185,000	6	11	17
Texas	182,000	280,000	8	14	13
Virginia	69,000	110,000	9	10	21

Source: Estimates based on official records, reports of the Southern Regional Council, other data: as reported in U. S. News & World Report, 10 December 1962.

A Century of Change: Negroes in the U. S. Economy, 1860-1960

Marion Hayes

[*From the* Monthly Labor Review, *December 1962.*]

When the Emancipation Proclamation went into effect on January 1, 1863, most Americans lived in the country, and lived by farming. One of the sharpest changes in the hundred years since then has been the move from farm to town for a livelihood, a break that was even sharper for Negroes than for whites. With the trend to the city have come gains for Negroes in health and education, in occupation level and income; these are the changes traced here.[1]

Population

In most decades since 1860, Negroes increased in number less rapidly than whites; in the last 30 years, however, the trend has changed. Negroes are estimated to have constituted 14 percent of the population in 1860, but were only 9.7 percent in 1930. By 1960, a relative recovery raised their number to 10.6 percent of the population. During the century ending in 1960, Negroes are believed to have increased in number 325 percent; whites, 489 percent. Negroes have formed the following percentages of the U.S. population:

Year	Percent	Year	Percent
1860	14.1	1920	9.9
1870	13.5	1930	9.7
1880	13.1	1940	9.8
1890	11.9	1950	10.0
1900	11.6	1960	10.6
1910	10.7		

Source: U. S. Bureau of Census, decennial censuses.

The recent faster increase in numbers of Negroes than of whites is due in large measure to a drop in the Negro death rate. The birth rate has long been higher among Negroes than among whites, but a higher death rate reduced or held constant the proportion of Negroes

[1]As Negroes constitute about 95 percent of the nonwhite population, information for all nonwhites is used where data are not available for Negroes alone.

Alaska and Hawaii are excluded throughout.

in the population. However, health measures, particularly those that led to near eradication of tuberculosis and typhoid and to big reductions in the deaths of mothers, infants, and children, have brought the overall Negro death rate to a point little above the rate for whites. Death rates from tuberculosis, for example, were three times as high among nonwhites in 1910 as among whites. By 1960, rates for nonwhites were still higher, but the rates for both groups had been cut about 97 percent—from 444.5 per 100,000 population to 13.2 for nonwhites and from 145.9 to 5.1 for whites. The years from 1940 to 1960 showed especially rapid progress.

Nonwhites' life expectancy at birth has risen in this century much more rapidly than that of whites: 28.4 years for nonwhite as compared with 20.7 for white men, and 32.7 years for nonwhite as against 25.2 for white women. But white males and females, in 1959, could still look for 6.4 and 7.7 more years of life than nonwhites. The latter had arrived by 1959 at about the longevity average attained by whites in 1940.

In early years, both Negroes and whites lived mainly in the country; the 1890 census found 80 percent of Negroes and over 60 percent of whites in rural areas (Chart 1). Both races have since shown, decade by decade, a preference for town life; the shift by Negroes has been even more rapid than that by whites. By 1960, about 30 percent of whites but only 27 percent of Negroes still lived in rural districts; only 8 percent of nonwhites lived on farms. Seventy-three percent of Negroes were now urban and 27 percent were rural residents, an exact reversal of the percentages in 1910.[2]

The past century has seen Negroes spread from the South to the North and West. The move began slowly (chart 2). In 1860, 92 percent of Negroes lived in the South; 50 years later, in 1910, 89 percent were still in the South (Table 1). By 1960, the percentage was 60.

The periods of rapid migration of Negroes were the World War I decade, the 1920's, and the years during and after World War II. According to observers, a need for laborers in the North—as the first war put a stop to immigration from Europe—joined with the Negroes' dissatisfaction with social and economic conditions in the South to produce the migration. Better wages offered in the North were the immediate inducement. One study indicated that about half the mi-

[2]Although the definition of urban has varied from one census to another, differences are not sufficient to invalidate the picture drawn here. In general, "urban" has meant residence in a place of 2,500 population or more.

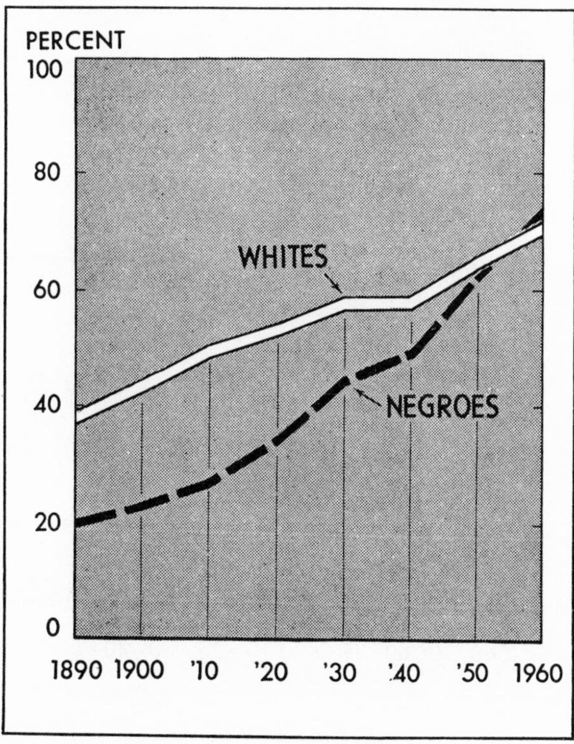

Chart 1: Percent of Population in Urban Areas 1890–1960

grants came from southern towns and mines, rather than from farms, their places then being taken by farm workers.[3]

Few Negroes went to Western States before the 1940's and 1950's; even then, the chief movement continued to be to the North. By 1960, 34 percent of the Negroes were in Northern and nearly 6 percent in Western States.

In the half century ending in 1960, the Negro population of the United States increased 92 percent, but less than 3 percent of the increase took place in the five Southern States which had had the largest Negro populations in 1910; nearly half the increase occurred in the States of New York, Illinois, California, Pennsylvania, and Ohio.

Negroes leaving the rural South, where nearly three-fourths lived

[3]Charles S. Johnson, "The Changing Economic Status of the Negro," *Annals* of the American Academy of Political and Social Science, November, 1928, p. 130; James H. Dillard, *Negro Migration in 1916-17* (U.S. Department of Labor, Division of Negro Economics, 1919), pp. 11-12.

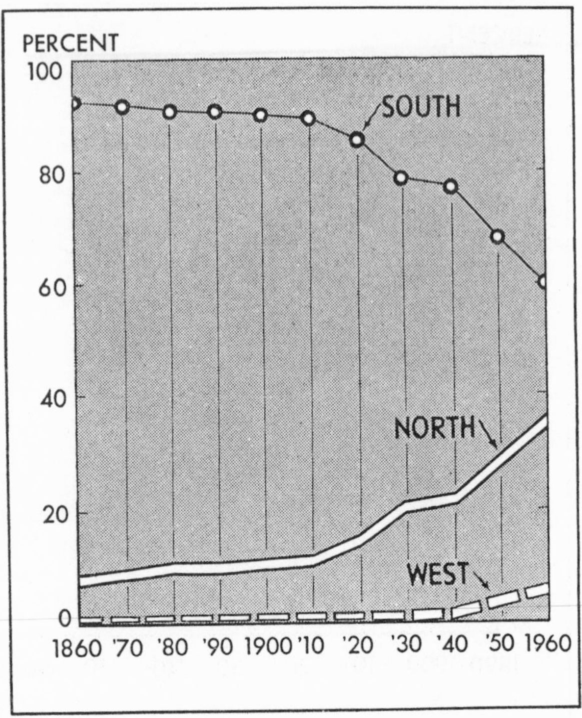

Chart 2: Negro Population in Each Region as Percent of U.S. Negro Population, 1860–1960

in 1900, went to towns and cities, both southern and northern; by 1960, only one-fourth remained in southern rural areas. More than a third were in southern, and 38 percent were in northern or western urban areas. Practically none had gone to northern or western farms.

Education

In education, as elsewhere, the problems of today would have surprised citizens of a century ago. In 1870, when most of the U.S. population lived on farms, less than 60 percent of children of all races aged 5 to 17 were in school. The move to the cities brought more time for school.

For Negroes particularly, the problem at first was basic elementary education. In 1863, about 90 percent were illiterate; at the end of 50 years, 38 percent; in 1947, 11 percent; and by 1960, possibly 5 percent.

TABLE I

PERCENT DISTRIBUTION OF NEGROES, BY REGION,[1] 1860-1960

Year	United States	North	South	West
1860 . . .	100.0	7.7	92.2	0.1
1870 . . .	100.0	8.4	91.0	.1
1880 . . .	100.0	9.3	90.5	.2
1890 . . .	100.0	9.4	90.3	.4
1900 . . .	100.0	10.0	89.7	.3
1910 . . .	100.0	10.5	89.0	.5
1920 . . .	100.0	14.1	85.2	.8
1930 . . .	100.0	20.3	78.7	1.0
1940 . . .	100.0	21.7	77.0	1.3
1950 . . .	100.0	28.2	68.0	3.8
1960 . . .	100.0	34.3	60.0	5.7

[1] The regions consist of the following States: South—Delaware, Maryland, District of Columbia, Virginia, West Virginia, North Carolina, South Carolina, Georgia, Florida, Kentucky, Tennessee, Alabama, Mississippi, Arkansas, Louisiana, Oklahoma, Texas; North—Maine, New Hampshire, Vermont, Massachusetts, Rhode Island, Connecticut, New York, New Jersey, Pennsylvania, Ohio, Indiana, Illinois, Michigan, Wisconsin, Minnesota, Iowa, Missouri, North Dakota, South Dakota, Nebraska, Kansas; West—Montana, Idaho, Wyoming, Colorado, New Mexico, Arizona, Utah, Nevada, Washington, Oregon, California.

Source: U.S. Bureau of the Census: Historical Statistics of the United States, Colonial Times to 1957, pp. 11-12; Statistical Abstract of the United States, 1961, pp. 24, 30.

Many early schools for Negroes in the South, where most Negroes lived, were established by churches and other private groups. They were far from providing for all children, and many were of a makeshift character. Shortly before the First World War the superintendent of schools of a southern State, in describing the Negro schools of his State, wrote: "The average length of the term ... is only 4 months; practically all schools are taught in dilapidated churches ... ; practically all the teachers are incompetent, possessing little or no education . . . ; the schools are generally overcrowded. . . ."[4]

Ensuing years brought rapid progress, and by 1930, 87 percent of the Negro children in the United States aged 7 to 13 were attending school. By 1961, practically all children of elementary school age were in school (nonwhites, 98.2 percent; whites, 99.5 percent).

For many years, while public elementary education for Negro children improved, secondary education lagged far behind. In 1866, there were 15 high schools and colleges for Negroes in the South. Progress was accelerated after the First World War. Public high schools for Negroes in 16 Southern and Border States and the District of Columbia were reported in 1917 and 1930 to be approximately as follows:[5]

	1916	*1930*
Number of public schools offering secondary work for Negro children	64	1,200
Negro high school enrollment	4,000	167,000

As late as 1930, however, only about 10 percent of the Negro children aged 15 to 18 in Southern and Border States were enrolled in public high school, as compared with 34 percent of white children. Many counties were without high school facilities for Negroes. Less than half the Negro high schools offered 4 years' work, and a relatively small percentage were accredited.

Differences in enrollment between whites and Negroes at the high school level still persist, but much less sharply. The percentages of children of high school age who were enrolled in school in October, 1961,[6] were—

	Nonwhites	*Whites*
Age 14 and 15	95.1	98.0
Age 16 and 17	76.8	84.5

Since World War I, Negroes have increasingly entered institutions of higher education. A survey published by the U.S. Bureau of Education in 1917 found most Negro colleges seriously handicapped

[4]Negro Education: *A Study of the Private and Public Higher Schools for Colored People in the United States* (U.S. Department of the Interior, Bureau of Education, Bulletin, 1916, 39), p. 15.

[5]*National Survey of Secondary Education: Summary* (U.S. Department of the Interior, Office of Education, Bulletin, 1932, 17, Monograph 1), p. 81.

[6]*School Enrollment: October, 1961* (U.S. Bureau of the Census, Current Population Reports, Series P-20, No. 117), p. 8.

both by inadequate funds and by the small number of pupils prepared for college work.[7] Opportunities have grown rapidly since that time. Proportionately fewer Negroes than whites go to college, but from 1947 to 1961 the number of nonwhites in college rose at a faster rate than the number of whites. The enrollment in colleges and professional schools was estimated as follows:[8]

	Nonwhites	*Whites*
1947	124,000	2,187,000
1961	233,000	3,498,000
Percent increase, 1947-61	87.9	60.0

The narrowing gap between whites and nonwhites is further reflected in the average number of years of school completed. Nonwhite men aged 25 and over in 1962 had averaged 8.3 years of schooling, compared with an average of 11.6 years for whites. But the nonwhite men in the age group 25 to 29 had averaged 11 years of schooling compared with 12.5 years for whites.[9]

Negroes in the Labor Market

Advances in education are reflected to some extent in the labor market. In 1910, a larger proportion of nonwhite than of white males were gainfully employed. By 1961, no great change had occurred in the percentage of white males in the labor force, but the percentage of nonwhites was clearly smaller (even allowing for lack of comparability in the statistics). This may indicate a greater increase among nonwhites in the number of years spent at school and in retirement.

Negro women have long appeared in the labor market to a greater extent than white women. In 1910, more than half the nonwhite women were gainfully employed, a proportion two and one-half times that for whites. By 1961, though far more white and comparatively fewer nonwhite women were in the labor market than 51 years before, the proportion of nonwhite women was still a fourth greater than the proportion of whites.

The move from agriculture, where underemployment is chronic but unemployment is comparatively rare, has brought new problems to Negroes; every recession now falls with special force upon them. According to T. J. Woofter, Jr.,[10] it took the Negro until 1925 to

7*Negro Education,* op. cit., Bulletin, 1916, 38, p. 11.

8*School Enrollment,* op.cit., p. 9, and unpublished data.

9*Educational Attainment: March, 1962* (U.S. Bureau of the Census Current Population Reports, Series P-20).

10*A Study of the Economic Status of the Negro* (June, 1930, mimeographed) p. 42.

regain what he lost in 1920-21, and certainly he lost both jobs and status during the thirties. When service trades newly entered by Negroes were sharply curtailed, the first to be laid off were the newer, less experienced workers. A question posed by Dr. Alba M. Edwards, in 1936, has not yet found its answer:

> If, with the further mechanization of industry, the machine takes over much of the unskilled work [Negroes] are now doing, will they be able to rise to higher pursuits, or will they replace white workers in the remaining unskilled pursuits, or, finally, will they largely fall into that permanently unemployed class certain writers have prophesied that we shall have in the future?[11]

Occupations

As already indicated, the history of Negro occupations shows the shift of men from farming and of women from farm and domestic work—a shift that was slow at first, but has accelerated in this century. New opportunities were most numerous during and after the two World Wars. By 1960, few were still in agriculture; but a third of the working women were still in domestic service work. Although the century showed a general advance, Negroes have not yet attained the occupational levels reached by whites.

The number of Negroes in agricultural work has shown the following trend:

As percent of all Negroes gainfully employed:	Male	Female
1890	60.8	44.0
1900	57.0	44.2
1910	56.1	52.2[1]
1920	46.7	38.9
1930	40.7	27.0
As percent of employed Negroes:		
1940	41.5	15.9
1950	23.7	8.9
1960[2]	11.5	3.6

[1]This figure is believed by the Bureau of the Census to be too high.

[2]All nonwhites. Source: U.S. Bureau of the Census: *Comparative Occupation Statistics for the United States, 1870 to 1940* (1943), p. 189; *1950 Census of Population: Nonwhite Population by Race* (P–E No. 3B), p. 27; *1960 Census of Population: United States Summary* (PC (1)–1C), pp. 217-218.

[11]*Journal of the American Statistical Association,* September, 1936, p. 529.

The decline from 1910 to 1930 reflected in part the shift of cotton from the older South to Texas and Oklahoma, where machines could be more extensively used. In general, the Negro did not operate machinery.

Throughout the century since 1863, Negroes leaving agriculture or domestic service have gone first into unskilled, often heavy jobs elsewhere. In the period after 1890, many men went into saw and planing mills, mining, or transportation jobs. Negroes were not hired as textile mill operatives.

World War I brought cessation of foreign immigration and, at the same time, a rapidly rising demand for industrial workers. In the South, there had been little immigration; factory operative jobs had been held largely by native whites. With the war, however, Negroes were brought in to some extent. Meanwhile, the first big movement to the North was under way. There the use of Negroes as machine operatives was regarded at first as an experiment; by the end of another decade, it had become a commonplace. Business and other opportunities expanded in the North, also.

Most Negroes, however, went into lower paid work requiring little or no skill or experience. Men became unskilled or semiskilled operatives in steel mills, automobile plants, foundries, and packing houses. Many took road or other construction jobs. Women found work as waitresses or in laundries; many entered the food industries or the needle trades, and some women became teachers or nurses.

Before the Civil War some Negroes were artisans, and as late as the turn of the century the southern Negro carpenter, mason, or blacksmith was a highly competent man, having served an apprenticeship under skilled craftsmen. The apprenticeship system had practically disappeared, however, and by the 1920's most Negro construction workers were men who had picked up their trade hurriedly, some in industrial courses in underequipped Negro high schools. They were no longer given preference for the well paid and steady construction jobs. In the North, Negro craftsmen began to gain a foothold during World War I.[12]

The net effect of the 1910 to 1930 shifts (Table 2) was a rapid rise in the proportion of Negroes in the white-collar group—professionals, proprietors, officials, and clerks—and the percentage of skilled and semiskilled workers (men, from 8.3 to 13.8 percent of all

[12]The situation among the skilled trades in the North was confusing, in part owing to union policies. Twenty-four international unions, most of them in the transportation field, were listed in the twenties as having constitutional provisions barring Negroes from membership. T. J. Woofter, Jr., *A Study of the Economic Status of the Negro,* op. cit., p. 53.

TABLE II

NEGROES AGE 10 AND OVER GAINFULLY EMPLOYED
BY OCCUPATION GROUP AND SEX,
1910, 1920, 1930

Occupation Group	Male			Female		
	1910	1920	1930	1910[1]	1920	1930
All occupations:						
Number (thousands)...	3,179	3,253	3,663	2,014	1,571	1,841
Percent	100.0	100.0	100.0	100.0	100.0	100.0
Professional -----------	1.1	1.2	1.5	1.4	2.4	3.3
Proprietors, managers officials, except farm	1.1	1.0	1.2	.3	.5	.6
Clerks, sales workers --	1.0	1.5	1.7	.3	1.0	1.1
Skilled workers, foremen	3.6	4.6	4.8	.1	.1	.1
Semiskilled, operatives -	4.7	7.0	9.0	5.4	9.0	10.1
Unskilled workers (except farm and service workers)-----	25.5	30.9	31.7	.8	2.7	1.7
Service workers--------	6.9	7.1	9.4	39.4	45.5	56.3
Farm workers ---------	56.1	46.7	40.7	52.2	38.9	27.0
Farm owners and tenants ------------	25.3	26.2	21.8	4.0	5.1	4.2
Farm laborers-------	30.8	20.5	18.9	48.2	33.8	22.8

[1] The figure is believed by the Bureau of the Census to be too high.

Source: U.S. Bureau of the Census, A Social-Economic Grouping of the Gainful Workers of the United States, 1930 (1938), p. 18.

Negro workers). Nonfarm laborer and service work also increased in importance, however, and despite the gradual movement of Negroes into higher economic groups, 6 out of 10 male and more than 8 out of 10 female Negro workers in 1930 were still in unskilled or service jobs. The percent was more than three times as great among Negroes as among native whites.

World War II brought further sharp changes, as many more Negroes left the farms for munitions and other factory work. The number of Negro skilled and semiskilled men doubled during the war years. Women in large numbers shifted from farms and domestic service to other types of personal services, to factories, and to clerical jobs. A considerable upgrading took place into more skilled, higher

TABLE III

MEDIAN ANNUAL WAGE AND SALARY INCOMES OF NONWHITE AND WHITE PERSONS, BY SEX, 1939, 1947, 1957, 1960

Sex and color	1939	1947	1957	1960	Percent rise, 1939-60
Male:					
Nonwhite------------	$ 460	$1,279	$2,436	$3,075	688.5
White---------------	$1,112	$2,357	$4,396	$5,137	362.0
Nonwhite as a percent of white -----------	41.4	54.3	55.4	59.9	-----
Female:					
Nonwhite------------	$ 240	$ 432	$1,019	$1,270	418.7
White---------------	$ 676	$1,269	$2,240	$2,537	275.3
Nonwhite as a percent of White -----------	36.4	34.0	45.5	50.3	-----

Source: U. S. Bureau of the Census, Income of Families and Persons in the United States (Current Population Reports, Series P-60, Nos. 5, 30, and 37.)

paid work and the professions. The postwar years showed continued advances in most regards. From 60 percent in 1930, the proportion of Negro men in unskilled or service jobs, including farm labor, was reduced by 1960 to 40 percent. For women, the reduction was from 80 percent to less than 60 percent.

Despite advances, however, proportionately fewer nonwhites than whites in 1960 were in the professional, managerial, other white-collar, or skilled groups. More men were in semiskilled, unskilled, or service jobs, and more were farm laborers. Many more women were in domestic service. But farm work, which in 1890 employed 61 percent of Negro men and 44 percent of the women, by 1960 employed less than 12 percent of the men who were working and less than 4 percent of the women.

Both men and women have entered Federal, State, and local government jobs. The ratio of nonwhites to all government employees, for April of each of the following years, has been estimated to be: 5.6 percent in 1940, 10.7 percent in 1960, and 12.1 percent in 1962.[13]

[13]Based on unpublished data from the household survey of the Bureau of Labor Statistics and the Bureau of the Census.

Income

Although data do not permit real comparison of incomes at any early period with those today, it is clear that there has been an advance. A move from agriculture to industry has meant, generally, the achievement of a higher income. From unskilled to semiskilled to skilled work in industry represents further progress. A move from blue-collar to white-collar work may not always mean a rise in income, but is considered by many, both Negro and white, to represent a rise in status.

Early studies of Negroes in the South suggest an economy operating with little cash: in rural areas, an exchange and subsistence economy; in the towns and cities, very low earnings, expended for bare essentials.

T. J. Woofter[14] reported in 1930 that, allowing for food raised and consumed on the farm and for other factors of difference, a southern farm family that moved to town improved its economic status if even one member could earn as much as $20 a week. Thus the low-wage situation and great natural increase of population in southern rural areas combined to set both whites and Negroes to seeking city jobs, at which they were willing to work for not much more than could be earned in agriculture.

According to another observer, there was little difference on unskilled work in the North, in 1930, between wages paid to Negroes and those paid to nonunion whites;[15] rates were also the same to both races for skilled work, but Negroes were not freely admitted to skilled jobs. In the South, rates were less for Negroes than for whites on both unskilled and skilled work, but Negroes were more readily admitted to skilled jobs than in the North.

Since earnings vary with occupation, the earnings of Negroes in recent years reflect both the relative rise in Negroes' occupational status and their continued disproportionate concentration in the less skilled jobs (table 3). Whites average much higher incomes than Negroes; but by 1960, the gap was less than in earlier years. Estimates for 1960 show incomes of Negroes closer to those of whites in the urban than in the rural areas. Yearly averages are reduced by the inclusion of many part-time or part-year workers, and such work is particularly frequent among Negroes.

Occupational differences are reflected in income differences among regions. The cash income from farming is low, and nearly all

[14]Op. cit., pp. 23, 26.

[15]Charles S. Johnson, *The Negro in American Civilization* (New York, Henry Holt and Co., 1930), p. 53.

the Negroes still on farms are in the South, which tends to lower the southern nonwhite average income. Nineteen percent of southern nonwhite males were on farms in 1960. Only 8 percent of nonwhite males were in professional, managerial, or other white-collar work in the South, as compared with 18 percent in the Northeast. As a result of such differences, data for 1960 showed the following variation among regions in the median money incomes of nonwhite males:[16]

	Income of nonwhite males as percent of income of white males
U.S. Average	52.5
Northeast	76.3
North Central	75.8
South	37.3
West	73.2

When the slaves were freed, 99 percent of the Negroes in the South, where most Negroes lived, were penniless field hands and servants. In the century since, Negroes have vanquished illiteracy. They have moved decisively out of farming and up the ladder of urban skills; to a significant extent, they have moved from South to North. The ensuing adjustments were difficult; they are still going on. But in continuing to move, Negroes have shown that they find the shifts advantageous.

Decline in the Relative Income of Negro Men

Alan B. Batchelder (Appendix by Rashi Fein)

[*From the* Quarterly Journal of Economics, *August 1964, with permission.*]

Protests against racial discrimination have been featured in newspaper headlines for several years. News stories have described the existing discriminatory barriers, the protests, and—not infrequently—the removal of barriers.

It is a commonplace that racial barriers have put the American Negro in a position that has allowed him, on the average, to produce and to lay claim to a smaller per capita share of America's real output

[16]*Income of Families and Persons in the United States: 1960* (U.S. Bureau of the Census, Current Population Reports, Series P-60, No. 37), p. 51.

than the white American. This article examines statistical data showing the economic position of American Negroes relative to whites in 1949 and in 1959. The particular statistics used are the median annual income figures for Negroes and for whites. Two questions are raised and answered, at least in part; these are: First, given the racial turbulence of the 1950's, did the American Negro's relative income position decline, hold steady, or improve during the fifties? Second, what explanations can be found for the changes that took place, particularly the changes for men?

Ratios aside, the real per capita income of American Negroes has been rising on the wings of rising American productivity. However, assuming that income comparisons with a man's peers are more meaningful than income comparisons with his progenitors, the focus of attention in this article will be on secular changes in the Negro-white income ratio, rather than on secular changes in Negro income alone.[1]

Newspaper reports upon the elimination of racial barriers led most commentators, at least until recently, to conclude that the Negro's social-economic position was steadily improving. Well into 1962, this view was dominant. Fairly typical were these paragraphs in a 1962 *New York Times* article titled, "Washington: Administration's Commitment to Negro Rights Has Resulted in Major Gains":

> In almost every aspect of American life it is possible to point to dramatic improvement in the status of the Negro over the last twenty or ten or even five years. Overall it is clear that racial discrimination, which once seemed an immovable fact of life, is now everywhere on the defensive.
>
> *Voting* is widely regarded as the key to the entire race-relations program. With political power, the theory is, Negroes can effectively fight their own battles for an end to all kinds of discrimination.
>
> The *economic situation* of the Negro again shows striking progress in historical terms. In the last twenty years the median income of Negro families has multiplied by more than six while the figure for whites has gone up a little more than four times.[2]

The author wishes gratefully to acknowledge helpful suggestions from his colleagues, Diran Bodenhorn and Herbert S. Parnes.

[1]The comparative importance of trends in income as against trends in *relative* income can best be appreciated by any married male economist's recalling his wife's reaction to his rash assertion, "Honey, it's not what Jan and Ted Smith have; what's important is that your real income is three times your grandmother's."

[2]A. Lewis in *New York Times,* Sept. 30, 1962, p. E-3.

Despite this optimism, Negro protests waxed during the early 1960's, and, as they did so, this fulsome optimism waned. Then other voices were heard denying the claims of Negro progress. Prominent among these voices was that of Whitney Young, Jr., Executive Director of the National Urban League, who said, for example, in Columbus, Ohio, in 1962, "In spite of what we wishfully like to think and feel, there have been few strides for the American Negro in this country during the last 10 years. When one looks at this from a relative standpoint ... one sees that ... there have been very few gains."[3] Mr. Young then surveyed figures for 1960 relating to employment, housing, mortality rates, and education, in each case noting the pronounced disadvantage of the Negro when compared with the white. Finally he concluded, "In every case, these [relative] figures are almost exactly the same as they were in 1950. So from the standpoint of the basic needs of life—food, shelter, health—there has been very little gain in closing the gaps. This is reality in 1962."[4]

I. Occupational Data and Economic Position: 1910, 1940, 1950

Which of these two men provided the most accurate picture of developments during the fifties? Emotion appears so likely to color personal impressions of conditions affected by racial discrimination that quantitative measures become essential tools for study in this area. Income, as such a measure, was not available until quite recently.

In 1950 the Census Bureau began the decennial collection of personal income data. Only now, with income statistics available by race and region from the 1950 and 1960 censuses, is it possible to use income data to measure secular changes in the economic position of Negroes relative to whites.

Earlier, seeking a quantitative measure of changes over time in the Negro's relative economic position, Gary Becker and Elton Rayack pioneered in the use of occupation indices for this purpose.[5] Occupational data, however, proved difficult to use because of the diversity of activities included under such headings as "carpenters," or "painters, construction and maintenance," or "operatives and kindred work-

[3]Address to the 44th Annual Meeting of the Columbus Urban League, Columbus, Ohio, 1962, mimeographed, pp. 1–2.

[4]*Ibid.*

[5]G. S. Becker, *The Economics of Discrimination* (Chicago: University of Chicago Press, 1957). Elton Rayack, "Discrimination and the Occupational Progress of Negroes," *Review of Economics and Statistics,* XLIII (May 1961), 209–14.

ers (not elsewhere classified) in manufacturing."[6] Further, occupational data proved difficult to use because their synthesis into index numbers for secular comparisons raised all the usual index number problems associated with the selection of appropriate weights.

Becker constructed an income-weighted occupation index permitting him to compare the relative occupational position of Negroes in 1910, in 1940, and in 1950. He found evidence of substantial occupational advance by Negroes during the 1940's, but these gains appeared to have been little more than sufficient to offset the losses experienced by Negroes between 1920 and 1940. He concluded "that neither striking increases nor striking decreases in discrimination against Negroes have occurred during the last four decades."[7]

Elton Rayack criticized Becker's use of 1940 occupational income ratios to weight 1950 occupational data; for, Rayack argued, the ratios had changed substantially (the spread narrowing as among occupations) by 1950. Confining his own study to the decade of the forties and using 1950 income ratios to weight 1950 occupational data, Rayack found, as had Becker, that the 1950 "occupational position of the Negro relative to the white is substantially better than it was prior to World War II."[8]

This conclusion would surprise no one, nor would anyone be surprised by Rayack's observation that the improved relative position could be attributed to the labor shortages of World War II. He went on to speculate:

> It is conceivable that the continuous high levels of employment for the economy as a whole since 1941 might have permitted the Negro to sufficiently consolidate [sic] his occupational position so that it would not decline greatly relative to that of whites even in the face of a prolonged and severe depression. Only the future can provide a test of this hypothesis.[9]

There has been no depression, but there has been a decade of gently swelling unemployment, of persistent technological change, and of disproportionate growth of the service industries during which

[6]For a description of this cause of unreliability in census occupation data, see J. P. Henderson, "A Deviation in the Pattern of Relative Earnings for Production Workers and Office Personnel," *Journal of Business*, XXVIII (July 1955), 203. If one assumes similar bias in the Negro and in the white data, then there is less risk in using Negro-white occupation *ratios* than in using either Negro or white data alone.

[7]*Op. cit.*, p. 125. He did find that there had been a 5 per cent improvement in the North offset (in the national figures) by a 2 per cent decline in the South. Cf., pp. 113–14.

[8]*Op. cit.*, p. 214.

[9]*Ibid.*

the security of the Negro's 1950 economic position has been tested. Avoiding index number problems, Tables I and II show what happened to the average Negro man and woman income receiver in the milieu of the 1950's.

II. Income Data for Men, 1949 and 1959

In Table I the median income of Negro men is compared with the median income of white[1] men for the years 1949 and 1959. Dollar figures appear for each group, and the ratio of Negro to white income is also shown as a percentage. Separate figures are presented for the conterminous United States (a Census Bureau expression referring to the 48 States other than Hawaii and Alaska) and for each of the four major census regions.[2] The income concept used here comprises three parts: wage and salary income, self-employment income, and "other" income, the latter including rent, interest, dividends, and transfer receipts. The three parts are described in detail in footnote 1 of Table I.

Between 1949 and 1959, the median dollar income of each group in each area rose. However, attention here centers upon what happened to the ratio of male Negro to male white income; that is to say, what happened to the economic position in America of the Negro as compared with the white primary breadwinner. For the country as a whole, the Negro's position showed no change, standing at 52.52 per cent of the white's in 1949 and 51.96 in 1959. In both years Negro men were able to bring home, on the average, in earnings and other income only slightly more than one half of what white men were able to bring home. In income terms, the relative economic position of American Negro men was low in 1949 and no higher in 1959.[3]

[1]Negro and Caucasian are racial designations and, as such, are capitalized. White and nonwhite are noncapitalized color designations. There are non-Negro nonwhites. This article frequently compares whites and Negroes while omitting consideration of non-negro nonwhites.

[2]The Census Bureau regions are: Northeast: Maine, N.H., Vt., Mass., R.I., Conn., N.Y., N.J., and Pa.; North Central: Ohio, Ind., Mich., Ill., Wis., Minn., Iowa, Mo., Kans., Nebr., S. D., N. D.; South: Del., Md., D. C., W. Va., Va., N.C., S.C., Ga., Fla., Ala., Miss., Tenn., Ky., Ark., La., Texas, Okla.; West: all other.

[3]The reliability of the 1949 income data has been examined; the reliability of the 1959 income data is being examined. A study of matched questionnaires for persons who were enumerated in both the March 1960 *Current Population Survey* and the 1960 *Census* has been undertaken, but as yet, no report has appeared upon this study or upon any other regarding the reliability of the 1959 income data.

The March 1956 Conference on Research in Income and Wealth was devoted to a discussion of the 1949 income data obtained by the 1950 decennial census. The record of the conference proceedings has been published as Vol. 23

These are national data. When viewing them, one must bear in mind that, between 1950 and 1960, 1,457,000 nonwhites (most of whom were Negroes[4]) moved out of the South and into the North and West.[5] One must also remember, as Table I shows, that the 1949 data for regions (and the 1959 data as well) show the ratio of male Negro to male white income to have been much lower in the South than in the other three regions. Therefore, given the size of the Negro movement out of the South, where Negro income was and is quite small compared with white, and into the North and West, where the

in the National Bureau of Economic Research series, *Studies in Income and Wealth.* The third and fourth papers in Part II deal explicitly with the quality of the census data. H. P. Miller and L. R. Paley of the Bureau of the Census compare census and income tax data of identical families and conclude that if the "tax returns are accurate" then "the census income data are quite accurate." H. P. Miller and L. R. Paley, "Income Reported in the 1950 Census and on Income Tax Returns," in *An Appraisal of the 1950 Census Income Data,* Vol. XXIII of *Studies in Income and Wealth,* National Bureau of Economic Research (Princeton: Princeton University Press, 1958) p. 200. Selma F. Goldsmith argued that the income tax returns show only about 95 per cent of individuals' taxable income. "The Relation of Census Income Distribution Statistics to Other Income Data," in *An Appraisal of the 1950 Census Income Data, op. cit.,* pp. 78 and 81.

In September 1950 the Census Bureau undertook an evaluation of census results through detailed repeat interviews by carefully trained and supervised interviewers, with a random sample of some 25,000 households. When the median 1949 income for male nonwhites (not just Negroes) was computed from the reinterview data, the resulting figure of $1,350 was only $10 greater than the median 1949 income for male nonwhites computed from the initial interviews. For white males, the reinterviewing median estimate was $30 above the median based upon the initial interviews. L. Pritzker and A. Sands, "The 1950 Census and the Post Enumeration Survey," in *An Appraisal of the 1950 Census Income Data, op. cit.,* p. 217. The reinterview technique is described in E. S. Marks, W. P. Mauldin, and H. Nisselson, "The Post-Enumeration Survey of the 1950 Census: A Case History in Survey Design," *Journal of the American Statistical Association,* Vol. 48 (June 1953), pp. 220–43.

It does seem likely that the census income data understate true income. The Negro income figure would be less inaccurate (on the low side) than the white income figure since income tax returns (and census data) understate proprietors' income, dividends, interest and rent more than wages and salaries. See Selma Goldsmith, *op. cit.,* pp. 78–81.

In short, inaccuracies in the data appear to understate everyone's dollar income and *over*state the Negro's relative position. A priori, one might expect this bias to be consistent over time and, therefore, to have no effect upon the change in ratios that are the subject of this study.

[4]In 1960, of America's nonwhite population, 94 per cent in the conterminous U.S. 96 per cent in the Northeast, 95 per cent in the North Central States, 98 per cent in the South, and 62 per cent in the conterminous West were Negroes. *U.S. Census of Population: 1960 General Characteristics, U.S. Summary,* pp. 1–164.

[5]U.S. Bureau of the Census, *Current Population Reports,* Series P-25, No. 247, p. 7.

TABLE I

MEDIAN INCOME OF NEGRO MEN AND MEDIAN INCOME OF WHITE MEN, 1949 AND 1959: DOLLAR AMOUNTS AND RATIOS, FOR THE CONTERMINOUS UNITED STATES AND BY REGION

Region	Dollar Income,[1] Negro over White		Income Ratio, Negro to White	
	1949[2]	1959[3]	1949	1959
Conterminous United States[4]	$1,334 / $2,572	$2,254 / $4,337	52.52	51.96
Northeast	2,061 / 2,759	3,326 / 4,623	74.70	71.94
North Central	2,210 / 2,721	3,468 / 4,525	81.22	76.64
West	2,049 / 2,786	3,395 / 4,773	73.55	71.13
South	1,033 / 2,065	1,643 / 3,524	50.02	46.62

1. For males 14 years old and over reporting 1949 or 1959 income. "Income" is the sum of wages, salaries, commissions, bonuses, and tips (wage and salary income); profits or fees from working in one's own business, professional practice, partnership or farm, net after business expenses (self-employment income); receipts from social security, pensions, veterans' payments, rent (minus expenses), interest, dividends, unemployment insurance, welfare payments or any other source not already stated (other income). The figures represent income before deductions for personal income taxes, Social Security, bond purchases, union dues, etc. Receipts from the following sources were not included: money from the sale of property, the value of income "in kind," tax refunds, gifts and lump sum inheritances or insurance benefits. U.S. Census of Population: 1950, II: Characteristics, of the Population, Part 1, U.S. Summary, p. 63. U.S. Census of Population: 1960, Detailed Characteristics, U.S. Summary, p. XXXIX.

2. Conterminous United States: U.S. Census of Population: 1950, II: Characteristics of the Population, p. 1-297; regions: white income-same volume, pp. 1-413-414; Negro income computed by the author from data for individual states—same volume, Table 87 of Parts for the several states. Based on a 20 per cent sample.

3. U.S. Census of Population: 1960, Detailed Characteristics, U.S. Summary, pp. 1-578, and 1-734-736. Based on a 25 per cent sample.

4. The forty-eight states other than Hawaii and Alaska.

income ratio is nearer unity, one would expect, *ceteris paribus*, a substantial rise in the Negro-to-white ratio for the nation as a whole simply as a consequence of the shift in weighting. That this rise did *not* follow was the consequence of a *decline* in the relative income position of Negro men within every one of the four major census regions.

The values of these declines were 2.42 points in the West, 2.76 in the Northeast, 3.40 in the South, and 4.58 in the North Central States. Thus it may be said of any particular region that in income terms the relative position of Negro men was low in 1949 and still lower in 1959.[6]

Furthermore, these statistics do not result from averaging together figures for many states, in some of which the Negro position declined, in some of which the Negro position improved. Herman P. Miller, Special Assistant to the Director of the Bureau of the Census, appeared before a Congressional committee in July 1963. He said that in the 26 states (including the District of Columbia) which have 100,000 or more Negroes, the ratio of Negro to white income for males increased between 1949 and 1959 in only two states (District of Columbia and Florida).[7] In two others (New Jersey and Oklahoma), it was unchanged. In every other state there was a widening of the gap between the incomes of whites and Negroes, and in some cases the increase was fairly substantial. Given this consistent decline throughout America in the relative income position of Negro men, it may seem surprising that the income experience of Negro women during the 1950's was quite different.

III. Income Data for Woman, 1949 and 1959

During the 1950's, there was a narrowing of the gap between the income of Negro women and the income of white women. Table II presents the dollar figures for median income of white women and Negro women in 1949 and in 1959 for the conterminous United States and for each census region. Table II also presents the Negro-white income ratios for women in each region in 1949 and in 1959. For the

[6]Since both the 1949 and the 1959 data were based on samples (20 and 25 per cent respectively), the effects of sampling error must be considered. If the 1959 white median incomes were lowered two standard errors while 1959 Negro median income rose two, the conclusions regarding decline in ratio values would remain. Therefore, the probability that the regional declines were due to sampling error was judged too slight to merit more extensive consideration in this paper.

[7]H. P. Miller, *Statement before the Subcommittee on Employment and Manpower, U. S. Senate Committee on Labor and Public Welfare,* U.S. Bureau of the Census, mimeo (Washington, 1963), p. 6.

TABLE II

MEDIAN INCOME OF NEGRO WOMEN AND MEDIAN INCOME OF WHITE WOMEN, 1949 AND 1959: DOLLAR AMOUNTS AND RATIOS, FOR THE CONTERMINOUS UNITED STATES AND BY REGION

Region	Dollar Income,[1] Negro over White		Income Ratio, Negro to White	
	1949[2]	1959[2]	1949	1959
Conterminous United States	$ 581 / $1,137	$ 905 / $1,509	51.10	59.97
Northeast	1,165 / 1,407	1,724 / 1,748	82.80	98.63
North Central	938 / 1,086	1,355 / 1,393	86.37	97.27
West	920 / 1,008	1,543 / 1,612	91.27	95.72
South	440 / 947	732 / 1,317	46.46	55.58

1. For females 14 years old and over reporting 1949 or 1959 income.
2. Source: Same as Table I.

nation, the Negro position advanced from 51 to 60 per cent of the white. In the three non-Southern regions, Negro women's income drew within three or four percentage points of white women's income. Even in the South, the percentage gap between Negro and white woman was reduced.[8]

[8]A warning: Census Bureau estimates of median income are based upon the assumption that income earners are distributed evenly within each class of the frequency distributions used in publishing census results. This assumption, combined with a change between 1950 and 1960 in the width of income classes, led to a 20 per cent difference between the 1950 census report and the 1960 census report on median 1949 income of Southern Negro women (the 1960 report recalculated this figure from 1950 data). In 1950, class intervals of $500 were used for income groups below $5,000; in 1960, $1000 intervals were used. Applied to 1949 data, the former method gave an estimate of median 1949 income of Southern Negro women of $581 (the figure used in Table II); the latter method gave an estimate of $703 because it failed to recognize that in 1949 there were more Negro women in the less than $500 income group than in the $500–999 income group.

Although the two methods give answers 20 per cent apart for median 1949 income of Southern Negro women, the results differ by less than 1 per cent for all other race-sex-regional groups.

TABLE III

INCOME RATIO BETWEEN WOMEN AND MEN:
BY RACE AND BY REGION,
1949 AND 1959

Area	Negro			White		
	1949	1959	Change in Percentage Points	1949	1959	Change in Percentage Points
Conterminous United States	43.6	40.2	-3.4	44.2	34.8	- 9.4
Northeast	56.5	51.8	-4.7	51.0	37.8	-13.2
North Central	42.4	39.1	-3.3	39.9	30.8	- 9.1
West	44.9	45.4	.5	36.2	33.8	- 2.4
South	42.6	44.6	2.0	45.9	37.4	- 8.5

Source: Tables I and II above.

IV. The Ratio of Female Income to Male Income

Recognition of the contrasting income experience of Negro men and of Negro women immediately raises questions regarding change in the relative incomes of Negro women and Negro men. The rising income position of Negro relative to white women and the falling income position of Negro relative to white men in each region might lead one to anticipate that, among Negroes, the ratio of female to male income would rise. That this was not everywhere the case was the consequence of another major change occurring during the 1950's.

This change was the decline in the income ratio between white women and white men. This decline was 9.4 points for the conterminous United States, from 44.2 to 34.8 per cent. Within each region, as Table III shows, similar changes occurred.

Table III shows that in the South and West, where 60 per cent of American Negroes lived in 1960,[9] the income of Negro women gained on that of Negro men while in the Northeastern and North Central States, Negro women slipped back a bit. Yet even in the latter two regions, the declines of 3 to 5 points were much smaller than the declines of 9 to 13 points for white women in the same regions.

[9] *U.S. Census of Population: 1960, General Characteristics, U.S. Summary* p. 1164.

Two conclusions follow: First, the "changing role of American women in the 1950's" was different for Negro than for white women. Second, the income of Negro women became increasingly important during the 1950's relative to the income of Negro men, first, as Table III shows, because Negro women in the South and West earned more relative to Negro men and, second, as the next paragraph will show, because a substantially larger per cent of Negro women worked in 1960 than had worked in 1950.

Between 1950 and 1960, increasing percentages of Negro (and white) women left their kitchens to enter the labor force. In 1950 women made up 37 per cent of the Negro labor force, in 1960, 42 per cent;[10] over the same decade white women increased their share of the white labor force from 27 to 32 per cent.[11] In each of the four regions, the figures were nearly the same as for the nation.

Thus both the female Negro and the female white labor force grew relative to the male labor force during the fifties. but it was the Negro woman's income, rather than the white woman's, that held up best against the income of men. Something in the labor market permitted Negro, but not white, women to increase their share of the labor force without depressing their incomes relative to men's.

Throughout American history matriarchy has been more common among Negroes than among whites. Slavery contributed to this by leaving young children with their mothers when splitting families. White bigotry regarding free Negroes contributed by showing greater willingness to employ Negro women than Negro men. In the nineteenth century the Negro washerwoman was "in many instances the sole breadwinner of the family"; in 1849 in Philadelphia, as an extreme example, there were more female than male Negroes in gainful occupations.[12]

Here in our own time, we find the income of Negro women becoming increasingly important relative to the income of Negro men. One is left to speculate upon the social implications of this trend.

Evidence that the trend continued into the sixties appears in data regarding trainees in Manpower Development and Training Courses. Among white women in these training courses in August 1963 only 28

[10] *U.S. Census of Population: 1950*, Vol. IV: *Special Reports*, Part 3, *Nonwhite Population by Race* (Washington, 1953), pp. 3–B–27–31. *U.S. Census of Population: 1960, Subject Reports, Nonwhite Population by Race* (Washington, 1963), pp. 101–2.

[11] *U.S. Census of Population: 1960, Detailed Characteristics, U.S. Summary*, pp. 1–499.

[12] Lorenzo Greene and Carter Woodson, *The Negro Wage Earner*, Association for the Study of Negro Life and History (Washington, 1930), pp. 3–4.

per cent came from among the 22–34 year old age group, so few, presumably, because women of that age stay home caring for their small children. In contrast, 53 per cent of female Negro trainees came from this age group,[13] as Negro women, with small children or not, were obliged to seek work.

V. Why the Relative Decline for Negro Men?

This article has begun with an examination of the changes occurring during the 1950's in the relative income position of American Negroes. This examination has shown that the changes occurring within census regions were unfavorable for Negro men. The second half of this article will have as its objective the identification of the causes of the regional declines in the relative income position of Negro men, particularly of the decline relative to white men.

It seems useful initially to catalogue some possible causes of this decline and to distinguish between those that will be considered in detail here and those that, because of a lack of statistics, will not be here considered.

As mentioned earlier, the income data comprise three parts: wage and salary income, self-employment income, and "other income," the latter including dividends, interest, rent, and transfer payments. It is upon the first two parts that the present inquiry will now concentrate. This concentration does not imply any lack of interest by the author in the income flows included in the third income component. Rather it is that the national and regional data deriving from the Census Bureau are limited to variables chiefly affecting wages, salaries, and (this to a lesser extent) self-employment income. Property income and transfer payments may have been important as causes of the relative decline in male Negro income, but they will not be examined here. It is to be hoped that some other researcher will be able to report soon upon recent trends in the division of property income and transfer payments as between Negroes and whites.

Considering variables operating chiefly through wages and salaries, the 1949–59 regional declines in the income position of Negro men relative to that of white men could have been due to a decline in the quality of the male Negro as compared with the male white labor force; it could have been due to an increase in the quantity of the male Negro as compared with that of the male white labor force; or it could have been due to increased discrimination against Negroes by white employers. An explanation may also be sought in more immedi-

[13] U.S. Department of Labor, "Form MT-101," Office of Manpower Automation and Training, mimeo. (Washington, 1963).

ate causes; as compared with white men, Negro men may have experienced greater growth in unemployment, greater growth in the importance of part-time workers, greater growth in the importance of casual and intermittent workers, or shifts from more to less well paid jobs.

In the sections below, median age of men in the labor force and median years of school completed by men aged 16 and over will be used to measure relative trends in the quality of the male Negro and the male white labor forces. To measure relative quantity, the size of the Negro labor force will be compared with the size of the entire labor force. Finally, consideration will be given to unemployment rates, part-time workers, and occupational distribution as immediate causes of the decline in the relative income status of Negro men.

The results of this examination will indicate for each region particular variables associated with the 1949–59 decline in the relative income position of Negro men. In the South growing unemployment among Negro men relative to white men and increased concentration of Negro men in laboring and service occupations will appear as the chief reasons for the decline.

In the North and West the explanatory variables derive from the Negroes out-migration from the South. This movement increased the supply of Negroes relative to the supply of whites in the Northern and Western male labor force and, quite possibly, depressed the educational level of Northern and Western Negro men relative to Northern and Western white men. It is curious, however, to find that similar causes for Negro women did not result in similar income effects as between Negro and white women. In the North and West no evidence of declining economic status for Negro men is to be found in the occupational data. Together, therefore, the occupational and income data suggest that in the North and West job changes unfavorable to Negro men occurred within rather than among the occupational categories used by the Census Bureau.

VI. Education

Labor force quality depends to a great extent upon the educational attainments of the labor force. It is pertinent here to ask what happened between 1949 and 1959 to the ratio between the average educational attainment of American Negroes and American whites? For the nation as a whole the Census Bureau computed in 1950 and again in 1960 the median years of school completed by persons 25 years of age and over. Separate medians were computed for male whites, male nonwhites, female whites and female nonwhites. The data for nonwhites will be used here to approximate the figures for Negroes. From 70.0 per cent of the male white median in 1950, the male nonwhite median rose to 74.5 per cent in 1960. The female nonwhite median rose from 72.0 per cent of the female white median in 1950 to 77.3 per cent in 1960.[14]

The regional medians computed by the Census Bureau for 1950 were for persons aged 25 and over; the regional 1960 medians were for persons aged 16 and over. Consequently, it is not possible to calculate comparable 1950 and 1960 Negro-to-white or nonwhite-to-white regional ratios. One may guess that in each region, as in the nation as a whole, there was in increase in the Negro (nonwhite) to white educational attainment ratios during the 1950's. Because of the lack of comparable quantitative data, one cannot be sure. Yet quantitative data may be less important than historical deductions that allow for qualitative as well as quantitative factors.

Among the 8,993,860 nonwhites in the North and West in 1960, there were 1,457,000 who had come to these regions from the South between 1950 and 1960.[15] Most of these people had attended schools markedly inferior to those of the non-South. Several sets of statistics support the latter assertion. First, average expenditure per standard classroom unit (30 children) in, for example, 1939–40 for Mississippi white schools: $784; for Mississippi Negro schools: $154. Second, average salaries paid public school teachers in, for example, 1939–40 in Mississippi white schools: $821; in Mississippi Negro schools: $235;[16] in New York schools: $2,604.[17]

Money is not everything in education; but, as an important catalyst, it was available to do far more for New York children than for Mississippi children. Nonfinancial statistics further illustrate the low level of education offered Southern Negroes in 1940. In that year, 11 per cent of Mississippi's white teachers had failed to complete two years of college and 84.7 per cent of Mississippi's Negro teachers had failed to complete two years of college.[18]

Many of the Negro in-migrants to the North and West in the 1950's received their educations in these Southern schools of the 1940's. Assuming that a year of school completed in the South by

[14]*U.S. Census of Population: 1960, Detailed Characteristics, U.S. Summary*, pp. 406–10.

[15]*Ibid.*, pp. 1–613. *Current Population Reports, op. cit.*, p. 7.

[16]J. P. Guzman (ed.), Negro Year Book, *A Review of Events Affecting Negro Life, 1941–1946* (Tuskeegee, 1947), pp. 58–59.

[17]U.S. Office of Education, *Biennial Surveys of Education in the United States, 1938–40 and 1940–42*, Vol. II, Chap. III, Statistics of State School Systems (Washington, 1944), p. 15.

[18]Guzman, *op. cit.*, p. 61.

these migrants was substantially inferior to the same year of school completed by Negroes educated outside the South, this migration would lower the quality represented by any given median number of years of school completed by Negroes living outside the South. Further, this migration would reduce the educational level of non-Southern Negroes relative to non-Southern whites, for the latter were much less affected by infusions of ill-educated Southerners.

This conclusion that the non-Southern Negro's education level was eroded between 1950 and 1960 depends upon the assumption that a large percentage of 1950's Northern and Western Negroes were educated in the North. Many were, but the point must not be overstated, for 51.5 per cent of nonwhites living in the North and West in 1950 were born in the South.[19] Most of these, presumably, received at least part of their formal education in the South, possibly during the years in which Southern schools were even worse, relative to contemporary non-Southern schools, than those attended by Negroes leaving the South during the 1950's.

Speculating upon changes in the South, it is possible that Negro out-migrants from the South were better educated and more able than those who remained behind. If so, the migration would have tended to reduce the quality of Southern Negro labor relative to Southern white labor. This possibility merits investigation. For the present, the necessary data are not, to the knowledge of the author, available.

One may conclude for the decade of the 1950's that although nonwhites (and surely Negroes too) gained on whites in median years of school completed, in the country as a whole, the average quality of a year of school completed by Negroes living in the North and West was reduced. Although assurance on this score must wait upon further research, it is the author's guess that, in educational attainment, quality dilution exceeded quantitative gains for Negroes in the North and West.

Beyond this it would be desirable to assemble data that would permit one to estimate what the median income of each age-sex group would have been in each region if there had been no change between 1950 and 1960 in the median education figures for each group. But without more data, this computation is not possible.

VII. Age

Age is a second variable that changed during the 1950's and that was potentially able to influence Negro-to-white income ratios by affecting

[19] *U.S. Census of Population: 1950*, Vol. IV: *Special Reports*, Part 4, *State of Birth* (Washington, 1953), p. 4A-12.

the quality of the labor force. American Negroes are younger than American whites. This was so in 1950 and it was more so in 1960. For males of all ages in the conterminous United States, the median age of Negroes was 25.8 in 1950 and 22.3 in 1960; the median age of whites was 30.1 in 1950[20] and 29.3 in 1960,[21] yielding a Negro-white ratio of .86 in 1950 and .76 in 1960. Statistics for women are similar. Negroes have remained younger than whites; and, between 1950 and 1960, all age medians fell while the difference between whites and Negroes increased.

But these figures refer to everyone in the population. For present purposes, the important figures are those for the working population.

Since the Census Bureau has published no data that would permit computation of median ages for the Negro labor force, figures for the nonwhite employed civilian labor force will be used here to approximate figures for the Negro employed civilian labor force. Table IV shows that between 1950 and 1960 the median age of every group rose. For men the increases for whites and for nonwhites were very nearly the same in each region. In contrast the median age for nonwhite women rose less than the median age for white women.

The age period in which income peaked in 1959 was 35–44 for white and nonwhite men and for nonwhite women and 45–55 for white woman.[22] Thus the greater aging of white than nonwhite women might have tended, *ceteris paribus,* to increase the Negro-white income difference for women. However, the changes in the average age of the employed white and nonwhite male populations were so nearly the same that the age factor, as measured by medians, cannot be credited with having had any part in causing the decline in the relative economic status of Negro men.

VIII. Negroes in the Labor Force

Between 1950 and 1960, as Table V shows, there was a decline in the Negro portion of both the male and the female labor force in America as a whole, in the South as a whole, and even in Southern cities. But in each non-Southern region, as Table V also shows, there was an increase in the Negro portion of the labor force. One may speculate regarding the consequences of this change. An initial hypothesis might

[20] *U.S. Census of Population: 1950,* Vol. II: *Characteristics of the Population,* pp. 1–166 and 1–173.

[21] *U.S. Census of Population: 1960, Detailed Characteristics, U.S. Summary,* pp. 1–358–359.

[22] *Ibid.,* p. 1–580.

TABLE IV

NONWHITE TO WHITE RATIO OF THE MEDIAN AGE OF THE EMPLOYED CIVILIAN LABOR FORCE, 1950 AND 1960: FOR THE CONTERMINOUS UNITED STATES AND FOR REGIONS, BY SEX

Area	Men			Women		
	Year		1950 to 1960	Year		1950 to 1960
	1950[1]	1960[2]	Change in Median Age	1950[1]	1960[2]	Change in Median Age
Conterminous United States	37.8 / 39.5	38.8 / 40.6	1.0 / 1.1	36.2 / 36.4	38.8 / 40.8	2.6 / 4.4
Northeast	37.6 / 40.6	38.5 / 41.7	.9 / 1.1	35.8 / 36.2	38.8 / 41.9	3.0 / 5.7
North Central	37.7 / 39.9	39.0 / 40.7	1.3 / .8	36.1 / 36.5	38.3 / 41.1	2.2 / 4.6
West	38.2 / 39.4	39.1 / 40.0	.9 / .6	34.6 / 37.9	37.5 / 40.5	2.9 / 2.6
South	37.4 / 38.0	38.9 / 39.8	1.5 / 1.8	36.5 / 35.4	39.3 / 39.4	2.8 / 4.0

[1] Calculated from U.S. Census of Population: 1950, Vol. II: Characteristics of the Population, pp. 1-247-248 and 1-366.
[2] Calculated from U.S. Census of Population: 1960, Detailed Characteristics, U.S. Summary, pp. 1-488-489 and 1-685-691.

be that the relative growth of the Negro labor force in the non-South would tend to depress Negro income relative to white. This would follow from a situation in which the number of jobs open to Negroes tended to remain the same (at least as a per cent of all jobs) while the Negro labor force grew relative to the white. This may have been the case in the North and West during the fifties.

IX. Negro-White Unemployment Ratios

The chief immediate determinant of income levels is the employment-unemployment pattern of the labor force. The unemployment, part-time employment, and occupation characteristics of that pattern will now be considered.

Unemployment data are available from the decennial census for April 1950 and April 1960 by region for Negroes and for whites.

TABLE V

NEGROES AS A PER CENT OF THE MALE CIVILIAN LABOR FORCE AND AS A PER CENT OF THE FEMALE LABOR FORCE: FOR THE CONTERMINOUS UNITED STATES BY REGIONS: 1950 AND 1960

Area	Male Civilian Labor Force: per cent Negro 1950[1]	Male Civilian Labor Force: per cent Negro 1960[2]	Female Labor Force: per cent Negro 1950[1]	Female Labor Force: per cent Negro 1960[2]
Conterminous United States	9.0	8.8	12.4	12.1
Northeast	5.6	5.9	7.2	8.7
North Central	4.7	5.7	6.4	7.5
West	2.8	3.3	4.3	4.6
South	20.2	17.5	27.7	23.4
Urban South	19.9	17.8	27.5	24.3

1. Calculated from all-labor-force data in U.S. Census of Population: 1950, Vol. II, Characteristics of the Population, pp. 1-247 and 1-366-373 and Negro data in U.S. Census of Population: 1950, Vol. IV: Special Reports, Part 3, Nonwhite Population by Race, pp. 3-B-27-31.

2. Calculated from all-labor-force data in U.S. Census of Population: 1960, Detailed Characteristics, U.S. Summary, pp. 1-499 and 1-685-691, and Negro data in U.S. Census of Population: 1960, Subject Reports, Nonwhite Population by Race, pp. 101-2.

Unemployment data are also available from the *Current Population Survey* for April 1950 and April 1960 and, as twelve month averages, for the years 1949 and 1959 but only for the United States as a whole (not for regions) and only for nonwhites (not Negroes) and for whites. Neither source of data is perfectly satisfactory for present purposes since the basic statistics here are 1949 and 1959 regional income figures for Negroes and for whites. Unemployment data from both sources are presented in Table VI as ratios of either Negro to white or nonwhite to white unemployment percentages.

The first row in Table VI shows that between 1949 and 1959 the ratio of nonwhite to white unemployment percentages rose by nearly one-half for men and by more than one-third for women. The decennial census data avoid the large sampling error associated with the *Current Population Survey* but err by understanding unemployment totals and percentages.[23] Computations based upon decennial census data appear on line two of Table VI for April 1950 and April 1960. Here the ratio of Negro to white unemployment percentages rose only one-tenth for men while declining slightly for women. Line three, as a *Current-Population-Survey* check on the decennial census data, also gives the nonwhite-to-white ratios for April 1950 and April 1960 and shows a one-quarter increase for men and a small increase for women. From all these figures, inconsistent as they are in part, one may conclude that between 1949 and 1959 unemployment did increase much more for Negro men than for white men and somewhat more for Negro women than for white women.

However, before leaping from national data to the conclusion that the regional declines in the relative economic position of Negro men can be explained by the growth of male Negro unemployment relative to male white unemployment percentages, the regional unemployment data must be considered.

It would be best to have data for 1949 and 1959, the years to which the income figures refer. Unfortunately, the only available regional data are decennial census figures for April 1950 and April 1960. Still, these may suffice as indicators, since, as Table VI shows,

[23] "The notion that a figure derived from a sample survey could be more nearly correct than a complete count received confirmation again in the 1950 Census comparisons. The Census count of employment was 5 per cent below the survey estimate and the count of unemployment 20 per cent below." Gertrude Bancroft, "Current Unemployment Statistics of the Census Bureau and Some Alternatives," in *The Measurement and Behavior of Unemployment,* a report of the National Bureau of Economic Research (Princeton: Princeton University Press, 1957) p. 75.

TABLE VI

NEGRO TO WHITE AND NONWHITE TO WHITE UNEMPLOYMENT PERCENTAGE RATIOS: BY SEX

Color or Racial Characteristic, Geographic Region, Time Points	Men		Women	
	Earlier Time	Later Time	Earlier Time	Later Time
Nonwhite to white, 1949 and 1959, for entire United States[1]	1.7	2.5	1.4	1.8
Negro to white, April 1950 and April 1960, conterminous United States[2]	1.7	1.9	1.9	1.8
Nonwhite to white, April 1950 and April 1960, entire United States[1]	1.8	2.3	1.7	1.9
Negro to white, April 1950 and April 1960[2]				
Northeast	2.7	2.0	2.0	1.6
North Central	3.1	2.8	3.5	2.6
West	5.0	2.3	2.2	1.8
South	.9	1.7	1.9	1.7

1. For 1949-50, calculated from U.S. Bureau of the Census, Current Population Reports, Series P-57. Table 11; for 1950-60 calculated from U.S. Department of Labor, Employment and Earnings, Table A-6.

2. Calculated from the same sources as Table V.

for each sex group in each region (except for men in the South) the Negro to white unemployment percentage ratio fell substantially, by one-tenth to one-half, between 1950 and 1960. Thus, the increase between 1950 and 1960, in the national ratio for men appeared because of the rise in the South and despite the decreases throughout the non-South.

What do the figures mean for the South? Assuming the April figures to be closely related to the true figures for the preceding year yielding the income statistics, it follows that the greater growth of unemployment among Negro men than among white men in the South contributed to the decline in the relative economic status of Southern Negro men. Yet, even this would not follow if the Southern rise in Negro unemployment were due to the transformation of disguised, uncounted, rural employment into visible, counted, urban unemployment.

Whatever the explanation of the Southern figures, the important point here is the evidence that outside the South there was no increase in the ratio of male Negro to male white unemployment percentages. And if there was no increase in this ratio, then changing unemployment rates will not help explain the decline in the relative income of Negro men in the North and West.

X. Part-time Employment

The Census Bureau and the Bureau of Labor Statistics define a part-time worker as one working fewer than 35 hours a week. Among persons employed in nonagricultural industries, the per cent working part time persistently increased during the 1950's. As Table VII shows, the increase appeared among nonagricultural workers in each color-sex group.

Concerned with regional Negro-white income ratios, it would be most helpful here to be able to compare the per cent working part time in each Negro or white sex group in 1949 with the per cent working part time in the same group in 1959 in each region. However, figures are not available for Negro men or Negro women, for regions, or for 1949. The existing data do permit some comparisons that will be used here to approximate the character of the changes between 1949 and 1959 in the importance of part-time work for each race-sex group in the nation as a whole.

To this end, the percentage employed part time in 1950 is compared with the percentage employed part time in 1959 in each color-sex group. The bottom row in Table VII shows the excess of the 1959 figure over the 1950 figure for each group. Across this row the figures are nearly the same although the increase for white women exceeds the increase for any other group. If, instead of comparing the single years 1950 and 1959, one computes an average figure for each color-sex group for the first two or three or four or five years in Table VII and compares that average with the average for the same color-sex group for the last two or three or four or five years in Table VII, the same conclusions emerge: (1) the part-time employment rate rose for each group, (2) the points by which the rate increased were nearly the same for each group, although, (3) the increase was greater for white women than for any other color-sex group.

The greater growth in the portion of employed white women than in the portion of employed white men working part time in nonagricultural industries may partly explain the decline, over the

TABLE VII

PERSONS EMPLOYED IN NONAGRICULTURAL INDUSTRIES, PER CENT WORKING PART TIME (1–35 HOURS), ANNUAL AVERAGES OF WEEKLY FIGURES: BY COLOR[1]

	Males		Females	
Years[2]	Nonwhite	White	Nonwhite	White
1950	14.8	8.3	31.1	21.5
1951	13.6	7.4	37.8	19.9
1953	9.4	7.2	30.0	19.1
1954	20.3	8.6	27.6	21.9
1955	15.3	9.5	35.2	27.7
1956	18.6	11.6	37.4	24.9
1957	18.1	12.0	36.4	25.8
1958	20.5	13.3	37.0	27.0
1959	21.8	14.7	38.6	29.6
1960	20.1	13.7	37.3	29.4
1961	19.0	12.8	35.9	28.1
Points of change 1950–1959	+ 7.0	+ 6.4	+ 7.5	+ 8.1

1. 1950–54, Current Population Reports, Series P50, Work Experience of the Population in 1950, in 1951, and 1954. 1955–58, Current Population Reports, Series P50, Annual Report of the Labor Force for 1955, 1956, 1957, and 1958. 1959–60, U.S. Department of Labor, Special Labor Force Report, No. 3, 1960, and No. 14, 1961. 1961, Employemnt and Earnings, op. cit. June 1962, p. 84.

2. Data are not available for 1949 or for 1952.

decade, in the ratio of white female to white male median income. The small differential in the growth of part-time employment rates of white and nonwhite men, provides slim evidence that differential growth in this factor kept Negro men's income from advancing relative to white men's income. It would be most helpful if one could reprocess decennial census data in a way that would reveal regional trends in part-time employment for Negroes and for whites between 1950 and 1960. This remains to be done.

XI. Negro-White Occupational Distribution

Occupational distribution and unemployment rates of Negroes represent at once the consequence of all supply and demand factors, qualitative and quantitative, and the chief determinants of income levels. Passing from unemployment data to measures of the relative occupational status of the employed Negro labor force requires the construction of index numbers, like Becker's and Rayack's, merging into one number the many occupations weighted by their various and, over decades, changing income levels. Herman P. Miller constructed such index numbers for male whites and nonwhites (not for Negroes or females) for 1940, 1950, and 1960. Using the 1959 income weights, he concluded:

> Although the occupational status of nonwhites relative to whites has improved for the country as a whole, in most States the nonwhite male now has about the same occupational distribution relative to the whites that he had in . . . 1950.[24]

Only in the West did he find a large gain. The advance of four points in the national figure was due to the growing weight attaching to non-Southern areas with relatively high Negro occupational status.

Using both median 1950 incomes and the 1950 median education of experienced workers in each occupation group as weights, Norval D. Glenn computed index numbers for 1940, 1950, and 1960 for males and for females by region and by color. For women, his index, measuring the occupational position of nonwhites relative to whites, increased between 1950 and 1960 for each of the four census regions. For the Northern and Southern regions, he found the index for men nearly constant as between 1950 and 1960. There was an increase in the West, but this Glenn attributed to the entry of Alaska and Hawaii between 1950 and 1960. In the end he concludes, as did Miller, that

[24] *Op. cit.*, p. 3.

"the rather pronounced improvement in the relative status of nonwhite males as a whole was mainly a function of the movement of nonwhites from the South to other regions."[25] Neither Miller nor Glenn turned up more than a very slight decline in the index number for men in any region.

One can also examine regional trends in Negro-white occupational patterns by the relatively easy process of dividing the percentage of all employed Negroes in a particular occupational group by the percentage of all employed whites in that group and comparing the resulting ratio for 1950 with the ratio for 1960. Table VIII shows these Negro-white percentage ratios for men in each of several occupation groups.

The trends are consistent as among occupational groups (including those not shown) and among non-Southern regions. Between 1950 and 1960, the per cent of employed Negro men in high-paid, high-status occupational groups rose more rapidly than the per cent of employed white men in those occupations while the per cent of employed Negro men in low-paid occupation groups declined relative to the per cent of employed white men in those occupations (to this the South was an exception). Similar computations for women yield similar results.

Judging from the income data showing male Negro decline and from the occupational data showing male Negro stagnation or advance relative to whites, it would appear to have been the inside-each-occupation story that was important, at least for men outside the South. It would appear that Negro men moved into the lowest income end of each "high-income" occupation while whites continued to monopolize the jobs at the increasingly distant upper-income end of the occupation. Neither occupation indexes nor Table VIII's ratios detect the character of movements within occupations. Yet, the income of individual Negroes would reflect the consequences of such movements.

XII. Trends in the Sixties

What has happened since 1959? On the basis of a sample, the Census Bureau, once each year, estimates median annual money income for men and for women, for whites and for nonwhites. These data are published in the *Current Population Reports* Series, P-60. If use is made of three year averages centering upon 1949 and upon 1959, the

[25] N. D. Glenn, "Some Changes in the Relative Status of American Non-whites, 1940 to 1960," *Phylon,* XXIV (Summer 1963), 115.

TABLE VIII

RATIO BETWEEN THE PER CENT OF EMPLOYED NEGRO MEN IN PARTICULAR OCCUPATIONS AND THE PER CENT OF EMPLOYED WHITE MEN IN THOSE OCCUPATIONS: BY REGION, 1950 AND 1960

Region	Clerical and Kindred Workers		Craftsmen, Foremen, and Kindred Workers		Service Workers		Laborers, except Farm and Mine	
	1950	1960	1950	1960	1950	1960	1950	1960
Northeast	.89	1.05	.50	.55	3.0	2.4	3.2	2.7
North Central	.78	1.00	.55	.55	3.9	3.1	4.0	3.2
West	.89	1.12	.54	.63	4.0	3.1	3.3	2.8
South	.28	.44	.34	.42	2.9	3.2	4.0	4.4

Source: 1950 figures calculated from U.S. Census of Population: 1950, Vol. II: Characteristics of the Population, pp. 1- 397-401; 1960 figures calculated from U.S. Census of Population: 1960, Detailed Characteristics, U.S. Summary, pp. 1-717-718.

figures from this source yield nonwhite-to-white income ratios of .52 for 1949 and .50 for 1959 for men and of .45 for 1949 and .61 for 1959 for women.[26] These figures are remarkably similar to those shown in Tables I and II. The two sources for income data agree in showing a decline, during the fifties, in the Negro-to-white (or nonwhite-to-white) income ratio for men and an increase for women.

And in more recent years? The nonwhite-to-white income ratio for men averaged .50 for 1958–60 and fell to .49 for 1962. The ratio for women averaged .61 for 1958–60 and rose to .67 for 1962.[27] The trends of the 1950's continued.

And what of the ratio of nonwhite women's to nonwhite men's median income? Table III (for Negroes rather than nonwhites) showed a rise for the South from .43 in 1949 to .45 in 1959. For the nation as a whole, Table III showed a decline from .44 in 1949 to .40 in 1959. The *Current Population Report's* three year average for Negroes for the nation was .36 for 1948–50 and rose to .38 for 1958–60. Since then, it has continued to rise and stood at .41 in 1962.[28] This trend toward matriarchy seems also to be continuing.

XIII. Conclusion

Becker and Rayack used occupational indices to show that during the 1940's, a decade distinguished by its tight labor market, the Negro's occupational position moved nearer that of whites. During the 1950's, the press reported the fall of many racial barriers. Yet income data show that during this decade of relatively weak demand (and despite the migration of 1,457,000 Negroes out of the South and into the relatively high income North and West) there was no increase between 1949 and 1959 in the national Negro-to-white median income ratio for men. This because within each of the four census regions, there was a decline in the Negro-to-white median income ratio for men.

It remains to be seen what the decade of the sixties will permit. The current population report samples indicate that the trends of the fifties continued at least through 1962. Whatever happens, economists will continue to be interested in the Negro-to-white median income ratio because, given the assumption that the average male white and the average male Negro are born with equal ability, an "efficient" allocation first of resources to education and second of men to work

[26] *Current Population Reports,* Series P-60, issues with titles mentioning "Income of Persons."

[27] *Ibid.*

[28] *Ibid.*

would result in an equal average contribution to production by (and equal income for) Negro men and white men. The data presented in this paper indicate that the equal-contribution ideal grew more rather than less chimerical during the decade of the fifties.

The social significance of that decade lay in the circumstance that while the press spoke of progress the gap grew between the income of Negro and white men, and the Negro man's economic dependence upon Negro women increased. Surely this talk of progress added to the frustration of men who experienced no progress.

Great moral fervor was directed against discrimination in the 1950's, but the labor market was much weaker in the fifties than in the forties. Therefore the question: Can exhortation ever be as effective a means to Negro advance as is buoyant demand? The trends of the sixties seem to remain those of the fifties. In the years ahead, buoyant demand may return, civil rights legislation may exert unprecedented leverage, or exhortation may gain in effectiveness; but if none of these possibilities materializes, the trends of the sixties may remain the trends of the fifties. If so there will be an economic justification for the "fire next time."

Appendix
Relative Income of Negro Men: Some Recent Data[1]

Rashi Fein

An article by Alan B. Batchelder entitled, "Decline in the Relative Income of Negro Men," containing data through 1962, appeared in the November 1964 issue of this *Journal.*[2] It is now possible to carry the relative income data forward for two additional years, 1963 and 1964.[3] Since the relative income of nonwhites has changed in these two years (particularly for males where we witnessed a reversal of trend), such an updating is of value.

Batchelder noted that the ratio of Negro to white income declined for males (while increasing for women) during the fifties and that "The nonwhite-to-white income ratio for men averaged .50 for 1958–60 and fell to .49 for 1962."[4] This trend, however, has sharply

[1]Reprinted with permission from *The Quarterly Journal of Economics,* May, 1966.

[2]Alan B. Batchelder, "Decline in the Relative Income of Negro Men," *The Quarterly Journal of Economics,* 78 (Nov., 1964).

[3]U.S. Bureau of the Census, *Current Population Reports,* series P-60, Nos. 43 and 47.

[4]Batchelder, *op. cit.,* p. 547.

reversed itself. In 1963 the ratio rose to .52 and in 1964 it rose further to .58. Improvement has replaced decline.

For females the ratio which "averaged .61 for 1958–60 and rose to .67 for 1962" stayed at .67 in 1963 and rose further to .71 in 1964.

These changes are substantial and help to answer Batchelder's query concerning possible trends in the sixties. They do not tell us to which of the three potential pressures discussed by Batchelder (buoyant demand, civil rights legislation, exhortation) to attribute the rise from .49 to .58. All pressures were present in the period 1962–64. The timing of the change does suggest that one should not underrate the impact of increasing demand. But since increase in relative incomes, while substantial, is not sufficient, a relaxation of the various pressures would be most unfortunate.

Changing Patterns in Employment of Nonwhite Workers

Joe L. Russell

[*From the* Monthly Labor Review, *May 1966.*]

Employment of nonwhite workers increased from 6.4 million to 7.7 million between 1955 and 1965, a substantially faster rate of growth than for white workers. As a result, the ratio of nonwhite workers to total employment rose from 10.2 to 10.7 percent. The increase in employment of nonwhite workers occurred in nearly all the major occupational groups, but—even more important—nonwhite workers made significant strides in entering occupational fields formerly unavailable to them in large numbers.[1] Nevertheless, nonwhite workers continue to be disproportionately concentrated in the less skilled blue-collar and service occupations. Their concentration in these occupations characterized by low educational requirements and high unemployment rates is significant in accounting for their high levels of unemployment (since 1955, the unemployment rate of nonwhites has averaged twice or more that of whites).

Moreover, looking to the future, because of the changing occupational structure in the American economy, the occupations in which

[1]The faster rate of growth in employment of nonwhites can be attributed to a faster rate of population growth and a small decrease in the unemployment rate. The nonwhite population rose by over 25 percent, the white population by 16 percent.

nonwhites are now concentrated will be growing more slowly than other occupations. Thus, even if nonwhites should continue to increase their share of jobs in the higher skilled occupations at the same rate as in recent years, the present unemployment gap between nonwhite workers and white workers would not be narrowed appreciably. Therefore, if nonwhite workers are to continue to improve their employment situation in the future, they will have to gain a larger proportion of the white-collar and skilled occupations even faster than heretofore. There are a number of programs, both governmental and private, which are designed to help nonwhites and other disadvantaged persons to gain access to these growing fields. Some of the programs are designed to provide education, training, and retraining opportunities to qualify persons for higher level fields (e.g., Manpower Development and Training Act, Vocational Educational Act, and various legislation providing for improvement and expansion of education and for financial aid for students). Other programs such as that included in recently passed and enacted civil rights legislation and programs of private employers are aimed at reducing racial discrimination in hiring. Only if such programs are successful in having a further major impact, and if nonwhite youth are motivated and assisted to take advantage of educational opportunities, can we expect a substantial reduction in the disparity between unemployment rates of whites and nonwhites.

Nonwhite Employment in 1965

In 1965, there were approximately 8½ million nonwhites in the civilian labor force in the United States—11.2 percent of the total. Nonwhite workers, however, constituted a smaller proportion of the employed (10.7 percent) and a much larger proportion of all unemployed persons (20.3 percent).

Nonwhite workers are concentrated in occupations which have limited growth prospects. They are employed less than proportionately in the professional, managerial, technical, clerical, sales, and craft occupations, with brighter growth prospects. The only rapidly growing major occupation group in which nonwhites are concentrated is service (except private households); even within this major group, nonwhites are usually concentrated in occupations with limited growth prospects.

In 1965, more than one-fourth of employed nonwhite men were in semiskilled occupations, such as drivers and factory operatives, compared with one-fifth of employed white men. More than one-fifth

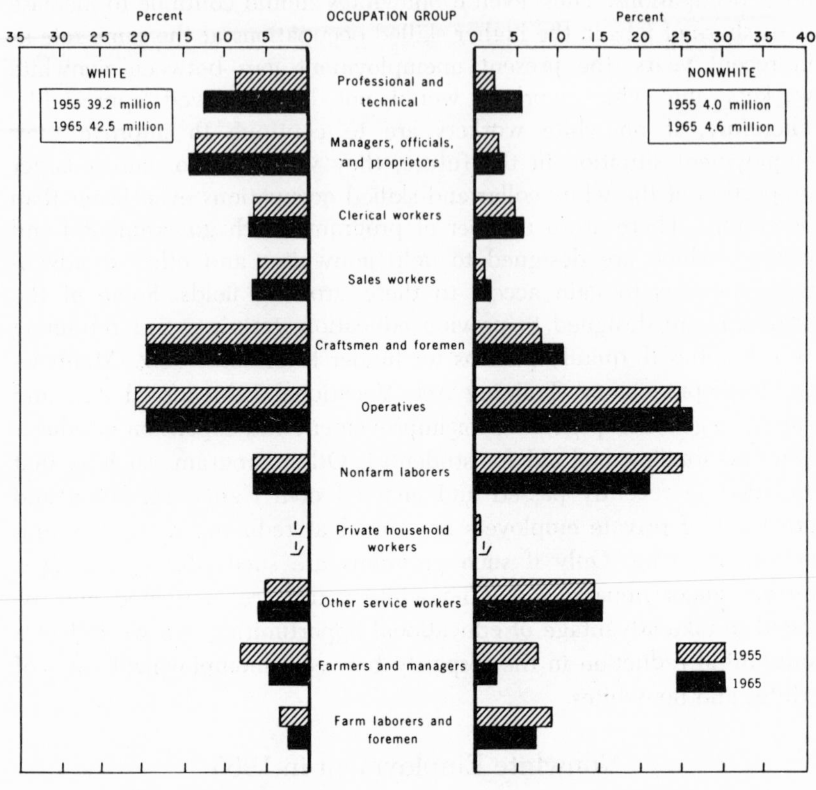

Chart 1: Percent Distribution of Employed Men, by Occupation Group and Color, 1955 and 1965

[1]Less than 0.5 percent.

of the nonwhite males were nonfarm laborers, in contrast with about one-fifteenth of the white males (See chart 1.)

In the same year, almost one-third of the employed nonwhite women worked in private household service occupations. (See chart 2.) One-fourth worked in other service occupations such as attendant, chambermaid, cleaner, cook, and dish washer. These two groups thus accounted for over one-half of all employed nonwhite women. In contrast, only one-fifth of the employed white women were employed in these two groups, many of them as babysitters and waitresses. Three-fifths of the employed white women were in white-collar jobs, compared with less than one-fourth of the employed nonwhite women.

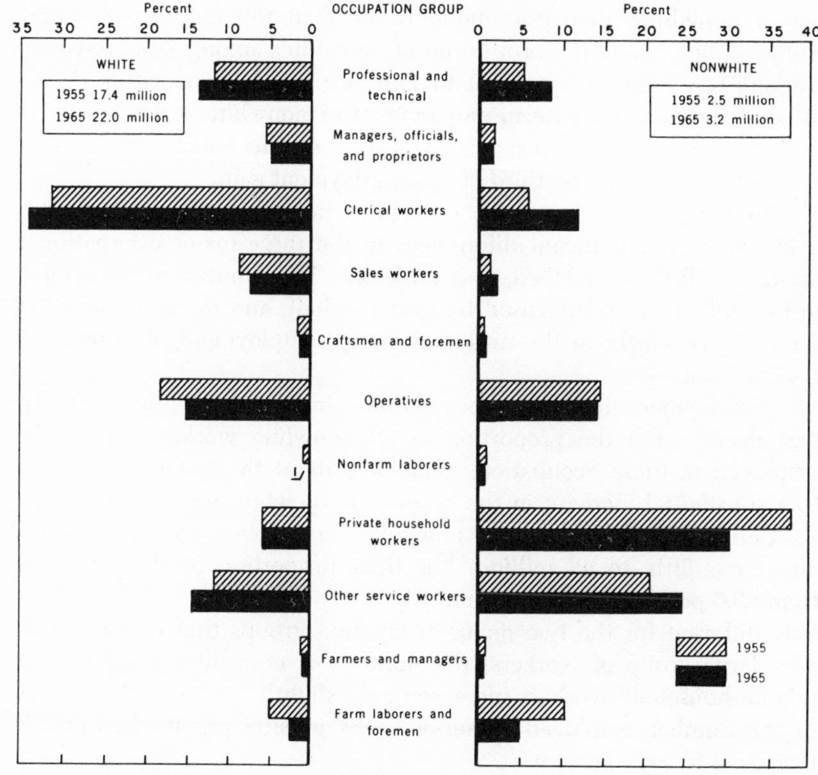

Chart 2: Percent Distribution of Employed Women, by Occupation Group and Color, 1955 and 1965

[1]Less than 0.5 percent.

Occupational Progress

Occupational patterns of nonwhite workers have changed markedly over the last decade. (See table 1.) In white-collar occupations, the proportion that nonwhite workers made up of total employment increased from 3.2 percent in 1955 to 4.7 percent in 1965, representing an increase of almost three-quarters of a million workers. This was more than one-half of the total increase during the decade in employment of nonwhites.

Even so, nonwhites are still employed less than proportionately in white-collar jobs. For example, less than one-fifth of all employed nonwhites are in white-collar jobs, compared with almost one-half of all employed whites.

In the blue-collar occupations, between 1955 and 1965, the number of nonwhites increased much faster than the number of white workers. As a result, the proportion of nonwhites among all blue-collar workers rose from 10.9 percent to 11.9 percent. Approximately three-fifths of the total increase in employment of nonwhite males occurred in blue-collar occupations; for whites, the blue-collar occupations accounted for about one-third of the employment gain.

In the progress made by nonwhites in entering the blue-collar field, there are significant differences in the three major occupational groups: skilled, semiskilled, and unskilled. The number of nonwhites in the skilled group increased by over one-half, and in the semiskilled group by one-fifth; in the unskilled group, employment of nonwhites declined somewhat.

Employment in service occupations increased rapidly over the past decade, but the proportion of all nonwhite workers who were employed in these occupations remained about the same, in contrast to a substantial increase in the proportion of white workers. Between 1955 and 1965, the number of nonwhite service workers increased by about one-fifth, to 2½ million, but their proportion of the total fell from 28.6 percent to 26.3 percent. The rates of increase were considerably different for the two major occupation groups that compose this very large group of workers; the number of nonwhites employed as private household workers increased only slightly (3 percent), whereas the number employed in service jobs outside private households increased by 35.7 percent.

Nonwhite farm workers as a proportion of all farm workers (including farmers, farm managers, farm laborers, and foremen) remained about the same. Between 1955 and 1965, the number of nonwhite farm workers declined by about one-third—the same rate of decline as for white farm workers.

Occupational Changes

Within the broad occupational groups, the increase in penetration rates (i.e., nonwhite workers as a proportion of all workers) was higher in some occupations than in others.

Employment of nonwhites in professional, technical, and kindred occupations has increased sharply over the past decade, more rapidly than in any other major occupation group, and much faster than employment of white workers in these fields. As a result, nonwhites as a proportion of all workers in professional jobs increased from 3.9 percent in 1955 to 5.9 percent in 1965, the major portion of this increase occurring since 1961.

Between 1957 and 1965, nonwhites made particularly rapid gains in teaching and in the medical and health service occupations.[2] The number of nonwhite teachers (below the college level) increased considerably faster than the number of white teachers in the same field, and as a result, the proportion of nonwhite workers employed as elementary and secondary teachers is now about equal to the proportion of white workers so employed.

Employment of nonwhite managers, officials, and proprietors has increased over the past decade, although not as rapidly as employment of nonwhite workers in other white-collar jobs. Nonwhite workers increased their share of jobs in this occupation group from 2.3 percent in 1955 to 2.8 percent in 1965. Between 1957 and 1965, the number of nonwhite proprietors increased by about one-fifth (most of the increase occurring outside the retail trade sector), while the number of white proprietors declined by about one-fifth.

The rate of increase in employment of nonwhite clerical and kindred workers has been sharper than that in any other major occupation (except the professional) group. This has resulted in a substantial rise in the proportion of nonwhites among all clerical workers—an increase from 3.8 percent in 1955 to 5.7 percent in 1965. Significant gains were made in the proportion of nonwhite postal clerks, telephone operators, stock clerks, office machine operators, and cashiers; however, the proportion of nonwhites among stenographers, typists, and secretaries increased very little.

The number of nonwhites employed as sales workers has risen by more than three-fourths during the past decade, and their proportion among sales workers from 2 percent to 3.1 percent. Even with these substantial gains, however, less than 2 percent of all the nonwhite workers were employed in sales occupations—less than one-third the proportion of white workers so employed.

Employment of nonwhite craftsmen, foremen, and kindred workers increased by nearly three-fifths, raising their proportion of total craftsmen employment from 4 percent in 1955 to 5.6 percent in 1965. Construction craftsmen made up a considerable part of this growth, especially over the past few years.

During the 1955–65 period, more nonwhites were employed as operatives and kindred workers than in any other major occupation group. Although the rate of increase of nonwhite employment in this occupation was less than in most others, it exceeded the rate of increase for whites. As a result, the proportion of nonwhites increased from 10.6 percent in 1955 to 12.3 percent in 1965.

A slight decline has taken place in the number of nonwhites employed as industrial laborers, so that their proportion in this occu-

[2]For the more detailed occupations, data are available since 1957.

TABLE 1

NONWHITE EMPLOYED WORKERS AS A PERCENT OF TOTAL EMPLOYMENT, BY OCCUPATION GROUP AND SEX, 1955-65[1]
(Annual averages)

Occupation group and sex	1965	1964	1963	1962	1961	1960	1959	1958	1957	1956	1955
All employed nonwhite workers	10.7	10.6	10.5	10.5	10.4	10.6	10.3	10.2	10.4	10.3	10.2
White-collar workers	4.7	4.5	4.2	4.0	3.9	3.9	3.5	3.3	3.3	3.0	3.2
Professional and technical workers	5.9	5.8	5.3	4.6	4.1	4.4	4.3	3.8	3.8	3.7	3.9
Managers, officials, and proprietors	2.8	2.6	2.6	2.5	2.5	2.5	2.3	2.3	2.1	2.2	2.3
Clerical Workers	5.7	5.4	5.1	5.1	5.4	5.2	4.4	4.3	4.4	3.8	3.8
Sales workers	3.1	3.1	3.0	2.6	2.5	2.6	2.1	2.1	1.9	1.8	2.0
Blue-collar workers	11.9	11.8	11.5	11.5	11.4	11.6	11.4	11.2	11.2	11.1	10.9
Craftsmen and foremen	5.6	5.8	5.2	4.9	4.9	4.9	4.5	4.5	4.4	4.2	4.0
Operatives	12.3	11.8	11.8	11.7	11.9	11.8	11.2	11.3	11.3	11.2	10.6
Nonfarm laborers	25.6	26.9	26.2	27.0	25.7	26.4	27.7	26.6	27.4	26.7	27.6
Service Workers	26.3	26.0	26.3	26.4	26.3	26.8	26.7	27.6	28.3	28.2	28.6
Private household	43.6	43.6	44.9	44.4	43.5	45.3	45.3	45.6	48.0	46.4	48.8
Other	20.8	20.2	19.9	19.9	20.0	20.1	19.7	20.5	20.8	21.2	21.0
Farm workers	14.7	14.6	15.3	16.1	15.7	16.2	15.5	14.9	15.3	14.9	14.3
Farmers and farm managers	6.1	6.3	7.0	7.5	7.5	7.9	7.7	7.8	8.3	8.5	8.6
Farm laborers and foremen	24.3	23.8	24.2	25.8	24.8	25.1	24.6	23.6	23.9	22.9	21.8

TABLE 1 (continued)

Occupation group and sex	1965	1964	1963	1962	1961	1960	1959	1958	1957	1956	1955
All employed nonwhite men	9.7	9.6	9.5	9.4	9.3	9.5	9.2	9.0	9.3	9.3	9.2
White-collar workers	4.2	4.0	3.8	3.6	3.7	3.6	3.2	3.0	3.0	2.8	3.0
Professional and technical workers	4.6	4.6	3.9	3.5	3.3	3.3	3.1	2.7	2.9	2.5	2.7
Managers, officials, and proprietors	2.5	2.3	2.4	2.3	2.1	2.1	1.8	1.9	1.7	1.9	2.0
Clerical workers	7.9	7.1	7.2	7.3	8.3	7.8	6.8	6.9	6.5	6.0	6.3
Sales workers	2.9	2.8	3.1	2.5	2.4	2.6	2.1	1.8	1.8	1.6	1.9
Blue-collar workers	11.9	11.9	11.5	11.5	11.2	11.5	11.4	11.1	11.3	11.1	11.0
Craftsmen and foremen	5.6	5.8	5.2	4.8	4.9	4.8	4.5	4.4	4.3	4.1	3.9
Operatives	12.4	11.8	12.0	11.7	11.7	11.8	11.1	11.2	11.4	11.3	10.7
Nonfarm laborers	25.7	27.1	26.4	27.1	25.7	26.6	27.9	26.7	27.5	26.8	27.8
Service workers	21.6	21.6	22.3	22.0	21.7	22.0	21.0	21.8	22.2	22.9	22.3
Private household	29.8	27.0	33.3	36.7	29.0	33.3	34.7	41.5	39.1	40.0	47.6
Other	21.5	21.5	22.1	21.7	21.6	21.8	20.8	21.4	21.9	22.6	21.9
Farm workers	13.1	12.8	12.9	14.1	13.8	13.7	13.1	12.7	13.2	13.0	12.4
Farmers and farm managers	5.8	5.8	6.4	7.2	7.1	7.5	7.5	7.6	7.9	8.2	8.4
Farm laborers and foremen	24.4	23.4	22.9	25.0	24.2	23.3	23.1	22.2	23.1	22.3	20.9

TABLE 1 (continued)

Occupation group and sex	1965	1964	1963	1962	1961	1960	1959	1958	1957	1956	1955
All employed nonwhite women	12.6	12.6	12.5	12.5	12.5	12.7	12.5	12.5	12.6	12.4	12.4
White-collar workers	5.3	5.2	4.8	4.5	4.2	4.3	3.9	3.7	3.7	3.3	3.4
Professional and technical workers	8.1	8.0	7.7	6.7	5.6	6.3	6.4	5.5	5.4	5.6	5.9
Managers, officials, and proprietors	4.4	4.2	4.0	3.9	4.1	4.7	4.9	4.4	3.9	3.4	3.9
Clerical workers	4.8	4.6	4.2	4.0	4.0	4.0	3.2	3.1	3.4	2.7	2.6
Sales workers	3.4	3.4	3.0	2.9	2.5	2.5	2.3	2.5	2.2	2.1	2.2
Blue-collar workers	12.2	11.5	11.3	11.9	12.2	11.8	11.4	11.7	10.9	11.0	10.3
Craftsmen and foremen	8.5	7.2	6.2	7.6	7.4	6.8	5.2	7.6	7.7	7.2	7.0
Operatives	12.2	11.6	11.4	11.8	12.2	11.9	11.5	11.6	10.8	11.0	10.2
Nonfarm laborers	20.7	18.7	21.3	25.6	23.8	19.5	19.8	22.0	23.3	21.6	21.7
Service workers	28.8	28.5	28.5	28.8	28.8	29.3	29.8	30.8	31.9	31.4	32.4
Private household	43.9	44.1	45.2	44.6	43.9	45.6	45.6	45.7	48.2	46.5	48.8
Other	20.2	19.0	18.1	18.3	18.7	18.5	18.8	19.7	19.7	19.8	20.0
Farm workers	22.0	22.9	25.2	25.4	24.7	27.3	25.6	24.7	24.1	22.6	22.2
Farmers and farm managers	11.4	14.4	16.8	12.9	15.4	16.2	12.6	13.0	17.1	14.8	14.3
Farm laborers and foremen	24.1	24.5	26.7	27.6	26.2	28.6	27.3	26.4	25.2	23.8	23.2

[1] Data through 1956 have not been adjusted to reflect changes in the definitions of employment and unemployment adopted in January 1957.

pation group fell from 27.6 percent in 1955 to 25.6 in 1965. However, nonwhites are still more than proportionally employed in unskilled jobs—in 1965, 1 in 5 nonwhite men, 1 in 15 white men.

In 1955, 48.8 percent of the private household workers were nonwhite. By 1965, this had fallen to 43.6 percent, even though employment of nonwhite private household service workers had increased by about 3 percent.

Employment of nonwhites as service workers (except private household) rose 35.7 percent between 1955 and 1965, reaching almost 1.5 million. But since these occupations as a whole expanded rapidly in this period, the proportion of jobs in this field held by nonwhites was unchanged—21 percent in 1955, 20.8 percent in 1965. The proportion of workers employed in service occupations increased at about the same rate for whites and nonwhites. However, nonwhites are still concentrated in the less desirable of these service occupations, such as porters and attendants.

The number of farmers and farm managers declined substantially over the past decade, but employment of nonwhites in this category fell even more rapidly—by 57 percent. Consequently, the nonwhite proportion of the total fell from 8.6 percent in 1955 to 6.1 percent in 1965. In contrast, employment of nonwhite farm laborers and foremen declined less rapidly than the employment of white workers in this group, so that the proportion of nonwhites in these occupations rose from 21.8 percent to 24.3 percent—even though their number decreased by about one-fifth.

Estimates of Future Patterns

The changing occupational structure of the economy will be working against nonwhites, since by and large the occupations in which they are now concentrated will grow more slowly than other occupations.[3]

To look into the implications of these changing occupational requirements, two illustrative hypothetical estimates for 1975 were made.[4]

[3]For a discussion of future trends in a wide variety of industries and occupations, see *America's Industrial and Occupational Manpower Requirements, 1975,* a report prepared by the Bureau of Labor Statistics for the National Commission on Technology, Automation and Economic Progress.

[4]Nonwhites will constitute almost 12 percent of the work force by the end of the next decade, compared with 11.2 percent in 1965 and 10.7 precent in 1955. This faster rate of growth for the nonwhite labor force will be accompanied by several dramatic changes in composition, one factor being that much of the increase will be in the younger age groups.

TABLE 2

PROJECTED EMPLOYMENT OF NONWHITE WORKERS IN 1975, ASSUMING THAT THEIR PROPORTION OF EMPLOYMENT IN EACH OCCUPATION WILL REMAIN THE SAME AS IN 1965 [1]

(Numbers in thousands)

Occupation group	1965					1975				
	Total		Nonwhite			Total		Nonwhite		
	Number	Percent	Number	Percent	Nonwhite as a percent of total	Number	Percent	Number	Percent	Nonwhite as a percent of total
All employed persons	72,179	100.0	7,750	100.0	10.7	88,700	100.0	9,130	100.0	10.3
White-collar workers	32,104	44.5	1,510	19.5	4.7	42,800	48.3	2,050	22.5	4.8
Professional and technical workers	8,883	12.3	530	6.8	5.9	13,200	14.9	790	8.6	6.0
Managers, officials, and proprietors	7,340	10.2	200	2.6	2.8	9,200	10.4	260	2.8	2.8
Clerical	11,166	15.5	630	8.2	5.7	14,600	16.5	830	9.1	5.7
Sales	4,715	6.5	150	1.9	3.1	5,800	6.5	180	1.9	3.1
Blue-collar workers	26,466	36.7	3,160	40.7	11.9	29,900	33.7	3,420	37.4	11.4
Craftsmen and foremen	9,221	12.8	520	6.7	5.6	11,400	12.9	640	7.0	5.6
Operatives	13,390	18.6	1,650	21.3	12.3	14,800	16.7	1,830	20.0	12.3
Laborers, excluding farm and mine	3,855	5.3	990	12.7	25.6	3,700	4.2	950	10.3	25.5
Service workers	9,342	12.9	2,450	31.7	26.3	12,500	14.1	3,140	34.4	25.1
Private household	2,251	3.1	980	12.7	43.6	2,400	2.7	1,050	11.5	43.6
Other	7,091	9.8	1,470	19.0	20.8	10,100	11.4	3,000	23.0	20.8
Farm workers	4,265	5.9	630	8.1	14.7	3,500	3.9	520	5.7	15.0
Farmers and farm managers	2,244	3.1	140	1.8	6.2	1,800	2.0	110	1.2	6.2
Laborers and foremen	2,021	2.8	490	6.3	24.3	1,700	1.9	410	4.5	24.3

1 The projections of total employment in this article were developed by the Bureau of Labor Statistics in the course of its continuing occupational outlook research program, especially its work for the 1966-67 edition of the Occupa-

TABLE 2 (continued)

tional Outlook Handbook. The projections assume a national unemployment rate of 3 percent in 1975.

Nonwhite employment is rounded to the nearest 10,000 and total employment to the nearest 100,000 for 1975; the percentages are based on unrounded data.

The computations were done separately for the following occupational categories: Medical and other health; teachers except college; other professional and technical; managers, officials, and proprietors; stenographers, typists, and secretaries; other clerical workers; retail trade sales workers; other sales workers; carpenters; construction craftsmen, except carpenters; mechanics and repairmen; metal craftsmen, except mechanics; other craftsmen and kindred workers; foremen, not elsewhere classified drivers; and deliverymen; other operatives; nonfarm laborers; private household workers; service workers, except private household; farmers and farm managers; and farm laborers and foremen.

NOTE: Because of rounding, sums of individual items may not equal totals.

TABLE

PROJECTED EMPLOYMENT OF NONWHITE WORKERS
EMPLOYMENT IN EACH OCCUPATION WILL INCREASE

(Numbers

Occupation group	1958				
	Total		Nonwhite		
	Number	Percent	Number	Percent	Nonwhite as a percent of total
All employed persons	63,966	100.0	6,520	100.0	10.2
White-collar workers	27,056	42.3	900	13.7	3.3
Professional and technical workers	6,961	10.9	260	4.0	3.8
Managers, officials, and proprietors	6,785	10.6	150	2.4	2.3
Clerical	9,137	14.3	390	6.0	4.3
Sales	4,173	6.5	90	1.3	2.1
Blue-collar workers	23,510	36.8	2,640	40.4	11.2
Craftsmen and foremen	8,469	13.2	380	5.8	4.5
Operatives	11,441	17.9	1,300	19.9	11.3
Laborers, excluding farm and mine	3,600	5.6	960	14.7	26.6
Service workers	7,809	12.2	2,150	33.0	27.6
Private household	2,204	3.4	1,000	15.4	45.6
Other	5,605	8.8	1,150	17.6	20.5
Farm workers	5,591	8.7	830	12.8	14.9
Farmers and farm managers	3,083	4.8	240	3.7	7.8
Laborers and foremen	2,508	3.9	590	9.1	23.6

[1]See footnote 1, table 2.

3

IN 1975, ASSUMING THAT THEIR PROPORTION OF
OR DECREASE AT THE SAME RATE AS IN 1958-65[1]

in thousands)

1965					1975				
Total		Nonwhite			Total		Nonwhite		
Number	Percent	Number	Percent	Nonwhite as a percent of total	Number	Percent	Number	Percent	Nonwhite as a percent of total
72,179	100.0	7,750	100.0	10.7	88,700	100.0	10,150	100.0	11.4
32,104	44.5	1,510	19.5	4.7	42,800	48.3	2,840	28.0	6.6
8,883	12.3	530	6.8	5.9	13,200	14.9	1,190	11.7	9.0
7,340	10.2	200	2.6	2.8	9,200	10.4	310	3.0	3.4
11,166	15.5	630	8.2	5.7	14,600	16.5	1,070	10.5	7.3
4,715	6.5	150	1.9	3.1	5,800	6.5	280	2.7	4.8
26,466	36.7	3,160	40.7	11.9	29,900	33.7	3,740	36.9	12.5
9,221	12.8	520	6.7	5.6	11,400	12.9	860	8.4	7.5
13,390	18.6	1,650	21.3	12.3	14,800	16.7	1,970	19.4	13.3
3,855	5.3	990	12.7	25.6	3,700	4.2	920	9.1	24.9
9,342	12.9	2,450	31.7	26.3	12,500	14.1	3,080	30.3	24.6
2,251	3.1	980	12.7	43.6	2,400	2.7	980	9.7	40.9
7,091	9.8	1,470	19.0	20.8	10,100	11.4	2,100	20.7	20.8
4,265	5.9	630	8.1	14.7	3,500	3.9	490	4.8	13.8
2,244	3.1	140	1.8	6.2	1,800	2.0	70	.7	3.8
2,021	2.8	490	6.3	24.3	1,700	1.9	420	4.1	24.4

Under the first hypothesis, it was assumed that in 1975 nonwhites would hold the same proportion of the jobs in each occupation that they held in 1965. (See table 2.) Under the second, it was assumed that between 1965 and 1975 nonwhites would continue to increase their penetration into each occupation at the same rates that occurred between 1958 and 1965. The 1958–65 period was chosen because most of the major changes occurred during this period and a review of recent data does not indicate that any substantial changes in the trend have occurred. (See table 3.)

If nonwhites merely continue to hold the same proportion of the jobs in each occupation that they held in 1965, nonwhite employment will increase from 7.8 million in 1965 to 9.1 million in 1975. Despite this growth, however, the nonwhite proportion of total employment would decline, simply because of the slower growth of the occupations in which nonwhite workers are now concentrated.

To see what this slower growth in employment could mean in relation to unemployment rates, this estimate of nonwhite employment in 1975 was compared with the nonwhite labor force projected for that year. Preliminary projections show a total nonwhite labor force of about 11 million in 1975, or almost 12 percent of the work force.[5] Making allowance for the number of workers who would be in the Armed Forces in 1975, the above projections imply a nonwhite unemployment rate of about 15 percent—about five times the unemployment rate assumed for the whole labor force in the same set of projections.

On the other hand, if the proportion of nonwhite workers in each occupation should continue to change between 1965 and 1975 the same rate as during the 1958–65 period, employment of nonwhite workers would increase from 7.8 million in 1965 to 10.2 million in 1975, and the proportion of nonwhites among all employed workers would rise from 10.7 percent to 11.4 percent. Thus, the combined effect of changing penetration ratios and changing occupational requirements would mean an increase of about one-third in the employment of nonwhites—an annual average rate of increase more than one-half greater than that of the past decade.

Nonwhite employment in white-collar occupations would increase by 88 percent, the most rapid increase occurring in the professional and technical jobs (125 percent). Nonwhite blue-collar employment

[5]For purposes of this article, preliminary projections of the labor force by color were used. These are consistent with the projections prepared by Sophia Cooper and Denis F. Johnston in "Labor Force Projections for 1970–80," *Monthly Labor Review*, February 1965, pp. 129–140. Detailed projections of labor force by color will be published by the Bureau later this year.

would rise by 18 percent, and employment in service occupations by 26 percent. The only decline would be in employment as farm workers (22 percent). Even with this more rapid progress, however, the 1975 unemployment rate for nonwhites would still be twice that for the labor force as a whole, and nonwhite workers would continue to be disproportionately employed in less skilled occupations.

Thus, the hypothetical estimates show that nonwhite workers will have to gain access to the rapidly growing skilled and white-collar occupations at a faster rate than in recent years if their unemployment rate is to be brought down toward the same level as that of white workers. The achievement of this increase in the rate of penetration is in part a matter of providing education and training opportunities; in part, of reducing racial discrimination in hiring.

Suggested Additional Readings

1. Becker, Gary. *The Economics of Discrimination.* Chicago: The University of Chicago Press, 1957.
2. Cummings, Laurie D. "The Employed Poor: Their Characteristics and Occupations," *Monthly Labor Review* (July 1964).
3. Hiestand, Dale L. *Economic Growth and Employment Opportunities for Minorities.* New York: Columbia University Press, 1964.
4. Kahn, Tom. *The Economics of Equality.* New York: League for Industrial Democracy, 1964.
5. Miller, Herman P. "Poverty and the Negro," *Poverty Amidst Affluence,* ed. Leo Fishman. New Haven: Yale University Press, 1966.
6. "The Negro American," *Daedalus* (Fall 1965 and Winter 1966). Entire issues.
7. Orshansky, Mollie. "Recounting the Poor—A Five Year Review," *Social Security Bulletin* (April 1966).
8. Ross, Arthur M. and Hill, Herbert, eds. *Employment, Race and Poverty.* New York: Harcourt, Brace and World, 1967.
9. Silberman, Charles. *Crisis in Black and White.* New York: Random House, 1964.
10. U.S. Department of Labor, Bureau of Labor Statistics. *The Negroes in the United States: Their Economic and Social Situation.* Bulletin No. 1511. June 1966.

Chapter 2

Background Factors in Negro Inequality in Employment

Introduction

There has always been controversy in this country about the "causes" of Negro disadvantagement in the labor market. The crude biologistic theories of the pre-1930's have given way to a series of more sophisticated, yet no less controversial, explanations. Each of these rests on a distinct set of assumptions about the nature of society and the relative importance of cultural and class factors in determining behavior. Three views in particular have gained increasing prominence in the last few years, and the current debate on "causes" has emphasized the divergence of these explanations. Although we discuss each of these views separately, we do so for analytical purposes, recognizing the overlap that exists between the explanations.

The first explanation assumes that lower income Negroes have a subculture with a distinctive set of values and behaviors that isolate them from the culture of the wider white community. It is argued that this subculture had its origins in (1) the many forms of discrimination that resulted in restricting Negro opportunities for participation in the social and economic life of the larger society, and (2) the cultural heritage of slavery that resulted in distinctive institutional styles and traditions (e.g., family structure) that have persisted and set Negroes apart from whites. The proponents of this view see three value themes as dominant in Negro subculture: a set of beliefs that favor a social dependency role for the Negro rather than one of independence; norms and values that support female role dominance as against males; and low aspiration patterns that set limited achievement goals. These values, supposedly at the core of lower-class Negro life, are transmitted from one generation to the next and set sharp limits on the development of the personal qualities necessary for success in the labor market.

One of the difficulties of this explanation is its inability to account for the extensive variation in family life styles even within a single Negro neighborhood. Thus, some Negro families show amazing resiliency in meeting social obligations (e.g., the education of the children) in the face of deprivatory, economic conditions. Other Negro families have members in prime economic roles, requiring considerable independent thought and action. A subculture explanation would have to explain these exceptions.

In contrast to this first explanation for Negro disadvantagement, others argue that the Negro is confronted by a restricted opportunity structure that denies him access—intentionally or unintentionally—to adequate jobs, training, education, and housing. It is not that the Negro does not have the proper goals, values, or motivations, but rather that these exist, unlike in the case of whites, within the framework of an opportunity structure that renders impossible the fulfillment of these basic social drives. Thus, while the first analysis stresses the need to *prepare* the Negro for the labor market by giving him *new* values, goals, and motivations, the second thesis argues that the major problem is one of *providing access* to adequate opportunities in the labor market.

A third view, implicit in the recent U. S. Department of Labor report on the Negro family, assumes that the major factor in disadvantagement is a growing deterioration of the fabric of Negro life—particularly the family. While this report recognizes the need to expand the opportunity structure for Negroes through increased federal and state legislation, it suggests that this program will not be successful unless coupled with intensive efforts to improve the quality and available resources of Negro family life. Daniel P. Moynihan, the author of the report, argues that the socio-economic context within which Negroes live in this country has seriously impaired the capacity of the family to provide important sources of social control during the development years and stable models for psychological identification and support. The "Moynihan Report" sees one source of Negro family instability in the patterns of matriarchal family dominance that relegate the Negro male to a secondary authority and economic role. This dominance, it is contended, is a reflection both of a heritage of slavery, when the family was female-centered, and current employment patterns that favor the wage-earning potentials of Negro women rather than Negro men. These patterns contribute to higher rates of desertion, divorce, and illegitimacy among Negroes. They create a climate of instability and unpredictability which makes it difficult for Negro youth to acquire a set of personal values and norms that will provide guidelines for access to the memberships, rewards, and services that characterize success in the larger society. The argument proposed by Moynihan is not new; it is simply a restatement of observations made by earlier sociologists. However, a storm of controversy has resulted from the publication of the report. Two oft-cited objections to it are its failure to recognize the diversity of family types in the Negro community and its failure to examine alternative sources of social support (e.g., extended kinship structure) that may obviate apparent weaknesses in Negro family structure.

The intellectual proposition about causes being debated here is of more than passing interest. The resolution of this debate will determine the means to be used in reducing Negro disadvantagement. If the first view prevails, then better labor market *preparation* for Negroes is needed through vocational or compensatory education. The second view calls for a *broad reassessment* of how institutions function in our society and for creating strategies to remedy inequities in opportunity. The third view postulates the need to commit *more resources* (e.g., counseling, education) to strengthen and stabilize the Negro family.

These discussions must be seen in the broader perspective of the intellectual history of the United States. Programs that favor radical institutional change have been a popular cause with intellectuals, but have been received with less than enthusiasm by the shapers of public policy. The bureaucratic tradition has been to use education as a panacea for all social ills. The administration of the federal antipoverty program has certainly leaned heavily on the first causal model with consequent emphais on education-orientation (e.g., Headstart, Job Corps). The possibilities for any radical departure from this mode seem slight.

The articles in Chapter 2 span all three points of view, but share the outlook that Negroes have been shortchanged by the society in terms of housing, education, medical care, opportunities for psychological growth, and control over their own destinies. The riots in the Northern ghettoes were spawned in neighborhoods characterized by similar conditions: poor housing, unemployment, inadequate transportation to industrial centers, complaints of police brutality, control of the neighborhood economy by whites, lack of political power, and alienation from the whole misery-producing "system." The combination of economic repression and racial suppression has culminated in a feeling of powerlessness within many Negroes. As Kenneth Clark pointed out in *Dark Ghetto*, "The poor are always alienated from normal society, and when the poor are Negro, as they increasingly are in American cities, a double trauma exists."

"Not lack of knowledge, but a sense of powerlessness is a key to the Negro reaction to the caste-class system," St. Clair Drake comments in his analysis of the Negro ghettoes. Ghettoes, he holds, are created by the white middle class to protect their own neighborhoods from behavior patterns of which it disapproves. Ghetto residents are victimized economically and psychologically by the spatial isolation from white communities, the profit potential in residential segregation, and the increased consciousness of a separate subordinate position. Many who aspire to leave the ghetto are trapped. The job ceiling and income gap set limits for realization of class values, since a given life style demands a minimum level of income.

As early as the preschool period, the Ausubels point out, Negro children learn to understand the negative implications of dark skin color for social status and personal worth. This process makes it difficult for them to identify with their parents and obtain from that identification the derived status that constitutes the principle basis of self-esteem during childhood. During adolescence many segregated Negro children characteristically develop low aspirations for academic and vocational achievement. This problem stems from existing social class and ethnic values, the absence of suitable models, marked educational retardation, restricted vocational opportunities, lack of parental and peer group support, and the cultural impoverishment of many Negro homes. The seeming hopelessness of attaining adequate vocational status in the wider culture induces many Negro youths to withdraw from competition with whites and to seek psychological shelter in their segregated subculture.

Deutsch and Brown found that Negroes participate much less in the cultural mainstream and that Negro life in this caste society is considerably more homogeneous than is life for the majority group. Children with fathers in the home exhibit higher IQ's than youngsters from fatherless families, although both groups score significantly higher on intelligence tests as the result of preschool experiences. The Negro groups which the authors studied showed greater deprivation on most of the social variables used in their analysis.

The syndrome of environmental insults is also discussed by Striner and Sheppard, who focus on the relevance of family structure to the individual's motivations to succeed, aspire, and obtain better jobs. They suggest that Negroes of working ages carry a greater burden of dependency than whites, citing the relationship between high birth rates among low-income Negro families and the perpetuation of inferior occupation levels and high unemployment.

Lower-class Negro youths face a difficult transition in moving from their home life to the workshop or office, Joseph Himes points out. Work-related cultural deprivations lessen the chances for successful job performance of many young Negroes entering the job market.

The traditional exclusion of Negroes from the work life of the community adversely affects a young Negro's ability to acquire a job or to perform adequately in many work roles. Since many jobs above the service level have been closed to Negroes, and traditional "Negro jobs" are often uninspiring and fatiguing, the child perceives work as an unpleasant condition of life which brings with it no promotion, no avenue for mobility, and which has in itself no intrinsic value.

The Ghettoization of Negro Life

St. Clair Drake

[From "Social and Economic Status of the Negro," Daedalus, *Fall 1965, with permission of The American Academy of Arts and Sciences.]*

The "Ghettoization" of Negro Life

Pressure upon Negroes to live within all-Negro neighborhoods has resulted in those massive concentrations of Negro population in Northern metropolitan areas which bitter critics call "concentration camps" or "plantations" and which some social scientists refer to as "Black Ghettos."[1] Small town replicas exist everywhere throughout the nation, for the roots of residential segregation lie deep in American history. In older Southern towns slave quarters were transformed into Negro residential areas after Emancipation—a few blocks here, a whole neighborhood there, often adjacent to white homes. In newer Southern towns and cities a less secure upwardly mobile white population usually demanded a greater degree of segregation from ex-slaves and their descendants. Prior to World War I, the residential patterns did not vary greatly between North and South, but the great northward migration of Negroes between 1914 and 1920 expanded the small Negro neighborhoods into massive Black Belts. Middle-class white neighbors used "restrictive-covenants" as their main device for slowing down and "containing" the expansion of Negro neighborhoods. Thus, with continued in-migration and restricted access to housing in "white neighborhoods," the overcrowded Black Ghetto emerged with its substandard structures, poor public services, and high crime and juvenile delinquency rates.

Scholars know from careful research, and increasingly wider circles are becoming aware of the fact, that Negroes do not depress property values, but that middle-class white attitudes toward Negroes do.[2] As long as Negroes, as a group, are a symbol of lower social status, proximity to them will be considered undesirable and such social attitudes will be reflected in the market place. The problem is complicated by the fact that a very high proportion of Negro Americans actually does have lower-class attributes and behavior patterns. The upward mobility of white Americans, as well as their comfort and personal safety, is facilitated by spatial segregation. (Older cities in the South have been an exception.) The white middle class could protect its values by acting solely in terms of class, letting middle-class Negro families scatter into white neighborhoods irrespective of race. Instead, the white middle class in American cities protects its own neighborhoods from behavior patterns it disapproves of and from chronic social disorganization by "ghettoizing" the Negro. Real-estate operators, black and white, have exploited the fears of the white middle class from the beginning of the northern migration by "block busting," that is, by buying property for less than its normal market value and reselling it at a higher price to Negroes barred from the open market or by charging them higher rentals. Eventually the profit-potential in residential segregation was maximized by the institutions which controlled mortgage money and refused to finance property for Negro residence outside of the Black Belts except under conditions approved by them.

In 1948, the Supreme Court declared racial restrictive covenants unenforceable in the courts, but this action tended to accelerate rather than reverse the process of ghettoization, for many whites proceeded to sell to Negroes at inflated prices and then moved to the suburbs, or they retained their properties, moved away, and raised the rents. The Court's decision was based partly upon a reevaluation of the concept of civil rights and partly upon a recognition of the fact that serious economic injustice was a by-product of residential segregation, a situation summed up by Thomas Pettigrew:

> While some housing gains occurred in the 1950's, the quality of Negro housing remains vastly inferior relative to that of whites. For example, in Chicago in 1960, Negroes paid as much for housing as whites, despite their lower incomes. . . . This situation exists because of essentially two separate housing markets; and the residential segregation that creates these dual markets has increased steadily over past decades until it has reached universally high levels in cities throughout the United States, despite significant advances in the socio-economic status of Negroes. . . .[3]

The trend has not yet been reversed despite F.H.A. administrative regulations and Supreme Court decisions.

The spatial isolation of Negroes from whites created Negro "communities." Within these Negro neighborhoods, church and school became the basic integrative institutions, and Negro entrepreneurs developed a variety of service enterprises—barbershops and beauty parlors, funeral homes and restaurants, pool parlors, taverns, and hotels—all selling to what came to be called "The Negro Market." Successful banking and insurance businesses also grew up within some Negro communities. A Negro "subculture" gradually emerged, national in scope, with distinctive variations upon the general American culture in the fields of literature, art, music, and dance, as well as in religious ritual and church polity.

The spatial isolation of Negroes from whites in "Black Belts" also increased consciousness of their separate subordinate position, for no whites were available to them as neighbors, schoolmates, or friends, but were present only in such roles as school teachers, policemen, and social workers, flat janitors and real-estate agents, merchants and bill collectors, skilled laborers involved in maintenance, and even a few white dentists and doctors with offices in the Black Belt. Such a situation inevitably generated anti-white sentiments (often with anti-Semitic overtones), and the pent-up feelings have occasionally erupted in anti-white riots. Normally, however, this intense racial consciousness finds expression in non-violent forms of social protest and is utilized by Negro leaders to sanction and reinforce Negro institutions and their own personal welfare. It has also lent powerful support to the segments of municipal political machines existing within Negro neighborhoods. As long as ghettos remain, race consciousness will be strong.

Residential segregation created the demographic and ecological basis for "balance of power" politics, since the possibility of a Negro bloc vote had to be recognized by both political parties. Northern Black Belt voters are not only occasionally the decisive factor in municipal elections, but have also sent a half-dozen Negroes to Congress. Indeed, it is ironic that one of the most effective weapons against segregation and discrimination in the South has been the political power generated in Negro precincts and wards of Northern Black Ghettos, thus reinforcing the direct action tactics of the civil rights movement. In the South, too, with the passage of the Civil Rights Act of 1964 and subsequent legislation, the political strength of newly enfranchised voters lies in their spatial concentration. There is some evidence that fear of this strength may operate as a factor in

Northern cities to support "open occupancy," desegregation being considered preferable to Negro dominance.[4]

While the development of machine politics has brought some gains to Negro communities, it has also resulted in various forms of indirect victimization. Local Negro leaders often co-operate with the city-wide machine in the protection of "the rackets"—policy, dope, and prostitution—and sacrifice group welfare to personal gain for self and party. They have not hesitated, in some places, even to drag their heels in the fight for residential desegregation rather than risk wiping out the base of their power. Being saddled with a "bought leadership" is one of the greatest burdens Black Ghettos have had to bear. Economic victimization is widespread, too. In the "affluent society" of the sixties, consumption-oriented and given to the "hard sell," Negroes like other Americans are under social pressure to spend beyond their means. Given the lack of sophistication of many recent migrants and the very low median income of those with less than a high-school education, it is not surprising that loan sharks and dubious credit merchants (of all races) make the Black Ghetto a prime target. Negroes pay a high price for "protection" of the white middle-class way of life, since those who aspire to leave the ghetto are trapped, and those who are content to stay develop a limited and restricted view of the world in which they live.

Folkways and Classways Within the Black Ghetto

Black Ghettos in America are, on the whole, "run down" in appearance and overcrowded, and their inhabitants bear the physical and psychological scars of those whose "life chances" are not equal to those of other Americans. Like the European immigrants before them, they inherited the worst housing in the city. Within the past decade, the white "flight to the suburbs" has released relatively new and well-kept property on the margins of some of the old Black Belts. Here, "gilded ghettos" have grown up, indistinguishable from any other middle-class neighborhoods except by the color of the residents' skin.[5] The power mower in the yard, the steak grill on the rear lawn, a well stocked library and equally well stocked bar in the rumpus room—these mark the homes of well-to-do Negroes living in the more desirable portions of the Black Belt. Many of them would flee to suburbia, too, if housing were available to Negroes there.

But the character of the Black Ghetto is not set by the newer "gilded," not-yet run down portions of it, but by the older sections where unemployment rates are high and the masses of people work with their hands—where the median level of education is just above graduation from grade school and many of the people are likely to be recent migrants from rural areas.[6]

The "ghettoization" of the Negro has resulted in the emergence of a ghetto subculture with a distinctive ethos, most pronounced, perhaps, in Harlem, but recognizable in all Negro neighborhoods. For the average Negro who walks the streets of any American Black Ghetto, the smell of barbecued ribs, fried shrimps, and chicken emanating from numerous restaurants gives olfactory reinforcement to a feeling of "at-homeness." The beat of "gut music" spilling into the street from ubiquitous tavern juke boxes and the sound of tambourines and rich harmony behind the crude folk art on the windows of store-front churches given auditory confirmation to the universal belief that "We Negroes have 'soul.'" The bedlam of an occasional brawl, the shouted obscenities of street corner "foul mouths," and the whine of police sirens break the monotony of waiting for the number that never "falls," the horses that neither win, place, nor show, and the "good job" that never materializes. The insouciant swagger of teen-age drop-outs (the "cats") masks the hurt of their aimless existence and contrasts sharply with the ragged clothing and dejected demeanor of "skid-row" types who have long since stopped trying to keep up appearances and who escape it all by becoming "winoes." The spontaneous vigor of the children who crowd streets and playgrounds (with Cassius Clay, Ernie Banks, the Harlem Globe Trotters, and black stars of stage, screen, and television as their role models) and the cheerful rushing about of adults, free from the occupational pressures of the "white world" in which they work, create an atmosphere of warmth and superficial intimacy which obscures the unpleasant facts of life in the overcrowded rooms behind the doors, the lack of adequate maintenance standards, and the too prevalent vermin and rats.

This is a world whose urban "folkways" the upwardly mobile Negro middle class deplores as a "drag" on "The Race," which the upper classes wince at as an embarrassment, and which race leaders point to as proof that Negroes have been victimized. But for the masses of the ghetto dwellers this is a warm and familiar milieu, preferable to the sanitary coldness of middle-class neighborhoods and a counterpart of the communities of the foreign-born, each of which has its own distinctive subcultural flavor. The arguments in the barbershop, the gossip in the beauty parlors, the "jiving" of bar girls and waitresses, the click of poolroom balls, the stomping of feet in the dance halls, the shouting in the churches are all *theirs*—and the white men who run the pawnshops, supermarts, drug stores, and grocery stores, the policemen on horseback, the teachers in blackboard jungles—all these are aliens, conceptualized collectively as "The Man," intruders on the Black Man's "turf." When an occasional riot breaks out, "The Man" and his property become targets of aggression upon which pent-up frustrations are vented. When someone during the Harlem riots of 1964 begged the street crowds to go home, the cry came back, "Baby, we *are* home!"

But the inhabitants of the Black Ghetto are not a homogeneous mass. Although, in Marxian terms, nearly all of them are "proletarians," with nothing to sell but their labor, variations in "life style" differentiate them into social classes based more upon differences in education and basic values (crystallized, in part, around occupational differences) than in meaningful differences in income. The American caste-class system has served, over the years, to concentrate the Negro population in the low-income sector of the economy. In 1961, six out of every ten Negro families had an income of less than $4000.00 per year. This situation among whites was just the reverse: six out of every ten white families had *over* $4000.00 a year at their disposal. (In the South, eight out of ten Negro families were below the $4000.00 level.) This is the income gap. Discrimination in employment creates a job ceiling, most Negroes being in blue-collar jobs.

With 60 per cent of America's Negro families earning less than $4000.00 a year, social strata emerge between the upper and lower boundaries of "no earned income" and $4000.00. Some families live a "middle-class style of life," placing heavy emphasis upon decorous public behavior and general respectability, insisting that their children "get an education" and "make something out of themselves." They prize family stability, and an unwed mother is something much more serious than "just a girl who had an accident"; pre-marital and extra-marital sexual relations, if indulged in at all, must be discreet. Social life is organized around churches and a welter of voluntary associations of all types, and, for women, "the cult of clothes" is so important that fashion shows are a popular fund raising activity even in churches. For both men and women, owning a home and going into business are highly desired goals, the former often being a realistic one, the latter a mere fantasy.

Within the same income range, and not always at the lower margin of it, other families live a "lower-class life-style" being part of the "organized" lower class, while at the lowest income levels an "unorganized" lower class exists whose members tend always to become *dis*organized—functioning in an anomic situation where gambling, excessive drinking, the use of narcotics, and sexual promiscuity are prevalent forms of behavior, and violent interpersonal relations reflect an ethos of suspicion and resentment which suffuses this deviant subculture. It is within this milieu that criminal and semi-criminal activities burgeon.

The "organized" lower class is oriented primarily around churches whose preachers, often semi-literate, exhort them to "be in the 'world' but not of it." Conventional middle-class morality and Pauline Puritanism are preached, although a general attitude of "the spirit is willing but the flesh is weak" prevails except among a minority fully committed to the Pentecostal sects. They boast, "We *live* the life"—a way of life that has been portrayed with great insight by James Baldwin in *Go Tell it on the Mountain* and *The Fire Next Time.*

Young people with talent find wide scope for expressing it in choirs, quartets, and sextets which travel from church to church (often bearing colorful names like The Four Heavenly Trumpets or the Six Singing Stars of Zion) and sometimes traveling from city to city. Such groups channel their aggressions in widely advertised "Battles of Song" and develop their talent in church pageants such as "Heaven Bound" or "Queen Esther" and fund-raising events where winners are crowned King and Queen. These activites provide fun as well as a testing ground for talent. Some lucky young church people eventually find their fortune in the secular world as did singers Sam Cooke and Nat King Cole, while others remain in the church world as nationally known gospel singers or famous evangelists.

Adults as well as young people find satisfaction and prestige in serving as ushers and deacons, "mothers," and deaconesses, Sunday-school teachers and choir leaders. National conventions of Negro denominations and national societies of ushers and gospel singers not only develop a continent-wide nexus of associations within the organized lower class, but also throw the more ambitious and capable individuals into meaningful contact with middle-class church members who operate as role models for those talented persons who seek to move upward. That prestige and sometimes money come so easily in these circles may be a factor militating against a pattern of delaying gratifications and seeking mobility into professional and semi-professional pursuits through higher education.

Lower-class families and institutions are constantly on the move, for in recent years the Negro lower class has suffered from projects to redevelop the inner city. By historic accident, the decision to check the expansion of physical deterioration in metropolitan areas came at a time when Negroes were the main inhabitants of sub-standard housing. (If urban redevelopment had been necessary sixty years ago immigrants, not Negroes, would have suffered.) In protest against large-scale demolition of areas where they live, Negroes have coined a slogan, "Slum clearance is Negro clearance." They resent the price in terms of the inconvenience thrust upon them in order to redevelop American cities,[7] and the evidence shows that, in some cities, there is no net gain in improved housing after relocation.

At the opposite pole from the Negro lower class in both life styles and life chances is the small Negro upper class whose solid core is a group in the professions, along with well-to-do businessmen who have had some higher education, but including, also, a scattering of individuals who have had college training but do not have a job commensurate with their education. These men and their spouses and children form a cohesive upper-class stratum in most Negro communities. Within this group are individuals who maintain some type of contact—though seldom any social relations—with members of the local white power élite; but whether or not they participate in occupational associations with their white peers depends upon the region of the country in which they live. (It is from this group that Negro "Exhibit A's" are recruited when white liberals are carrying on campaigns to "increase interracial understanding.") They must always think of themselves as symbols of racial advancement as well as individuals, and they often provide the basic leadership at local levels for organizations such as the N.A.A.C.P. and the Urban League. They must lend sympathetic support to the more militant civil rights organizations, too, by financial contributions, if not action.[8]

The life styles of the Negro upper class are similar to those of the white upper *middle* class, but it is only in rare instances that Negroes have been incorporated into the clique and associational life of this group or have intermarried into it. (Their participation in activities of the white upper class occurs more often than with those whites who have similar life styles because of Negro upper-class participation as members of various civic boards and interracial associations to which wealthy white people contribute.) Living "well" with highly developed skills, having enough money to travel, Negroes at this social level do not experience victimization in the same fashion as do the members of the lower class. Their victimization flows primarily from the fact that the social system keeps them "half in and half out," preventing the free and easy contact with their occupational peers which they need; and it often keeps them from making the kind of significant intellectual and social contributions to the national welfare that they might make if they were white. (They are also forced to experience various types of nervous strain and dissipation of energy over petty annoyances and deprivations which only the sensitive and the cultivated feel. Most barbershops, for instance, are not yet desegregated, and taxi drivers, even in the North, sometimes refuse Negro passengers.)

The Negro upper class has created a social world of its own in which a universe of discourse and uniformity of behavior and outlook are maintained by the interaction on national and local levels of members of Negro Greek-letter fraternities and sororities, college and alumni associations, professional associations, and civic and social clubs. It is probable that if all caste barriers were dropped, a large proportion of the Negro upper class would welcome complete social integration, and that these all-Negro institutions would be left in the hands of the Negro middle class, as the most capable and sophisticated Negroes moved into the orbit of the general society. Their sense of pride and dignity does not even allow them to imagine such a fate, and they pursue their social activities and play their roles as "race leaders" with little feeling of inferiority or deprivation, but always with a tragic sense of the irony of it all.

The Negro middle class covers a very wide income range, and whatever cohesion it has comes from the network of churches and social clubs to which many of its members devote a great deal of time and money. What sociologists call the Negro middle class is merely a collection of people who have similar life styles and aspirations, whose basic goals are "living well," being "respectable," and not being crude. Middle-class Negroes, by and large, are not concerned about mobility into the Negro upper class or integration with whites. They want their "rights" and "good jobs," as well as enough money to get those goods and services which make life comfortable. They want to expand continuously their level of consumption. But they also desire "decent" schools for their children, and here the degree of victimization experienced by Negroes is most clear and the ambivalence toward policies of change most sharp. Ghetto schools are, on the whole, inferior. In fact, some of the most convincing evidence that residential segregation perpetuates inequality can be found by comparing data on school districts in Northern urban areas where *de facto* school segregation exists. (Table 1 presents such data for Chicago in 1962.)

Awareness of the poor quality of education grew as the protest movement against *de facto* school segregation in the North gathered momentum. But while the fight was going on, doubt about the desirability of forcing the issue was always present within some sections of the broad Negro middle class. Those in opposition asked, "Are we not saying that our teachers can't teach our own children as well as whites can, or that our children can't learn unless they're around whites? Aren't we insulting ourselves?" Those who want to stress Negro history and achievement and to use the schools to build race pride also express doubts about the value of mixed schools. In fact, the desirability of race consciousness and racial solidarity seems to be taken for granted in this stratum, and sometimes there is an expression of contempt for the behavior of whites of their own and lower income levels. In the present period one even occasionally hears a remark such as "Who'd want to be integrated with *those* awful white people?"

Marxist critics would dismiss the whole configuration of Negro folkways and classways as a subculture which reinforces "false consciousness," which prevents Negroes from facing the full extent of their victimization, which keeps them from ever focusing upon what they could be because they are so busy enjoying what they are—or rationalizing their subordination and exclusion. Gunnar Myrdal, in *An American Dilemma,* goes so far as to refer to the Negro community as a "pathological" growth within American society.[9] Some novelists and poets, on the other hand, romanticize it, and some Black Nationalists glorify it. A sober analysis of the civil rights movement would suggest, however, that the striking fact about all levels of the Negro community is the absence of "false consciousness," and the presence of a keen awareness of the extent of their victimization, as well as knowledge of the forces which maintain it. Not lack of knowledge but a sense of powerlessness is the key to the Negro reaction to the caste-class system.

Few Negroes believe that Black Ghettos will disappear within the next two decades despite much talk about "open occupancy" and

TABLE 1

COMPARISON OF WHITE, INTEGRATED AND NEGRO SCHOOLS IN CHICAGO: 1962

Indices of Comparison	Type of School White	 Integrated	 Negro
Total appropriation per pupil	$342.00	$320.00	$269.00
Annual teachers' salary per pupil	256.00	231.00	220.00
Per cent uncertified teachers	12.00	23.00	49.00
No. of pupils per classroom	30.95	34.95	46.80
Library resource books per pupil	5.00	3.50	2.50
Expenditures per pupil other than teachers' salaries	86.00	90.00	49.00

Adapted from a table in the U.S. Commission on Civil Rights report, Public Schools, Negro and White (Washington, D.C., 1962), pp. 241–248.

"freedom of residence." There is an increasing tendency among Negroes to discuss what the quality of life could be within Negro communities as they grow larger and larger. At one extreme this interest slides over into Black Nationalist reactions such as the statement by a Chicago Negro leader who said, "Let all of the white people flee to the suburbs. We'll show them that the Black Man can run the second largest city in America better than the white man. Let them go. If any of them want to come back and integrate with *us* we'll accept them."

It is probable that the Black Belts of America will increase in size rather than decrease during the next decade, for no city seems likely to commit itself to "open occupancy" (although a committee in New York has been discussing a ten-year plan for dismantling Harlem).[10] And even if a race-free market were to appear Negroes would remain segregated unless drastic changes took place in the job ceiling and income gap. Controlled integration will probably continue, with a few upper- and upper-middle-class Negroes trickling into the suburbs and into carefully regulated mixed neighborhoods and mixed buildings within the city limits.[11] The basic problem of the next decade will be how to change Black Ghettos into relatively stable and attractive "colored communities." Here the social implications of low incomes become decisive.

Social Implications of the Job Ceiling and the Income Gap

Nowhere is direct victimization of Negroes more apparent than with respect to the job ceiling and the income gap; but indirect victimization which is a consequence of direct victimization is often less obvious. For instance, it has been mentioned that family incomes for Negroes are lower than for whites; but family income figures are inadequate tools for careful sociological analysis unless we know which, and how many, members of a family labor to earn a given income. In 1960, half of the white families were being supported by a husband only, while just a few more than a third of the Negro families could depend solely upon the earnings of one male breadwinner. In six out of ten nonwhite families where both a husband and wife were present, two or more persons worked; yet less than half of the white families had both husband and wife working. But even in those families which commanded an income of over $7,000.00 a year, twice as many nonwhite wives had to help earn it as white.[12] One not unimportant consequence is that a smaller proportion of Negro than white wives at this income level can play roles of unpaid volunteers in civic and social work, a fact which should be remembered by those who criticize Negroes in these income brackets for not doing more to "elevate their own people."

One of the most important effects of the income gap and the job ceiling has been the shaping of social class systems within Negro communities which differ markedly in their profiles from those of the surrounding white society. Negro class structure is "pyramidal," with a large lower class, a somewhat smaller middle class, and a tiny upper class (made up of people whose income and occupations would make them only middle class in the white society). White class profiles tend to be "diamond shaped," with small lower and upper classes and a large middle class. Unpromising "life chances" are reflected in inferior "life styles," and Black Ghettos are on the whole "rougher" and exhibit a higher degree of social disorganization than do white communities.

The job ceiling and the income gap do not create classways—for these reflect educational levels and cultural values, as well as the economic situation—but job ceiling and income gap do set the limits for realization of class values. It is a fact of American life (whether one approves of it or not) that as long as Negroes are predominantly lower-class they will, as a group, have low esteem. Yet, Negroes are victimized in the sense that the job ceiling and the income gap make it more difficult for them than for whites to maintain middle-class standards equivalent to those obtaining among whites. A given life style demands a minimum level of income, but it is evident that Negroes are victimized in the sense that their effort as reflected in the acquisition of an education does not bring equal rewards in terms of purchasing power, for they have less to spend than their white counterparts at any given educational level. Nonwhite family heads in 1960 had a smaller median income than whites for every educational level. (See Table 2.)[13]

In a sense, getting an education "pays off" for Negroes as for all other Americans; but while some individuals "get ahead" of other Negroes, education has not yet raised their earning power to the level of whites with equivalent training. In fact, the average income for a nonwhite family with a male head who had finished high school was less than that of a white male head who had finished only the eighth grade. Since any aspects of the caste-class system which make it more difficult for Negroes than for whites to achieve middle-class norms of family behavior retard the process of eventual "integration," the income differential and the necessity for more members of the family to work operate in this negative fashion. Even more serious in determining deviations from general middle-class family norms is the manner in which both income distribution and the occupational structure function to reinforce the number of families without fathers and to lower the prestige of Negro males *vis-à-vis* their mates, prospective mates, and children. Thus a pattern of male insecurity which originated under slavery persists into the present. In fact, the struggle of Negro men, viewed as a group, to attain economic parity with Negro women has, up to the present, been a losing fight. Norval Glenn, in an exhaustive study of this problem,[14] has concluded that "Among full-time workers, non-white females were, in 1959, less disadvantaged relative to whites than were non-white males." Women were obtaining employment at a relatively faster rate than men and sustained a more rapid proportionate increase in income between 1939 and 1959. According to Glenn, there was an actual reversal in the income growth pattern of Negro males and females during a twenty-year period, and he notes that if their respective rates remain the same it will take twice as long for Negro males to catch up with white males as for Negro women to catch up with white women (93 years to achieve occupational equality and 219 to achieve equality of income). This is a case of *relative* deprivation, of course, but is significant nevertheless. An impressive body of evidence indicates that rather serious personality distortions result from the female dominance so prevalent in the Negro subculture, since the general norms of the larger society stress the opposite pattern as more desirable.

The interplay between caste evaluations and economic and ecological factors has tended not only to concentrate a low-income Negro population within ghettos, but has also concentrated a significant proportion of them in vast public housing projects—sometimes "high

TABLE 2

WHITE AND NONWHITE MEDIAN FAMILY INCOME BY EDUCATIONAL LEVEL, 1960: U. S. A.

Amount of Education in Yrs. of School Completed	White	Nonwhite
Elementary School		
Less than 8 years	$3,656	$2,294
8 years	4,911	3,338
High School		
1-3 years	5,882	3,449
4 years	6,370	4,559
College		
1-3 years	7,344	5,525
4 or more years	9,315	7,875

rise." In the 1930's public housing projects were often exciting experiments in interracial living, but there has been a tendency in many cities for them to become ghettos within ghettos. Within housing projects as well as out, a small hard core of mothers without husbands and a larger group of youth without jobs are developing a pattern which social psychologist Frederick Strodtbeck has called "the poverty-dependency syndrome." Here and there an integrated program of professional family services has proved its usefulness, but, in general, family case-work becomes a mere "holding operation."

Only the future will tell whether a large-scale "Poverty Program" coordinated through federally sponsored agencies will break the interlocking vicious circles which now victimize urban Negro populations. The dominant pattern in the American economic system has never been one of racial segregation. In fact. the racial division of labor has always involved considerable close personal contact, while demanding that Negroes play subordinate occupational roles carrying the lesser rewards in terms of economic power and social prestige. Doctrines of racial inferiority originated as dogmas to defend the use of African slave labor and were later used by white workers to defend their own privileged position against Negro competition. Trade union restrictionism reinforces employer preference in maintaining a job ceiling. Often, even when an employer decided it was profitable to use Negro labor, white workers used intimidation or violence against both white employer and black employee.

Access to new roles in the economic structure has occurred during periods of a great shortage of labor, as in the North during both world wars. Negroes entered at the bottom of the hierarchy, but were "last hired and first fired." Yet the job ceiling *was* raised, and, beginning with the organization of industrial unions in the 1930's and reaching a climax in the civil rights movement of the 1960's, ideological factors have reinforced economic interest in breaking the job ceiling. Now, for the first time in American history the full weight of top leadership in labor, industry, and government has been thrown in the direction of "fair employment practices," and public opinion is tolerating an all-out drive against job discrimination (partly because the economy is still expanding). Yet so drastic are the effects of the past victimization of the Negro that any decisive alteration in the caste-class structure without more drastic measures seems remote. Thomas Pettigrew, after an analysis of recent changes, concludes:

> At the creeping 1950–1960 rate of change, non-whites in the United States would not attain equal proportional representation

among clerical workers until 1992, among skilled workers until 2005, among professionals until 2017, among sales workers until 2114, and among business managers and proprietors until 2730![15]

Insofar as the job ceiling, the income gap, and Ghettoization preserve and reinforce lower-class behavior patterns among Negroes to a greater extent than in the general society, the general health status of the Negro will be affected. For instance, a less adequate nutritional level than is found among whites is one factor often cited in accounting for the poorer average health status of Negroes. It is conceivable that Negroes could improve their nutritional status immediately by altering their present patterns of food consumption, but this is likely to occur less as a result of education and propaganda than as a by-product of changes in the caste-class situation. Except in wartime or during depressions, food habits are among the most difficult to change, unless change is related to mobility strivings. Maximizing the opportunity for Negroes to achieve the values and norms of the general American middle class is likely to do more to change the eating habits of the Negro population than all of the written or spoken exhortations of home economists or the most seductive of television commercials. A shift in social class supplies the motivation to change, and such a shift is dependent upon an increase in the number and proportion of Negroes entering white-collar occupations.

Maintaining a style of living consonant with any occupational roles demands a minimum level of income. Success in improving the health status of the Negro population may ultimately depend upon an indirect rather than a frontal assault. One student of the problem gives us a clue to the strategy when he observes that "... the much lower income level of the American Negro, to the extent that it is a measure of standard of living, explains, in part at least, the differences in health status and longevity between whites and non-whites in the United States.[16] Carefully controlled studies "point up the intimate relationship between physical illness and economic . . ."[17] to use Dr. Ann Pettigrew's expression. Economic factors not only partially explain, or serve as indices of, the causes of divergent morbidity and mortality rates, but they also give us the clues to a strategy for change, namely, working toward a continuously rising standard of living. Whether hope or pessimism is warranted depends upon the possibility of drastically changing the economic status of the Negro over the next decade, of eliminating economic "victimization."

Closing the income gap is crucial, or alternatively, the provision of a subsidy for medical services. Large masses of Negroes will never become members of the white-collar class, but better job opportunities in commerce and industry will place many of them in a position to benefit from privately sponsored health and insurance plans. These will be of maximum benefit, however, only if hospital discrimination is eliminated. Also, the wider extension of adequate medical care to all citizens through the use of public funds, and the more effective use of social workers and educators, will automatically benefit those Negroes who are not upwardly mobile.

Chronic illness, as well as frequent periods of sickness, not only results in loss of man-hours of production, but also increases stress and strain in interpersonal relations and deprives individuals of the maximum amount of pleasure to be derived from a sense of physical well-being and from recreation and pleasurable interaction with other human beings. Insofar as the general health level of Negroes is lower than that of whites they suffer more from these deprivations. Tendencies to escape from pain and its consequences by habitual use of alcohol and drugs, or the anodyne of excessive preoccupation with the supernatural world, may be related to the general health situation within the Negro lower class. These less tangible and immeasurable disabilities are as real as the financial burdens imposed by sickness.

Notes

1. St. Clair Drake and Horace R. Cayton, in *Black Metropolis* (New York, 1962), use the term "Black Ghetto" to refer to the involuntary and exploitative aspect of the all-Negro community and "Bronzeville" to symbolize the more pleasant aspects of the segregated community. Robert C. Weaver, another Negro scholar, called his first book *The Negro Ghetto* (New York, 1948). The term is widely used by contemporary Negro leaders with pejorative implications. See also Kenneth Clark, *Dark Ghetto* (New York, 1965).

2. The most careful study of the effect of Negro entry into all-white neighborhoods is to be found in a book published by the University of California Press in 1961 which reports upon the results of research in Detroit, Chicago, Kansas City, Oakland, San Francisco, Philadelphia, and Portland, Oregon—Luigi Laurenti's *Property Values and Race* (Berkeley, Calif., 1961).

3. Thomas F. Pettigrew, *A Profile of the Negro American* (Princeton, N. J., 1964), p. 190. His wife, Dr. Ann Pettigrew, M.D., collaborated with him on the chapter dealing with health.

4. Though based upon only one community in Chicago, *The Politics of Urban Renewal*, by Peter Rossi and Robert A. Dentler (Glencoe, Ill., 1961) analyzes basic processes to be found in all Northern cities.

5. Professor Everett C. Hughes makes some original and highly pertinent remarks about new Negro middle-class communities in his introduction to the 1962 edition of Drake and Cayton's *Black Metropolis.*

6. Pettigrew, *op. cit.*, pp. 180-181.

7. The issue of the extent to which Negroes have been victimized by urban redevelopment is discussed briefly by Robert C. Weaver in *The Urban Complex: Human Values in Urban Life* (New York, 1964). See also Martin Anderson, *The Federal Bulldozer: A Critical Analysis of Urban Renewal: 1949-1962* (Cambridge, Mass., 1964).

8. Drake and Cayton, *op. cit.*, Chap. 23, "Advancing the Race."

9. See section on "The Negro Community as a Pathological Form of an American Community," Chap. 43 of Gunnar Myrdal, *An American Dilemma* (New York, 1944), p. 927.

10. A report appeared on the front page of *The New York Times,* April 5, 1965, stating that a commission was at work trying to elaborate plans for "integrating" Harlem by 1975. Columbia University was said to be cooperating in the research aspects of the project.

11. A successful experiment in "controlled integration" has been described by Julia Abrahamson in *A Neighborhood Finds Itself* (New York, 1959).

12. Jacob Schiffman, "Marital and Family Characteristics of Workers, March, 1962," in *Monthly Labor Review,* U. S. Department of Labor, Bureau of Labor Statistics, Special Labor Force Report No. 26, January 1963.

13. *Ibid.*

14. Norval D. Glenn, "Some Changes in the Relative Status of American Non-whites: 1940-1960," *Phylon,* Vol. 24, No. 2 (Summer 1963).

15. Pettigrew, *op. cit.*, p. 188.

16. Dr. Ann Pettigrew cites a study carried out in Chicago, using 1950 data, in which, when Negroes and whites of the same economic level were compared, mortality rates were about the same although the rates for Negroes as a group when compared with those for whites as a group were higher. Other studies using the same body of data indicate sharp differences in mortality rates as between laborers and skilled workers among Negroes, a situation similar to that found among whites (Pettigrew, *op. cit.*, p. 98).

17. *Ibid.*, p. 80.

Ego Development among Segregated Negro Children

David P. Ausubel and Pearl Ausubel

[From Education in Depressed Areas *(New York, copyright 1963) by permission of the Columbia University Teachers College Press.]*

Ego development refers to the orderly series of changes in an individual's self-concept, self-attitudes, motives, aspirations, sources of self-esteem, and key personality traits affecting the realization of his aspirations as he advances in age in a particular cultural setting. It obviously varies from one individual to another within a particular culture or subculture in accordance with significant temperamental traits and idiosyncratic experience. Nevertheless, it manifests a certain amount of intracultural homogeneity or intercultural difference because of culturally institutionalized differences in interpersonal relations; in opportunities for and methods of acquiring status; in prescribed age, sex, class, and occupational roles; in approved kinds of personality traits; and in the amount and types of achievement motivation that are socially sanctioned for individuals of a given age, sex, class, and occupation.

For all of these reasons the ego development of segregated Negro children in America manifests certain distinctive properties. Negro children live in a predominantly lower-class subculture that is further characterized by a unique type of family structure, by specially circumscribed opportunities for acquiring status, by varying degrees of segregation from the dominant white majority, and, above all, by a fixed and apparently immutable denigration of their social value, standing, and dignity as human beings because of their skin color. Hence, it would be remarkable indeed if these factors did not result in significant developmental differences in self-esteem, in aspirations for achievement, in personality adjustment, and in character structure. In fact the Supreme Court decision of 1954 outlawing school segregation was based primarily on considerations of ego development. It recognized that school and other public facilities cannot be "separate and equal" because enforced and involuntary separateness that is predicated on purely arbitrary criteria necessarily implies an inferior caste status, and thereby results in psychological degradation and injury to self-esteem.

In the context of this conference on the education of culturally disadvantaged groups in depressed urban areas, our interest in the ego development of segregated Negro children obviously transcends mere theoretical considerations. Recent technological and sociological changes are confronting the American Negro with significant new challenges to his traditional role and status in our society. In the past it was possible for him to achieve some measure of stable adjustment to his inferior caste position, unsatisfactory though it was. He more or less accepted his devalued social status and second-class citizenship, aspired to low-level occupational roles requiring little education and training, found work in unskilled and menial occupations, and lived within his segregated subculture shunning contact and competition with whites. But two important changes are currently rendering this type of adjustment less and less tenable. In the first place, automation is rapidly decreasing the need for unskilled and uneducated labor in America. The poorly trained and poorly educated Negro youth who drops out of secondary school as soon as he reaches the minimum legal age, or fails to acquire some post-high-school technical training, finds himself at a much greater disadvantage in today's job market than was true of his father and older brother just a decade ago. He now lives in a wider culture in which a much higher level of educational and vocational training is a prerequisite for occupational adjustment, but he still grows up in a subculture that neither fosters aspirations for such education and training, nor provides the moral and material support necessary for their realization. Second, there are many indications that the Negro is no longer content with his segregated caste status and second-class citizenship. At the same time, however, he possesses a character structure and a repertoire of educational and vocational skills that, on the whole, do not prepare him to compete adequately with whites in the wider culture. In short, he is more desirous of participating in the unsegregated American culture, but lacks the personality traits and intellectual attainments that would enable him to do so effectively.

As educators, our job is to help the Negro child fill the new and more desirable place in American society that technological change and his elders' aspirations for equality are creating for him. Essentially this means altering his ego structure so that he desires and is able to achieve a level of educational and vocational training that would make it possible for him to compete successfully with whites in modern industrial society. It is true, of course, that the Negro's ego structure is largely a reflection of the actual social and legal status he enjoys in our culture; and as citizens it is our obligation to help him achieve equality of opportunity and equality before the law. But status and its reflection in self-esteem depend as much on real achievement as on equality of rights and opportunity. A changed ego structure, as manifested in higher educational and vocational aspirations, in the development of personality traits necessary for realizing these aspirations, and in the actual achievement of higher educational and vocational qualifications, can do as much to improve the Negro's status in society, and hence enhance his self-esteem, as can amelioration of his social and legal status. If, on the other hand, the Negro community cannot obtain our support in helping to mold the Negro youth's ego structure in ways that will eventually improve his competitive position in the employment market, he can only look forward to becoming permanently unemployable and subsisting on public assistance. This latter state of affairs would not only tend to perpetuate the Negro's lower-class and inferior caste position with its attendant adverse effects on ego development, but would also increase racial tensions and encourage anti-social behavior.

In this paper we propose to do three things. First, we would like to consider the personality development of the segregated Negro child as a special variant of the more typical course of ego development in our culture. Here the approach is normative, from the standpoint of a personality theorist interested in subcultural differences. In what ways does the ego development of segregated Negro children differ from that of the textbook child growing up in the shadow of our dominant middle-class value system? Second, we would like to consider some kinds of and reasons for individual differences within this underprivileged group. Do all Negro children in the Harlem ghetto respond in the same way to the impact of their segregated lower-class environment? If not, why not? Are there social class, sex, and individual differences among Negro children? Questions of this type would be asked by a personality theorist concerned with idiosyncratic and group variability within a subcultural setting, or by a psychiatrist treating the behavior disorders of such children in a Harlem community clinic. Finally, we propose to consider the implications of this material for such practical issues as educational practice and desegregation.

Overview of Ego Development in White Middle-Class Children

Before turning to a description of ego development in segregated Negro communities, it may be helpful to examine briefly the typical middle-class model with which it will be compared. In doing this we do not mean to imply that the developmental pattern in suburbia is necessarily typical of the American scene. Obviously only a minority of America's children live in the ecological equivalent of suburban culture. Nevertheless it is still a useful model for comparative purposes because it reflects the value system that dominates such official socializing institutions in our society as the school, the church, the youth organizations, the mass media, and the child-rearing manuals. Hence, it is the most widely diffused and influential model of socialization in our culture. It is the official model that most parents profess to believe in regardless of whether or not they practice it. It is the model that would most impress foreign anthropologists as typical of American culture.

The infant in suburbia, as in many other cultures, may be pardoned for entertaining mild feelings of omnipotence (7). Out of deference for his manifest helplessness, his altruistic parents are indulgent, satisfy most of his needs, and make few demands on him. In view of his cognitive immaturity, it is hardly surprising then that he interprets his enviable situation as proof of his volitional power than as reflective of parental altruism. As he becomes less helpless and more responsive to parental direction, however, this idyllic picture begins to change. His parents become more demanding, impose their will on him, and take steps to socialize him in the ways of the culture; and by this time the toddler has sufficient cognitive maturity to perceive his relative impotence and volitional dependence on them. All of these factors favor the occurrence of satellization. The child surrenders his volitional independence and by the fiat of parental acceptance and intrinsic valuation acquires a derived or attributed status. As a result, despite his marginal status in the culture and manifest inability to fend for himself, he acquires feelings of self-esteem that are independent of his performance ability. He also internalizes parental values and expectations regarding mature and acceptable behavior.

In suburbia, derived status constitutes the cornerstone of the child's self-esteem until adolescence. Beginning with middle childhood, however, forces are set in motion which bring about preliminary desatellization from parents. Both in school and in the peer group he is urged to compete for a primary status based on his academic proficiency, athletic prowess and social skills. School and peer groups legislate their own values, impose their own standards, and also offer him a subsidiary source of derived status insofar as they accept him for himself in return for his loyalty and self-subordination. All of these factors tend to devalue the parents and to undermine their omniscience in the child's eyes. The home becomes only one of several socializing agents that foster the development of aspirations for academic and vocational success and of the pattern of deferred gratification necessary to achieve them. Nevertheless, until adolescence, parents remain the major socializing agents and source of values in the child's life. Compared to the derived status obtained from parents, the primary status available in school and peer group plays only a subsidiary role in the total economy of ego organization.

Ego Development in Young Negro Children

Social-class factors. Many of the ecological features of the segregated Negro subculture that impinge on personality development in early childhood are not specific to Negroes as such, but are characteristic of most lower-class populations. This fact is not widely appreciated by white Americans and hence contributes to much anti-Negro sentiment: many characteristic facets of the Negro's value system and behavior pattern are falsely attributed to his racial membership, whereas they really reflect his predominant membership in the lower social class. Nevertheless, these characteristics are commonly offered as proof of the alleged moral and intellectual inferiority that is supposedly inherent in persons of Negro ancestry and are used to justify existing discriminatory practices.

Lower-class parents, for example, are generally more casual, inconsistent, and authoritarian than middle-class parents in controlling their children, and resort more to harsh, corporal forms of punishment (30, 31, 70, 71, 74). Unlike middle-class fathers, whose wives expect them to be as supportive as themselves in relation to children, the lower-class father's chief role in child rearing is to impose constraints and administer punishment (74). Even more important, lower-class parents extend less succorant care and relax closely monitored supervision much earlier than their middle-class counterparts (29, 30, 35, 54). Lower-class children are thus free to roam the neighborhood and join unsupervised play groups at an age when suburban children are still confined to nursery school or to their own backyards. Hence during the pre-school and early elementary-school years, the lower-class family yields to the peer group much of its role as socializing agent and source of values and derived status. During this early period lower-class children undergo much of the desatellization from parents that ordinarily occurs during middle childhood and preadolescence in most middle-class families. They acquire earlier volitional and executive independence outside the home and in many cases assume adult responsibilities such as earning money and caring for younger siblings. Abbreviated parental succorance, which frustrates the dependency needs of middle-class children and commonly fosters overdependence (100), has a different significance for and effect on these lower-class children. Since it reflects the prevailing subcultural norm, and since the opportunity for early anchorage to a free-ranging peer group is available, it tends to encourage the development of precocious independence.

This pattern of precocious independence from the family combined with the exaggerated socializing influence of the peer group, although characteristic of both white and Negro lower-class children, does not necessarily prevail among all lower-class minority groups in the United States. Both Puerto Rican (3) and Mexican (75) children enjoy a more closely-knit family life marked by more intimate contact between parents and children. In Mexican families, maternal and paternal roles are also more distinctive, masculine and feminine roles are more clearly delineated in childhood, and the socializing influence of the peer group is less pronounced (75).

The working-class mother's desire for unquestioned domination of her offspring, her preference for harsh, punitive, and suppressive forms of control, and her tendency to maintain considerable social and emotional distance between herself and her children are probably responsible in part for the greater prevalence of the authoritarian personality syndrome in lower-class children than in middle-class children (36, 53, 69). Lower-class children tend to develop ambivalent attitudes toward authority figures and to cope with this ambivalence by making an exaggerated show of overt, implicit compliance, by maintaining formally appropriate social distance, and by interacting with these figures on the basis of formalized role attributes rather than as persons. Their underlying hostility and resentment toward this arbitrary and often unfair authority is later expressed in such displaced forms as scape-goating, prejudice, extremist political and religious behavior, ethnocentrism, and delinquency (36, 53, 69).

Much of the significant relationship between social-class status and school achievement undoubtedly reflects pervasive social-class differences in cognitive orientation and functioning that are operative from early childhood (15). Middle-class children are trained to respond to the abstract, categorical, and relational properties of objects, whereas lower-class children are trained to respond more to their concrete, tangible, immediate, and particularized properties. This difference in perceptual disposition is carried over into verbal expression, memory, concept formation, learning and problem-solving. Hence, since schools place great emphasis on the learning of abstract relationships and on the abstract use of language, lower-class children, on the average, experience much greater difficulty than middle-class children in mastering the curriculum.

Racial factors. All of the foregoing properties of the lower-class environment also apply to the segregated Negro community. Most authorities on Negro family life agree that well over 50 per cent of

Negro families live at the very lowest level of the lower-class standard (56). In addition, however, Negro families are characterized by a disproportionate number of illegal and loosely connected unions (56). Illegitimacy is a very common phenomenon and is associated with relatively little social stigma in the Negro community (20); nevertheless, illegitimate Negro children, especially at the older age levels, are significantly inferior to their legitimate counterparts in IQ, school achievement, and personal adjustment (59).

Negro families are much more unstable than comparable lower-class white families. Homes are more apt to be broken, fathers are more frequently absent, and a matriarchal and negative family atmosphere more commonly prevails (25, 28, 34, 56). Thus the lower-class Negro child is frequently denied the benefits of bi-parental affection and upbringing; he is often raised by his grandmother or older sister while his mother works to support the family deserted by the father (34). One consequence of the matriarchal family climate is an open preference for girls. Boys frequently attempt to adjust to this situation by adopting feminine traits and mannerisms (28).

Negro family life is even more authoritarian in nature than is that of the lower social class generally. "Children are expected to be obedient and submissive" (56), and insubordination is suppressed by harsh and often brutal physical punishment (28, 31, 56). "Southern Negro culture teaches obedience and respect for authority as a mainspring of survival" (51). Surveys of high-school and college students show that authoritarian attitudes are more prevalent among Negroes at all grade levels (50, 51, 108).

Being a Negro also has many other implications for the ego development of young children that are not inherent in lower-class membership. The Negro child inherits an inferior caste status and almost inevitably acquires the negative self-esteem that is a realistic ego reflection of such status. Through personal slights, blocked opportunities, and unpleasant contacts with white persons and with institutionalized symbols of caste inferiority (segregated schools, neighborhoods, amusement areas, etc.)—and more indirectly through mass media and the reactions of his own family—he gradually becomes aware of the social significance of racial membership (45).

As a consequence of prejudice, segregation, discrimination, inferior status, and not finding himself respected as a human being with dignity and worth,

> . . . the Negro child becomes confused in regard to his feelings about himself and his group. He would like to think well of himself but often tends to evaluate himself according to standards

used by the other group. These mixed feelings lead to self-hatred and rejection of his group, hostility toward other groups, and a generalized pattern of personality difficulties (58, p. 146).

Segregation

> . . . means that the personal worth, of either a white or Negro person, is measured solely by group membership regardless of individual merit. Such a measure is realistically false and of necessity distorts the developing self-image of Negro and white children as well as their view of each other. Under these psychological circumstances the Negro child, for example, is burdened with inescapable inferiority feelings, a fixed ceiling to his aspiration level which can constrict the development of his potentialities, and a sense of humiliation and resentment which can entail patterns of hatred against himself and his own group, as well as against the dominant white group (14, p. 151).

The Negro child perceives himself as an object of derision and disparagement (45), as socially rejected by the prestigeful elements of society, and as unworthy of succorance and affection (34); and having no compelling reasons for not accepting this officially sanctioned negative evaluation or himself, he develops a deeply ingrained negative self-image (14, 123).

It does not take long for Negro children to become aware of the unfavorable implications of their racial membership. In interracial nursery schools, most children show some type of racial awareness at the age of three (115), and this awareness increases rapidly between the ages of 3 and 7 (116). Once aware of racial differences, they soon learn that "skin color is important, that white is to be desired, dark to be regretted" (68). Very significantly, racial self-recognition develops later in Negro than in white children (77, 116); in the light of doll play evidence indicating that they resist identifying with their own stigmatized racial group (23), this delay in racial self-recognition can only be interpreted as reluctance in acknowledging their racial membership.

All of the sociometric rejection and maltreatment experienced by Negro children in a mixed group cannot, of course, be attributed to their inferior caste status alone. Some of the victimization undoubtedly reflects the dynamics of a majority-minority group situation. Thus, when white children are in the minority, the values, judgments, and verbal expression of the Negro majority tend to prevail (96). Under these conditions, Negroes curse whites but the latter do not openly retaliate despite revealing anti-Negro prejudice to white investigators (96).

In addition to suffering ego deflation through awareness of his inferior status in society, the Negro child finds it more difficult to satellize and is denied much of the self-esteem advantages of satellization. The derived status that is the principal source of children's self-esteem in all cultures is largely discounted in his case since he can only satellize in relation to superordinate individuals or groups who themselves possess an inferior and degraded status. Satellization under such conditions not only confers a very limited amount of derived status but also has deflationary implications for self-esteem. We can understand, therefore, why young Negro children resist identifying with their own racial group, why they seek to shed their identities (34), why they more frequently choose white than Negro playmates (116), why they prefer the skin color of the culturally dominant caste (23, 47, 68), and why they tend to assign negative roles to children of their own race (116). These tendencies persist at least into late adolescence and early adult life, insofar as one can judge from the attitudes of Negro college students. These students tend to reject ethnocentric and anti-white ideologies and to accept authoritarian and anti-Negro propositions (114).

Ego Development in Older Negro Children and Adolescents

Social-class factors. During middle childhood and preadolescence the ego development of the segregated Negro child also reflects the influence of both general social class factors and of more specific racial factors. As already pointed out, early experience in fending for himself both in the wider culture and in the unsupervised peer group, as well as in exercising adult-like responsibilities, accomplishes precociously much of the desatellization from and devaluation of parents characterizing the ego development of middle-class children during this period.

In these developments, the school plays a much less significant role among lower-class than among middle-class children. The lower-class child of school age has fewer illusions about parental omniscience for the teacher to shatter, and is coerced by the norms of his peer group against accepting her authority, seeking her approval, or entering into a satellizing relationship with her (30). School can also offer him very little in the way of either current or ultimate primary status. His parents and associates place no great value on education and do not generally encourage high aspirations for academic and vocational success, financial independence, or social recognition (30,

54, 97). It is hardly surprising, therefore, that lower-class children are less interested in reading than are middle-class children, have lower educational aspirations, take their schoolwork less seriously, and are less willing to spend the years of their youth in school in order to gain higher prestige and more social rewards as adults (30, 54 97).

Even if they equalled middle-class children in these latter respects, academic achievement would still be quite a valueless reward for a child who soon comes to realize that professional status is beyond his grasp (30). Hence, anxiety regarding the attainment of internalized needs for vocational prestige does not drive the lower-class child to excel in school (30). Also, because of low achievement and discriminatory treatment, he fails to obtain the current rewards of academic success available to middle-class school children (30). On what grounds could a child immersed in an intellectually impoverished environment be expected to actualize his genic potentials for verbal and abstract thinking, when he is unmotivated by parental pressures, by ambitions for vocational success, or by the anxiety associated with realizing these ambitions?

Lower- and middle-class adolescents differ markedly both in their social value systems and in their vocational interests. Middle-class youths and their parents are more concerned with community service, self-realization, altruistic values, and internalized standards of conduct (60, 112), and prefer demanding, responsible, and prestigeful occupational pursuits (88, 89, 103). They also make higher vocational interest scores in the literary, esthetic, persuasive, scientific and business areas than do lower-class adolescents. The latter adolescents and their parents, on the other hand, place greater stress on such values as money, security, respectability, obedience, and conformity to authority, and tend to prefer agricultural, mechanical, domestic service, and clerical pursuits (88, 89, 103).

The lower-class child's *expressed* levels of academic and vocational aspirations often appear unrealistically high (34), but unlike the analogous situation in middle-class children, these do not necessarily represent his *real* or functional levels of striving. They more probably reflect impairment of realistic judgment under the cumulative impact of chronic failure (99) and low social status (48), as well as a compensatory attempt to bolster self-esteem through the appearance rather than the substance of aiming high. Lacking the strong ego involvement which the middle-class child brings to schoolwork, and which preserves the attractiveness of academic tasks despite failure experience (98), he quickly loses interest in school if he is unsuccessful. Finally, since he does not perceive the eventual rewards of striving and self-denial as attainable for persons of his status, he fails to develop to the same degree as the middle-class child the supportive traits of ego maturity necessary for the achievement of academic and vocational success (30). These supportive traits include habits of initiative and responsibility and the "deferred gratification pattern" of hard work, renunciation of immediate pleasures, long-range planning, high frustration tolerance, impulse control, thrift, orderliness, punctuality, and willingness to undergo prolonged vocational preparation (30, 54, 86, 97).

Despite having less deep-seated anxiety with respect to internalized needs for academic achievement and vocational prestige, children of lower-class families exhibit more signs of personality maladjustment than do children of middle-class families (4, 6, 57, 101, 102, 111). This greater degree of maladjustment is largely a response to the greater vicissitudes and insecurities of daily living; to the greater possibility and actual occurrence of failure in an educational and vocational world dominated by middle-class standards in which they are greatly disadvantaged; to inner tensions engendered by conflict between the values of the family and those of the dominant middle-class culture; to feelings of shame about family background that are associated with impulses to reject family ties; to feelings of guilt and anxiety about these latter impulses (102); and to the personal demoralization and self-derogation that accompany social disorganization and the possession of inferior social status (5, 7, 111). In most instances, of course, the symptoms of maladjustment are uncomfortable rather than disabling; but the generally higher level of anxiety, and the more frequent occurrence of motivational immaturity in lower-class children and adolescents, also increase the incidence of such serious disorders as schizophrenia, drug addiction, and anxiety neurosis and its various complications (7, 57, 111). Proneness to delinquency is, of course, higher among lower-class adolescents because of greater family and social disorganization, the deep-seated resentments and aggressive impulses attributable to socio-economic deprivation, the influence of organized, predatory gangs, and the tacit encouragement offered by the lower-class value system and the slum-urban teen-age cult of thrills, kicks, self-indulgence, violence, and non-conformity.

Racial factors. All of the aforementioned factors inhibiting the development of high level ego aspirations and their supportive personality traits in lower-class children are intensified in the segregated Negro child. His over-all prospects for vertical social mobility, although more restricted, are not completely hopeless. But the stigma of his caste membership is inescapable and unsurmountable. It is inherent in his skin color, permanently ingrained in his body image, and enforced by the extra-legal power of a society whose moral, legal, and religious codes proclaim his equality (123).

It is proper to speak of a stigma as being "enforced" when the stigma in question is culturally derived rather than inherent in the physical existence of the mark per se (that is, a mark of inferiority in *any* culture such as lameness or blindness). Dark skin color is a stigma in our culture only because it identifies a culturally stigmatized caste. When we speak of the stigma being "inherent in his skin color," we mean that it is a stigma which the Negro inherits by virtue of being born with that skin color in a culture that places a negative valuation on it. Hence the stigma "inheres" in the skin color. But this does not imply that dark skin color is inherently (that is, apart from a particular set of cultural values) a mark of inferiority; the stigma is only inherent for the individual insofar as he acquires it by cultural definition rather than by anything he does.

Hence, since a culturally derived stigma refers to an identifying characteristic of a group which has been relegated to an inferiority status position in society, the stigma can only be perpetuated as long as the culture provides some mechanism for *enforcing* the low status position of the group in question. In the absence of cultural enforcement the stigma would vanish in as much as it is not inherent in the characteristic itself but is merely a symbol of membership in an inferior caste. In our society (unlike the Union of South Africa), there are no laws which explicitly create an inferior caste status for the Negro; even segregation statutes accord him a separate rather than an inferior status. Hence the "mark" is enforced extra-legally by preserving through informal social practices the social inferiority of which the mark is but a symbol.

If this situation exists despite the authority of God and the Constitution, what basis for hope does the Negro child have? It is not surprising, therefore, that, in comparison with lower-class white children, he aspires to jobs with more of the formal trappings than with the actual attributes of social prestige; that he feels impotent to strike back at his tormentors; that he feels more lonely and scared when he is by himself; and that he gives more self-deprecatory reactions when figuratively looking at himself in the mirror (34). He may have less anxiety about realizing high-flown ambitions than the middle-class child, but generalized feelings of inadequacy and unworthiness make him very prone to overrespond with anxiety to any threatening situation. In view of the general hopelessness of his position, lethargy, apathy, submission, and passive sabotage are more typical than aggressive striving of his predominant reaction to frustration (95, 105).

Rosen (95) compared the educational and vocational aspirations of Negro boys (age 8 through 14) and their mothers to those of white, Protestant Americans, French Canadians, American Jews, Greek-Americans, and Italian-Americans. The mean vocational aspiration score of his Negro group was significantly lower than the mean scores of all other groups except the French Canadian. Paradoxically, however, 83 per cent of the Negro mothers aspired to a college education for their sons.[1] Rosen concluded that although Negroes have been

> ... exposed to the liberal economic ethic longer than most of the other groups ... their culture, it seems, is least likely to accent achievement values. The Negro's history as a slave and depressed farm worker, and the sharp discrepancy between his experience and the American Creed, would appear to work against the achievement values of the dominant white group. Typically, the Negro life-situation does not encourage the belief that one can manipulate his environment, or the conviction that one can improve his condition very much by plannning and hard work (95, p. 55).

> ... Negroes who might be expected to share the prevalent American emphasis upon education, face the painfully apparent fact that positions open to educated Negroes are scarce. This fact means that most Negroes, in all likelihood, do not consider high educational aspirations realistic, and the heavy drop-out in high school suggests that the curtailment of educational aspirations begins very early (95, p. 58).

Ethnicity was found to be more highly related to vocational aspirations than was social class; sizable ethnic and racial differences prevailed even when the influence of social class was controlled. These results are consistent with the finding that white students tend to prefer "very interesting jobs," whereas Negro students are more concerned with job security (106).

The relatively low vocational aspirations of Negro children are apparently justified by the current facts of economic life. Negroes predominate in the unskilled occupations, receive less pay than whites for equivalent work, and exceed the percentage figured for whites in degree of unemployment (43, 105). In skilled occupations, Negroes

[1]Another datum at variance with the general trend of the evidence is Grossack's finding that female Negro students in the South score significantly higher on need achievement measures than do comparable white females, and that the males of both groups are not significantly different (52).

are excluded at all educational levels (120): higher educational qualifications in Negroes are less frequently associated with higher-level vocational pursuits than they are in the case of whites (119). Thus,

> ... from long experience Negroes have learned that it is best to be prepared for the absence, rather then the presence of opportunity—or, at most, to prepare and strive only for those limited opportunities which have been open in the past.... Like most other people, Negroes tend to accept the views that prevail in the larger society about their appropriate role in that society, [and aspire and prepare] for only those positions where they are confident of acceptance (110, p. 461).

Negro children and lower-class white children who attend schools with a heterogeneous social class and racial population are in a more favorable developmental situation. Under these conditions, the unfavored group is stimulated to compete more aggressively, even to the point of unrealism (16, 109), with the more privileged group in every-day contacts and in aspirational behavior (16). In their self-judgments they compare themselves with *actual* models, who in fact are only slightly better off than they are, and hence do not feel particularly inferior (34). Negro children in segregated schools, on the other hand, are not only deprived of this stimulation, but in comparing themselves to other children paradoxically feel more depressed and less able to compete adequately (34), despite the fact that their actual contacts are confined to children in the incapsulated community who share their socio-economic status. Apparently then, they must use idealized mass media models as the basis for comparison.

Negro children are placed in the same ambivalent, conflictful position with respect to the achievement values of western civilization as are the children of many native peoples experiencing acculturation and the socio-cultural impact of rapid industrialization. On the one hand, exposure to the new value system and its patent and alluring advantages makes them less able to accept the traditional values of their elders; on the other hand, both loyalty to their families and the excluding color bar established by the dominant group make it difficult for them to assimilate the new set of values (9, 11, 12, 35, 81). Resentment and hostility toward the rejecting whites, as well as disillusionment regarding white middle-class values and institutions, predispose them arbitrarily and indiscriminately to repudiate the aspirations and personality traits valued by the dominant culture. These negativistic tendencies are even manifested in speech patterns: minority group children tend to reject the accepted model of speech that is symbolic of superordinate status in a social order that accords them only second-class membership (2).

Further abetting these tendencies toward resistive acculturation are many organized and institutionalized forms of nationalism and counter-chauvinism. Among the Maori, "resistance took the form of unadaptive but adjustive messianic and magical cults, emphasis on moribund and ceremonial features of the ancient culture, and indiscriminate rejection of progressive aspects of European culture" (9, p. 221). Numerous parallels can be found among the American Negro—for example, the Father Divine and Black Muslim movements.

One of the most damaging effects of racial prejudice and discrimination on the victimized group is that it provides an all-embracing rationalization for personal shortcomings, lack of striving, and antisocial conduct.

> Some Negroes use the objective injustice of [creating scapegoats] as an opportunity to relieve or ward off feelings of personal inadequacy, self-contempt, or self-reproach by projecting all the blame onto white prejudice and discrimination. For other Negroes, however, reaction-formation becomes a main defense against the negative racial image.... Thus they may develop extremes of moralistic, prudish, and compulsively meticulous attitudes [to disprove the stereotype] (14, p. 152).

> The Negro child is offered an excuse for anti-social behavior and evasion of social responsibility through feeling deprived of the social rewards for self-denial which are part of a healthy socialization process. But since these reactions are at variance with the democratic ideal of many other teachings to which children of both races are exposed at home, at church, and at school, they arouse of necessity feelings of inner conflict, confusion, anxiety, and guilt. These constitute liabilities for optimal adjustment (14, p. 152).

> A continuing set of small incidents, closed doors, and blocked opportunities contribute to feelings of insecurity and mistrust and lead to the building of faith only in immediate gratifications and personal possessions (14, p. 148).

Withdrawal from Competition. An important factor helping to perpetuate the Negro's inferior social status and devalued ego structure is his tendency to withdraw from the competition of the wider American culture and to seek psychological shelter within the segregated walls of his own subculture. Such tendencies are particularly evident among middle-class Negroes who, instead of providing the necessary leadership in preparing their people to take advantage of new vocational opportunities in the emerging desegregated culture, often seek to protect their own vested interests in segregation. Negro businessmen, professionals, and teachers, for example, largely owe their clientele, jobs, and incomes to the existence of segregated institutions; furthermore, in the segregated community they do not have to meet the more stringent competitive standards prevailing in the wider culture (42, 93, 120). An additional complication is the fact that even though they "cannot escape altogether the discrimination and contempt to which Negroes are generally subjected" (42, p. 299), they tend to identify with the values and ideology of the white middle-class and to dissociate themselves from other Negroes (42, 93, 107, 110, 114). Together with pride of race and grudging affirmation of their racial identity, members of intellectual Negro families "are led to assert their superiority over other Negroes, and look down on those who are 'no account,' shiftless, and 'mean' " (93, p. 240).

The degree to which Negro potential can be developed in America depends, according to Smuts (110),

> . . . not only on the willingness of the white community to grant greater opportunity to Negroes in the struggle for integrated schools and equal access to jobs; but it also depends at least as much on what the Negro community does to help its own members prepare themselves for new opportunities. . . . In a democracy, how well the individual develops and utilizes his potential depends not only on the opportunities that come his way as a youth and a man, but equally on his own determination to seek and make the most of opportunity (p. 456).
>
> In the past the real world that Negroes had to adjust to included segregation, discrimination, absence of opportunity. But the facts are changing and a new kind of adjustment is called for (p. 461). . . . The development of high ambition and firm self-confidence among Negro youth is one prerequisite for the fuller development of Negro potential (p. 462). . . . In a competitive society integration means competition, and successful competition requires at least equal preparation (p. 458). . . . Negroes will not be able to take full advantage of [new] opportunities unless they improve their preparation for work (p. 458). . . . Negro children cannot develop an image of themselves as free and equal members of American society unless they see their elders actually living that role (p. 463).

Educational aspirations and achievement of Negro children. Partly as a result of unequal educational opportunities, Negro children show serious academic retardation. They attend school for fewer years and, on the average, learn much less than white children do (5, 17, 21, 82, 110, 113). One of the chief reasons for this discrepancy is the inferior education and training of Negro teachers who themselves are usually products of segregated education. The inequality of educational facilities exists not only in the South (5, 17, 127), but also in the urban North as well, where, for the most part, de facto segregation prevails (110, 113). Eighty-four per cent of the top 10 per cent of Negro graduates in one southern high school scored below the national mean on the Scholastic Aptitude Test (17). Thus the incentive of reaching the average level of proficiency in the group is not very stimulating for Negro children, since the mean and even the somewhat superior child in this group are still below grade level. Teachers in segregated schools also tend to be overly permissive and to emphasize play skills over academic achievement; they are perceived by their pupils as evaluating them negatively, and as more concerned with behavior than with schoolwork (34).

Even more important perhaps as a cause of Negro educational retardation is the situation prevailing in the Negro home. Many Negro parents have had little schooling themselves and hence are unable to appreciate its value. Thus they do not provide active, wholehearted support for high-level academic performance by demanding conscientious study and regular attendance from their children. Furthermore, because of their large families and their own meager schooling they are less able to provide help with lessons. Keeping a large family of children in secondary school constitutes a heavy economic burden on Negro parents in view of their low per capita income and the substantial hidden costs of "free" education. The greater frequency of broken homes, unemployment, and negative family atmosphere, as well as the high rate of pupil turnover (25, 104), are also not conducive to academic achievement.

Negro pupils are undoubtedly handicapped in academic attainment by a lower average level of intellectual functioning than is characteristic of comparable white pupils. In both northern and southern areas, particularly the latter, Negro pupils have significantly lower IQs (19, 39, 80, 82), and are retarded in arithmetic, reading, language usage, and ability to handle abstract concepts (17, 82). The extreme intellectual impoverishment of the Negro home *over and above* its lower social-class status reflects the poor standard of English spoken in the home and the general lack of books, magazines, and stimulating conversation. In view of the educational and psychological inequality of segregated schools, the inferior intellectual status of Negro homes, and the negative motivational effects of membership in a socially stigmatized group, any inferences from the lower IQ's and educational retardation of Negro pupils regarding *innate* differences in intelligence are obviously unwarranted. Organic brain damage, however, is a more frequent occurrence in Negro children because of inadequate prenatal care and nutrition and because of the higher incidence of prematurity (85).

Similar kinds of family and community factors depress the vocational strivings and accomplishments of Negro youth. Practically all of the following description of the occupational aspirations of Maori adolescents in New Zealand applies to the Negro in America:

> Maori parents are less sophisticated than their [European] counterparts about vocational matters and are accordingly less capable of assisting their children with appropriate information, advice, and guidance. . . . In view of their smaller incomes and larger families, Maori parents are also more reluctant to commit themselves to supporting plans requiring long-term vocational preparation (9, p. 623).
>
> . . . Maori parents tend to adopt more permissive and laissez-faire attitudes than [European] parents toward their children's vocational careers. Despite occasional and inconsistent displays of authoritarianism in this regard, they are usually content to let them drift. They apply fewer coercive pressures and extend less support and encouragement in relation to the long-term occupational ambitions of their children. Their own values concerning vocational achievement and the example they set their children also tend to encourage the adoption of a short-term view. In practice they make few demands for the deferment of immediate hedonistic satisfactions and for the internalization of supportive traits consistent with high academic and occupational attainment (p. 623).
>
> . . . [Still] another factor limiting the vocational achievement of Maori youth is the relatively low occupational status and morale of Maori adults. Young people lack the encouragement [of visible emulatory models], of a tradition and a high current standard of vocational accomplishment in the ethnic group. They are also denied the practical benefits of guidance and financial backing that would follow from the existence of such a standard and tradition. On the other hand, they are discouraged by the marginal economic position of their elders [and] by social demoralization (p. 624).

> Maori pupils also receive less encouragement from their peers than [European] pupils do to strive for vocational achievement. Not only is occupational success less highly valued in the Maori than in the European peer culture, but the greater availability of *derived status*—based solely on membership in and intrinsic acceptance by the group—also removes much of the incentive for seeking *primary status* based on individual competence and performance. In districts where community morale is low and juvenile delinquency flourishes, vocational achievement tends to be negatively sanctioned (p. 624).

Low vocational aspirations, of course, are in large part a reflection of the distressingly high rate of unemployment among Negro youth in the urban slums. Conant reports that in one large city 48 per cent of male Negro high school graduates and 63 per cent of non-graduates were unemployed (25).

> The tone is not one to encourage education or stimulate ambition. One often finds a vicious circle of lack of jobs and lack of ambition; one leads to the other. It is my contention that the circle must be broken both by upgrading the educational and vocational aspirations of slum youth and, even more important, by finding employment opportunity for them, particularly for high school graduates. It does no good whatever to prepare boys and girls for non-existent jobs (25, p. 36).

Finally, because of their precocious desatellization and emancipation from parents, Negro youths have greater needs for *immediate* financial independence. They therefore find psychologically more intolerable a prolonged period of psychological dependence on parents, such as would be required in preparing for a profession.

Personality adjustment. The destructive impact of prejudice, discrimination, segregation, an inferior caste status on self-esteem, in addition to the usual mental hygiene consequences of lower social class membership, result in a much higher incidence of behavior disorders in Negroes than in whites (51, 111, 128). Personality disturbance is also more highly correlated with intelligence test scores in Negroes than in whites (94). Quite understandably, both high anxiety level (83, 94) and suppressed feelings of aggression (61) are prominent symptoms of Negro maladjustment. Overt expression of these same aggressive impulses leads to a juvenile delinquency rate that is two to three times as high as among white teen-agers (37, 38). The occurrence of delinquent behavior is abetted by the high rate of unemployment (25) and by many characteristic features of lower-class Negro family life, such as illegitimate births, broken homes, desertion, neglect, employment of the mother, intra-familial violence, harsh punishment, and tolerance for minor dishonesties (20). Under these circumstances, aggressive antisocial behavior may be considered both a form of individual and social protest (38), as well as an effective means of obtaining and maintaining status in the peer group of the lower-class Negro subculture (22). Drug addiction, on the other hand, represents a particularly efficient type of "dead-end" adjustment for the hedonistic, motivationally immature adolescent who refuses to face up to the responsibilities of adult life (10, 41).

Sex Differences

One of the most striking features of ego development in the segregated Negro community is the relatively more favored position enjoyed by girls in comparison to the middle-class model. It is true that middle-class girls have certain advantages over boys in early ego development. Since girls perceive themselves as more highly accepted and intrinsically valued by parents (13) and have a more available emulatory model in the home (84), they tend to satellize more and longer. In addition to enjoying more derived status in the home, they can also acquire more primary status from household activities (84) and from school achievement. The opportunity for acquiring primary status in school is greater for girls than for boys because of their superior verbal fluency and greater conformity to adult authority, and because school success is less ambivalently prized by their peers. In general, girls are less negativistic (46), more amenable to social controls (66), and less alienated from adults.

Middle-class boys, however, are not excessively disadvantaged. Their mothers tend to prefer them to girls (100), and their fathers are responsible and respected status figures in the home and the principal source of economic security. Furthermore, although girls enjoy more current primary status during childhood, boys have higher ultimate aspirations for primary status; their aspirational level both for laboratory tasks (121) and for possessions and achievement (24) are higher. Unlike boys, girls do not *really* expect to prove their adequacy and maintain their self-esteem as adults by means of their vocational accomplishments. Their fathers are satisfied if they are "pretty, sweet, affectionate, and well-liked" (1). Finally, the superordinate position of men in our society, and the accompanying male chauvinism, is reflected in childhood sex roles. From an early age boys learn to be contemptuous of girls and their activities; and although girls retaliate in kind by finding reasons for deprecating the male sex, they tend to accept in part the prevailing view of their inferiority (65). Whereas boys seldom if ever desire to change sex, girls not infrequently wish they were boys (124). The male counterpart of a "tomboy" who relishes sewing and reads girls' books is indeed a rarity.

In contrast to this picture, we find girls in the *segregated* Negro community showing much greater relative superiority in academic, personal, and social adjustment (34). They not only outperform boys academically by a greater margin, but do so in all subjects rather than only in language skills (34). These girls have higher achievement needs (44, 52) and a greater span of attention; they are more popular with classmates; they show more mature and realistic aspirations; they assume more responsible roles; and they feel less depressed in comparing themselves with other children (3). Substantially more Negro girls than Negro boys complete every level of education in the United States (110). Adequate reasons for these differences are not difficult to find. Negro children in this subculture live in a matriarchal family atmosphere where girls are openly preferred by mothers and grandmothers, and where the male sex role is generally deprecated. The father frequently deserts the family and in any case tends to be an unreliable source of economic and emotional security (28, 34). Hence the mother, assisted perhaps by her mother or by a daughter, shoulders most of the burdens and responsibilities of child rearing and is the only dependable adult with whom the child can identify. In this environment male chauvinism can obtain little foothold. The preferential treatment accorded girls is even extended to opportunities for acquiring ultimate primary status. If the family pins all of its hopes on one child and makes desperate sacrifices for that child, it will often be a daughter in preference to a son.[2] Over and above his handicaps at home, the Negro boy also faces more obstacles in the wider culture in realizing his vocational ambitions, whatever they may be, than the Negro girl in fulfilling her adult role expectations of housewife, mother, nurse, teacher, or clerical worker (34).

It seems, therefore, that Negro girls in racially incapsulated areas are less traumatized than boys by the impact of racial discrimination. This is precisely the opposite of what is found in studies of Negro children from less economically depressed and less segregated environments (45, 117). The discrepancy can be attributed perhaps to two factors: (1) the preferential treatment accorded girls in the

[2]In lower-class Puerto Rican and Mexican families, just the opposite situation is to be found; that is, male dominance and superiority prevails (40, 49, 75).

incapsulated community is more pervasive, unqualified, and continuous, and (2) the fact that, unlike Negro girls in mixed neighborhoods, these girls are less exposed to slights and humiliation from white persons. However, because of less tendency to internalize their feelings and greater openness in their social organization, Negro boys are able to adjust more easily than girls to the initial impact of desegregation (18).

Individual Differences in Reactions to the Segregated Negro Environment

Only extreme cultural determinists would argue that all children in the incapsulated Negro community necessarily respond in substantially identical ways to the impact of their social environment. Although common factors in cultural conditioning obviously make for many uniformities in personality development, genically determined differences in temperamental and cognitive traits, as well as differential experience in the home and wider culture, account for much idiosyncratic variations. Would it be unreasonable, for example, to anticipate that an intellectually gifted Negro child in this environment might have a different fate than an intellectually dull or average youngster; that an active, assertive, outgoing, and tough-skinned child might react differently to discriminatory treatment than one who is phlegmatic, submissive, sensitive, and introverted?

Differences in early socializing experience with parents are probably even more important, especially since they tend to generalize to interpersonal behavior outside the home. At this point it is worth noting that, generally speaking, racial discrimination affects children indirectly through their parents before it affects them directly through their own contacts with the wider culture. This indirect influence is mediated in two ways. (1) General parental attitudes toward the child are undoubtedly determined in part by the parent's own experience as a victim of discrimination. Some racially victimized parents, seeking retribution through their children, may fail to value them intrinsically and may place exaggerated emphasis on ego aggrandizement. Others may be so preoccupied with their own frustrations as to reject their children. Still others may accept and intrinsically value their children, and through their own example and strength of character encourage the development of realistic aspirations and mature, self-disciplined behavior. (2) Parents transmit to their children some of their own ways of responding to discrimination, such as counter-aggression, passive sabotage, obsequious submission, or strident counter-chauvinism. Individual differences such as these undoubtedly explain in part why some Negroes move into unsegregated neighborhoods and transfer to unsegregated schools when these opportunities arise, whereas other members of the race choose to remain in the segregated environment. The decision to transfer or not to transfer to an unsegregated school, for example, was found to be unrelated to both social class status and academic ability (27).

Much inter-individual variability therefore prevails in the reactions of children to minority group membership. Fortunately, sufficient time is available for establishing some stable feelings of intrinsic adequacy within the home before the impact of segregation on ego development becomes catastrophically destructive. It was found, for example, that Negro children who are most self-accepting also tend to exhibit more positive attitudes toward other Negro and white children (117), and that Negro college students who identify most with their own race tend to be least prejudiced against other minority groups (64). Hence, while appreciating the generally unfavorable effects of a segregated environment on all Negro children, we may conclude on the more hopeful note that the consequences of membership in a stigmatized racial group can be cushioned in part by a foundation of intrinsic self-esteem established in the home (7, 76) . . .

Summary and Conclusions

The ego development of segregated Negro children in the United States manifests various distinctive properties, both because Negroes generally occupy the lowest stratum of the lower-class subculture, and because they possess an inferior caste status in American society. Their inferior caste position is marked by an unstable and matriarchal type of family structure, by restricted opportunities for acquiring educational, vocational, and social status, by varying degrees of segregation from the dominant white majority, and by a culturally fixed devaluation of their dignity as human beings. The consequences of this regrettable state of affairs for Negro children's self-esteem and self-confidence, for their educational and vocational aspirations, and for their character structure, interpersonal relations, and personality adjustment, constitute the characteristic features of their ego development.

Beginning in the pre-school period, the Negro child gradually learns to appreciate the negative implications of dark skin color for social status and personal worth. Hence he resists identifying with his own racial group and shows definite preference for white dolls and playmates. This reluctance to acknowledge his racial membership not only results in ego deflation, but also makes it difficult for him to identify with his parents and to obtain from such identification the derived status that universally constitutes the principal basis of self-esteem during childhood. Much of the derived status that white children obtain from their parents is made available to the Negro child by virtue of his membership in an unsupervised peer group, which accordingly performs many of the socializing functions of the white-middle-class home. This is especially true for the Negro boy who often has no adult male with whom to identify in the frequently fatherless Negro family, and who finds maleness deprecated in his matriarchal and authoritarian home. Early experience in fending for himself results in precocious social maturity, independence, and emancipation from the home.

During pre-adolescence and adolescence, segregated Negro children characteristically develop low aspirations for academic and vocational achievement. These low aspirations reflect existing social class and ethnic values, the absence of suitable emulatory models, marked educational retardation, restricted vocational opportunities, lack of parental and peer group support, and the cultural impoverishment of the Negro home. Because of loyalty to parents and rejection by the dominant white group, Negro adolescents develop ambivalent feelings toward middle-class achievement values and the personality traits necessary for their implementation. In many instances they use the objective facts of racial prejudice and discrimination as a rationalization for personal inadequacies, apathy, lack of striving, and anti-social behavior. The seeming hopelessness of attaining adequate vocational and social status in the wider American culture induces many Negro youths to withdraw from contact and competition with whites, and to seek the psychological shelter of their own segregated subculture. Girls tend to develop a more mature ego structure than boys because of their favored position in the home, but face greater adjustment problems during desegregation. The detrimental effects of segregation and inferior caste status on Negro ego development naturally vary from one child to another depending on ability, temperament, and the degree of intrinsic self-esteem and ego maturity that can be acquired with the home environment.

The problem of raising aspirational and achievement levels among Negro youth is presently acute because Negroes can no longer adjust comfortably to their segregated caste status, and because automation has eliminated many of the unskilled jobs which formerly made some type of stable economic adjustment possible. Two different but complementary approaches are available in dealing with this problem. The more general approach, which primarily applies to educators in their role as citizens, involves the elimination of existing racial barriers in housing, education, employment, religion, and civil rights. The more specific educational approach is to attempt, through various family, school and community measures, an upgrading of the Negro child's aspirational level, standards of achievement, and character structure that will both enhance his self-esteem and enable him to take advantage of new opportunities.

In the educational sphere, school desegregation is an indispensable prerequisite for raising aspiration and achievement levels, but obviously cannot compensate, in and of itself, for the long-standing educational handicaps of the Negro child or for existing inadequacies in schools, teachers, curriculums, and counseling services. Before we can expect any permanent improvement in the educational performance of Negro children, we must strengthen Negro family life, combat the cultural impoverishment of the Negro home, and enlist the support and cooperation of Negro parents in accomplishing this objective. More intensive guidance services, utilizing Negro personnel, are required to provide the socializing and supportive functions that are currently lacking in many Negro homes. Other important needs are smaller classes, specially trained teachers, abundant remedial facilities, the provision of expanded and more realistic vocational education, and a public works program to alleviate the explosively dangerous problem of unemployment among urban Negro youth.

References

1. Aberle, D. F., and Naegele, K. D., "Middle-Class Fathers' Occupational Roles and Attitudes Toward Children," *Amer. J. Orthopsychiat.*, 1952, 22:366-378.

2. Anastasi, Anne, and Cordova, F. A., "Some Effects of Bilingualism upon the Intelligence Test Performance of Puerto Rican Children in New York City," *J. educ. Psychol.*, 1953, 44:1-19.

3. Anastasi, Anne, and DeJesus, C., "Language Development and Nonverbal IQ of Puerto Rican Preschool Children in New York City." *J. abnorm. soc. Psychol.*, 1953, 48:357-366.

4. Angelino, H., Dollins, J., and Mech, E. V., "Trends in the 'Fears and Worries' of School Children as Related to Socioeconomic Status and Age," *J. genet. Psychol.*, 1956, 89:263-276.

5. Ashmore, H. S., *The Negro and the Schools*, Chapel Hill, N.C.: University of North Carolina Press, 1954.

6. Auld, B. F., "Influence of Social Class on Personality Test Response," *Psychol. Bull.*, 152, 49:318-332.

7. Ausubel, D. P., *Ego Development and the Personality Disorders,* New York: Grune and Stratton, 1952.

8. ———, "Ego Development Among Segregated Negro Children," *Ment. Hyg.*, 1958, 42:362-369.

9. ———, "Acculturative Stress in Modern Maori Adolescence," *Child Develpm.*, 1960, 31:617-631.

10. ———, "Causes and Types of Drug Addiction: a Psychosocial View," *Psychiat. Quart.*, 1961, 35:523-531.

11. ———, "The Maori: A Study in Resistive Acculturation," *Soc. Forces,* 1961, 39:218-227.

12. ———, *Maori Youth,* Wellington, New Zealand: Price, Milburn, 1961.

13. ———, et al. "Perceived Parent Attitudes as Determinants of Children's Ego Structure," *Child Develpm.*, 1954, 25:173-183.

14. Bernard, Viola W., "School Desegregation: Some Psychiatric Implications," *Psychiatry,* 1958, 21:149-158.

15. Bernstein, B., "Some Sociological Determinants of Perception: an Enquiry into Sub-cultural Differences," *Brit. J. Sociol.,* 1958, 9, 159-174.

16. Boyd, G. F., "The Levels of Aspiration of White and Negro Children in Non-segregated Elementary School," *J. soc. Psychol.*, 1952, 36:191-196.

17. Bullock, H. A., "A Comparison of the Academic Achievements of White and Negro High School Graduates," *J. educ. Res.*, 1950, 44:179-192.

18. Campbell, J. D., and Yarrow, Marian R., "Personal and Situational Variables in Adaptation to Change," *J. soc. Issues,* 1958, 14:29-46.

19. Carson, A. S., and Rabin, A. I., "Verbal Comprehension and Communication in Negro and White Children," *J. educ. Psychol.*, 1960, 51:47-51.

20. Cavan, Ruth S., "Negro Family Disorganization and Juvenile Delinquency," *J. Negro Educ.*, 1959, 28:230-239.

21. Clark, K. B., "The Most Valuable Hidden Resource," *Coll. Bd. Rev.*, 1956, No. 29, 23-26.

22. ———, "Color, Class Personality, and Juvenile Delinquency," *J. Negro Educ.*, 1959, 28:240-251.

23. ———, and Clark, M. P., "Racial Identification and Preference in Negro Children," *in* T. M. Newcomb and E. L. Hartley (Eds.), *Readings in Social Psychology,* New York: Holt, 1947, pp. 169-178.

24. Cobb, H. V., "Role-Wishes and General Wishes of Children and Adolescents," *Child Develpm.*, 1954, 25:161-171.

25. Conant, James B., *Slums and Suburbs: A Commentary on Schools in Metropolitan Areas,* New York: McGraw-Hill, 1961.

26. Cothran, T. C., "Negro Conceptions of White People," *Amer. J. Social.,* 1951, 56:458-467.

27. Crockett, Harry J., "A Study of Some Factors Affecting the Decision of Negro High School Students to Enroll in Previously All-White High Schools, St. Louis, 1955," *Soc. Forces,* 1957, 35:351-356.

28. Dai, B., "Some Problems of Personality Development in Negro Children," *in* C. Kluckhohn and H. A. Murray (Eds.), *Personality in Nature, Society and Culture,* New York: Knopf, 1949, pp. 437-458.

29. Davis, A., *Deep South: a Social Anthropological Study of Caste and Class,* Chicago: University of Chicago Press, 1941.

30. ———, "Child Training and Social Class," *in* R. G. Barker, J. S. Kounin, and H. F. Wright (Eds.), *Child Behavior and Development.* New York: McGraw-Hill, 1943, pp. 607-620.

31. ———, and Dollard, J., *Children of Bondage,* Washington, D. C.: American Council on Education, 1940.

32. Davis, A., and Havighurst, R. J., Social class and color differences in child rearing. *Ameri. sociol. Rev.,* 1946, 11:698-710.

33. Deutsch, Martin P., Minority group and class status as related to social and personality factors in scholastic achievement. *Soc. appl, Anthropol. Monogr.,* 1960, No. 2.

34. ———, et al. "Some Considerations as to the Contributions of Social, Personality, and Racial Factors to School Retardation in Minority Group Children," paper read at American Psychology Association, Chicago, September 1956.

35. De Vos, G., and Miner, H. "Algerian Culture and Personality in Changes," *Sociometry,* 1958, 21:255-268.

36. Dickens, Sara L., and Hobart C., "Parental Dominance and Offspring Ethnocentrism," *J. soc. Psychol.,* 1959, 49:297-303.

37. Dinitz S., Kay, Barbara A., and Reckless, W. C., "Group Gradients in Delinquency Potential and Achievement Score of Sixth Graders," *Amer. J. Orthopsychiat.,* 1958, 28:598-605.

38. Douglass, J. H., "The Extent and Characteristics of Juvenile Delinquency Among Negroes in the United States," *J. Negro Educ.,* 1959, 28:214-229.

39. Dreger, R. M., and Miller, K. S., "Comparative Psychological Studies of Negroes and Whites in the United States," *Psychol. Bull.,* 1960, 57:361-402.

40. Fernandez-Marina, R., Maldonado-Sierra, E. D., and Trent, R. D., "Three Basic Themes in Mexican and Puerto Rican Family Values," *J. soc. Psychol.,* 48:167-81, 1958.

41. Finestone, H., "Cats, Kicks, and Color," *Soc. Probl.*, 1957, 5:3-13.

42. Frazier, E. F., "The Negro Middle Class and Desegregation," *Soc. Probl.*, 1957, 4:291-301.

43. Frumkin, R. M., "Race, Occupation, and Social Class in New York," *J. Negro Educ.*, 1958, 27:62-65.

44. Gaier, E. L., and Wambach, Helen S., "Self-evaluation of Personality Assets and Liabilities of Southern White and Negro Students," *J. soc. Psychol.*, 1960, 51: 135-143.

45. Goff, R. M., *Problems and Emotional Difficulties of Negro Children*, New York: Bureau of Publications, Teachers College, Columbia University, 1949.

46. Goodenough, F. L., "Anger in Young Children," *Inst. Child Welf. Monogr.*, 1931, No. 9.

47. Goodman, M. E., *Race Awareness in Young Children*. Cambridge, Mass.: Addison-Wesley, 1952.

48. Gould, R., "Some Sociological Determinants of Goal Strivings," *J. soc. Psychol.* 1941, 13:461-473.

49. Green, Helen B., "Comparison of Nurturance and Independence Training in Jamaica and Puerto Rico with Consideration of the Resulting Personality Structure and Transplanted Social Patterns," *J. soc. Psychol.* 1960, 50:27-63.

50. Greenberg, H., Chase, A. L., and Cannon, T. M., "Attitudes of White and Negro High School Students in a West Texas Town Toward School Integration," *J. appl. Psychol.*, 1957, 41:27-31.

51. Greenberg, H., and Fane, D., "An Investigation of Several Variables as Determinants of Authoritarianism," *J. soc. Psychol.*, 1959, 49:105-111.

52. Grossack, M. M., "Some Personality Characteristics of Southern Negro Students," *J. soc. Psychol.*, 1957, 46:125-131.

53. Hart, I., "Maternal Child-Rearing Practices and Authoritarian Ideology,"*J. abnorm. soc. Psychol.*, 1957, 55:232-237.

54. Havighurst, R. J., and Taba, H., *Adolescent Character and Personality*, New York: Wiley, 1949.

55. Herr, D. M., "The Sentiment of White Supremacy: an Ecological Study," *Amer. J. Sociol.*, 1959, 64:592-598.

56. Hill, M. C., "Research on the Negro Family," *Marriage fam., Living*, 1957, 19:25-31.

57. Hollingshead, A. B., and Redlich, F. C., *Social Class and Mental Illness*, New York: Wiley, 1958.

58. Jefferson, Ruth B., "Some Obstacles to Racial Integration," *J. Negro Educ.* 1957, 26:145-154.

59. Jenkins, W. A., "An Experimental Study of the Relationship of Legitimate and Illegitimate Birth Status to School and Personal Adjustment of Negro Children," *Amer. J. Sociol.*, 1958, 64:169-173.

60. Kahn, M. L., "Social Class and Parental Values," *Amer. J. Sociol.*, 1959, 64:337-351.

61. Karon, B. P., *The Negro Personality*, New York: Springer, 1958.

62. Kelly, J. G., Ferson, J. E., and Holtzman, W. H., "The Measurement of Attitudes Toward the Negro in the South," *J. soc. Psychol.*, 1958, 48:305-317.

63. Killian, L. M., and Haer, J. L., "Variables Related to Attitudes Regarding School Desegregation Among White Southerners," *Sociometry*, 1958, 21:159-164.

64. Kirkhart, R. O., "Psychological and Socio-psychological Correlates of Marginality in Negroes," *Dissert Abstr.*, 1960, 20:4173.

65. Kitay, P. M., "A Comparison of the Sexes in Their Attitudes and Beliefs About Women: a Study of Prestige Groups," *Sociometry*, 1940, 3:399-407.

66. Koch, H. L., "Some Personality Correlates of Sex, Sibling Position, and Sex of Siblings Among Five- and Six-Year-Old Children," *Genet. Psychol. Monogr.*, 1955, 52:3-51.

67. Kvaraceus, W. C., "Culture and the Delinquent," *NEA J.*, 1959, 48:14-16.

68. Landreth, C., and Johnson, B. C., "Young Children's Responses to a Picture and Inset Test Designed to Reveal Reactions to Persons of Different Skin Color," *Child Develpm.*, 1953, 24:63-79.

69. Lipset, S. M., "Democracy and Working-Class Authoritarianism," *Amer sociol. Rev.*, 1959, 24:482-501.

70. Maas, H., "Some Social Class Differences in the Family Systems and Group Relations of Pre- and Early Adolescents," *Child Develpm.*, 1951, 22:145-152.

71. Maccoby, Eleanor, Gibbs, P. K., et al., "Methods of Child Rearing in Two Social Classes," *in* W. E. Martin and C. B. Stendler (Eds.), *Readings in Child Development*. New York: Harcourt, Brace, 1954, pp. 380-396.

72. McLure, W. P., "Challenge of Vocational and Technical Education," *Phi Delta Kappan*, 1962, 44:212-217.

73. Mann, J. H., "The Effect of Interracial Contact on Sociometric Choices and Perceptions," *J. soc. Psychol.*, 1959, 50:143-152.

74. Markley, Elaine R., "Social Class Differences in Mothers' Attitudes Toward Child Rearing," *Dissert. Abst.*, 1958, 19:355-356.

75. Maslow, A. H., and Diaz-Guerrero, R., "Delinquency as Value Disturbance," *in* J. G. Peatman and E. L. Hartley, (Eds.), *Festschrift for Gardner Murphy*, New York: Harper, 1960, pp. 228-240.

76. Milner, Esther, "Some Hypotheses Concerning the Influence of Segregation on Negro Personality Development," *Psychiatry*, 1953, 16:291-297.

77. Morland, J. K., "Racial Recognition by Nursery School Children in Lynchburg, Virginia," *Soc. Forces*, 1958, 37:132-137.

78. Neprash, J. A., "Minority Group Contacts and Social Distance," *Phylon*, 1953, 14:207-212.

79. *The New York Times*, Sunday, March 11, 1962.

80. North, R. D., *The Intelligence of American Negroes*, New York: Anti-Defamation League of B'nai B'rith, 1954.

81. Omari, T. P., "Changing Attitudes of Students in West African Society Toward Marriage and Family Relationships," *Brit. J. Sociol.*, 1960, 11:197-210.

82. Osborne, R. T., "Racial Differences in Mental Growth and School Achievement: a Longitudinal Study," *Psychol Reps.*, 1960, 7:233-239.

83. Palermo, D. S., "Racial Comparisons and Additional Normative Data on the Children's Manifest Anxiety Scale," *Child Develpm.*, 1959, 30:53-57.

84. Parsons, T., "Age and Sex in the Social Structure of the United States," *Amer. sociol. Rev.*, 1942, 7:604-616.

85. Pasamanick, B., and Knobloch, Hilda, "The Contribution of Some Organic Factors to School Retardation in Negro Children," *J. Negro Educ.*, 1958, 27:4-9.

86. Pawl, J. L. H., "Some Ego Skills and Their Relation to the Differences in Intelligence Between the Middle and Lower Classes," *Dissert. Abstr.*, 1960, 21:368.

87. Phillips, W. B., "Counseling Negro Students: an Educational Dilemma," *Calif. J. educ. Res.*, 1959, 10:185-188.

88. Pierce-Jones, J., "Socio-economic Status and Adolescents' Interests," *Psychol. Reps.* 1959, 5:683.

89. ———, "Vocational Interest Correlates of Socio-economic Status in Adolescence," *Educ. psychol. Measmt*, 1959, 19:65-71.

90. Pompilo, P. T., "The Relationship Between Projection and Prejudice with a Factor Analysis of Anti-Semitic and Anti-Negro Attitudes," unpublished doctoral dissertation, Catholic University, Washington, D.C., 1957.

91. Prothro, E. T., "Ethnocentrism and Anti-Negro Attitudes in the Deep South," *J. abnorm. soc. Psychol.*, 1952, 47:105-108.

92. Raab, E., and Lipset, S. M., *Prejudice and Society,* New York: Anti-Defamation League of B'nai B'rith, 1959.

93. Record, W., "Social Stratification and Intellectual Roles in the Negro Community," *Brit. J. Sociol.,* 1957, 8:235-255.

94. Roen, S. R., "Personality and Negro-White Intelligence," *J. abnorm. soc. Psychol.,* 1960, 61:148-150.

95. Rosen, B. C., "Race, Ethnicity, and the Achievement Syndrome," *Amer. sociol. Rev.,* 1959, 24:47-60.

96. Rosner, J., "When White Children Are in the Minority," *J. educ. Sociol.,* 1954, 28:69-72.

97. Schneider, L., and Lysgaard, S., "The Deferred Gratification Pattern: a Preliminary Study," *Amer. sociol. Rev.,* 1953, 18:142-149.

98. Schpoont, S., "Some Relationships Between Task Attractiveness, Self-evaluated Motivation, and Success or Failure," unpublished doctoral dissertation, University of Illinois, Urbana, Ill., 1955.

99. Sears, P. S., "Levels of Aspiration in Academically Successful and Unsuccessful Children," *J. abnorm. soc. Psychol.,* 1940, 35:498-536.

100. Sears, R. R., et al., "Some Child-Rearing Antecedents of Aggression and Dependency in Young Children," *Genet. Psychol. Monogr.,* 1953, 47:135-234.

101. Sewell, W., and Haller, A. O., "Social Status and the Personality Status of the Child," *Sociometry,* 1956, 19:113-125.

102. ———, "Factors in the Relationships Between Social Status and the Personality Adjustment of the Child," *Amer. sociol, Rev.,* 1959, 24:511-520.

103. ———, and Strauss, M. A., "Social Status and Educational and Occupational Aspiration," *Amer. sociol. Rev.,* 1957, 22:67-73.

104. Sexton, Patricia C., "Social Class and Pupil Turn-over Rates," *J. educ. Sociol.,* 1959, 33:131-134.

105. Siegel, A. I., and Federman, P., *Employment Experiences of Negro Philadelphians: A Descriptive Study of the Employment Experiences, Perceptions, and Aspirations of Selected Philadelphia Whites and Non-Whites.* Wayne, Pa.: Applied Psychological Services, 1959.

106. Singer, S. L., and Stafflre, B., "A Note on Racial Differences in Job Values and Desires," *J. soc. Psychol.,* 1956, 43:333-337.

107. Smith, B. F., "Wishes of High School Seniors and Social Status," *J. educ. Sociol.,* 1952, 25:466-475.

108. Smith, C. U., and Prothro, J. W., "Ethnic Differences in Authoritarian Personality," *Soc. Forces,* 1957, 35:334-338.

109. Smith, M. G., "Education and Occupational Choice in Rural Jamaica," *Soc. econ. Stud.,* 1960, 9:332-354.

110. Smuts, R. W., "The Negro Community and the Development of Negro Potential," *J. Negro Educ.*, 1957, 26:456-465.

111. Srole, L., Langner, T. S., Michael, S. T., Opler, M. K., and Rennie, T. A. C., *Mental Health in the Metropolis: the Midtown Manhattan Study*, New York: McGraw-Hill, 1962.

112. Stafflre, B., "Concurrent Validity of the Vocational Values Inventory," *J. educ. Res.*, 1959, 52:339-341.

113. *The Status of the Public School Education of Negro and Puerto Rican Children in New York City*, New York: Public Education Association, 1955.

114. Steckler, G. A., "Authoritarian Ideology in Negro College Students," *J. abnorm. soc. Psychol.*, 1957, 54:396-399.

115. Stevenson, H. W., and Stevenson, N. G., "Social Interaction in an Interracial Nursery-School," *Genet. Psychol., Monogr.*, 1960, 61:37-75.

116. Stevenson, H. W., and Stewart, E. C., A developmental study of racial awareness in young children. *Child Develpm.*, 1958, 29:399-409.

117. Trent, R. D., "An Analysis of Expressed Self-Acceptance Among Negro Children," unpublished doctoral dissertation, Teachers College, Columbia University, New York, 1954.

118. Tumin, M. M., "Readiness and Resistance to Desegregation: a Social Portrait of the Hard Core," *Soc. Forces*, 1958, 36:256-263.

119. Turner, R. H., "Negro Job Status and Education," *Soc. Forces*, 1953, 32:45-52.

120. ———. "Occupational Patterns of Inequality," *Amer. J. Sociol.*, 1954, 59:437-447.

121. Walter, L. M., and Marzolf, S. S., "The Relation of Sex, Age, and School Achievement to Levels of Aspiration," *J. educ. Psychol.*, 1951, 42:285-292.

122. Webster, S. W., "The Influence of Interracial Contact on Social Acceptance in a Newly Integrated School," *J. educ. Psychol.*, 1961, 52:292-296.

123. Wertham, F., "Psychological Effects of School Segregation," *Amer. J. Psychother.*, 1952, 6:94-103.

124. West, J., *Plainville, U. S. A.*, New York: Columbia University Press, 1945.

125. Westie, F. R., "Negro-White Status Differentials and Social Distance," *Amer. Sociol. Rev.*, 1952, 17:550-558.

126. ———, and Howard, D., "Social Status Differentials and the Race Attitudes of Negroes," *Amer. sociol. Rev.*, 1954, 19:584-591.

127. Wilkerson, D. A., "Conscious and Impersonal Forces in Recent Trends Toward Negro-White School Equality in Virginia," *J. educ. Sociol.*, 1959, 32:402-408.

128. Wilson, D. C., and Lantz, E. M., "The Effect of Culture Change on the Negro Race in Virginia as Indicated by a Study of State Hospital Admissions," *Amer. J. Psychiat.*, 1957, 114:25-32.

129. Yarrows, Marian R., Campbell, J. O., and Yarrow, L. J., "Acquisition of New Norms: a Study of Racial Desegregation," *J. soc. Issues*, 1958, 14:8-28.

130. Young, R. K., Benson, W. M., and Holtzman, W. H., "Change in Attitudes Toward the Negro in a Southern University," *J. abnorm. soc. Psychol.*, 1960, 60:131-133.

Social Influences in Negro-White Intelligence Differences[1]

Martin Deutsch and Bert Brown[2]

[From The Journal of Social Issues, *April 1964, with permission.]*

This paper reports on some aspects of experience that influence the development of intellective functions in children. The social experiential variable is often treated in the psychological literature in a most macroscopic manner. It has been one of our purposes to break down the attributes of social experience along what might be called social environmental and developmental dimensions.

As regards the social environmental, the attempt has been to analyze racial group membership by some of its psychological properties, to determine some of the components of social class, and to determine something of the interaction of the two, particularly as it impinges on intellectual achievement and growth.

On what we are calling the developmental dimension, the focus has been on identifying "experience groups" in terms of language, perception, learning, general intellective functioning, and to a lesser extent, self, attitudinal, and motivational variables. These variables, in

[1]The data reported here were collected as part of studies supported by the Taconic Foundation, by Research Grant No. MH-1098 from the U.S. Department of Health, Education, and Welfare, and by Project #908 of the Cooperative Research Program of the Office of Education. The research was carried out at the Institute for Developmental Studies, Department of Psychiatry, New York Medical College.

An earlier version of this paper was read at the biennial meeting of the Society for Research in Child Development, Berkeley, California, April, 1963.

[2]We should like gratefully to acknowledge the assistance of Dr. Martin Whiteman specifically, and of all the other members of the staff of the Institute who worked on the Verbal Survey.

turn, have been broken down into more specific components for measurement and for evaluation of interrelationships.

The data have been collected on cross-sectional samples, but the work is closely associated with a large-scale longitudinal study which attempts to manipulate mediating environmental variables and to measure any subsequent behavioral modification or facilitation in intellectual growth. The cross-sectional study referred to is a large social class and race analysis, involving first and fifth grade children, which we colloquially refer to as "The Verbal Survey"—a term which is something of a misnomer, as the range goes beyond verbal measures.

This report is concerned with the intellectual test differences between Negro and white first and fifth graders of different social classes—though the focus in this report is largely on the lower class. Two more specific independent variables of special significance are presence or absence of father in the home, and whether the child had an organized pre-school experience.

The data reported in this paper are from a sample of 543 urban public school children stratified by race, grade level (first and fifth graders) and social class, as measured by the Institute's twelve point SES scale. This scale is derived both from prestige ratings of occupation as well as education of main breadwinners and yields a weighted index of these factors for each subject in the sample. The distribution of index scores is broken down into twelve levels and subsequently trichotomized into three socio-economic strata. SES comparisons reported in this paper are made among three distinguishable social class levels, I, II, and III, where level I represents the lowest group on the continuum and III the highest. Housing condition for these S's, was evaluated along a six point continuum from "Sound, with all plumbing facilities" to "Dilapidated" following from the technique suggested by the U.S. Census of Housing.[3] The weighted SES index score correlates .27 with the housing condition index for a sample of 292 children within the larger group of 543. The magnitude of this correlation is low but significant for the sample size on which it was obtained.

The intelligence test used was the Lorge-Thorndike, Level I, Primary Battery for first graders, and Level 3 for fifth graders. Both forms, as described by the authors, are essentially non-verbal (Lorge-Thorndike, 1959). Level I uses pictorial items only to measure abstract thinking, pictorial classification and pictorial pairing. Level 3 uses picture classification, pictorial analogies, and numerical relation-

[3]U.S. Bureau of the Census, *U.S. Census of Housing*, 1960, Nos. 274-276.

ships. This test was selected because of the inclusion in its standardization population of a much better than usual representation of the lower social class categories. It was given in small groups, during school hours, by trained examiners on the Institute's research staff.

The SES data were gathered by mailed questionnaires and home interviews. The SES items were only a part of the interview schedule. The rest of the items had to do with home conditions, daily routine, and aspirations of both parents and children. The appropriate items here are now being collated into a "deprivation index" for purposes of identifying the sources of inter- and intra-class variation.

Table 1 presents results of a three-way analysis of variance using Lorge-Thorndike I.Q. scores as the dependent variable. It can readily be seen that fifth grade I.Q. scores do not differ significantly from scores achieved by first grade children. Differences between scores of Negro and white children can be seen to be highly significant (p .0001) and are equally strong between SES levels. Examination of the secondary tables of means and sigma's for subgroups within each of these variables indicates the direction and magnitude of these differences. Clearly, the means for white children are significantly higher than are mean I.Q scores for their Negro counterparts and the relationship is documented by t-test differences between race groups reaching significance at $p < .01$. Similarly, inter-level differences are significant for SES groups at $p < .01$. While the analysis of variance does not indicate a significant race by SES interaction, inspection of the means shows: (1) that Negro children at each SES level score lower than white children, and (2) that Negro-white differences increase at each higher SES level. While children in each racial group show gain in I.Q. with ascending SES level, gains for the white group appear to be considerably greater.

These results are consistent with other data (Kennedy, 1963; Anderson, 1962; Eells, 1951) and could reflect the ascending isomorphism between social class and the item content of intelligence tests. Nevertheless, such results are usually predictive of school achievement, although their meaning with regard to individual potential may be questionable.

It is extremely interesting to note this more sharply defined escalation of the white majority group child's I.Q. through the three social class steps. In the lowest class, where social deprivation is most homogeneous and the influence of race is attenuated by the pervasiveness of poor living conditions, there is somewhat less difference, as has been mentioned, between Negro and white.

To summarize: (1) a linear relationship exists between SES and performance level for both Negro and white groups, and (2) within

TABLE 1

ANALYSIS OF VARIANCE* AND CELL MEANS
ON LORGE-THORNDIKE INTELLIGENCE TEST PERFORMANCE
BY GRADE, RACE AND SOCIAL CLASS (N = 543)

Source	Sum of Squares	d.f.	F	Sig.
Grade	634.429	1	3.153	N.S.
Race	10,119.416	1	50.296	P<.0001
SES	14,429.344	2	35.859	P<.0001
Within	106,834.966	531		
Total	137,656.866	542		

*Note—Interaction terms have been omitted from the table, as none reached significance.

MEAN LORGE-THORNDIKE I.Q. SCORES FOR SES GROUPS,
RACE GROUPS WITHIN SES GROUPS AND TOTAL RACE GROUPS

Group	$\overline{X}$	S.D.	N
SES I			
White	97.24	15.35	104
Negro	91.24	13.25	157
Total	93.63	14.43	261
SES II			
White	105.59	14.88	68
Negro	94.87	14.70	111
Total	98.94	15.67	179
SES III			
White	114.92	12.05	52
Negro	102.57	14.53	51
Total	108.81	14.70	103
Total Race Groups			
White	103.88	16.12	224
Negro	94.32	14.53	319

Note—Two-tailed t-tests for differences between total race groups and SES levels significant at P<.01.

this linear relationship the absolute increase in I.Q. is greater for the white group than it is for the Negro.

The interpretation put forth here for these data is that the influence of racial membership tends to become increasingly manifest and crucial as the social class level increases. The hypothesis we would advance has to do with increased participation in the cultural mainstream, and the differing conditions under which Negroes and whites participate (Deutsch, 1963). The weight of color and resulting minority status, it is postulated here, results in much less participation by the Negro, while the lowest class status operates similarly for the white as well as for the Negro. In other words, it is much more difficult for the Negro to attain identical middle or upper-middle-class status with whites, and the social class gradations are less marked for Negroes because Negro life in a caste society is considerably more homogeneous than is life for the majority group. This makes it extremely difficult ever really to match racial groups meaningfully on class status as the context and history of social experience are so different.

There is support for the "participation" hypothesis in some social background data. These data indicate that there are fewer variegated family activities, such as eating together or taking trips, in the Negro as opposed to the white group. These differences are especially apparent at the lower SES levels. It may well be that such family experiences operate differentially at the higher SES levels, but our current data for the SES III group are incomplete and there is no indication that the differences would reach statistical significance.

This information demands that we probe even more carefully into background variables as possible sources of some of the variation in intelligence scores found in different population groups.

One of the most striking differences between the Negro and white groups is the consistently higher frequency of broken homes and resulting family disorganization in the Negro group. Indeed, Table 2 indicates that this phenomenon varies directly with social class and with race, both at $p < .001$ by X^2 test.

We are *not* here considering the very real historical, social and economic antecedents of this condition, but are instead simply making an empirical observation. Since in the vast majority of cases, the home is broken by the absence of the father, this is used as a rough indicator of family cohesiveness. The absence or presence of the father has been shown in other studies to relate to need achievement and aspiration levels, especially of boys (Ausubel, 1963; Deutsch, 1960).

Table 3 presents the results of a four-way analysis of variance of Lorge-Thorndike scores, using sex, grade, race, and presence of father as independent variables.

As can be seen, significant differences are obtained on the race and presence of father variables, with white children scoring higher

TABLE 2

INCIDENCE OF FATHER'S PRESENCE IN THE HOME BY RACE WITHIN SES GROUP
(N = 543)

Condition	SES I				SES II				SES III			
	White		Negro		White		Negro		White		Negro	
	N	%	N	%	N	%	N	%	N	%	N	%
Father present in home	(88)	84.6	(88)	56.1	(61)	89.7	(80)	72.1	(52)	100.0	(44)	86.3
Father not present in home	(16)	15.4	(69)	43.9	(7)	10.3	(31)	27.9	---	0.0	(7)	13.7
N =	(104)		(157)		(68)		(111)		(52)		(51)	

Note—x^2 for SES x father condition = 28.01, 2d.f., p = < .001
x^2 for Race x father condition = 39.152, 1d.f., p = < .001

than Negro, and children coming from homes where fathers are present having significantly higher scores than children from fatherless homes. None of the interaction terms was statistically significant. (SES could not be included in the analysis of variance because in our Class III sample there were no white fatherless families. Thus, by dropping SES III's from this analysis, the N here becomes 440.)

To get at the influence of father's presence on intelligence score within groups, several additional comparisons were made. Because the absence of significant interactions in the data might relate to the strong pull exerted on the scores by race differences, the data from the Negro sample were subjected to specific analysis within grade and SES. Special attention was paid to lower SES, as the number of homes without fathers was largest in this group, and the comparisons, thus, were more meaningful.

Table 4 presents the comparisons for first and fifth grade Negro children in the lowest two SES groups.

As is seen from Table 4, a consistent trend within both grades at the lower SES level appears, and in no case is there a reversal of this trend: for males, females, and the combined group, the I.Q.'s of children with fathers in the home are always higher than those who have no father in the home. In addition, a constricted range of performance, as reflected in standard deviation units is found among fifth graders without fathers in the home, as opposed to both first and fifth graders in homes where fathers are present.

Differences between first and fifth grade children, controlling for father in home, are not significant, and they are not reported here in tabular form. Within the Negro lower-class, there is a consistent decrement in I.Q. level from the first to fifth grade, there again being no reversals in direction in sex or father-in-home categories. (In comparisons made between first and fifth graders in the white lower-class sample, there is a non-significant increment in score from first to fifth grade.)

While the specific interaction term for this break in the previous four-way analysis of variance did not reach statistical significance, the data in Table 4 are presented for the purpose of identifying cells in which I.Q. differences, as predicted by family stability, are greatest. Also the specific descriptive data are revealing in that there is no reversal of trend even though the analysis of variance did not yield statistically significant results.

Further analysis will reveal if the Negro score decrement from first to fifth grade is accounted for by the greater proportion of broken Negro homes. This also might account for some of the differences between Negro and white intelligence scores.

TABLE 3

ANALYSIS OF VARIANCE* ON LORGE-THORNDIKE INTELLIGENCE SCORES BY SEX, GRADE, RACE, AND PRESENCE OF FATHER IN THE HOME (SES GROUPS I AND II ONLY, N = 440)

Source	Sum of Squares	d.f.	F	Sig.
Sex	8.726	1	< 1.000	N.S.
Grade	404.317	1	1.882	N.S.
Race	2,580.069	1	12.013	< .01
Father in Home	954.073	1	4.442	< .05
Within	91,490.127	424		
Total	101,313.415	439		

*Note—Interaction terms have been omitted from the table, as none reached significance. The obtained F value in each case was less than 1.00.

MEANS FOR RACE GROUPS**

Group	$\overline{X}$	S.D.	N
Negro	92.75	14.02	268
White	100.72	15.91	172

MEANS FOR FATHER CONDITION **
(Combined Race Groups)

Condition	$\overline{X}$	S.D.	N
Father in Home	97.83	15.25	317
No Father in Home	90.79	14.18	123

**Note—t-tests for differences between race groups and father condition significant at $p<.01$.

A weakness in these cross-sectional data is that there is no reliable way of knowing how long the fifth grade children have lived in homes without fathers, or whether this has been a recurrent or a consistent condition. But it is reasonable to assume that on the average the fifth graders have had more fatherless years than the first graders. If this is tenable, then what we might be tapping is the cumulative effect of fatherless years, and if so, this might explain why the first grade differences are not significant: they are simply not significant *yet.* This hypothesis is supported by the limited variance reported in Table 4 for fifth grade children from fatherless homes in contrast to the greater variance shown among children on the same grade level but coming from homes in which fathers are present.

A second, and perhaps more parsimonious, explanation for this finding is that I.Q. tests at the fifth grade level may tap more responses which directly relate to the role of the father in the family structure for both boys and girls. This might have particular reference to the cohesiveness of the family and the variety of activities in which the family participates, and most specifically simply reflect the quantity of verbal interaction engendered through the medium of family organization and activity.

Another background variable which might relate to intelligence test performance is the amount and timing of schooling the child has had. As with the father variable, it was thought that the more oppor-

TABLE 4

PERFORMANCE ON THE LORGE-THORNDIKE INTELLIGENCE TEST AMONG LOWER AND LOWER MIDDLE (SES I AND II) NEGRO CHILDREN WITH AND WITHOUT FATHERS PRESENT IN THE HOME

	Father Present			Father Absent		
Group	$\overline{X}$	S. D.	N	$\overline{X}$	S. D.	N
Grade 1						
Male	95.55	15.74	31	87.71	21.70	28
Female	94.50	10.39	10	88.20	12.19	5
Total	95.24	14.51	41	87.78	20.40	33
SES I						
Grade 5						
Male	90.81	13.14	26	83.41	9.65	17
Female	95.19	14.73	21	87.70	9.75	20
Total	92.77	13.89	47	85.73	9.81	37
Grade 1						
Male	98.35	12.18	26	92.80	18.64	10
Female	99.27	12.99	15	-----	-----	--
Total	98.68	12.33	41	92.80	18.64	10
SES II						
Grade 5						
Male	94.78	15.12	23	91.75	15.67	16
Female	90.25	17.19	16	93.00	12.27	5
Total	92.92	15.89	39	92.05	14.65	21

tunity the child has for adult-child contact, conversation, and experiential variety, the more positive the influence on his performance. Also Fowler's analysis (1962) pointed out the importance for the child of cognitive stimulation and practice in the early years. As was seen in Lee's study (1951) of I.Q. differences between Negro children born in Philadelphia and those who migrated there from the South, consistently higher I.Q. test scores were obtained by children who had the longest residence in the presumably more fostering northern environment. Lee's data also show a consistent difference in favor of Negro children who had a kindergarten experience, as compared with those

TABLE 5

ANALYSIS OF VARIANCE ON LORGE-THORNDIKE INTELLIGENCE SCORES BY SEX, RACE, AND PRE-SCHOOL EXPERIENCE (Grade 5, SES I and II only, N = 246)

Source	Sum of Squares	d.f.	F	Sig.
Sex	128.204	1	<1.000	N.S.
Race	1,785.477	1	7.873	<.01
Pre-School Experience	1,619.750	1	7.143	<.01
Within	43,083.956	238		
Total	50,027.132	245		

Note—Interaction terms have been omitted from the table, as none were significant. The F value in each case was less than 1.00.

MEANS FOR RACE GROUPS

Group	$\bar{X}$	S.D.	N
Negro	90.90	13.89	144
White	99.82	16.40	102

MEANS FOR PRE-SCHOOL CONDITION*

Condition	$\bar{X}$	S.D.	N
Pre-School Experience	97.42	15.72	152
No Pre-School Experience	90.65	14.32	53

*Note—N's for Pre-School Condition reduced from total N for fifth grade due to missing data.

who did not. Therefore, an experiential variable selected for analysis in the present study was whether or not the child had any formal pre-school educational experience. Because of the variety of types of pre-school experience—some children had nursery and no kindergarten, others reversed—the variable was treated dichotomously as "some pre-school experience" or "no pre-school experience."

Table 5 reports results of a three-way analysis of variance of Lorge-Thorndike scores for fifth-grade children by sex, race, and pre-school experience.

As can be seen, race differences are significant at the $p < .01$

TABLE 6

ANALYSIS OF VARIANCE ON LORGE-THORNDIKE INTELLIGENCE SCORES BY SEX, RACE, AND PRE-SCHOOL EXPERIENCE (Grade 1, SES I and II only, N = 194)

Source	Sum of Squares	d.f.	F	Sig.
Sex	17.283	1	<1.000	N.S.
Race	1,152.579	1	5.817	<.05
Pre-School Experience	609.235	1	3.074	<.10
Within	25,162.214	186		
Total	27,148.326	193		

Note—Interaction terms have been omitted from the table, as none were significant.

MEANS FOR RACE GROUPS

Group	$\overline{X}$	S.D.	N
Negro	94.90	13.92	124
White	102.01	15.27	70

MEANS FOR PRE-SCHOOL CONDITION*

Condition	$\overline{X}$	S.D.	N
Pre-School Experience	100.03	13.99	112
No Pre-School Experience	94.48	16.24	23

*Note—N's for Pre-School Condition reduced from Total N due to missing data.

level, and so are pre-school experience differences. Those children who have had pre-school experience score significantly higher than those without. Again, the interaction terms were not significant.

Table 6 presents the same analysis for the first grade group. Here, while the significant race difference in test performance prevails ($p < .05$), the difference as predicted by pre-school experience is not significant, although *directionality* is still apparent. In other words, presence or lack of pre-school experience at grade 5 more highly differentiates intelligence test scores than it does at grade 1. Nevertheless, at grade 1 it is still differentiating ($p < .10$), though not within the conventional limits of statistical significance.

This finding is consistent with those for the father-in-home variable, and, therefore, lends support to the cumulative deficit hypothesis previously advanced: that deprivational influences have a greater impact at later developmental stages than at earlier ones.

The effect of the father-in-home variable on I.Q. for this sample has been shown in the data presented here. What is less easily measurable, but may nonetheless exist, is the potential systematic lowering of Negro children's I.Q. by the greater prevalence of broken homes in Negro SES groups I and II. In our samples, for example, there is a significantly greater frequency of broken homes among the Negro group, as compared with the white, and it is hard to estimate what the overall effect may be of this family instability in the development of the Negro child. From these data, it is quite conceivable, if not probable, that one effect would be the systematic lowering with age of I.Q. scores of the children where markedly unfavorable social conditions exist.

The data presented here represent only a small portion of those we have collected on the children in the various samples. When one surveys the entire mass of data, what is striking is the fact that on most of the *social* variables, the Negro group shows greater deprivation. This is true within social class categories, with the possible exception of Social Class II, and even here the factors associated with racial discrimination and caste are still quite operative; the class and caste discussion of Dreger and Miller (1960) is an adequate recognition of this problem. The conclusion is inescapable that the Negro group is a socially deprived one, and that whatever other measures and functions are sensitive to social effects will also reflect this deprivation.

We are now attempting to measure the ingredients of deprivation with the aim of developing a typology of deprivation which organizes experience in developmentally relevant groupings that can be related to sources of socially determined group variation in I.Q. performance.

It would seem probable that when behavioral scientists have been able to classify and measure the elements and variables in social deprivation, the observed differential in intelligence test scores between Negro and white samples will be accounted for.

The present data on family cohesion and pre-school experience represent two possible environmental modifiers of intelligence test performance that would seem to account for a portion of differences found between ethnic, class or experiential groups. If these are influential variables a positive implication is that they are amenable to social intervention and change.

References

Anastasi, A. *Differential psychology*. New York: Macmillan, 1958.

Anderson, W. F. Relation of Lorge-Thorndike Intelligence Test Scores of public school pupils to the socio-economic status of their parents. *J. exp. Educ.*, 1962, 31 (1), 73-76.

Ausubel, D. P., and Ausubel, Pearl. Ego development among segregated Negro children. In A. H. Passow (Ed.), *Education in depressed areas.* New York: Teachers College Bureau of Publications, Columbia Univer., 1963, pp. 109-141.

Deutsch, M. Minority group and class status as related to social and personality factors in scholastic achievement. Society for Applied Anthropology, Monograph Number 2, 1960.

Deutsch, M. The disadvantaged child and the learning process: Some social, psychological and developmental considerations. In A. H. Passow (Ed.), *Education in depressed areas.* New York: Teachers College Bureau of Publications, Columbia Univer., 1963, pp. 163-179.

Dreger, R. M., and Miller, K. S. Comparative psychological studies of Negroes and whites in the United States. *Psychol. Bull.*, 1960, 57, 361-402.

Eells, K. et al. *Intelligence and cultural differences.* Chicago: Univer. of Chicago Press, 1951.

Fowler, W. Cognitive learning in infancy and early childhood. *Psychol. Bull.*, 1962, 59, 116-152.

Kennedy, W. A. et al. *A normative sample of intelligence and achievement of Negro elementary school children in the southeastern United States.* Monogr., Soc. for Res. in Child Development, 1963 (20) Number 6.

Klineberg, O. *Negro intelligence and selective migration.* New York: Columbia Univer. Press, 1935.

Klineberg, O. The intelligence of migrants. *Amer. sociol. Rev.*, 1938, 3, 218-224.

KLINEBERG, O. Negro-white differences in intelligence test performance: A new look at an old problem. *Amer. Psychologist,* 1963, 18, 198-203.

LEE, E. S. Negro intelligence and selective migration: A Philadelphia test of the Klineberg hypothesis. *Amer. sociol. Rev.,* 1951, 16, 227-233.

LORGE, I., AND THORNDIKE, R. I. *Lorge-Thorndike Tests of Intelligence,* Specimen Test Booklet. New York: Houghton-Mifflin, 1959.

SCHWEBEL, M. Individual differences in learning abilities. *Amer. J. Orthopsychiat.,* 1963, 33, 60-71.

U.S. Bureau of the Census. *U.S. Census of Housing,* 1960, 3, City Blocks, Series HC (3), Nos. 274-276.

WHITEMAN, M. Intelligence and learning. Paper presented at the Arden House Conference on Pre-School Enrichment of Socially Disadvantaged Children, Arden House, Harriman, N.Y., December 17, 1962.

Family Structure and Employment Problems

Harold L. Sheppard and Herbert E. Striner

[From Chapter 3 of Civil Rights, Employment, and the Social Status of American Negroes *(the W. E. Upjohn Institute for Employment Research, 1966), with permission.]*

This report places strong emphasis upon the relationship of family structure and size to the problems of employment and job status for many Negroes. At the outset, it should be stressed that there is no such thing as *the* Negro family and that there is nothing intrinsically pathological about different family structures or sizes. Because of the great lack of research and data concerning the relationship of family structure and size to employment and economic opportunity, much of what follows is necessarily inferential. There is great need for gathering data explicitly for the purpose of more systematic research on this subject. Recent discussions of this topic have tended to engender acrimonious debate instead of needed research. Unless a calmer, more empirical analysis is undertaken, a solution to the employment problems of Negroes will not be found.

The large-scale migration of Negroes during the forties and fifties has had a profound effect on their families. This impact on the families is heaped upon repercussions from the plantation and slavery system. In any evaluation of differences between the Negro family and the white family, it is quickly apparent that the former is much more frequently identified with the poverty population. But an even closer look is required. Nonwhite poverty families have, on the average, more children than white poverty families. There is a direct relationship between a large number of children in a family and frustrating experience; and this correlation provides a pessimism base, an unconscious or conscious disposition to believe that "we just can't beat the game." The problem of planning family size, unfortunately, is being faced very late. But it is being faced at last; and the issue of employment and economic security cannot be divorced from the outcome of present and future family planning programs.

The following table presents the comparative distribution of large size families among whites and Negroes, and the relationship of size to poverty:

Distribution of Negro and White Families in Poverty, by Number of Children Under 18, 1963*

All families with children under 18 (percent)	*Families with 1 child (percent)*		*Families with 6 or more children (percent)*	
	Negro	*White*	*Negro*	*White*
22	33	10	77	35

**Based on the less rigorous "economy" level criteria established by the Social Security Administration (Mollie Orshansky, "Counting the Poor: Another Look at the Poverty Profile,"* Social Security Bulletin, *January* 1965).

Such comparisons show that the larger the family the greater the poverty. Furthermore, there is a greater proportion of larger families among Negroes than among whites. *Given the continuing differential in birth rates between poor whites and Negroes, it is possible for the problem to become even more acute among Negroes.* As Philip Hauser has pointed out, "The Negro, like the inhabitant of the developing regions in Asia, Latin America, and Africa, in his new exposure to amenities of twentieth-century living, is experiencing rapidly declining mortality while fertility rates either remain high or, as in urban areas, actually increase."[1]

Furthermore, for every 100 Negroes between the ages of 20 and 64 in 1960, there were 94 under 20, while the corresponding ratio for whites in the same year was only 75. In other words, Negroes of

[1]"Demographic Factors in the Integration of the Negro," *Daedalus,* Fall 1965, p. 864.

working ages carry a greater burden of dependency than whites. As of 1965, there were 103 Negroes under 20 for every 100 aged 20-64.

In 1960, one-third of all nonwhite children under the age of 14—as contrasted to only one-twelfth of white children in the same age group—were living and being reared in the absence of one or both parents, usually the absence of the father. About 20 percent of all nonwhite children were living with mothers only, as contrasted with less than 6 percent of white children. There are no data on how many Negroes have lived in fatherless families during all of their childhood. Living in a fatherless family is especially difficult for boys in their developmental years. The emergence of this type of pattern as an urban phenomenon is suggested by the fact that, in 1965, 25.5 percent of nonfarm Negro families were headed by females, in contrast to only 15.3 percent among farm families, according to the Bureau of the Census.

With one-third of Negro children under 14 being reared in families with one or both parents absent, economic equality with whites for large numbers of Negroes (perhaps growing numbers) can only be a pious wish. There is nothing intrinsically immoral about fatherless or motherless family structures—unless we view as immoral in our type of society and economy high unemployment rates, low income, and exhausting occupations. Nor is there anything intrinsically immoral about matriarchal families if there is an adequate role for the husband and son to perform in such families and in the general society.

As long as there are large families in low-income, low-skilled, poorly schooled populations—white or Negro—we must strive to design more effective means of attaining progress in income and occupational status. Low-income rural-origin families with large numbers of children have a high rate of dropouts. And dropouts have a higher unemployment rate than high school graduates. Thus, there seems to be a definite correlation between birth in a large low-income, rural-origin family and low job status and high unemployment. In other words, the nature and size of the family can become a condition for poor jobs and unemployment. Generally speaking, birth rates actually have declined in periods of unemployment in our history; that is, extended unemployment has tended to be followed by declines in birth rates. It would be interesting, incidentally, to trace historically white-Negro differences, if any, in birth rate "adjustments" to changes in nonfarm unemployment rates.

The fact that in urban centers Negroes currently have a higher proportion of low-income recent migrant persons and larger families than whites creates the impression of a "Negro problem." Many Negroes become sensitive to such a description. Many whites use the description as a defense against any action that would change such a fact, thus indulging in a self-fulfilling prophecy. It may also be possible that some Negro leaders, by refusing to cope with these facts, are also participating in self-fulfilling of the prophecy.

In years past, we witnessed the reluctance on the part of whites and Negroes alike to accept the proposition that education is a crucial variable in the life chances of Negroes. Prejudiced whites insisted that biology was the sole underlying cause of Negro inequality, while many Negroes insisted that discrimination was the sole cause. Biology certainly was not and is not the explanation, but discrimination on the basis of skin color alone is no longer as crucial as it was in the past (although it is far from being eradicated). The main point, however, is that Negroes and whites now accept the importance of educational improvements as one of the means or conditions for equality.

Since education and training are recognized today as making a difference between success and failure in the world of work, it has become almost trite and platitudinous to state that Negroes must be given better and more education and training. What has not been recognized sufficiently is that one—and *only one*—of the obstacles to rapid progress toward this goal for more Negroes is the nature of the family structure in a significant minority of the Negro population in urban areas. This minority has a greater birth rate, and it may thus be on the way to becoming a larger minority than before—*the result of which can be a perpetuation of the very crisis we are trying to prevent or mitigate.* One statistical aspect of this differential birth rate is that 64 percent of all the nonfarm, nonwhite poor population living in families are 21 years of age or younger—a proportion 21 percent higher than that among white poor persons living in nonfarm families. Among the nonwhites who were not poor, about one-half were 21 or younger.

The modern American urban world encompasses a caste system that has emerged out of the migrations of the descendants of 19th century slavery. As St. Clair Drake has pointed out:

> . . . the character of the Black Ghetto is not set by the newer "gilded," not-yet run down portions of it, but by the older sections where unemployment rates are high and the masses of people work with their hands—where the median level of education is just above graduation from grade school and many of the people are likely to be recent migrants from rural areas.

The "ghettoization" of the Negro has resulted in the emergence of a ghetto subculture with a distinctive ethos, most pronounced,

> perhaps, in Harlem, but recognizable in all Negro neighborhoods. ... The spontaneous vigor of the children who crowd streets and playgrounds ... and the cheerful rushing about of adults, free from the occupational pressures of the "white world" in which they work, create an atmosphere of warmth and superficial intimacy which obscures the unpleasant facts of life in the overcrowded rooms behind the doors, the lack of adequate maintenance standards, and the too prevalent vermin and rats.[2]

About 60 percent of Negro families in the United States earn less than $4,000 per year, while 60 percent of white families earn more than that amount. Within the Negro low-income segment there is naturally a heterogeneity of social strata and styles of life. Many low-income Negroes behave within a system of what has come to be called "middle class" values, including a stress on respectability and decorum; getting an education (if not for themselves, at least for their children); family stability; and a reasonable family size. To quote Drake, "For both men and women, owning a home and going into business are highly desired goals, the former often being a realistic one, the latter a mere fantasy."[3]

But within this same income category there are other types of families and individuals. This part of the urban Negro population and its style of life provide the flesh-and-blood world from which spring the statistics of the "Moynihan" Report:

> ... an "unorganized" lower class exists whose members tend always to become disorganized—functioning in an anomic situation where gambling, excessive drinking, the use of narcotics, and sexual promiscuity are prevalent forms of behavior, and violent interpersonal relations reflect an ethos of suspicion and resentment which suffuses this deviant subculture. It is within this milieu that criminal and semi-criminal activities burgeon.[4]

The maintenance of a middle class style of life requires more than sheer perseverance and will power. It also calls for a certain level of income (more precisely, a certain level of purchasing power) and perhaps even a certain kind of family structure. Purchasing power is not distributed and occupational and family structure are not organized among Negroes to the same degree as they are among whites. The issue is, can one be changed without changing the others?

[2] "The Social and Economic Status of the Negro in the United States," *Daedalus*, Fall 1965, pp. 771-772.

[3] *Ibid.*, p. 779.

[4] *Loc. cit.*

In this respect, a vicious circle continues to pervade the social world of many Negroes in which the number of families without fathers and a lower prestige of males among their female associates and their children are dominant features. The pattern of Negro male insecurity, sustained by other current conditions, continues to be a major obstacle to effectuating a distinct break from the disadvantaged position of a large part of the Negro population today. For one thing, "An impressive body of evidence indicates that rather serious personality distortions result from the female dominance so prevalent in the Negro subculture. . . ."[5] What is not sufficiently recognized is the link between the nature of the social status of many Negro males today and their problems of employment and occupational status. Indeed, this link is often vehemently denied.

The low esteem of the Negro male, especially in the lower income strata, must be given prime attention in any serious effort to change the social structure of American Negro society which is much more like a pyramid than the white social structure. Negro occupational structure, for example, consists of a miniscule capstone of upper class families, a larger stratum of middle class families under that, and the largest class at the bottom. Conversely, white social structure is shaped more like a diamond, with a large middle class bulge.

This situation of a large number of Negro males warrants further comment. For example, Negro boys in lower income families receive less and even inferior education compared to Negro girls. Smaller proportions enroll in college-preparatory and commercial classes in the high schools. Even if the girls in such classes do not actually enter college, they at least become more qualified for white-collar jobs—the occupational sector which is expanding at a greater rate than manual jobs. As one study has pointed out:

> When more white-collar occupations open up for Negroes, the girls will be better prepared and more motivated to fill them than the boys. This is true for clerical and sales positions, but also for semi-professional and professional ones. Under these conditions Negro girls, especially those of a working class background, can be expected to achieve higher occupational status than the boys from their socio-economic category. This kind of development would tend to perpetuate the high prestige position of Negro women with the Negro group.[6]

[5]*Ibid.*, p. 787.

[6]Jetse Sprey, "Sex Differences in Occupational Choice Patterns among Negro Adolescents," *Social Problems,* Summer 1962, p. 22.

The author of that study also confirms one of the major theses of this bulletin, namely, that the disadvantaged position of Negroes can persist even when discrimination itself declines or is actually eliminated, especially in the case of Negro males. If this is so, the civil rights movement and the drive for equal job status face some severe frustrations. Unless major changes can be brought about in the demography, sociology, and psychology of lower income Negro families, and of males in particular, civil rights legislation for fair employment practices will not soon achieve its goal. At best, the only kinds of jobs available for unskilled Negro males born and reared in such family settings are actually declining, and the large numbers involved cannot possibly be absorbed.

The adverse character of families in substantial parts of the Negro population is certainly due in large part to (1) the heritage of past decades and (2) the nature of their present environmental setting. In other words, it may be looked upon as an effect, a result. But effects can assume a causative role in human affairs.[7] Illegitimacy, many children in a family, and unstable parental relations have their effects, too; they should not be looked upon merely as results of other factors if we intend to deal with the problem and not just continue to look for someone or something to blame.

A large number of children is obviously an insuperable burden for a low-income family, regardless of racial background. In this particular instance, just on the aggregate level, the average income of Negro families is about 50 percent of the average income of white families, but the average number of children in Negro families is 30 percent more than in white families. Putting it even more dramatically, while the average number of children in upper income nonwhite families has fallen below that of whites with comparable economic characteristics, the average number of children for lower income nonwhites is above that for comparable whites. According to the 1960 Census, for every 1,000 nonwhite females aged 15-19 who had ever been married, 1,247 children had been born unto them. For comparable white females, the corresponding figure was 725.

The basic point is that the growth in the Negro population is concentrated among those with low income, inadequate education, employment insecurity, and unstable family structure.

[7]The family problem does exist and also does affect efforts to move the Negro into the economy and the society on a comparable footing with the white. But to be really effective, one must see the family factor not as the sole or major focus of our efforts, but as one of many crucial focuses. We are faced with a social simultaneous equation where the solution can only result if all factors are dealt with in the solving process.

If we are sincere in our statements about the crisis nature of Negro income, employment, and occupational status, it is not enough to be comforted by long-run predictions that, like others before them, Negroes will decrease their rural exodus to urban areas and thus eventually produce a population "increasingly similar to others in the areas to which they have come."[8] For one thing, there is nothing inevitable about such a prediction. Even if it were inevitable, the current rate of change is actually so slow that it could take more than 100 years to reach "parity." Certainly, recent trends in income and occupational status do not point to any optimistic conclusion about the future.

Hauser points to the impact of the higher birth rate among Negroes on their socioeconomic status:

> High fertility with its consequent large family size handicaps the Negro by limiting the investment the family can make in human resources—that is, in the education and training of the child. Under economic pressure the Negro child, on the one hand, has little incentive to remain in school and, on the other, is often forced to leave even when he desires to obtain an education. Thus, the Negro child tends to be the high school drop-out rather than the high school graduate. Even if much more is done to remove the Negro family from the bitter consequences of raw poverty, large numbers of children will tend to set limits on the education each child in the Negro community will receive. Certainly, the family with two or three children will, for some time to come, be in a better position to support its children through high school than the family with six or more children.
>
> The poverty of the Negro family must rank as the single most important factor preventing the Negro from developing those abilities which could help him to assume both the rights and obligations of being a first-class American citizen. . . . the large proportion of Negro children now under eighteen cannot possibly be expected to participate fully in the mainstream of American life so long as they are steeped in the morass of poverty.[9]

Since education is becoming a much more important requirement for eliminating Negro-white economic differentials and for increasing job opportunities, and since "large numbers of children will tend to set limits on the education each child in the Negro community will

[8]Hauser, *Daedalus*, Fall 1965, p. 865.
[9]*Ibid.*, pp. 865-866.

receive," we must come face to face with the subject of family structure and size. This matter is more than a spurious factor in the issue of Negro progress in employment and occupational status. To put it more directly by quoting Hauser, "As a result of a high birth rate, the Negro population retains characteristics such as inferior occupations, low income, and a style of life precluding association and social interaction with the dominant white society—all of which retard assimilation."[10] This statement underscores the authors' view that a high birth rate among low-income families can itself serve to perpetuate inferior occupations and high unemployment rates.

The vicious circle of poverty, large family size, poor education and skills, and high unemployment rates must be broken. It *can* be broken. And a vicious circle can be entered and broken at many points of its circumference. One of these points of entry relates to family size. We need a massive effective program aimed at helping "the relatively uneducated and impoverished Negro family to restrict its size." If all Negroes were in the upper 5 percent of the income distribution, concern about family size would, of course, be irrelevant (or indicative of fears of Negro dominance). Millionaires—Negro or white—can afford to have families of six or more children. The only adverse effect would be smaller inheritances for each child. Low-income persons—Negro or white—cannot afford large families, at least in the current stage of human history.

Poverty, poor education, punitive welfare policies (such as the "man-in-the-house" rule), and even pathological discrimination, have all contributed to the economic and social-psychological frustrations of our Negro citizens. Such frustrations are a result of these and other patterns created and sustained by dominant white beliefs and practices. But again, results can, in turn, become causes. Today, the inferior role and status of low-income Negro males contribute to the perpetuation of Negro inequality in general. "There is a great need for special efforts to enhance the role of the Negro male in the family, to concentrate on providing him with the capabilities of taking on his expected functions, responsibilities, and obligations as husband, father, and provider."[11] These capabilities also depend on the less understood, but nevertheless real, psychological phenomena such as self-identity, ego strength, etc. These factors are among the causes, as well as among the effects, of the employment problem.

The psychological literature is replete with findings about the unique personality problems of Negro males from lower income

[10] *Ibid.*, p. 866.
[11] *Ibid.*, p. 867.

families. Department of Labor and Bureau of the Census data on economic and demographic characteristics offer only partial–and hence inadequate–information and "explanations" about the employment problem of Negroes. Furthermore, the data too frequently understate the problem by being reported in the category of nonwhites instead of Negroes specifically and exclusively.

The research findings on Negro males in particular, as well as on the impact of fatherless situations on basic behavior patterns and motivations, have been summarized by Thomas Pettigrew. One of his passages supports the authors' position that the employment problems of Negroes (males in particular) cannot be separated from family structure.

> . . . eight-and-nine-year-old children whose fathers are absent seek immediate gratification far more than children whose fathers are present in the home. For example, when offered their choice of receiving a tiny candy bar immediately or a large bar a week later, fatherless children typically take the small bar while other children prefer to wait for the larger bar. This hunger for immediate gratification among fatherless children seems to have serious implications. Regardless of race, children manifesting this trait also tend to be less accurate in judging time, less "socially responsible," less oriented toward achievement and more prone to delinquency. Indeed, two psychologists maintain that the inability to delay gratification is a critical factor in immature, criminal, and neurotic behavior.
>
> ... Various studies have demonstrated the crucial importance of the father in the socialization of boys. Mothers raising their children in homes without fathers are frequently overprotective, sometimes even smothering, in their compensatory attempts to be a combined father and mother. . . . boys whose fathers are not present have initially identified with their mothers and must later, in America's relatively patrifocal society, develop a conflicting, secondary identification with males. . . .
>
> Several studies point to the applicability of this sex-identity problem to lower-class Negro males.[12]

Lower income Negroes have experienced difficulty in the learning process, as Martin Deutsch pointed out.[13] He also described how

[12]*A Profile of the Negro American* (Princeton: Van Nostrand, 1964), pp. 17-19.

[13]The Disadvantaged Child and the Learning Process," *in* A. H. Passow, ed., *Education in Depressed Areas* (New York: Teachers College, Columbia University, 1963), pp. 163-179.

the economic and social experiences of the low-income Negro male have influenced his "concept of himself and his general motivation to succeed in competitive areas of society where the rewards are the greatest. . . . the lower-class Negro child entering school often has had no experience with a 'successful' male model or thereby with a psychological framework in which effort can result in at least the possibility of achievement. . . . A child from any circumstance who has been deprived of a substantial portion of the variety of stimuli which he is maturationally capable of responding to is likely to be deficient in the equipment required for learning." Deutsch and Brown have also shown that even when income is held constant, the IQ's of Negro pupils from families without a father present are lower than the IQ's of those from families with a father.[14]

The large urban areas of the United States are fostering and are subject to a set of adverse social conditions affecting young Negroes—especially the males. These boys are too frequently in fatherless and/or unemployed families; they lack adequate stimulation for achievement, adequate occupational guidance (often nonexistent) in the families and the schools and sufficient occupational training; and they obtain only blind-end jobs, if any. The "choice" of a first job is itself a vital variable; an unskilled (or nonskilled) worker typically takes the only job he knows about when entering the labor market, and this job is stigmatized by a low wage and/or frequent spells of layoffs. If young Negroes are not poorly motivated to begin with, they inevitably lower their aspirations and efforts at self-improvement as a result of the syndrome of environmental insults. Even the pernicious system of easy credit and exorbitant interest operates to discourage their active jobseeking once unemployed, since their income from jobs would only be garnisheed by their creditors. The unemployed have their own version of cost-benefit analysis too.

David McClelland, of Harvard University, who has studied extensively the role of motivation in economic behavior, has pointed out that the conditions of slavery influenced the nature of American Negro adjustment conducive to obedience but not to achievement and self-betterment; and that it should not be surprising to find that many of the descendants of slavery—even though "free"—still show the effects of such adjustment. It is significant that for those few Negroes who have become middle and upper class, their achievement motivation (as measured by McClelland's projective test approach) is conspicuously high—"Reflecting once again the fact that individuals who

[14] Martin Deutsch and Bert Brown, "Social Influences in Negro-White Intelligence Differences," *Social Issues,* April 1964, p. 27.

have managed to move out of a low . . . achievement [motivation] group tend to have exceptionally high motivation."[15]

The relevance of the family structure to the individual's motivations to succeed—to aspire to and obtain better jobs, more education, and training—should be made clear to persons concerned with the job and income status of Negroes. A number of studies have indicated that people whose fathers were absent during their childhood tend not to develop such motivations.[16] Neither Negroes nor the nation as a whole will benefit if we create the conditions for greater opportunities in employment without preparing Negroes to take actual advantage of these conditions and opportunities. Part of this preparation must include a full-scale program of restructuring the motivational conditions of Negroes, again especially Negro males. This attack must enlist the active leadership of Negroes themselves, with the financial and organizational support from public and private sources. Some Negro leaders have already taken the initiative in the formulation of part of the issue in these terms, notably Whitney Young, Jr., of the Urban League. Since he has professional background in the field of social work and community organization, this is to be expected. We must, however, persuade others that these considerations are involved in the economic problems of Negroes, not merely as effects but as causes.

In a 1963 study, in Philadelphia,[17] it was found that lower status Negro mothers had lower educational and job aspirations for their sons than did higher status Negro mothers; they were less certain about aspirations for their sons than for their daughters (which was not true of higher status mothers). Compared to higher status mothers, a much higher percentage of these mothers said that 21 years of age or under is the best age for their sons to marry and 19 years of age for their daughters. This finding is crucial because "if a mother holds high educational and occupational aspirations for her children and at the same time thinks they should marry young and have a large family, there is often, by implication, a contradiction in her aspirations." And the younger the age at marriage, the greater the chances for bearing more children. If one keeps in mind the high

[15]*The Achieving Society* (Princeton: Van Nostrand, 1961), p. 377.

[16]For example, W. Mischel, "Father-Absence and Delay of Gratification," *Journal of Abnormal and Social Psychology,* Vol. 63 (1961), pp. 116-134; R. L. Nuttall, "Some Correlates of High Need for Achievement among Urban Northern Negroes," *Journal of Abnormal and Social Psychology,* Vol. 68 (1964), pp. 593-600.

[17]Robert R. Bell, "Lower Class Negro Mothers' Aspirations for their Children," *Social Forces,* May 1965, pp. 493-500.

percentage of mother-dominated families (even in families where the father is present) in Negro urban lower income groups, these findings have a significant bearing on the occupational and employment progress of Negro males. Given the importance of the mother in Negro lower income urban families, her aspirations can adversely influence the future of her offspring—even in the face of rising job opportunities as a result of economic growth and fair employment legislation:

> . . . the relative positions of Negro mothers in the lower class may be related to different aspirational values transmitted to their children, and may also contribute to a way of life which makes any alternative aspirational levels difficult for their children to internalize and possibly achieve.[18]

If such lower aspirations operate at the lower end of the lower income group's values system, the greater is the need for agencies and institutions to exercise a positive role in reshaping the goals of Negro youths who lack such motivation. The schools, training programs, the employment service, OEO, and other agencies in the community have much to do. If they fail, the less likely will it be that values conducive to occupational upgrading can be injected into the thinking and behavior of these groups of Negroes, especially the males. Negro adults must not be excluded from such attention, either.

Much of this reshaping must be carried out by the larger society, too. Once opportunities are available, the larger society and the government in general cannot simply stand aside and watch. What whites do in addition will also play a role in the motivational environment of Negroes. What motivation is there for a young Negro to graduate from high school when he sees that whites with high school diplomas earn one-third more than Negroes with similar schooling? How can a young Negro aspire to enter an apprenticeship program when he might be required to serve for four to seven years before he enjoys the fruits of such training? How can a young Negro adult with a family to support enter a training program, instead of taking a job as a laborer, for 16 to 52 weeks if the training allowance is less than the immediate income as a common laborer, and if the job for which he may be trained seems to be a dead-end one?

The responsibility for helping low-motivated Negroes to improve themselves lies partly in community institutions such as the schools. But the teachers are not yet equipped with the appropriate techniques to perform this task. Any program aimed at raising the motivations and aspirations of those Negro youths who are frustrated, and

[18] *Ibid.*, p. 500.

who often have ample reason for frustration, will in and of itself be a motivating factor in their lives. If someone pays attention to them and is sincerely concerned about their future, a large number of them will respond favorably. There is a great urgency for a vast program to train large numbers of Negro male "motivators" to serve in this role.[19]

Some Work-Related Cultural Deprivations of Lower-Class Negro Youths

Joseph S. Himes

[From the Journal of Marriage and the Family, *November 1964, by permission of the National Council on Family Relations.]*

For lower-class Negro youths just entering the labor market, three conditions are institutionally depriving: age, race, and social class. Since age tends to affect white and Negro youths alike, it may be omitted in the following discussion. Race and social class are, of course, not the same. For Negroes, however, race tends to determine class, and, in fact, the two are almost inseparable.

In the present discussion, cultural deprivation is understood to refer to residual personality characteristics that issue from socialization under specific institutionalized preconditions. In the case of lower-class Negroes, the significant institutionalized preconditions include, among others, color segregation, material discrimination, inferior or collateral social status, disparaging social evaluations, chronic social frustrations, and a substantively distinct subculture. From socialization under such preconditions, the individual emerges as a functioning member of his social world. Certain dimensions of the functional adjustment to his effective social world, however, constitute cultural deprivations in terms of the standards and demands of the larger world from which he is more or less excluded.

The work-related residual cultural deprivations of lower-class Negro youths taken at the point of entering the labor market have both judgmental and realistic dimensions. Judgmentally, deprivation refers

[19]In this connection, David McClelland now believes that he and his associates at Harvard (Sterling Livingston, George Litwin, and others) have techniques for increasing the achievement motivation of individuals. His proposals deserve serious consideration by public and private agencies concerned with the issue of employment progress among Negroes. See "Achievement Motivation Can Be Developed," *Harvard Business Review*, November-December 1965.

to the absence or distortion of those knowledges, social graces, and levels of sophistication that "typical" young people are expected to exhibit. For example, culturally deprived young Negroes are said to be awkward and ill-at-ease, loud and boisterous, uncouth or gauche in manner, improperly dressed, limited in general knowledge, unsophisticated, and the like. These and similar phrases indicate that Negro youths differ in many respects from a generally accepted model or standard.

Stated judgmentally, deprivations signify cultural deviation rather than absolute cultural lacks. Lower-class Negro youths reveal the knowledge, social traits, and personality characteristics of the racial group and social class from which they emerge. Such characteristics seem to have more relevance for social acceptance than for specific job performance. For example, gauche manners or lack of sophistication may have little or no relevance for operating a machine or performing a technical task. However, such behavior may decisively influence the individual's chances of securing a job or his relations with associates in the work situation.

In terms of the reality dimension, some cultural deprivations represent genuine lacks as defined by minimal demands of the economy and specific occupations. For example, inability to read and to understand and follow directions is decisively handicapping for many modern jobs. Functional illiteracy of this kind is not limited, of course, to lower-class Negroes, although their race and social class make them peculiarly vulnerable to this cultural deprivation.

A number of studies have examined the nature, extent, and consequences of realistic cultural deprivations such as functional illiteracy, lack of basic education, inadequacy of mathematical and scientific skills, adolescent character defects, and so on.[1] Some other work-related cultural deprivations constitute incidental residual consequences of exclusion of Negroes from the basic work life of the economy. They appear as group-linked, trained incapacities and function to handicap youthful Negroes when they enter the labor market.

Two local situations may serve to symbolize the institutionalized exclusion of Negro workers from important sectors of the national work force. In Piedmont, North Carolina, furniture and textile manufacture are basic, traditional industries. Historically, virtually no Negro workers are employed in production jobs in either industry. In

[1]Among other sources, see Michael Harrington, *The Other America,* New York: Macmillan, 1962; and James Bryant Conant, *The American High School Today,* New York: McGraw-Hill, 1959.

Durham, within Piedmont, North Carolina, although some Negroes work as insurance executives and bankers in all-Negro concerns, none is employed as stock broker or advertising executive. The extent of Negro exclusion from the nation's work force is well known and has been documented elsewhere.[2] In the following paragraphs, three residual work-related cultural deprivations issuing from job exclusions of Negro workers are examined briefly.

Irrelevant Work Models. Lower-class Negro children are denied the experience of daily association with parents, relatives, neighbors, friends, and peers who manufacture textiles and furniture and who deal in securities or plan advertising campaigns. There is none of the casual talk and informal interaction that imperceptibly and inadvertently introduce the child to the role of the worker and the world of work in factory and office. Unlike their lower-class, poor white cohorts, such Negro children cannot, in routine socialization, acquire and identify with the roles of workers in factory and office. Rather they must rely on the formal institutions, the mass media and second-hand gleanings of Negro servants for glimpses into the world of work symbolized by the furniture factory and the brokerage office. In a revealing comment on transmission of the female role in American families, Talcott Parons stresses the importance of the availability of the mother model in casual informal contacts with girl children in the home: ". . . it is possible from an early age to initiate girls directly into many important aspects of the adult feminine role. Their mothers are continually about the house and the meaning of many of the things they are doing is relatively tangible and easily understandable to a child. It is also possible for the daughter to participate actively and usefully in many of these activities. . . ."[3]

Excluded from casual though meaningful contacts with modern workers, the lower-class Negro child cannot identify by internal role taking and anticipatory socialization with the worker models that are symbolized by the furniture maker and stock broker. Such experiences are as much beyond his social reach as if they were prohibited by law. Whatever knowledge and skill and character he may bring to the modern labor market, he cannot present those fringe cultural characteristics that come from being "bred to the job."

However, it must not be thought from the foregoing that the

[2]See E. Franklin Frazier, *The Negro in the United States,* New York: Macmillan, 1957, Chapter XXIII; and Robert C. Weaver, *Negro Labor,* New York: Harcourt, Brace, 1946.

[3]Talcott Parsons, "Age and Sex in the Social Structure of the United States," *Amercian Sociological Review,* 7 (October 1942), p. 605.

lower-class Negro youth comes to the job market culturally empty handed. He brings with him the residues of learning and the precipitates of identification with those occupational models that exist in reality within his racial and class world. For most, casual and informal childhood experiences have been with unskilled and service workers in city and country. But terms like "technology," "automation," and "white collar" tend to show how irrelevant this Negro youth's work-related cultural baggage is for the modern labor market.

Exclusion From Work Ethos. Workers who are restricted to the fringes of the occupational structure tend to be excluded from the tenets and rationalizations of the work ethos. They cannot perceive the linkage between effort and advancement. For example, the Negro janitors and maids in furniture factories and brokerage offices cannot expect to become production, office, or managerial workers as a result of hard work and self-improvement. The lower-class Negro child sees none of his parents, relatives, neighbors, friends. and peers moving up the occupational ladder. Hard work and extra effort may be a necessary condition of keeping a job. But neither hard work nor self-improvement leads to a promotion. What then is the value of hard work, extra effort, and self-improvement?

The work reserved for Negroes has no intrinsic goodness or importance. The worker does not have a sense of the relation of his job to any total scheme or large goal of the enterprise. Both he and his job are marginal to the aims of the business and to the philosophy of business. If he is loyal or dedicated, and many are, his reaction is likely to be personal rather than ideological. Such work is often uninspiring, fatiguing, and sometimes even deadening.

In family and neighborhood, Negro lower-class workers are prone to act out negative responses to the job. In casual talk and informal relations with their children, they say in effect that work is neither good nor promiseful of better things. In spite of the teachings of the social institutions and the mass media, they believe that work is simply work, an unpleasant though necessary condition of staying alive. They go to the job in the morning with reluctance and escape from it at day's end with relief.

Such workers and their children are often alleged to be "apathetic" or "lazy." But these words are social evaluations, not real explanations. From one perspective, they mean that lower-class workers and their children have not entered into the Protestant middle-class work ethos. They have not seen that work is good, that more education leads to greater opportunities, and that increased effort results in job advancements. From another perspective, such judgments reveal a pragmatic realism. The experiences of many lower-class Negroes demonstrate that self-improvement and increased effort tend to multiply and intensify their frustrations and unhappiness.

The lower-class Negro child relies upon the formal institutions, the mass media, and various adventitious personal experiences to acquire the tenets and rationalizations of the work ethos. In this respect, he is disadvantaged *vis à vis* his white cohort, whose childhood observations demonstrate the validity of hard work and self-improvement as preludes to advancement in the world of work. When he enters the labor market, therefore, the lower-class Negro youth is initially handicapped by a cultural deprivation with consequences which may accumulate with the passage of time.

Alienated From Job Ways. Family and neighborhood experiences of lower-class Negro children tend to alienate them from the distinctive ways of factory and office. They do not overhear relatives, neighbors, and friends in the "shop talk" about incidents, people, and things of the job. They cannot acquire familiarity with office and factory tools by playing with daddy's briefcase or tool kit. No casual talk and informal relations introduce them to the jargon, costumes, bearing, manners, and attitudes of office and shop. They have no childhood experiences that acquaint them with the general layout, daily routines, general atmosphere, and occupational *dramatis personae* of an industrial workshop or business office.[4]

Furthermore, lower-class Negro children cannot acquire from their occupationally marginal parents the ideologies and values of labor unions. Thus, they do not apprehend the sense of structured competition and cooperation that marks awareness of labor-management relations. They are not bred to that robust labor union conviction that the worker, if not his work, is good and dignified and important. These children are alien to the experience of group solidarity and secular collective destiny that distinguish the American labor movement. They cannot acquire from daily experience the definitions and justifications of legitimate individual and collective goals and values that are transmitted by the labor movement.

Finally, family patterns and daily habits of lower-class Negroes and their children are seldom conditioned by the long arm of production and office jobs. Work shifts, pay periods, overtime requirements,

[4]I still remember vividly how alien and unprepared I felt the first days in the aircraft factory during the war. The overwhelming and incessant racket, the inescapable glaring lights, and the sense of frantic perpetual motion distracted and terrified me. Everything and everybody was strange. The jargon—socket wrench, bonding cable, duralium, lock nut, etc.,—was a foreign tongue. It took me days to find my way around and to feel at home in the factory. My experiences were duplicated by many other novices to the production line.

vacation schedules, and the like, seldom shape the routines of family life and daily activities. The climate of family relations is not affected by the vagaries of the politics of the job, for Negro workers are outside the occupational power system. These children and their families are passed by in the drama of the strike, the diversions of the industrial recreational program, or the securities and protections of pension systems.

Exclusion from these and other social extensions of the factory and office job tends to induce a further cultural deprivation among lower-class Negro youths. It appears as a trained unreadiness for smooth transition from family, school, and neighborhood to the social world and technical roles of work. For these youths, the workshop or the business office is a world apart, an alien and intimidating social milieu.

Conclusion. Race and class establish institutionalized preconditions under which lower-class Negro youths are socialized to certain work-related cultural deprivations. Some are judgmental in character and influence the individual's acceptance as a worker. Realistic deprivations, however, tend to handicap the individual in actual job performance. Exclusion of lower-class Negroes from important sectors of the work force constitutes one institutionalized precondition and eventuates in a series of work-related cultural deprivations. The three examined here briefly include socialization to irrelevant job models, exclusion from the prevailing work ethos, and alienation from the culture of the modern factory and office.

Suggested Additional Readings

1. Billingsby, Arthur and Amy T. "Negro Family Life in America," *Social Service Review* (September 1965).
2. Clark, Kenneth. *Dark Ghetto.* New York: Harper and Row, 1965.
3. Clift, Virgil A., Anderson, Archibald W., and Hullfish, Gordon G., eds. *Negro Education in America: Its Adequacy, Problems and Needs.* New York: Harper and Brothers, 1962.
4. Herzog, Elizabeth. "Is There a 'Breakdown' of the Negro Family?" *Social Work* (January 1966).
5. Lewis, Hylan. *Child Rearing among Low Income Families.* Washington, D. C.: Center for Metropolitan Studies, 1961.
6. McEntire, Davis. *Residence and Race.* Berkeley: University of California Press, 1960.
7. Newman, Dorothy K. "The Negro's Journey to the City," *Monthly Labor Review,* Part I (May 1965); Part II (June 1965).

8. Passow, A. Harry, ed. *Education in Depressed Areas.* New York: Columbia University, Teachers College Press, 1963.

9. Pettigrew, Thomas F. *A Profile of the Negro American.* Princeton: D. Van Nostrand Co., Inc., 1964.

10. Schorr, Alvin L. *Slums and Social Insecurity.* U.S. Department of Health, Education, and Welfare, Social Security Administration, Division of Research and Statistics. Research Report No. 1, 1963.

Chapter 3

Institutional Barriers to Negro Equality in Employment

Introduction

In this chapter we are concerned with institutional patterns that sustain Negro disadvantagement in employment by creating obstacles to changes in the Negro's occupational status. There are two basic ways to deal with this topic. One way is to look at the Negro's status and participation in institutional sectors of society that affect his preparation for the labor market as well as his access to job opportunities. The other is to examine barriers directly related to labor market structure and experiences in work organizations. Here we primarily consider the former.

Patterns of residential segregation between Negro and white, particularly in the large metropolitan communities, are more pronounced today than they were a decade ago. The exodus of whites to suburban areas and the uninterrupted urban migration of Negroes have continued to spawn inner city ghettoes. To date, efforts to break the "ghetto lock" have been largely unsuccessful.

For present purposes it is not simply the spatial ghettoization of Negroes that is important, but the employment effects associated with residential concentration, conditions of life, and quality of community services. In the ghetto children grow up in an environment largely lacking in adequate educational, recreational, and social facilities; it is an environment more productive of alienation and hostility than of aspiration.

Abundant evidence shows that low-income areas, particularly those with a predominance of Negro residents, share unequally in the educational investments of the community. Yet, the educational system is the mechanism that prepares the individual for the labor market, especially today when formal educational attainment has become a prime requisite for job security and mobility. A lack of education may disadvantage a worker in numerous ways. It may bar him from higher status jobs. It may reduce his opportunities for promotion. It can certainly restrict his access to company training programs. The question is not whether high educational standards are desirable or undesirable in the labor market. Such standards exist and have a marked influence on employment opportunities.

In view of the important relationship between education and job opportunities, current interest in the educational status of Negroes in the United States is understandable. The Negro who receives an inferior education or lacks adequate educational preparation will be limited in the job market even under the best conditions of "equal employment opportunity."

In a recent Urban League publication, *Education and Race,* the educational gap between Negroes and whites is examined in terms of current data on their educational differences. The picture which emerges is curiously dynamic and static at the same time. On the one hand, the data point to important educational gains in recent years, particularly on the part of nonwhite youths, as indicated by years of school completed. The narrowing of educational differences, however, has not resulted in any impressive reduction of the income gap and of job inequalities between white and Negro.

In discussing the education gap it is not sufficient to refer only to quantitative differences in educational attainment between white and Negro, for this would omit entirely the question of the quality of education received. Although there are no nationwide studies of qualitative differences, there are numerous smaller studies which reveal glaring deficiencies in the overall quality of education offered nonwhites. One thing is clear from the available information: The interlinkages between persistent and increasing school segregation, the concentration of Negroes in urban ghettoes, and the experiences of Negro children with inferior educational facilities hardly bespeak quality education. The closing educational gap is a promising, though in some ways illusory, sign of progress.

Thus, the ghetto is not merely a place of residence. In its internal organization it is a set of interacting influences which frustrate ambition, thwart aspiration, and sustain apathy. Viewed in the context of the larger community, it is part of a total pattern which may exclude the Negro from effective participation in its economic life. The organization of institutional patterns in American society is generally such that Negroes are easily denied access to resources and facilities for economic improvement; the ghetto is the clearest expression of that denial.

On a more general scale the Negro has been a key victim of technological changes, particularly in those job categories hardest hit by industrial adaptation to machine technologies and automated production systems. Most affected have been the unskilled and semiskilled job levels, those with notable Negro concentrations. Technological changes tend to erode clusters of jobs, and in many cases these affect occupational categories in which Negroes predominate. When this occurs the changing structure of labor demands adds to the disadvantagement of Negroes and underscores the necessity for increased attention to formal schooling and development of skills.

The foregoing are only a few examples of the institutional barriers and community conditions which sustain Negro disadvantagement in employment. In the readings which follow, several of these and related issues are examined. In the first article Puryear notes that automation and technological change have both good and bad effects for the Negro, though, on balance, barring significant advances in formal education and job information systems, the net effect can be expected to be negative. Strauss and Ingerman examine the adequacy of vocational education programs today, with particular reference to urban Negro youths. They suggest the need for an updating of curricula to bring them more into line with the realities. The article by Patricia Sexton deals with the issue of community resource-allocations for public education and demonstrates that schools in predominantly Negro neighborhoods are shortchanged. Kain focuses on the relationship between urban ecological and transportation patterns and the Negro's access to job opportunities and places of work. The selection from the HARYOU report deals with three important barriers to parity in employment especially affecting Negro youths. Finally, Senator Kennedy presents a picture of the urban ghetto which is both a cause for shame and a challenge.

All of these articles converge on a common point, viz., the need to break the vicious circle of discrimination and disadvantagement in which the Negro is trapped. Furthermore, the following three points emerge as corollaries to this general proposition: (1) Extensive changes are not going to occur automatically and probably not at all apart from the intervention of outside agencies and massive inputs of fiscal and human resources. (2) Changes will necessitate not only the development of programs of instruction and training to improve the Negro's educational and skill levels but also alterations in the political, economic, and social structures which affect his access to opportunities for employment, job security, and job mobility. (3) Although the ultimate goal of ending racial ghettoization should not be discarded, the magnitude and immediacy of the problems faced by Negroes in the center city are such that programs aimed toward the improvement of social and economic conditions *within* ghetto boundaries must be given top priority.

The concept of "intervention strategies" is not new. In recent years there have been many programs developed to ameliorate conditions facing disadvantaged groups in American society. Some of these have failed, others have been partly effective, but none can be counted as an outstanding success. It may not be possible to create a single set of guidelines for dealing with conditions which sustain Negro inequalities in employment, but based on information presented in this and preceding chapters several critical reference points can be noted:

1) There must be a massive investment of resources—of money, time, skills, and talents—to reshape the opportunity structure which confronts the majority of Negro workers.

2) The programs developed from such investments should be planned and projected on a long-term basis to change some of the underlying conditions of ghetto life rather than as short-range efforts to keep the lid on ghetto unrest.

3) Existing organizations attuned to the economic problems of the Negro ghetto, must be strengthened and in some cases new organizations must be created to meet special needs.

4) The ghetto must be recognized as a distinctive unit of social organization with leadership patterns and channels of influence.

5) The programs developed should seek active involvement and a broad base of support from residents within the community rather than reliance on the traditional dependency relationship between the helper and the helped.

Technology and the Negro

Mahlon T. Puryear

[*Prepared for the National Commission on Technology, Automation, and Economic Progress, February 1964.*]

I. Automation and Technology and the Impact of the Negro Worker

The Extent of the Problem

No one can deny that automation will increasingly affect the Nation's unemployment and economic structure in the years ahead. President

Meany of the AFL–CIO recently reported to a congressional subcommittee on the pace at which technology is automating jobs out of existence: From 1953 to 1960, 200,000 mining jobs were lost, 400,000 railroad jobs, and 1,500,000 jobs in factory production and maintenance. This job disappearance was taking place at the same time that the labor force was increasing by 6,500,000 workers.

The story is not all negative. Technological changes and automation, in fact, have provided many Negroes job opportunities in manufacturing, machine production, and services. This is evidenced by the large numbers of those, many with limited educational backgrounds, who found jobs in urban areas after migrating from farms and rural areas. Increased productivity and job expansion have helped the Negro worker. But unfortunately, in many instances gains have been offset by major problems in education, job opportunity, and related areas. These problems, coupled with the high incidence of Negroes being replaced as technological changes make jobs less physically taxing, make for continuing concern regarding the plight of Negro workers.

The most recent study of the impact of automation and technological changes on Negro employment was done by the writer in 1962. Included in this report are data on 40-odd cities where local Urban Leagues were familiar with the problems. A recent recheck with executives in selected cities indicates little change. I, therefore, shall rely heavily on these data.

At this time we do not have adequate statistical data concerning the impact of automation on the employment structure generally, nor on the Negro labor force in particular. However, we do know that automation and related technological change tend to create the greatest displacements in those occupational classifications where the bulk of the Negro labor force is concentrated. Furthermore, when we place automation in its proper context within the total employment structure and examine the status of the Negro worker within that structure, the information is ample to make a crystal clear picture—and dismal it is. Job opportunities for the Negro worker have traditionally been, and are now, severely restricted. Predictions for the immediate and long-range future indicate that the plight of the Negro worker is very likely to get worse instead of better unless drastic countermeasures are instituted now to offset current trends. This is no wild-eyed alarm stemming from irresponsible visionaries. It is a plain, honest, though unpleasant fact, supported by nationwide figures from the U.S. Employment Service and by regional estimates from local Urban League affiliates.

The Plight of the Negro Worker—Selected Cities

Reports from selected cities across the Nation define the problem by census regions and local community areas. In addition to illustrating the extent of the problem, these reports note limited remedial measures currently being undertaken by government, business and industry, labor, and local communities, and evaluate their relevance and effectiveness. No apologies are made for the fact that statistics are often based on limited, or are not derived from primary sources, and are often presented as estimates; every available source of information was tapped even though much remains to be desired in technical sophistication in some instances. These estimates are educated guesses of professional staff closely in touch with conditions in their respective communities and will, we are certain, be found to compare favorably with more "scientific" data when and as these data become available. The thoroughness and dedication with which the reports were prepared are evident in the extracts.

In Rhode Island, a depressed and labor surplus area, the Negro unemployment rate has been twice that of the general population in every census since 1930. The enormity of the retraining problem is indicated by the fact that 67 percent of unemployed Negroes in 1960 were in semiskilled and unskilled occupations.

There has been a heavy increase in Negro population in Atlanta, Ga.—from 165,816 in 1950 to 231,790 in 1960—largely due to displacement of farm workers by automation and other technological advances.

The extent of the problem in Baltimore, Md., is not known statistically. However, 90 percent of dropouts in Baltimore public schools are Negroes. The major instrument for improving job opportunities for local youth is the Joint Apprenticeship Council, from which Negroes are excluded and around which there appears to be an aura of secrecy.

Tampa, Fla., is a critical unemployment area with expectations of a worsening situation. Statistics are not available by race, but the size of the problem is indicated by (1) a decline in the tobacco industry due to automation and Government embargo, (2) the appreciable decrease in number of work permits in the period 1959–61, (3) a heavy decrease in employment on docks, a major job source for Negroes, due to the use of automated material handling equipment, and (4) exclusion of Negroes from apprenticeship programs.

Automation has displaced thousands of Negro workers from farms and crafts in Louisiana, Mississippi, and Alabama, creating an unemployment problem of major proportions. In 1961, 70 percent of the

40,000 unemployed in metropolitan New Orleans were Negroes, and an estimated 50 percent of Negroes were underemployed.

Unprecedented opportunities were made available for Negro youth qualified in such fields as engineering, mathematics, accounting, drafting, stenography, and typing at the NASA-Michoud operation which, in 1965, employed 8,000 to 10,000 people. An additional 8,000 to 10,000 will be employed in new related operations.

Racial barriers are being lowered in area Federal service, in such companies as Western Electric and IBM, and generally in industries under Federal Government contracts.

A major disruption created by automation in Stark County, Ohio, has resulted from reduction in plant size and plant relocation. A good example is provided by Republic Steel Corp. and Timken Roller Bearing Co., two firms which together account for approximately one-third of the total manufacturing employment in the area. Republic recently consolidated four divisions and removed top administrative personnel to Youngstown, Ohio. Timken has established plants in France and Australia.

Paradoxically, along with these reductions and relocations, the number of new firms in Stark County increased by 18 from 1954 to 1962. Yet, with this increase, the number of persons employed decreased by 4,215 in the period 1954–57.

The World War II period (1942–46) saw Detroit, Mich., industry recruit extensively in the rural South, bringing to the area thousands of individuals with low academic attainment. Around 1952, Detroit's total employment configuration began to change. Intensification of labor-management conflicts, sharpening of political differences, increasingly crowded schools, poor housing, reduced per capita income, and reduced recreational outlets combined to form attitudes which continue to cripple intelligent attempts to eliminate the negative effects of automation on the work force. The Negro worker, a needed asset in 1942, was caught in the middle of a sociopolitical maelstrom in 1962, and presents an economic and racial problem of the first magnitude.

It is difficult to measure the extent of the problem statistically. However, of the approximately 101,000 people unemployed in the Detroit area in March 1962, approximately 59 percent were Negroes.

Underemployment of Negroes in Detroit has been traditional, with conservative estimates placing the proportion of the Negro work force underemployed at 35 percent.

Many individuals seeking a solution to Detroit's hard core unemployment problem emphasize the need for retraining workers displaced by automation or other causes. But job retraining is not simple.

> (1) Seventy percent of those presently unemployed are not academically prepared to master short-term retraining programs.
>
> (2) The assumption is false that the untrained want to be trained, and further that they want to be trained for jobs with skills that could be attained in a short period of time.
>
> (3) The factor of racial discrimination, still present in the manipulations of Detroit's labor force, precludes any "open sesame" policy as regards the placement of a retrained worker in the newer jobs being created.

In the period 1956–60, Trumbull County, Ohio, lost 15 plants which had employed an average of 4,000 workers annually. A 1960 study of the higher skill potential of unemployed persons receiving extended unemployment insurance claims payments showed many to be retrainable, and a skills survey in Trumbull and Mahoning Counties showed expected labor shortages in 22 of 33 key skills.

The Cudahy case in Omaha, Nebr., dramatically exemplifies not only the effects of automation and technological change on the employment structure of a community, but also the salubrious effects that concerted, well-planned, and carefully executed community effort may have on resolving inherent problems. Of 1,000 persons involved in the Cudahy automation layoff in 1962, approximately 675 were dislocated totally from their type of work. The joint efforts of the Nebraska State Employment Service, Cudahy Packing Co., Omaha School system, Mayor's Committee on Automation, and Local 60 UPWA, AFL-CIO, resulted in the selection of 150 persons for retraining who were receiving unemployment insurance. An additional 90 qualified for Cudahy-financed training. Ninety-five more were retrained, and 160 have been placed in jobs. Thus 495 out of the original 675 displaced have been retrained or reemployed.

In Phoenix, Ariz., the large pool of workers displaced by mechanization need retraining. For example, in 1958, 46 percent of the cotton harvested was machine-picked. By 1959, the percentage had increased to 60 percent. In 1960, a total of 1,921 machines picked 70 percent of the cotton, while in 1961, the number of machines had risen to 2,019, harvesting 83 percent of the cotton produced. More startling is the revelation that during the 10-week period from October 20 to December 15, 1961, 2,019 machines picked 484,000 bales, while a mere 64,000 bales were hand-picked by 9,000 workers. The peak harvester force in 1960 numbered 21,000 as compared with 13,600 in 1961.[1]

Unemployment problems in the San Diego area are generated less by automation than by layoffs in the aircraft industry and termination or expiration of Government programs in the missile field. Of the approximately 24,900 unemployed, an estimated 20 percent are Negroes. The State market analyst estimates that the total unemployed group are retrainable.

Negroes comprise 8.6 percent of the total population of 2,783,359 in the six-county San Francisco, Calif., area. Of these, 29 percent are skilled workers, 21.2 percent are semiskilled and unskilled workers, 17.3 percent are city, county, or State government workers, and 6.4 percent are professional workers. Restrictions based on race as we have known them traditionally do not exist, and the highly trained Negro has relatively little difficulty in securing a good job. However, relatively few Negroes are prepared to enter the new high labor demand occupations, such as chemists, electromicrowave and electronic designers, digital programers, technical writers, technical salesmen, secretaries, and insurance and related workers.

Generally speaking, the problem of displacement by automation has been relatively slow in coming to the Northwest, especially Seattle, Wash. It is true that over the past half dozen years, men and women have lost jobs in areas where automatic equipment has been brought in. In some of the larger banks, checkproof readers have been displaced by machines that do the job much more quickly. Here and there an industry will also put in a machine or some equipment which will displace a half dozen or so persons. These, of course, are usually absorbed in the work force in other capacities.

To recapitulate:

(1) The present intolerable plight of the Negro worker in America is becoming worse and will become permanent unless constructive measures are immediately undertaken.

(2) Critical areas exist in every census region.

(3) Current and projected unemployment trends hold out little hope of better times for Negro workers who look for improvement of their lot.

(4) Repeatedly it was said that "little is being done." This is reported as fact, not in a desire to defame character or disparage the positive accomplishments thus far of government, industry, labor, and education. We cannot state too strongly, however, our

[1]Source: Farm Labor Office—Arizona State Employment Service.

conviction that all good work to date, however lofty in motive, however progressive in intention, however effective in accomplishment, is not yet enough.

Problems in Education and Jobs

Discrimination. Discrimination is the most serious and fundamental problem confronting Negroes. This awesome monster crops up in training and education, and plays an important role in turning a poorly prepared product out into the work-a-day world. Most important, poor work backgrounds that result from discrimination make it impossible for Negroes to qualify for many jobs now available or that will appear during the coming years.

Even when there may be no discrimination in a particular job-related situation for a particular Negro, his difficulties in securing advancement or placement stem directly from past discrimination in education and training opportunities. The specifics may vary, but the fundamental disease is somewhere in his economic history. Discrimination is at the core of each problem discussed below.

Training. The net result of discrimination in training opportunities is the present glut of the market with millions of unskilled, unqualified Negro workers and jobseekers.

Lack of vocational and technical skills. Negroes have historically been denied equal opportunities for vocational and technical training. The feeling that Negroes should not be trained for jobs unless there were job possibilities has contributed to Negroes being unemployable because they were not given the chance to learn necessary skills. In the South, little or no vocational training was provided in areas other than gardening, cooking, sewing, or other traditional areas of employment. Technical educational opportunities were almost nonexistent until World War II, except in large cities or in the segregated land-grant colleges and other post high school institutions attended by Negroes.

New Negro workers find it difficult to find suitable employment, and the opportunities of older Negro workers are limited because no provisions have been made for them to learn new skills on the job or in organized educational programs. Only in recent years have positive steps been taken to give Negro workers an opportunity to apply for on-the-job training. Despite this opportunity, many find they very often lack the skills and educational requirements to make satisfactory progress in such training programs.

Lack of apprenticeship opportunities. Of all training barriers, those in apprenticeship programs have been most unyielding to the

Negro's efforts to upgrade his skills. Only recently has noticeable progress been made. The lack of apprenticeship opportunities constitutes one of the greatest tragedies facing Negro youth who wish employment. While participation in apprenticeship programs is considered the best way to involve large numbers of young people involved in craft skills, such opportunities will be difficult to attain: Apprenticeships are rigidly controlled by management, labor, and government, and it is absolutely necessary to understand that Negroes will be afforded greater opportunity only if these three groups step up their efforts. Another tragic fact must be faced: It is extremely difficult to develop opportunities for apprentices when many skilled craftsmen are on layoff or when there is substantial unemployment.

Inadequate educational and vocational counseling. Many of those counseling Negro youth are either not qualified or do not care about doing a genuine job. They know little or nothing about these youths, their ambitions, their aspirations, or their problems. Many of these counselors have advised Negro youth to accept early work permits or stop their educational programs any time a job became available, and honestly thought they were helping them.

While this situation has prevailed in so-called integrated educational settings, Negro youth in segregated schools with a full complement of Negro teaching personnel have had problems no less frustrating. Here any semblance of guidance and counseling services has been almost completely nonexistent, and the little there is has become the responsibility of teachers whose orientation to the world of work consisted only of what they had read, seen, or heard. Their own lack of experience with business, industry, government, and labor made it impossible for them to do anything resembling a realistic counseling job.

Recruiting

Unrealistic recruiting programs. As the number of Negro youth in colleges continues to rise and the quality of their education continues to improve, recruiting on college campuses should become a more fruitful medium for expanding job opportunities. Unfortunately, however, many Negro youths still are not able to move into the broader job market because recruiting and placement services available to them before they leave college are inadequate.

In predominantly Negro colleges, there is a grave shortage of placement services; in predominantly white colleges placement officials continue to be reluctant to believe that recruiters have a genuine interest in interviewing all qualified candidates, regardless of race. The use of interracial teams for visits to all campuses would show Negro and white youth alike that the present world of work can and does make use of the skills of all qualified workers. This would say to Negro youth, "Here is living proof that there are opportunities for you with my company."

Negro college youth do not readily accept mere statements that changes are taking place. They see too few examples of progress and too little evidence that opportunities are opening to them. Their skepticism is the direct outgrowth of the recruiting practices of businesses and firms which continue to overlook the Negro student or graduate as a prospective job applicant.

Lack of cooperation between Negro colleges and employers. Closely related to the problems of recruitment and placement is the lack of mutual information on the part of Negro colleges and industry. This ignorance can be removed only if industry and business offer teachers opportunities to obtain firsthand knowledge of business operations. Such knowledge can then be used to revamp curriculums to meet industry's needs. The colleges on their part should call on persons from business and industry for help in activities other than commencement and fundraising.

Misinformation about Negro jobseekers. The extent to which misinformation and distorted notions about Negroes and their work habits affect job opportunities can be measured in such phrases as "jobs for Negroes," "white jobs," "Negroes work best at jobs that require muscle and endurance," "Negroes like to work with other Negroes," "white people will not work with Negroes," "Negro men may not work with or around white women," and "Negroes cannot supervise white workers." In many instances, it has been almost impossible to change the attitudes of some employers because of such ingrained notions.

Inability of Negro youth to pass written examinations. Negro job applicants fail in alarming numbers to pass written and oral screening examinations. Admittedly, many Negroes have not had a great deal of experience with tests and examinations. However, the major problem appears to be only indirectly related to skills or abilities, and more a matter of attitudes toward tests and the belief that one will not be employed no matter how well one does on such tests. There is also evidence to support the contention that even if a Negro passes the written portion of the test, he is likely to be eliminated in the oral or personal interview. And then, passing the test only means that his name is placed on an eligibility list—then a candidate must wait to be selected over others also on the list. Until discrimination in the testing and selecting process is removed, Negroes will continue to have negative attitudes toward tests and as a result, will perform unsatisfactorily.

Advancement on the Job

Integrating the work force. The problem of integrating the work force requires the attention of top management and firm plans for implementation of policy at all levels below. Too often policy statements made at the top are considerably watered down by the time they reach the working level, causing many Negroes to lack faith in business, industry, government, and labor. Yet experience has shown that excellent working relationships do not change when well-planned steps are taken to assure Negroes opportunities for promotion and transfer to more responsible jobs.

Lack of opportunities for on-the-job training and retraining. Efforts must be made to give underemployed Negroes an opportunity to seek jobs at higher levels, with additional training available in or out of the plant. This is especially needed when a firm opens new plants in the same area and needs additional workers, or when layoffs are probable for employees not trained to more advanced operational techniques.

Special on-the-job training programs, sponsored with Federal funds, are just now beginning to have an impact on training and employment opportunities. Before they are laid off, workers at lower level jobs should be offered training opportunities to increase their skills and maintain seniority rights and other benefits.

Inadequate placement services. Jobseekers use a variety of job placement services. They may go directly to a firm's employment offices; they may seek assistance from friends or relatives employed in a firm where they hope to work; they may use whatever services are available to them in their schools; or they may use private employment agencies or the public employment service.

The biggest problem of firms that do their own hiring seems to be getting suitable applicants who are ready, willing, and able to meet job requirements. Firms that do massive hiring cannot rely on friends and relatives of the workers to provide suitable applicants. Records show that the private employment agencies have cooperated with employers in accepting applications and making referrals in an obviously discriminatory fashion. This has limited the use of private employment agencies except where there is a great deal of job activity at the service or low income levels.

What happens in the public employment service offices is another issue. For many years it has been illegal for those offices to accept job orders that indicate a racial preference or to make referrals on a racial basis. However, many offices of the public employment service are themselves segregated, either by race or by job classification, and discrimination is practiced. The public employment service does its greatest disservice to Negro applicants where it exercises no initiative in developing additional job opportunities within the service itself or among its employer clients. There are, for example, very few Negro managers on the staff of more than 2,000 public employment service offices across the country. While some progress has been made, the service has a very bad image in many communities, and many skilled or professionally trained Negroes do not register with it at all. Failure to use the service and its facilities very often robs the Negro of an opportunity to expand his field of possible job prospects.

Underemployment. Discriminatory hiring practices have resulted in extensive underemployment, especially in many branches of the Federal Government. Not long ago a Government study of employment practices among several Federal agencies operating in the Southeast revealed that only two Negroes were employed in grades as high as GS–12 (both were race relations representatives with the Housing Authority), none at GS–11, one at GS–10 (a social worker at the Federal Penitentiary in Atlanta), and none at GS–9 or GS–8. A large group were GS–7's which included mailroom supervisors and messengers who had been working for as long as 20 years. Many Negroes working at GS–7 and below were college graduates, and some had completed many courses above the college level. Some changes have been made, but much more needs to be done.

Discrimination in Federal employment is magnified in the light of civil service regulations in effect since 1873, which specifically forbid discriminatory practices. There is little doubt that this regulation has been ignored during all these years. Even now, when a great effort is being made to do a more equitable job, it is possible to indicate at least 11 ways of ignoring the well-known "rule of three," even when all three candidates are Negroes. The only way to achieve real change would be to declare a moratorium on all Federal jobs until a more equitable pattern is developed and fairer proportions of Negro workers are employed at all levels.

Special Problems in White Collar Job Areas. Whatever the status of Negro workers generally, the plight of those who work in or aspire to white-collar jobs is even more serious. In 1961, 14.1 percent of Negroes, compared to 45.6 percent of others, were employed in skilled white-collar and professional jobs. Included in this 14 percent are those employed in segregated school systems and colleges in the South, and Negro professionals who serve Negroes mainly. The remainder, in the general labor force, is then extremely small.

More specifically, the ratio of Negroes and others was found to be:

—for accountants and auditors, 3,662 to 463,934;
—for architects, 233 to 28,813;
—for dentists, 1,998 to 78,200;
—for physicians and surgeons, 4,706 to 218,904;
—for aeronautical, civil, and electrical engineers, 2,794 to 380,-273.
—In the area of business management, the ratio was 73,433 Negroes to 4,420,894 others, with 45,464 of the 73-odd thousand Negro managers listed as self-employed.

These figures prevailed in spite of increased efforts by employers during and after World War II.

In the area of private enterprise, we find that the Negro has made his greatest contributions in businesses that serve the Negro community—insurance, banking, and personal services. He is not a substantial participant in the overall business world because he qualifies as neither lender nor borrower of important monies.

When Negroes have an opportunity to participate in the overall economic development of this country, they are generally not given equal pay for equal work. That this difference in income had widened in recent years is reflected in the fact that today Negro workers as a whole earn only 53 percent as much as white workers, a drop of 4 percent since 1950. Also, 62.4 percent of Negro families earn less than $4,000, while 70.6 percent of white families earn more than $4,000. Among white-collar workers, college graduates as a whole may expect to earn $9,000 per year; but for Negro college graduates the figure is $5,400. Most Negroes, even in white-collar jobs, work at the lowest paying levels, and so far they have not had sufficient opportunity to work in as wide a variety of jobs as other groups.

Business, industry, government, labor, or education have not made full use of available manpower. In business there were, outside the Negro community, only one Negro corporation president, fewer than eight directors on major corporation boards, fewer than six vice presidents; and several of these deal with the "special Negro market." Most of us at the Urban League know personally all the Negroes who hold top-level jobs in industry and business, for there are not many.

In government, the situation presents a very dismal picture. Here fair employment programs date back 90 years; State and city ordinances guaranteed equal employment opportunities all those years. Yet, Negroes still hold few supervisory jobs in most government areas.

In higher education, other than in Negro colleges, we have not produced one president of a college or university, not one dean, and very few department heads. There are surprisingly few Negroes holding full professorships in major universities, and this is true despite the fact that Negroes have been graduating from these institutions for more than 100 years.

The opportunity to learn, to acquire meaningful experiences, to explore, to make mistakes and recover from them, to be a part of the whole and not just a segment, to be understood as having desires, aspirations, ambitions, and feelings for America has not typically been the lot of Negro citizens.

Lack of Community Concern. Motivation and stimulation of Negro youth are major responsibilities of the community at large and cannot be delegated to teachers and professional counselors alone. First, industry, business, government, and labor leaders alike must be made aware of the problems confronting the Negro worker and jobseeker; and, second, positive plans to bring about desired changes in the school and community must be developed and implemented. Counseling and teaching materials at all levels should be redesigned for teachers, counselors, and administrators to depict the true image and worth of the Negro in our economy.

Equally new and dramatic thinking on the part of parents is called for to motivate their children. A parent's own work experiences are reflected in the advice and information he passes on to his children; hence, it becomes doubly important that every effort be made to secure better jobs for adults.

Negroes should participate at all levels of policy-making and policy implementation—planning, advisory, consultation, operation, evaluation, and followup—in overall community programs, as well as those dealing specifically with the Negro and his employment problems.

Some Problems Created by Negroes

Failure to take full advantage of available resources. Some of the problems Negroes face in finding suitable work may be attributed to their failure to take full advantage of available resources. The number of State Fair Employment Practices Commissions has reached 25, and the number of municipal commissions is now more than 50. Although many of the Commissions do not have *real* authority for dealing with the problems they are confronted with, they report that they do not receive enough complaints from persons with genuine cases of discrimination or unequal treatment.

In most instances, however, the commissions require too much of the complaintant, with some of their procedures so complicated that they almost need a lawyer. While positive results have been produced in a number of situations, the major job is yet to be done. In addition to the power of investigation, persuasion, and counsel, these commissions need to be able to initiate investigations; penalties should be realistic and administered as soon as decisions are handed down; and they should have the authority to request information regarding progress in planning and executing fair employment programs. The Government should take immediate steps to cancel its contracts with businesses not complying with the intent and purpose of fair employment programs. State and municipal FEPC laws also need to be augmented by a Federal law.

Reluctance to move with plants that relocate in other communities. Despite their widely proclaimed mobility, Negroes are often not mobile, either at time of initial employment or when it is necessary to move with a firm which finds it necessary to relocate. For example, the Mack Truck Division of General Motors Corp. recently moved from its Newark, N.J., operations to Maryland, and not a single Negro worker has accepted a transfer. Despite the fact that many were making more than $125 a week in production shops, they have elected to remain in the Newark area and collect severance pay and unem ployment compensation.

Lack of interest in pursuing careers in new areas of work. Negroes shun employment where income is based on commissons; they feel that they are being asked to produce with no guarantee of security or regularity of income.

Many opportunities exist in accounting, yet a recent check of the catalogues of 30 of the leading Negro colleges reveals that undergraduate majors in accounting were offered in fewer than 6.

Attitude of Negroes regarding "prestige" jobs and status. For many years and until very recently, Negroes were builders, chauffeurs, porters, coal shovelers, and nurses. These were the traditional jobs held by Negroes, the parents of today's youth. However, they saw the schoolteacher, the social worker, the preacher, all with personal status, all accepted by the community. These became their symbols of success.

As a result, the Negro told his children about the disadvantages of "hard work," "outdoor jobs," "seasonal work," "serving other people," "working with your hands, " being "bossed by white people."

Teachers and administrators had little contact with workers, and unwittingly also helped develop negative attitudes toward manual and technical work. Available vocational programs provided training in limited areas, and technical offerings were virtually nonexistent. Vocational schools were used as dumping grounds for problem children and those who did not do well in English and mathematics.

Consequently Negroes today are not employed in skilled trades. While the need for professional, technical, business, and other white-collar jobs will increase in the years ahead, larger numbers of skilled workers will also be needed. Adults and youth alike would be wise to examine the possibility for achieving success in the skilled trades area.

Difficulty in getting Negroes to believe in changes. Many Negro youth simply do not accept the fact that changes are taking place, and that they are now at long last regarded as worthy of consideration for jobs at all levels in an integrated society. Part of the difficulty can be traced to parents who are still smarting from the evil effects of the situation just a few years ago. However, a really dramatic recruiting program conducted by management, coupled with improved counseling and guidance services at the school level, could change this quite rapidly. Young people do need more information about changes in the world of work and how to fit into this world. Educators and counselors must help youth explore opportunities made available through technological advances.

Status of Negro Women Workers. Negro women in the work force present special problems. Some must work to supplement the incomes of their husbands; others are the principal wage earners because there is no male head of the household. The percentage of Negro women who work is 45.6 percent, far greater than the 35.6 percent of white women. Unlike white women, however, Negro women are largely employed in low-paying jobs that make them vulnerable to unemployment and provide them with the least protection during illness, advancing years, and retirement. For example, 40 percent of all domestic jobs are held by Negro women. White women have priority of job opportunity over Negro men in many areas where Negro women never find employment; for example, in the transportation industry in such jobs as ticket sellers, drivers, and officeworkers.

Raising the status of Negro women who perform service work or other lower income jobs presents an almost insurmountable problem. There have been few efforts to organize these workers to give them leverage in raising wages, reducing hours of work, or setting standards of employment. Many of them know little about potential benefits through voluntary participation in the social security program.

In the many Negro families with working mothers the entire family can be together only on weekends. Where there is no father, boys are deprived of a male image and male counselor and companion.

Vocational Education for Negro Youth

George Strauss and Sidney Ingerman

One approach to the Negro youth's problems of preparing for the urban labor market is to increase his specific skill preparation through vocational schooling. In theory, vocational training provides work experience not normally available to the Negro youngster, increases his chances of well-paid employment after graduation, and provides a learning situation in which academic demands that he may be ill prepared for are minimized, thus increasing his chances of staying in school. Let us examine these notions.

Of the approximately 13 million youths of all colors in our nation's high schools, about 2.1 million are enrolled in vocational programs.[1] But of this figure well over half are in home economics classes and almost a quarter in vocational agriculture. Only 330,000, or less than 3 per cent of all high school students, are enrolled in programs relevant to Negro city youth—the so-called trade, industry, technical, distributive, and health occupations courses.

For Negroes the picture is somewhat different, particularly in the big cities. In New York 20 per cent of the Negro high school students are in vocational schools, compared with 34 percent of the Puerto Ricans and but 10 per cent of "others."[2] In Chicago the total vocational school enrollment is 53 percent Negro, a considerably higher figure than for academic high schools.[3] In many parts of the country, particularly the West, specifically vocational programs (as opposed to individual courses) are less common than they are in some Eastern cities. Yet, taking non-Southern metropolitan areas as a whole 28 per cent of the Negro twelfth graders reported have attended one or more vocational courses, compared with only 18 per cent among white students. (The difference is even higher in the South where the comparable figures for metropolitan areas are 23 per cent for Negroes and 9 per cent for whites.)[4]

How adequate is vocational schooling, particularly in training Negroes? Certainly vocational education has been the subject of great controversy recently. Among the charges made are that such schooling (1) marks too sharp a separation from academic schooling; (2) offers second class education; (3) serves as a dumping ground for educational misfits, and (4) does not provide useful training for the vast majority of occupations which provide most opportunity for Negroes.

Too Sharp a Separation

In the older programs which have separate vocational schools the student normally must make a decision as to whether to enter vocational school before the 9th or 10th grades (often at age 14 or 15) and frequently must, at the same time, pick a specific trade to study. Particularly for Negroes, who may have less knowledge of job opportunities than do white youths of the same age, this may be too young an age for so important a decision—all the more so since it is usually extremely difficult for a youngster to change trades or to return to an academic high school if he finds he has made a mistake. His only real alternative is to drop out of school altogether.

The traditional vocational school represents too sharp a break in another sense, for these schools are normally located in buildings geographically separate from academic high schools and they have a distinctly different course of study in that the student's time is rigidly divided half and half between academic and shop subjects.

School systems in the West are less prone to adopt so rigid a division between the two kinds of education. Indeed the trend nationally seems toward comprehensive high schools, as we shall discuss.

Second-Class Education

At least until recent substantial transfusions of federal money, vocational education was the step-child of the educational system. With the increasingly academic orientation of our high schools and junior colleges, vocational education and vocational educators fell to the very bottom of the ladder in terms of morale and status. Vocational educators were looked upon as second class citizens by the rest of the school system. Vocational instructors in general have less advanced education than academic instructors; presumably they make up for this through practical experience in the trades they teach. Nevertheless, they are often segregated, socially if not physically, from other teachers and understandably develop defeatist attitudes. Such attitudes are easily transmitted to students, particularly to those in overwhelmingly Negro vocational schools.

Vocational schools are often located in run down buildings. They rarely have an adequate athletic program—an important source of identification for the Negro boy and an important outlet for his energies and frustrations. Vocational schools have relatively few extracurricular activities, many are all-male and thus lack social life. For these reasons vocational school students are unlikely to develop a sense of pride in their school. Instead the school can develop into a symbol of degradation.

A Dumping Ground

Both students and educators too often look upon vocational schools as a dumping ground for rejects. Indeed many vocational courses (particularly those with large numbers of Negroes) seem to exist chiefly to provide custody of student misfits with disciplinary or learning problems who can't make out in academic high schools, or even in the college-directed "general course."

There is no inherent reason why this should be so. Many vocational courses are intellectually demanding. Particularly students in "technical" (as contrasted to ordinary vocational) high schools often go to junior or even senior college. Yet "today's theory of counseling and placement too often clings to the antiquated concept that the school trains either brain or brawn—not both—and therefore students with below-average academic ability should be placed either in vocational high schools or in the industrial arts course."[5]

With some students there may be an inverse correlation between academic and practical abilities. These are students who have done poorly in academic subjects but who settle down to study, once they are given practical, "meaningful," less abstract subjects in vocational schools. But there are many other students who do just as badly in one type of school as in the other. Indeed students with eight or nine years of "failure experience" in elementary and junior high school have often lost their motivation to learn. With low expectations that training will lead into jobs, such students develop self-images of being rejects and often become virtually unteachable. Feeling that they are getting nowhere, they leave school just as soon as they can.[6]

When classes contain many students with problems such as these, standards of accomplishment are naturally set low. Under these circumstances even well motivated students learn that they can get by with a minimum of effort and so they learn poor work habits. All this further lowers the reputation of vocational schools and frightens away many manually oriented students of average intelligence who might do well in a vocational setting.

Vocational educators are deeply sensitive to the charge that vocational education is a dumping ground and are understandably anxious to raise the status of their programs. A number of these programs have established screening examinations to prevent the slow learner from entering. Indeed in some school systems there seems to be a conflict between the vocational and academic high school, each competing for the middle range of students and seeking to reject the exceptionally slow learners—thus creating an additional problem for the underprivileged.

Inadequate Training for Jobs

How effectively does vocational school training fit Negroes for the demands of the urban labor market? Some training courses are quite useful—above all the classes provided for girls in secretarial skills and the "technical" training which leads to occupations in expanding fields such as electronics.

Despite these exceptions vocational education for most boys is concentrated on a comparatively few occupations, particularly in the skilled trades.[7] Few of these occupations are expanding rapidly (over the next decade the demand for craftsmen is expected to rise only as fast as the work force as a whole).[8] Relatively little training is provided for the vast majority of occupations, especially in the expanding sectors of the economy. Indeed vocational schooling, as presently conceived, is inappropriate for most occupations because these occupations are too small to warrant specific programs, because training can be obtained very quickly on the job, or because employers have well-developed training programs of their own. Federal aid has only recently been extended to courses leading to office, technical, or semi-professional jobs or to jobs in distribution.[9] With few exceptions, there is little training for government service, though this is an increasing source of jobs for Negroes. Though a high percentage of vocational students will not graduate from high school, there are few courses directed specifically for this group.

Historically, vocational schools have trained boys for the traditional skilled trades—in construction, printing, and automotive and machine shops. Outside of the automotive and printing trades, there is little evidence that going to vocational school gives a boy a significant advantage over his academic counterpart in terms of finding a skilled trades job.[10] As far as the building trades are concerned there is reason to believe that even white vocational graduates are at best likely to end up in the lower-paid, non-union sector of the industry. In the unionized sector many of the joint apprenticeship committees which select apprentices actually prefer applicants who have graduated from academic high schools and credit is rarely given for vocational classes.[11]

Admission to the trades, whether through apprenticeship or through the "back door" is to a considerable extent based on nepotism and personal contacts. Relatively few Negroes get by. Though Negro electricians, plumbers, and sheetmetal workers are turned out by vocational schools each year, in most communities these trades are almost lily-white. In addition, substantial numbers of Negroes are enrolled in courses such as woodworking and cabinet making, declining fields in which the remaining jobs (particularly those available for Negroes) are low paid. The real trouble with training Negroes, both for the skilled trades and for the declining occupations, is that this involves a kind of hypocrisy leading both teachers and students to become cynical about the whole process.

Despite the frequently made comment that students without specific vocational training face substantial hardships in getting a job, the vocational school is the normal form of preparation for work in only a few occupations. Many occupations can be learned on the job in a few days or at the most several weeks.[12] Milkmen, waiters, truckdrivers, and service station attendants are among these. In addition there are hundreds of other occupations for which vocational training might well be useful (furrier, terrazzo worker, mortician, ceramic caster, and so forth, endlessly), but since these jobs are held by but a handful of people in a given community there are rarely enough job openings in any specific occupation to warrant holding special classes for it. Yet together these occupations add up to a substantial proportion of the work force.

Finally there is a wide range of jobs for which industrial practice disregards vocational education since the employer provides on-the-job training in any case. In many instances, because of tradition or union contracts, new employees start at the bottom on totally unskilled jobs and gradually work their way up, learning through practice. For other jobs companies have their own formalized training programs. A Nassau County report concludes:

> "It is safe to say that if trade and industrial practices are taken into account, in the final analysis, certainly no more than 25% and probably less than 20% of the jobs available to male high school graduates are in occupations for which single-occupation trade, industrial, and technical vocational training in high school is conceivably relevant."[13]

Indeed many employers seem to look chiefly for abilities which can't be learned easily on the job—reading, writing, and mathematics—

plus social skills, such as making a good appearance, willingness to take orders, and to adapt to new situations. Given the poor reputation of vocational students some employers prefer graduates of academic high schools.

In any case, that vocational schools are not the open road for Negro opportunity is shown by two studies which suggest that Negro vocational school graduates earn substantially less than their white counterparts.[14]

The Value of Vocational Schools

Does this mean that vocational education should be abandoned as a worthless experiment? Some have suggested so, pointing out that though vocational education is considerably more expensive than academic education[15] it is far from clear that graduates of vocational schools do any better job-wise than do academic graduates. But this is hardly a fair comparison since the groups are not equal in other ways. Were it not for the existence of vocational schools many vocational graduates might not have finished school at all. Though drop out rates of vocational students are high, they might well have been higher yet had these students gone on to academic high schools. Even for drop-outs vocational schools may provide meaningful help; the discipline and work skills training picked up at school is likely to be better than none at all.

No, the evidence does *not* suggest that vocational education should be eliminated. What it does suggest is the wisdom of turning away from the old, rigid format, as is being done in many school districts already. In particular the following recommendations seem reasonable:

1. Less emphasis should be placed on training for specific jobs; greater emphasis should be given to providing a broad background of manual skills and academic training which would be useful in a range of occupations (dealing with engines, for instance, or working with electricity and electronics). Training for specific occupations should be avoided particularly since changes are so rapid, both in the nature of a given occupation and the number of job vacancies there may be for it.

2. More emphasis should be placed on general education. In a sense mathematics and English are vocational courses since they may be of more practical value in getting a job than training for a specific occupation.

3. The sharp line between vocational and academic high schools should be eliminated. The second class status of vocational education

can be reduced through establishing comprehensive high schools, as already exist in many communities, particularly in the West. Students should be given considerable freedom in deciding how to divide their time between academic and vocational studies. Instead of forcing students to choose a vocation in the ninth or tenth grades, greater attention should be given to "industrial arts" courses which are designed to prepare students for the world of work and give them some feeling for the range of occupations available.

4. Students of average ability or better should devote their high school years to academic education. The present trend toward providing training for specific skills in "post-secondary" junior colleges, area vocational schools, and junior colleges should be encouraged. Certainly there is evidence of increasing demand for junior college degrees for technical occupations.

5. For students not going on to post-secondary school—and most Negroes fall into this category—courses providing training for a *family* of jobs may be particularly useful, especially if such training can be tied in with cooperative "part-time" work. Greater emphasis should be given to clerical, service, and government employment. Specific training should deal with how to find a job and perhaps how to pass tests, such as civil service entrance examinations.

6. For the poorest, slow-to-learn students "vocational"[16] training may provide a sugar-coated form of general education. For such students the objective of education should be to provide at least a rudimentary ability to read, write, and calculate. School should also provide some training in industrial social skills and how to work and hold a job. For such students success may consist of landing an unskilled job. Although these students should be encouraged to stay in school as long as they can, it should be recognized that many will be dropouts.

Conclusion

Much current thinking emphasizes job training as a solution to the problems of Negro teen-age unemployment. It is often suggested that Negroes have a hard time finding jobs because they lack the specific vocational skills for which employers are looking. Expansion of vocational education at the high school level and attempts to provide underprivileged youth with immediately saleable skills through various manpower and poverty programs are the result of this thinking.[17]

Our thesis has been that the value of training for specific jobs at the secondary school level has been over-emphasized. A large number of firms do their own training, and in the skilled trades apprenticeship programs are the formal port of entry. In some cases, having attended a vocational school may be a poor recommendation for employment. In addition, vocational education for specific jobs is increasingly being left to post-secondary institutions where jobs with significant technical content can best be taught. This does not mean that vocational education serves no purpose. Quite the contrary. The evidence suggests that a youth with a high school vocational education is better off than if he had dropped out of an academic high school. For some jobs, particularly in the clerical field, automotive repair, and occupations performed in typically small enterprises, like those in the lady's garment industry, vocational training does lead to jobs.

Nevertheless, the critics of vocational education, as it exists in many eastern schools, seem to be largely justified. Little purpose is served by the sharp separation between vocational and academic education and the rigid format into which many vocational courses are bound. Indeed, as we have discussed, these factors tend to make vocational education second class education and give it the appearance of a dumping ground for misfits.

Because high school vocational education for specific occupations in fact prepares for so few jobs, it would seem that vocational education would serve its purpose better as an integral part of a comprehensive school program. The main purpose of vocational education should not be to train people for a particular occupation. For the average and better-than-average student it should be concerned primarily with providing some understanding of the range of occupations and how to get and hold a job. A limited amount of skill training may be useful—for example, typing for girls and the use of basic tools and machinery for boys. But at this stage theoretical knowledge (for example grammer, or understanding the principles of electric circuits) may be more important to them than manual skills.

For students of low academic ability who are potential dropouts greater emphasis might be given to manual work. But even here manual training should be tied in with substantial doses of job related reading, writing, and arithmetic presented in a "sugar coated" practical form. In any case, specific occupational preparation should be only part of a broad curriculum designed to provide youth with a feeling for the realities of working life.

Schools that make available both academic and vocational educational opportunities in a coordinated framework can help meet the needs of Negro youths in preparing for the world of work. The problems of organizing and administering schools that have more diverse goals and students with a wider range of achievement potential poses some difficult problems, but the needs and benefits seem well worth the undertaking.

Notes

1. Statistics are from the 1965 *Manpower Report of the President,* p. 263 and *Vocational and Technical Education,* Fiscal year 1964, U. S. Office of Education (Washington, 1966), p. 5.
2. *New York Times,* March 15, 1967, p. 11. These statistics indicate a considerable drop from those of 1960 when 30 per cent of the Negro high school students, almost half the Puerto Ricans and 12 per cent of the "others" were in vocational school. *Youth and Work in New York City* (New York: Taconic Foundation, 1962), p. i.
3. James S. Coleman and others, *Equality of Educational Opportunity* (Washington: U. S. Government Printing Office, 1966), p. 488.
4. *Ibid.,* p. 545. Note the figures here refer to students who have taken one or more courses—as opposed to the smaller number who are enrolled in vocational programs.
5. Robert J. Havighurst, *The Public Schools of Chicago* (Chicago: Board of Education, 1964), p. 252.
6. Dropout rates from vocational schools are high. In New York, during the early 1950's, over 60 per cent of the vocational high school students failed to graduate, compared to less than 40 per cent in academic high schools. *Youth and Work in New York City,* p. 9.
7. The following nine trades encompass over 80 per cent of the 1963 trade and industrial graduates from public vocational and technical high schools in the twelve Northeastern states: cabinet maker, carpenter, drafting, electronics, electrician, auto mechanic, aircraft mechanic, machinist, and printer. *Follow-up Study of 1963 Graduates, Trade and Industrial Programs in Public Vocational and Technical High Schools, North Atlantic Region* (Rutgers, New Jersey: Graduate School of Education, Rutgers University, n.d.). Of these trades only drafting and electronics are expected to expand as fast or faster than the work force as a whole. *America's Industrial and Occupational Manpower Requirements, 1964-1975,* U. S. Department of Labor, Bureau of Labor Statistics (Washington, 1966).
8. *America's Industrial and Occupational Manpower Requirements,* 1964-1975, p. 128.
9. An exception to this statement was a small "cooperative" program in distribution education for those holding part-time jobs in distribution.
10. For statistical evidence as to the low percentage of craftsmen who have had vocational training in high school, see U. S. Department of Labor, Office of Manpower, Automation, and Training, *Formal Occupational Training of Adult Workers,* Manpower/Automation Research Monograph No. 2 (December 1964), Tables 5 and 11.

11. A study of vocational training in Nassau County, New York concludes, "The percentage of apprentices for the skilled crafts among nonvocational high school graduates—5 per cent as compared to 6 per cent. Moreover, 35 per cent of the vocational graduates who became apprentices were in crafts totally different from what they learned in high school." *Preparing Youth for the World of Work* (New York: New York State Citizens Committee for the Public Schools, Inc., n.d.), pp. 12-13.

12. One study estimates that two-thirds of the jobs in New York State can be learned "on a full-time basis in a few days, a few weeks, or a few months." *Jobs, 1960-1970: The Changing Pattern of Manpower and Technological Change in New York State,* New York State Department of Labor (Albany, 1960), p. 3.

13. *Preparing Youth for a World of Work, op. cit.,* p. 15.

14. A Baltimore study indicates that the difference is more than 40 per cent for men and even more for women. Bernard Levenson and Edmund D. Meyers, Jr., *The Employment Situation of White and Negro Youth in the City of Baltimore* (New York: Bureau of Applied Research, Columbia University, 1963), p. 45. Among graduates of the New York High School of Fashion the difference runs about 20 per cent. *Selected Tabulations, High School of Fashion Industries, New York City, 1956-1963 Graduates,* Youth Employment Project, Bureau of Applied Social Research, Columbia University, March 22, 1966.

15. In New York the average vocational student costs 50 per cent more than his academic counterpart. In Chicago he costs 20 per cent more.

16. Although it may be a misnomer to call this vocational education since it is not directed toward a specific occupation.

17. Provision for such skills has been a major purpose of many of the manpower and poverty programs, particularly those under the Manpower Development and Training Act, the Job Corps, and the Community Action Programs. All these seek to provide underprivileged youths with immediately saleable skills. For the high school dropout the Job Corps and MDTA training is useful for no other reason than completing such training provides evidence to the employer that the youth is able to complete something. But dropouts are not likely to be motivated into this training unless it seems to be leading to some practical payoff, and specific training seems to the youth to be more practical than further general education.

City Schools

Patricia Cayo Sexton

[*From* The Annals of the American Academy of Political and Social Science, 352 *(March 1964), pp. 95–106.*]

To talk about urban education is to talk about an old fallen phrase in such disrepute during two postwar decades that it has hidden out from scholarly journals like a furtive sex criminal. The phrase "class struggle" now appears in black tie and softened aliases as "slum and suburb," "inequalities," problems of the "disadvantaged," of the "culturally deprived," of "integration." However Americanized or blurred the new image may appear, the basic fact seems simple enough: a remarkable "class struggle" now rattles our nation's schools and the scene of sharpest conflict is the city. Southern cities—and New York—were the scenes of first eruptions, but now almost every northern city, and many suburbs, are feeling the new tremors.

A high-ranking official in New Rochelle, New York, put it in these words: "It's not just race in our schools . . . it's class warfare!" Class conflict, of course, is not the only issue in city schools. There is ethnic conflict and the special status of Negroes—and of Puerto Ricans and other identifiable groups—at the bottom end of the ladder and the special Rickover pressure-cooked conformism and prestige-college frenzy at the upper end.[1] Nor are the sides in the conflict always clearly formed. But, usually, when the chaff and wheat are separated, what is left is the "haves" in one pile and "have-nots" in another, with some impurities in each—middle-class white "liberals," for example, who support some Negro demands and white have-nots who oppose them. Banfield and Wilson claim four important cleavages in city politics: (1) haves and have-nots, (2) suburbanites and the central city, (3) ethnic and racial groups, (4) political parties.[2] A reduction to more basic outlines might show that the first category would, with some slippage, cover the other three. Indeed, the authors acknowledge as much when they say: "These tend to cut across each other and, in general, to become one fundamental cleavage separating two opposed conceptions of the public interest."[3] When they refer to "... The fundamental cleavage between the public-regarding Anglo-

[1]Rickover supporters in the Council on Basic Education voice some misgivings about the Admiral's program to restrict higher education to an elite.

[2]Edward C. Banfield and James Q. Wilson, *City Politics* (Cambridge, Mass.: Harvard University Press and MIT Press, 1963).

[3]*Ibid.*, p. 35.

Saxon Protestant, middle-class ethos and the private-regarding lower-class, immigrant ethos," they seem to refer, though the phrase is unspoken, to one aspect of the class struggle.[4]

Other major urban school issues exist—finances, bureaucracy, and the unionization of teachers, among others—and may seem, on the surface, unrelated to class conflict. At second glance, the shortage of school funds can be seen as a product of the antitax ideology of haves. The behemoth bureaucracies may be seen everywhere as more accessible to and influenced by haves, and the decentralization of administration—to which New York's Superintendent Gross and others have devoted themselves—may be seen as a partial response to the growing arousal of have-not groups. The unionization of city teachers may be seen as a response to the hitherto rather rigid conservative control of school systems and the new thrust of liberalism in the cities and the schools, released by have-not votes and agitation, as well as a defense against the difficult conditions in have-not schools.[5]

Levels of Conflict

The class struggle in the schools and the struggle for power which is part of it are carried on at many levels. In some cases, it seems least visible under the spotlight—on the school boards. Through liberal and have-not activity, some city school boards are now composed of middle-class moderates who are more inclined to represent the educational interests of have-nots than were their more conservative predecessors. Some big-city boards, as New York's, seem exemplary public servants, superior in purpose and competence to higher political bodies. Their efforts on behalf of have-nots are limited by several personal as well as external characteristics: they are haves, a quality

[4]*Ibid.*, p. 329. Their ascription of a "public-regarding" ethos to the middle class and a "private-regarding" one to the "lower class" seems an extraordinary and questionable reversal of the usual association of the middle class with private efforts and the lower class with public efforts. It is most puzzling when contrasted with their summary statement: "If in the old days [of lower class ward politics] specific material inducements were illegally given as bribes to favored individuals, now much bigger ones are legally given to a different class of favored individuals . . ." (p. 340).

[5]In New York and Chicago especially, the popular political issues of "bossism" and "machine politics" have been referred to the school arena. In New York, 110 Livingston Street (the Board of Education headquarters) has appeared to many as the school equivalent of "city hall," the one place you "can't beat" and with which you often cannot even communicate. Now a proposal is being considered to divide the city schools into several fairly autonomous geographic units in order to scatter the shots at "city hall" and provide easier access.

that usually though not invariably limits zeal and identity with have-nots; they are moderates in contrast to those leading the more militant have-not groups. Among the limits set by school systems are: (1) the traditional conservative reluctance of boards to interfere in the operations of the bureaucracy; (2) the inertia and resistance of the bureaucracy to pressure from the board; (3) the usual tendency to become defensive of "their system" and to take criticisms of the system as personal affronts; (4) influences from middle-class interests which are usually more insistent and weighty than have-not pressure; (5) interference from outside groups—such as the unprecedented threat of the Northcentral Association to withdraw accreditation from the Chicago schools if the school board insisted on a step which forced Superintendent Willis into further desegregation. The external limits on the situation, however, seem more determining: (1) the difficulty of the job to be done, (2) the lack of sufficient money to do the job.

Services to have-nots within the city system, therefore, are limited by these conservative factors: (1) the moderate position of most liberal board members and the insufficiency of zeal or identification to drive home the grievances of have-nots; (2) conservatism and resistance within the bureaucracy; (3) conservative influence which acts to shut off funds to the schools.

In the movement of the class struggle from one end of the continuum, where a small elite holds total power, to the other extreme, where have-nots share proportionate influence, there are many points of compromise, and public officials tend to pursue ever more liberal ends and means. The white liberals who sit on some city boards may begin to push for more rapid change or may be replaced soon by representatives who will.

The claim that the city and its school system are so constrained by outside conservatism, especially at the state level, that they can do little seems largely true, though partially exaggerated. Too often outside interference is made an excuse for inertia. City schools have not given adequate service to have-nots largely because the have-nots were underrepresented in decision-making positions. As cities go, New York's school board seems unusually enlightened, appointed as it is by a relatively responsive mayor and served by two unusually alert citizen groups—the Public Education Association and the United Parents Association. Yet a nine-member board includes only one Negro and no Puerto Rican, although these groups together compose 40 percent of the city's public school enrollment. Nor is there any blue-collar worker or person of modest means or position on the board, but, then, such individuals are rare specimens on city boards. One trade unionist, himself a university graduate and member of a professional union, sits on the board. Of some 777 top officials in the system—

board members, superintendents, and principals—it appears that only six are Negroes, 0.8 per cent of the total.[6]

Although it is sometimes asserted that the interest-group identity of board members does not affect their decision-making, what may be more nearly the case, given present knowledge of group dynamics, is that the group interests of the lone have-not representative may be submerged in a board's moderate consensus.

Perhaps the "equality lag" within city systems may be more directly attributable to deficiencies in have-not organization than to lack of good faith among liberals and board members. Many cities could nearly be "possessed" by Negroes who approach a majority in some cases, but Negroes do not vote their numerical strength and may be evicted from the city limits by urban renewal before they catch up with their potential. Nor do labor unions use their full authority in school affairs. A major weakness of have-nots is their limited understanding of power, who has it and how to get it; they also lack the time, money, and organization often needed to purchase it.[7]

Beyond the City Limits

Local class conflict seems only a dim reflection of a larger conflict. The main drama of class conflict and thrust of conservatism are seen in full dimension in a larger arena—at the federal and state levels. The national scene cannot be ignored in any consideration of the city school situation. Only at this level does there appear a possibility of releasing the funds needed to support high-quality education and the high-level job opportunity that goes with it. The claim that federal aid to education is the *only* school issue and that other concerns are simply distractions is given substantial support by any cursory study of city school budgets and revenue limitations.[8]

[6]Daniel Griffiths and Others, *Teacher Mobility in New York City* (New York, 1963).

[7]Banfield and Wilson, *op. cit.*, p. 282: "Organized labor—even if it includes in its ranks the majority of all the adult citizens in the community—is generally regarded as a 'special interest' which must be 'represented'; businessmen, on the other hand, are often regarded, not as 'representing business' as a 'special interest,' but as serving the community as a whole. Businessmen, in Peter Clark's term, often are viewed as 'symbols of civic legitimacy.' Labor leaders rarely have this symbolic quality, but must contend with whatever stigma attaches to being from a lowerclass background and associated with a special-interest group. . . . Labor is handicapped not only by having imputed to it less civic virtue but also by a shortage of money and organizational skills."

[8]This seems to suggest that social scientists could much more profitably study the political mechanisms by which such aid could be released rather than the often esoteric and "academic" studies of culture, personality, and the like which now tend overly to occupy many who are concerned with have-nots.

Nationally, the conflict seems shaped by at least two major factors:

(1) The congressional system is biased against have-nots and their representatives. The bias results from at least two forms of conservative manipulation: (a) manipulation of rural and small-town interests, North and South, and, through them, congressional apportionment and votes; (b) the additional manipulation of southern rural conservatism—which is given unusual congressional power by the committee seniority system—through the exchange of votes on the race issue.

The superior effective power of haves at this top level serves to block federal legislation in general but specifically those measures that might ensure rapid economic growth through federal expenditures, full employment, and the extension of power to have-nots—measures that would give significant relief to the city's distress. More directly relevant, it has blocked any substantial aid to urban areas and held up the transfer of political power from rural to urban areas.[9]

Moreover, largely by the manipulation of conflicting religious interests, this coalition has prevented the passage of the federal aid that seems indispensable to urban schools. At the same time, it has continued, through extension programs, copious aid to rural education.

(2) Seriously deprived have-nots have failed to enter their full power into the political arena.

The State

If direct federal aid seems distant and the aid formula unlikely to provide much assistance to the cities, fiscal aid from the state may be closer at hand, depending upon how quickly reapportionment will be enforced in the states. New York City received $197 in school aid for each student in its public schools in 1961–1962, while the average in the rest of the state was $314. Miami, Florida paid $47 million in state taxes in one recent year and got back only $1.5 million in grants-in-aid. With sympathetic legislatures, cities may be able to call on other revenues, including an income tax on suburbanites working in the city such as has been adopted in Philadelphia and Detroit.

[9] The assumption that a proper apportioning of representatives, giving a proper share to the city's suburban areas, will result in an accretion of power to haves may not be warranted inasmuch as have-nots are also being rapidly suburbanized yet, contrary to expectation, seem to be maintaining their political identity.

Inequalities

The consequences of local, state, and national class conflict are seen in the school inequalities and class-biased training given to children even within the most liberal city systems. Only in the past few years has the concern of some unionists, academicians, liberals, and many Negroes brought the full range of inequities to public attention. The "spoils" of the city school, limited as they are by outside controls, are usually divided according to the crude formula "them as has gets." Only now in some cities is there any insistence on the more radical "compensatory" formula—"to each according to need."

Documentary evidence about class inequalities, past and present, is now weighty. My own study of one large city school system, *Education and Income,* describes the various forms of class inequities within one system.[10] I will refer here only to a few facts about Chicago and New York (not the cities of my study). In 1955, following Dr. Kenneth Clark's demand for attention to Negro schools, an "outside" study found that Negro and Puerto Rican schools in New York City were generally inferior to "Other" schools.[11] In a group of Negro and Puerto Rican schools (the *X* Group), 50.3 percent of teachers were on tenure, compared to 78.2 percent in the "Other" group (the *Y* Group); 18.1 percent in the *X* group and only 8.3 percent in the *Y* group were "permanent substitutes." On the average, facilities in Group X schools were older, less adequate, and more poorly maintained than *Y* schools. The costs of operating *Y* schools were higher than costs in *X* schools. Though the New York Board of Education now claims that Negro and Puerto Rican schools are equal or superior to "Other" schools, Dr. Kenneth Clark still says Harlem schools reflect "a consistent pattern of criminal neglect."

In the absence of cost-accounting, comparative expenditures in have and have-not schools in New York cannot be checked. Certainly efforts are being made by New York schools to provide better education for deprived minorities, especially in "certain" schools where extra services tend to be over-concentrated, but the schools still do not seem to approach full equality, and the cost estimates do not measure the *full* cost of education—the differences in nursery and kindergarten education, the last two years of high school missed by the low-income dropout, and the costs of higher education—not to mention the low-

[10] Patricia Cayo Sexton, *Education and Income* (New York: Viking Press, 1961).

[11] *The Status of the Public School Education of Negro and Puerto Rican Children in New York City,* October, 1955.

quality and segregated "ability" tracks into which have-not children are often placed.

Though New York permitted an outside study of school inequalities in 1954, the Chicago Superintendent of Schools, Benjamin Willis, has only in the past year agreed to a three-man study committee of which he will be a member. In 1962 John E. Coons, Northwestern University law professor, prepared for the United States Commission on Civil Rights a report on segregated schools in Chicago.[12] Ten schools in each of three groups were selected—white, integrated, Negro—and the findings were as follows:

1961–1962	*White*	*Integrated*	*Negro*
Number of pupils per classrooms	30.95	34.95	46.8
Appropriation per pupil	$342	$320	$269
Number of uncertified teachers	12%	23%	27%
Average number of books per pupil	5.0	3.5	2.5

In 1963 a *Handbook of Chicago School Segregation* claimed that 1961 appropriations for school operating expenses were almost 25 percent greater per pupil in white than in Negro schools, that teacher salaries were 18 percent higher, that nonteaching operating expenses—clerical and maintenance, salaries, supplies, textbooks—were 50 percent higher, and that only 3 percent of Chicago's Negro population finishes college.[13]

The reluctance of Chicago schools to move as far as New York on the race issue seems to derive from at least these sources: (1) the centralization of power in the person of the mayor; (2) the praise of Dr. Conant—probably the most influential person in American education—for Mr. Willis and the Chicago method and his concurrent criticism of the New York method; (3) the presence in New York of large numbers of unusually concerned and articulate white middle-class liberals; (4) the inordinate influence in Chicago schools and civic affairs of State Street, tax-conscious financial interests; (5) the past failures of have-not organization in Chicago.

An example of influential conservatism in relation to have-nots and the schools is seen in this passage from the Chicago *Tribune:* "Let's Throw the Slobs out of School":[14]

[12]John E. Coons, *Civil Rights USA, Chicago, 1962,* A Report to the United States Commission on Civil Rights.

[13]*Handbook of Chicago School Segregation,* 1963, compiled and edited by the Education Committee, Coordinating Council of Community Organizations, August 1963.

[14]Reprint from *Chicago Tribune Magazine,* "Let's Throw the Slobs out of School," as it appears in *Human Events,* September 21, 1963, a weekly magazine distributed to social-studies classes in schools throughout the nation.

> The ignoramuses have had their chance. It is time to make them responsible for their actions. . . . Sweep through the school house with a fiery broom. Remove the deadwood, the trouble-makers, the no-goods, the thugs. . . .
>
> [The teacher can tell on the first day] which students are the dissatisfied, the misfits, the illiterate [*sic,*] undeserving, *non compos* nincompoops.
>
> We have become the victims of the great transcendental fraud, a deceit put upon us by a generation of psychiatrists, guidance counselors, and psychologists, none of whom spends any more time in the classroom dealing with these apes than he has to.

Despite the fact that median income in Chicago is higher than in New York, Chicago in one recent year spent $410 per pupil while New York spent $761.52.[15]

Inequalities and the compensatory formula now being advocated—reverse inequality—produce only one kind of conflict, one which may be more easily resolved than other disputes because it involves simply the redistribution of money. The "concept" of equality itself seems far less susceptible to change—the notion that, with proper attention, the abilities of have-not children may prove roughly equal to those of haves and that, therefore, they should not be separated, sent off at an early age on different tracks, or given disproportionate access to higher education.

In New York City, fiscal inequality, segregation, and the "concept" of inequality resulted in the following racial distribution of recent graduating classes in New York's special high schools for "gifted children" drawn from the whole city:

	Negroes	*Puerto Ricans*	*Others*
Bronx High School of Science	14	2	863
Stuyvesant High School	23	2	629
High School of Music and Art	45	12	638
Brooklyn Technical School	22	6	907

In one recent year, Negroes and Puerto Ricans were about 14 percent of the graduating class in the city's academic high schools and about 50 percent in the city's vocational high schools. In the vocational schools, Negroes and Puerto Ricans tend to be heavily concentrated

[15]While 21.3 percent of Chicago's population have incomes over $10,000 annually, only 18.5 percent of New Yorkers are in this category. In Chicago, 26.3 percent of whites are in this bracket and only 8.7 percent of Negroes; at the same time, 9.9 percent of whites and 28.4 percent of Negroes have incomes less than $3,000 per year.

in inferior manual trade schools and seriously underrepresented in the technical schools. For example, in a class of 361 in the aviation school (a high-level technical school), 26 were Negroes, 51 were Puerto Ricans, 284 were "Others." In the class at the New York printing school, 4 were Negroes, 16 were Puerto Ricans, and 183 were "Others." At the Clara Barton school for hospital workers, Negroes were a clear majority. Vocational schools have been "tightening standards" recently and sending minorities to "academic schools where, if neglected, they may be no better off.

Higher Education

A developing conflict centers on higher education. Though ethnic records are not kept, one expert estimate is that about 2 percent of students at the University of the City of New York (formerly the city's free colleges) are Negro. One branch of the University is located at the edge of Harlem and is more integrated and accessible to Negroes than other branches, yet less than 5 percent Negro enrollment is reported there.

In New York, Negroes tend to fall between the free city colleges and the dominant and expensive private universities (New York University, Columbia, and their like). They can neither qualify for the former nor afford the latter. Needs tests are not applied to city-college admissions, and free tuition is extended to the affluent with an 85 high school average and denied the impoverished with an 84 average; enrollments are reported to be now predominantly middle class.[16]

Some critics now say that the only equitable system of tuition charges, in all types of institutions, is a sliding scale based on ability to pay. New York does not have a single state university; what is called the University of the State of New York is simply a scattered collection, mainly in nonurban areas, of teachers colleges, agricultural schools, a few technical schools.[17] Recently, the state gave a 40 percent subsidy to New York's city colleges, converted by some gradu-

[16]A recent admissions change at the city university from sole reliance on high school averages to inclusion of college boards scores is expected further to lighten the skin of enrollees. The Board of Higher Education, however, is now discussing a change of admissions standards to accommodate more Negroes.

[17]California spent $33 million on community and junior colleges in 1961–1962 and $214 million on other types of higher education. New York State spent $5.7 million on community and junior colleges and $111 million on other types of higher education. M. M. Chambers, Joint Office of Institutional Research, "Appropriations of State Funds for Operating Expenses of Higher Education, 1961–62," Washington, D. C., January 1962.

ate offerings into the University of the City of New York. The importance of federal funds to education is seen in federal research and development investments in California and the pervading effect such funds have had in underwriting and stimulating growth of educational institutions there.

New York City's effort through the years to provide free college education and to compensate for the void at the state level has been extraordinary. No other city appears to have made any comparable effort. Still the city seems not to have deployed its college resources equitably, and the gathering debate over the city colleges suggests a conflict of view—or interest—between the city's have-nots and its numerous liberal middle class.[18]

The compilation and release of information about ethnic and social class enrollments in institutions of higher education, as well as the postsecondary experiences of students, appear to be the first step out of the college inequities which have, in turn, imposed inequities on lower educational levels. Equality of opportunity in higher education will probably come only through a national network of community colleges—low in cost and located within easy commuting distance—and available to all "average"-or-above students who want further education.[19] Perhaps Britain's proposed experiment with televised university instruction will provide an alternative, or supplementary model, to the community college.

Class and Ethnic Roles

Within the city itself, at least these elements seem to have some separate, though often overlapping, identity: (1) Negroes; (2) labor unions; (3) white have-nots; (4) white liberals; (5) the Jewish community; (6) the Catholic community; (7) business organizations and their allies in city silk-stocking areas.

The roles and activities of these groups in relation to the schools have never been adequately defined, but impressionistic observation seems to indicate the following outlines: The main white support for

[18]None of the New York Board of Education's three community colleges (where admissions standards are such that Negroes can, and often do, qualify) are located in Negro areas. One is now scheduled for Manhattan, but the tentative location is between 23rd and 42nd streets, a white area—one of the few in Manhattan. One high ranking public-school official is quoted as saying "the municipal colleges are not equipped to operate vestibule courses for students who have to be civilized."

[19]The so-called "Russell Report" (Columbia Teachers College) to the Michigan legislature reported that the college enrollments by area rose and fell in proportion to the distance from the state's colleges.

civil rights in the past several decades has unquestionably come from the leadership within the labor and Jewish communities—with some major assists from middle-class liberal and church groups, particularly in the last several years. The rank-and-file within the labor-union and Jewish communities, more personally threatened by Negroes, have tended to lag some distance behind on civil rights.[20]

In the schools, the class and ethnic lines are distinct, even though less clearly drawn than in the larger community. Some political allies of Negroes have been largely outside the school conflict: unions and large numbers of white have-nots, notably the Poles, Italians, and Irish who have tended to use parochial schools. Some feel it is fortunate that these have-not groups have tended to be outside the public school controversy; others feel that the parochial-public school separation has worked hardships on the public schools and delayed a crisis that would, in the long run, be beneficial to the public schools. Union leaders have been less involved in the schools than in other political affairs because of what seems to be a rather basic alienation from the schools and frequently because of their own parochial background. They have, however, supported school expansion, improvement, financing, and their organized political power, as in New York, has given important direct assistance to the schools and to the claims of Negroes on the schools.

The organized business community has traditionally opposed tax increases for public education, the leadership in these groups usually residing in the suburbs where they have provided ample funds for good schools. Powerful real-estate groups have opposed property taxes as well as school and housing integration. The "swing" group has been the Jewish community and, to some extent, the white liberal. The Jewish community, even middle and upper income, has consistently given solid support to the public schools,[21] but its own heavy stress on education and the fact that it is one of the largest remaining white middle-class groups within many cities have produced some ambiva-

[20] On general political and economic issues, class lines seem quite clearly drawn: Negroes, unions, white have-nots, and a preponderance of the Jewish community appear on the have-not side, and the organized business, middle-class, and upper-class groups on the have side. Strangely, perhaps, and to some large extent understandably, Negroes chose two groups closest to them politically for their first-line offense: unions and the Jewish community. Both were vulnerable, having made continuing proclamations, accompanied by considerable effort, on behalf of equality and brotherhood, yet having done much less than their best to provide equality for Negroes within their own jurisdictions.

[21] In Detroit, a recent school-tax election was won, informed observers report, by majorities rolled up in the Negro and Jewish precincts.

lence in its role and some conflict in unexpected places. The confrontation of these two allies in the city public schools is a source of growing distress to both groups. Because the Jewish community has tended to remain in the city and to use the public schools, it is generally contiguous, geographically and emphatically, with the Negro community and located in the middle of the integration cross fire.[22] Negroes point to Jewish predominance in the "better" high schools, the top "ability" groups, the free city colleges, and in public school administration. In many of the "integrating" areas of the city, the two groups have joined in open conflict, though in other areas they have integrated without friction. Thus, the Jewish community, because it has not fled like others from the city, often finds itself in the same situation as the labor movement with regard to Negroes: competition within a family of mutual interest for a scarcity of opportunities—in the schools in one case and in the job market in the other.[23] Perhaps for this reason, among others, the International Ladies Garment Workers Union has been a particularly sensitive target.[24]

Acculturation and Integration

The urban schools now confront the most difficult task they have attempted. Never before has a major *racial* minority been integrated into a nation's school or society. In fact, such integration within a

[22]If the Jewish community is represented in the schools in proportion to its numbers in the population (one quarter of the New York population), then together with Negroes and Puerto Ricans (40 percent) it would represent at least 65 percent of public school enrollments.

[23]On the nine-man New York City school board, three representatives are traditionally selected for each of the three religious communities: Catholic, Protestant, Jewish. Though the Jewish community is represented by three board members, plus a Jewish-Unitarian superintendent of schools, the Negro and Puerto Rican communities, who constitute 40 percent of the public school population, have only one representative (a Negro) on the board.

[24]The Negro struggle seems to have an interacting effect on other have-not groups. In Detroit, the civil-rights movement is supported by the auto workers' union. In battle-torn Chicago, where the class struggle appears in its more primitive form, unembellished by righteous platitudes, the school board seems to have had two lone dissenters on equality and class issues: a steelworker representative (the only unionist on the board) and a Negro (another Negro member has consistently voted with the more conservative majority). The civil-rights drive, however, comes at a time when white workers feel insecure about jobs and their place in society and fear Negro competition in an already glutted job market. In areas of the nation where white have-nots are not organized (as in the South) and therefore do not have this broad view, racial conflict among have-nots is maximum.

dominantly non-Latin European population is unprecedented in history, the Soviets having settled their racial affairs by geographic separation.

The urban school, whose heavy job has always been the acculturation of immigrant and foreign-speaking ethnic groups, is now taking its first large bite of racial acculturation, as a giant reptile tries to swallow a whole animal. The city is accustomed to educating the immigrant: In New York City in 1960, 48.6 percent of the population was either foreign-born or had at least one foreign-born parent; in Chicago, the figure was 35.9; in Detroit, 32.2; in San Francisco, 43.5. But the Negro group is unique in these respects: (1) it is the largest "immigrant" group of low-income, public-school-using Protestants (many other recent immigrations have skirted the public schools); (2) it is the first large racial minority to come to the city schools and the first large group with non-Western origins; (3) it has had a unique history of educational and social deprivation.

The active demand of Negro parents for integration perhaps cannot be fully appeased. Negro—and Puerto Rican—students are approaching a majority in many city public schools and any demand for total, one-for-one integration—which few would make—may be impossible in view of the increasing shortage of white public school students. Rather large-scale integration seems possible, however, as New York City is now beginning to demonstrate. Perhaps the issue will finally be settled by integrated urban renewal, or by setting up superschools and superservices in Negro areas—such as the Amidon school in Washington, D. C.—that will attract white students into Negro areas. Mainly, the urban school integration movement has served the latent function of calling attention to Negro education and arousing concern over the quality of Negro schools. The hope is held by many that, if Negro schools are improved, Negroes will not be so eager to integrate.

Among the newer racial demands in urban schools are: (1) compensatory treatment to balance past inequities; (2) "reverse" integration of schools and the busing of whites into Negro schools in order to "equalize" sacrifice (in New York, the demand has been for compulsory busing of both groups; on this most controversial point, Dr. Kenneth Clark has objected that Harlem schools are not fit either for Negroes or for whites and that busing should be "out" only); (3) heterogeneous grouping to scatter Negroes throughout the school population in any given school, rather than segregating them into slow-moving, homogeneous "ability" groups. In New York City and elsewhere, homogeneous grouping has proceeded so far that children in some places are "ability grouped" in kindergarten, based on whether or not they have been to nursery school; these groups; starting almost in the cradle, tend to perpetuate themselves throughout the child's school life.

Some Ways Out

In this author's view, major breakthroughs in urban education may come via any or all of the numerous possible routes.

Outside the school, the possibilities include: (1) a political breakthrough of have-nots at the congressional and state legislative levels; (2) increasing civil-rights activity and pressure; (3) organization of have-nots at the following levels: political community, ethnic (civil rights), on the job (union), out of a job (unemployed); (4) federal aid programs—either through direct federal aid or around this bottleneck and through special funds, job retraining, Health, Education, and Welfare funds, urban-renewal domestic peace corps, vocational education; (5) massive infusions of voluntary aid to the schools and assistance from private foundations.

Inside the schools, the break-through might come from such sources as: (1) massive enlargement of college opportunities through the introduction of new funds or new methods of teaching; (2) technological innovation in public school, especially educational television; (3) the unionization of teachers and the arousal of the professional group with the greatest stake in improved schools (organized teachers, it has been demonstrated in New York City, can have an electric effect on the schools, attracting qualified teachers through improved salaries and working conditions, reduced class size, improved curriculum, and quality of school administration and instruction); (4) decentralization of city school systems to encourage greater participation of have-nots and clearer and closer channels of communication.[25]

Recent months have seen a spectacular burst of citizen interest in the schools, perhaps unparalleled by anything in the history of public education. Women's clubs, youth groups, civil-rights organizations, settlement houses, churches, local government, private funds, and foundations have taken up "tutorials" in deprived areas, and the more imaginative and energetic groups have moved out from there into community organization. The intrusion of nonschool groups into the

[25]In New York, the new community school boards, serving as advisory groups, have already geometrically increased the flow of new ideas, spirit, and activity into the schools from the local communities and cleared the clogged lines of communication.

learning process has injected some new excited spirit into the institutional drabness.

Accompanying this new citizen concern with the "disadvantaged" is a new wave of interest among educators, writers, and scholars in the problems of poverty and equality, a current that has in recent months washed over previous concentration on the "gifted" and almost swept the word out of the educator's vocabulary.

Another source of backdoor assistance to the schools will be the decongestion of cities—a desperate need of New York especially—by: (1) the natural attrition of a suburban-bound, affluent population, and a Negro population pushing ever outward; (2) the forced decentralization of urban renewal, thinning out populations and bringing back into central areas a more taxable balance of middle and lower income grups. Renewal, intelligently, humanely, and artfully carried on, has the potential, of course, to remake urban life—by decentralizing, rebuilding, rehabilitating, and creating a truly heterogeneous class and ethnic community.

The Big Cities' Big Problem

John F. Kain

[*From* Challenge, The Magazine of Economic Affairs, *a publication of Challenge Communications, Inc., New York. September/October 1966.*]

Last summer's riots in our big city ghettos, plus the heated Congressional debate over open housing legislation have focused national attention on two sides of the same coin: Negro residential segregation and our declining central cities. Costly government programs have been failures because they treat symptoms rather than basic causes and because they frequently, though unintentionally, aggravate the more fundamental causes of metropolitan disorders. Negro residential segregation is the most important of these fundamental causes.

I share the concern of numerous commentators, journalists and academic researchers about ghetto housing and living conditions. However, there are other equally grave, more indirect, and largely unperceived, consequences of housing segregation whose ultimate costs to society may be even greater. As these effects are more subtle and indirect, they are also more difficult to document. Much of what follows is highly speculative and even hypothetical. But the questions evaluated below are too important to be ignored even if they are difficult and the answers necessarily uncertain.

The so-called commuter crisis is a leading example of an urban problem that derives much of its complexity from housing segregation. Huge expansions of centrally oriented rail rapid transit systems are under way or being demanded in nearly every large metropolitan area. Yet travel to certain areas has declined or remained constant, substantial declines in transit use have occurred, and there have been huge expansions of highway capacity serving central areas. Why these apparent contradictions?

The answer is found in the changing composition and characteristics of travel to central workplaces. Increasingly these trips are being made to ever more distant and lower density residential areas located beyond existing transit facilities and/or in areas with densities too low for economic transit services. As a result peak-hour automobile trips to central areas have increased rapidly, keeping pace with highway construction and leading to continued demands for even more construction. Thus the commuter crisis is the result of changes in the residence patterns of centrally employed workers and their more frequent dependence on, or choice of, private automobile commutation.

The response of public officials to the commuter crisis has taken two forms: construction of additional expensive and heavily subsidized peak-hour highway capacity into central areas and/or increased subsidization of transit systems serving central areas. Yet it is apparent that residential location decisions are affected by transportation costs, and that existing residential patterns of centrally employed workers are at least partially the result of prior subsidization. These postwar changes in residential location are also due to increased real incomes, accumulations of wartime savings, improved and easier to obtain mortgage credit, and a seemingly strong preference of U.S. families for lower density residential services. These same factors are largely responsible for the postwar suburbanization of metropolitan populations as a whole.

But the rapid growth of Negro ghettos may have been even more important. The ghetto in most Northern cities rings the central business district like a collar, or as some have suggested, a noose. The ghetto's expansion, crudely illustrated by the table on page 242, has pushed white residential areas farther and farther from central workplaces.

While additional middle- and high-income whites are forced by the steady expansion of Negro ghettos to move farther away from their centrally located workplaces, more low-income and low-skilled Negroes find it necessary to commute longer distances from central residence areas to jobs in outlying areas. Moreover as jobs shift from central ghettos, Negroes have more difficulty acquiring and holding jobs, and employment in marginal jobs becomes less attractive.

Estimates by the author suggest segregation may cause Detroit Negroes the loss of as many as 9,000 jobs and Chicago Negroes as many as 30,000. While these estimates must be considered as only suggestive, they do indicate residential segregation may be an important and largely overlooked cause of Negro unemployment. Moreover, employment decentralization is proceeding steadily, while Negro residential centralization is increasing relatively. Thus, the problem is likely worsening and may already be far more serious than the estimates for Detroit (1952) and Chicago (1956) suggest.

The McCone inquiry into the causes of the Watts riots strongly emphasized the importance of high unemployment as a cause and pointed to inadequate public transit as a prime reason. The Commission recommended vastly improved and subsidized transit *from* Watts, and the Department of Housing and Urban Affairs has approved a transit demonstration project for this purpose.

Low-income white workers adapt their residential choices to their job locations and to available transit services. When their jobs are in suburban areas, an increasing trend, they invariably live in suburban areas. When Negro jobs are located in suburban areas, they must either be foregone or they represent difficult, costly, and time-consuming trips from central residence areas to suburban workplaces.

The McCone Commission Report virtually ignores the question of residential integration. Yet the problem of Negro access to jobs could be solved equally well by improved transportation or by housing integration. The McCone Report strongly urges the former, but is strangely silent on the latter, which appears far less costly economically (but perhaps not politically).

The Commission's recommendations and observations suggest another indirect contribution of housing segregation to the urban transportation problem. Housing segregation creates a need for several more or less independent yet overlapping systems.

A system is needed to transport central city white "captive" transit users (low-income, childless and elderly white households) between high-density origins and other destinations.

An entirely different transit system is needed for ghetto Negroes. Since they are much less able to change their places of residence, this second system must be (1) largely confined to the ghetto, (2) very indirect and thereby slow (usually requiring one or more transfers from the ghetto system to other parts of the metropolitan transit system), or (3) very extensive, expensive and heavily subsidized (if it is to provide reasonably direct and fast service to the rest of the metropolitan area).

The choice noted for Watts, of a largely independent ghetto system with poor or no service to other parts of the metropolitan area, is not typical.

Finally, a third system is needed to transport centrally employed whites through the steadily expanding ghettos to white garrison suburbs. Since the distances between home and work are so great and steadily growing, this white commuter system must be high performance (special purpose and expensive) and subsidized.

Determination of what the demand for and price of centrally located housing would be in the absence of Negro residential segregation is a nearly impossible task. However, estimates by the author suggest as many as 40,000 Detroit Negro workers might move from central to outlying residential areas, *if they were free to choose locations* similar to those of low-income whites employed at the same workplaces. Using similar methods and assumptions, it is estimated that as many as 112,000 Negroes might move from Chicago's ghetto, and a majority of these might choose suburban residences. These estimates are based on the existing distribution of Negro employment.

But housing segregation affects the location of Negro jobs. If housing segregation were reduced, more Negroes would work in suburban areas and many of these would live there. Moreover, these findings are consistent with others indicating that very little of existing housing segregation can be explained by socioeconomic differences.

If housing segregation had not existed, new suburban housing still would have attracted many higher income white residents. In the absence of encroaching racial ghettos, many central city home-owners might have been encouraged to renovate their existing properties rather than buy new houses in outlying areas.

Certainly employment dispersal provided strong incentives for many whites to move to suburban residence areas nearby their new workplace locations where their housing dollars would buy more and better housing. But the jobs of many whites remained in central cities, and these individuals often would have reduced their combined housing and travel outlays by not moving. Moreover, many Negro jobs also shifted to suburban locations; others were located there all the while; and if Negroes had free access to surburban housing markets, both the number of Negroes employed in suburbs and the number of whites employed in central cities would be larger.

Negro residential segregation also frustrates efforts at central city renewal by increasing the proportion of low-status residents and thereby reducing middle- and high-income residential demand. Effects on demand are partly psychological. Central cities are simply viewed as an inferior place to live because they contain so many low-income and dark-skinned persons. Of possibly even greater importance, given existing methods of municipal finance, it appears impossible to provide high-quality public education and other services for the entire city.

Urban policy makers have refused to even recognize this problem. Yet central city residential renewal for middle- and high-income families requires that a way be found either to increase substantially the quality of public services in central cities as a whole (while at the same time distributing most of these costs outside of the central city), or to permit larger allocations of public services in favor of middle- and high-income central city residents.

As with all other urban problems, the many causes of the crisis in local public finance are complex and interrelated. However, decentralization of commercial and industrial activity must be counted among the most important. Central cities have always contained a disproportionate number of the poor. But they also contained a disproportionate share of nonresidential real property. In a rough way these nonresidential properties subsidized public services for the poor and usually provided some surplus to pay for regional public goods, such as museums, zoos, parks and the like.

Postwar trends upset this rough balance. Metropolitan decentralization sharply reduced the share of taxable nonresidential wealth located in central cities. Higher incomes sharply increased the demand for public services, and the tax base (value of real property) increased more slowly. Most importantly, the central city had the Negro ghetto which accelerated the flight of higher income whites.

It would be foolish to contend that all postwar problems of central city finance would have disappeared if housing had been unsegregated. The technological and economic forces underlying much of the metropolitan decentralization would have remained, and central cities would have lost a substantial part of the nonresidential wealth which had previously subsidized public services for the poor. However, they almost as certainly would have retained a larger proportion of middle- and high-income households were it not for the artificially created Negro demand. And while suburban communities would have had the same incentives to exclude lower income tax payers, Negro and other low-skilled, low-income members of the population would have been more equally distributed throughout metropolitan areas.

Population and employment dispersal have almost certainly been affected by housing segregation as well. Rapid growth of Negro populations has been a powerful force underlying the white exodus from the central city. But Negro residents have taken the place of displaced whites and, while the resulting pattern is an inefficient one, central city populations are almost certainly larger than if racial segregation had not existed. Central city populations would be lighter in color, more affluent and reside closer to work, but they also would be smaller in number and less densely housed.

Housing segregation, directly or indirectly, may also have been a factor in the choice of suburban locations by some firms. Everything else being equal, employers prefer locating nearby the homes of their employees and particularly their more highly skilled and difficult to replace ones. As these increasingly move to outlying areas, centrally located firms must partially compensate them for their increased commutation costs (either through higher wages or shorter working hours) or lose them to firms nearer suburban residential areas. These factors may be decisive for employers without compelling reasons for choosing central locations. The converse of this is that some firms employing large numbers of low-skilled workers may be encouraged to remain or to move to central locations to take advantage of the ghetto's large pool of low-skilled Negro labor.

Much retailing decentralization must also be credited to the suburbanization of higher income populations. Had central cities kept more of these residents, downtown might have held its supremacy.

High central city taxes, which must be at least partially credited to housing segregation, is another reason given by firms for choosing suburban location. The best publicized conflict over central city taxes is the threat by the New York Stock Exchange to move to Hoboken. While this conflict has been a boon to cartoonists and pundits, it is anything but a laughing matter to Mayor Lindsay.

The increased problems of maintaining civil order may influence the thinking of many entrepreneurs about the advisability of locating in central areas. Claims of this kind are obviously difficult to evaluate. Yet annual references to a "long, hot summer" are unlikely to cause a wavering businessman to choose in favor of a central location.

If these speculations about the indirect and largely unperceived costs of housing segregation contain only a germ of truth, they would appear to point to a single conclusion. Racial segregation is "*the* urban problem," and some modification of historic patterns of racial segrega-

Change in White and Nonwhite Central City and Suburban Ring Populations 1950-60 (thousands).

	Central City		*Suburban Ring*	
	White	*Negro*	*White*	*Negro*
Baltimore	−113	100	324	7
Boston	−130	23	278	3
Chicago	−399	320	1,076	34
Cleveland	−142	103	367	2
Detroit	−363	182	904	19
New York	−476	240	1,777	67
Philadelphia	−225	153	700	38
Pittsburgh	− 91	18	257	7
St. Louis	−168	61	429	18
San Francisco	−148	67	554	25
Washington, D.C.	−173	131	553	18

tion in metropolitan housing is necessary to achieving reasonably efficient solutions to an ever increasing array of related problems. The alternative would appear to be greater distortions of metropolitan development and continued failure of government policies intended to solve urban problems.

Recognition of high rates of Negro unemployment, low incomes and other undesirable conditions found in central city ghettos have led to widespread demands for corrective action. A majority of practical men seem to have concluded that residential integration is either impossible or will take too long. They contend the problems of the urban Negro are current and real and that while residential integration might be desirable as a long-range goal, such a course for the immediate future is uncertain, difficult and politically dangerous. Still there are growing demands to do something right now for Negroes entrapped in central city ghettos.

Proposals to patch up the ghetto and make it a better place to live and to create jobs there are heard with increasing frequency. The concept of immediate and direct attacks on Negro low incomes, unemployment and poor housing has obvious appeal. But there are several serious questions that need to be raised about ghetto improvement and job-creation schemes. These programs would reduce pressures for residential integration and would tend to perpetuate existing patterns and practices of racial segregation. In fact, a cynic might look here for some of the very considerable support for these ideas. Such an approach would certainly be a costly and inefficient solution since it would not reduce, and in fact might aggravate, several of the problems identified here.

But, the most telling objection is that such policies might well fail altogether. There are strong links between Northern ghettos and the still vast pools of rural, Southern Negroes. Ghetto improvement and particularly ghetto job creation programs might well have as their principal result increased migration of Southern Negroes to Northern metropolitan areas. Growth rates of Northern ghettos might increase severalfold, greatly aggravating the problems, while leaving the existing levels of income and unemployment unchanged. Undoubtedly the well-being of many Southern Negroes might be enhanced; but just as assuredly the distortions of metropolitan growth would be magnified, and the goal of assimilating and integrating the Negro into urban society would be made far more difficult. Better, more direct means of improving the conditions of Southern Negroes exist.

While I personally would prefer a truly integrated society, with fully integrated housing markets as a principal building block, many of the costs of Negro residential segregation would disappear or be greatly mitigated by a substantially altered, but still segregated, housing pattern. This alternative would satisfy those who contend that much racial segregation is self-segregation, and that most Negroes prefer segregated housing. The indirect costs of Negro residential segregation result principally from the continued growth of a single massive central city ghetto. If this single, or overwhelmingly dominant, Negro ghetto were replaced by numerous smaller and widely dispersed Negro settlements, in a large number of political jurisdictions, most of the indirect costs of housing segregation would either be mitigated or disappear entirely.

Regardless of whether Negroes would choose many small segregated communities or a more integrated housing pattern, there is no alternative but vastly increased *suburbanization* of Negro populations, if we are to avoid unnecessary economic waste and growing social and political conflict. Human resource programs such as Head Start, increased grants for slum schools, and manpower retraining can make major contributions to solving urban problems. However, suburbanization of Negro populations should have priority, since solution of so many other urban problems would be simplified by changes in existing patterns of housing segregation.

Recognition of the serious difficulties created by Negro residential segregation and its direct relationship to other urban problems implies a reorientation of existing government programs. These programs should emphasize the strengthening of the Negro's ability to break out of the ghetto (education and job retraining) and the expansion of suburban housing opportunities. By contrast, ghetto improvement and job-creation programs are likely to have far different consequences than first imagined, and central city redevelopment programs are likely to remain costly and inefficient.

While there is great resistance to integration in the suburbs, suburbanization of Negroes is the only long-run solution to the massive urban problems stemming from housing segregation. Even with strenuous efforts these changes will require decades and will be difficult. But there is no alternative.

Barriers to Parity in Employment

Harlem Youth Opportunities Unlimited, Inc.

[*From Chapter 7 of* Youth in the Ghetto *(New York, 1964) by permission of Harlem Youth Opportunities Unlimited, Inc., copyright 1964.*]

Barriers to Parity of Employment

Many complex factors operate to produce the discrepancies between the white and non-white labor force. These vary in their impact in specific kinds of situations. The factors may be grouped under three general headings. It must be recognized, however, that the specifics under each of the headings tend to be interrelated among the categories. The occupational retardation of the residents of the community, and of Negroes in general, can be perceived as stemming from: (1) racial discrimination, (2) inadequacies in education and preparation for employment, and (3) the process, itself, of obtaining jobs.

Racial Discrimination

Overt denial of a job on the basis of skin color is usually cloaked under a variety of publicly defensible reasons for rejection. The complaint that Negro applicants lack the qualifications necessary for a particular job is often used to mask discrimination. Entry into many jobs is controlled by a series of requirements which are *guides* to the skills needed to enter the job. For the Negro applicant, however, these guides become a rigid set of qualifications and failure to meet one is grounds for rejection of the applicant. Often working against the Negro applicant, but sometimes in his favor, are ethnic quotas applied to certain types of jobs. When the quota is filled, the Negro applicant, no matter how well qualified, is told that there are no openings. Such quotas are often employed with the conscious intent of maintaining an "ethnic balance" in the work force. While the manifest intent of the quota may not be to restrict the number of openings to Negroes, there is no doubt that in many instances this is the practical effect. Much more subtle, although no less discriminatory, is the practice employed by some unions of having a member of the union vouch for an applicant. When the union has no Negro members, the possibility of finding someone who will vouch for the applicant is extremely remote. The role of management attitudes in racial discrimination towards Negro apprentices and craftsmen is described explicitly in the report of the Labor Department of the National Association for the Advancement of Colored People, "The Negro Wage-Earner and Apprenticeship Training Programs":

> There appears to be an inordinate fear on the part of management that white employees will not accept Negro workers in such occupations. This appears to hold true whether or not management has actually received this opinion from its employees, and is given additional significance because of the known contrary experiences through the nation and in contrast to management's usual insensitivity to other relevant employee attitudes and opinions. . . .
>
> Management may not be motivated to train Negro apprentices or hire Negro craftsmen because the principal reasons for such a course of action—labor shortages, legal obligation, realistic personnel administration, public relations and special appeals by interest groups may not be operative in a given industrial situation or for a particular firm. In addition, employers may be especially wary of placing skilled Negroes in public contact positions because of other anxieties regarding social mores.[1]
>
> A variety of studies show that management sources do not employ Negroes in artisan occupations because . . . it just isn't customary to hire Negroes for skilled-craft jobs. It is believed, by many management groups, that Negroes are just not interested in this type of work. Even if they were, management personnel will often state that they are not sufficiently trained, self-reliant or are careless in their work habits. Given such a set of beliefs, it is not surprising that apprenticeship opportunities are denied to many Negro youth by employers so motivated.
>
> Another factor limiting the apprenticeship skilled craftsmanship opportunities of Negroes is management's belief relative to the

[1]*The Negro Wage-Earner and Apprenticeship Training Programs: A Critical Analysis with Recommendations,* 1959, p. 22.

employment of Negroes in supervisory positions. In the New Haven-Charlotte analysis, it was the consensus of opinion that Negroes were not competent to supervise; but if they were, they would not fit into the work group; but if they did, customers and other firms would object. Other studies tend to confirm the prevalence of this stereotype in the thinking of management about Negroes.[1]

Some forms of discrimination flow from the way the occupational system operates. Much angry comment has resulted from the practice of guidance counselors advising Negro students not to prepare for jobs where employment opportunities for Negroes are limited. More often the counselor follows this practice in the belief that the best interests of the youth are being protected. So the reasoning goes, it is far better to steer the youngster toward those occupations in which he can find employment, even if his potentials are far greater, than to encourage him to pursue a career which is likely to end in bitter frustration and in not finding work at all. The priority here placed upon adjustment produces Negro youngsters unprepared to take advantage of jobs newly opened to Negroes.

Also built into the occupational system is the practice in many industries of relying upon specialized employment agencies for new personnel. This is particularly true of banking and finance, also insurance and real estate concerns, in New York City. Although reliance upon these employment specialists perhaps facilitates the flow of applicants sent into these particular fields, the fact that the specialties of these agencies are unknown to the general public means that Negroes do not apply and, consequently, do not enter the occupations these agencies control. But probably the most significant factor in restricting employment opportunities for Negroes in certain skilled crafts and certain other high paying occupations is due to the phenomenon of the "ethnic lock"[2] on jobs.

Through historical processes certain ethnic or religious minority groups come to predominate in certain kinds of jobs: the waterfront for the Italian, the police force for the Irish, the school system for Jews, and the personal services for Negroes. In addition, most skilled garment workers in New York are Jewish and of eastern European origin, or Italian. Many tool and die makers are of British and German extraction. The "ethnic lock" held by these groups over certain

[1]Ibid., p. 22.

[2]A similar conception has been formulated by Eli Ginsberg in *A Policy for Skilled Manpower,* Columbia University Press for the National Manpower Council, 1954, especially p. 249.

jobs means that employment opportunities in these fields, and the saliency of these fields as future occupations, are known and restricted primarily to members of these ethnic groups.

Even when persons of other ethnic origins succeed in entering one of these fields, chances are that they do not advance as rapidly, not so much because of overt discrimination, but for not being part of the in-group.

In a detailed study of employer attitudes toward young workers made by the Bureau of Social Science Research, Inc., as reported by Kohler and Fontaine, the findings showed that for Negroes jobs are harder to get. The larger companies, it appears, are more ready to hire non-whites than the small companies. And on jobs where the worker has to deal with the public, prejudices of the public were cited as the reason for *not being able* to hire Negroes. According to Kohler and Fontaine, "practical discrimination was shown most often by the familiar tactic of characterizing some jobs, usually the lowest, as 'Negro' jobs—so while these employers did hire Negroes, they did not offer the same chance for advancement that they did to whites."[1]

The deep consequences of the exclusion policies of industry and labor are well documented in the aforementioned report of the National Association for the Advancement of Colored People. Roy Wilkins, executive secretary of the NAACP, states this view based on the findings of that report:

> At present there is a broad exclusion of Negro youth from major apprenticeship training programs jointly conducted by industrial management and labor unions in the North as well as in the South. For many occupations the only way a worker can be recognized as qualified for employment is to complete the apprenticeship training program. This is true for the printing trades, among machinists and metal workers, the various crafts in the building and construction trades industry and many others. The role of the labor union in these occupations is decisive because the trade union usually determines who is admitted into the training program and, therefore, who is admitted into the union. This results in a loss to the entire economy when basic human resources are not utilized. This discrimination directly relates to the future status of Negro wage earners throughout the United

[1]Mary Conway Kohler and Andre Fontaine, "We Waste a Millions Kids a Year," *Saturday Evening Post,* March 10, 17, and 24, 1962, reprinted in *Hearings before Subcommittee on Employment and Manpower of the Senate Committee on Labor and Public Welfare,* Feb. 14, 1963.

States. Given a continuation of present rates of advance, it will take Negroes 138 years, or until the year 2094 to secure equal participation in skilled craft training and employment.[1]

The financial losses incurred through the many forms of racial discrimination practiced in the American economy have been conservatively estimated by the Council of Economic Advisers at about $30 billion a year in lost Gross National Product. At the National Urban League Equal Opportunity Day Dinner, November 19, 1963, Secretary of Commerce Luther Hodges indicated that this "is about equal to the gap which economists estimate exists between the productive potential of our economy and our actual annual production in the last five or six years."

There is no doubt that racial discrimination is a major factor in the occupational retardation of Negroes, yet the plethora of ineffective anti-discrimination and equal opportunities legislation leads one to suspect that the manner in which discrimination operates makes it relatively immune to the laws which have abolished crass discrimination. It would appear therefore that in addition to legislation and enforcement, effective techniques for reducing discrimination in employment must be as specific, subtle, and as pervasive as the evil which they seek to overcome.

Inadequacies in Education and Preparation for Employment

Under this heading are classified the educational preparation of Negroes, their job orientation, and their work motivation. Each of these determines, in a particular way, the nature of the youth as he enters the job market. It is generally known that the Negro enters the job market unprepared for the tasks which will be assigned to him. The crucial question is why are the bulk of Negroes so woefully unprepared.

All of the available data on the educational achievements of Negro youth show that many of them enter the job market equipped only for the most menial tasks. In fact, the data for the Central Harlem schools suggest that the youth are not being prepared for anything but the most menial work.

Clearly, the projected trends in employment point to the necessity for a thorough and comprehensive education for a place in tomorrow's world. Those jobs which are due to expand within the next

[1] *The Negro Wage-Earner and Apprenticeship Training Programs*, as cited, p. 3.

decade are those which will require considerable mathematical and verbal skills, plus a broad knowledge of science, literature, history, and social science. Concomitantly, those jobs requiring few of these skills are rapidly disappearing as machines and automation take over. The uniformly low level of performance of the pupils in Central Harlem schools has been noted in the chapter on education. Evidence of massive deterioration in academic achievement was presented showing that the further students progress in school, the larger the proportion who are performing below grade level. City-wide standard tests in the Central Harlem elementary schools revealed that students exhibited a uniformly low level of reading comprehension, word knowledge, and mathematics with a rather rapid relative deterioration from the third to the sixth grades.

Although about four out of five of Central Harlem's pupils enter an academic high school, this does not mean that they constitute an academicaly proficient group. While the vocational schools have raised their standards in recent years, many of the academic high schools, especially those that do not require an examination for admission, have become dumping grounds for the non-achieving student. The poor preparation of Central Harlem students is attested to by the fact that only 1 percent of them entered an academic high school requiring an admission examination.

An analysis of data from a study of Manhattan high school drop-outs conducted by the New York State Division of Youth indicates that the drop-out rate for Central Harlem high school students is consistently higher than that for students living elsewhere in Manhattan.

It goes without saying that in tomorrow's world a high school diploma will be the minimum requirement for entry into an increasing number of jobs. Yet, the high proportion of drop-outs in Central Harlem is not the whole story. On this, the findings from a Connecticut drop-out study are pertinent:

> With limited education, and virtually no experience, these drop-outs, whether white or Negro, must accept employment requiring a minimum of skills. In this respect, Negro dropouts seemed to operate at even a greater disadvantage than whites. They found it more difficult to get *any* type of job, and if successful, they were channeled more frequently into unskilled, non-white-collar jobs. Negro girls in particular did not enter clerical or sales jobs nearly as frequently as white girls. There is probably a hard core of racial discrimination involved even after we exclude the larger proportion of Negro girls who married early and therefore

> were not seeking gainful employment. Our findings on the gainful employment of dropouts, wherein lack of experience is constant for both whites and Negroes, seem to indicate the presence of racial discrimination during the earliest years of the Negro's entrance into the labor market.[1]

While it is true that lack of skills as manifested by the absence of a high school diploma plays a major role in the inability of the Central Harlem population to achieve parity of employment, the fact of racial discrimination aggravates the problem, but the story on the educational preparation of Negroes transcends the drop-out problem.

As indicated, even those youngsters who graduate from high school are so deficient in basic skills like reading and writing that for all practical purposes they have not received an education. This is especially true for youngsters brought up through the Harlem schools. The lower educational attainment of Harlem's youth means that few will enter those jobs which require competitive testing, and the number of jobs requiring such tests is increasing.

It has been charged over and over again that Negro youth lack motivation to undertake the training that is required to succeed in many fields. To the extent that this is true, it is related to the generally low socio-economic status of Negroes. At an early age Negro youth must frequently share in the support of the family unit. They do not have the financial support needed to sustain extended periods of training. In addition, it has been pointed out that a background of family poverty may force the young Negro, as soon as possible, to seek employment with little or no regard for the long-run factors of any given occupation. Thus, the prospect of earning a minimum wage in marginal employment is far more attractive than remaining in school and securing the necessary training for higher-paying employment at a later date. It has also been charged that Negroes are not motivated to break new ground in the employment field, preferring to walk the same old path that their ancestors and friends have trod. Fear of the unknown is not peculiar to one racial group, and the fact that Negroes have had traumatic experiences in seeking employment cannot be ignored. Further, in treading new paths, the lone Negro lacks the group support and encouragement which is available to other ethnic groups with friends and relatives already in the occupation.

Finally, in regard to the job preparation of Negroes, comment

[1] *Comparative Study of Negro and White Dropouts in Selected Connecticut High Schools,* State of Connecticut Commission on Civil Rights, 1959, pp. 45-46.

must be made about the repeated observation that Negro youth tend, much more than whites, to orient themselves to the white-collar occupations and shun the skilled trades. In large part this orientation is produced by an "ethnic lock" on jobs, which tends to reduce the saliency of the skilled trades for Negro youth. The import of this constricted perception is that those youngsters who fail to realize their white-collar aspirations (and inferior education insures that most will fail) have no alternative but to accept the low-paying, low-prestige jobs which remain open to them.

The foregoing indicates that, in a variety of ways, Negro youth enter the job market unprepared to fill a substantial proportion of the better jobs. The two major sources for this lack of preparation are the poor education they receive and the constraints of low socio-economic status. What is operative is a vicious cycle wherein poor preparation means poor jobs and low socio-economic status, resulting in poor preparation for the next generation to come.

The Process of Obtaining a Job

There are two general approaches to securing employment: through formal channels (employment agencies, newspaper ads, and professional associations) and through informal channels (parents, relatives, friends, and neighbors). The kind of employment obtained through formal channels is heavily dependent upon the amount and kind of formal education of the applicant. Employment obtained through informal channels depends upon the occupational contacts of the youth's friends, neighbors, and relatives. It appears that a large percentage of the jobs obtained by youth are through informal channels. A study of the early employment experiences of youth in seven communities[1] reports that 43 percent of drop-outs found jobs through friends and relatives, compared with 27 percent of high school graduates. The next most frequent method of obtaining a job was through personal application (33 percent of graduates and 31 percent of drop-outs). However, fewer than 6 percent of the students in this study were non-white. In the case of high school students looking for summer work,[2] a survey conducted by the New York City Youth Board found that two-thirds of the students secured employment through efforts of friends and relatives. In only 10 percent of

[1]*The Early Employment Experience of Youth in Seven Communities, 1952-1957,* Bureau of Labor Statistics, 1960, Table D-12, p. 83.

[2]*Report on a Special Youth Board Project,* Federation Employment and Guidance Service, April 1958. See also, *The Early Employment Experience of Youth in Seven Communities, 1952-1957,* as cited, Table D-12, p. 83.

the instances did schools, employment agencies, or guidance services help in finding jobs.

The fact that many young people find jobs through informal channels, however, operates to restrict the job opportunities available to Negro youth, for whites have wider contacts (if only by virtue of their numerical superiority) and more available resources. As the data on the occupations of Negroes show, the jobs they have, and consequently can make available to Negro youth, are those requiring little skill and offering little monetary reward.

In view of the greater enforced reliance of the Negro upon formal public channels, it is important to examine the effectiveness of the principal youth employment resources in the Central Harlem area.

About two years ago, the New York State Employment Service established the Youth Employment Service Program (YES) in order to provide a more accessible neighborhood employment service for the high school drop-out 16 to 18 years of age. Serving the Central Harlem community are five YES Centers, two of which are physically located within Central Harlem. One Center serves more than half of the Central Harlem area, the area from 130th to 164th Streets between St. Nicholas Avenue and the Harlem River. The other Centers serve sections of the remaining Central Harlem area as well as young people from outside the Central Harlem area.

The consequence of token staffing and the restricted availability of these Centers can be seen from the number of desk interviews, referrals, and placements made over an 11-month period.[1] The main YES Center in Central Harlem, staffed by one counselor and open four days a week (from 9:30 a.m. to 2 p.m.), placed 81 persons out of 448 referred during the 11-month period, a ratio of less than one in five or fewer than eight a month. In two of the Centers, where one counselor divides her time between them (one is open for two days a week, the other the remaining three days of the week), the ratio of placements to referrals was one in four. That a more adequate staff and wider availability of the facility would affect positively the effectiveness of the service is clear from the degree of activity of another Center having a staff of two counselors (and open from 9 a.m. to 5 p.m.) on a five-day-week basis. Desk interviews in this Center were more than seven times that of the main Central Harlem YES Center, while

[1]Analysis based on statistics contained in a letter dated August 26, 1963 from Alex Altheim, manager of Youth Placement Service, New York State Employment Service.

placements in this Center were made for nearly half of the young people referred to a job.

The number of desk interviews can be considered an index of the needs of young people for employment, even though the same person may be represented in the data several times during a year. The counselor at the most active of the Centers reported that many young people hold jobs for one or two months only, while the majority do not hold jobs for more than three months. Most of them dislike the kinds of jobs they get and do not remain beyond their period of immediate financial need. This can probably be explained by the fact that most of the jobs in which the youth were placed were low-level jobs in service industries which do not hold the promise of any future—jobs such as delivery boy, messenger, dishwasher, counter girl, checker, stock clerk, laundry worker, and factory worker. A few girls were placed as typists, salesgirls, file clerks, proofreaders, and sewing machine operators.

The ratio of referrals to desk interviews, then, is indeed of interest. On an average, referrals were made for half the applicants receiving a desk interview. Somewhat less than four out of every ten applicants referred actually got jobs. In three of the Centers, this ratio was considerably less (18, 24, and 26 percent, respectively). Placements in relation to the total number of desk interviews indicate that about one out of six desk interviews culminated in employment.

To compensate either for the lack of a job referral or for the lack of job skills or job preparation, counseling interviews are held with the applicant. The overall ratio of counseling interviews to desk interviews was one in five. It is significant that the two Centers having the lowest ratio of placements to referrals had the higher ratios of counseling interviews.

It seems that the counselors were particularly active in the case of boy drop-outs for whom the highest percentage of referrals and placements were made. This may have been due to the fact that those seeking service had some kind of work experience and were not entering the job market for the first time. According to a survey conducted at one of the Centers, three-fourths of the boys and a majority of the girls had held jobs previously. It is clear that the jobs secured for them were, however, still of a marginal nature. Subsequent contacts at the YES Center after placement indicated that more than one-fourth of those placed held their jobs for one month or less, while many had been placed in two or three jobs within the previous period.

A detailed study of the characteristics of the applicants in one of the part-time Centers showed that two-thirds were boys. Furthermore, a higher proportion of the boy applicants were drop-outs (two out of three boys compared to one out of three girls). Of those who were not drop-outs, most were still in school and sought part-time, after school, or summer jobs. High school graduates represented 10 percent of the male applicants, but better than a fourth of the female job-seekers. Almost half of the drop-outs had taken a general course in high school while a third of the boys, and a fourth of the girls, had taken vocational courses. Of interest is the fact that while YES technically is supposed to serve young people between the ages of 16 and 18, one-fourth of the job seekers from the Central Harlem area were 19 and 20 years of age, which points to a need for service to this age group as well.

On the basis of the available data, it appears that YES Centers serve about 7 percent of the youth population, 16 to 20 years of age, from the Central Harlem area. This figure is lower although close to that of 10 percent obtained by the Youth Board study on the proportion of youth looking for summer work who are served by formal agencies.

In summary, the impact of the YES program upon the youth in the Central Harlem community appears to be minimal, since it touches a very small percentage of the youth population. A matter of even greater concern is that the YES program does not secure more regular employment leading to some kind of occupational career.

However, the efforts of the staff, in attempting to serve the youth in the face of such limited resources, do reflect a glimmer of hope in regard to what might be accomplished in a program better staffed and with provisions for more effective training, counseling, and job development.

Program Implications

A comprehensive employment program for Central Harlem's youth must be geared toward revamping the various systems which feed upon one another. It is not enough to understand the framework within which we must move but also, and most crucial, we must challenge the existing situation by training youngsters for more than marginal positions, and at the same time demand the removal of racial barriers.

For such a program to be effective, it must deal directly with the factors or forces which are responsible for these inequalities. It must upgrade the educational system which spawns functional illiterates and helps perpetuate personnel practices which exclude Negro youth, thereby making it impossible for them to be incorporated into the economy. In a real sense, the employment problem of Negro youth reflects the woeful inadequacy of the education of Negro youngsters. In effect, it is not necessary for even a most prejudiced personnel officer to discriminate against Negro youth because the schools have done the job for him. The massively gross inefficiency of the public schools has so limited the occupational possibilities of Negro youth that, if not made mandatory, a life of menial status or unemployment is virtually inevitable.

A second chance to secure compensatory education must be given to those Negro youth who are already the victims of educational deficiencies, to enable them to improve their occupational possibilities. In other words, given the staggering educational inefficiency, it is *now* mandatory to give the present casualties the type of crash educational preparation which can permit them to profit from specific skill training.

Barriers to the employment of Negro youth, enforced by the unions in apprenticeship programs, must be removed. By being less defensive and rigid, the unions could make a positive contribution to the training of Negro youth, helping them to learn, and eventually to earn, thereby carrying their weight in their communities and in our complex industrial system. The establishment of pre-apprenticeship and apprenticeship training courses under the leadership of skilled craftsmen, could give Negro youth new incentives to work and to achieve by teaching them skills and devotion to the job.

Crucial to an effective and realistic training and employment program for the youth of Central Harlem is actual work experience, which teaches basic job requirements and lays the foundation for later and more intensive skilled training. It also provides experience that youth can sell to employers when seeking other than marginal employment.

Emphasis must also be given to helping Negro youth to a broadened view of the labor market. It has been suggested elsewhere in this chapter that the general ignorance among Negro youth of employment opportunities and job requirements demanded by our complex world of work is just as powerful a deterrent to employment as is outright racial discrimination. With such a diversity of employment opportunities open to the qualified, it is crucial that some systematic procedure exist through which Central Harlem youth can be informed about the occupations for which they might qualify and be told how to prepare for them.

Included in a realistic and comprehensive occupational training and employment program should be a counseling program which is administered within the context of expanded work opportunities. The goals of this program should be the development not only of a positive self-image, motivation, and an understanding of the world of work, but also realistic perceptions of dress, comportment, and approach to employers.

Also involved is agitation and pressure for expanded job opportunities for Negroes, not in terms of a single job here and there, but in terms of a realistic program designed to open up massive numbers of jobs everywhere. A final task involves inducing corporations, especially those employing Negroes for the first time, to develop procedures which will enable the Negro to qualify for employment. It is certain that for some jobs the number of fully qualified Negroes willing to enter the occupation will remain minuscule until education's basic job is accomplished, but the opening of new opportunities cannot wait for the proper preparation of the next generation of Negro youth.

The Urban Ghetto and Negro Job Problems: A Diagnosis and a Proposed Plan of Action

Senator Robert F. Kennedy

[*From a statement given before the Senate Subcommittee on Executive Reorganization, August 15, 1966.*]

What the City Should Provide

What should we expect from our cities? A great historian of urban life, Lewis Mumford, has written: "What makes the city in fact one is the common interest in justice and the common aim, that of pursuing the good life." He drew, in turn, upon Aristotle, who wrote that the city "should be such as may enable the inhabitants to live at once temperately and liberally in the enjoyment of leisure." If we add the objective of rewarding and satisfying work, we have a goal worthy of the effort and energy of this entire generation of Americans.

Therefore, the city is not just housing and stores. It is not just education and employment, parks and theaters, banks and shops. It is a place where men should be able to live in dignity and security and harmony, where the great achievements of modern civilization and the ageless pleasures afforded by natural beauty should be available to all.

The beginning of action is to understand the problem. We know riots are a problem. We know that poverty is a problem. But underneath these problems and all the others are a series of converging forces which rip at the fabric of life in the American city.

By city, we mean not just downtown, or the central city, but the whole vast sprawling organism—covering dozens of communities and crossing State lines. It is not a political unit, but a living social and economic body—extending into suburbs and beyond into tens of thousands of outlying acres, to be covered all too soon with homes and shops and factories.

Five Forces Which Disrupt the City

One great problem is sheer growth—growth which crowds people into slums, thrusts suburbs out over the countryside, burdens to the breaking point all our old ways of thought and action—our systems of transport and water supply and education, and our means of raising money to finance these vital services.

A second is destruction of the physical environment, stripping people of contact with sun and fresh air, clean rivers, grass and trees—condemning them to a life among stone and concrete, neon lights and an endless flow of automobiles. This happens not only in the central city, but in the very suburbs where people once fled to find nature. "There is no police so effective," said Emerson, "as a good hill and a wide pasture * * * where the boys * * * can dispose of their superfluous strength and spirits." We cannot restore the pastures; but we must provide a chance to enjoy nature, a chance for recreation, for pleasure and for some restoration of that essential dimension of human existence which flows only from man's contact with the natural world around him.

A third is the increasing difficulty of transportation—adding concealed, unpaid hours to the workweek; removing men from the social and cultural amenities that are the heart of the city; sending destructive swarms of automobiles across the city, leaving behind them a band of concrete and a poisoned atmosphere. And sometimes—as in Watts—our surrender to the automobile has so crippled public transport that thousands literally cannot afford to go to work elsewhere in the city.

A fourth destructive force is the concentrated poverty and racial tension of the urban ghetto—a problem so vast that the barest recital of its symptoms is profoundly shocking:

> Segregation is becoming the governing rule: Washington is only the most prominent example of a city which has become overwhelmingly Negro as whites move to the suburbs; many other cities are moving along the same road—for example, Chica-

go, which, if present trends continue, will be over 50 percent Negro by 1975. The ghettoes of Harlem and Southside and Watts are cities in themselves, areas of as much as 350,000 people.

Poverty and unemployment are endemic: from one-third to one-half of the families in these areas live in poverty; in some, male unemployment may be as high as 40 percent; unemployment of Negro youths nationally is over 25 percent.

Welfare and dependency are pervasive: one-fourth of the children in these ghettoes, as in Harlem, may receive Federal Aid to Dependent Children; in New York City, ADC alone costs over $20 million a month; in our five largest cities, the ADC bill is over $500 million a year.

Housing is overcrowded, unhealthy, and dilapidated: the last housing census found 43 percent of urban Negro housing to be substandard; in these ghettoes, over 10,000 children may be injured or infected by rat bites every year.

Education is segregated, unequal, and inadequate: the high school dropout rate averages nearly 70 percent; there are academic high schools in which less than 3 percent of the entering students will graduate with an academic diploma.

Health is poor and care inadequate: infant mortality in the ghettoes is more than twice the rate outside; mental retardation among Negroes caused by inadequate prenatal care is more than seven times the white rate; one-half of all babies born in Manhattan last year will have had no prenatal care at all; deaths from diseases like tuberculosis, influenza, and pneumonia are two to three times as common as elsewhere.

Fifth is both cause and consequence of all the rest. It is the destruction of the sense, and often the fact, of community, of human dialog, the thousand invisible strands of common experience and purpose, affection and respect which tie men to their fellows. Community is expressed in such words as neighborhood, civic pride, friendship. It provides the life-sustaining force of human warmth and security, a sense of one's own human significance in the accepted association and companionship of others.

Negro Problem in Cities is Paramount

But of all our problems, the most immediate and pressing, the one which threatens to paralyze our very capacity to act, to obliterate our vision of the future, is the plight of the Negro of the center city. For this plight—and the riots which are its product and symptom—threaten to divide Americans for generations to come; to add to the ever-present difficulties of race and class the bitter legacy of violence and destruction and fear.

The riots which have taken place—and the riots which we know may all too easily take place in the future—are therefore an intolerable threat to the most essential interests of every American, black or white—the mind's peace and the body's safety and the community's order, to all that makes life worthwhile. None of us should look at this violence as anything but destructive of self, community, and nation. But we should not delude ourselves. The riots are not crises which can be resolved as suddenly as they arose.

First, it is clear that our present policies have been directed to particular aspects of our problems—and have often ignored or even harmed our larger purposes. For example, Federal housing and highway programs have accelerated the move of middle-income families and business to the suburbs, while virtually ignoring the cities' needs for new revenue and declining tax base. Our welfare programs have helped people to subsist. But after 30 years of Federal welfare programs, we have just begun our first effort to help these people become independent of welfare. And this effort—the work experience program of the Economic Opportunity Act—is so new and so meager that last year, it managed to spend less than half of its $160 million budget.

Our public housing has been built in the center cities, on our highest-cost land, further reinforcing the segregation of the city; in 1962, 80 percent of all federally assisted public housing projects were occupied solely by members of one race.

Public housing was once thought of as the answer to the problems of slums. Therefore, it became another of those programs, addressed to some symptomatic shortcoming, which has ignored the wider problem, the other needed government action. Our housing projects were built largely without either reference or relevance to the underlying problems of poverty, unemployment, social disorganization, and alienation which caused people to need assistance in the first place.

Too many of the projects, as a result, become jungles—places of despair and anger for their residents, and for the cities they were designed to save. Many of them are preserved from this fate only by screening, such as is practiced in New York City, to keep the "problem" families—who, of course, are most in need of help—out of public housing projects, while families with incomes as high as $9,000 a year may live there.

And, therefore, it has been, too often, a failure. For no single program, no attempted solution of any single element of the problem, can be the answer.

In recent years, education has come to be regarded as the answer. But past efforts to improve life conditions simply by the expenditure of more money on education have not been notably successful: A recent Brookings Institute study finds that in only 5 percent of all cases is there any observable correlation between increased expenditure on education in the ghetto and better jobs later in life. And the major study prepared for the Office of Education has also found that other factors—family, home, general environment and motivation—determine whether a child can benefit at all from the best schools we provide. Education has failed to motivate many of our young people because of what they could see around them: the sharply restricted opportunities open to the people of the ghetto, whatever their educatoin. The Negro college graduate earns, in his lifetime, no more than a white man whose education ended at the eighth grade.

Now we have begun, with Project Headstart, to reach further back toward infancy, in an effort to equalize educational opportunity where it counts most—at the beginning of life. But we have not carried that insight to its point of greatest importance: the family in which the child first finds itself, its vision of the world, shaping its response to all that follows for the full threescore and 10.

Importance of Family Life

We know the importance of strong families to development; we know that financial security is important for family stability and that there is strength in the father's earning power. But in dealing with Negro families, we have too often penalized them for staying together. As Richard Cloward has said:

> Men for whom there are no jobs will nevertheless mate like other men, but they are not so likely to marry. Our society has preferred to deal with the resulting female-headed families not by putting the men to work but by placing the unwed mothers and children on public welfare—substituting checkwriting machines for male wage earners. By this means, we have robbed men of manhood, women of husbands, and children of fathers. To create a stable monogamous family, we need to provide men (especially Negro men) with the opportunity to be men, and that involves enabling them to perform occupationally.

And here we come to an aspect of our cities' problems almost untouched by Federal action: the unemployment crisis of the Negro ghetto.

The White House Conference on Civil Rights placed employment and income problems of Negroes at the head of its agenda for action in the United States.

Negro unemployment, it said—

> is of disaster proportions. Even in today's booming economy, the unemployment rate for Negroes is about 7 percent—more than twice the average for whites. * * * The gap between whites and non-whites is even greater for married people and heads of households who are most in need of a job to support their families. * * * In some areas, such as Watts in Los Angeles, the rate of unemployment among Negroes is as high as 40 percent. * * *

Negro Unemployment is Crucial Problem

Any attempt to discuss the problems of the cities, and the ghettoes which presently threaten their future, cannot ignore the findings of commission after commission, student after student, public official after public official. The McCone Commission looked into the Watts riots—and said that the most serious problem in Watts is unemployment. The Wall Street Journal looked at Oakland—and said that the core of Oakland's plight is unemployment. Kenneth Clark's pioneering Haryou study looked at Harlem—and said that Harlem's key problem is unemployment.

This should not be strange to us.

In an age of increasing complaints about the welfare state, it is well to remember that less than 25 percent of those living in poverty receive public assistance. We earn our livings, support our families, purchase the comforts and ease of life with work. To be without it is to be less than a man—less than a citizen—hardly, in a real sense, to be a father or brother, or son, to have any identity at all. To be without function, without use to our fellow citizens, is to be in truth the "invisible man" of whom Ralph Ellison wrote so eloquently—the man who, John Adams said a century and a half ago, suffers the greatest possible humiliation—"he is simply not seen."

The crisis in Negro unemployment, therefore, is significant far beyond its economic effects—devastating as those are. For it is both measure and cause of the extent to which the Negro lives apart—the extent to which he is alienated from the general community. More than segregation in housing and schools, more than differences in attitudes or life-styles, it is unemployment which marks the Negro of the urban ghetto off and apart from the rest of us—from Negroes who have jobs (including Negro leaders) almost as much as from whites. Unemployment is having nothing to do—which means having nothing to do with the rest of us.

A Million Invisible People

It is a shocking fact—but it is a fact nonetheless—that we are literally unaware even of the existence of more than a million Negro Americans. Our census system—our social security system—the whole array of Government computers which threaten to compile on some reel of tape every bit of information ever recorded on the people in this room—this system nowhere records the names or faces or identities of a million Negro men. Seventeen percent of Negro teenagers, 13 percent of men in the prime working age of the thirties, are uncounted in our unemployment statistics, our housing statistics: simply drifting about our cities, living without families, as if they were of no greater concern to our daily lives than so many sparrows or spent matches.

Some are "found" in later life, when they may settle down. Some reappear in our statistics only at death. Others remind us of their presence when we read of rising crime rates. And some, undoubtedly, became visible in the riots which will be much discussed before this committee.

In my judgment, the question of employment and income is central to the solution of the problems of the city. But I do not stress it so strongly here because I believe it to be the only solution, or to be a solution by itself. There are and must be many other elements to any truly comprehensive defense (we are not in an attacking position) against the ill which afflicts us. Rather I stress employment here for the following reasons:

Priority of Employment

First, it is the most direct and embarrassing—and therefore the most important—of our failures. Whatever people may feel about open housing or open schools—though I myself am deeply committed to both—still there can be no argument at all, no sense for even a committed segregationist, in the maintenance of Negro unemployment. Making sure men have jobs does not by itself mean that they will live with you, or that their chldren will go to school with you. It does not mean, in the long run, higher taxes or welfare costs; indeed, it means far less, and lessened costs of crime and crime prevention as well. It means the use of unused resources, and greater prosperity for all. Meeting the unemployment problem can only be to the benefit of every American of every shade of opinion.

But we have not done it.

Second, employment is the only true long-run solution; only if Negroes achieve full and equal employment will they be able to support themselves and their families, become active citizens and not passive objects of our action, become contributing members and not recipients of our charity. This is not to say that education, for example, is not critical to future employment and self-sufficiency; of course it is. But it is to say that unless we achieve employment, by whatever means or programs, we will never solve the problem. People with jobs can buy or rent their own housing; people with adequate incomes can see that their children are educated; people with jobs can mark out their own relationships with their fellows of whatever color. But without employment, without basic economic security and self-sufficiency, any other help we provide will be only temporary in effect.

Third, there are Government programs which seem at least to have some promise of ameliorating, if not solving, some of the other problems of the Negro and the city. But no Government program now operating gives any substantial promise of meeting the problem of Negro unemployment in the ghetto. The Manpower Development and Training Act, the Vocational Development Act—these and similar efforts have been going on for 5 years. Yet in those same 5 years, while family income nationwide was increasing 14 percent, and family income of Negroes nationwide was increasing 24 percent, family income in Watts dropped by 8 percent. Just from last June to this, says the Labor Department, 950,000 new jobs were created for young men—but only 33,000, about 3.7 percent, went to Negroes—so that Negro youth unemployment is still, at a very minimum 26.9 percent. A Labor Department spokesman explained that Negro youth "just don't have the connections."

That remark sums up what is wrong with our cities. It capsules as well the consequences of our past errors of omission and commission. And it sets the agenda for a program for the cities today.

Comprehensive Attack on Ghetto Needed

The program must contain certain elements.

It must attack the fundamental pathology of the ghetto—for unless the deprivation and alienation of the ghetto are eliminated, there is no hope for the city. And it must attack these problems within a framework that coordinates action on the four central elements: employment, education, housing, and a sense of community.

This is not to say that other problems and programs are not

important—questions of police relations, recreation, health and other services, and the thousands of other factors that make life bearable or a thing of joy. It is to say that these other questions can only be properly dealt with in concert with action on the major problems. A police force, for example, can exert every possible effort, and imagination, and will to better relations with the community. But it still must enforce the law. And if the conditions of the ghetto produce stealing—for which people must be arrested—or the nonpayment of rent—for which people must be evicted, even if they have no place to go—then the police will inevitably bear the brunt of the ghetto's resentment at the conditions which the police, through no fault of their own, enforce. For another example, recreation is good and necessary for all of us. But a donated swimming pool will not replace an absent father; nor will it produce income for the father's son, who may have to steal a pair of swimming trunks to use the pool.

Libraries are for those who can read, and sports for those strong enough to participate in them. Each strand we pick up leads us further into the central web of life, coming closer to every other thread of thought and action. The web must be grasped whole.

Plan For Dealing With Urban Condition

The plan begins with a perspective: that questions of technical or surface integration are far less important now than is the building of self-sufficiency and self-determination within the Negro community; in fact, that what is too often an undifferentiated mass must be helped to form a coherent and cohesive community. Thus it is important that Negroes who have achieved financial and social security should have complete freedom to choose where to live. But it is far more important that the vast majority of Negroes be enabled to achieve basic financial and social security where they live now. It will be the work of years, and of all Americans, white and black, to decide whether most people will live in substantially homogeneous neighborhoods. But there should be no question that black neighborhoods, as well as white, must be places of security and dignity and achievement and comfort.

Needs of the Cities

It begins with a base of employment, in a vastly expanded and accelerated program of urban reconstruction. Our cities are in dire need of rebuilding, especially at the core; in spite of the largest slum clearance and rebuilding program in the United States, the number of unsound housing units in New York, for example, increased from 420,000 in 1960 to 520,000 in 1965. In most major cities, great stocks of housing built to accommodate the influx of migrants, from rural areas and abroad, in this early part of this century are long overdue for rehabilitation or replacement.

Our public facilities are in similar need of repair. In New York City, for example, the Commissioner of Hospitals said even before medicare that the city-owned hospitals alone required $50 million worth of renovation in each of the next 10 years; and the dozens of private hospitals are in similar need. Center city schools and colleges are notorious for the physical deterioration of their physical plant.

Our cities' beaches are polluted and parklands eroded, parks and playgrounds inadequate to the minimum demands of our people.

And in the coming years, these needs will multiply almost beyond measure. Just in the next 40 years, the urban population of the United States will double—which means we must build homes and hospitals, schools and shops and factories, roads and railways and airports, equal to everything we have managed to build in the 200 years of this Republic.

The Labor Department estimates that even without major government stimulation, employment in construction will expand more rapidly than in any other field in the next 10 years. Given, then, the known needs of the next four decades, it is clear that if we begin now, with proper initiative and stimulation, to repair the decay of the past and meet the needs of the future, we can create hundreds of thousands of new jobs directly, and through the new demands stimulated by this addition, millions more indirectly.

But let us not make the mistake of regarding these just as jobs; and let us not erect buildings for their own sake. Our needs, and the programs we will now undertake to meet them, are in fact an opportunity to make every Government program, and many private efforts, more effective than ever before. In any program of rebuilding now begun, therefore, I urge the following:

First, priority in employment on these projects should go to residents of the areas in which they are undertaken. The fathers and young men of Harlem need work—and this is the best kind of work we could possibly offer them.

For this is man's work—work which is dignified, which is hard and exacting, which is at the same time rewarding to the man who does it and rewarding to the community around him. Much of it is work which can be done by unskilled workers, who now have the most difficult time finding jobs; but in such programs there would be jobs of all kinds, including those requiring administrative and managerial skills.

Jobs Bring Hope

Creating these jobs would say to the residents of Harlem that there is hope—that there is a future—that all of us are truly determined to change the conditions under which they live. In my judgment, it is not too much to say that the ready availability of jobs in Harlem would make a major change in the entire environment in which its young people grow up.

Second, public and private training programs should concentrate their funds and their efforts in on-the-job training on these projects. Not only will job training be needed to make initial employment possible for many of the ghetto's residents; just as important, the availability of jobs will make many of our training programs more meaningful than they have been before. Construction work has traditionally been taught through a system of apprenticeship—which means a 1-to-1 teacher-student ratio, a system of learning by doing, a system in which learning has immediate rewards and the relationship of skill to increased earning power is clear. In a very real sense, these projects could be a vast new educational institution—teaching skills, but teaching pride of self and pride of craft as well.

Third, our conventional educational system should be directly integrated with the rebuilding effort; for many of our most serious educational problems, there is real hope of solution within such a program.

Stimulate Motivation of Youth

The central problem of motivation, for example, would be directly confronted. Any high school student who so desired—whether for financial or other reasons—could be allowed to leave school to work on such a project. The schools would maintain jurisdiction over these students; and they would, as a condition of employment, be required to continue schooling at least part time until the requirements for graduation were met. In fact, all jobs on these projects should require part-time study to remedy educational deficiencies, and advancement on the job should be directly related to school credits gained, just as it is in the Armed Forces. Without the need to discipline unmotivated students, the schools would find it far easier to educate students who wish to learn. And the young men who work on these projects will learn that the ability to read a blueprint or a specification is worth returning to school to acquire.

Indeed, it would be possible to open up new opportunities for every level of education. A young man showing supervisory abilities, for example, should be encouraged to study business or public administration at the college level, either part time or full time. Strawbosses should be able to become superintendents, and perhaps receive engineering training. Appropriate branches of city and State universities could be established in the immediate neighborhoods to allow maximum participation in this process.

Fourth, present social service programs, particularly welfare, should be integrated with the rebuilding effort. The program I envision would make it possible for families to turn dependence into self-sufficiency; but we must work to make possibilities into fact—for example, by using a man's new employment as an aid to reuniting him with his family.

For another example, the rebuilding program should focus in significant degree on unmet social needs—such as by constructing clinics and physicians' group practice facilities in the ghettos, which are notoriously short of medical services.

Using the building program as a base, occupational opportunities and training should be opened up in all related ways. As building takes place, for example, some should learn and then operate building supply businesses; small furniture manufacturing establishments; and other neighborhood shops. As health clinics are established, young people should be trained as medical aids. Buildings should be decorated and embellished by art students; housing should contain facilities in which students of music and drama could put on entertainments.

It should be clear that the possibilities of such a program are limited only by our imagination and daring. For it does no more—and no less—than apply to the needs of the ghetto the same entrepreneurial vision which has brought the rest of us to our present state of comfort and strength.

Community Development Corporation

And to fulfill that entrepreneurial vision—to bring the people of the ghetto into full participation in the economy—which is the lifeflood of America—it will be necessary to create new institutions of initiative and action, responding directly to the needs and wishes of these people themselves. This program will require Government assistance, just as nearly all American growth has depended on some Government assistance and support. But it cannot and should not be owned or managed by Government, by the rules and regulations of bureaucracy, hundreds of miles away, responding to a different constituency.

The measure of the success of this or any other program will be the extent to which it helps the ghetto to become a community—a functioning unit, its people acting together on matters of mutual concern, with the power and resources to affect the conditions of their own lives. Therefore the heart of the program, I believe, should be the creation of community development corporations, which would carry out the work of construction, the hiring and training of workers, the provision of services, the encouragement of associated enterprises.

Such corporations might be financed along these lines: They would receive an initial contribution of capital from the Federal Government; but for their ongoing activities, they should need and receive no significantly greater subsidy than is ordinarily available to nonprofit housing corporations under present law. As with all other housing and commercial construction, the bulk of funds would come as loans from the great financial institutions—banks, insurance companies, corporations. Government would enter by way of the common devices of loan repayment insurance, some subsidization of the interest rate, and in some cases, assistance in the acquisition of land.

Partnership with Private Sector

These community development corporations, I believe, would find a fruitful partnership with American industry; many firms, of which U.S. Gypsum is perhaps the furthest along, have actively undertaken the search for ways to bring the ghetto into the national economic market. Loans and technical cooperation from industry and commerce; trained manpower and organization from labor unions; academic and educational partnership with the universities; funds for education and training such as those provided under many present Federal programs: these would be resources thus far unknown to the ghetto, resources sufficient to mount a real attack on the intertwined problems of housing and jobs, education, and income.

Citizen Participation Necessary

But a further and critical element in the structure, financial and otherwise, of these corporations should be the full and dominant participation by the residents of the community concerned. Through purchase of cooperative and condominium apartments; through subscription to equity shares; through receiving part of their pay on these projects in equity shares; such as has been done in farsighted private enterprises such as Sears, Roebuck—in these ways, residents of the ghettos could at once contribute to the betterment of their immediate conditions, and build a base for full participation in the economy—in the ownership and the savings and the self-sufficiency which the more fortunate in our Nation already take for granted.

Such corporations, each devoted to improving the conditions of a single community, could go far to changing, perhaps in revolutionary ways, our techniques for meeting urban needs—for developing and coordinating the many services and facilities, necessities and comforts, which community living requires. For example, there is in the entire area of Watts, not one movie theater; and the notorious lack of public transportation in between Watts and the rest of the city makes theaters elsewhere virtually unavailable to most of the area's residents. A corporation with minimal capital, engaged in and experienced in construction work, could build a theater and either lease it out for operation or operate it as a community venture, with revenues paying off the mortgage—thus creating, at once, employment and recreation for the community. For another example, medical care is a more pressing need in many ghettos. But a community development corporation could build the facilities—and carry the cost—of a physicians' group practice facility in a housing project, and rent the completely furnished offices to young, active practitioners.

Present Organization of Social Services is Inadequate

The point is that—in the supposed interests of efficiency—we have thus far provided municipal services only on a citywide basis: using the same kind of organizational structure whether the city had 2,000 people or 2 million. This technique has proved unable to meet the special needs of the ghetto, and should now be replaced by a system which allows a recognizable community to organize and secure those services which meet its own unique needs. But we may well find that this system would have benefits for nondeprived neighborhoods within the city—allowing each to determine what kind of services, recreational facilities, perhaps even what kind of zoning and planning it will have. At least for matters of immediate neighborhood concern these community development corporations might return us part way toward the ideals of community on a human scale which is so easily lost in metropolis: but as Jefferson said when describing a somewhat similar institution, "elementary republics of the wards," which he urged, "begin them only for a single purpose; they will soon show for what others they are the best instruments."

Plan Would Reduce Alienation of Negro Youth

One purpose for which they must be an instrument, however; and one purpose which must be served by every aspect of the program I have proposed, or any other program—is to try to meet the increasing alienation of Negro youth. In a sense, young urban Negroes are only a particular case of a situation which prevails all over the world—a gap between generations so broad and deep that it can lead to the most fundamental rejections of society by the young, or the most terrible revolutions in society, worked by the young. Here in America, white young people as well as Negroes are finding their own answers, their own paths to the future which is theirs. And this is as it should be; the future is theirs, though it may be very different from what we would wish for ourselves. But among Negro youth we can sense, in their alienation, a frustration so terrible, an energy and determination so great, that it must find constructive outlet or result in unknowable danger for us all. This alienation will be reduced to reasonable proportions, in the end, only by bringing the Negro into his rightful place in this Nation. But we must work to try and understand, to speak and touch across the gap, and not leave their voices of protest to echo unheard in the ghetto of our ignorance.

Suggested Additional Readings

1. Coleman, James S. *Equality of Educational Opportunity.* U.S. Department of Health, Education, and Welfare, Office of Education, 1966.
2. Dentler, Robert A. "Barriers to Northern School Desegregation," *Daedalus* (Winter, 1965).
3. Goldberg, Miriam. "Factors Affecting Educational Attainment in Depressed Urban Areas," *Education in Depressed Areas,* ed. A. Harry Passow. New York: Columbia University Teachers College Press, 1963.
4. Grier, George and Eunice. *Equality and Beyond: Housing Goals in the Great Society.* Chicago: Quadrangle Books, 1966.
5. Harlem Youth Opportunities Unlimited, Inc. *Youth in the Ghetto.* New York: Harlem Youth Opportunities Unlimited, Inc., 1964.
6. Harrington, Michael. "Economics for the Minority," *IUD Agenda,* 1 (September, 1965).
7. Hill, Herbert. "Demographic Change and Racial Ghettos: The Crisis of American Cities," *Journal of Urban Law* (Winter, 1966).
8. National Urban League. *Education and Race.* New York: National Urban League, 1966.

9. Schwartz, Michael, and Henderson, George. "The Culture of Unemployment: Some Notes on Negro Children," *Blue-Collar World*, ed. Arthur B. Shostak and William Gomberg. Englewood Cliffs, N.J.: Prentice-Hall, Inc., 1966.

10. Sexton, Patricia C. *Education and Income: Inequalities in our Public Schools*. New York: Viking Press, 1961.

Chapter 4

Labor Market Structure and Negro Employment

Introduction

In the preceding chapters, various authors have presented an impressive array of evidence to substantiate the economic distress of lower-class Negroes. It seems obvious that these Negroes are disadvantaged both in preparation for the labor market and participation in it. Less obvious are the components that contribute to and sustain this problem. Granted that Negro lower-class life may not adequately prepare the Negro for a productive role in the economy, one can marshal considerable evidence to support the thesis that the structure of the economy and the labor market imposes formidable barriers to the economic advancement of the Negro. We can identify five elements of our industrial society that act to sustain economic inequalities between Negroes and whites: (1) labor force participation trends, (2) management-white worker attitudes and perspectives toward the Negro, (3) the attitudes and policies of labor union leaders, (4) employment policies of the firm, and (5) technological changes in the economy. Let us discuss each of these in turn.

(1) Labor Force Participation Trends

The structure of the labor market is ever changing. Some groups are participating more today than in other years, other groups are participating less. The most significant long-term trend in the labor market has been a general increase in labor-force participation, i.e., of those able to work, a greater proportion are working today than in years gone by. However, this increase has not been characteristic of all groups. For example, since the Korean War, the rate for men in prime working years (ages 35-44) has remained stable for whites but has declined for nonwhites.

At least four labor-force participation trends have disadvantaged Negroes. First, the rate of increase of female labor-force participation has been higher than the rate of increase for males. Among Negroes this sex difference has been very striking. Negro females have a higher rate of participation than do Negro men, and the gap has been widening. At a time when Negro female participation is at an all-time high and steadily increasing, labor-force participation for Negro males is declining. This difference reflects the unprecedented demand for female workers in the clerical and service occupations. While Negro females have been making significant gains in semiprofessional occupations (e.g., practical nursing) and continue to dominate in domestic employment, Negro males have found themselves in occupations—largely in heavy commodity manufacturing—where significant productivity gains have eroded job opportunities. Thus, even the sharp gains in female labor-force participation have been offset by the sharp decrease in unskilled jobs for Negro males.

A second trend has also disadvantaged the Negro male. A number of studies show that once displaced from a job, he finds it harder than do whites to become reemployed. This may be a consequence of discrimination, or an inability to qualify for training programs, or a failure to meet rising job requirements in the market place. Between 1950 and 1960 there was a significant drop in labor-force participation for Negro males in all age groups, suggesting that many Negroes become discouraged in job hunting and withdraw from the labor force. The majority of these Negro men still have the potential for a long work life but find themselves relegated to nonproductive, dependency roles in our industrial society.

A third consideration in Negro disadvantagement is the sharp rise in the labor market demand for highly educated workers. Both the employed and unemployed of today have higher levels of education than did their predecessors of a decade ago. The rise in education is apparent among all groups, but the education gap between Negroes and whites persists. Thus, although Negroes now invest more time in education than in the past, they still find themselves overshadowed by the higher educational levels of whites.

Finally, the introduction of labor-saving technology together with the entrance of large numbers of youths into the labor market has exerted considerable pressure for early retirement from the labor force. Although older whites have felt this pressure, older Negro workers are particularly disadvantaged by such retirement. Such displaced workers in seeking new jobs must contend with a double handicap, age and race. Since few older Negro workers have high levels of educational attainment, opportunities for retraining also tend to be minimal.

These observations suggest that if current trends continue, more and more, lower class Negro families will depend on female rather than male wage earners for financial support. The pressures to concentrate decision-making and wage earning in female roles appears to be strong. There are also indications that a substantial number of lower-class Negro males will find themselves in nonproductive, dependency roles without any meaningful attachment to work or society.

(2) Management-White Worker Attitudes and Perspective Toward the Negro

The attitudes of corporate policy makers are key variables explaining differences in employment opportunities for Negroes. Should there be compensatory training programs for Negroes? Should basic company personnel policies be altered to give Negroes a greater opportunity for jobs or promotions? Such attitudes will be reflected in the type of employment policies that the decision maker adopts and in the zeal with which such policies are applied. Attitudes will also play a part in shaping the behavior of subordinate managerial decision makers who make many choices for which they have only general guidelines. They operate within constraints not all of which can be satisfied. The priority given to equalizing employment opportunities for Negroes is a function not only of the organizational requirements but of personal attitudes as well.

The most obvious limitations on Negro job opportunities are the stereotypes of Negro capabilities held by corporate or local plant decision makers. These may range from a very general hostility toward the Negro workers ("he is lazy, shiftless, or ignorant") to very specific notions of his limitations ("Negro workers cannot stand office discipline," "Negro workers cannot stand heights," "Negro workers can stand heat better than white workers"). The origins of these stereotypes are usually lost in the socialization and background experiences of the decision makers. These stereotypes usually exist where there is a lack of *real* acquaintance or contact with Negro workers, and they are susceptible to modification when the decision maker engages in personal contact with Negro workers. There is an obvious circularity here insofar as the stereotypes impose a limitation of contact that, in turn, further reinforces the stereotypes. One further point about the stereotypes of corporate and local plant decision makers should be noted. A frequent barrier to Negro employment is management *anticipation* of the negative reactions of customers or white coworkers to Negro jobholders. The desire to avoid an unpleasant situation frequently causes hesitation in assigning Negroes to nontraditional jobs (e.g., sales or white collar) that present opportunities for economic advancement.

The attitudes and perspectives of white workers should not be overlooked as a source of Negro economic disadvantagement. Once employed, the Negro worker is part of a network of social relationships present in the work place, and the pressures and hostilities of these relationships can influence his job progress. Coworkers can significantly improve or impair the Negro worker's opportunities in the work situation in a number of ways. First, opportunities for promotion or job advancement depend to some extent on informal learning practices. The worker—white or black—who is shown the intricacies of technological processes or machine operation by friendly coworkers has significantly advanced his opportunities for promotion, particularly if no formal training program exists. Similarly, the worker who lacks access to such learning finds his opportunities for advancement limited.

Second, bidding for jobs and training opportunities may well depend on two kinds of support given by the work situation—informational and psychological. Access to inside information about the availability of openings and requirements for mastering the job may be as important as seniority in helping the worker to progress. This information is rarely available on a formal basis, but exists as part of informal group knowledge open only to workers who are psychologically identified as belonging to the group. Bids for advancement are often encouraged or discouraged depending on the extent of psychological support given or withheld to the potential candidates or pressures transmitted to the supervisor through informal work groups. The opportunities of the Negro worker must be measured against the friendliness or hostility of his work environment.

(3) The Attitudes and Policies of Labor Union Leaders

The union can exert considerable influence in protecting its members from discriminatory practices. The union may affect the lives of Negro workers in several ways. It can set conditions of membership to facilitate or impede Negro membership in the union. Such membership may be crucial in gaining access to rewarding and desired jobs. In this sense the union may control the labor market and place restrictions on Negro employment. The union may also exert influence to protect members inside a shop, making it easier in the case of the Negro to insulate himself against disadvantagement. The attitudes of union leaders in defining these opportunities or rights for Negroes become important to an understanding of the dynamics of Negro employment opportunities.

(4) Employment Policies of the Firm

The employment policy of any company is viewed by its management as the end product of a rational trial and error process by which certain employment activities become accepted as legitimate and need-fulfilling to the organization. To examine or to modify such employment practices is to challenge seriously the company's unique way of getting things done. For example, the company that relies on new job referrals from its own work force and finds this a successful recruiting practice is apt to resist a change in the practice, even if it results in the exclusion of Negroes. It is necessary to understand that unintentional forms of discrimination are usually linked to employment practices that are viewed by the management as being necessary, if not vital, to the firm's successful operation (e.g., vocational testing, recruitment through the private employment agency). These employment practices become routinized and beyond question—the "well-worn Indian pathways." This may explain why it is so difficult to reduce forms of unintentional discrimination.

Several forms of unintentional discrimination may be noted. Many firms require a stable work record, minimum educational standards (e.g., a high-school diploma), health certification, and a certificate of good moral standing (e.g., no police record or good credit experience). These requirements for work may or may not be related to success on the job, but they act as reference points for employment. Frequently, there is the assumption that a job applicant must qualify for a career in the company rather than a specific job. The end result of many of these requirements is to erect barriers to Negro employment. The economic deprivations of lower-class Negro life often produce the social characteristics—unstable work histories, for example—that make qualification for many of these jobs impossible.

It is an oversimplification to say that all firms practice exclusion or discrimination against Negroes to the same extent. There is a spectrum of discriminatory-nondiscriminatory practices. At one extreme are the firms with overtly discriminatory employment policies, who are unwilling to undertake any remedial action. At the other extreme are firms that have made a concerted effort to examine and eliminate discriminatory practices—intentional or unintentional—from their employment policy. Most business organizations fall between these extremes, having an employment policy which has both intentional and unintentional discriminatory features.

(5) Technological Changes in the Economy

The sweeping changes in technology and productivity, coupled with geographical shifts in plant locations have influenced job opportunities. The greatest gains in productivity through mechanization have been in industries in which Negroes have been disproportionately employed—heavy commodity manufacturing such as automobiles and steel. In 1953 and 1964 the automobile industry manufactured about 7.5 million cars, but with one-third less workers in the latter year. The jobs most susceptible to elimination through automation and mechanization are the semiskilled and unskilled jobs in which Negroes are disproportionately represented. It is ironic that the entry jobs most available to lower-class Negroes at present are those most likely to be eliminated through technological gains.

The pattern of geographical redistribution of industry has also added to the Negro's job problems. Trapped in the ghetto or inner-city area, he finds it harder to commute to the new plant locations in the suburbs or the semirural areas. This spatial isolation means that he must accept jobs in the services industries near his home that may be limited in mobility opportunities and monetary rewards.

These components of our industrial society in some measure sustain patterns of Negro economic disadvantagement. Thus, an educational and technical upgrading of Negro workers will not immediately remove all traces of disadvantagement. The more subtle barriers to Negro economic progress are lodged in the fabric of our society and demand a concerted measure of our attention.

In this chapter, the selections discuss a wide variety of institutional arrangements in the labor market that *intentionally* or *unintentionally* result in discrimination against Negro job applicants and workers. Ray Marshall details a number of formal and informal exclusion mechanisms that dominate in the trade unions. Strauss and Ingerman analyze apprenticeship systems and the problems of entry for Negroes. Robert Guion discusses the use of employment tests in industry and the barriers that they raise to Negro employment. Finally, Daniel Fusfeld analyzes the race factor in early MDTA training programs.

Racial Practices of Unions

Ray Marshall

[*From chapters 5 and 6 of* The Negro and Organized Labor *(New York, 1965), by permission of John Wiley and Sons, Inc., copyright 1965.*]

If unions could be arranged along a continuum according to their racial practices, organizations that would not accept Negroes could be placed on one end and those with perfectly equalitarian practices at the other, with various degrees of discrimination represented by the organizations along the continuum. As might be expected, in reality very few unions are to be found at either extreme. Almost no unions have completely equalitarian policies in the sense that they pay no attention whatsoever to their members' or potential members' racial composition. A number of organizations bar Negroes from membership, but the tactics used to accomplish this vary considerably. In classifying union racial practices, moreover, it is necessary to distinguish the practices of federations, national or international (unions are called "international" if they have foreign affiliates) unions, and locals.

Although it is not possible to obtain the necessary information to classify union racial practices according to precise degrees of discrimination, there have been certain discernible trends and patterns. The trend has been toward more equalitarian racial practices. Many unions have moved through a series of stages beginning with formal exclusion and followed by auxiliary locals for Negroes, segregated locals, and finally the elimination of segregated locals. These practices will be discussed in this article. Unions have also adopted various informal policies and procedures that restrict or promote the Negro's job opportunties. Because they are the main economic units in the labor movement and their practices differ considerably from the more politically oriented federations, the racial practices of international unions and their local affiliates will be discussed in this paper.

Formal Exclusion

The number of national unions with formal race restrictions in their constitutions or rituals declined markedly between 1930 and 1963, when the last AFL–CIO affiliate removed its race bar. In 1930, for example, there were perhaps twenty-seven unions with formal race bars, though the exact number is not certain.[1] By 1943 mergers and changing racial practices had reduced the number of restrictive unions to about fourteen, eight of which were AFL affiliates.[2] When the Brotherhood of Locomotive Firemen (BLF) removed its ban in 1963, for the first time since 1895 when the International Association of Machinists (IAM) was admitted to the AFL, the major American labor federation had no affiliates with formal race bars.

The forces that caused unions to abandon exclusion by formal means, or to adopt more subtle forms, will be analyzed at greater length later, but may be summarized as follows: expansion of Negro employment in jurisdictions covered by these unions, especially during the First and Second World Wars; competition between unions for Negro votes in representation elections; embarrassment of exclusionist union leaders at conventions and in the press by criticism from Negro and white union leaders, especially the moral castigations from within the AFL by the Negro leaders of the Brotherhood of Sleeping Car Porters; action by such governmental agencies as the wartime and state FEP committees; and fear of the loss of exclusive bargaining rights, union shop provisions, or other legal privileges under the Railway Labor Act or the Taft-Hartley Act.

Auxiliary and Segregated Locals

A number of international unions which did not bar Negroes from membership restricted them to auxiliary locals. This arrangement was usually adopted in lieu of formal exclusion and was sometimes the next stage following the elimination of formal restrictions. As illustrated by the IAM, the BRSC, and the Boilermakers, however, an intermediate stage between outright exclusion and auxiliary locals frequently was the organization of federal locals for Negroes. Sometimes, however, this intermediate stage was skipped altogether and auxiliaries were fused with exclusion.

Segregated locals[3] are theoretically different from auxiliaries in that the segregated locals have equal status and separate charters. This distinction is often more theoretical than real, however, because the whites might in fact bargain for the Negro locals. Moreover, white locals and employers sometimes take measures affecting Negroes in segregated locals without even consulting the colored workers.[4]

It is also common to refer to locals as "segregated" when they in fact have mixed memberships. In cities with large Negro populations, building-trades locals were established in Negro areas, but many of these later took in some white members. This pattern was followed, for example, by locals of the Carpenters, International Longshoremen's Association, Bricklayers, Musicians, Hod Carriers and Common Laborers, and Painters. In Washington, D. C., for example, the previously segregated Negro local had about 10 per cent white membership in 1964 and the "white" local had about 200 Negroes. Sometimes the locals were in occupations—like hod carriers and common laborers—which were traditionally "Negro" jobs but into which whites moved during depressions or when wages or working conditions in those occupations improved. Of course, some jobs, like sleeping car porters, "red caps," laborers, freighthandlers, cotton warehouse and compress workers, fertilizer workers, and some chemical operations are held almost exclusively by Negroes in many places, so the unions tend to be all-Negro. Although segregated locals have existed throughout the country, most of these have been in the South and sometimes were insisted upon by the Negroes as a condition for joining the unions. Segregation also was imposed by local laws against integrated meetings. Even where there were no segregation laws, community pressures frequently required segregation. Indeed, about the only union with a long history in the South which did not establish segregated locals was the United Mine Workers, whose members were isolated and relatively impervious to community pressure. Even so, UMW frequently was attacked in the South because of its integrated meetings.

There are, however, actually relatively few segregated locals if by this we mean that there are separate unions in the same plant or craft. A few unions almost invariably were segregated in the South. A survey by the Jewish Labor Committee in 1957 found that of 110 locals from thirty-two internationals, two-thirds had Negro membership, but that two-fifths of the biracial unions had less than 10 per cent Negro membership. Figures for unions affiliated with various state federations of labor yield similar conclusions. Of 1500 locals in Texas, with 290,000 members in 1957, only fifteen, with 10,000 members, were all-Negro and nine of these were segregated; and of twenty-two locals affiliated with the Montgomery, Alabama, Central Labor Union, with 13,000 members, six were all-Negro and three of these were auxiliaries. In Tennessee, of 650 locals affiliated with the AFL–CIO in 1958, 425 were integrated, 200 were all-white and twenty-five all-Negro; there were about 700 locals affiliated with the Tennessee State Labor Council, so the racial composition of only 50 locals was unknown. Finally, in September 1963, the AFL Civil Rights Committee reported that only 172 of its 55,000 locals were segregated.

Segregated local unions have encountered increasing opposition from Negro and civil-rights groups since the Second World War. The Negro community is convinced that segregated unions like other forms of segregation contribute to the Negro's economic disadvantages and should therefore be abolished. Consequently, those Negro union leaders who favored segregation as a means of preserving the advantages of union leadership and giving Negroes some control over their own affairs find themselves out of harmony with the mainstream of Negro opinion. The Negro community's opposition to segregated locals is perhaps instinctively hardened by the alacrity with which some white labor leaders seize upon Negro opposition to merger as a justification for segregation.

In truth, however, there was apparently very little opposition to integration by white union leaders, especially where the government or some other outside force could be blamed for the change. International union leaders apparently were less opposed to integration per se than afraid of the problems involved in merging long-established local unions. Union leaders were naturally fearful of opposition from rank-and-file whites, but this rarely seems to have been a very difficult problem, though a few unions—National Association of Letter Carriers (NALC) and the American Federation of Teachers (AFT)—have lost Southern locals who refused to obey ultimatums to integrate. However, though some general tendencies seem to be supported by the evidence, it is not possible to lay down hard-and-fast principles for white reactions to integration. A key factor seem to be the proportion of Negro to white membership in the locals. Almost invariably, North or South, whites have resisted integration when they would be in the minority in the merged organizations. Indeed, even some locals in unions like the United Packinghouse Workers and the United Automobile Workers, which have relatively equalitarian policies, have tended to become almost all-Negro in attendance at union functions when Negroes were in the majority. White opposition also will be great either where whites expect to lose their relative seniority positions in integrated rosters, or where Negroes will acquire previously all-white jobs. This, for example, was a problem in the tobacco, aircraft, and paper industries in the South when the federal government caused the integration of seniority rosters and local unions. Finally, where groups like the Ku Klux Klan or White Citizens Councils raise the issue, white members are likely to resist integration—at least publicly.

Some problems in merging locals affect Negroes and whites alike. The attitudes of Negro and white rank-and-file members are likely to be shaped, for example, by their interpretation of the economic advantages and disadvantages of integration. In some occupations (longshoremen, bricklayers, and musicians in the South) Negroes feel that their economic conditions will not be improved by integration. Indeed, there is even some apprehension that Negro job opportunities might actually deteriorate if integration destroys protected markets. Negroes and whites will also be concerned with the disposition of union property. In a Tennessee Boilermakers' merger, for instance, the Negroes spent all of their money on an elaborate party before merging with the white local. Similarly, a white local of the Oil, Chemical, and Atomic Workers in Texas distributed some $80,000 in its strike fund among its members before merging with the Negro local. Initially, the most successful mergers of Musicians, Longshoremen, Tobacco Workers, and Machinists seem to have required that Negroes, who will usually be in a minority, be given some official positions in the merged organizations. Although such special treatment for Negroes signifies that the groups really are not "integrated," union officials consider these important first steps toward integration. That these arrangements are considered temporary is suggested by the fact that they are rarely formalized or stated as official policy.

Just as the white workers usually will be concerned about community reaction to integration, Negro workers must be concerned about the prevailing attitudes of the Negro community. Indeed, one of the most important forces against segregated locals has been the mood of the Negro community, translated into political power and reinforced by moral condemnations of segregation by the nation's opinion makers. These pressures have put the Negro leader of a segregated local in the position of being ostracized by the Negro community if he resists integration. However, some Negro union leaders in the South have buttressed their traditional economic arguments against integration with the contentions that Negroes can better promote the civil-rights movement through segregated locals. In New Orleans, for instance, an ILA Negro local owns several business establishments, operates a political organization, and conducts a school to teach Negroes how to register and vote. Negro leaders of this local oppose integration because, they argue, it would restrict their civil-rights activities.

Although the number of segregated locals is declining, they are not likely to disappear completely for many years. Several international unions, such as the Machinists, the Bricklayers, Longshoremen, Paper Makers, and various railroad unions, have policies encouraging merger but, respecting local autonomy, apparently will not employ sanctions to enforce mergers. Similarly, although the 1959 AFL–CIO convention adopted a policy against segregated locals, no sanctions were imposed for violations of that policy. Finally, the President's Committee on Equal Employment Opportunity (PCEEO) and the NLRB apparently are moving to cripple segregated locals, but the courts and many state civil-rights commissions have refused to compel mergers of separate locals if whites and Negroes can transfer freely into either local. In these circumstances, and barring new legal measures against segregation, the resistance from Negroes and whites will be sufficient to perpetuate some segregated locals for many years.

The most important forces tending to eliminate segregated locals have been: prevailing moral sentiment against segregation; opposition from the Negro community as contrasted with Negro union members; some state FEP laws; and finally the Kennedy and Johnson administrations' policy of not permitting segregated locals to bargain for government employees and strongly discouraging them among federal contractors. Moreover, almost all international unions have signed pledges with the PCEEO agreeing to abolish discrimination, including segregated locals, within their locals.

We should note, however, that to call a local "integrated" might not mean very much. It might mean that one or two Negroes belong to the organization but never participate other than by paying dues. Those few Negroes might be janitors in the plant or they might have been admitted to the local or plant as "tokens" to prove the absence of discrimination. "Integration" might mean that Negroes are members of the industrial union and if they attend meetings they segregate themselves or are segregated by whites. In other cases, like some Woodworkers' locals, Negroes and whites ostensibly are integrated, but actually meet at different times.

Informal Exclusion

The decline in formal exclusion by international unions does not mean that discrimination has declined by the same degree, of course, because of local variations from these policies. Locals of internationals with race bars sometimes accepted Negroes, and the locals of some international unions that do not have formal race bars have barred Negroes by informal means. The variety of ways in which this is done include agreements not to sponsor Negroes for membership; refusal to admit Negroes into apprenticeship programs; refusal to accept applications from Negroes, or simply ignoring their applications; general "understandings" to vote against Negroes if they are proposed (for example, as few as three members of some railroad lodges have barred applicants for membership); using examinations to refuse Negroes journeyman status which either are not given to whites or are rigged so that Negroes cannot pass them; exerting political pressure on governmental licensing agencies to see to it that Negroes fail the tests; and restricting membership to sons, nephews, or other relatives of members.

International Unions

We should note the distinction between the policies of international and local unions. Both the United Association of Journeymen and Apprentices of the Plumbing and Pipefitting Industry (UA) and the IBEW, for example, have become concerned about the adverse publicity they are receiving, which has caused their actions to be carefully scrutinized by civil-rights and government agencies and which jeopardizes their control of apprenticeship and job referral procedures.

The UA established a committee in 1959 to study charges of racial discrimination against its locals, and in 1962 the international union included a non-discrimination clause in its national agreement covering large contractors. Similarly, the 1958 IBEW convention adopted a "Resolution on Civil Rights," whch resolved that it was the "enduring goal of our Brotherhood to assure to all workers their full share in the benefits of union organization without regard to race, creed, color or national origin."[5] Although there is frequently a vast difference between resolutions and practices, at least the international officers are moving—or being forced to move—toward more equalitarian policies.

1963 Demonstrations

Although the absence of Negroes from these occupations is due to a host of other factors, discrimination by building-trades unions has been too well documented to be successfully denied by even the most vigorous defenders of those unions. Indeed, the admission of discrimination has frequently been made by ex-plumber George Meany himself.[6]

The Negro community's smoldering resentment against racial discrimination by building-trades unions produced a number of demonstrations at construction sites in several major cities during the spring and summer of 1963. The building trades were logical targets for these more militant measures, not only because these unions had acquired unfavorable images in the Negro community, but also because their work was frequently on government projects, conspicuous, and in Negro neighborhoods.

Almost simultaneously, therefore, building projects in Philadelphia, New York, and other cities were subjected to picketing, laydowns, and sit-ins, devices which had already been tested by civil-rights groups in the South and, ironically, by the unions themselves. The earliest demonstrations appear to have occurred in Philadelphia, where NAACP pickets halted work on an $18 million building project in May.[7] There were a number of injuries in Philadelphia when police attempted to escort workmen through demonstrators on a school construction site. Some Negroes among those workers being escorted to the construction site were photographed and the president of the Philadelphia branch of the NAACP declared that they would be "ostracized by the Negro community."[8] The Philadelphia unions agreed to admit Negro apprentices only after the mayor halted work on the school project. The unions against whom these demonstrations were primarily directed—the Electricians, Plumbers, and

Steamfitters—had been under attack from civil-rights groups and the Philadelphia Human Relations Commission for some time. Indeed, members of the Philadelphia AFL–CIO even "... testified before the Commission giving evidence of discriminatory practices in membership, rules and apprenticeship programs."[9] Of course, the building trades argued that "they do not discriminate on account of race, creed, or color; that their membership rules are of old standing and were not directed to keep out any particular section of the population . . . faced with unemployment . . . they are not willing to give nonunion Negroes super-seniority over unemployed white union members."[10] However, the Philadelphia Sheet Metal Workers have adopted what appears to be a completely nondiscriminatory method of selecting apprentices. There is no "father-son" clause, tests are announced in advance and are administered by the public schools. In one group, there were 302 applicants to the program, 55 of whom were Negroes. Of these, 32 Negroes of 190 eligible took the test. Seven Negroes and 95 whites passed the test.

In New York hundreds of demonstrators were arrested as various civil-rights groups halted work on state and city construction projects for as long as four months. In one project alone—the $23.5 million Harlem Hospital—the City of New York incurred costs of between $800 and $900 a day while the project was closed by pickets, and by early August the demonstrations are reported to have cost the city over $250,000 for overtime payments to police.[11] A ministers' group in Brooklyn succeeded in halting work on the Downstate Medical Center in Brooklyn,[12] and sit-ins protesting building-trades discrimination were conducted at the New York governor's and mayor's offices and in the city hall at Newark, New Jersey.[13] There also were scores of injuries and arrests during demonstrations in Brooklyn; Elizabeth, Paterson, and Newark, New Jersey; Detroit; Chicago; and other cities.[14]

In most of these situations, there were several civil-rights organizations with conflicting tactics and demands. In New York six major civil-rights groups[15] sought to present a united front by forming the Joint Committee on Equal Employment Opportunity (JCEEO), but there were several other competing groups, including the Greater New York Coordinating Committee for Equal Opportunity, the Blue Ribbon Organization for Equal Opportunity Now, and the Ministers Committee on Job Opportunities for Brooklyn. These groups demonstrated independently of the JCEEO, and asked that Negroes be assigned quotas of the jobs on construction projects. The JCEEO, for example, asked that unions admit all qualified Negro and Puerto Rican journeymen to the unions and open apprenticeship programs to

Negroes and Puerto Ricans at twice their proportion in the City's population "because the unemployment rate of these groups is twice that of white workers and because the historical exclusion of non-whites from these trades has created an imbalance that needs correction."[16]

City and state officials usually responded to these demonstrations by closing the projects and attempting to get the building-trades unions to accept more Negroes. Mayor Wagner appointed a so-called "action panel" to seek a solution to the problem, but its recommendations were rejected by both the Negroes and the unions.[17] The Building and Construction Trades Council (BCTC) announced that it would not discriminate but would not lower its standards to accommodate anyone and would not accept "dictation by outside groups." The unions said they would launch their own program to get non-white journeymen and apprentices and threatened to "start picketing ourselves" if demonstrators stopped union members from going to work.[18] Union leaders also thought the demonstrations unfair to them because there were usually a number of Negroes on the picketed projects.[19]

After the action panel's recommendations were rejected, Mayor Wagner launched a program to recruit Negroes and Puerto Ricans for construction jobs by opening some twenty recruiting stations throughout the city; the Brooklyn ministers group, who seem to have had the support of Governor Rockefeller, opened four competing offices. Indeed, one of the mayor's stations was opened in the same building where the Brooklyn ministers had been recruiting.[20]

Political pressure also apparently was focused directly on some of the unions with poor reputations among Negroes. For example, it was reported that Plumbers Local 1, whose jurisdiction covered Brooklyn and Queens, agreed to "work out a procedure for identifying qualified minority apprentices." This agreement came "after meetings with various subcommittees of the Democratic Executive Council." Local 1 denied that minorities would be "jumped over whites" but said that the waiting list would be "mixed in at the top of the list." The union had six Negroes among its 3000 members, but all of the Negroes held "B" cards which permitted them to work on alterations at $3.25 an hour, whereas those with "A" cards worked on new construction at $5.15 an hour.[21]

The results of these recruiting drives proved disappointing to all concerned. After about a month, Mayor Wagner announced that the drive had resulted in only 2600 applications for jobs or union apprenticeship training, 60 per cent of which were from Negroes, 37 per cent from Puerto Ricans, and 3 per cent from people not included in the program.[22] The Brooklyn ministers' group had received about 1000 applications and a BCTC screening committee had referred only about 100 applicants to various unions.[23] Three months later it was reported that only 3121 had applied, and of these 1003 were not seeking apprentice or journeyman status, but were looking for positions as typists, printers, diamond cutters, elevator operators, janitors, and other jobs outside the building field. Only 849 of the applicants met minimum standards for journeymen or apprentices, and 167 of these were rejected for various reasons. Of the 682 remaining applicants, 537 qualified as apprentices and 109 as journeymen and were referred to local unions. The unions accepted 111 of the applicants, rejected two, and 28 failed to appear. A spokesman from the Referral Committee of the Building Industry noted that "We fully expect that all qualified applicants will be accepted consistent with job opportunities and openings in apprentice programs."[24] He also claimed that the report tended to show that the charges of discrimination against the building-trades unions was unjustified. "We had been led to believe," he said, "that there were thousands who couldn't gain admittance into the building trades unions. As a committee we felt that the numbers who came forward were small and that those qualified were even smaller in number."[25] A spokesman for the JCEEO branded the committee's report "an obvious and transparent attempt to blame the Negro community for a broad pattern of racial discrimination that characterizes the AFL–CIO building trades unions in this city."[26] The Brooklyn ministers' group also voiced their disappointment with efforts to get more building-trades jobs for Negroes. The ministers criticized city, state, industry, and union representatives for failing to take vigorous action "in opening union membership to non-white persons."[27] The ministers reported that of over 2000 applicants, only 31 workers had actually received jobs.[28]

An investigation of the building industry by the New York City Commission on Human Rights during these demonstrations found "a pattern of exclusion in a substantial portion of the building and construction industry which effectively bars nonwhites from participating in this area of the city's economic life."[29] The CHR placed responsibility for this discrimination on employers, who "turned over the right to hire to others, notably to the trade unions under collective bargaining agreements with builders," and the unions, which imposed "almost insurmountable barriers" to non-whites seeking union membership in a substantial number of the construction trades unions."[30] The Commission noted that "whenever the employer had control over hiring some nonwhites were employed. But in those trades where contractors traditionally relied upon the locals for referrals, nonwhites were effectively excluded from construction trades employment." Nonwhite journeymen were found by the CHR to face the union barriers of sponsorship requirements, discrimination in referrals, and priority given to out-of-town workers. Apprentices faced obstacles in the historical "for white only" clauses, "father-son" clauses, sponsorship requirements, withholding of apprenticeship information, restrictive recommendations, and apprenticeship-journeymen ratios.[31]

While these developments were taking place, civil-rights groups in Cleveland adopted a more orderly and perhaps more important strategy to get Negroes into building-trades unions in that city. Of course, the Cleveland officials were influenced by repugnance at the demonstrations in other communities. Moreover, as we have seen, the effort to get Negroes into the Cleveland building-trades unions had been going on for some time. But the militant mood of the Negro community affected Cleveland no less than New York, Philadelphia, Chicago, and other places. And Cleveland Negroes generally considered construction unions to be among the worst anti-Negro organizations in the city.

However, a number of factors caused the Cleveland experience to be different from New York. Perhaps most important was the leadership of Cleveland's mayor, Ralph S. Locher, who had been involved (as a law officer) in the earlier efforts to get Negroes admitted to IBEW Local 38 and who therefore already had some experience in dealing with union racial practices. Indeed, Locher felt that one of the difficulties in 1963 was that "more Negro apprentices weren't encouraged to enter the crafts," after the 1957 settlement; the mayor argued that if they had, "we wouldn't have this problem today."[32] Moreover, Cleveland officials were particularly concerned about the possible adverse effects of racial demonstrations. "I have seen this picketing in New York," Mayor Locher said, "and I do not want it to happen here."[33]

Cleveland civil-rights organizations not only presented a relatively solid front through the United Freedom Movement (UFM) but also presented specific and clear-cut demands to city officials and unions. This contrasts vividly with the dissension within the civil-rights movements in and around New York.

The role of various international unions in the Cleveland experience is not clear, but it appeared for a while that the main union involved, the UA, would use sanctions against its Cleveland affiliate, and though the international apparently backed down after being defied by its Cleveland local, the sanctions threatened were plausible enough to have at least given pause to the local's leaders. At the request of Mayor Locher, a high-ranking official of the U. S. Department of Labor who was highly regarded by building-trades unionists, and Donald Slaiman, assistant director (later director) of the AFL–CIO Civil Rights Department also were involved in the Cleveland negotiations.

Although the Cleveland settlement was reached without the violence that occurred in other places, and probably has greater potential for gaining Negro entry into unions, we do not mean to imply that there was no difficulty in Cleveland or that that settlement was not reached without trouble. But let us take a closer look at the events in Cleveland.

In July 1963 the UFM announced that it would picket the Mall, a city building project, unless three Negro electricians and two Negro plumbers were hired.[34] This threat led to negotiations by representatives of the AFL–CIO, the UFM, the Community Relations Board (CRB), the U.S. Department of Labor, and the unions and contractors. During the first series of negotiations, the IBEW said that it had only two Negro electricians (of 1400 members) so would not be able to supply the UFM's demands (though it later turned out that three Negroes were members of the local).[35] The Plumbers (who had no Negroes in a local of 1300 members) were considering the applications of six Negro journeymen and a master plumber, but their applications were being delayed by procedural problems. Mayor Locher felt that Negroes should be hired on the project because it was being built with public funds. When the first negotiations failed to produce satisfactory results, the UFM announced that it would place 1000 pickets at all entrances to the Mall project, and seek to have city and federal funds withdrawn from the apprenticeship training programs of all discriminating unions. After this threat the IBEW agreed to accept two Negro apprentices on the Mall project, and the Plumbers agreed to accept two Negro journeymen and to process other Negro applications in its regular manner.[36] All parties expressed dissatisfaction with this compromise, but it was generally considered to have ended the conflict.[37]

The matter was far from settled, however, because rank-and-file union members still had to be reckoned with. When two Negro plumbers (who were described as "house plumbers") were hired on the Mall project, eleven Plumbers union members walked off the job, and were followed by forty-four pipe fitters and asbestos workers. However, 200 union members stayed on the job when they were told by their leaders that this dispute was none of their business.[38] A general organizer for the UA came to Cleveland and announced that the whole thing was a mistake, and had occurred mainly because the contractor had not given the workers sufficient notice that the Negroes were being hired. However, the Plumbers local later voted to declare a "holiday" to begin Monday, July 29, obviously to protest the hiring of the Negro workers on the Mall project. The Plumbers' general organizer announced that "There'll be no holiday—nor any other day—it's not being recognized. Any union plumber taking it takes it on his own, and he may be fired."[39] Only 700 of the city's 1400 plumbers went to work on Monday and the boycott of the Mall project continued thereafter. Faced with this obvious defiance by the local union, the general organizer announced that the international had "no problem" and that it was up to the contractor to "move the situation." Company and union representatives suggested that the dispute be settled by making the two Negroes apprentices instead of journeymen, but the UFM objected, since the July 20 agreement called for two journeymen. The UFM renewed its threat to picket the Mall project.

The local Plumbers' leaders naturally denied that their actions were dictated by racial bias. The local's secretary-treasurer claimed that membership was open to all who qualified and that six Negro applications were being processed. The union had to carefully screen applicants, he argued, because "We believe that eventually every plumber will get into the home, and it is for the protection of the general public that we require character reference."[40] Another local official said that the Negroes' lack of union membership was the main issue in the "holiday," because no "self-respecting union man would work alongside nonunion men. The fact that the two men were Negroes had nothing to do with it."[41] The Plumbers' general organizer felt that the whole thing was caused by a "few rabble-rousers" in the union who had persuaded the others. He felt that the chief issue was international intervention in a local matter; in his opinion, the holiday's main purpose was "to express a little dissatisfaction."[42] A spokesman for the plumbing contractor being boycotted thought the "holiday" represented increasing disenchantment by the union's rank-and-file against the union leaders who were urging them to return to work.[43]

After lengthy negotiations, the dispute was settled on August 4, 1963, by representatives of the United Freedom Movement, Plumbers Local 55, the company, the City of Cleveland, John F. Henning, Under Secretary of Labor, and Donald Slaiman, Civil Rights Department, AFL–CIO. The terms of this agreement are sufficiently important to be quoted in full:

1. Local 55 agrees to sign labor contracts with the Negro Plumbing contractors and as of the date of the signing of the contract

by the contractors and the union, *all Negro journeymen who are employed by such contractors will be admitted to membership in Local 55 as journeymen, upon successful passage of the journeyman's examination given by the Examining Board of Local 55;* and all apprentices who are employed by such contractors will be admitted as apprentices upon successful passage of the apprentice examination given the Joint Apprentice Committee in accordance with the Constitution of the United Association of Journeymen and Apprentices.

In the event an applicant for status as a journeyman feels that the examination given to qualify him for such status was unfairly administered or graded, *a review committee composed of a nominee of the U.S. Department of Labor, a nominee of the* United Association International Union of Journeymen and Apprentices, and a third member nominated by the United Freedom Movement shall have the right to review the administration and grading of the examination.

2. It is further agreed that a part of the Mall Construction job relating to plumbing will be sublet to a Negro contractor who will employ Messrs. Hilliard and Baker [the Negro plumbers involved in the dispute] as journeyman plumbers and Messrs. Hilliard and Baker in turn will be *admitted to membership in Local 55 in accordance with the Constitution* of the United Association of Journeymen and Apprentices.

3. Local Union 55 agrees that the Apprenticeship Training Program will be open to Negro applicants on the same basis as all other apprentices starting with the acceptance of applications on August 7, 1963.

4. The foregoing agreement was entered into in the presence of a representative of the Negro Plumbing Contractors who agreed to undertake the obligation required of the Negro Plumbing Contractors. [Emphasis added.]

The Cleveland agreement was suggested as a model for other settlements by Herbert Hill, NAACP labor secretary, who called it "the most significant breakthrough that we have had anywhere in the country."[44] It was generally recognized that this compact not only resolved the immediate conflict of the plumbers on the Mall project, but also opened up the possibility of a large influx of Negroes into the union. It is particularly noteworthy that the Negroes who were rejected could appeal to an outside agency. On August 15, Local 55 admitted a Negro contractor with his four journeymen and two apprentices.

The Plumbers' settlement was no sooner announced, however, than efforts to get a Negro into the local Sheet Metal Workers Union again threatened to close the Mall project. When fourteen white sheet metal workers refused to work with a newly hired Negro, the contractor let him stay in a company trailer on the project, and the local's executive board ordered the sheet metal workers back to work.[45] The UFM again threatened to picket the project, but, in an apparently stormy meeting, was persuaded by a Negro trade unionist—who was also labor advisor to the UFM—and another UFM leader to wait until the local had a chance to act on the Negro's application.[46] When the Negro was considered by the union at its September meeting, however, he was denied membership on the ground that he had not passed the examination. The UFM, however, did not protest the union's action and apparently considered the Negro's failure legitimate.

The 1963 experiences suggest several conclusions. First, although civil-rights organizations are able to draw public attention to racial discrimination through these demonstrations, they also involve some dangers, the most important of which is that they might lead to violence, especially where union members feel that they are being unjustly accused. Moreover, these experiences indicate that negotiations will be more effective if the objectives sought are specific and clear. There is also a danger in a proliferation of demonstrating organizations, each seeking to impress the Negro community that it is more militant than the others. Demonstrations can provide bases for negotiations, but effective negotiations presuppose organizations on both sides with power to speak for and bind their constituents. There was a marked contrast between the United Freedom Movement in Cleveland and the numerous organizations in New York and New Jersey. In Cleveland the more disciplined UFM produced jobs for Negroes through negotiations with less difficulty. In New York negotiations were impossible because no organization spoke for Negroes. This problem was solved in industrial relations through the representation elections supervised by the National Labor Relations Board. It might not be feasible to provide similar machinery for Negroes, but there is an obvious need for unity among civil-rights groups during demonstrations. There also is room for competition among civil-rights groups, but the contests should be judged on such relevant standards as who can achieve specific objectives and not, as is presently too often the case, on the basis of which organization can make the most noise and claim the most credit for the few successful breakthroughs that do occur.

Several conclusions concerning unions that bar Negroes from membership by informal means should be noted.

1. Racial exclusion by informal means is not restricted to any particular geographic area. Though restriction is undoubtedly more rigid in the South, there are some unions that have more Negro members in the South than some other places: the trowel trades, Longshoremen, Teamsters, Roofers, Hod Carriers and Common Laborers, and Hotel and Restaurent Employees. These trades have been practiced by Negroes in the South because they have been traditionally regarded as "Negro work" and because Negroes have sufficient supplies of labor to protect their interest and to protect employers who might be boycotted by whites. These occupations also have relatively old and stable techniques, making it difficult for unions to exclude Negroes by monopolizing the latest technology, as they have in electricity and plumbing. It has been common practice in some industries and occupations in the South for Negroes to be displaced when operations are mechanized.

2. Some of the craft unions have had equalitarian racial policies and some industrial unions have refused to admit Negroes, but as a rule the unions that practice exclusion are craft organizations. Craft locals have the ability to exclude Negroes from membership and from the trade if they can control the labor supply. Industrial unions, on the other hand, organize workers after they are hired. In addition, craft unions at the local level consider it to their advantage to exclude workers, whereas industrial unions consider it to their advantage to organize extensively.

3. These factors, however, are not sufficient to identify the general character of excluding unions. We have already noted some of these factors as they relate to formal exclusion by railroad unions, but there are other considerations. Because of the equalitarian trend in race relations, older unions, other things being equal, seem more likely to exclude minorities than new unions. When the employer determines the hiring policy and therefore decides whether Negroes are to be hired, Negroes are likely to be excluded from such jobs as plumbing, milk delivering, and electrical work, which require home deliveries or repairs; apparently there have been widespread "understandings" that Negro males should not be permitted to work on jobs where they are likely to come in contact with the public. Whites are also likely to attempt to exclude Negroes from certain status jobs. And, in some cases, exclusion is directed against all except a particular nationality group; it has been common practice in the building trades and some garment unions, for instance, for locals to be restricted to a particular nationality group.

4. The foregoing evidence demonstrates widespread racial discrimination, but it should be emphasized that racial restrictions by the building-trades unions are not due entirely to racial reasons. Craft unionists are likely to have strong feelings of property rights in their crafts and their unions. They feel that these property rights have been won through years of training and fighting to build and strengthen unions. Any encroachment on either their jobs or their traditional union practices are likely to be resented—whether the encroachment comes from the international union, governments, or civil-rights organizations. There seem to be a pervasive belief among building-trades unionists that civil-rights groups are striving for special treatment for Negroes at the expense of the unions' members. Many craft union members have strong depression-created fears of unemployment; these fears are reinforced by the casual nature of the construction industry. In short, much of what appears to be discrimination by building-trades unions is in reality resentment at outside pressures. In these circumstances, discrimination is obviously also a factor, but union members are less likely to be motivated by racial prejudices than determination to win the contest against outside interference.

Notes

1. Abram L. Harris, in *The Negro Worker* (New York: Conference for Progressive Labor Action, 1930, p. 8), listed the following AFL unions with formal race bars in 1930:

1. Brotherhood of Railway Carmen (BRC)
2. The Switchmen's Union of North America (SNA)
3. The Order of Sleeping Car Conductors (OSCC)
4. The (International) National Organization of Masters, Mates and Pilots of North America (MMP)
5. The Railway Mail Association (RMA)
6. American Wire Weavers Protective Association (WWPA)
7. Commercial Telegraphers (CT)
8. The Boilermakers, Iron Shipbuilders and Helpers Union (BIS)
9. The International Association of Machinists (IAM)
10. The Order of Railway (Railroad) Telegraphers (ORT)
11. Brotherhood of Railway and Steamship Clerks (BRSC)

Harris listed the following unaffiliated unions as having race bars in 1930:

1. American Federation of Express Workers (AFEW)
2. American Federation of Railway Workers (AFRW)

3. Brotherhood of Railway Station Employees and Clerks (BRSEC)

4. [American] Train Dispatchers [Association] (ATDA)

5. Railroad Yard Masters of America (RYA)

6. Neptune Association (NA)

7. Brotherhood of Locomotive Engineers (BLE)

8. Brotherhood [Order] of Railway Conductors (ORC)

9. Brotherhood of Locomotive Firemen and Enginemen (BLF)

10. Brotherhood of Railroad Trainmen (BRT)

11. Order of Railroad Telegraphers (ORT)

12. Brotherhood of Dining Car Conductors (BDC)

13. Order of Railway Expressmen (ORE)

Harris said that there were 26 unions with racial bars, 10 of which were AFL affiliates, though he listed only 24 unions, 11 of which were AFL affiliates. The U. S. Department of Labor, Bureau of Labor Statistics, in its 1926 *Handbook of American Trade Unions,* listed the following unions with race bars: BDC, AFRW, ORE, AFREW, BRSEC, RYA, the Railroad Yard Masters of North America (RYNA), NA, BRT, ORC, BLE, and BLFE. In addition, Spero and Harris (*The Black Worker,* New York: Columbia University Press, 1930, p. 57) listed the following AFL organizations with race bars in 1929, which also probably had race bars in 1926: BRC, SNA, BRSC, CT, OSCC, ORT, MMP, RMA, WWPA, BIS, and the IAM. Between 1926 and 1930, however, the ORE and the AFEW returned to the BRSC, and in 1929 the BRSE no longer limited membership to whites. Thus, Spero and Harris concluded "... in 1930 there are nine unions affiliated with the Federation and ten unaffiliated unions whose constitutions debar Negro members." (*Ibid.,* p. 58). In addition, an AFL affiliate, the Sheet Metal Workers' International Association (SMW), was reported by the New York State Commission on Human Rights in 1964 to have barred Negroes from membership for the previous 76 years of its existence and to have had a constitutional race bar until 1946. (*New York Times,* March 4, 1964.) It appears, however, that the SMW's bar was not absolute, but restricted Negroes to auxiliary locals governed by whites.

2. IAM, SNA, MMP, ORT, RMA, WWPA, and the Airline Pilots Association (ALPA). See Herbert Northrup, *Organized Labor and the Negro,* New York: Harper, 1944, p. 3. The unaffiliated organizations listed by Northrup in 1943 were: BLE, BLFE, BRT, RYA, RYNA, ORC, ATDA. The SMW also had a race bar in 1943. (New York Times, March 5, 1964.)

3. Although the list is not complete, the following international unions have or have had segregated locals: Brotherhood of Maintenance of Way Employees (BMWE); Brotherhood of Painters, Decorators and Paperhangers of America (BPDP); Brotherhood of Railway Carmen of America

(BRC); Brotherhood of Railway and Steamship Clerks, Freight Handlers, Express and Station Employees (BRSC); Iron Workers; International Brotherhood of Boilermakers, Iron Ship Builders, Blacksmiths, Forgers and Helpers (BIS); International Union of Pulp, Sulphite and Paper Mill Workers (PPS); Aluminum Workers; Sheet Metal Workers International Association (SMW); United Brotherhood of Carpenters and Joiners of America (UBCJ); International Brotherhood of Teamsters, Chauffeurs and Warehousemen; United Brotherhood of Paper Makers and Paperworkers (UPP); The National Federation of Rural Letter Carriers (independent); International Chemical Workers (ICW); American Federation of Musicians (AFM); American Federation of Teachers (AFT); National Association of Letter Carriers (NALC); International Association of Machinists (IAM); Tobacco Workers International Union (TWIU); the Bricklayers, Masons and Plasterers (BMP); the Journeyman Barbers International Union; the Oil, Chemical and Atomic Workers (OCAW); State, County and Municipal Workers; the Textile Workers Union (TWU); the United Textile Workers (UTWA); the International Longshoremen's Association (ILA); The Molders; the Glass and Ceramic Workers; the Amalgamated Clothing Workers (ACWA); and the International Ladies' Garment Workers Union (ILGWU).

4. See my "Independent Unions in the Southern Petroleum Refining Industry—the Esso Experience," *Labor Law Journal,* September 1961.

5. See Chapter 8, *Union Racial Practices and Problems.*

6. See, for example, speech delivered to the Sixth National Legislative Conference of the Building and Construction Trades Department of the AFL-CIO, Washington, D. C., March 14, 1960; the N. Y. State Commission Against Discrimination, "Apprentices, Skilled Craftsmen and the Negro: An Analysis," 1960; Ben D. Segal, "The Practices of Craft Unions in Washington, D. C., with Respect to Minority Groups," in *Civil Rights in the National Capital,* Washington National Association of Intergroup Relations Officials, November 1959, p. 35; Memo to the writer from David Sawyer, executive director of the Commissioners' Council on Human Relations, Washington, D. C., June 3, 1959; Herman D. Bloch, "Craft Unions—a Link in the Circle of Negro Discrimination," *Phylon,* Fourth Quarter, 1958; "Craft Unions and the Negro in Historical Perspective," *Journal of Negro History,* January 1958; Herbert Northrup, *Organized Labor and the Negro,* New York: Harper, 1944, Ch. 2; National Planning Association, Committee on the South, *Negro Employment in the South,* New York, 1955; Herbert Hill, "Organized Labor and the Negro Wage Earner," *New Politics,* Winter 1962, and "Labor Unions and the Negro," *Commentary,* December 1959; National Urban League, "Negroes and the Building Trades Unions," New York, Industrial Relations Department, mimeo, n.d.; U. S. Commission on Civil Rights, Reports on Apprenticeship, January 1964; New York City Commission on Human Rights, *Bias in the Building Industry, An Interim Report to the Mayor,* December 13, 1963.

7. *New York Times,* May 16, 1963.

8. *Ibid.*, May 30, 1963.

9. Daniel Neifeld, "Civil Rights: Philadelphia," *Labor Today*, August-September, 1963, p. 18.

10. Ibid.

11. *Cleveland Plain Dealer*, August 8, 1963.

12. *New York Times*, August 13, 1963.

13. *Ibid.*, August 7, 1963.

14. *Ibid.*, June 30, 1963; July 10, 20, 25, and 30; August 13 and 15, 1963.

15. NAACP, Urban League, Association of Catholic Trade Unionists, Workers Defense League, Congress of Racial Equality, and the Negro-American Labor Council.

16. *New York Times*, July 8, 1963.

17. *Ibid.*, July 13, 1963.

18. *Ibid.*, July 18, 1963.

19. *Ibid.*, July 4 and 17, and November 14, 1963.

20. *Ibid.*, August 20, 1963.

21. *Ibid.*, June 21, 1963.

22. *New York Times*, September 14, 1963.

23. *Ibid.*

24. *Ibid.*, December 19, 1963.

25. *Ibid.*

26. *Ibid.*, December 20, 1963.

27. *Ibid.*, January 30, 1964.

28. *Ibid.*

29. N.Y. City Commission on Human Rights, *Bias in the Building Industry, An Interim Report to the Mayor*, December 13, 1963, p. 10.

30. *Ibid.*, pp. 11-12.

31. *Ibid.*, pp. 12-16.

32. *Cleveland Press*, July 18, 1963.

33. *Cleveland Plain Dealer*, July 19, 1963; see also *Plain Dealer* editorial, July 22, 1963.

34. *Cleveland Press*, July 30, 1963.

35. *Cleveland Plain Dealer*, July 30, 1963.

36. *Ibid.*, July 21, 1963.

37. *Ibid.*

38. *Ibid.*, July 24, 1963.

39. *Ibid.*, July 28, 1963.

40. *Ibid.*, July 29, 1963.

41. *Ibid.*

42. *Ibid.*, July 28, 1963.

43. *Ibid.*, July 31, 1963.

44. *New York Times*, August 9, 1963.

45. *Cleveland Plain Dealer*, August 8, 1963.

46. *Ibid.*, August 20, 1963.

Public Policy and Discrimination in Apprenticeship

George Strauss and Sidney Ingerman

[*From* The Hastings Law Journal, *February, 1965, by permission.*]

Negro action groups have given high priority to the elimination of discrimination in apprenticeship.[1] Sharp declines in the number of unskilled jobs which Negroes have traditionally filled, the high percentage of Negro youth unable to find work, and the often publicized forecast of shortages of skilled tradesmen provide an important part of the motivation for making the responsible well-paying jobs of the apprenticeable trades available to Negro youth. A. Philip Randolph, international president of the Brotherhood of Sleeping Car Porters has declared: "It is an understatement to observe that the elimination of racial discrimination from all apprenticeship training programs involves the economic life and death of the black laboring masses."[2]

[1]The research reported here is part of a larger study of apprenticeship which has been supported by a Ford Foundation grant to the Institute of Industrial Relations, University of California, Berkeley, for Research on Unemployment and the American Economy. Research methodology includes interviewing, observation, and examination of relevant documents. Uncited quotations are from the authors' confidential interviews. For an early report of this research see Strauss, *Apprenticeship: An Evaluation of the Need in* EMPLOYMENT POLICY AND THE LABOR MARKET 299-322 (Ross Ed. 1965). This report is based also on previous research in upstate New York see Strauss, UNIONS IN THE BUILDING TRADES (1958). The authors wish to thank Barry Silverman for research assistance.

[2]*Hearing on H. R. 8219 Before the Special Subcommittee on Labor of the House Committee on Labor and Education,* 87th Cong., 1st Sess. 121 (1961). [hereinafter cited as *House Hearings*].

There is little question that Negroes are badly represented in apprenticeship. According to the 1960 census, only 3.3 per cent of all apprentices are Negro, while in the two largest and often considered the most progressive states in the Union, California and New York, the percentage falls to 1.9 and 2.0 respectively.[3] Even where government agencies have a maximum amount of leverage available to implement equal employment policies, evidence of discrimination in the training of Negro apprentices persists. A spot survey of 47 federal construction projects indicated that of 303 apprentices, only 16 were Negro.[4]

At first glance, such imbalance may seem incongruous. George Meany, the Executive Council of the AFL-CIO, and the AFL-CIO Building Trades Department have all taken positions against continued discrimination in apprentice training programs. Discrimination in apprenticeship, as in all forms of employment, is now contrary to public policy and would seem to be particularly susceptible to governmental remedy, since government agencies are especially charged with promoting and regulating apprenticeship, and since "related training" classes necessary for the programs are typically conducted in public school systems. Furthermore, there is no a priori reason why Negroes should not make good apprentices. Over one hundred years ago substantial numbers of Negro slaves and freemen were trained as skilled tradesmen in the ante-bellum South.

Why, then, are there so few Negro apprentices? What explains the relatively limited success of governmental anti-discrimination efforts to date? Can we prescribe more effective regulatory mechanisms? These are the questions which this paper will attempt to answer.

Our emphasis will be primarily in the building trades, since this is the field where the largest amount of current apprentice training occurs (as of January 1, 1963, out of 158,616 registered apprentices in the United States, 103,046 were in construction).[5] Our discussion of governmental regulatory activities will be focused on the efforts of the

[3]California Division of Apprenticeship Standards, Survey of Active Apprentices 5 (1962); NEW YORK STATE COMMISSION AGAINST DISCRIMINATION, APPRENTICES, SKILLED CRAFTSMEN, AND THE NEGRO 15 (1960) [hereinafter cited as APPRENTICES, SKILLED CRAFTSMEN, AND THE NEGRO.] The California study was based on a sample which is probably not representative.

[4]N.Y. Times, June 28, 1963, p. 13.

[5]*The Role of Apprenticeship in Manpower Development: United States and Western Europe,* in 3 SUBCOMM. ON EMPLOYMENT AND MANPOWER, SENATE COMM. ON LABOR AND PUBLIC WELFARE, SELECTED READINGS IN EMPLOYMENT AND MANPOWER, 88th, Cong., 2d Sess. 1216 (1964).

federal government and of our two largest states, California and New York.

We will first discuss the present pattern of racial imbalance in apprenticeship. We then seek to explain why there are so few Negro apprentices. Next we examine why Negro action groups place so high a priority on opening apprenticeships to Negroes, and why the building trade unions (the ones primarily involved) resist outside intervention so strongly. Finally, we seek to appraise the effectiveness of governmental efforts, and suggest the major problems of legal engineering involved in developing a meaningful public policy in this area.

Patterns of Imbalance

The South

The South has traditionally been the training ground for Negro craftsmen,[6] and the bulk of Negro journeymen in the building trades are still employed in that region.[7] It is therefore appropriate to begin by stressing that events in the South have had and continue to have an important bearing on the skilled craft employment pattern of Negroes throughout the nation.

Paradoxically, in view of the difficulties Negroes now face in entering the skilled trades, Negro slaves and freemen provided a significant source of trained artisans in the ante-bellum South. "Al-

[6]Individual histories suggest that a high percentage of Negro building tradesmen in New York City have obtained their training in the South. A study dealing with Detroit explains, "Generally speaking, the majority of Negro building artisans have been trained in the lower Southern border States. In an interview in 1941, Mr. Joseph Meyer, Secretary of Detroit Local No. 2 of the Brick Masons and Plasterers' International Union, stated that 'practically all' of the Negro members in his local organization had been trained in the South. He said that the practice in Detroit was to admit 'the cream of the crop' of the highly skilled bricklayers migrating from the southern areas. This was said to work out 'better' for the union and the trade than training Negro apprentices locally. Mr. Meyer also said that southern-trained mechanics in the trowel trades tended to be superior to those who enter the trade in the North because the southern recruit had a somewhat better chance to gain valuable experience through steady employment at his trade." Meyers, The Building Workers, A Study of Industrial Sub-Culture 118-119 (1945) (unpublished Ph.D. thesis in University of Michigan Library).

[7]In 1960, 75% of all Negro carpenters, 72% of Negro brickmasons, tile layers and stone cutters, 68% of Negro plasterers and cement finishers, and 56% of Negro painters were employed in what the census defines as the South. U. S. CENSUS OF POPULATION 1960, U. S. SUMMARY, DETAILED CHARACTERISTICS, 1-544, 1-717.

TABLE 1

SELECTED CRAFTSMEN AND APPRENTICES IN CHARLESTON, SOUTH CAROLINA, 1848

Occupations	Male Slaves	Free Negroes	White Males
Apprentices	43	14	55
Carpenters	120	27	119
Masons & Bricklayers	68	10	60
Painters & Plasterers	16	4	18
Tinners	3	1	10
Ship's Carpenters & Joiners	51	6	52
Printers	5	0	65
Coachmakers & Wheelwrights	3	1	26
Cabinetmakers	8	0	16
Upholsterers	1	1	10
Blacksmiths & Horseshoers	40	4	51
Millwrights	0	5	4

Sources: Dowson & De Saussare, Census of Charleston for 1848, at 31-36 (1849), cited in Evans, The Economics of American Negro Slavery, 1830-1860, in Aspects of Labor Economics 189 (National Bureau of Economic Research ed., 1962).

though occupational census data were not tabulated by race until 1890, it is generally believed that in the ante-bellum South, the bulk of the building work was performed by Negroes."[8] Negroes were frequently trained as apprentices.[9]

The city of Charleston, South Carolina, with about half its population Negro in 1848, used, employed, and trained Negro craftsmen in what we would now consider "racially balanced" proportions. Table 1 shows that more than half of the city's carpenters, masons and bricklayers, painters and plasterers, ship carpenters and joiners, and blacksmiths and horseshoers were Negroes, as were 57 of 112 apprentices.[10]

[8]Myrdal, Sterner & Rose, An American Dilemma 1100-01 (1944).

[9]For a good discussion of ante-bellum Negro apprenticeship see Apprentices, Skilled Craftsmen and the Negro ch. 2. See also Kelsey, *The Evolution of Negro Labor,* 21 Annals 55 (1903).

[10]With a Negro population of about 20,000 the city of Charlotte, South Carolina, had 57 Negro apprentices in training in 1848. The 1960 Census of Population reports 829,291 Negroes in the *State* of South Carolina and a total of 61 Negro apprentices in training.

Following reconstruction, southern Negro craftsmen were excluded from some positions they had previously held[11] and were prevented from developing skills in the newly emerging electrical, pipe, and metal trades, or from obtaining training in the newer aspects of traditional trades. Although census data on apprenticeship is notoriously unreliable because of the difficulty in defining an apprentice, Table 2 illustrates both the relative and absolute downward trend of apprenticeship openings for Negroes in the South.

At present, we find Negro apprentices are relatively scarcer than Negro journeymen in the South. For example, as of the spring of 1963, there were no Negro apprentices in Dade County (Miami), while there are at most 30 in the whole State of Tennessee. Of these, 4 were on AEC sponsored projects and the rest were being trained in carpenter, roofers and trowel trades locals.[12]

One reason for the small number of Negro apprentices is the existence of segregated schools. There were no related training classes for Negroes in Dade County and only one (a roofing class) in Memphis. Another reason is that Negro journeymen, already faced with restricted work opportunities throughout the South,[13] are rarely willing to train Negro apprentices. Practically all Negro apprenticeship in the South is restricted to carpentry and the trowel trades, and is so-called "family apprenticeship," conducted on an extremely informal basis and in many ways inferior to the more formalized union-sponsored training which normally includes related instruction in the schools.[14]

Outside the Deep South

It has been easier for Negro journeymen to gain building trade training and union membership in some Southern States than in most Northern Cities.[15] Outside the deep South, Negroes have never been able to penetrate apprentice training programs in any significant numbers. This situation has as yet not changed markedly. In early 1963, of 2,400 apprentices in Maryland, only 20 at most were Negro,

[11]"In Maryland it is reported that the Negroes controlled the skilled trades in 1860. By 1890 they had been largely reduced to the status of hod carrier." Meyers, *op. cit. supra* note 6, at 107.

[12]COMM'N ON CIVIL RIGHTS, REPORTS ON APPRENTICESHIP 57, 127, 128 (1964) [hereinafter cited as REPORTS ON APPRENTICESHIP].

[13]NORTHRUP, ORGANIZED LABOR AND THE NEGRO 20 (1944).

[14]Wheeler, *The Impact of Race Relations on Industrial Relations in the South*, 15 LAB. L.J. 474 (1964).

[15]MARSHALL, THE NEGRO AND ORGANIZED LABOR 101 (1965).

TABLE 2

TOTAL APPRENTICES, NEGRO APPRENTICES, AND PERCENTAGE OF NEGRO APPRENTICES IN FOUR SELECTED SOUTHERN STATES FOR THE YEARS 1890, 1920, 1950, AND 1960

	1890	1920	1950	1960
Alabama				
Total	331	817	1,090	913
Negro	73	118	115	48
Percent Negro	22.1	14.4	10.6	5.3
Florida				
Total	237	420	1,851	2,386
Negro	67	43	54	103
Percent Negro	28.3	10.2	2.9	4.3
Georgia				
Total	779	952	1,087	1,243
Negro	247	130	113	75
Percent Negro	31.7	13.7	10.4	6.0
Virginia				
Total	964	1,397	2,118	1,705
Negro	186	107	94	76
Percent Negro	19.3	7.7	4.4	4.4

Source: U.S. Census of Population

and of these, 9 were carpenter apprentices in a Jim Crow local.[16] In Montgomery County, Maryland, outside of Washington, there was not a single Negro among 122 apprentices in related training. Even token integration on government construction was not obtained in Baltimore until Negro demonstrations took place in the summer of 1963.[17] The situation in Washington D.C. was little different and has only recently improved somewhat as a result of strenuous pressure by the federal government.

As we have seen, reports indicate that in California only 1.9 per cent of the apprentices were Negro, in New York 2 per cent. In Connecticut[18] and New Jersey there were less than 0.5 per cent.[19] (The starkness of the racial imbalance in New Jersey can be appreciated when we note that at the same time, 30 percent of vocational

16 REPORTS ON APPRENTICESHIP 67-68.

17 *Id.* at 78.

18 Connecticut Commission on Civil Rights, Civil Rights Bulletin 2 (Aug. 1953).

19 REPORTS ON APPRENTICESHIP 92.

school enrollment was non-white.)[20] A recent report indicates that there are no Negro apprentices in the building or printing trades of Milwaukee.[21] Herbert Hill, labor secretary of the National Association for the Advancement of Colored People, testified in 1961 that roughly similar conditions existed in St. Louis, Minneapolis, and Newark, New Jersey, while in Philadelphia less than four per cent of the apprenticeable trades were open to qualified Negroes.[22]

Since 1960 breakthroughs have been made in Jim Crow apprentice programs in many major cities, but even in these cities many apprenticeships are still effectively closed to Negroes. For example, let us look at New York City: Plumbers Local 2 (Manhattan and the Bronx), George Meany's home local, was lily-white until forced by picketing and political pressure to admit a token number of Negro apprentices in the summer of 1964.[23] Ironworkers Local 40 (Manhattan) admitted its first and, up to September 1964, only Negro apprentice in 1963; it had no Negro journeymen, while its Brooklyn sister Local 361, had no Negroes in either category.[24] Sheet Metal Workers Local 28 remained adamant until the summer of 1964, refusing to admit any Negro apprentices or journeymen, even in the face of a formal order by the State Human Relations Commission.[25] In 1961 Electricians Local 3 had but eight Negroes in construction work, but in 1962 it lived up to its reputation for being different: after winning its twenty-five hour week, unprecedented in the construction industry, Local 3 recruited 1,000 new apprentices, 140 of whom were Negro and 60 Puerto Rican. "This dramatic result and Local 3's broad recruiting effort is, so far as we know, without parallel in any building trades union in the country."[26]

Somewhat equivalent patterns of imbalance exist outside the building trades. Two studies of General Motors, for example reported there was but 1 nonwhite among 289 apprentices in the Detroit area

[20] *Id.* at 91.

[21] *Id.* at 145.

[22] *House Hearings* 91.

[23] *Reports on Apprenticeship* 116; N.Y. Times, Aug. 14, 1964, p. 25.

[24] N.Y. Times, Sept. 3, 1964, p. 22.

[25] Lefkowitz v. Farrell, C-9287-63 (N. Y. State Commission for Human Rights, 1964 (mimeo.)).

[26] REPORTS ON APPRENTICESHIP 117. Another study suggests the possibility that these new apprentices "are not apprentices in the ordinary sense of the word but in fact are a special force to do heavy work and are not expected to advance through the apprenticeship program to full membership, become 'A' card holders, and receive full pay and benefits." Shaughnessy, A Survey of Discrimination in the Building Trades Industry 35 (1963) (unpublished ms. in Columbia University Library).

in 1960 and but 2 nonwhites out of 171 apprentices in the Central Atlantic area in 1963.[27] A 1958 report indicates that the 19 railroads operating in New York and New Jersey employed a total of 594 apprentices, and only 4 were Negro.[28]

Overall Picture

The South has historically been the primary training area for Negro building craftsmen. The long-term decline in training opportunities in the South, coupled with the fact that young Negro workers are not being trained in significant numbers in *any* part of the country, tends to have a deleterious effect on overall Negro participation rates in skilled-craft employment. Negro apprentices and craftsmen have for the most part been excluded from the expanding electrical, pipe, and metal trades, and have found work mainly in the trowel trades, carpentry, and painting, where employment has been either growing slowly or contracting during the past decade.[29]

Pressure from the civil rights movement, governmental agencies, and the AFL–CIO national leadership has resulted in a few major steps toward equal employment opportunities in apprentice training, but for the most part, only a token number of Negroes have been able to penetrate traditionally Jim Crow apprentice training programs.

Why Negroes Don't Become Apprentices

We have already indicated the pervasive national pattern of Negro exclusion from the skilled trades and especially from apprentice training opportunites. There is little doubt that this pattern is to a considerable extent the result of outright racial discrimination.[30] Little more will be said about it here. However, in a subsequent section we

[27]Bloch, The Employment Status of the New York Negro, 1920-60, at 10 (1964) (typescript). These studies report 67 nonwhites out of 11,125 skilled tradesmen in the Detroit area and 230 nonwhites out of 11,314 skilled tradesmen in the Central Atlantic area. See also STEIBER, GOVERNING THE UAW 125 (1962).

[28]Cited in APPRENTICES, SKILLED CRAFTSMEN, AND THE NEGRO, *passim.*

[29]Of 7 major building trades in only 4 were there more than 4% Negro in 1960. In 3 of these, the carpenters, plasterers, and painters, employment declined from 1950 to 1960. Only in the bricklayers did employment rise. On the other hand, the 3 "mechanical trades," the electricians, plumbers, and sheetmetal workers, all had rising employment and a Negro representation of less than 4%. See U. S. CENSUS OF OCCUPATIONS, 1950 & 1960.

[30]*House Hearings passim.*; APPRENTICES, SKILLED CRAFTSMEN, AND THE NEGRO 91-96.

will examine the specific motivations and mechanisms that make this problem a particularly difficult one in the building trades.

Other factors are also at work. These include environmental and educational influences primarily affecting Negroes and barriers that obstruct Negroes in the same manner as all potential craftsmen who do not have relatives, friends or "connections" in the trades. At least five barriers to Negro participation may be noted: (1) qualified Negroes rarely perceive the skilled trades as a potential occupation; (2) Negroes have little information as to how to apply for apprenticeship openings; (3) Negroes often cannot meet the formal qualifications required for entry into apprenticeship; (4) even where they meet the formal qualifications, they do not have the proper "connections" or "sponsors"; (5) even after winning formal acceptance into the program, they find it difficult to win social acceptance on the job.

Not Perceived as a Potential Occupation

Youths usually become interested in apprenticeship and skilled craft employment because a parent, relative, friend, or neighbor provides the necessary encouragement and aid that makes such a choice seem desirable and feasible. Adults frequently provide "role models" which influence youths to enter an occupation; a high percentage of white apprentices report that they entered apprenticeship upon the advice of friends or relatives already in the trade.[31] The chances of Negroes receiving this kind of encouragement are slight.

To be sure, Negroes working as laborers and helpers in and around the building trades are well aware of the desirability of skilled-craft jobs. However, because of their first hand experience with discrimination in these trades, this knowledge is seldom converted into positive efforts to encourage youngsters to prepare for apprentice programs. Vocational-guidance counsellors often tend to steer Negro and other nonwhite youths away from training for occupations known or believed to be racially restricted.[32] Negro adults also discourage these tendencies because of their own employment experiences and pessimistic view of the present occupational environment.[33] Thus,

[31]GINZBERG *et al.*, OCCUPATIONAL CHOICE (1951); Schuster, *Career Patterns of Former Apprentices in the Construction Trades,* 5 CONSTRUCTION REV. 4 (1959); Swerdloff & Bluestone, *Backgrounds and Career Choice of Tool and Die Makers,* 76 MONTHLY LABOR REV. 8 (1953).

[32]Babow & Howden, A CIVIL RIGHTS INVENTORY OF SAN FRANCISCO (Part I, Employment) 89 (1958).

[33]"The Negro child, moreover, is also likely to respond to the attitudes of the dominant white population toward the work role of his race. Seeing his elders

because an early interest in apprenticeship is not normally a part of a Negro youth's background, relatively few consider applying for apprentice positions.

Negro students with better than average grades and high motivation are more likely to prepare for the professions and white collar work than are their white counterparts. "Over the years, Negroes have not been able to rationally plan their life work and usually have badly skewed occupational goals. 'As a result of his background, the ambitious young Negro is even more likely than the white youth to scorn skilled work and to overestimate the importance of achieving status through white-collar or professional employment.'"[34] A report on high school graduates in Milwaukee concludes that "Negro students with better grades overwhelmingly chose academic courses, while Negroes who chose vocational training had grade averages so low as to indicate no potential for the apprenticeable trades. The brighter youths understandably seek training in employment they know to be open without regard to race."[35]

Lack of Information

Negroes are often at a disadvantage because they do not know how to apply for apprenticeship. White applicants normally learn about vacancies from relatives or friends working in the trade. "Since Negroes have been excluded from many unions and trades over a period of time, there is no one on whom the young Negro may rely for information about apprentice openings. . . ."[36]

Union after union reports that few if any Negroes apply for apprenticeship. For example, the business agents of the Washington,

holding down poor jobs and sensing that the white community takes this for granted, the Negro child is not likely to develop high aspirations for himself." GINZBERG, THE NEGRO POTENTIAL 99 (1956). It is also suggested that since Negro youths rarely have families able to support them during the early periods of apprenticeship, when wages may be half that of journeymen (and often are themselves primary sources of support for their families), Negroes just cannot afford to enter apprenticeship. *Cf.* APPRENTICES, SKILLED CRAFTSMEN AND THE NEGRO 72-74. However, apprentice starting wages of $2.00-$2.25 (and sometimes much more) per hour are somewhat higher than the wages on jobs the average Negro youth can get. Consequently, this is probably not an important factor.

[34] *Id.* at 72 citing GINZBERG, THE NEGRO POTENTIAL 108 (1956); see also Antonovsky & Lerner, *Negro and White Youth in Elimira,* in DISCRIMINATION AND LOW INCOMES 134 *passim* (New York State Commission Against Discrimination ed. 1959).

[35] REPORTS ON APPRENTICESHIP 147.

[36] *Id.* at 146.

D.C. locals of the Plumbers and Ironworkers both ascribed the lily-white conditions of their locals at least in part to the fact that they had *never* received a Negro application.[37] The business agent of the Ironworkers in New York testified that only two Negroes had ever applied for membership in his local.[38] Until the summer of 1963, Sheet Metal Workers Local 28 had never received a Negro applicant.[39] The New York State Commission Against Discrimination asked 170 representatives of firms or joint committees indenturing apprentices why they did not have any or many Negro apprentices. Of the 142 who answered, 58 explained in terms of "no Negro applicants; few or none apply."[40] And many other examples might be cited.

Roughly the same story was told us during our interviews. One business agent, for example, made the following comment:

> I know you have a question you haven't asked yet. We don't have any Negroes in our local. During my time as business agent I have never had one apply. Well, there was a fellow who called over the phone; his voice sounded like a Negro's. I told him the truth—that we weren't accepting any applications and I told him to call again next month and maybe we would have different news for him. That's all.

Certainly, unions make little effort to publicize their openings. It is assumed that those who are "around" the trade will know the proper procedure and there is apparently little concern about anyone else. Outsiders are often given the cold shoulder.

The Wisconsin Advisory Committee to the United States Commission on Civil Rights describes this problem vividly.

> It was difficult even for our Advisory Committee in a day-long session with experts in the apprenticeship field to get a clear picture of how one actually does apply for an apprenticeship. One fact that emerged, however: a youngster trying to break into the field without expert assistance would find it discouragingly difficult to get the necessary information.
>
> The Wisconsin Industrial Commission publishes a guide for school counselors on apprenticeship, which lists seven sources of further information on opportunites. Among these are three government agencies, the Industrial Commission itself, the State

[37] *House Hearings* 140, 148.
[38] N.Y. Times, Aug. 5, 1963, p. 19.
[39] N.Y. Times, Aug. 17, 1963, p. 8.
[40] APPRENTICES, SKILLED CRAFTSMEN AND THE NEGRO 64.

Employment Service, and the Federal Bureau of Apprenticeship and Training. . . . [But] none of these agencies engage in . . . hiring. [Nor do the schools.] . . . The local trade union is also suggested, but the union officials told us that employers do the hiring. Employers are suggested, but if there is a trade association, it is suggested that it be contacted. If there is a joint apprenticeship committee, it is suggested as a source of information. From the testimony we did get the idea that if the applicant succeeds in locating the joint apprenticeship committee (the committees are not listed in the telephone directory) he would at least have found the place where the actual selection is made. The final suggestion ... is "Friends and/or relatives already engaged in the trade." This seemed to the Committee to be the contact most likely to produce results. But since this means is open only to those having friends or relatives in the skilled trades, it is obvious that the practical result is to exclude most nonwhites.

There exist no means by which the Negro youth or the general public may receive notice of specific apprenticeship openings.[41]

Lack of Qualifications

To be eligible for the better apprentice programs an applicant must now have a high school diploma and pass a formal screening examination that typically stresses knowledge of elementary mathematics. High school dropouts,[42] students educated in second-rate segregated Southern schools, and *de facto* segregated schools outside of the South often cannot meet these educational requirements.[43] We checked examination records and verified the claim by one union that none of the few Negroes who had applied for its apprentice program had received a passing score on the school-administered ad-

[41]REPORTS ON APPRENTICESHIP 145-146.

[42]"Only 40 percent of non-whites—compared to 70 percent of whites—complete high school." 1964 ECONOMIC REPORT OF THE PRESIDENT 16.

[43]The year's best plumbing graduate from Thomas Edison Vocational High School, Queens, New York, scored but 63 out of 400 points in the examination for admission into the apprenticeship program of Plumbers Local No. 1. On this test, which was administered by New York University, "the best prospective plumber in a New York City vocational school had been equipped by his teachers to rank less than a point above the *lowest five percent of American high school graduates* in alertness, mechanical capacity, and skill with numbers." Kempton, *The Meritocracy of Labor,* New Republic, Feb. 6, 1965, pp. 14, 15.

missions examination, even though a number of these applicants had satisfactory grades in Southern high schools.

Indeed, civil rights organizations sometimes find it difficult to recruit qualified applicants when apprenticeship vacancies are made available to Negroes.

> When one of the [New York] locals in the pipe trades did agree to accept a Negro apprentice at the request of the Civil Rights Bureau, it proved difficult to locate a qualified, interested Negro youth. In the summer of 1960, when Local 2 indicated to the Civil Rights Bureau [of the State Department of Law] that it would make two places available to Negro boys, it was only after great difficulty that the Bureau obtained the names of two interested and qualified youths, and one of these resigned from the program before he was inducted.[44]

A report from Las Vegas, Nevada tells of a Negro official of the Bureau of Apprenticeship and Training interviewing 50 Negro applicants in that city and determining that only 7 met the minimum educational requirements for apprenticeship. One factor that ruled out Las Vegas Negro applicants educated in the South was that they had no training in mathematics.

Lack of "Connections"

Apprentices are selected in the building trades normally by a joint union-management Joint Apprenticeship Committee (JAC), though sometimes by the union acting alone. JAC's are usually dominated by their union members; in any case, the question of whom to admit to apprenticeship is rarely one about which union and employer members split. In many cases there is implicit or explicit agreement that preference should be shown to friends and relatives. Thus, "discrimination for" is as important a problem as "discrimination against."

Not having a relative, friend, or "connection" already implanted in an apprenticeable craft is most likely the most serious barrier to

[44]Shaughnessy, *op. cit. supra*, note 26, at 23. Members of this same local walked off a New York City construction site recently when three nonunion Negro plumbers and a nonunion Puerto Rican plumber were hired onto the job as a result of efforts by the New York City Commission on Human Rights. After great pressure was exerted by the Mayor, the NAACP, and George Meany, President of the AFL-CIO, Local 2 agreed to accept these men into membership if they passed the standard journeyman's test. Three of the four men took the test. All failed the written examination that is a prerequisite to taking the examination on practical applications. N.Y. Times, May 1, 1964, p. 1; May 20, 1964, p. 33.

any potential applicant for apprentice training—whether he be Negro or white (though the extent of preference will differ from one community or trade to another and is probably stronger in construction than outside it). "It has been historic over the years," C. J. Haggerty, president of the AFL-CIO Building and Construction Trades Department, told a Congressional Committee, "that you become an apprentice boy in a given trade . . . by being a brother or a son or a cousin of a member, or of the employer or management. . . ."[45] Haggerty estimated that at least fifty per cent of apprentices fell into this class.[46]

In a number of cases apprentices to a given training program must be "sponsored," thus guarantying that "outsiders" are excluded. As a result, some building trades locals are dominated by one nationality. Sometimes being non-Italian or non-Irish is almost as sufficient cause for exclusion as being Negro. Of course, the general pattern of exclusion of Negroes, especially from the more desirable trades, makes the possibility of sponsorship for a Negro apprentice quite poor.[47]

Members of some minorities (such as the Irish and the Italian) have been provided jobs by members of their own group who have become entrepreneurs. However, there are relatively few Negro business concerns and even fewer Negro contractors who can provide apprenticeship openings.[48]

Apprenticeship openings are scarce compared to the number of workers desiring them.[49] Most apprenticeship programs have long waiting lists, and in some areas applicants must wait more than a year from the time they have been approved for a program until they actually begin training. The reason for this is simple: apprentice

[45]*House Hearings* 138.

[46]*Id.* at 133.

[47]An exception that proves the "rule" is Local 134 of the I.B.E.W. in Chicago which "opened its ranks to Negroes 35 years ago to protect itself from nonunion labor. About 200 of its 8,000 journeymen electricians are Negroes and it has 20 Negro apprentices. "They are the sons of journeymen,' Mr. Murray [the local's president] points out. 'That's how they got there,' " N.Y. Times, Aug. 26, 1963, p. 16.

[48]GLAZER & MOYNIHAN, BEYOND THE MELTING POT 31, 39 (1963), citing KINZER & SAGARIN, THE NEGRO IN AMERICAN BUSINESS (1950).

[49]There are presently fewer than 160,000 apprentices in training in programs registered with state apprenticeship agencies or the Federal Bureau of Apprenticeship and Training, and there were an estimated 225,000-250,000 apprentices in all programs during 1962. In that year there were only 55,321 new registrants in all registered programs, and of these 36,994 were in the construction trades. § 3 SUBCOMM. ON EMPLOYMENT AND MANPOWER, SENATE COMM. ON LABOR AND PUBLIC WELFARE, SELECTED READINGS IN EMPLOYMENT AND MANPOWER, 88TH CONG., 2d SESS. 1216, 1233 (1964).

training can lead to relatively high economic rewards for the worker with only a high school education. A 1961 survey of California journeymen who had completed apprentice training in 1955 showed that 52.4 per cent earned more than $8,000 per year; another 19.6 per cent earned between $7,000-$8,000 per year, and 84.5 per cent of these men reported buying or already owning their own homes.[50] If we couple the scarcity of these apprentice openings and the economic prize they represent with the fact that unemployment has become a principal problem facing high school graduates entering the labor force, we can readily understand why union members and contractors often give preference to sons, relatives, and friends when apprentice trainees are chosen.

Discrimination on the Job

Finally, even when a Negro is able to overcome all the hurdles thus far described, his troubles are hardly over. How fast an apprentice learns on the job depends to a large extent on the social relations he is able to develop. If other men ignore him, he learns little.[51] Thus, discrimination on the part of his co-workers may seriously hamper the Negro apprentice's training progress.

To sum up: all of the above barriers to Negro admission into apprentice training are directly or indirectly related to discrimination. The fact that there are few Negro sons of members is caused by the fact that there are few Negro members. Lack of knowledge of how to apply, lack of experience, lack of education—all are due largely to discrimination.

In view of the formidable complex of barriers to Negro entrance into apprentice training, and thereby the skilled trades, and considering the relatively small number of potential openings in existing apprenticeship programs even if racial discrimination were nonexistent, it is now relevant to consider why abolition of discrimination in apprenticeship has been given such high priority by civil rights action groups throughout the country.

[50]California Division of Apprenticeship Standards, Survey of Completed Apprentices Certified by the California Apprenticeship Council in 1955, at 6, 7, 18 (1961).

[51]"It is so easy to deep-freeze an apprentice out, in view of the relationship that exists between him and his journeymen mentors, and the master-pupil situation, which should give encouragement to the apprentice and help him over his troubles . . . . [T]here is a hostility which the Negro apprentice encounters, which is an added handicap when he is finally admitted to achieving journeyman status." Testimony of Francis A. Gregory, Assistant Superintendent of Education, Public Schools System, Washington, D. C., in *House Hearings* 119.

Civil Rights Pressures

Racial discrimination in apprentice training became an issue for the civil rights movement during the late 1950's.[52] At that time the National Association for the Advancement of Colored People tried to convince governmental agencies and union officials of the importance of eliminating Jim Crow apprentice training programs.[53] Other activities by civil rights leaders during this period included efforts to influence federal and state legislation in the area of apprentice training, and attempts by the Urban League to make placements of Negroes into apprentice programs.[54] All of these efforts produced, at best, only a few token openings for Negro apprentices in trades that had previously barred them.

By the spring and summer of 1963, deep-seated resentment against racial bias in the construction industry that had been smoldering in many Negro communities merged with employment demands of diverse civil rights groups to produce mass demonstrations at building sites throughout the country. The first major demonstration appears to have occurred in Philadelphia, in May of 1963, when pickets closed down an 18 million dollar project because of the longstanding Jim Crow policies of the electricians, plumbers, and steamfitters in that city.[55] Sit-ins, lie-ins, and picket lines soon be came the order of the day at construction sites in Harlem, Brooklyn, Elizabeth, Patterson, Newark, Cleveland, Detroit, Chicago, and Washington, D. C.[56] In each of these actions the fundamental de-

[52]As late as April 1960 the New York State Commission Against Discrimination was able to report that in regard to apprenticeship there was "an apparent sense of apathy on the part of the minority community. With one exception, no Negro group in New York State has raised the apprenticeship issue with the Commission Against Discrimination. Indeed, it appears that the efforts of these groups are aimed primarily at eliminating discriminatory employment policies and practices in white-collar occupations." APPRENTICES, SKILLED CRAFTSMEN, AND THE NEGRO 102.

[53]LABOR DEPARTMENT, NATIONAL ASSOCIATION FOR THE ADVANCEMENT OF COLORED PEOPLE, THE NEGRO WAGE EARNER AND APPRENTICESHIP TRAINING PROGRAMS 39-49 (1960?).

[54]Testimony of Herbert Hill, labor secretary of the National Association for the Advancement of Colored People, *House Hearings* 88; Testimony of A. Philip Randolph, president of the Negro American Labor Council, *House Hearings* 121; Testimony of Richard C. Wells, director of job development, Washington Urban League, *House Hearings* 159.

[55]Lees, *Philadelphia, Pennsylvania: A Process of Fragmentation,* Reporter, July 4, 1963, p. 18.

[56]N.Y. Times, July 10, 1963, p. 1; July 20, 1963, p. 1; July 25, 1963, p. 1; July 30, 1963, p. 1; Aug. 7, 1963, p. 1; Aug. 13, 1963, p. 1; Aug. 15, 1963, p. 1; Cleveland Plain Dealer, July 21, 1963, p. 1.

mand was for jobs for Negroes in the skilled crafts; and since, in theory at least, apprenticeship is the port of entry into these trades, the virtual exclusion of Negroes from apprenticeship in some trades soon became a central issue in these struggles.

Why have civil rights groups been especially concerned with racial barriers to skilled-craft opportunities? Negroes have been militant all through the 1960's, and the tragically high unemployment rate for Negro youth has made the need for jobs desperate. Yet given the pervasive patterns of job discrimination that have existed in all desirable areas of employment, why did the construction industry receive such particularly heavy emphasis from Negro protestors?[57]

1. The traditional sources of Negro employment in manual occupations seem to be drying up—particularly the relatively well paying jobs in the mass production industries and on the railroads. White-collar occupations are largely closed to Negroes because, among other reasons, of their poor education. On the other hand, educational attainments have been less frequently required for the skilled trades.[58]

2. Thousands of Negroes work as construction laborers; to move into the skilled trades seems like a promotion one step into a world they already know, not a jump into a world which is completely foreign. Many of these men have picked up a smattering of construction skills working as helpers, handymen, or on non-union jobs, and they feel capable of mastering a trade. In addition, significant numbers of northern Negro youth study subjects such as plumbing or electricity in vocational schools and have expectations of entering the skilled trades, expectations which are frequently frustrated.[59]

3. With a great deal of construction taking place in central sections of cities, in or near Negro communities, the high visibility of all-white crews of skilled tradesmen provides an open irritant to the Negro community. The antagonism is accentuated when these crews

[57]According to civil rights leaders to whom we have talked, the 1963 construction protests aroused greater support from the Negro masses than has any other activity previously or since.

[58]But the last few years have seen such requirements become considerably more prevalent.

[59]In Baltimore, 74% of the graduates from the predominantly white vocational high school found jobs in trades at least closely related to their field of study, while only 15% of the graduates from the all Negro vocational high school went into such trades. REPORTS ON APPRENTICESHIP 74-75. Five vocational high schools in New York City provide training in construction skills, yet "their better graduates, year after year, [are] forced to take low-paying, non-union jobs or else abandon the skills for which they are trained." Shaughnessy, *op. cit. supra* note 26, at 9.

work on urban renewal projects which displace present Negro slums for middle and upper income white housing.

4. Discrimination in construction has been ascribed largely to unions, and yet unions are presumably more democratic and more representative of the underdog than is management. The failure of many unions to meet these expectations has been particularly frustrating to Negro leaders.

5. Since a high percentage of new construction is supported by the government, and apprentice training programs often use public school facilities, there are obvious political possibilities here.[60]

6. Finally, Negro unemployment is particularly concentrated among youth, and Negro action groups look upon the apprenticeship programs as an opportunity to find work for thousands of unemployed Negro teenagers.

All these factors, and possibly others we are unaware of, combined to produce picketing, violence, and civil disobedience aimed at winning jobs for Negroes in the apprenticeable construction trades. In addition, as we shall discuss, the general level of governmental pressure for equal opportunity for Negroes in apprenticeships has markedly increased. With a few notable exceptions, the results of this pressure have been largely symbolic. In most instances a few Negro journeymen were hired onto disputed projects, and pledges were made to open apprenticeships in hitherto lily-white programs.[61] Only time will tell whether these minimal breakthroughs will be enlarged.

For an explanation of why the cumulative pressures of the Government, civil rights groups, and AFL-CIO leaders have produced so little payoff to date, we must look at some of the attitudes and characteristics of the building trades unions and the construction industry.

[60]During the 1963 demonstrations, related sit-ins took place at the New York Governor's office and the mayor's office in New York City and Newark, New Jersey. Many of the action groups made demands directed at local government.

[61]Token breakthroughs were made in New York in the plumbers, lathers, iron-workers and elevator constructors. N.Y. Times, Nov. 15, 1963, p. 22; Sept. 3, 1964, p. 22. Data as to the numbers admitted are hard to get. In September 1963 the Acting City Labor Commissioner said that as yet not a single Puerto Rican or Negro had been hired as a result of the demonstrations. N.Y. Times, Sept. 30, 1963, p. 1. Yet in December the union-management Referral Committee of the Building Industry, established as a consequence of the summer's demonstrations, reported that 111 minority group applicants referred by them had been accepted by New York construction unions. (The committee had received 3121 applications of which 849 met minimum standards.) N.Y. Times, Dec. 19, 1963, p. 22.

Craft Resistance

Building tradesmen have reacted strongly against the efforts of civil rights groups and the government to force them to change their traditional selection practices. Although racial prejudice is involved, the problem is more complicated than this. Building tradesmen have traditionally resisted all forms of outside control of the collective bargaining relationship; they look upon apprenticeship as a form of job protection; and they feel that nepotism is both moral and proper. These attitudes make them especially resistant to pressures for change.

Resistance to Outsiders

The building trades form a tight-knit social group. They have a strong sense of pride and identification with their craft and with the construction industry as a whole. The rough, dirty, dangerous nature of their job tends to draw them together and, in a way, to isolate them from the rest of the community. They have a sense of being different which is perhaps accentuated by the fact that the rest of the community tends to look down on them as "rough and dirty" and to treat them as "lower class," while their income is unquestionably middle class.

In any case, over the years, the construction community (both employees and contractors) have developed a tradition of self-regulation, particularly in regard to labor relations; they feel proud of their apprenticeship programs as institutions which they have developed by themselves; and they resent any outsiders meddling in what they feel to be a matter of purely private concern. Under the circumstances, union members are as likely to be motivated to win the battle against outside interference as they are by racial prejudice.[62]

Certainly many building tradesmen feel that the outside world has treated them unfairly. "The school counselors don't know our needs; they think any dumbbell can be an apprentice," a business agent charged. "They send us the trash and then charge us with discrimination if we don't take them." There is a great deal of resentment against outsiders who give unwanted advice. "The bullets are flying fast and furious," exclaimed a union official. "There are people coming out of the woodwork who you've never seen before; and they all set off pot shots at you." Discrimination is a fact of life, they argue, and other groups discriminate as well.

President Peter Schoemann of the Plumbers Union is an eloquent

[62]See MARSHALL, *op. cit. supra* note 15, at 129.

spokesman for one wing in the building trades which wishes to resist new regulations strongly. Though the temptation to quote him at length is great, we will cite but three passages:

> There comes a time when free citizens must stand up against government pressures and dictation, or succumb. So far as our apprenticeship program is concerned, that time has now arrived.
>
> We are convinced that our program is fair and just and successful. It is endangered today from one source—those who in public or private life, no matter how well intentioned, who want to use our program [for purposes] completely foreign to its reason for existence.
>
> To these theorists, to these social experimenters, to these impractical reformers, we say as to a child reaching toward a buzzsaw: "Hands Off."[63]

> [W]e resent the use of the equal employment campaign as a reason for a federal takeover in an area where the federal government does not belong.[64]

> Our apprenticeship programs are private enterprises. . . . [T]he committee members ... are not agents of the federal government, for we do have a free enterprise economy. . . . [T]hey must be allowed free scope in choosing the young men they want in their apprenticeship program. . . . If the federal government wishes to run its employee selection process on the civil service merit system, that is the business of the federal government. . . . but ... trade unions ... are not part of the government—at least not as yet.[65]

Protection of Job Control

Government efforts to regulate apprenticeship strike at "job control," the right to restrict entry into the trade which has traditionally been the heart of the craft unions' power. These unions have always been acutely conscious of the real or potential scarcity of job opportunities, particularly in an industry as subject to cyclical and seasonal fluctuations as construction. They have based their strength on controlling both the number of workers in a craft and access to available

[63]Pipe Lines, April 1964, p. 2 (publication of Plumbers' Local 38, San Francisco).

[64]Schoemann, *Report of the General President,* United Ass'n J., Sept. 1963, p. 56.

[65]*Id.* at 57.

work. "The Government's assertion that it should have a voice in who gets into the craft undercuts the traditional basis of union strength, in the eyes of union officials,"[66] and unions object to government regulations "mainly on the ground that they make the Government the final judge of who is qualified for apprenticeship."[67] Indeed, the Government's action threatens what are viewed as property rights in the job, rights which "have been won through years of training and fighting to build and strengthen unions."[68]

Building tradesmen in general exhibit a tendency to underestimate the long-run demand for their trade. As a consequence they resist outsiders' efforts to expand the size of their apprenticeship programs. Great pressure was placed on New York union leaders during the summer of 1963, at the height of the civil rights demonstrations designed to open their unions' doors to all qualified Negro journeymen and to begin an active program to recruit Negro apprentices. Union leaders argued at the time (the peak of the summer construction season) that there were over 12,000 unemployed construction workers in the city and building permits were sharply declining.[69]

The building trades unions reacted violently to a portion of President Kennedy's *Manpower Report* for 1963 which included a Department of Labor forecast of manpower needs in construction and called for a substantial increase in apprenticeship. This report, President Haggerty of the AFL-CIO Building Trades Department charged, can only "succeed in raising the hopes of and causing disillusionment in thousands of young boys. . . ."[70] The apprenticeship program has been turning out an adequate number of journeymen, Haggerty added, "and will continue, without government domination, to do it on schedule in the years ahead."[71]

Belief in Nepotism

Building tradesmen do not feel that family favoritism is immoral. Quite the contrary. They believe that the right to work in a trade is a property right that a man should be able to pass on to his children as

[66]N.Y. Times, July 31, 1963, p. 13.

[67]N.Y. Times, July 27, 1963, p. 8.

[68]MARSHALL, *op. cit. supra* note 15, at 129.

[69]N.Y. Times, August 1, 1963, p. 12. At the same time the New York Advisory Commission to the U.S. Commission on Civil Rights was suggesting that the long run prospects for construction employment were good.

[70] 3 SUBCOMM. ON EMPLOYMENT AND MANPOWER, SENATE COMM. ON LABOR AND PUBLIC WELFARE, SELECTED READINGS IN EMPLOYMENT AND MANPOWER, 88TH CONG., 2D SESS. 1158 (1964).

[71]*Id.* at 1159.

part of his estate. The point has been aptly made in a number of building trades journals[72] by coupling a quotation from the Talmud, "Any father who does not give his son a trade steals from him," with a quotation from Ben Franklin, "He that hath a trade hath an estate."

"The father-son tradition is no invention by us," a business agent wrote.

> The father-son tradition is just about as old as the country and . . . has been carried on by all classes, in every . . . aspect of American life. . . .
>
> Civil War General Arthur McArthur saw to it that his son, the late General Douglas McArthur, got into West Point, likewise Ex-President Eisenhower, a West Pointer, saw to it that his son got there too. . . . And yet, when a craftsman wants to do the same thing and help his son, he gets the business. . . .
>
> What really bugs me about this beefing against the father-son tradition, in the building trades, is the fact that because of this tradition, the skill developed by craftsmen was passed down through the years, all, of course, to the great benefit of the country.[73]

The attitudes of employers in the building trades reflect the attitudes of small business generally. It should be noted that the values of professional management, which dominate large corporations, are very different from those of small businessmen.[74] Though nepotism, apple polishing, and office politics undoubtedly continue to exist in a big business, these are universally condemned as unethical. The small businessman, on the other hand, typically feels under a moral obligation to do special favors for his friends; to him it is only right and proper that the better jobs be reserved for sons. And so employers tend to support the system of nepotism just as strongly as do the unions.[75]

For the above reasons, the bulk of the skilled trades have been antagonistic to efforts by the government and civil rights groups to open their ranks to outsiders, and particularly to Negro youth.

AFL-CIO policy is now unequivocally opposed to discrimination

[72]Pipe Lines, April 1964, p. 2.

[73]Mazzola, *Memo to the Members,* Pipe Lines, April 1964, p. 1.

[74]See Strauss, *How Management Views Its Race Relations Responsibilities,* in EMPLOYMENT, RACE, AND POVERTY (Ross & Hill eds. 1967).

[75]According to an employers' association, the right of an electrician to train his own son is "the most basic of human rights." CASCADE EMPLOYERS ASSOCIATION, WHAT'S WRONG WITH APPRENTICESHIP TRAINING 5 (1964?).

in employment,[76] and President George Meany has urged that racial discrimination in apprentice selection be made illegal.[77] In two critical cases where the Cleveland and Washington locals of the Electricians defied strong governmental and union pressures to permit qualified Negroes to work in their jurisdiction, President Meany threatened to remove these locals' charters and in the Washington case personally to recruit non-union Negroes to work on government projects.[78]

As these two cases illustrate, "local unions do resist and, sometimes, even reject policies laid down by the parent organization. If the action of the local union arises from the determined conviction of its membership, it is not easy for a democratic organization, like a trade union, to reverse that action—even if it is wrong."[79]

There is reason to believe that the rank and file feel more strongly about barring Negroes from apprenticeship than do local leaders, and that local leaders feel more strongly than do those on the state and national level. Rank and file leadership led the 1964 strike in New York when a contractor hired four Negro plumbers, upset an agreement reached to hire Negro plumbers in Cleveland in 1963, and made it difficult for the Detroit Electricians leadership to comply with an FEPC integration order in 1957. And, . . . local leadership revolted against the moderate leadership of state officers at the 1964 meeting of the California Conference on Apprenticeship.

The bitterness of the feelings expressed by building tradesmen should help us understand the difficulties from which government regulation of apprenticeship suffers.

Conclusions

Though apprenticeship would seem to provide a natural opportunity for Negro youth who are unable to find jobs, Negroes are seriously underrepresented in all but the least desirable trades, while the three most desirable ones are almost entirely white. Contrary to what we might expect, the imbalance of employment in the building trades (where most apprenticeship exists) is roughly the same, North and South, and over the last seventy years the overall pattern of exclusion has gotten worse, if anything, rather than better. Unless this pattern changes, Negro employment is likely to decline still further, since the trades in which Negroes are best represented are contracting, while

[76]Testimony of George Meany, *House Hearings* 6.
[77]*Ibid.*
[78]Marshall, *op. cit. supra* note 15, at 113-114.
[79]Testimony of George Meany, *House Hearings* 6.

those in which they are poorly represented are expanding. Underrepresentation is due not so much to discrimination *against* Negroes as it is to discrimination *for* relatives and friends. In addition, lack of motivation to enter apprenticeship, lack of knowledge of how to apply, and inadequate training and education all contribute to the present imbalance. All this suggests that simple remedies cannot do the job.

State fair employment practice laws have been generally ineffective in this area because of the difficulties of fixing responsibility and proving discrimination in each particular case. The state experience suggests that discrimination cannot be prevented until JAC's are required to establish objective standards for selection, standards which are susceptible of review. Since the promulgation of 29 C.F.R. 30, the federal apprenticeship agency has required that such standards be established. The problem here is one of enforcement, since the agency's only weapon, deregistration, is hardly a convincing deterrant. Government purchasing agencies may withdraw contracts where discrimination exists, but this means little in a situation where the union controls the labor market. Apprenticeship information centers cannot perform their function as long as JAC's refuse to cooperate.

Nevertheless, there has been some progress over the last two years. The combined impact of government regulations, Negro demonstrations, unofficial political pressures, and the efforts of AFL-CIO leaders has forced apprenticeship officials to be significantly more objective and formalistic in making selection, and has led to a significant number of previously lily-white unions opening their doors to at least token Negro representation. Precedents have been set which probably will not be broken.

One should view this problem in perspective, however. Understandably, Negro action groups have given high priority to the elimination of all barriers to employment. One wonders, however, whether their efforts may be somewhat misplaced. Though apprenticeship is the traditional means of entry into the building trades, particularly for the better jobs, it should be emphasized that only a small proportion of building tradesmen have ever completed apprenticeship.[80] Approximately 30,000 registered apprentices complete their training each year.[81] Were 12 per cent of these apprentices Negro, the proportion of Negroes to the population as a whole, 3,600 jobs per year would be available—only a drop in the bucket in terms of total Negro unemployment.

[80]Strauss, *Apprenticeship: An Evaluation of the Need, op. cit. supra* note 1.

[81]Statistics as to non-registered apprentices are not reliable, in part because of difficulties in defining who is an apprentice. The best estimate is that two-thirds of all apprentices are registered.

The advantages of apprenticeship to the industry as a whole are quite substantial, but from the point of view of the individual employer, these advantages barely outweight the disadvantages—and it is the individual employer who does the hiring. Within the union there are always strong pressures for restricting the size of membership and therefore for keeping apprenticeship programs small. Fear of government control is so great that were the government to attempt strict enforcement of anti-discrimination rules, the trades might well decide to restrict or abandon apprenticeship altogether rather than admit more Negroes.

Successful governmental action to eliminate discrimination in the building trades requires control over more than apprenticeship. It requires control over *all* forms of entry. An effective law would require that admission to closed-shop unions and dispatch to jobs be entirely on the basis of the non-discriminatory application of objective standards susceptible of review.[82] And since the trades would undoubtedly try to evade the law—as they have done with regard to the closed-shop and secondary boycott provisions of the Taft-Hartley Act—effective regulation would require a government enforcement agency with the power to regulate every step of the selection procedure.[83] It would practically require a government take-over in this area, and would drastically change the nature of collective bargaining in construction.

Over the years building tradesmen (both union and management) have developed a private government which has set regulations governing entry into a significant number of occupations. Though this arrangement has tended to exclude outsiders, it has worked reasonably well in terms of supplying adequately trained skilled craftsmen. The law suggested would substitute government regulation for grass roots participation. In a pluralistic society this would be a substantial loss. The choice is not easy to make. One can only hope that self-interest and an expanding economy may motivate the trades to take the initiative in eliminating unjustifiable barriers to entry.

[82]It might also be sound public policy to consider expanding vocational training programs in the school system.

[83]The New York State Advisory Commission to the U.S. Commission on Civil Rights recommends that if other forms of regulation fail, "Congress enact legislation declaring that admission to apprenticeship in the construction trades is a matter affecting interstate commerce and that such admission be vested in a suitable agency empowered to adopt and enforce procedures analogous to those employed by the Civil Service Commission." REPORTS ON APPRENTICESHIP 123.

Employment Tests and Discriminatory Hiring

Robert M. Guion

[*From* Industrial Relations, *February 1966, by permission.*]

The celebrated *Myart* v. *Motorola* case focused attention dramatically on the possibility that employment tests might be used, deliberately or inadvertently, as instruments of racial discrimination.[1] Paradoxically, the evidence of the case suggests that the test score apparently played only an obscure role in influencing the employment decision.

Nevertheless, many testers jumped to an immediate and often irrational defense of testing, and many critics of testing began to regard the employment test as the clever subterfuge of confirmed racists. Both reactions are unfortunate, and it is to be hoped that they will be superseded by a more realistic and moderate view. A less emotional appraisal of the current state of the art should bring forth certain admissions from both camps. Testers must admit that most companies using psychological tests in their employment procedures do not use them competently; more often than not tests are used with no knowledge at all of their validities for a particular situation. Conversely, critics must admit that other employment procedures are also typically misused and accepted on faith.

These remarks are devoted to test technology to the virtual exclusion of other employment procedures—with, I think, sufficient reason. Any procedure which can be used to discover, disprove, or verify claims of unfair discrimination through testing can also be applied to such other employment tools as interviewers' judgments, reference statements, or work histories. And let me clearly assert at the outset that despite many pitfalls, both obvious and hidden, competent psychological testing is better than any other hiring practice currently available. Such employment tools are designed to reduce the frequency of wrong decisions—hiring applicants who cannot do the job or rejecting those who could have done it well. Where tests have been used competently, they have been far more successful in reducing the number of mistakes than have, for example, such venerated practices as employment interviews.

The task of the tester is not to argue, but to develop procedures for reducing the mistakes still further. Now that our attention has been directed to the problem, it seems likely that many employment

[1]"Hiring tests wait for the score: Myart vs. Motorola," *Business Week*, February 13, 1965, pp. 45–46. Less easily obtainable, but much more detailed and complete is the account by Robert L. French, "The Motorola Case," *Industrial Psychologist*, II (August, 1965), 20–50.

decision errors attributable to tests have resulted in unfair discrimination. There is no virtue in arguing whether this is so; investigation, not argument, is necessary for the task of minimizing such errors. The word is minimizing, not *eliminating;* it is unreasonable and unrealistic to expect perfection.

It should also be clearly understood at the outset that the target of this article is *inadvertent* discrimination. As Ash has pointed out, any competent psychologist who wishes to do so can easily develop a selection process that will discriminate in illegal ways.[2] The dedicated discriminator, like an assassin, will find a way, and it may be through testing. However, we can leave it to judicial process to deal with blatant, deliberate discrimination. Our first concern must be with the fact that it is so easy to stumble into illegal discrimination inadvertently. It is when there is uncertainty—when one honestly does not know whether a test is an instrument of illegal discrimination—that tester and adjudicator alike need guides to follow.

Unfair Discrimination: Nature of the Problem

The employment plight of the Negro—"last hired, first fired"—is well-documented. During the last half century there have been advances in Negro employment opportunities without corresponding increases in relative incomes; in fact, the gap between Negro and white income seems to have widened during the fifties.[2]

This is not, by itself, direct evidence of discrimination. The fact is that Negro applicants are often less qualified than their white counterparts. The 1963 Report on Civil Rights listed such reasons for Negro unemployment as "inadequate education, inferior job training, discrimination by private employers, and discrimination in the state and local administration of federal programs."[3] A survey conducted under the auspices of Industrial Relations Counselors identified four areas in which Negro applicants generally seemed to be deficient: scores on achievement and aptitude tests, attentiveness to grooming and general attitudes during selection interviews, educational background, and work experience.[4] It has been observed that few Negroes are employed at higher organizational levels. Once again, this is partly due to the scarcity of Negro personnel qualified for managerial and executive work. However, the shortage can be attributed to the

[2]Daniel E. Diamond, "Occupational Shifts in Negro Employment," *Business Topics*, XII (Summer, 1965), 32–44.

[3]*Civil Rights '63*, U.S. Commission on Civil Rights (Washington, D.C.: 1963), p. 90.

[4]Paul H. Norgren, Albert N. Webster, Roger D. Borgeson, and Maud B. Patten, *Employing the Negro in American Industry: A Study of Management Practices*, Industrial Relations Monograph No. 17 (New York: Industrial Relations Counselors, 1959).

fact that capable Negroes have rarely seen much point in preparing themselves for executive positions; as Whitlow has put it, "The teaching professions grew in interest to the Negro because of the fact that there were no alternatives. We either went into teaching or nothing."[5] Now that many companies are actively, and many quite sincerely, seeking Negro managerial personnel, they must reckon with the consequences of the dry years which preceded the present situation in which it is a distinct advantage to be an intelligent Negro interested in professional management.[6]

That there is a vicious cycle is evident, and some employers are supporting or sponsoring programs to compensate for deficiencies in early experience. This is commendable, but neither law nor sound business practice demands it. However, both law and good sense demand that employers cease practices of unfair discrimination, including those that are inadvertent, which lead to unemployment. Perhaps the best way to break the cycle is to be sure that qualified Negroes get jobs they are qualified for.

Employment practice is by nature discriminatory, and it must be so. An employer cannot be expected to take on all applicants regardless of their qualifications; he is expected to be able to distinguish between those who are qualified and those who are not. The test of Table 1 is discriminatory; it discriminates between those with high and those with low probability of success. For a different illustration, women characteristically score lower than men on tests of mechanical aptitudes. Where such tests are used in making employment decisions, the effect is that women are less likely to be hired than men. The effect of the mechanical aptitude test is therefore discriminatory, but it can hardly be said to be discriminating against women unfairly unless low scoring women can actually perform the job as well as higher scoring men.[7]

[5]Edward W. Whitlow, "The Placement of Negro College Graduates in Business Organizations," in *Selecting and Training Negroes for Managerial Positions* (Princeton, N.J.: Educational Testing Service, 1964), pp. 41–50.

[6]Robert Mallory, "On-the-Job Experiences of Negro Managers," *ibid.*, pp. 131–134.

[7]Sometimes a generalization stemming from research on tests becomes the basis for employment decisions, even if the research had nothing to do with an employment problem. In the present example, such a generalization might be the basis for a general policy that a woman cannot be hired, no matter how high her score, because women are in general inferior (in this regard!) to men. An analogous illustration might be a verbal test on which the mean score of nonwhites is lower than the mean of whites, with the resulting policy being the automatic rejection of all nonwhite applicants. In either case, the prejudicial discrimination is manifestly unfair, but the fault is not with the test or with the use of tests in general. This kind of policy is simply not followed where there is competent use of tests.

In talking about discrimination, then, a clear distinction must be made between discrimination which is necessary and right and discrimination which is unfair. *Unfair discrimination exists when persons with equal probabilities of success on the job have unequal probabilities of being hired for the job.*

Civil Rights Act of 1964: Title VII. It is against the law to discriminate on the basis of race, color, religion, national origin, or sex.[8] Despite some of the static from the Motorola incident, tests cannot be considered unlawful unless "intended *or used* to discriminate because of race, color, religion, sex, or national origin."[9] The phrase "or used" is especially interesting. When the courts interpret this phrase, a test will probably be considered unlawfully discriminating in any situation in which the effect is unlawful discrimination. The basic question is what constitutes an unlawful discriminatory effect. I propose that a reasonable interpretation of the law will hold a test to be illegally discriminatory only when a specified group exhibits inferior performance on the test, but *not* on the job for which the test is a predictor. Conversely, a test is not unlawfully discriminatory when a group characteristic that depresses test scores also tends to depress job performance.

Much is heard about the effect of cultural deprivation on test performance, but less is heard about the effect of cultural deprivation on job performance. As Ash has pointed out, "neither the Illinois Fair Employment Practices Act nor any other similar act protects 'culturally deprived persons' as such from discrimination in employment"[10] He went on to say that it is likely that complaining applicants, their attorneys, and the courts will become sophisticated enough to distinguish between standards of *test* performance and standards of *job* performance.

The principal implication of Title VII, then, seems clear enough: test specialists had better be able to make the same distinction! People using employment tests had better gather data to demonstrate that their tests are valid as predictors of relevant aspects of job

[8]People who have not bothered to look at the provisions of the law have been making some rather unfunny jokes about female attendants in men's rooms or male "bunnies" in nightclubs or Nordic blondes playing the parts of African tribal rulers—as if all of these absurdities were made necessary by adherence to the law. Special requirements of sex, religion, or national origin are clearly permitted in circumstances where they are explicitly relevant and necessary for a particular lawful enterprise.

[9]Tower amendment to the 1964 Civil Rights Act, as quoted by Ash, *op. cit.*, italica mine.

[10]Ash, *loc. cit.*

behavior for all classes of applicants. And if these tests are found to be invalid, they ought not to be used.

Smoke screens. The basic issue of validity has been obscured by a vast smoke screen of irrelevancies. The solution to the problem of eliminating unfair discrimination through testing is obscured by these smoke screens, some of which are identified and commented on below.

1. *Debate over the reality of racial differences.* Even if it could be unambiguously demonstrated that one racial group is inherently inferior to another, the problem of unfair discrimination would persist. The overlap in any set of distributions showing ethnic differences is such that many people in the "inferior" group score higher than the average member of the "superior" group.

2. *Debate over whether race or cultural deprivation is the villain.* Many whites are culturally deprived; many nonwhites are not. It is not sensible to jump to the conclusion that cultural deprivation is the source of unfair discrimination. Such a jump is scientifically unjustified. Since racial identification is one variable and deprivation is a different one, both deserve study. The linking of the two is also legally of questionable use: the mere demonstration that a test does not discriminate unfairly against the culturally deprived may not be deemed competent evidence in court that it does not discriminate against racial groups.

3. *Debate over moral values.* The word "unfair" admittedly implies a moral judgment. However, if one can accept the definition of "unfair discrimination" offered here and can agree that the aim is to discover whether a test is or is not acting as an instrument of unfair discrimination within that definition, then the whole thing becomes more a technical than a moral matter, regardless of whether one's motive is to stay clear of the law, to redress earlier wrongs done by one segment of society to another, or to achieve a more complete utilization of society's manpower resources.

4. *Questions about why nonwhites are underemployed or unemployed more often than whites.* Answers are needed; the questions are important. Too often, however, the answers offered are unsubstantiated opinions serving as excuses for denying the problems of unfair discrimination.

5. *Concern over the social consequences of integration in employment.* Even where the concern is genuine, it does not solve the problems. Moreover, the predicted dire consequences seem never to materialize in organizations actually providing equal opportunities.

Research on Discrimination

Thorough, competent validation is not especially easy. Research which combines the ordinary task of validation with the less charted task of research on discrimination accents ordinary problems and finds some new ones.

Perhaps the most serious problem is the almost universal willingness to use unvalidated tests. An utterly disgusting phrase is all too common: "We feel that our tests are very good." Such feelings may be comforting, but they serve neither as evidence nor as a substitute for knowing what one is doing. Even many companies that routinely validate their tests shy away from any kind of research dealing with racial discrimination; it is a potato that is much too hot. Whether because of fear or inertia, testers seem to be hoping that they will never be called upon for evidence that their tests are nondiscriminatory, rather than doing something to seek evidence one way or the other.

The criterion problem is stickier in research on discrimination than in ordinary validation. Most personnel research relies on ratings; the ratings of a potentially prejudiced supervisor can hardly be used in research on discrimination. Fortunately, some special criterion variables have been provided by folklore and some of them are not too difficult to measure. In the selection of salesmen or other public-contact personnel, for example, customer reaction may well be one criterion. Here ratings of customers seem justified, although observations of customer behavior would be better. Or it may be said that minority group applicants are more likely to quit their jobs; turnover is an appropriate criterion measure, as are other personal variables: absenteeism, lateness, health and accident data, and so on. In general, however, one should develop objective measures of the same criterion variables that would be used in any other validation research. Other considerations aside, the current emphasis on equal opportunity in employment will have immeasurable value simply because it will cause organizations to consider carefully the outcomes they seek through all of their employment practices.

Another problem is that there are differences in test performances of different ethnic groups. Although this fact should not be used as a smoke screen to obscure the matter of predictive validation, it does pose special problems—principally because of the lack of scientific understanding of the basis of such differences. Group differences are often attributed to cultural deprivation. This is probably due to contemporary concern with Negro applicants who, a century after the Emancipation Proclamation, still carry with them the vestigial remains of slavery. Test differences are also found, however, for Jewish, Oriental, and certain national groups. Some of these groups may be culturally favored in some respect; others may have their own rich, through different, sorts of cultures. Can these differences be attributed to "cultural deprivation"?

Too much has been said about cultural *deprivation,* not enough about cultural *difference.* Certainly the ghetto and its attendant lack of communication with the outside—even when schools are integrated—fossilizes cultural differences. Some of the population differences may be due to suspiciousness; what has passed for cultural deprivation may be better described as cultural alienation. While the choice of term—deprivation, difference, or alienation—becomes relatively unimportant for the search for evidence of predictive validity, the question of cause poses genuine, long-range research problems.

For one thing, the nature of the differences in test performance needs to be better established. One should be rather cautious, for example, about such statements as "on the average, Negroes score lower than whites." The fact that this has generally been true may be more a reflection of test specialists' lack of imagination than of any underlying reality. It has been noted for several years that research on individual differences has been done with a rather archaic notion of the nature of intelligence. Dreger and Miller cite a study showing (among four ethnic groups each divided into low- and middle-class subgroups) differential patterns of scores on factorial test batteries.[11] The direction of differences between groups may prove to be much less important in future research than the kinds or patterns of differences that exist.

A further research problem is that of recruiting. In many organizations, there will be no opportunity to do any research at all unless there is a special effort to recruit from minority groups. For example, it has been shown that there is often a discrepancy between the attitudes of top management toward hiring Jewish college graduates and the actual practice of campus recruiters.[12] Clearly, managements must take unusual steps if they are to convince their recruiters that they are sincere in an equal opportunity program.

If a manager is embarking on a new push to hire Negroes, he must advertise in Negro periodicals, he must make direct contact with

[11]Ralph Mason Dreger and Kent S. Miller, *Recent Research in Psychological Comparisons of Negroes and Whites in the United States,* presented at the convention of the Southeastern Psychological Association in Atlanta, April 2, 1965.

[12]Lewis B. Ward, "The Ethnics of Executive Selection," *Harvard Business Review,* XLIII (March–April, 1965), 6–8.

local Negro organizations, and he should have personal contact with leaders of the Negro community. These are extraordinary recruiting procedures: the result is an extraordinary applicant population. If there are differences in validity, should these differences be attributed to racial differences or to differences in the recruiting procedures?

Despite the many problems and questions, the research must be done if an organization is to know whether it is guilty of unfair discrimination in its employment tests. There are several research models which can be used.

The use of moderator variables. A moderator variable may markedly influence validity. Most moderator variables have been used to describe or define differences between two or more groups which may have different patterns of validity. In a pioneer study, for example, Frederiksen and Melville[13] classified college students as either compulsive or noncompulsive and found interest test scores significantly more valid for the noncompulsive group. Compulsiveness in this example is a moderator variable; it "moderates" the effect of interest on academic performance.

Elsewhere, I have advocated investigating race as a moderator variable and suggested that different expectancy tables be developed for Negro and white applicants.[14] Table 1 offers, in schematic form, the kinds of results that might be found if expectancies were distinctly different for the two groups. It is designed to illustrate several possible research results and inferences: (1) that scores of the Negro sample may actually be systematically lower than those of the white sample, (2) that the kinds of relationships may be different for the two groups (linear for whites and nonlinear for Negroes), (3) that interpretations of very low scores may be the same for the two groups, while the interpretation of scores at another range may need to be different, and (4) that hiring standards can be expressed in terms of probabilities of success rather than in terms of test scores. Where distinctly different validities are found, hiring standards expressed as minimum test scores constitute unfair discrimination.

Table 2 offers a slightly different set of plausible results; it is like Table 1 only in that it assumes that scores in the Negro sample may actually be systematically lower than scores in the white sample. However, the kinds of relationships are the same and the interpreta-

[13]Norman Frederiksen and S. Donald Melville, "Differential Predictability in the Use of Test Scores," *Educational and Psychological Measurement,* XIV (Winter, 1954), 647–656.

[14]Guion, *op. cit.,* pp. 491–493. This is not an unusual suggestion; however, it is usually offered in terms of different regressions rather than different expectancies.

TABLE 1

RELATIONSHIP OF TWO HYPOTHETICAL DISTRIBUTIONS TO SPECIFIED EXPECTANCIES OF JOB SUCCESS WHERE STANDARDS MAY BE DEFINED ONLY BY EXPECTATIONS

Expectancy	Minimum test score for each expectancy White distribution	 Negro distribution
80	100	78
70	85	60
60	70	45
50	55	32
40	40	22
30	25	15
20	10	10

tions of individual scores are the same. Where the validities are this similar, there is no evidence of unfair discrimination, even if hiring standards are expressed in terms of test scores.

These two different kinds of results have important implications for employment practice. If one wishes to hire only the applicants whose expectancy of success is of the order of 50 per cent, the situation in Table 1 calls for different cutting scores for the two groups

TABLE 2

TEST SCORE INTERPRETATIONS FOR TWO HYPOTHETICAL DISTRIBUTIONS

Test score	Percentile rank		Expectancy	
	White	Negro	White	Negro
100	99	--	95	--
90	80	99	83	85
80	65	90	76	75
70	55	72	65	63
60	50	60	50	50
50	45	52	41	42
40	35	48	37	36
30	20	40	27	28
20	1	28	19	20

(55 for whites and 32 for Negroes), whereas the situation depicted in Table 2 calls for the same score (60) in each group.

Other moderator variables could be substituted for race—with, of course, the proviso that they can be shown to be relevant to the legal issues as well as to scientific investigation. Measures of cultural deprivation should certainly be investigated; Lockwood has proposed the use of personal history or motivational variables as potential moderators.[15] Ignoring the pressure of the legal issues for the moment, it seems likely that some of these might ultimately serve better than race as moderators.

There are several objections to, or potential restrictions on, the moderator variable approach. If race is to be the moderator, one stumbles immediately over the scientific difficulty of establishing clear yardsticks by which people can be classified into convenient racial categories. Returning to the legal pressures, however, and to the social problems which precipitated them, such yardsticks do not seem to be a really serious problem for the test specialist. He can classify as Negro anyone whom an employment interviewer so identifies; and he can do the same in classifying others as whites. Discrimination is not such a big problem to those Negroes who can be identified as such only by their own statements, genetic histories, or anthropological measurements!

A more general limitation to the moderator variable approach has been identified by Campbell. He distinguishes between indirect validity, where the trait measured is related to job success but not essential to it, and intrinsic validity, where any factor changing test performance (such as training) also changed job performance. He points out that the value of moderator variables is probably limited to situations of indirect validity.[16] Parenthetically, it might be noted that most employment tests fit this category—a fact of which employment testers are not very proud.

A practical objection is that the moderator variable approach intensifies two ordinary and difficult validation problems. The first of these is the frequent inability to identify the criterion variables; the second is the more prosaic problem of finding enough cases. It is not easy to find situations in which both Negroes and whites are being hired to do the same type of work at a rapid enough rate to gather the kind of data that one would desire. In one organization which

[15]Howard C. Lockwood, "Testing Minority Applicants for Employment," *Personnel Journal,* XLIV (July–August, 1965), 356–360.

[16]Joel T. Campbell, "The Problem of Cultural Bias in Selection: I. Background and Literature," *Selecting and Training Negroes . . .*, pp. 57–64.

attempted research on discrimination in employment testing, the design called for at least 60 Negro applicants. In a full year they were unable to find that many, despite systematic recruiting efforts—and their research, not involving validation, utilized all applicants whether hired or not.

A social or ethical objection sometimes offered is that the moderator variable approach establishes different standards for applicants of different ethnic groups. This objection does not deserve to be taken seriously, since it betrays a confused refusal or inability to make the necessary distinction between standards of test performance and standards of job performance.

Use of culture-free tests. Some investigators, assuming that unfair discrimination has cultural deprivation at its roots, are looking for ways to utilize the so-called culture-free tests. The use of such a test by itself does not seem to be very promising; however, culture-free tests might be used as something other than straightforward predictors. For example, such tests might be used where scores are marginal on ordinarily valid tests. The procedure would be to identify, probably in standard error terms, the range of scores around a cutting score in which additional information should be sought. That information would include the score on a culture-free test. The original test and the culture-free test, expressed in standard score units, would be compared. The degree of discrepancy between the two could be a measure of cultural deprivation; such a measure could be a moderator or it could, by itself, prove to be a valid predictor. Since these tests are typically measures of intelligence, their use seems especially worth considering where the criterion is trainability.

Krug has suggested two other classes of predictors, not intended to measure mental ability, which he considers to be relatively culture-free.[17] One of these is biographical information—a category more commonly thought to be especially biased. His argument is that the biographical inventory usually seeks indication of achievement or achievement motivation, of leadership experience, of breadth of interest, or of self-sufficiency. Items that reflect these variables, he says, have cultural equivalents. That is, whether one went to a Negro school, a white school, or an integrated school, questions about class offices held or subject matter clubs joined are essentially unbiased. The biographical inventory items that Krug is looking for, then, are those in which there is a "relative standard imbedded in the item"—i.e., the response is relative to the culture from which the applicant

[17]Robert E. Krug, "The Problem of Cultural Bias in Selection: III. Possible Solutions to the Problem of Cultural Bias in Tests," *ibid.*, pp. 77–85.

has come. Although the idea seems worthy of investigation, I would personally have serious reservations about the validity of the assumption of the unbiased relative standard.

Krug's second suggestion is the use of situation tests, which, he asserts, have high promise of validity, partly because of their realism and partly because of their novelty.[18] This is a depressing point of view; it suggests that any effort in employment testing is probably self-defeating. The argument is that ordinary paper-and-pencil tests are easier for the white applicant than for the culturally deprived Negro because the white applicant has encountered them quite frequently in the past; they are in no sense an unusual experience for him, whereas the situational test is novel to both. Unanswered is the question of what happens to situational tests, however, when they become commonplace enough so that they are no longer novel.

Compensatory models. Traditional prediction through multiple regression has been essentially compensatory; a deficiency in one characteristic can be overcome in the equation by an overabundance of some other characteristics. The compensatory model has worked in a wide variety of situations; it might well be the most useful solution to the problem of unfair racial discrimination in testing. Essentially, what is needed is an identification of the variables through which an individual can overcome an initial handicap that he may have, from whatever cause.

Traditional multiple regression can also be combined with the moderator variable idea for a different sort of compensation. That is, a variable might be identified that is relevant to one group and not to another; it might, where it is relevant, compensate for "underqualification." For example, commitment to the civil rights movement might, for a Negro youth, be the sort of motivational variable that could be called "the Avis syndrome"—being number two, he tries harder! Perhaps the discrepancy between an applicant's level of aspiration and the father's occupational level could be measured and used in multiple prediction equations for one or both groups.

[18]A situation test is one in which a person is placed in some kind of problem situation and his performance in that situation is observed and scored. A characteristic feature of the test is that the subject either does not know he is being observed or is unaware of the nature of the observations. For example, the subject might be placed in a situation in which he is supposed to exercise leadership in getting a task completed; at the same time, one might create in the situation essential obstacles to the completion of the task. The subject would probably be aware that he is being observed, but would not be aware that the obstacles were deliberately introduced for the sake of observing his reactions to them.

Coaching. Although the idea of coaching people on tests is usually repugnant to test specialists, there have been some indications that it might be useful. Hay once developed a "warm-up" test that served somewhat as a coaching device.[19] In an unpublished study, this writer once improved the validity of a psychomotor test by providing enough preliminary practice trials so that learning tended to level off by the time a trial was officially "scored." Perhaps more to the point, it has been shown in Israel (where there are wide individual differences in exposure to test and test-like situations) that straightforward coaching increases the validity of intelligence tests.[20]

Developmental models. Personnel research is typically concerned with static measurement. In effect, the researcher takes two snapshots, one of the individual as an applicant and another when his performance is evaluated. Perhaps it would be better to take movies: look at patterns of change, identify processes of change, and measure the magnitudes of changes that have occurred. With such an approach, perhaps an applicant's future growth could be predicted from the kinds of choices he had made earlier in certain sorts of inevitable situations, or from persistent reactions to identifiable challenge situations. This concept is vague, but it seems worth some thought.

A slightly different developmental approach integrates selection with training. Here the argument is that full utilization of Negro manpower resources cannot be achieved without establishing extraordinary training programs to compensate for the effects of a history of discrimination. The selection problem is to identify those who will profit most from such training. There are two prediction problems: (1) to identify variables in the training situation (grades, rate of learning, etc.) that are valid predictors of later performance, and (2) to find employment tests that are valid predictors of these variables in training.

The outlook in research. There is no evidence now available to indicate which models will be most useful for finding and eliminating unfair discrimination in testing; nor will such evidence become available until more equal-opportunity employers conduct the necessary research and publish the results. It is easy to be pessimistic and wonder whether the research will get done. If it is done, however, one can say quite optimistically that one by-product will be a general improvement in the state of test technology. At the very least, such research

[19]Edward N. Hay, "A Warm-up Test," *Personnel Psychology,* III (Summer, 1950), 221–223.

[20]Gina R. Ortar, "Improving Test Validity by Coaching," *Educational Research,* II (June, 1960), 137–142.

should result in a technically defensible individualization of employment testing in contrast to the more conventional group orientation. Furthermore, it is reasonable to hope that such research will move toward the identification of predictors with intrinsic validities.

Postscript

The point of view of this article may be identified by its omissions as well as by the topic discussed. For example, the concept of clinical prediction, as distinguished from statistical prediction, was given no place in the discussion of competence.

There are two reasons. First, clinical prediction is most necessary in hiring for positions where statistical validation is impossible because of the small numbers of people hired, e.g., executives. While discrimination is indeed a problem at these levels, the more pressing problem is probably at levels requiring less in the way of personal and background qualifications. The income gap between white and Negro, for example, is unlikely to be closed by intensive efforts to recruit executives from the centers of cultural deprivation; it is more likely to be closed first in the blue-collar and office occupations where "underemployment" is a numerically greater problem and where the necessary skills can soon be learned. At these levels, statistical prediction is possible, preferable, and essential.

In the second place, statistical prediction provides actual data—data which can be unambiguously presented to fair employment commissions or to courts as the legal issues relating to testing are examined. In contrast, clinical prediction depends on "expert judgment"—a less demonstrable quality.

Another important omission from this article is the lack of serious mention of discrimination against women, Jews, the Irish, American Indians, Spanish-Americans, Unitarians, and Seventh Day Adventists. Such discrimination can exist and is illegal whether deliberate or not. The models suggested for identifying it in testing apply to these groups as well as to Negroes. Moreover, such discrimination may well pose serious social problems; probably all—and more—that has been said about the plight of the Negro can be said about the plight of the American Indian.

The focus on employment opportunities of the Negro may be attributed, first of all, to the trend of the times. There is a special urgency about Negro employment. Contemporary civil rights movements are essentially Negro civil rights movements. The moral issues of discrimination against Negroes are known and vehemently debated, although both the moral decisions and the technical ones may be as applicable to other objects of unfair discrimination as to Negroes.

More than this, however, the focus on Negro employment may partly be due to a fear that time is running out, if indeed it has not already done so.[21] The civil rights movement is more aptly described as a civil rights revolution; all segments of the American community may be thankful that it has been, in the main, a nonviolent revolution.

Industry, the source of jobs, tends to be concentrated in northern communities—communities that have observed but have not participated in the upheavals of sit-ins, freedom rides, and voter registrations. Despite the drama of sit-ins, however, the basic issue has never really been equality in eating or riding as much as equality of economic opportunity. That means jobs—jobs in the industrial North as well as in the South. Civil rights leadership in the South has been nonviolent. Will it also be nonviolent in the North?

I doubt it. Nonviolence has not been a tradition in many industrial communities, and one can already observe parallels between today's civil rights movement and the labor strife of the thirties.[22] If major, catastrophic upheaval is to be avoided, there must be a concerted, intelligent effort to eliminate pretense and defense of the status quo—to seek out and to develop job competence and employment stability among Negro citizens. This means that industrial leaders—as individuals or as corporations—must take the initiative in (1) removing any removable causes of the lack of qualified Negroes in responsible positions and (2) removing the obstacles society has placed between the qualified Negro and the job he can do. Specifically, industrial leaders must take the initiative in the elimination of hope-destroying ghettoes, in the development of better schools for all children, and in the creation of technical and apprenticeship training centers where none now exist. Not the least of the needs is for industrial leaders to take the lead in authorizing or sponsoring research on possible discriminatory employment practices and seeing that it gets done.

It seems unfortunate that much industrial leadership must wait for demonstrations, laws, or riots to stimulate it to do what it ought to have done long ago; it seems unfortunate that efforts to eliminate the

[21]Consider the pessimism of Stewart Alsop who, following his trip to the scene of the Watts riot, said that America's racial problem may not have a solution; he compared it to a painful, incurable disease. "Watts: The Fire Next Time," *Saturday Evening Post,* November 6, 1965, p. 20.

[22]Robert B. McKersie, "The Civil Rights Movement and Employment," *Industrial Relations,* III (May, 1964), 1–21.

evils of unfair discrimination may take on the coloration of self-protection rather than concern for the welfare of others in a common society. Regardless of the motives, however, appropriate actions must be taken. But first they must be identified, and this calls for programs—crash programs—of research.

It is also to be hoped that the effect of the Negro civil rights movement will be more general, and that the broader question of unfair discrimination against those groups specifically included in the Civil Rights Act of 1964—women and other racial or ethnic groups—and against groups not specifically named in the act (e.g., recent high school graduates, older workers, epileptics) can be approached more effectively.

Training for Minority Groups: Problems of Racial Imbalance and Segregation*

Daniel R. Fusfeld

Although there are no provisions in the 1962 Manpower Development and Training Act which specifically refer to fair employment practices or nondiscriminatory training, the two federal departments involved in the Manpower Program decided from the beginning to operate the program on a nondiscriminatory basis. Following considerable discussion by top policy makers in the two departments, both the Department of Health, Education, and Welfare and the Department of Labor developed and adopted rules and regulations for the administration of integrated MDTA training courses although there was fear that such regulations might cause some southern states to stay outside the Program.

Nevertheless, the views of those who wished to move cautiously prevailed to the extent that the two departments did not include provisions for nondiscrimination in the training program in their individual agreements with the various states. Under these agreements, the state employment services determine the occupations for which training shall be offered and provide the testing, counseling, selection and placement of trainees in MDTA classes administered by the state vocational education agencies. This compromise was designed to

*The bulk of the data in this article is from the U.S. Office of Education, and was developed when the author was Director of the Manpower Evaluation Staff of that office in 1963-64. A grant from the Institute of Public Administration, The University of Michigan, enabled the author to complete the study.

soothe the sensitivities of southern politicians who would not be required to agree in a formal contract that integrated MDTA classes be carried on in their states.

As a result, the nondiscrimination policy for the MDTA Program was interpreted differently in the southern states than it was in Washington, D. C. In some states, training projects were established on a racially segregated basis although whites and Negroes were taking the same training for which they had been selected by identical criteria. In one Alabama city, for example, two classes for stenographers which operated concurrently and covered the same material were held in adjacent classrooms. One class was for Negroes, the other for whites. In other states some projects were set up for Negroes and entirely different ones for whites.

As civil rights issues loomed larger on the national scene and racial unrest in Montgomery and Birmingham made headlines, pressure was put on both the Department of Health, Education, and Welfare and the Department of Labor to run a "color blind" Manpower Program. Because of incomplete compliance with the nondiscriminatory training policy for MDTA Programs and misunderstanding of what it implied, the two federal departments made their policies and regulations more explicit on March 29, 1963.

As of that date, the Department of Labor required that all selection of trainees should be made without regard to race. The Department of Health, Education, and Welfare notified the state vocational education agencies that groups referred for training were likely to be racially mixed, that if the local training agency refused a racially mixed group the state agency should make other arrangements for training, and if the state agency could not do so the Department of Health, Education, and Welfare "will take appropriate action to have the required training provided on an integrated basis." The state vocational education agencies were required to provide assurances on all projects reviewed for approval on and after March 29, 1963, that designated training would provide training without regard to the racial composition of the traineee groups. If the training agency refused to accept a student because of his race, all expenditures made by the training agency in preparation for the project would be disallowed and other arrangements for training would be made.

In order to stress the nondiscriminatory policy for MDTA Programs, early in April 1963 the Department of Health, Education, and Welfare established guidelines for dealing with borderline situations as well as projects already underway which had not properly complied with the regulations for integrated training. These guidelines reaffirmed the policy that MDTA projects would be operated on an integrated basis both in the assignment to training as well as in the training itself. MDT field representatives of the U.S. Office of Education were instructed to make sure that state vocational education directors were aware of the policy and were selecting training institutions willing to take integrated groups. Unless these federal regulations were observed, field representatives could not approve new projects although existing programs were not to be disturbed since it was felt that students currently in training should not have their classes interrupted or terminated because of past failure on the part of state and local administrators to follow the nondiscrimination policy. No further federal funds were to be expended on segregated projects and the field representatives were asked to report to the Commissioner of Education if they found that a state would not arrange for integrated training according to regulations.

At the time the 1963 guidelines were under discussion, the advisability of including a nondiscrimination clause in MDT training contracts with the states was again considered and again felt to be unwise. Louisiana had already refused to take part in the Manpower Program and it was anticipated that such a clause would force other southern states out of the Program because of political conditions and public opinion. Moreover, it was felt that a nondiscriminatory program could be maintained on the basis of existing regulations and their reinforcement with the new guidelines. The April 1963 guidelines would not have been necessary if the two departments has rigorously enforced a policy of equal and integrated training opportunities from the start of the MDT Program. The position of the federal departments had been compromised, and it was clear to state and local administrators that minimum compliance with the letter of the regulations would be acceptable. The heritage of a weak position hung over the Program, particularly in the South.

Selection of Trainees

During 1963, data became available for the first time on the participation of minority groups in the manpower training programs. Over 40,500 trainees were enrolled in MDT training classes which started in 1963. Of these, almost 30,000 were white (71 percent), 9,200 were nonwhite (23 percent), and racial data were not obtained for about 2,600 (6 percent). Negroes accounted for 93 percent of the nonwhites, including 91 percent of the nonwhite men and 94 percent of the nonwhite women.

TABLE I

RACE OF MANPOWER TRAINEES ENROLLED IN COURSES STARTED IN 1963

Race	Total Trainees Number	Percent
Total	40,684	100.0
White	28,921	71.1
Nonwhite	9,191	22.6
Negro	8,502	20.9
Not obtained	2,572	6.3
Negro as percent of nonwhite		92.5

Over the nation as a whole, the Manpower Program provided adequate training opportunities for nonwhites. Since the trainees were selected primarily from the ranks of the unemployed, a simple measure of the racial balance of the Program is the proportion of nonwhites among the trainees as compared with the proportion of unemployed nonwhites in the population. The Program passed this test well. In 1963, 24.1 percent of the trainees whose race was known were nonwhite as compared with 21 percent of the unemployed.[1]

When the characteristics of the Manpower Program trainees are examined in detail, however, it becomes apparent that the Program tended to apply somewhat stricter standards of selection for nonwhites than for whites. In general, the Program tended to "skim the cream" of the unemployed and did so to an even greater extent for nonwhites.

1. *Age.* Over half the nonwhite trainees were in the prime working age group of 22 to 34 years, as compared with only three out of eight white trainees. Relatively few nonwhites were in the lowest age group (under 19) or in the oldest (45 and over).

2. *Education.* As compared with whites, relatively few poorly educated nonwhites were selected for training. As Table III points out, only 5.9 percent of the nonwhite trainees had 8 years or less of schooling although 43.8 percent of the nonwhite unemployed are in that category. In contrast, 10.2 percent of the white trainees had 8 years or less of schooling although 33.9 percent of the white unemployed are at the lower educational level. Furthermore, 11.9 percent

[1] 1964 Manpower Report of the President, p. 95.

of the nonwhite trainees had some education beyond high school, although that was true for only 5.3 percent of the nonwhite unemployed. On the other hand, 9.2 percent of the white trainees had had some college level training against 10.5 percent of the white unemployed.

TABLE II

AGE DISTRIBUTION OF WHITE AND NONWHITE MANPOWER TRAINEES, 1963
(percent)

Age	White	Nonwhite
Less than 19	9.5	5.0
19 - 21	20.4	22.2
22 - 34	37.5	53.0
35 - 44	20.0	16.2
45 and over	12.6	3.6
Total	100.0	100.0

TABLE III

EDUCATIONAL ATTAINMENT OF WHITE AND NONWHITE MANPOWER TRAINEES, 1963 AND THE UNEMPLOYED, MARCH 1962
(percent)

Years of Education	Manpower Trainees		Unemployed[1]	
	White	Nonwhite	White	Nonwhite
Less than 8	2.6	2.3	17.5	29.4
8	7.6	3.6	16.4	14.4
9 - 11	28.1	33.3	26.1	29.4
12	52.5	48.9	29.5	21.5
More than 12	9.2	11.9	10.5	5.3
Total	100.0	100.0	100.0	100.0

[1]Includes unemployed age 18 and older as of March 1962. From U.S. Department of Labor, Special Force Report No. 30, Table L.

This greater selectivity for nonwhites was shown at both ends of the educational scale. In the middle—9-12 years of education where the bulk of the nonwhite and white trainees fall—there was little difference between the two groups. Although the differences overall were not great and suggest that the chief educational determinants of selection are the standards set by schools and employers, nevertheless, a greater degree of selectivity did prevail for nonwhites than for whites chosen for training in the MDT Manpower Program.

3. *Prior Employment.* With respect to length of unemployment, there appeared to be no extra selectivity factors applied to nonwhites. Indeed, a higher proportion of nonwhite trainees were long-term unemployed. The Program served the long-term unemployed rather effectively, as shown in Table IV. However, in reaching out to the nonwhite hard core unemployed, the Program's good record may have been more apparent than real. Over half the nonwhite trainees (52 percent) were women, and women made up 61 percent of the long-term unemployed (27 weeks or more) among the nonwhite trainees. As a whole, the Program tended to draw women back into the labor force after their substantial periods of unemployment. This was more true of the nonwhite trainees than others and the apparent emphasis on the long-term unemployed nonwhites may be due to this factor.

TABLE IV

PRIOR EMPLOYMENT STATUS OF WHITE AND NONWHITE MANPOWER TRAINEES, 1963 AND UNEMPLOYED, 1962
(percent)

Prior Employment Status	Manpower Trainees White	Manpower Trainees Nonwhite	Unemployed[1] White	Unemployed[1] Nonwhite
Unemployed				
Under 5 weeks	26.4	20.1	44.6	39.7
5 - 14 weeks	23.4	21.2	28.6	27.3
15 - 26 weeks	13.9	14.7	13.1	14.1
27 - 52 weeks	10.8	13.9	13.4	18.9
Over 52 weeks	16.0	21.6	----	----
Family Farm Worker	0.9	0.7	----	----
Underemployed	8.6	7.7	----	----
Total	100.0	100.0	100.0	100.0

[1]14 years and over, 1962. From U.S. Department of Labor, Special Labor Force Report, No. 31, Table G-2.

4. *Sex.* Wider opportunities for MDT training were provided to nonwhite women than to nonwhite men. Only 19 percent of all male trainees were nonwhite, while 28 percent of all female trainees were nonwhite. Disparities in training opportunities between nonwhite men and women are revealed in data from Table V which show that although 62 percent of the white trainees were men, nonwhite males constituted only 48 percent of nonwhite trainees. However, in spite of the greater training opportunities for nonwhite women, training opportunities for nonwhite men were adequate. As of December 1963, nonwhite men comprised 19 percent of all unemployed men and 19 percent of all male Manpower Program trainees in 1963. Nonwhite women, in contrast, constituted 28 percent of all women trainees but only 24 percent of all unemployed women.

By providing more training for Negro women than for Negro men, however, the Manpower Program reinforced those patterns which lead to a matriarchal household and to psychological problems for Negro males who are unable to support their families. Although a better record was made in training Negro women, the Program should have made special efforts to train and place male Negro household heads.

Types of Training

The Manpower Training Program made a major effort to open employment opportunities to Negroes and other nonwhites by training them for higher level jobs. Nevertheless, the Program has been limited

TABLE V

RACE AND SEX OF MANPOWER TRAINEES ENROLLED IN COURSES STARTED IN 1963

Race	Male		Female	
	Number	Percent	Number	Percent
Total	23,821	100.0	16,863	100.0
White	17,881	75.1	11,040	65.5
Nonwhite	4,428	18.6	4,763	28.2
Negro	4,017	16.9	4,485	26.6
Not obtained	1,512	6.3	1,060	6.3
Negro as percent of nonwhite		90.8		94.2

in what it can do. Many skilled occupations have been closed to nonwhites because of employer attitudes, union restrictions and community pressures. In the South, for example, even many semi-skilled factory jobs are closed for the most part to Negroes, especially in the smaller towns in such important industries as textiles and furniture manufacturing. Similar situations exist in other parts of the nation as well. Training programs alone cannot break down these barriers but must be coordinated with other programs of community action, such as the federal government's efforts to assure equal opportunity in employment with government contractors.

Furthermore, the generally low educational attainment of many nonwhites has made it difficult to train them for more highly skilled employment. Qualifications for entry into Manpower Program classes tend to keep out a larger proportion of nonwhites than whites. The upgrading of basic educational skills that can be accomplished by the Manpower Program is meager.

In spite of these difficulties, the record of the Manpower Program in 1963 was good in the types of training courses offered. Table VI shows the racial breakdown of the trainees in each type of training. Over three-quarters of the trainees were in skilled, semiskilled and clerical-sales occupation classes, and a negligible proportion in unskilled and agricultural occupations. A little better than one in ten trainees was trained in professional and managerial occupations and a little less than one in ten in service occupations.

Nonwhites made up about one-fourth of the total number of trainees whose race was known. They were heavily represented among those trained in service occupations (over 40 percent) and semiskilled occupations (about 30 percent), and were less well represented in the skilled occupations (16 percent) professional-managerial occupations (20 percent) and clerical-sales occupations (21 percent). The figures on the proportion of nonwhites in the various occupational classifications of training is given in Table VII, which looks at the racial composition of the trainees in the various occupational groups for which training was offered.

Several cautions should be kept in mind in interpreting these figures. A wide variety of skill levels, ranging from unskilled to highly skilled and trained, are implied in such categories as "professional and managerial," "clerical and sales," and "services." Even so, formal academic education is usually more necessary in those occupations which involve verbal and writing skills rather than the manual-manipulative abilities needed in the skilled, semi-skilled and unskilled training categories. Many nonwhite unemployed lack the schooling

TABLE VI

MDTA TRAINEES ENROLLED IN COURSES STARTED IN 1963, BY RACE AND OCCUPATION OF TRAINING

OCCUPATIONAL GROUP	Race				Racial Data Not Obtained
	Total	White	Nonwhite	Negro	
Professional and Managerial	4,288	3,265	821	763	202
Clerical and Sales	8,621	6,311	1,818	1,700	492
Services	3,913	2,040	1,587	1,512	286
Agricultural	700	535	116	80	49
Skilled Occupations:	13,281	10,411	1,982	1,757	888
Manufacturing	5,276	4,268	707	634	301
Nonmanufacturing	955	683	130	73	142
Misc. Occupations	7,050	5,460	1,145	1,050	445
Semiskilled Occupations:	9,420	6,112	2,703	2,530	605
Manufacturing	8,442	5,616	2,327	2,163	499
Nonmanufacturing	544	196	273	268	75
Misc. Occupations	434	300	103	99	31
Unskilled Occupations (MFG)	234	137	76	76	21
D.O.T. not reported	227	110	88	84	29
Total	40,684	28,921	9,191	8,502	2,572

TABLE VII

TOTAL U.S. MDTA TRAINEES ENROLLED IN COURSES STARTED IN 1963 PERCENT NONWHITE IN EACH OCCUPATIONAL GROUP
(exclusive of those for whom racial data was not obtained)

OCCUPATIONAL GROUP	All Trainees		Nonwhite Trainees as a Percent of all Trainees in each occupational group
	Number	Percent	
Professional and Managerial	4,288	10.5	20.1
Clerical and Sales	8,621	21.2	21.1
Services	3,913	9.6	43.8
Agricultural	700	1.7	17.8
Skilled Occupations:	13,281	32.6	16.0
Manufacturing			
Nonmanufacturing			
Misc. Occupations			
Semiskilled Occupations:	9,420	23.2	30.7
Manufacturing			
Nonmanufacturing			
Misc. Occupations			
Unskilled Occupations:	234	0.6	35.7
D.O.T. not reported	227	0.6	44.4
Total	40,684	100.0	24.1

Note: Table VII shows that 24.1 percent of all trainees whose race was known were nonwhites, 20.1 percent of professional and managerial trainees were nonwhite. etc.

necessary to qualify for admission to training classes in these areas.

Another way of assessing the training opportunities provided for nonwhites is to compare the two racial groups in terms of the proportion of trainees in the various occupational categories. Data show that a slightly higher proportion of whites than nonwhites were trained in professional-managerial and clerical-sales occupations and a considerably higher proportion received training for skilled occupations. On the other hand, a considerably higher proportion of nonwhites than whites were trained in semiskilled and service occupations.

These comparisons indicate that the Manpower Program was not

TABLE VIII

PERCENT DISTRIBUTION OF WHITE AND NONWHITE TRAINEES AMONG OCCUPATIONAL GROUPS, CLASSES STARTED IN 1963

OCCUPATIONAL GROUP	White	Nonwhite
Professional and Managerial	11.3	8.9
Clerical and Sales	21.8	19.8
Services	7.1	17.3
Agricultural	1.8	1.3
Skilled Occupations:	36.0	21.6
Manufacturing	14.8	7.7
Nonmanufacturing	2.4	1.4
Misc. Occupations	18.9	12.5
Semiskilled Occupations:	21.1	29.4
Manufacturing	19.4	25.3
Nonmanufacturing	0.7	3.0
Misc. Occupations	1.0	1.1
Unskilled Occupations	0.5	0.8
D.O.T. not reported	0.4	1.0
Total	100.0	100.1

able to achieve racial equality in its training activities. Nevertheless, effective training and placement programs can significantly upgrade the nonwhite unemployed, and the Manpower Program is providing training for nonwhites in more highly skilled and white collar occupations to a much greater extent than those jobs are currently held by Negroes in the U. S. labor market.

Integration and Segregation in the Classroom

The Manpower Program has only moderate success in providing integrated training classes. Of all classes started in 1963, some three out of eight (37.5 percent) were either all white or all Negro. The remainder (62.5 percent) included white and nonwhite trainees.

There were several reasons for the relatively large number of all white classes. First, there were very few nonwhites in some states and areas within states. As a result, any training program that seeks to serve the unemployed will inevitably have some classes composed entirely of white trainees. Second, nonwhites in general have lower levels of educational attainment than whites, and educational requirements for entry into some training courses will eliminate many non-

TABLE IX

RACIAL COMPOSITION OF MANPOWER TRAINING CLASSES STARTED IN 1963

	Number of Classes	Percent
All white	753	35.1
All nonwhite	62	2.4
White and nonwhite	1,330	62.5
Total	2,145	100.0

whites from consideration. Third, discrimination by employers and/or unions may make it unwise to select nonwhites for training for some occupations in certain areas, even though employment opportunities for trained workers are present.

Not all classes wholly composed of nonwhite students resulted from efforts to maintain segregation. Many developed through efforts to reach the hard core unemployed in large urban areas where a high proportion of the jobless are from minority groups. For example, the largest number of all nonwhite classes in 1963 was in Illinois (12 classes) and the District of Columbia (10 classes) where a major effort was made to reach and train the long-term unemployed. On the other hand, there was a smaller number of all nonwhite classes in the Southern states simply because training opportunities for nonwhites in those areas were limited.

The Program in Individual States

Two groups of states did not provide adequate training opportunities for nonwhites. In 11 southern states with relatively large Negro populations and in six western states with significant Indian populations, the Program was notably limited in meeting the training needs of the minority group unemployed. The inadequacy of training opportunities for nonwhites in these states was assessed by comparing the proportion of nonwhites in the training program with the proportion of nonwhites among the unemployed: in each case nonwhites were significantly underrepresented in the training Program. Data on these states are given in Table XI.

The trend toward underrepresentation of nonwhites in these states may be due to a variety of factors. First, attitudes of employers undoubtedly play a significant role. If nonwhites are not normally hired in certain types of jobs, it would be foolish to train them unless special placement efforts and arrangements for them were made. Second, in many areas the educational level of nonwhites is significantly below that of whites and with the entrance requirements for training classes established by the training institutions, many more nonwhites than whites would be excluded on this basis. Third, cultural patterns within the community may militate against training for nonwhites and make it difficult for the schools to train them and for the state employment services to place them. Fourth, there may be a disproportionate number of nonwhites living in rural rather than urban areas, making it difficult to recruit, train and place them in jobs. Finally, there may be a deliberate effort on the part of the local employment service and school to exclude nonwhites in spite of the

TABLE X

STATES IN WHICH SEGREGATED MANPOWER TRAINING CLASSES OUTNUMBERED INTEGRATED CLASSES, CLASSES STARTED IN 1963

Region and State	Number of All White and/or All Nonwhite Classes	Number of Mixed Classes
South		
Alabama	36	7
Arkansas	24	9
Georgia	15	5
Mississippi	3	0
South Carolina	11	2
West		
Idaho	8	0
Montana	13	2
North Dakota	15	2
Oregon	11	7
Utah	8	4
Wyoming	3	1
New England		
Maine	71	6
New Hampshire	33	6
Rhode Island	10	5
Vermont	9	0
Other		
District of Columbia	10	7
West Virginia	14	13

national policy of nondiscrimination adopted for the Program. All of these factors are undoubtedly more significant in the South where employment opportunities for Negroes are limited, where the disparities in educational attainment is greatest, and where a larger proportion of nonwhites live in rural areas.

Throughout the South, problems in providing training for Negroes have been prevalent. Negroes were trained for lower skilled occupations than whites. In several states (Louisiana and northern Florida) no training was given for either Negroes or whites and in the most southern states the number of Negroes receiving training was disproportionately low. In many localities, classes were segregated and in other areas there was only token integration. On the other

TABLE XI

STATES PROVIDING INADEQUATE TRAINING OPPORTUNITIES FOR NON-WHITES IN THE MANPOWER PROGRAM, 1963

State	Number of Trainees, 1963	Nonwhite Trainees (percent)[1]	Nonwhite Unemployed (percent)[2]
Southern States			
Alabama	627	17.3	40.5
Arkansas	489	8.6	28.1
Delaware	33	15.6	28.8
Florida	680	17.9	26.5
Georgia	327	16.9	37.3
Louisiana	No Participation		
Mississippi	55	31.4	49.0
North Carolina	696	12.4	37.0
South Carolina	222	28.2	42.4
Tennessee	807	9.4	19.6
Texas	1814	15.6	19.8
Western States			
Alaska	88	18.4	30.7
Idaho	134	0.0	1.6
Montana	221	1.9	8.1
North Dakota	217	1.0	4.4
South Dakota	82	6.6	13.0
Wyoming	90	2.3	2.8

[1]Excluding trainees for whom racial data was not obtained.
[2]Data from 1960 Census. No later data are available for individual states.

hand, in some parts of the South Negroes were well represented in the Program and classes were integrated. In some localities an originally segregated program moved to token and then full integration. The situation was worst in smaller cities and rural areas, somewhat better in larger urban areas. Progress was made, but it was spotty, and it is obvious that a special effort should have been made in the South if all the factors which prevent adequate training opportunities for Negroes are to be overcome.

Some idea of problems encountered by the Program in the South may be obtained by looking at some representative states.

In *Florida,* the Manpower Program developed into a nondiscriminatory and integrated one. Negroes, however, were underrepresented: 17.9 percent of the trainees were nonwhite, but nonwhites made up 26.5 percent of the state's unemployed in 1960. In addition, there were wide areas of the state that had no projects.

Experience in Orlando and Pensacola showed that progress can be made in racial matters. In Pensacola the first two projects were started in January and April of 1963. One was for waitress training and enrolled 19 white women. The second trained chambermaids and enrolled 17 Negro women. A third project, training automobile mechanics, was begun in June; 21 whites and one Negro were enrolled. The next step was to move to something more than token integration, with a project for secretarial training begun in June with 13 white and 3 Negro trainees.

The situation in Orlando was somewhat similar. Six projects begun in March and April were segregated, providing classes only for whites, although one Negro who did not enroll was referred to one class. No new classes were begun in Orlando until August, when a class for cooks enrolled 3 whites and 12 Negroes.

Both Orlando and Pensacola indicated that a policy of segregation could be changed to one of integration within a relatively short period of time.

Some areas in Florida had integrated projects from the beginning, including Tampa, St. Petersburg. Miami, and Fort Lauderdale. On the other hand, there were no projects at all in Jacksonville, one of the largest cities in the state, and aside from those in Pensacola none in any city in the northern half of the state. Florida had a substantial program, but only in six cities. A large portion of the state—the "old South" part—was left untouched.

In *Arkansas,* outside Little Rock the Manpower Program in 1963 was largely segregated, although in the last half of the year some effort was made to achieve token integration in other parts of the state. Of the 24 sections of MDTA projects started in 1963, 14 had white trainees only. In four of the projects, including two classes in Little Rock, one Negro each had been referred to the class but had not enrolled. One project enrolled only Negroes: located at Benton, it trained practical nurses and no white trainees were referred to it for training. Nine classes were integrated. Two in Fort Smith for stenographer training had 30 white and 3 Negro trainees, which is hardly more than a token. One in Jonesboro to train machinists had 18 white trainees and one Negro. The other six integrated classes were all in Little Rock, and one of those had only one Negro.

Training opportunities for Negroes in the Manpower Program were practically non-existent outside of Little Rock, and even these were available chiefly for women. Only 9 Negro men received training in the entire state in 1963, compared with 242 white men. Among the women trainees 183 were white and 31 were Negro. The pattern of inadequate training opportunities for Negroes in Arkansas is indicated by the fact that 28.1 percent of the unemployed in 1960 were Negroes, as against only 8.6 of the trainees.

Conclusions

In the early years of its development, the Manpower Program reflected the inconsistencies and ambiguities of the nation's attitudes and policies toward racial minorities. Administrators of the Program were caught between two social forces, the drive for full racial equality and the traditions of racial discrimination in the South and in other parts of the country. Federal administrators were forced into a compromise position while trying to set in motion a new program to get manpower training projects started in as many states as possible, in the shortest possible time. In seeking this goal, a nondiscrimination policy was announced but not pushed vigorously where local resistance was expected to be strong. In addition, the desire to have a "successful" program with a good record of placements seems to have been behind the tendency throughout the country to apply more vigorous selection standards to nonwhites than to whites.

Early in 1963 when preparations for the civil rights March on Washington were being made, a stronger stand was taken on integrated training opportunities for minority groups. After the new federal directives of April 1963, noticeable progress was made toward elimination of segregated training classes. But in most Southern states only token changes were instituted, involving, for the most part, the referral of a single Negro to an otherwise all white class. There is little evidence that significant further progress toward integrated and nondiscriminatory programs has been made in most parts of the South.

One important reason for these problems is administration of the Manpower Program at the local level by state, rather than by federal, agencies. State employment services are responsible for selection and placement of trainees, and state vocational education authorities administer the training programs. These agencies are more sensitive to local attitudes and community political pressures than a federal agency would be.

In addition, the federal agencies themselves—the Bureau of Employment Security of the Department of Labor, and the Division of Vocational Education of the Office of Education—are imbued with a philosophy of localism and look upon themselves as service organizations which assist, rather than lead, the state agencies with which they deal. A long heritage of policy and politics made these agencies reluctant to pursue vigorously and unequivocally the stated policies on full integration of training programs. Too much leeway has been given to the states; partial compliance with regulations was winked at and token desegregation of classes permitted. The full power of the federal government to develop projects and classes outside the aegis of the state agencies was not used.

More can and should be done to provide greater equality in training opportunities and to enforce vigorously an equal opportunity policy throughout the entire Manpower Program. Nevertheless, and in spite of its shortcomings, the Manpower Program has had a significant impact in upgrading skills, providing new training opportunities, and opening new areas of employment for nonwhite workers.

Suggested Additional Readings

1. Caplan, Nathan. *Job Holding Among Negro Youth.* Ann Arbor, Michigan: The University of Michigan, Institute for Social Research, April, 1967.
2. Grier, Eunice S. *In Search of a Future: A Study of Career-Seeking Experiences of Selected Negro High-School Graduates in Washington, D.C.* Washington, D.C.: Center for Metropolitan Studies, 1963.
3. "Hiring Negro Workers," *Conference Board Record,* Vol. 1 (June 1964).
4. Killingsworth, Charles C. "Negroes in a Changing Labor Market," *Employment, Race and Poverty.* Ed. Arthur M. Ross and Herbert Hill. New York: Harcourt, Brace and World, 1967.
5. *Manpower Report of the President and a Report on Manpower Requirements, Resources, Utilization, and Training.* Transmitted to Congress, April 1967. Part 2, pp. 73-98.
6. U. S. Department of Commerce. *Hard-Core Unemployment and Poverty in Los Angeles.* Washington, D.C.: U.S. Department of Commerce, Government Printing Office, 1965.
7. Zeitz, Leonard. "Survey of Negro Attitudes Toward Law," *Rutgers Law Review,* 19 (Winter 1961).

Chapter 5

Negro Experiences in the Labor Market

Introduction

Considering the recent attention given to Negro employment problems, we know very little about the *actual* experiences of Negroes in the labor market. How do Negroes find jobs? What job mobility patterns characterize Negro workers? What patterns of interpersonal relations emerge between whites and Negroes in a work situation? Do Negroes avail themselves of federal, state, and local resources to redress their job grievances? To what extent do Negro labor market experiences and attitudes resemble those of whites? The answers to these questions, and many others, are yet to be determined by future research.

The articles in this chapter represent many different kinds of situations and themes and in no sense form a basic unity of the labor market experiences of Negro workers. The presentations range from the work, or nonwork, patterns of a streetcorner group of Negro men in Washington, D.C., to the job-seeking experiences of Negroes in a small Connecticut town. We also include an article describing the integration of Negroes into the armed services, an institution that is increasingly offering occupational roles to Negroes in an environment in which equality of opportunities between the races has been proceeding at a rapid rate. Each article represents a slice of the attitudes and labor market experiences of Negro workers and yields some insight into the job problems of the Negro.

It may very well be that the main value of the articles in this chapter is to suggest questions for future research, rather than to supply definitive answers on the labor market experiences of Negroes. Systematic research of Negro labor market experiences has barely begun. With few exceptions what we know of Negro work and nonwork experiences has been made available largely through official agency records, studies of fair employment agency experiences, and interviews with management personnel on equal employment policies. There have been remarkably few attempts to question Negroes themselves about their experiences or their perceptions of employment problems.

We suggest five research propositions as reference points for a research program on Negro labor market experiences and attitudes:

1. *Is the labor market organized differently for Negroes than for whites?* The Lurie-Rayack study, reported in this chapter, suggests that in some ways it is, and in other ways it is not. Apparently, the majority of Negroes seeking jobs use the same techniques as do whites—informal leads from friends and relatives. But in obtaining information for job mobility or for the labor market in general, Negroes fall back on the expertise or wisdom of formal organizations (e.g., the state employment service or the Urban League), while whites continue to rely on white peers who know the "white man's labor market." Although the labor market behavior of numerous groups of whites is well documented in research, little is known of the corresponding labor market patterns among Negroes. It would be valuable to know how different groups of Negroes attach themselves to the labor market, and what their points of reference are for such attachments.

2. *Does the Negro ghetto have an economy of its own with a distinct network of occupational trades?* It is a common observation that unemployment in Negro ghettoes exceeds that of contiguous metropolian areas. For example, the unemployment rate in the Hough section of Cleveland was 15.6 percent in November, 1966, whereas the 1966 annual average unemployment rate for the Cleveland metropolitan area was 3.5 percent. To assume, however, that the unemployed in these ghettoes are without work does not fit the observations made in a number of recent studies. An unemployed person is officially described as "one who is without a job and is actively seeking employment." In the ghetto, work opportunities exist, but the jobs frequently fall outside of any official listing of occupational specialities. In other words, the "unemployed" label frequently disregards the fact that the ghetto may have an occupational network of its own which provides meaningful work opportunities to ghetto residents. A study of this network would provide important insights into the conditions—psychological and structural—that tie an individual to ghetto life and make him resist work opportunities in the regular economy.

3. *Do Negroes have access to information about legal safeguards against job discrimination, and if they have this information, what use do they make of it?* Recent findings suggest that Negroes have a low level of information about legal safeguards against employment discrimination. They are neither aware of community agencies with a

legal mandate to redress employment inequities nor aware of equal employment opportunities or practices within companies for which they work. Furthermore, there is an apparent reluctance to use legal means to redress grievances even if such information is available. These findings suggest that the strategy of placing the legal responsibility on the victim of job discrimination leaves much to be desired. We do not know with any certainty why this information never reaches the Negro, nor the psychological pressures that result in nonuse of the information.

4. *Do Negroes really want access to the major institutions of a white society or would they prefer to utilize institutions indigenous to the Negro community?* Both Jan Dizard and Elliot Liebow suggest in their articles that Negroes are hard to reach because they reject institutional ties to the larger society. Dizard draws a picture of Negro men who view the institutions of the whites with scorn and hatred, while Liebow's streetcorner men are apathetic toward linking ties to institutions outside the Negro ghetto. Does this suggest that some Negroes do not seek access to white society? If so, what does the Negro want? The assumption in the drive for equal employment opportunities in the 1960's has been that Negroes wanted greater participation in the system as against leaving the system. The Negro workers portrayed by Lurie and Rayack in a small Connecticut town obviously strove to achieve rewards within the white system, although they used slightly different means to look for work than those used by white job seekers. For the most part, intervention strategies have assumed that the Negro "wants in." If this assumption is wrong, then new strategies will have to be developed. At this time, we simply do not know what different groups of blue-collar and service Negro workers want, since no large scale, national study has ever been executed to answer the question.

5. *What is the impact of military service on Negro job opportunities in the civilian labor market?* Increasingly, large numbers of Negro youth are entering military service as a result of military manpower demands in the Viet Nam War. For many of these youth, military experience is a sharp break from the economic deprivation of ghetto life. Military service might have an impact on the post-service occupational careers of these youths. First, sophisticated advances in weaponry require a higher level of training and education for military personnel. In the present emergency the military institution is one of the few institutions able to mobilize considerable resources to upgrade the potential of Negro youth. A great deal of this basic investment in human resources will undoubtedly be carried over to civilian life. Second, the military experience provides a setting in which mobility is

possible and motivation can be maximized. It represents to disadvantaged Negro youth one of the few opportunities to be in a motivation-reward structure, an important set of experiences in the development of a work self-image. Finally, the resources available from military service (e.g., the "G.I. Bill") provide new opportunities for training in civilian life. There is a need to assess the military experience and its impact on Negro youth.

The research possibilities suggested are intriguing and, undoubtedly, constitute significant reference points in developing a comprehensive research program to help determine meaningful social policy to reduce Negro job problems.

Racial Differences in Migration and Job Search: A Case Study

Melvin Lurie and Elton Rayack*

[From The Southern Economic Journal, *July 1966, by permission.]*

I. Introduction

Unemployment and underemployment harass the Negro in American labor markets. During the past decade, the unemployment rate among Negro workers has been persistently double that of white workers. Even when the Negro is successful in securing employment, the job found is often not commensurate with his skill and ability; in the economist's terms, he is underemployed.

The causes of the Negro's disadvantaged position in the labor market are many—inadequate education, both quantitatively and qualitatively, poor and misdirected vocational training, barriers erected by employers and unions, segregation in ghettos, general cultural deprivation—and through them all runs the powerful thread of racial discrimination. The effects of all of these elements have been or are now being analyzed by students of our society.

One factor, however, that has not been analyzed in any depth with respect to the Negro worker is how he goes about looking for a job—his "job search." The critical role that the search process plays in the labor market is evident by the large number of labor mobility

*We gratefully acknowledge a grant from the Unemployment and the American Economy project, University of California (Berkeley), which made this study possible. The questionnaire survey was conducted with the invaluable assistance of Mr. Willard McRae of the Connecticut State Welfare Department.

studies conducted over the last three decades by economists and others. None of these studies, however, devoted any significant attention to the Negro worker. Do the job hunting patterns of Negroes differ from those of whites? Is the job search of recent Negro and white migrants similar? What differences are there in the pattern of search of the recent migrant and the established resident of the same race? Are there any channels of job information open to whites that are not open to Negroes? Are there any ways that the efficiency of the Negro's job search may be improved so that his underemployment may be lessened? These are some of the questions we will try to answer in this paper.[1] The answers, we feel, may have important implications for public policy aimed at improving the position of the Negro in the labor market. To suggest answers to these questions, we studied the methods of job search of workers in a small New England labor market.

The Middletown Labor Market

This study of racial differences in migration and job search was conducted in the Middletown, Connecticut labor market area in the summer of 1964.[2] Middletown is, in many ways, a microcosm of the larger cities in this region. More than 40 per cent of the city's population consists of "foreign stock," i.e., the foreign born and first-generation Americans.[3] The three largest nationality groups are the

[1]This paper is not presented as a study providing definitive answers to these questions. We fully recognize that the small sample on which our analysis is based may contain considerable sampling error. This paper is offered as a pilot project with the belief that the technique employed and the answers given, while admittedly tentative, are highly suggestive.

[2]Middletown is located in eastern Connecticut, half way between New York and Boston, 15 miles south of Hartford and 24 miles north of New Haven. Hartford and New Haven are the two largest cities in the state and are major industrial centers. Middletown (1960 population: 38,837) is the principal city in the Middletown labor market area. The next largest city is Portland (1960 population: 5,587), which is adjacent to Middletown (lying on the opposite bank of the Connecticut River). The population and the labor force of the two cities constitute slightly over half of these totals for the entire labor market area.

Middletown is a city which is a center of light manufacturing industries, a college town (Wesleyan University), and a residential area. A state hospital, located in the area, is a major employer of Negroes. Although the majority of Middletown residents are employed in local enterprises, a part of the labor force living in Middletown is employed in the aircraft engine, foundry, and other heavy industries in and around Hartford.

[3]*Census of Population: 1960 Volume 1, Characteristics of the Population,* Part 8, Connecticut U. S. Department of Commerce, Bureau of the Census, 1963, p. 155.

Italians (35 per cent), the Polish (19 per cent), and the French-Canadians (11 per cent).

Over 90 per cent of the Negro population in the Middletown labor market area lives in the cities of Middletown and Portland. Although the Negro population is small, averaging 4 per cent of the total population, it grew by 134 per cent during the 1950's while the white population increased by 13 per cent.[4]

Table I presents the occupational distribution of employed males, by race, for Middletown in 1960. Negroes are under-represented in professional, managerial, white collar, and skilled blue collar occupations, and over-represented in the common labor and service classifications. Only 5.3 per cent of employed Negro males held professional, managerial, and white collar jobs, while 35.0 per cent of employed white males held such positions. White workers were evenly distributed in the craftsmen and operatives occupations. but 2.5 times as many Negroes held the lesser skilled operatives jobs as compared to their employment as craftsmen. Almost twice as large a fraction of Negroes held common labor positions as did whites.

The distribution of employed persons, in 1960, by industry group and race, is presented in Table II. These data show that Negroes are under-represented in those service industries where visibility is important. For example, the fraction of whites holding jobs in wholesale and retail trade was more than twice the fraction of Negroes in these positions.[5] No Negroes held jobs in the construction industry, in public utilities, and in finance, insurance and real estate while almost 13 per cent of the whites were employed in these industries. The pattern of employment for Negroes relative to whites in occupations and in industry groups, as outlined above, is *not* peculiar to Middletown. It is repeated in cities of all sizes throughout the country.

The primary data for this study were collected by interviewing workers in their homes. The sample size was 250; of this number, 150 were Negroes and 100 were whites. The sample was stratified to include only males who were members of the labor force, who were 45 years of age or less, and who were employed in non-professional and non-managerial occupations. The Negro workers interviewed

[4]Estimates indicate that the relatively rapid growth of the Negro population is likely to continue so that, by 1980, the percentage of Negroes in Middletown will be almost double what it is today. (Source: Middletown Redevelopment Agency.)

[5]Main Street in Middletown is the major shopping area for the city and the immediate surrounding area. There are two large department stores and many smaller variety and specialty stores. If one looks hard, one may find one or two Negro salesgirls.

TABLE I

OCCUPATIONS OF EMPLOYED MALES IN MIDDLETOWN, BY RACE, 1960

Occupation	Negro* No.	Negro* Percent	White No.	White Percent
Total	300	100.0	8,121	100.0
Professional, Technical and Kindred Workers	4	1.3	1,071	13.2
Farmers and Farm Managers	0	0.0	68	.8
Managers, Off. and Propr. excluding farm	8	2.7	701	8.6
Clerical and Kindred Workers	4	1.3	556	6.8
Sales Workers	0	0.0	454	5.6
Craftsmen, Foremen and Kindred Workers	49	16.3	1,842	22.7
Operatives and Kindred Workers	122	40.7	1,847	22.7
Private Household Workers	0	0.0	9	.1
Service Workers, except Private Household	35	11.7	722	8.9
Farm Laborers	0	0.0	104	1.3
Laborers, except Farm and Mine	32	10.7	364	4.5
Occupation not reported	46	15.3	383	4.7

*The figures in the Census are presented for "nonwhites." Over 95% of the nonwhites in Middletown are Negroes.

Source: 1960 Census of Population, Volume 1, Characteristics of the Population, Part 8, Connecticut, U.S. Department of Commerce, Bureau of the Census (Washington, D.C.: U.S. Government Printing Office, 1963).

comprised 62 per cent of the Negro labor force; the white workers were 3 per cent of the white labor force (as stratified).[6]

[6]The interviewers were carefully selected on the basis of their ability and their familiarity with the Middletown community. Negroes interviewed Negro workers and whites interviewed white workers. In constructing the questionnaire, primary emphasis was placed on obtaining factual information from the worker about his personal characteristics and his employment experiences. A copy of the questionnaire may be obtained by writing the authors.

One of the findings of this study is that the method of job search, and implicitly the success of the search, depends on the migratory status of the worker, particularly whether he is a new arrival from a distant and diverse labor market or whether he is a long term resident of the area. We have therefore devoted Section II to a discussion of the migration of Negro and white workers to Middletown. Section III analyzes the racial differences in methods of job search, primarily by

TABLE II

INDUSTRIES OF EMPLOYED PERSONS IN MIDDLETOWN, BY RACE, 1960

	Negro		White	
	No.	Percent	No.	Percent
Total	477	100.0	12,423	100.0
Agriculture, forestry and fisheries	8	1.7	199	1.6
Mining	0	0.0	11	.1
Construction	0	0.0	739	5.9
Manufacturing	211	44.2	5,019	40.4
Durable goods	105	22.0	3,044	24.5
Nondurable goods	106	22.2	1,975	15.9
Transport, Communication and other public utilities	0	0.0	344	2.8
Wholesale and retail trade	32	6.7	1,808	14.6
Finance, insurance and real estate	0	0.0	494	3.9
Business and repair services	4	.8	248	2.0
Personal services (including private household)	64	13.4	409	3.3
Entertainment and recreation services	0	0.0	20	.2
Professional and related services*	117	24.5	2,339	18.8
Public Administration	8	1.7	389	3.1
Industry not reported	33	6.9	404	3.3

*Includes hospitals, education, welfare, religious and nonprofit organizations.

Source: 1960 Census of Population, Volume 1, Characteristics of the Population, Part 8, Connecticut, U.S. Department of Commerce, Bureau of the Census, (Washington, D.C.: U.S. Government Printing Office, 1963).

migratory status. Section IV summarizes the results and presents some suggestions about the role of government in the job search process.

II. Migration to Middletown

The White Migration

Sociologists have used the term "chain migration" to describe "that movement in which prospective migrants learn of opportunities, are provided with transportation, and have initial accommodation and employment arranged by means of primary social relationships with previous migrants."[7] Most of Middletown's Italian and about half of its Negro population can trace its migration, settlement, and employment to this process.

Nearly all of Middletown's Italians came from Melilli, a town of 8,000 in southeastern Sicily, or are first generation descendants of those immigrants. The migration from Melilli to Middletown started in the 1890's; once the early immigrants were established, the chain from Melilli to Middletown was forged.[8]

The large majority of the Italian immigrants came from economically depressed laboring backgrounds. Very few had more than five years of education and most had less or none at all. A few had training as masons, barbers, shoemakers, or tailors. For the first few years, however, the early immigrants worked mostly on manual labor jobs in factories. A large proportion of those who first came found employment, through the *padroni* system, in a few specific firms and industries in which they still play a significant role. Not only did chain migration produce a "Little Italy" ghetto in Middletown, but it also led to "chain occupations"—"particular niches in the American em-

[7]John S. and Leatrice D. MacDonald, "Chain Migration, Ethnic Neighborhood Formation, and Social Networks," *The Milbank Memorial Fund Quarterly,* January 1964, p. 82.

[8]Some of the early migrants encouraged and assisted prospective male immigrants in order to profit from them. These *padroni* (bosses) exploited the new arrivals directly or were paid a commission for their efforts by American employers in need of labor. It was common for lone males to come to Middletown and, once reasonably established, to send for their wives, relatives, or friends. The more enterprising *padroni* often extended credit, provided tenement housing, and acquired jobs for the new arrivals. The new Italian immigrants were almost invariably faced with hostility and discrimination by the native Yankees and the established Irish and Polish immigrants. "Sicilians need not apply" was a common phrase in advertisements for jobs. See W. H. Sangree, *Mel Hyblaeum: A Study of the People of Middletown of Sicilian Origin,* unpublished M.A. thesis, Wesleyan University, 1962. The information in this section on the migration from Melilli was obtained from this thesis.

ployment structure to which successive immigrants directed their fellows on the basis of their own experience."[9]

The Negro Migration

Middletown's Negro population like that in the larger urban centers of the North, though on a much smaller scale, has been significantly affected by the migratory movements from the South.[10] While the 1960 Census indicates that 26 per cent of the city's white population were born in states other than Connecticut, 57 per cent of the Negro population were born in another state. That the migration has continued down to recent years is indicated by the fact that of Middletown's 1960 Negro population, 18 per cent lived in another state five years earlier, whereas the corresponding figure for the whites was 9 per cent. In addition to those who came directly from the South to Middletown, the city has a number of Negroes who have moved from other urban areas in the North.[11]

The long-term movement of the Southern Negro to Middletown is analogous, in many respects, to the "chain migration" that characterized the movement of Italian and other immigrants to this country. Our survey of Middletown Negro male migrants who had recently moved from the South revealed that 68 per cent came from two states, North and South Carolina, and 19 per cent from Virginia and Florida; thus a total of 87 per cent came to Middletown from Atlantic seaboard states.[12] Moreover, 60 per cent of the recent arrivals had migrated from three clusters of small towns in North and South Carolina, the towns in each cluster being located within a radius of 15 to 20 miles. The presence of "chain migration" was also supported by our survey of 310 Negro established residents (male and female)

[9]MacDonald, J.S. and L. D., *op. cit.*, p. 90.

[10]Despite the fact that most Negro migrants have settled in the large non-Southern cities like New York City, Chicago, Los Angeles, Philadelphia and Detroit, more than 2.5 million Negroes, about 13.5 per cent, live in the smaller urban places outside the large urbanized areas and central cities. *Census of Population: 1960, Part 1, U. S. Summary,* U. S. Department of Commerce, Bureau of the Census (Washington, D. C.: U. S. Government Printing Office, 1963), p. 144.

[11]*Census of Population:* 1960, Vol. 1, Part 8, *op cit.*, pp. 115, 150.

[12]This is consistent with Thornthwaite's finding in his pioneer study of Negro migration during the 1920's that "the northward movement (of Negroes) is roughly along meridians of longitude. The Negroes in New York City, Philadelphia, Baltimore and Washington have come almost entirely from the Atlantic seaboard states." (C. Warren Thornthwaite, *Internal Migration in the United States,* University of Pennsylvania Press, 1934, p. 13).

between the ages of 18 and 45 (62 per cent of the Negro labor force in 1964 in that age group).[13] Of those surveyed, 116, or 37 per cent, were born in the same three clusters of small towns from which 60 per cent of the recent migrants had come.[14]

Although the movement of the Southern Negro to the North is in many ways comparable to the great overseas migrations of yesteryear, there are at least three important dissimilarities. First, the Middletown labor market in the early 1900's was expanding rapidly and was able to absorb, in fact needed, the unskilled labor supplied by the immigrant; the Middletown labor market of 1964, while currently firm, has little prospect for major growth. Second, among the established residents in the Negro community, there is no institution performing the functions that the *padroni* performed in the early 1900's for the Italian immigrant. And third, as Taeuber has succinctly observed, "the barriers of color made assimilation for Americans who spoke English more difficult that it once was for those whose languages, religions, and cultures were alike alien, but whose skin color was technically white."[15]

[13]Those persons of both races who had come to Middletown before 1958 are referred to as the "established residents" whereas those who had come since 1958 are referred to as "recent migrants."

[14]In response to a question asking them why they came to Middletown, 19 of 21 (90 per cent) of the recent Italian migrants gave "be with relatives" as the reason; however, only 5 of 23 (22 per cent) of the recent white migrants from nearby cities in the Northeast responded in this way. Among recent Southern Negro migrants, 15 of 32 (46 per cent) replied "be with relatives" in response to this question while 3 of 23 (13 per cent) of the recent Negro migrants from the Northeast region gave relatives as the reason for their movement. The location of friends and relatives seems to have played a much stronger role in determining the precise geographic direction that migration took in the case of the migrants of both races who came from distant areas than the migrants who came from nearby cities in the Northeast. Others have found a similar pattern of Negro migration from the South. One study, using the school records of Norristown, Pennsylvania, found that a large proportion of the Negro migrants came from a single county of South Carolina–Saluda. (Sidney Goldstein, *Patterns of Mobility 1910–1950*, University of Pennsylvania Press, 1958, p. 38). In an earlier pathbreaking study it was found that a small nucleus of Negroes from St. Helena, North Carolina, had established a base in New York City in the latter part of the nineteenth century. Since that time, "their number was constantly augmented by the influence of these pioneers on friends and relatives." (Clyde V. Kiser, *Sea Island to City*, Columbia University Press, 1932, p. 163).

[15]Irene B. Taeuber, "Migration, Mobility and the Assimilation of the Negro," *Population Bulletin*, November 1958, pp. 129 to 134, and Paul F. Coe, "The Nonwhite Population Surge to our Cities," *Land Economics*, August 1959, p. 199.

III. Racial Differences in Job Search

The methods by which American workers search for jobs have been studied extensively by economists. We have prepared in the Appendix a summary of 9 major studies of job search, covering 17 labor markets. Neither in the research discussed in the Appendix nor, to our knowledge, in other studies, has more than passing notice been given to the job search of Negro workers.

Success in job search depends heavily upon knowledge—knowledge about the labor market, about job vacancies, and about new hiring. The longer a worker is employed or lives in a labor market, the more information he is likely to have about job opportunities in that market. However, even if residence or working time is the same, we believe that the white worker will have more knowledge about the job market than the Negro worker. Besides overt racial discrimination in hiring practices, there exists a more subtle form of discrimination—the white worker, even when his skill and ability are no greater than that of the nonwhite, is favored with a significant initial competitive advantage as he has access to more and better information concerning jobs. On the basis of our interviews and our own residence in Middletown, we do have some *a priori* judgments about the kinds of problems that a Negro worker faces when he looks for a job in this city. Middletown is a white man's labor market. The employers are white; the large majority of the work force is white, and the job information and placement intermediaries—in that they must respond to the needs and desires of white employers—are white-oriented. It does not surprise us that racial discrimination in employment exists in Middletown or that the Negro operates within the framework of a dual job system where some jobs are Negro jobs and others are reserved for whites. Middletown, in these respects, is no different from other non-Southern cities.

Not only is Middletown a white man's labor market, it is a market in which jobs and industries are to a significant extent stratified according to national origin. The predominant nationality group is Italian (more specifically, Sicilian) and people of Italian origin have familial ties in selected industries and the jobs within these industries; other areas of job and industry influence are reserved for people of other national origins. This division of jobs, by national origin, does not imply discrimination in the sense that a person of one national origin cannot obtain employment in an industry controlled by members of another nationality group. What the division does mean is that custom and informal home apprenticeship here and abroad does attract the young job seeker to those industries designated for his kind, and entry by others is difficult, but possible.

The Negro, however, stands outside of this job structure influenced by old country loyalties and skills cultivated by national origin. He is an easily identified interloper in a small city labor market. To find employment, the Negro's job search—his capacities not withstanding—must be directed towards the limited range of job opportunities open to him. If he comes to the market with any skill, it is quite likely that he will be underemployed.

Not only is the range of jobs open to the Negro worker restricted by the white man's labor market but this market also limits the number of methods that the Negro can use to look for a job. In keeping with previous work (see Appendix), let us define job search as consisting of the following methods:

I. *Formal Search* (or the Use of Institutional Intermediaries)
   A. Public Employment Service
   B. Private Employment Service
   C. Newspaper "Help Wanted" Ads
   D. Union

II. *Informal Search*
   A. Information Provided by Friends and Relatives
   B. Direct Application at the Plant Gate

Success in placement by some of these methods varies with race and the Negro worker finds out through his own experiences, or those of other Negroes, what sources are likely to lead him to the "right" job. The public employment service is legally committed to equal opportunity and the Negro feels that he is more likely to get equal treatment there. However, he suspects that the private employment service, the newspaper ads and the union are less likely to place him in "good" employment and furthermore, that any attempt by him to use these sources may result in embarrassment to him. Some Negroes do find employment through private institutional intermediaries but, as we shall see subsequently, Negroes use such services less frequently than whites. This is of some consequence, for the better jobs in a labor market are filled through institutional intermediaries, particularly the private employment service and the union; the less than full use of these job services by Negroes probably results in underemployment.

In what ways, if any, does a man's race affect the way he hunts for a job? In this analysis we must be certain, insofar as possible, to adjust for factors, other than race, that affect job search. It would be incorrect to attribute to racial differences, differences in job search that are, in fact, due to other factors; the impact of age, education, skill level, and length of time in a labor market on search are discussed subsequently.[16] Fortunately, there are a large number of factors affecting job search with which we need not be concerned; many of these affect the job search of *all* workers in much the same way and our interest is only in the *differences* in search patterns between Negro and white workers.[17]

An enumeration of the methods by which the 250 Negro and white workers surveyed found their current jobs is presented in Table III. These data support firmly the same overall conclusion arrived at by the studies in the Appendix—the majority of American workers found their current jobs through friends or relatives, or by applying directly to the firm.[18]

A second and more striking feature of these data is the reversed use of the private and public employment services, by race. Whereas 9 per cent of the Negro workers found their current jobs through the public employment service and 3 per cent through the private employment service, 10 per cent of the white workers used the private employment service while only 2 per cent used the public employment service. Third, no Negroes found their current jobs through the

[16]In the sample design for the analysis of job search, a strong effort was made to minimize the differences in the charactersitics of the workers interviewed so that the sample would be standardized. We excluded women and older workers (over age 45). To keep the skill and occupational mix as constant as possible, workers in professional and managerial classifications were also excluded.

[17]There is evidence, for example, from the studies discussed in the Appendix that city size has an impact on the method of job search; the data indicate that, in a small city like Middletown, institutional intermediaries will be used less frequently by workers than in larger cities. But in Middletown, this means that the search of both Negro and white workers will be affected in the same way by the size of the labor market and therefore no *differences* in the pattern of search will be evident from this factor. Similarly, other factors that may affect job search generally, but that will have no effect on *relative* search patterns, are the industrial structure of the city, the size of firms in the area, and the kind of products produced by the manufacturing industries in the city.

[18]If, in order to maintain race comparability, only the white workers in our sample were considered, the distribution of methods of job search in Middletown yielded a pattern which was very similar to that found for the workers with similar occupational and other characteristics in the studies of the 17 labor markets discussed in the Appendix. This suggests that, except for the minor differences in results caused by city size (the population of Middletown is one-tenth of the average population of the other cities studied), no substantial bias in methods of job search has been introduced either by our choice of the sample of workers interviewed or by our choice of Middletown, Connecticut as a labor market for study.

TABLE III

SOURCE OF CURRENT JOBS OF EMPLOYED MALES, BY RACE, MIDDLETOWN, 1964

	Negro		White	
	No.	Percent	No.	Percent
State Employment Service	13	9	2	2
Private employment service	5	3	10	10
Want-ads	4	3	3	3
Unions	0	0	4	4
Friends and relatives	48	32	36	36
Direct applications	80	53	45	45
Total sample	150	100	100	100

union while 4 per cent of the white workers did, despite the fact that 55 per cent of the Negroes were union members while only 36 per cent of the whites belonged to unions.[19] Finally, although our data show no difference in the use of newspaper want ads, our interviewers noted a reluctance expressed by Negroes to seek jobs in this way.

These differences in job search cannot be explained by differences in age or level of education, for the Negro and white workers surveyed were close to each other in both characteristics. Since the Negroes in our survey had relatively fewer skilled and clerical jobs than did the whites surveyed, it was possible that the job search pattern found was a product of occupational or skill differentials rather than race. In order to isolate the influence of race, comparisons were made between whites and Negroes in similar occupational classes. The results are presented in Table IV. In Table IV and Table V following, the reader is warned again, that, in the subdivisions of the sample, the sample size is small and that our conclusions are only suggestive.

No great differences between the races appeared in the relative use of direct plant application and friends and relatives. In addition,

[19]What is important here is that no Negroes found their current jobs with union assistance, despite their large membership. Negroes become union members after employment and joined unions that perform no employment service. The four white workers who found their current employment with union help were working in the construction industry. As noted in Table II, no Negro employment in construction is revealed by the 1960 Census.

TABLE IV

SOURCE OF CURRENT JOBS OF MALES, BY RACE AND SKILL, MIDDLETOWN, 1964

	Skilled and Clerical				Semiskilled and Unskilled			
	Negro		White		Negro		White	
	No.	Percent	No.	Percent	No.	Percent	No.	Percent
Private employment services, want ads and unions	4	15	11	28	5	4	6	10
State Employment Service	4	15	2	5	9	7	0	0
Friends and relatives	7	28	11	28	41	33	25	41
Direct application	11	42	15	39	69	56	30	49
Total sample	26	100	39	100	124	100	61	100

TABLE V

SOURCE OF CURRENT JOBS OF MALES, BY RACE AND PRIOR RESIDENCE, MIDDLETOWN, 1964

	Established Residents				New Migrants			
	Negro		White		Negro		White	
	No.	Percent	No.	Percent	No.	Percent	No.	Percent
Private employment services, want ads and unions	6	6	9	19	3	5	8	15
State Employment Service	7	7	1	2	6	11	1	2
Friends and relatives	29	31	13	28	19	35	23	43
Direct application	53	56	24	51	27	49	21	40
Total sample	95	100	47	100	55	100	53	100

as expected, both Negro and white clerical and skilled workers tended to use the formal methods of job search more than did either race in the semi-skilled and unskilled fields. Among clerical and skilled workers, 11 whites (27 per cent) obtained their current jobs through the private employment service, want-ads, and unions, while 4 Negroes (15 per cent) found their current jobs in this way. Negroes, however, used the State Employment Service to obtain their current jobs more often than whites. As Table IV shows, similar relationships exist among the semi-skilled and unskilled workers. Thus, even when workers in similar occupational and skill classes are compared, inverse differences in the use of private and public employment services, with respect to race, emerge.

We turn now to a consideration of the final variable that we suspect may affect the job search of Negro and white workers—the length of residence in Middletown and the kind of labor market from which the worker migrated. To analyze this variable, our sample was first divided into two groups, defining those workers who arrived in Middletown after 1958 as "new migrants" and those who came before 1958 or who were born in Middletown as "established residents." For the new migrants only, the further step was taken of placing into separate categories those who migrated from urban labor market areas in the Northeast and those who migrated from other, usually rural, labor markets. We have assumed that the newly-arrived were less familiar with the market than the older residents, and, among the new migrants, we assumed that those who migrated from Northeastern urban areas knew more about the kind of labor market they would face in Middletown than those who came from other kinds of labor markets. This division for Negro workers was made by defining as "other areas," the migrants from the South; the remaining Negro migrants were then classified as "Northeastern urban."[20] The white worker sample of new migrants was subdivided into those who came from Italy and those who came from other areas in the United States.[21] The sample of Negro and white workers who came to Middletown prior to 1958 was not subdivided on the assumption that, even if a worker had migrated from a non-urban area, he would have—in six or more years—acquired enough knowledge of the labor

[20]The Negro migrants from the South came largely from rural areas in North and South Carolina and the non-South Negro migrants came from cities in Connecticut, New York and Pennsylvania.

[21]The Italian migrants were, with two exceptions, from a small town (Melilli) in Sicily and, with very few exceptions, the white migrants from other parts of the United States originated in urban areas in the Northeastern region.

market to be considered as being on the same competitive footing in this respect as a worker who had come from a Northeastern city.[22]

Established Residents and New Migrants

About two-thirds of the total sample (142 Negro and white workers) were classified as established residents, for they arrived in Middletown before 1958. The age and years of education of workers of both races were essentially identical. Except for the finding made earlier for the total sample that there was an inverse use of the private and public employment service, by race, Table V shows that workers of both races with long attachment to a labor market have very similar search patterns.

In our sample, there were 55 Negro and 53 white workers, who were "new migrants," having come to Middletown since 1958. The Negro migrants had two more years of education, on the average, than the white migrants. The advantage that this seems to give to Negroes with respect to knowledge of the labor market is probably offset by the fact that the Negro migrants were six years younger. Again, inverse use of the employment services emerges. However, the informal search of new migrants seems to differ considerably from that of the established residents, with newly-arrived white workers depending more on friends and relatives and newly-arrived Negroes having more success in finding employment through direct application at the plant.

More insight into the search pattern of the migrants can be obtained by subdividing the new migrants into those that came to

[22]The question still arises as to whether, within these subdivisions, Negro and white workers have essentially the same knowledge of the Middletown labor market. To test this proposition, we asked all workers the following questions: (1) Did you know the specific kind of work and the wages to be paid before you were actually hired? (2) What are the best and worst firms in Middletown to work for? (3) Do you know whether there are any government training programs in the Middletown area? For all three subdivisions of workers by migratory status, white workers said they knew more about the jobs for which they were being hired than Negroes. This was particularly true among new migrants. Among the Italian migrants, 20 of 21 said that they knew before actual hiring the wages and working conditions; among Southern Negro migrants, only 16 of 32 said they knew their terms of employment. On the question of the best and worst firms, the majority of white workers classified the rubber companies (major employers of unskilled labor in Middletown) as the worst places to work, while a majority of Negroes thought they were the best places to have a job. There seemed to be no difference in knowledge about government training programs. Both races of workers knew little about them though, in the past year, the Office of Manpower, Automation and Training had offered a training program in Middletown.

Middletown from nearby cities in the Northeast and those that came from small towns or rural areas, far from Middletown.

Migrants from Northeastern Labor Market Areas

There were 23 Negro and 32 white workers who were recent migrants to Middletown from nearby areas. These workers had essentially the same median age and years of education. The search data collected from these workers indicated that there was little difference in the use of friends and relatives between the established residents and the urban migrants of both races. There was, however, a relative increase in direct application at plant gates by these Negroes; 16 of 23, or 70 per cent found their current employment by this method compared to 53 of 95, or 56 per cent, of the established Negro residents. The success of the urban white migrants at the plant gate showed no variation from that of the white established residents. A possible interpretation of this shift in search pattern is that Negro workers moved from neighboring areas when they heard that there were opportunities for general employment because of a new plant opening or the expansion of an existing plant. Our data also showed that these migrants used the public employment service hardly at all; for most moves from nearby areas, while not for specific jobs, were for general employment already known or suspected.

Southern Negroes and Italian Migrants

We interviewed 32 Negro males who had come to Middletown since 1958 from small towns and rural areas in the South and 21 white males who migrated recently from small towns (19 from Melilli) in Italy. These workers, of both races, knew very little about the operations of the labor market in an industrial city like Middletown. None of the Italian or Negro migrants indicated that their purpose in coming to Middletown was to accept a specific job. Most of the Italian migrants gave as their reason the desire to be with relatives while the Negro migrants mentioned relatives and better employment opportunities about the same number of times. The Negro migrants were almost eight years younger than the Italian immigrants and they had almost five years more of formal education.

The job search methods of the newly arrived workers of both races who came from distant regions with little or no knowledge about the operation of an urban labor market were quite different from the methods used by the workers previously discussed. The major difference was in the pattern of informal search. As one would expect, the Southern Negro and the migrant from Italy depended more heavily for their current employment on the information supplied by their sponsors—their friends and relatives—than on direct application at the plant. The fact that the Italian migrants relied more heavily on their relatives and friends than did the Southern Negroes may reflect the greater efficiency of the "chain occupation" placement service among the Italians than among the Negroes. A second difference was the heavy reliance of the Southern Negro on placement by the Connecticut State Employment Service. Almost three times as many Negro migrants, relatively (6 of 32), found their current jobs in this way as compared with Negro established residents (7 of 95). No Italian migrants used the public employment service; their alien status might have had a retarding effect on their use of a governmental agency but we should note that only two per cent of the entire sample of white workers found their current employment through the public employment service.

The fact that almost three in four placements of Italian workers resulted from friends and relatives as sources while less than one in two Southern Negro migrants and one in four workers in all other classes were placed in this way suggests that there is a more intimate relationship here than can be explained by differentials in age, education, or skill level. The "white man's market, by national origin" seems to offer some insight. The relatives and friends of Italian immigrants occupy important positions in the employment process. They are employers, workers, government officials and union leaders in Middletown and in cities like Middletown. They control jobs. Their recommendations count. Furthermore, the white community has assets of various kinds, including cash. They can begin the employment process by paying for the transportation of a friend or relative and can end it by placing him on a job for which there are no other candidates. Old country ties offer understandable opportunities to increase the welfare of a friend or relative.

The Southern Negro migrant comes to the Middletown labor market under very different circumstances. His friends and relatives have very little standing in the employment structure of a small Northern city. The migrant usually arrives without assets and the assistance given to him can amount only to room and lodging—and that for a short period of time. His benefactors are not so well situated that they can keep him while he makes a careful search of job opportunities. Their assistance in search must be minimal; they can always suggest, and do, firms that are hiring but the work is often arduous, seasonal and low-paying. It is stop-gap employment at best. The Southern Negro migrant also uses the public employment service, as the data indicate, but again he comes to the employer as a seller of labor for which there are few demanders.

The role of friends and relatives in the migration and subsequent employment of the job seeker is the crucial one. This, as we have indicated, from the outset places the Negro workers at a disadvantage relative to his competitors by virtue of the superior economic, political and social position of the white person in the Northern industrial community.

Our survey of the Negro migrants in Middletown has also yielded data on unemployment that are highly suggestive of what may well be an important source of the Negroes' higher rate of unemployment nationally. The unemployment rate for Middletown Negro migrants from the South—about 14 per cent—was by far the highest for any group in our survey. The rate was almost 2.5 times that found for all other Negroes and more than 3.5 times that of all whites surveyed. Looking at it another way, while the Southern Negro migrants made up only 14 per cent of our total sample, they were 31 per cent of the unemployed; although they were only 23 per cent of all the Negroes surveyed they were 42 per cent of the unemployed Negroes.

Between 1955 and 1960 more than a half-million Negroes over 14 years of age migrated from a Southern state in which they had lived in 1955.[23] All the available evidence indicates that this enormous wave of migration of Negroes from Southern states has been continuing for more than two decades. If the Southern Negro migrants are having similar difficulty nationally in finding employment as our survey found they were having in Middletown, then our study suggests that they may represent a significant share of the higher unemployment rates found among Negroes generally.

IV. Conclusions and Policy Proposals

The relatively poor employment record of Negroes may be explained in part by the less adequate sources of job information—in terms of both number and quality of sources—available to them than to whites of comparable skill. Our research shows that most jobs are obtained by workers of both races using informal methods of job search—direct plant application and information obtained from relatives and friends. Informal search, however, operates more effectively for white workers since their friends and relatives are already integrated within all levels of the occupational structure. The contacts that the job-seeking Negro must rely upon are, on the other hand, concentrated in the poorer-paying, less desirable occupations. The dependence of Negroes upon the kind of information available from friends or relatives tends to perpetuate the existing patterns of employment. Furthermore, in

[23]United States *Census of Population,* 1960, Detailed Characteristics, *op. cit.*

making direct application to plants, Negroes will tend to go to those firms where they have reason to believe there are "Negro jobs."

To break out of these existing patterns and find employment higher up on the occupational ladder, the Negro must turn to institutional intermediaries. However, these intermediaries, as they now function, do not hold out much hope for him. He gets relatively little assistance from private employment services and practically none from unions—both sources of information for many of the better paying jobs—and he also seems reluctant to use want-ads. The relationship between Negroes and unions is beyond the scope of this paper, and there seems to be little that can be done to make want-ads an important job source for Negroes. Neither is it likely that anything significant can be accomplished through regulation of private employment services. Since they are profit-making institutions and their profits depend on placements, there is no reason to expect that they will ever act as vehicles of social change in opening up a wider range of jobs opportunities for Negroes.

Since Negroes get little help from private institutional intermediaries, they are compelled to rely much more heavily than whites on the public employment service. Unfortunately, state employment services, as they are now organized and operating—even in the North—do little more than maintain existing discriminatory patterns, for the budgets of the state employment services depend largely on the number of placements. Therefore, the Negro job-seeker is likely to be referred to jobs where there is little chance of rejection, i.e., to "Negro jobs."[24]

The critical role that the informal search plays in employment and the inability of the Negro, through his own efforts, to break out of the dual job system leaves little alternative other than the assumption of a more vigorous policy position by the federal government. As a minimum, the United States Employment Service should discard, temporarily at least, the formula for allocating funds on the basis of the number of placements. This action, along with strong federal proscriptions against discriminatory placement practices, should break down some of the barriers to better jobs for Negro workers.

Once the dual job system has been breached, the informal search can then provide the Negro with knowledge about jobs throughout

[24]Furthermore, the employment service may be understandably reluctant to risk cutting off channels of communication that have been assiduously developed with white employers and, as a result, they will be cautious in making Negro referrals to jobs which have been generally closed to them. See, for example, Paul H. Norgren and Samuel E. Hill, *Toward Fair Employment*, Columbia University Press, 1964, pp. 38–39.

the occupational structure. However, to accelerate integration within the labor force, along with the action taken by the USES, it would help considerably if the Negro community could develop an informal structure in some measure similar to the informal job information and placement services that other minority groups have used. The National Urban League has already moved along these lines by establishing a national registry of Negroes with skills for managerial and professional positions. This registry, of course, can assist only a small segment of the Negro labor force, but we feel that it is a step in the right direction.

The relatively heavy use of the state employment services by Negroes and their massive and continuing migration from the South suggests another vital role for the USES—the provision of much more adequate job information than is now provided about spatially separated labor markets. As our data show, the Southern Negro comes to a city like Middletown without information other than what he can obtain from his sponsors—and they may be recent migrants themselves. If "following one's relatives" is the only criterion for choosing a labor market, the migrant will often come into an area in which there are no real prospects for the long term growth of job opportunities or wage levels. The public employment service should have offices in the South which could provide potential migrants with information concerning economic opportunities in other parts of the country so that their chances of moving into areas where they would experience unemployment or underemployment would be lessened.

Appendix

Previous work on job search has consisted largely of the study of the methods by which the unemployed worker intended to find employment, or, if already employed, how he intended to find a better job; and the methods by which he actually found a job or a new job. We are here concerned only with the last of these areas of investigation—how workers actually found their current jobs. Table A has been prepared showing a distribution of the methods of job search, tabulated from the data presented in these studies, based on the workers' responses to the question of how he found his current job.

We have presented these responses under four headings: "formal" job search, "informal" job search, employer recall or recruitment, and "other" methods of job search. Formal job search is restricted to the search that uses the following specific employment intermediaries: the public employment service, the private employment services and placement by unions. The informal job search is less well-defined. It includes the search that results in employment based on the leads, tips and suggestions that come to the attention of the job seekers from his relatives, friends, and even casual acquaintances, as well as the search that involves direct application at the plant gate or the personnel office. It is possible, even likely, that the methods of informal search are not independent of each other; for some gate hiring is probably derived from information that the worker, when asked, is unable to attribute to particular sources. In some markets, however, it is common knowledge among workers that some firms are always hiring and that employment depends only on application, and it is also very possible that random application at plant gates will result in employment. The third category is reserved for employment due to employer recall; this is really not the result of job search at all, but only a resumption of permanent employment interrupted by seasonal or other usually predictable fluctuations in the demand for labor. We also had a fourth catch-all category for a few methods of search, used so infrequently by workers that separate classification was not appropriate, e.g., civil service examination, high school placement.

From this earlier work there is evidence that job search is affected by the level of unemployment in the local labor market; therefore these studies have been divided into those made in labor markets with a high level of unemployment and those made in labor markets with firm or expanding employment conditions. The majority of studies fall in the high unemployment group; for the stimulus to find out about the deficiencies in the operation of the labor market increases with rising unemployment..

There are 9 studies represented in Table A, covering 17 labor market areas. Thirteen of these labor market areas have been classified by us as areas of high unemployment at the time of the studies; three markets could be considered as firm or expanding; and one, the Philadelphia labor market—the first market to be studied for job search—although depressed in 1930, has been classified separately because the date of the study preceded the establishment of the public employment service in this country. The labor force in 15 of the 17 cities studied depended for their employment on manufacturing industries. Furthermore, the employees interviewed in all of the labor markets, except one, were predominantly male and only a small percentage of the workers, and these in a few markets, were nonwhite.

A striking feature of these data is that, irrespective of the level of unemployment, only a small percentage of workers found their current jobs by using formal methods of job search. In high unemploy-

TABLE A

SUMMARY OF JOB SEARCH STUDIES
HOW CURRENT JOB WAS FOUND

Authors	Date of Study	Labor Market	Population (000*)	Methods of Job Search (% distribution)								
				"Formal" Search				"Informal" Search				
				(1)	(2)	(3)	(4)	(5)	(6)	(7)	(8)	(9)
High Unemployment												
1. Wilcock-Franke	1960-62	Columbus, O.	670	4				12	37	32		15
		Oklahoma City, Oklahoma	500	4				3	33	40		20
		E. St. Louis, Illinois	500	3				7	53	22		15
		Peoria, Ill.	290	5				5	43	31		16
		Fargo, N.D.-Moorhead, Minn.	70	9				7	31	35		18
2. Miernyk	1951-53	Lowell, Mass.	100	9		9	2		36	35		9
		Lawrence, Mass.	80	3		7	1		50	35		4
		Fall River, Mass.	100	5		3	1		59	29	1	2
		New Bedford, Mass.	100	3		0	3		39	42	11	2
		Providence, R.I.	800	3		7	3		32	42		13
3. Adams-Aronson	1949-50	Auburn, N.Y.	70	2					22	52	12	12
4. Myers-Schultz	1948-49	Nashua, N.H.	50	5		3	3		38	16	33	2
5. Myers-Maclaurin	1937-40	Fitchburg, Mass.	60	1	1	2			39	33	22	2
6. de Schweinitz	1930	Phila., Penna.	2,000		2	3			58	23		14

TABLE A (continued)

Expanding or Firm Employment

7. Wilcock-Sobel	1952	Kankakee, Illinois	100	8		19			46	23	3	1
8. Reynolds-Shister	1947	New Haven, Connecticut	350	13		13	5		28	20	13	8
9. Heneman-Fox-Yoder	1947-48	Minneapolis, Minn.	500	6	5	14	7		30	32		6
Lurie-Rayack	1964	Middletown, Connecticut	35	2	10	3	4		36	45		

* Population at time of study.
Code for Methods of Job Search:
(1) Public Employment Service
(2) Private Employment Service
(3) Newspaper "help wanted" ads
(4) Trade Union
(5) Company assistance in finding new employment
(6) Friends and relatives
(7) Application at plant gate
(8) Recall or recruited by company
(9) Other or unknown

SOURCES

1. Richard C. Wilcock and Walter H. Franke, Unwanted Workers, the Free Press of Glencoe, 1963.
2. William H. Miernyk, Inter-Industry Labor Mobility, Northeastern University, 1955.
3. Leonard P. Adams and Robert L. Aronson, Workers and Industrial Change, Cornell University, 1957.
4. Charles A. Myers and George P. Shultz, The Dynamics of a Labor Market (Englewood Cliffs, N.J.: Prentice-Hall, 1951).
5. Charles A. Myers and W. Rupert MacLaurin, The Movement of Factory Workers (New York: John Wiley, 1943).
6. Dorothea de Schweinitz, How Workers Find Jobs, University of Pennsylvania Press, 1935.
7. Richard C. Wilcock and Irvin Sobel, Small City Job Markets, University of Illinois, 1958.
8. Lloyd G. Reynolds and Joseph Shister, Job Horizons (New York: Harper, 1949).
9. H. G. Heneman, Harland Fox, and Dale Yoder, Minnesota Manpower Mobilities (University of Minnesota, 1950).

ment labor markets, 10 per cent used employment intermediaries; in the firm or expanding markets, the number increased to 30 per cent. One expects greater placement by formal methods in tight labor markets, for employers are forced to recruit actively in order to hire the number and quality of workers needed. These data also show that placement by the public employment service accounted for very few jobs. Only 4 per cent of the workers in high unemployment labor markets found their jobs in this manner; while, in the tighter labor markets, placements were increased to an average of 9 per cent.

From these data, one concludes that informal search is the way most workers have found their current jobs. In the high unemployment markets, 74 per cent of those interviewed who were currently employed found their jobs through their relatives or friends, or by applying directly at the plant gate; in firm labor markets, 60 per cent of the workers employed found their jobs in this manner.

The 1930 de Schweinitz study of the job search of Philadelphia hosiery workers (not included in the results cited above) showed a very similar pattern of job search; for at that economically-depressed time prior to the establishment of the public employment service, 81 per cent of the workers found jobs through informal methods and 5 per cent found their jobs through the private employment service or help wanted ads.

Negro-White Differences in Geographic Mobility

Eva Mueller and William Ladd

[*From* Negro-White Differences in Geographic Mobility. *U. S. Department of Commerce, 1964.*]

Introduction

This report focuses on differences in geographic mobility between the white and the Negro population. It contrasts the rate and geographic pattern of mobility between Negro and white heads of families, distinguishing between Negroes born in the 11 Southern States which formed the Confederacy[1] and those born elsewhere. After highlight-

[1]For our purposes it seemed appropriate to distinguish the eleven States of the Confederacy (Alabama, Arkansas, Florida, Georgia, Louisiana, Mississippi, North Carolina, South Carolina, Tennessee, Texas, and Virginia), from the five border areas (District of Columbia, Kentucky, Maryland, Oklahoma and West Virginia). As our analysis shows, the pattern of migration is substantially different among the two groups of southern states.

ing these differences, it attempts to answer the question—Why are Negro families geographically less mobile now than white families?

For purposes of this study mobility has been defined to include all moves across labor market area boundaries. These boundaries are defined by the Department of Labor. In many cases the labor market area is a single county. In other cases a few counties are grouped into one labor market area. For those parts of the country where labor market areas are not designated, county boundaries are used. A person is not regarded as having moved if he changes his place of residence within a labor market area.

The findings presented here are based on 2,669 personal interviews taken between September and December, 1962. These interviews represent a probability sample of all families living in private dwelling units in the conterminous United Statess. Of the 2,669 respondents, 2,406 were white and 263 non-white. About 86 percent of the non-white respondents in the survey were Negroes. Only the latter are included in this report. In families where the head was married, the head was interviewed in half of the cases, the wife in the other half. In other households the head was always the respondent.[2]

Patterns of Mobility

At the present time geographic mobility is considerably lower among Negro than among white families of the U. S. This finding emerges clearly from the Survey Research Center study and is confirmed by Census surveys. The Census data, available annually since 1950, have registered a lower rate of inter-county moves ever since 1950 for the Negro than for the white population. Such data as are available for earlier periods suggest that during World War II, and probably earlier too, the opposite was true: Negro workers seemed to be more mobile than white workers. Therefore, in comparing mobility, the time period under review becomes crucial.

Lifetime mobility: Comparisons of the proportion of Negro and white adults who have moved at some time during their lives are affected both by the high mobility of the Negro population prior to 1950 and its relatively low mobility since then. Looking at the present adult population, we find that nearly equal proportions of Negro and white family heads—about 35 percent—are now living in the same labor market area in which they were born. However, the Negro

[2]For further detail on the methods of this study, see John B. Lansing, Eva Mueller, William Ladd, and Nancy Barth, "The Geographic Mobility of Labor: A First Report," Survey Research Center, University of Michigan, 1963.

population does not fit a single pattern of life-time mobility. Of those Negroes who were born in the South of the Confederacy, only slightly more than 1 in 4 are currently living in the area of their birthplace. This group has a decidedly greater lifetime mobility than the white population. By contrast, roughly one-half of the Negroes born outside the South of the Confederacy are still living in the area where they were born. Thus, the northern-born Negro represents a particularly immobile group in the populaton, and one which is growing in importance.[3]

As is commonly known, migration toward the West and from rural to urban areas has been characteristic of the white population in recent decades; Negro migration has taken place from the South to all other areas of the country and also from farms to urban areas. Lifetime mobility patterns reflect these major population movements. Chart II illustrates the geographic shifts of the white and Negro population insofar as these shifts have resulted from the migration of the present adult population. Those changes in the distribution of the population which result from the migration of children and any regional race-specific differences in fertility and mortality rates between racial groups are not reflected here. Only the West shows a net gain in white population in the sense that a higher proportion of the present white adult population lives there than was born there; all other regions show no significant net change due to migration. All regions except the eleven States of the Confederacy have gained population through Negro migration. Fully three-fourths of present Negro family heads were born in these eleven southern States but only 43 percent of Negro family heads remain there now. Conversely, 6 percent of present Negro family heads were born in the North Central States, but 23 percent live there now.

The differential impact of the farm-urban migration on race groups is illustrated by the following tabulation, which shows the origin of family heads living in metropolitan areas at the time of interview. Slightly over a third of the present white adult population in metropolitan areas was born on a farm or lived for at least a year on a farm.

Among Negroes born in the South of the Confederacy and now residing in metropolitan areas, 56 percent have a farm background. Among Negroes born outside the South and now residing in a metro-

[3]Because of the relatively small number of Negro respondents, figures for Negroes in this report are indicative of orders of magnitude but should not be read too closely. Of the 226 Negro heads of families, three-fourths were born in the eleven States of the Confederacy.

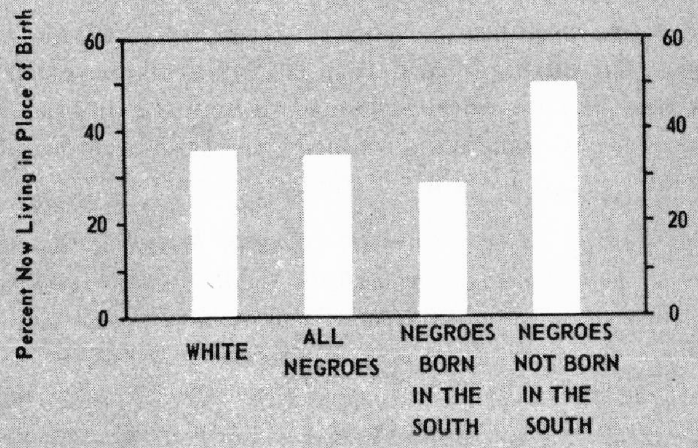
CHART I
Percent of White and Negro Heads of Families
Now Living in Area in Which They Were Born.
Percent Now Living in Place of Birth
60
40
20
0
WHITE
ALL NEGROES
NEGROES BORN IN THE SOUTH
NEGROES NOT BORN IN THE SOUTH

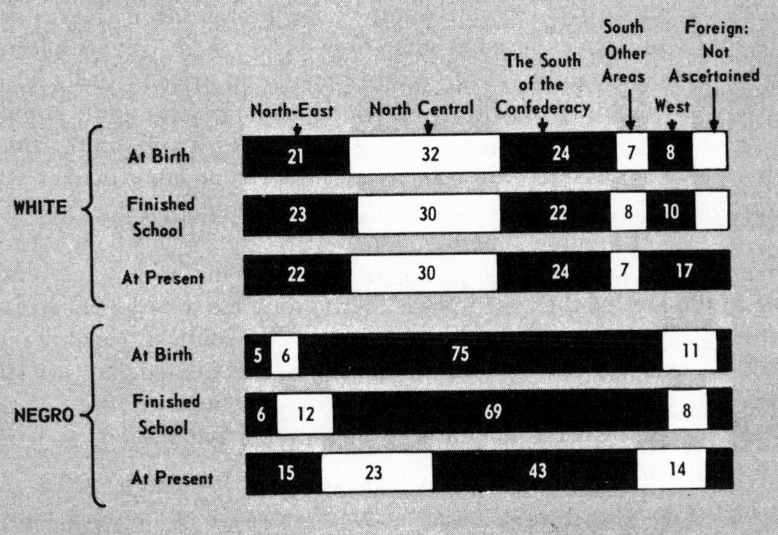
CHART II
Percent of White and Negro Heads Living in Specified Regions.
North-East
North Central
The South of the Confederacy
South Other Areas
West
Foreign: Not Ascertained
WHITE
At Birth
21
32
24
7
8
Finished School
23
30
22
8
10
At Present
22
30
24
7
17
NEGRO
At Birth
5
6
75
11
Finished School
6
12
69
8
At Present
15
23
43
14

Race	*Percent of heads of families now living in metropolitan areas who once lived on a farm for a year or more*
Negro	43
Born in South	56
Born elsewhere	18
White	36

politan area, this percentage is much lower: only about 18 percent have a farm background. It is also interesting to note that among white adults who have lived in rural areas, about 44 percent remain rural residents while among adult Negroes with a rural background, only about 30 percent are still in rural areas.

Race	*Percent of all heads of families having a rural background who are now living in rural areas*
Negro	30
Born in the South.	31
Born elsewhere	*
White	44

* Too few cases.

Mobility Since 1950: Data on more recent mobility show that since 1950 the proportion of white family heads who have moved between labor market areas has been nearly as high as the proportion of Negroes who have made such moves. Also, since 1950 there has been no significant difference in mobility rates between Negroes born in the South and outside the South. However, since northern-born Negroes are younger and better educated, on the average, than those born in the South, their low geographic mobility remains particularly noteworthy.

For the most recent period, the five years from 1957-1962, the contrast between the mobility of the white and that of the Negro population is even greater. As Chart III shows, nearly three times as large a proportion of the white as of the Negro population moved from one labor market area into another during that time. Annual Census data for the years since 1950 confirm this declining trend in Negro migration rates. During the three years 1950-1953, the average annual inter-county migration rate for Negroes was 5.6 percent: for 1958-1961, it was down to 4.2 percent. Over the same period the migration rate for the white population declined only from 6.9 to 6.6 percent.

In addition to the proportion of each racial group who moved, the survey measured the number of moves made by each migrant since 1950. Of those who moved since 1950, on the average, white people made multiple moves more often than Negroes. About 17 percent of white family heads have moved four or more times since 1950; for Negroes the corresponding figure is 5 percent.

Besides making more or less permanent moves, people work away from home on a temporary basis. Migratory farm laborers, construction workers, and some types of sales workers are groups for which this kind of mobility is characteristic. Long distance commuting is another sort of recurrent mobility which affects a community's labor supply, but in this case no change of residence is involved. Both temporary moves and long distance commuting have occurred less frequently since 1950 among Negro than among white family heads.

The survey shows that since 1950 about 7 percent of white family heads, as compared with 2 percent of Negroes, have gone away temporarily to work and then returned to their former place of residence.[4] Similarly about 9 percent of white workers, as against 4 percent of Negroes, have commuted 50 or more miles to work for some period since 1950. These figures are another manifestation of the apparently greater mobility of the white than the Negro population, as is shown below:

Race	*Went away temporarily to work*	*Commuted 50 or more miles to work*
Negro	2%	5%
Born in the South.	2	4
Born elsewhere	3	6
White	7	9

The regional pattern of migration rates since 1950 does not differ greatly from the pattern of lifetime mobility. Among the white population the movement to the West has slowed down since 1950, and immigration and outmigration are nearly in balance for all regions. For Negroes, all regions but the South continue to be destinations of moves more often than origins of moves; the South shows a substantial net loss of Negro migrants.

Of all moves since 1950, about 20 percent are returns to a place of previous residence. Roughly one-half of the return moves are moves

[4]Migratory workers are not fully covered by the survey since the sample excludes people housed in temporary dwellings and those living in large rooming or boarding houses.

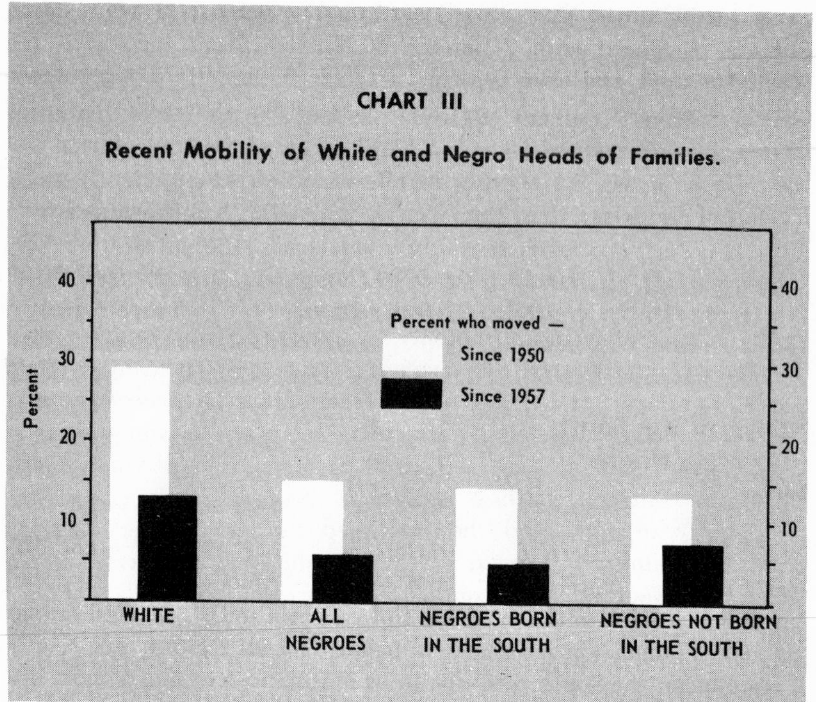
CHART III
Recent Mobility of White and Negro Heads of Families.
Percent
40
30
20
10
Percent who moved —
Since 1950
Since 1957
WHITE
ALL NEGROES
NEGROES BORN IN THE SOUTH
NEGROES NOT BORN IN THE SOUTH

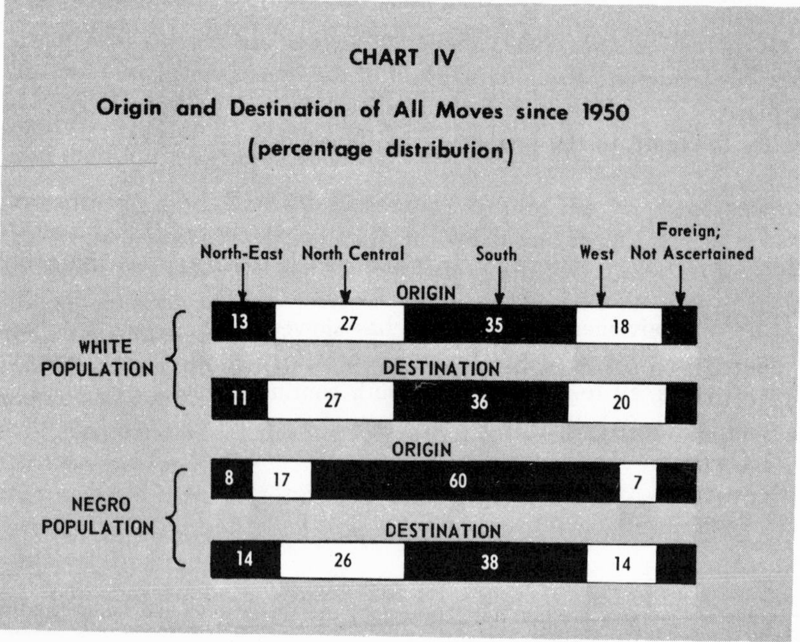
CHART IV
Origin and Destination of All Moves since 1950
(percentage distribution)
North-East
North Central
South
West
Foreign; Not Ascertained
WHITE POPULATION
ORIGIN
13 27 35 18
DESTINATION
11 27 36 20
NEGRO POPULATION
ORIGIN
8 17 60 7
DESTINATION
14 26 38 14

back to place of birth. There is little, if any, difference between Negroes and whites in regard to the proportion of moves that are returns.

Return moves	*Race* White	Negro
Proportion of all moves	22%	19%
Return to place of birth	9	10
Return to places lived during childhood excluding place of birth	11	8
Return to other place of previous residence	2	1

Future mobility: In addition to asking about past mobility, the survey inquired into the likelihood that people might move in the near future. A likelihood of moving might be indicated by dissatisfaction with one's present place of residence or by actual plans to move. A disposition to move in the near future, according to these indicators, was found much less frequently among Negroes than among white people.

People were asked—"If you could do as you please, would you like to stay in . . . or would you like to move?" In their replies, Negroes indicated a greater attachment to the community in which they are now living than did white citizens. The proportion of people reporting a preference for moving away from their present place of residence is nearly twice as high for white adults as it is for Negroes, as is shown in the following:

Preference	*Race* White	Negro
Prefers to move	20%	11%
Not sure	3	*
Prefers to stay	73	87
Not ascertained	4	2
	100%	100%

* Too few cases.

Subsequently, respondents were asked whether there was any chance that they might move away from the area of their present residence in the next year. Only a small proportion of Negroes had any moving plans, however uncertain; 97 percent saw no possibility of moving in the 12 months following the 1962 interview. On the other hand, about one in every ten white adults thought they would or might move to another labor market area in the coming year. Negroes who were born outside the eleven States of the Confederacy, the younger and better educated part of the Negro population, expressed moving plans more often than Southern-born Negroes; although since 1950 the two groups have not differed significantly in mobility rates. The data on expressed moving plans below include those who said they would or might move in the following 12 months:

Race	*See chance of moving*
Negro	3%
Born in the South.	1
Born elsewhere	7
White	11

Why Are Negro Families Geographically Less Mobile Than White Families?

The lesser geographic mobility of the Negro than of the white population now and in the recent past requires explanation. We shall examine in turn a number of possible reasons for the observed difference in mobility.

Demographic Factors: In the American population as a whole three demographic factors—age, occupation, and education—account for a large part of the difference in mobility between individuals. Young people, college graduates, and those in professional and managerial occupations are much more mobile than people who do not have these characteristics.

With respect to the age distribution, the white and Negro populations resemble each other closely. Negro family heads are slightly younger on the average than white family heads; but the difference is small and should, if anything, lead to higher mobility among Negroes.

Differences in education and occupation between white and Negro family heads are extensive. Data for the population as a whole indicate that a person with a college education is at least three times as likely to have moved in the past five years as a person who has attended only grammar school. Therefore, it is highly relevant that 27 percent of white family heads, but only 12 percent of Negroes, have had some college education. Conversely, only 28 percent of white family heads, as against 59 percent of Negroes, have had 8 years or less of schooling.

Since education and occupation are closely related, it is not surprising that those occupations which require more education are also characterized by a higher level of geographic mobility. Looking at the adult population as a whole we find that the proportion of movers was about twice as high in the last five years among families headed by managerial and professional workers as among those headed by operatives, laborers, and service workers. Negroes are predominantly in the less mobile occupations: 55 percent of them are operatives, laborers, and service workers and only 6 percent are professional workers or salaried managers. The corresponding percentages for white family heads are 19 and 18.

In brief, in a modern economy geographic mobility occurs in part because people with highly specialized knowledge and highly differentiated skills must be matched with job openings which call for specific types of knowledge and training. To use his special qualifications to best advantage, a person may have to move across county or even State lines to the most suitable job opening. This matching of specialized jobs and people affects primarily people in professional, managerial, or skilled technical work. Often it takes place within large companies which "transfer" personnel from one location to another. Since only a small proportion of Negroes are in highly specialized or skilled occupations, this reason for geographic mobility is not applicable to most of them. For example. among recent white movers 15 percent were transferred by their companies, among recent Negro movers only 1-2 percent.

Do educational and occupational differences between the Negro and the white population account fully for the observed differences in recent geographic mobility? The following tabulations show that the answer to this question is clearly—no. Even if we compare Negro and white adults having the same education or occupation, the Negro groups still appear considerably less mobile than the corresponding white groups. It is necessary to search for additional explanations.

Demographic Characteristics	*Percentage In Each Group Who Have Moved in the Past 5 Years*	
Education	White	Negro
8 grades or less	8%	5%
9-12 grades	14	8
College	28	11
Occupation	White	Negro
Professional, Managerial	30%	8%
Laborers, Service workers, Operatives	15	6
Other	13	6

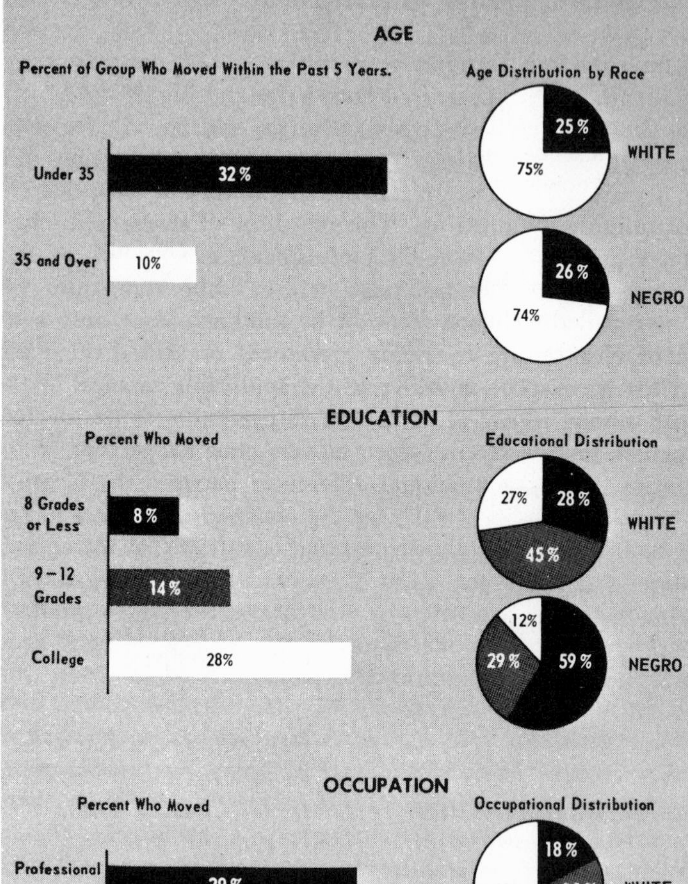

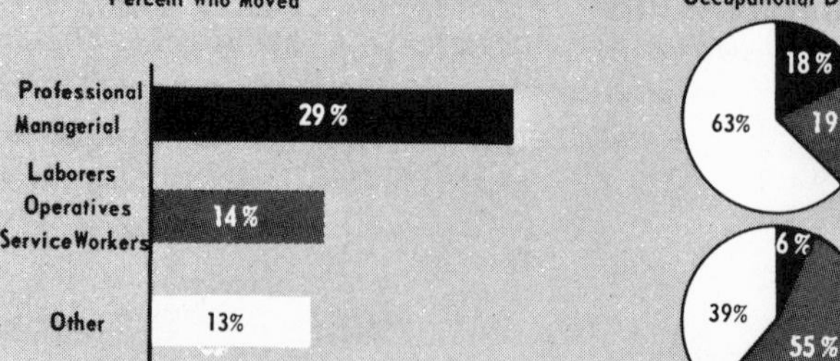

Note: Data relate to family heads.
The "other" occupation group includes families whose head is not in the labor force.

Financial Factors: A striking difference between the Negro and the white population lies in the larger proportion of Negroes with very low incomes and no savings or reserve funds. In 1962, 24 percent of Negro families compared with 9 percent of white families, earned less than $2000. People in this bottom income bracket are considerably less mobile than others. However, low income is associated with low levels of education and occupational skills and with old age, and it seems to reflect primarily the low mobility associated with those factors.

Regarding financial reserves, these is no evidence, for the population as a whole or for racial groups, that lack of such funds reduces geographic mobility significantly. Although one might suppose that poverty would make it more difficult to meet the expenses and the financial risks involved in moving, the survey data do *not indicate* that the relatively low income and reserve funds of the Negro population constitute *per se* a barrier to mobility. Low-income Negro movers studied in the survey usually reported that their moving expenses were small (the price of a bus ticket) and that they had nothing to take along but their clothes.

Poverty may lead to dependence on some form of public assistance or private charity. Among the white population with incomes below $4000, mobility was significantly lower in recent years if a family received public assistance than if it did not receive such support. However, if both private and public assistance are considered, it would appear that dependence on financial aid on the whole does not have an important negative effect on mobility. Among low-income Negro families mobility was, if anything, more frequent among recipients of financial aid than among non-recipients. Thus, frequent dependence on private welfare or public assistance among the low-income Negro population does not help to explain their low geographic mobility.

Community and Family Reasons: Despite the large movements of the Negro population from South to North and from rural to urban areas within the South during the first half of the 20th Century, Negroes on the whole seem to have stronger emotional and family ties to their current place of residence than the white population. We have noted already that, in reply to the question—"If you could do as you please, would you like to stay here in . . . or would you like to move?"—87 percent of Negroes compared with 73 percent of white adults indicated a decided preference for staying in their present community. When asked further whether there might be any disadvantages in staying "here" only 29 percent of Negroes, but 44 percent of whites, mentioned some disadvantages. Interestingly, economic or

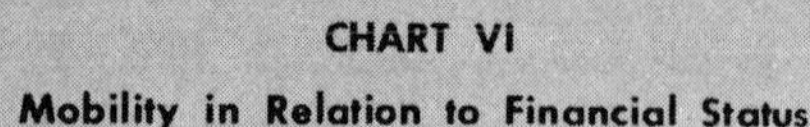

CHART VI
Mobility in Relation to Financial Status

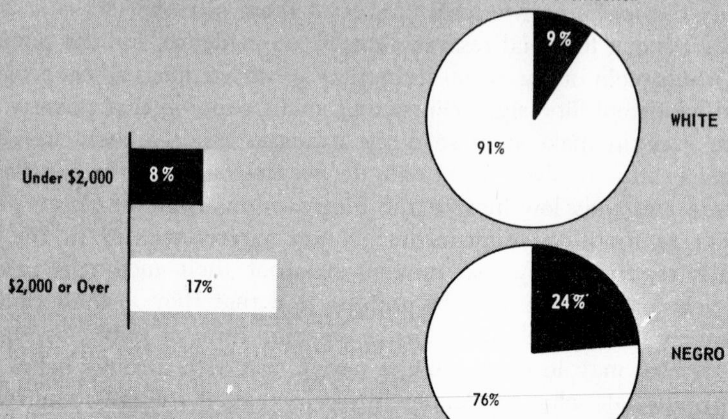

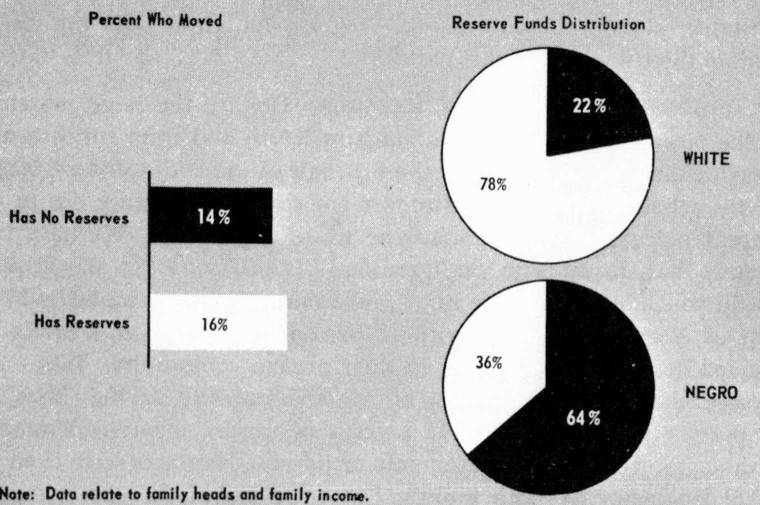

Note: Data relate to family heads and family income.

job disadvantages were cited with equal frequency by both groups; but criticisms of the community—its size, climate, schools, traffic congestion, and the like—were voiced much less frequently by Negroes than by white respondents.

The ties of the Negro to the community seem to be to an important extent family and friendship ties. Apparently the Negro migrant from the rural South, like the immigrant from Europe before him, often sent for or was followed by other members of his family. As a result we find that, even though only one-third of Negro adults are still living in the county where they were born 59 percent have all or most of their relatives living near them now in the same community. Most of the remaining Negro families reported that "some" relatives are living in the same community where they are. The survey shows that only 6 percent of Negro families, in contrast to 21 percent of white families, have no relatives in the community where they are now residing. It should be added that 48 percent of Negro families, but only 37 percent of white families, reported that *all* their close friends are living in their current place of residence. These contrasts between the Negro and the white populations are important since the survey shows that both past geographic mobility and moving plans are particularly low among families who have all or most of their relatives living near them.

When a family does decide to move, relatives may play a further role in facilitating and guiding the move. In discussing their most recent move across county lines, most Negro as well as most white families mentioned job or economic factors as the primary reason for moving. However, among Negroes who were born in the South and have moved North or West, family reasons were mentioned with considerable frequency. A third of this group said that they moved in order to be closer to a relative who had moved earlier. A closer look at cases of recent Negro migrants in the survey suggests that job and family considerations tend to be inseparable in many instances, since relatives are the major source of job information and often help the migrant to find work. For example:

> A 51 year-old Negro and his wife moved from Arkansas to California where their daughter and her family lived. The son-in-law told him he could get work there as a common laborer and in fact helped him to locate his first job as a janitor.
>
> A young Negro moved from Louisiana to the West Coast to join a brother who urged him to come. The brother then helped him to find a job in a shipyard by sending him to the appropriate union.

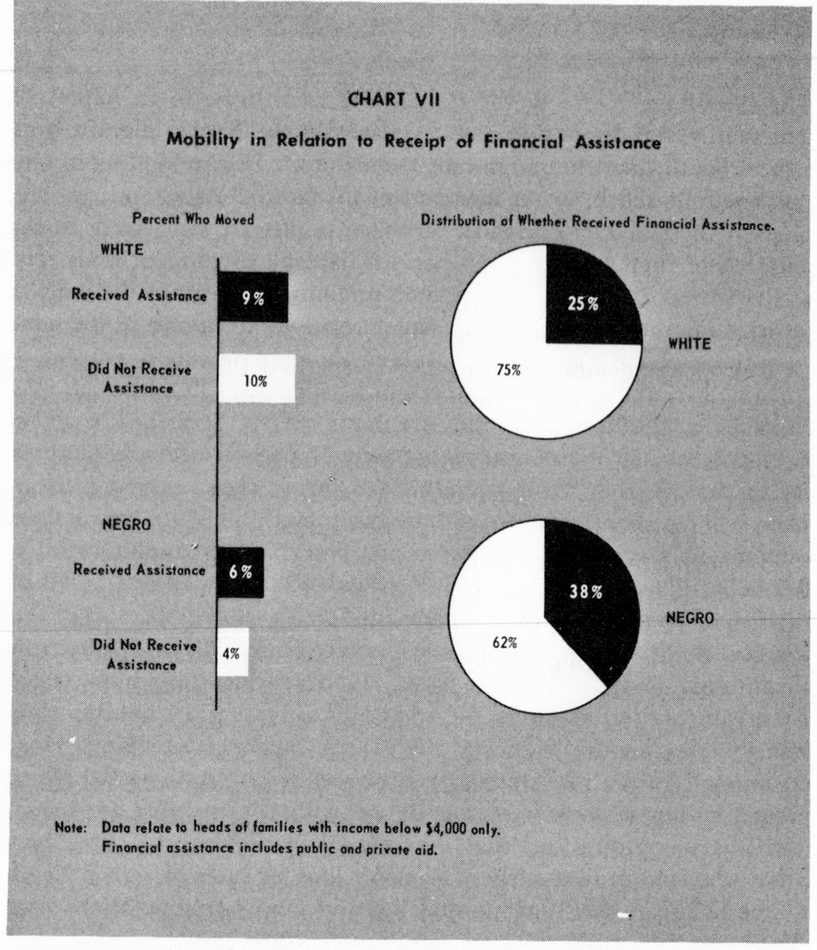

A 30 year-old single Negro had moved from Kansas to California and had made several moves in California in an attempt to find suitable work. Then he heard that his father was in San Francisco and he joined him there. The father had an apartment and took him in until he had work; the father also took him around in his car to look for a job. He is now a waiter.

Similarly, in the case of return migrants to the South:

A young Negro woman, domestic worker, who had been living in New York with her mother, returned to North Carolina when her mother died. All her other relatives were living in North Carolina.

A middle-aged Negro born in the South had migrated to New York City in the early 1950's. In 1959 his boss died, and he became unemployed. He and his family returned to his wife's home town in the South. A friend there gave him a job as a farm laborer.

It seems then that family ties and emotional ties to a place and to friends are a greater barrier to mobility among Negro than among white families. Furthermore, such geographic moves that do occur, particularly among unskilled workers, in many instances seem to be guided by the location of relatives as much as by job opportunities. The role which relatives play in determining Negro moves may help to solve the difficult problems of adjustment to a new environment which the Negro migrant faces. But this system hardly provides an effective mechanism for guiding Negroes into areas of new opportunities or expanding employment.

Economic Incentives: The history of Negro migration during recent decades demonstrates clearly that the Negro population *does* move in reponse to strong economic incentives. According to Census data, the growing inadequacy of employment opportunities in South-

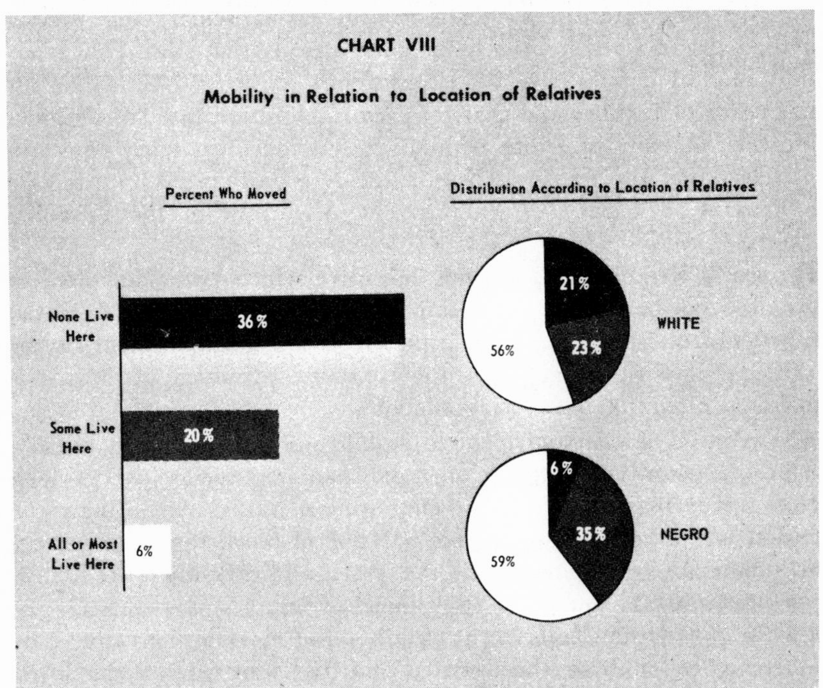

ern agriculture induced a net migration from the South of over 700,000 Negroes between 1920 and 1930. During the 1930's, when few job openings were beckoning, net Negro migration out of the South fell below 350,000. During the decade of World War II large numbers of job openings for unskilled workers at rising rates of pay led an unprecedented 1,200,000 Negroes to leave the South. The migration rate during World War II was higher for Negro than for white men; it was particularly high among unskilled Negro workers. We have noted already that since 1950 intercounty migration rates have been consistently lower for Negro than for white heads of families and that the Negro migration rate has declined while the rate for the white population has remained fairly constant. It is likely that the recent decline in the Negro migration rate reflects the growing deficiency of employment opportunities for unskilled workers.

For many Negroes the economic incentive which persuades them to move need not be a higher wage somewhere else; it might simply be the prospect of steady work. At least at present, when unemployment among unskilled Negro workers is high, the economic advantage of moving is stated most often in terms of available jobs.

The relation of unemployment to mobility is best studied by classifying people according to their unemployment experience over a long period rather than their current employment status. Accordingly the question was asked—"Some people are out of work for a time every year, others are unemployed every few years, and still others are almost never unemployed. What has been (head of family's) experience?" In the white population, both recent mobility and moving plans were only slightly higher for those who reported that they were often unemployed than for those who had never or rarely been unemployed. Among Negro families, on the other hand, mobility seems to be much higher if the head suffered repeated unemployment than if he experienced steady employment. In fact, it appears that the contrast in past mobility between Negroes and white people is pronounced only for that part of the population which has not suffered unemployment. That is, Negroes with steady jobs are considerably less likely to move than white workers who are continuously employed. But Negro families subject to repeated unemployment do not have an appreciably lower mobility rate than white families in a similar unemployment situation.

Thus it appears that emotional or family ties to a place, or uneasiness about unfamiliar surroundings, are barriers to mobility among the Negro population primarily when economic incentives to move are weak. Unemployment creates an economic incentive to

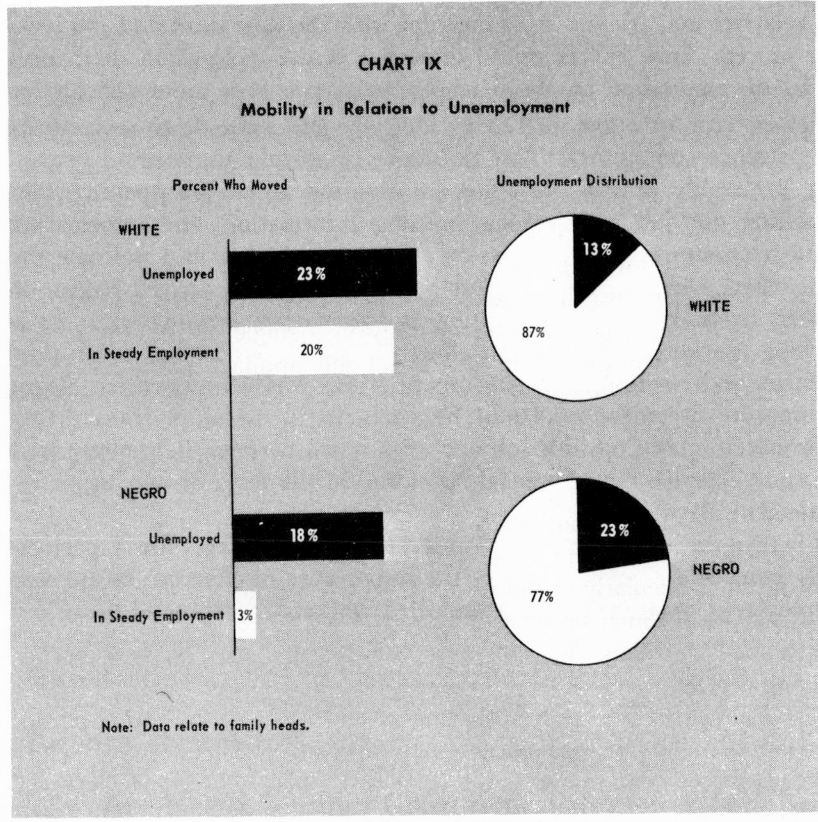

move, yet most of the unemployed—Negro or white—remain in the same labor market area. Having relatives elsewhere may bring better job opportunities to the Negro worker's attention; and at the same time it may lower his reluctance to leave a familiar place of residence.

Policy Implications: The policy implications of this study may be considered with the assumption that greater geographic mobility on the part of the Negro population would enhance its economic welfare and would make for a more efficient utilization of the labor force generally. We have seen that the relatively low rate of geographic mobility of non-white workers is related to their low level of education and occupational skills. An improvement in education, vocational training, and employment opportunities for Negroes in skilled occupations of itself should lead to greater mobility. Secondly, racial discrimination may be responsible for the disinclination of Negroes to leave family, friends, and a familiar place of residence. Most likely, the elimination of discrimination (together with better education) would lessen the Negro's uneasiness about finding a job and suitable housing in a new community.

Besides these longer range objectives of national policy, direct steps might be taken to overcome the dependence of potential Negro migrants on relatives and friends in connection with the migration and job seeking process. Such efforts would grow out of the recognition that, until racial discrimination has been wholly overcome, it is more difficult for Negroes than for other workers to find jobs and settle down successfully in a strange community. This assistance could take the form of providing, preferably in a single office, information about job openings, aid in filling out job applications, housing information, and information about community and religious organizations which would welcome the newcomer. One could go even further in aid to newly arrived Negro job seekers by providing transportation and temporary housing while he is looking for work. For such an effort close cooperation between public agencies and Negro community organizations would be essential. Negro community organizations could be particularly useful in transmitting information about possible job openings. Such personal help might well be more effective than financial subsidies, in the form of moving or resettlement allowances.

Finally, the recognition that unskilled Negro workers are a particularly immobile group underlines the importance of efforts to create new employment opportunities for unskilled workers in depressed areas.

Why Should Negroes Work?

Jan E. Dizard*

With the publication of Myrdal's monumental work, *An American Dilemma,* a new interpretation of race relations gained currency. Prior to this, social scientists, primarily under the influence of Robert E.

*The author wishes to record his appreciation to R. A. Gordon, Margaret Gordon, and Charles Y. Glock for discussing many of the ideas in this paper and cooperating in making the research discussion possible. Lloyd C. Street and Bruce Johnson have read earlier drafts of this paper and their comments and suggestions have also been invaluable. This paper represents the initial formulation of guidelines for a research project on Negro unemployment supported by a grant from the Ford Foundation and co-sponsored by the Institute of Industrial Relations and the Survey Research Center, both of the University of California, Berkeley.

Park, had viewed race relations problems as part of a process eventually leading to racial assimilation in the dominant society. When two different races meet, Park had argued, conflict ensues.[1] Once hegemony of one over the other is established, conflict is gradually superceded by accommodation. According to this view, the United States had been in the accommodation phase. In order to move from accommodation to assimilation and to the elimination of caste inferiority and discrimination, Park saw the role of urbanization as central. Education and self-help could flourish in the urban setting. Since the Negro community produces values and institutions that parallel those of the dominant white society,[2] it would ultimately come to a complete parallel with the whole range of statuses in white society. Assimilation would then take place between strata in the white and Negro communities, strata which shared the same life styles, values and occupational talents.

Myrdal's work, if not in spirit then surely in substance, refuted much of this mechanistic view of race relations. While there were some obvious parallels between white and black communities, according to Myrdal Negroes were "exaggerated Americans," and generations of slavery and Jim Crow had severely distorted the viability of their community.[3] In Myrdal's words, the Negroes had a "pathological community." They had come to believe what they had been told for years—that black was bad and white was right—and were thus, for all practical purposes, rendered immobile. Self-help had no basis: as soon as a Negro managed to accumulate some capital, instead of using it for the good of the Negro community, he tried frantically to dissociate himself from other Negroes. Negroes turned upon Negroes—stealing from one another, maiming one another—and, ultimately, they turned on themselves, using skin lighteners and hair straighteners in an attempt to rid themselves of the onus, black. These observations and others pointing in the same general direction, made Myrdal

[1]See, for example, Robert E. Park, *Race and Culture,* Glencoe, Illinois: The Free Press, 1950. pp. 189-195.

[2]To be sure, Park recognizes differences between the white and Negro communities, both in terms of values and institutions. However, these differences are generally ascribed to the Negro "folk culture" which was, like all folk cultures in the presence of a growing urban society, essentially anachronistic and soon to disappear. On this and the idea of parallel communities, see *Ibid.*, especially Part Two. For greater elaboration on this point in Park's view of race relations, see the essays by Ernest W. Burgess and Everett C. Hughes in Jitfuichi Masuoka and Preston Valien (eds.), *Race Relations,* Chapel Hill, North Carolina: University of North Carolina Press, 1961.

[3]Gunnar Myrdal, *An American Dilemma,* New York: Harper and Row (20th Anniversary Edition), 1962. pp. 927-994.

less optimistic than Park. Not only do whites have to be shaken free of their prejudice and discriminatory behavior, he claimed, Negroes too, have to shake themselves free of their own disorganization. The accommodation that Park saw merging into assimilation was seen by Myrdal as sustaining a self-fulfilling prophecy, that led nowhere. Positing the now famous "vicious circle" concept, Myrdal viewed black and white action and reaction as interdependent and held that as soon as whites ceased discrimination, Negroes would look up.[4]

The nature of this vicious circle is simple. Prejudiced whites discriminate against Negroes and, as a result of this discrimination, Negroes are forced to adapt to deprivation in ways that serve to reinforce white prejudice, e.g., by dropping out of school to seek employment ("See, they can't do well in school"). Thus, each generation of whites and Negroes responds in ways that serve to perpetuate the status quo. What is required is for one generation of Negroes to sacrifice its adaptations and plunge ahead as if there were no prejudice and discrimination (e.g., get educated even though the "payoff" for being educated will not be forthcoming for them) or for a generation of whites to refuse to fall into the trap of stereotyping, even though Negroes, using the above example, may achieve at lower levels in schools. The difficulties in effecting one or the other of these "sacrifices" (the difficulties in accomplishing both simultaneously are even greater) are attested to in the emergence of a third "school" of race relations. This group has no one spokesman such as Park or Myrdal but its position is clear nonetheless. After "feeding on itself" for years, the vicious circle has become a vicious *spiral* in which one generation's pathological adaptations are compounded in the next generation. Things get worse instead of staying the same.[5] Unemployment leads to welfare and, ultimately, to welfare dependency; family instability and illegitimacy lead to inadequate socialization of children and, thus, a perpetuation of family instability and illegitimacy.

Each of these interpretations has been more or less carefully

[4]*Ibid.*, pp. 75-78. In theory, the vicious circle works both ways so that Negroes could initiate the breaking of the circle. However, Myrdal places greatest emphasis on the role of whites in initiating changes.

[5]The idea of progressive deterioration is most clearly stated by Daniel P. Moynihan in "Employment, Income and the Ordeal of the Negro Family," *Daedalus*, Fall, 1965. pp. 745-770, especially pp. 758, 766-69. The idea, however, is implicit in many recent studies, especially those focusing on family and personality. This follows from the overdeterminist bias in these studies. See for example, Thomas Pettigrew, *A Profile of the American Negro*, New York: Van Nostrand, 1964.

researched and documented. But although each rests on facts, the interpretations themselves and the assumptions underlying these interpretations are not fact and are only convenient ways of ordering facts and providing, implicitly or explicitly, guidelines for action. It is the purpose of this paper to investigate current thinking on the issue of race and employment and offer a tentative alternative interpretation. Specifically, we wish to take issue with the assumption, common to all three of the above approaches, that Negroes and whites share the same basic evaluations of the "system"—occupational, social, and political. It seems to us that the preponderant view of the Negro community is far too undifferentiated, and that academic as well as programmatic approaches to the problem of Negro unemployment ignore one basic feature of ghetto life—a dislike, ranging from mild to intense hatred, of whites, and ambivalence toward the institutions of white society. Euphemisms such as "the hard-to-reach" only serve to avoid this basic—and basically discomfiting—fact that has, we think, important implications for understanding employment patterns and strategies for easing Negro unemployment. For the sake of explication, let us examine more thoroughly the vicious circle-spiral thesis and, in the process, elaborate an alternative approach which we think more closely encompasses the realities of the ghetto.

Identity, "Pathology," and Employment

In simplified form, the vicious circle-spiral theses run as follows:[6] slavery stripped the Negro of his culture and identity and left little but self-hatred and a rejection of blackness. Negro men were prevented from asserting traditional masculine prerogatives, such as the elemental right to care for and protect wife (or wives) and children, making the identity of Negro males especially problematic. Moreover, women under slavery tended to enjoy a more favorable position vis-a-vis whites and, hence, in the slave context, vis-a-vis Negro men. The fact that Negro women have continued, for a variety of reasons, to hold a more favorable economic position than Negro men has led to the development and perpetuation of a matrifocal family structure in which the male is frequently treated as a useless, or worse, disuseful appendage. Children reared under these circumstances are either without a father, as a result of marital instability, or with a father who is continually subservient to his wife. Boys, especially, are seen to suffer. Failing to develop positive self-definitions, they are unable to

[6]This synopsis is based primarily on Moynihan, *op cit.* and Pettigrew, *op. cit.* Also see Nathan Glazer and Daniel P. Moynihan, *Beyond the Melting Pot*, Cambridge, Massachusetts: M.I.T. Press, 1964.

assume adequately roles demanded of adult males. One generation's problems are thus passed on to the next, perpetuating (or increasing) family instability, unemployment and other symptoms of a pathological adjustment to past and present discrimination. The key elements of this analysis are, typically, identity (masculine), family instability, and unemployment. Let us examine these elements of the argument.

Relative to whites, the Negro family is unstable; men do have a harder time than women (e.g., men have higher rates of mental illness than do women in the Negro community); Negro women do tend to be more dominant in their families than white women are in theirs, and so forth. But do these facts necessarily lead to the conclusion that the Negro male is rendered functionless and psychologically emasculated—i.e., unable to assume adult male roles? Or could it be the case that only if the Negro male accepts the dominant society's definitions of masculinity and Negro inferiority is he thereby left without masculine identity and function? Could not these same phenomena, typically attributed to the society's withholding of manhood and its prerogatives, be seen as an attempt on the part of the male to *assert his own sense of dignity and manhood?*

There are several observations that have been made regarding the status differences accorded men and women in both Negro and white society. In the dominant white society, women are the social inferiors of men. This is reflected in familial roles, educational patterns (women go less far in school), and, of course, in work force roles. By contrast, the Negro woman typically goes further in school than the Negro male, has enjoyed steadier, if lower paying, work that brings her into closer and more intimate contact with *socially* superior whites (i.e., wealthier families who can afford domestic help, office staffs made up primarily of white, middle-class people, and so forth). As we have noted, she also enjoys more authority, if not outright dominance, in her family. Thus, Negro women, more than Negro men, are more likely to identify with and aspire to middle-class values and life styles. If nothing else, they are more exposed to these values and life styles than are Negro men. Moreover, it appears as if Negro women have a different perspective on the social order, compared to Negro men. Parker and Kleiner report that: "Significantly more females than males in the community population [non-institutionalized Negro population of Philadelphia] feel that being a Negro does not constitute a barrier to achievement."[7] Following from this, it does

[7]Seymour Parker and Robert J. Kleiner, *Mental Illness in the Urban Negro Community,* New York: The Free Press of Glencoe, 1966. p. 162. The institutional population refers to those in mental hospitals at the time of the study.

not seem unreasonable to conjecture that the instability of the Negro family might be the result of a refracted conflict between Negroes and whites, in this case the wife being the symbolic representative of the demands of white society. Insofar as adherence to the dominant society's definitions of self-worth place the Negro male in a problematic position, the issue is clear: marriage will be difficult if the wife is insistent on her demands that her husband conform to the definitions of self-worth of the dominant society. If this is true, the desertion of the husband, instead of indicating his emasculation, would represent an *assertion* of his masculinity as he sees and defines it.

This conclusion rests on the assumption that, for the Negro male, adherence to the standards of performance of white society is untenable. Again, data from the Parker and Kleiner study are illuminating. The authors concluded that mental illness rates were highest for those Negro men holding most firmly to the standards of success and mobility of the general society. Negro males who perceived an open mobility structure and who believed in mobility goals were most likely to be (or become) ill.[8] In addition, their data suggest that self-esteem is highest among those men who rejected mobility as a goal and perceived the social system as closed to Negroes.[9] Given these facts, coupled with the already noted tendency for women to perceive a more open mobility structure, it is not surprising that Parker and Kleiner also found that Negro males had higher self-esteem than did Negro females.[10] This is the exact opposite of what we are led to expect in the "vicious circle"-spiral theses.

There are two additional observations relating to the issue of masculinity and family structure that are worthy of note. First of all, the marriage rate for Negro women is considerably lower than that for white women, even when age, education and occupation are standardized.[11] There is, however, an interesting exception to this general pattern: Negro women with low levels of education (eighth grade or less) have a higher marriage rate than similarly educated white women, and, more importantly, they have a higher marriage rate than better educated Negro women.[12] This latter pattern is just the reverse for white women—the higher the education of the woman, the

[8]*Ibid.*, pp. 50-61; also Chapter 4.

[9]Parker and Kleiner do not present data bearing directly on this issue. However, at several points they discuss this relationship for specific strata in their sample. See pp. 174-175; 307-308.

[10]*Ibid.*, p. 181.

[11]Paul Glick, *American Families*, New York: John Wiley and Sons, 1957. p. 131.

[12]*Ibid.*, p. 133.

higher the marriage rate. Taken together, these observations indicate that Negro women may indeed be threatening to Negro men (hence they are less likely to marry) and that this threat increases as the Negro woman's education increases and as she becomes more exposed to the models of man in the larger society. As the Negro woman moves further in the direction of white society she is either less able to find a mate who shares her outlook on life or Negro men are less willing to place themselves in a situation in which "measuring up" is made structurally difficult. Either way, the implication is clear: Negro men are less likely than Negro women to share the values of whites, and there are numbers of men and women who choose to define themselves in terms other than those extant in the dominant society.

Secondly, a few words regarding the matriarchy of the Negro family is in order. The general assumption in the prevailing "vicious circle"-spiral theses is that matriarchy is most prevalent in lower-class Negro families and that as Negro couples more closely approximate the occupational and income attributes of the white middle-class, family structure also more closely approximates that of whites. Thus, the less secure masculinity of lower-class Negro males. In a study of Detroit families, however, Blood and Wolfe found the opposite to be true. Higher income Negro husbands endured a more subordinate position vis-a-vis their wives than did Negro husbands with lower income, and this was the reverse of the pattern for whites.[13] Once again, we see data suggesting that the Negroes who are at least moderately successful occupationally, presumably those who have accepted the values of white society, are those who evince difficulties with masculine roles.

These considerations raise the question whether the unemployment of the Negro male and his propensity to sever marital bonds by leaving his wife indicates the absence or the assertion of positive masculine self-identity. While this question may appear to be a scholastic exercise it seems probable that quite different evaluations of the future course of race relations depend on the answer to this question. It is also clear that quite different programs aimed at alleviating poverty and unemployment may be required. If the Negro male judges himself and is judged by his peers in terms of criteria that, in one degree or another, deny the efficacy of the criteria of the dominant society, then programs based on the values of the dominant society are clearly going to meet resistance. Witness, for example, the "revolts" in various Job Corps training camps across the country, the

[13]Robert O. Blood, Jr., and Donald M. Wolfe, *Husbands and Wives,* New York: The Free Press of Glencoe, 1960. p. 99.

most spectacular of which occurred in a supposedly model—i.e., successful—camp in New Jersey one day after an inspection visit by Sargent Shriver, O.E.O. chief.[14]

Not all resistance takes so open a form, however. Even after completion of training program and placement in a job, nominally the mark of a "successful" program, indications are that trainees do not stay on these jobs for long. Absenteeism leading to firing has been cited as one of the principal problems involved in post-training job histories. While there are many possible explanations for this phenomenon, it seems at least plausible that among these reasons one is likely to find resistance to subordination in work contexts where a Negro traditionally has been forced to accept "his place." One way out of this demeaning circumstance is to play the "system" for what it is worth—to "hustle." Reports from various people involved in training programs on the West Coast indicate that many trainees refer to their internship as "the poverty hustle," indicating that their interest is hardly one of getting into the occupational structure and beginning the long trek to the American Dream. They are not making it in the system—they are, in their eyes, beating the system.[15] This is one way of psychologically withholding commitment and thus avoiding experiences that to Negroes, after centuries of experience, must seem certain to end in disapointment. Beating the system is also a way of asserting one's own autonomy and sense of dignity by denying the efficacy of the dominant society.

Of course Negroes do, like whites, desire a decent job, education, home and all of the other things that they have so long been deprived of. It is something else again, however, to assume that all Negroes are committed to obtaining these desiderata by the same means as whites. What is being suggested here as an alternative to the assump-

[14]Discussions of the strengths and weaknesses of the various programs aimed at alleviating unemployment are proliferating. For two critical views see Edward Moscovitch "Finding Jobs for the Poor," *The New Republic,* November 5, 1966; and Patrick Anderson, "Job Corps—What Boys will it Take?" in Hanna H. Meissner (ed.) *Poverty in the Affluent Society,* New York: Harper and Row, 1966. pp. 219-220. For a more optimistic, though cautious, view see Gerald G. Somers, "Retraining the Unemployed: A Preliminary Survey" in Stanley Lebergott (ed.) *Men Without Work,* Englewood Cliffs, New Jersey: Prentice-Hall, 1964. pp. 152-160.

[15]These comments are based primarily on informal conversation with persons involved in the Neighborhood Youth Corps programs in Los Angeles and Oakland. On the Oakland program, a paper by David Wellman ("Putting on the Youth Opportunity Center," mimeoed, Department of Sociology, University of California, Berkeley) goes into depth on this phenomenon. Mr. Wellman's discussions with the author on this and several other issues have been most helpful.

tions of the vicious circle-spiral theses is that much of what is commonly taken as social pathology is, perhaps, attributable to the dynamic of antagonistic models of man. Having been kept out of the mainstream for so long, it may be that Negroes have rejected this mainstream and created "streams" of their own. This, of course, is not a new suggestion. Discussions of the "culture of poverty," and "deviant subcultures" have long been in the literature and are well known to all who are concerned with "reaching the 'hard-to-reach'." But recognition and understanding are two quite different things. Altogether too frequently, this recognition becomes translated into attempts to inspire motivation—i.e., to convince the "hard-to-reach" of the basic fairness and worth of the American Way. Many Negroes, apparently, are not buying this argument. But what are a few of the alternative "streams" that seem open to Negroes in this society and how might each affect work?

Subcultures, Commitment and Work

In the first instance, obviously, the Negro can opt for identifying with the broader society and pattern his aspirations and behavior after the models provided therein. Many do just this, but we should not be overly eager to include in this stratum all Negroes who do have steady jobs and are, ostensibly, successful. Events such as those in Watts clearly indicate that a job, while perhaps necessary, is certainly not sufficient cause for subscribing to the dominant society's norms and values. If unemployed, individuals in this stratum are very likely to be the successful job finders, for having a job is central. Having a job places the individual in the "system" and, given a belief in the "system," this means that there will be some chances, real or imagined, of getting ahead. This holds true even if getting ahead means only minor promotions. To the extent that one's *raison d'etre* is based on the values and assumptions of the dominant society, even a "foot in the door" is important.

There is a second alternative open to Negroes, an alternative that many take in spite of its obvious destructiveness—*viz.*, rejection of the values of white society and retreat into a highly privatized world. A recent study of ethnic groups in Chicago revealed that fully 20 percent of the Negro respondents indicated having no friends with whom they associated—they were social isolates. Comparable figures for whites indicated that only six percent had no friends whatever.[16]

[16]Jan E. Dizard, "Ethnic Groups in the Metropolis," unpublished paper, Community and Family Study Center, University of Chicago, 1965. The status reports were based on a sample survey of 1,800 families in Chicago.

Unfortunately, employment patterns for this stratum were not investigated. It would, however, be surprising if the employment patterns of this stratum were anything approaching satisfactory. Unemployment can reasonably be expected to be high and length of unemployment long. Without even a modicum of social contacts and people to rely on, it is difficult to see how the socially isolated individual can avoid this fate.[17]

A third possibility is a rejection of the dominant society, accompanied by the substitution of collective alternatives—i.e, the creating of a more or less viable subculture in which dignity and self-worth are sustained on the basis of criteria variant from the criteria of the general society. The various Black Nationalist movements are examples of this stratum. The important feature of this option is that the institutions, including the occupational structure, of the dominant society are devalued and participation in the broader society is restricted. This may not mean unemployment is the rule—money is still essential—but labor considered demeaning is probably ruled out (as it should be). The key issue here is what is considered demeaning labor? This is an answer yet unknown. Some indications are available, however, and are worthy of consideration. There are increasing reports of men unwilling to work for less than about $2.00 per hour. This has caused a good deal of consternation in white communities essentially hostile to welfare in the first place. I think the answer may lie in a consideration of the role of work for one who does not accept the notions of mobility within the occupational structure. Working for less than a perceived living wage makes little sense unless the individual sees the work as leading to something more desireable, unless he believes in or aspires to mobility. To the extent that this stratum of Negroes do not believe in or aspire to mobility (mobility in the sense defined by the dominant society), a job is only valuable for the money it pays now. If it does not pay enough, the social and psychological costs involved in submitting to what is seen as an essentially corrupt and evil society are simply too great.

This perspective also sheds light on the problem of absenteeism mentioned above. Even when a job pays well enough, if the Negro worker is forced to submit to what he perceives as discriminatory behavior—a very likely occurrence, we might add—the job and its

[17]This is not to say that isolation necessitates poverty and unemployment. Several studies have shown, however, that the isolated are disproportionately represented among the lowest socio-economic strata of society. See for example, Morris Axelrod, "Urban Structure and Social Participation" in Paul K. Hatt and Albert J. Reiss, Jr. (eds.) Cities and Society, rev. ed., Glencoe, Illinois: The Free Press, 1957, pp. 722-729.

pay may simply not be worth it. Working becomes a very immediate and real challenge to his sense of dignity and self-worth, and it gets harder and harder to face work each morning. The lower the initial commitment to the occupational values of the society, the less time it takes for this process to culminate either in quitting or firing.

This matter points up an essential feature of the strata we have been discussing. They are not fixed; an individual can move in or out of any of them and into any other. The career of the late Malcolm X is a vivid example of a clearly exceptional individual who, in his short life, managed to move through three strata—from an honor student, to hustler, to leading spokesman for black nationalist sentiment.[18] Although, obviously, his labor force participation is not to be taken as archtypal, his career does limn the essential fluidity—or volatility—of Negro life and labor.

While there are no doubt individuals who cling stubbornly to, say, the occupational values of the society, it is reasonable to expect that many become disillusioned and radically alter their commitments. A more humble example of this is provided in a recent paper by Lee Rainwater in which he describes a sequence of events leading up to the marital breakup of a young Negro couple ostensibly doing reasonably well. They had no children and both worked, aspiring to the usual bigger apartment, better car, newer furniture, et cetera. Then he was fired. Rainwater quotes the man's description of the event:

> I went to work one day and the man told me that I would have to work until 1:00. I asked him if there would be any extra pay for working overtime and he said no. I asked him why and he said, 'If you don't like it you can kiss my ass.' He said that to me. I said 'Why do I have to do all that?' . . . I wanted to fight him but I said to myself I don't want to be that ignorant. I don't want to be as ignorant as he is, so I just cut out and left.[19]

The boss called later (it was the boss' son in the exchange above) and fired him. Rainwater then goes on to relate the change that took place in the man's attitudes toward race. Before the firing, he maintained that some Negroes were just not ready for integration yet and he couldn't figure out what all the civil rights activity was about. After the firing (his wife left him shortly after he lost his job), his attitude changed markedly—he condemned whites, saying in part:

[18]Malcolm X, *The Autobiography of Malcolm X,* New York: Grove Press, 1965.

[19]Lee Rainwater, "The Crucible of Identity," *Daedalus,* Winter, 1966. p. 193.

We do believe that man was put here to live together as human beings; not one that's superior and one that's a dog, but as human beings. And if you don't want to live this way then you become the dog and we'll become the human beings.[20]

This man may have little trouble getting another job, but it is clear that his commitment to the world of work is not what it was and that his behavior on the next job will be markedly different. The process can work the other way. A favorable response from a teacher or respect from an employer can provide the basis for a positive change in an individual's attitudes toward work and toward the larger society. In Claude Brown's autobiography, *Manchild in the Promised Land,* a psychiatrist provided the impetus for just such a shift.[21]

It would be unnecessary to point out the essential anecdotal character of much of the "evidence" we have used in discussing the range of alternative models of man open to the Negro were it not for the fact that anecdotal information is just about all that is available. What is needed if we are to understand fully the relationships between race and employment is to have empirical studies of the range of alternatives open to Negroes, the numbers making these choices, and the extent to which some options place the individual in opposition to the dominant society. Moreover, it is necessary that data be collected on the kinds of shifts in an individual's relationships to the occupational structure and the broader society and the nature of the causes of these shifts.

Our discussion of Negro unemployment has not focused on the question of why Negroes have higher rates of unemployment than do whites. Rather, we have taken for granted the fact of high Negro unemployment and raised another question: Why do some Negroes find themselves without work while others do not? We would like to redress this imbalance somewhat and briefly consider one of the most frequently cited factors contributing to high Negro unemployment—low skills among Negroes.

Discussions of the role skills play in employment tend to assume an unreasonable degree of rationality in hiring. For many, if not most blue collar jobs, skill requirements are quite flexible and are determined more by general criteria than by the specific tasks required by the job.[22] Chief among these general criteria are education and prior

[20]*Ibid.*, pp. 193-194.

[21]Claude Brown, *Manchild in the Promised Land,* New York: The Macmillan Company, 1966.

[22]For a brief discussion of this and the way in which skill requirements fluctuate with the demand for labor, see James Tobin, "Improving the Economic Status of the Negro," *Daedalus,* Fall, 1965. pp. 883-884.

job experience. Steadiness in the latter and persistence in the former—both indications of dependability and commitment—probably suffice for many employers' purposes. In times of labor shortage, even these general criteria are waived. This is not to deny that more specific skills are preferable; nevertheless the "fit" between the skills one has and the skills one might need for a specific job is usually loose enough that workmen, foremen and employers alike rely heavily on general skills at hiring time. With regard both to steadiness of work history and education, subcultural values play an extremely important role. Thinking of the work history for a moment, it seems more than reasonable to hypothesize that the weaker the commitment to occupational values and the less one invests in work, the greater the likelihood of a chaotic work history, marked by firings, resignations and lay-offs. In short, it seems likely that those Negroes who do not sustain a commitment to work usually have job records that make potential employers hesitant to hire them.

Education in many ways is more important than prior job experience in determining employability, especially for the higher paid blue collar and white collar jobs. As we have mentioned earlier, it is through education that occupational values are transmitted and sustained; and justifiably, education is seen by most whites as the primary path to upward mobility. How do Negroes feel about education? James Coleman's recent investigation of educational achievement indicates that the educational achievement of Negroes is heavily dependent upon their perception of the extent to which education pays off—i.e., educational achievement depends upon the extent to which the individual feels the society is just. A few examples of Coleman's results are worth citing in this regard. Among twelfth graders in the northeastern region of the U. S., 88 percent of the whites and 70 percent of the Negroes felt that hard work was more important than luck in determining success; in the West, the figures are 84 and 58 percent respectively.[23] While the majority of Negroes believe in the essential rationality of the society, the differences between whites and Negroes are impressive and confirm our earlier comments—there is a large number of Negroes who have little or no faith in the "system" and, thus, little reason to believe that working hard will make any difference. In discussing this and other related findings, Coleman concludes:

> For children from advantaged [white] groups, achievement or lack of it appears closely related to their self-concept: what they

[23] James S. Coleman, *Equality of Educational Opportunity,* Washington, D.C: Government Printing Office, 1966. p. 289.

believe about themselves. For children from disadvantaged [non-white] groups, achievement or lack of it appears closely related to what they believe about their environment: whether they believe the environment will respond to reasonable efforts, or whether they believe it is instead merely random or immovable.[24]

Coleman's findings call into question prevailing assumptions about the self-esteem of Negroes as related to achievement. They also indicate clearly that the issue of skills, insofar as education is concerned, cannot be treated adequately without serious consideration being given to the processes by which skills are obtained and the ways in which commitment to the values of work and success affects obtaining skills.

Thus far, we have made little mention of discrimination as a determinant of unemployment differentials between whites and Negroes. Indeed, were we not to mention discrimination, much of what we have argued could be (mistakenly) interpreted as placing responsibility for Negro unemployment at the door of the Negro himself. Nothing is further from our intent. Were it not for the hostility of whites, the estrangement we have been discussing would not be. The attempts on the part of many Negroes to seek alternatives for realizing themselves and affirming their dignity can only be understood in the context of their being shut out from the institutions that provide whites the means of self-realization and validation of self-worth. It is true, of course, that this search for alternatives is not easy and it frequently can result in frustration, despair, and apathy. It is also true that many alternatives are, ultimately, self-destructive—e.g., the subculture of the addict. But this is simply to state the obvious; it is hard to be a Negro in this society. However hard being a Negro is, though, it should not obscure the fact that alternatives are continuously sought. From the slave revolts, to the Garvey movement, to the contemporary expressions of black pride, Negroes have asserted themselves.[25] That, hitherto, these assertions have failed is important; but failure and resultant apathy is not to be confused with acquiescence in or acceptance of white domination.

[24]*Ibid.*, pp. 320-321.

[25]Negro resistance has usually been treated as epiphenomenal, an eddy in the major current of acceptance of and adjustment to white superiority. That this way of thinking is a mistaken reading of both the historical and contemporary record does not need re-emphasis. For material on Negro slave revolts see Herbert Aptheker, *American Negro Slave Revolts,* New York: Columbia University Press, 1943; on Garvey, see Edmund David Cronon, *Black Moses,* Madison: University of Wisconsin Press, 1955.

By way of summary, a few final comments seem in order regarding the meaning of apathy. Given discrimination and deprivation, there are analytically two types of apathy: 1) the apathy of one who is rejected by or a failure in the society he aspires to become a part of but who shares the society's judgements of success and failure; 2) the apathy of one who rejects the society's standards of judgement and is waiting and looking for a way to change those standards by either creating his own or changing the society's. Unemployment and underemployment may characterize both but, it should be clear, they do so for quite different reasons. These differences, it would seem, require different responses from the broader society. For the first, retraining programs and the like may suffice to restore self-esteem and an ability to function in the society. For the second, individual treatment would seem to be doomed from the start. For him, problems are not of his own making since society, and not he, has failed. The society has failed in justly distributing its rewards. This issue, the distribution of rewards, is not resolved by training or retraining for the "simple" reason that real interests are at stake and are likely to conflict.

What is clearly called for is a very hard look at our contemporary "crisis in black and white." It may yet not be too late to resolve this conflict within the context of political democracy.

Tally's Corner: Work Patterns of Negro Streetcorner Men

Elliot Liebow

[*From Chapter 2 of* Tally's Corner: A Study of Streetcorner Men *(Boston, 1967) by permission of Little, Brown and Company, copyright 1967. The data were collected as part of the Child Rearing Study of the Health and Welfare Council of the National Capital Area.*]

A pickup truck drives slowly down the street. The truck stops as it comes abreast of a man sitting on a cast-iron porch and the white driver calls out, asking if the man wants a day's work. The man shakes his head and the truck moves on up the block, stopping again whenever idling men come within calling distance of the driver. At the Carry-out corner, five men debate the question briefly and shake their heads no to the truck. The truck turns the corner and repeats the same performance up the next street. In the distance, one can see one man, then another, climb into the back of the truck and sit down. In starts and stops, the truck finally disappears.

What is it we have witnessed here? A labor scavenger rebuffed by his would-be prey? Lazy, irresponsible men turning down an honest day's pay for an honest day's work? Or a more complex phenomenon marking the intersection of economic forces, social values and individual states of mind and body?

Let us look again at the driver of the truck. He has been able to recruit only two or three men from each twenty or fifty he contacts. To him, it is clear that the others simply do not choose to work. Singly or in groups, belly-empty or belly-full, sullen or gregarious, drunk or sober, they confirm what he has read, heard and knows from his own experience: these men wouldn't take a job if it were handed to them on a platter.[1]

Quite apart from the question of whether or not this is true of some of the men he sees on the street, it is clearly not true of all of them. If it were, he would not have come here in the first place; or having come, he would have left with an empty truck. It is not even true of most of them, for most of the men he sees on the street this week-day morning do, in fact, have jobs. But since, at the moment, they are neither working nor sleeping, and since they hate the depressing room or apartment they live in, or because there is nothing to do there,[2] or because they want to get away from their wives or anyone else living there, they are out on the street, indistinguishable from those who do not have jobs or do not want them. Some, like Boley, a member of a trash-collection crew in a suburban housing development, work Saturdays and are off on this week day. Some, like Sweets, work nights cleaning up middle class trash, dirt, dishes and garbage and mopping the floors of the office buildings, hotels, restaurants, toilets and other public places dirtied during the day. Some men work for retail businesses such as liquor stores which do not begin the day until ten o'clock. Some laborers, like Tally, have already come back from the job because the ground was too wet for pick and

[1]By different methods, perhaps, some social scientists have also located the problem in the men themselves, in their unwillingness or lack of desire to work: "To improve the underprivileged worker's performance, one must help him to learn *to want* . . . higher social goals for himself and his children. . . . The problem of changing the work habits and motivation of [lower class] people . . . is a problem of changing the goals, the ambitions, and the level of cultural and occupational aspiration of the underprivileged worker." (Emphasis in original.) Allison Davis, "The Motivation of the Underprivileged Worker," in William F. Whyte, ed., *Industry and Society*, New York: McGraw-Hill, 1946, p. 90.

[2]The comparison of sitting at home alone with being in jail is commonplace.

shovel or because the weather was too cold for pouring concrete. Other employed men stayed off the job today for personal reasons: Clarence to go to a funeral at eleven this morning and Sea Cat to answer a subpoena as a witness in a criminal proceeding.

Also on the street, unwitting contributors to the impression taken away by the truck driver, are the halt and the lame. The man on the cast iron steps strokes one gnarled arthritic hand with the other and says he doesn't know whether or not he'll live long enough to be eligible for Social Security. He pauses, then adds matter-of-factly, "Most times, I don't care whether I do or don't." Stoopy's left leg was polio-withered in childhood. Raymond, who looks as if he could tear out a fire hydrant, coughs up blood if he bends or moves suddenly. The quiet man who hangs out in front of the Saratoga apartments has a steel hook strapped onto his left elbow. And had the man in the truck been able to look into the wine-clouded eyes of the man in the green cap, he would have realized that the man did not even understand he was being offered a day's work.

Others, having had jobs and been laid off, are drawing unemployment compensation (up to $44 per week) and have nothing to gain by accepting work which pays little more than this and frequently less.

Still others, like Bumdoodle the numbers man, are working hard at illegal ways of making money, hustlers who are on the street to turn a dollar any way they can: buying and selling sex, liquor, narcotics, stolen goods, or anything else that turns up.

Only a handful remains unaccounted for. There is Tonk, who cannot bring himself to take a job away from the corner because, according to the other men, he suspects his wife will be unfaithful if given the oportunity. There is Stanton, who has not reported to work for four days now, not since Bernice disappeared.

And finally, there are those like Arthur, able-bodied men who have no visible means of support, legal or illegal, who neither have jobs nor want them. The truck driver, among others, believes the Arthurs to be representative of all the men he sees idling on the street during his own working hours. They are not, but they cannot be dismissed simply because they are a small minority. It is not enough to explain them away as being lazy or irresponsible or both because an able-bodied man with responsibilities who refuses work is, by the truck driver's definition, lazy and irresponsible. Such an answer begs the question. It is descriptive of the facts; it does not explain them.

Moreover, the don't work-and-don't-want-to-work minority is especially significant because, despite their small numbers, they represent the strongest and clearest expression of those values and attitudes associated with making a living which, to varying degrees, are found throughout the streetcorner world. These men differ from the others in degree rather than in kind, the principal difference being that they are carrying out the implications of their values and experiences to their logical, inevitable conclusions. In this sense, the others have yet to come to terms with themselves and the world they live in.

Putting aside, for the moment, what the men say and feel, and looking at what they actually do and the choices they make, getting a job, keeping a job, and doing well at it is clearly of low priority. Arthur will not take a job at all. Leroy is supposed to be on his job at 4:00 P.M. but it is already 4:10 and he still cannot bring himself to leave the free games he has accumulated on the pin-ball machine in the Carry-out. Tonk started a construction job on Wednesday, worked Thursday and Friday, then didn't go back again. On the same kind of job, Sea Cat quit in the second week. Sweets had been working three months as a busboy in a restaurant, then quit without notice, not sure himself why he did so. A real estate agent, saying he was more interested in getting the job done than in the cost, asked Richard to give him an estimate on repairing and painting the inside of a house, but Richard, after looking over the job, somehow never got around to submitting an estimate. During one period, Tonk would not leave the corner to take a job because his wife might prove unfaithful; Stanton would not take a job because his woman had been unfaithful.

Thus, the man-job relationship is a tenuous one. At any given moment, a job may occupy a relatively low position on the streetcorner scale of real values. Getting a job may be subordinated to relations with women or to other non-job considerations; the commitment to a job one already has is frequently shallow and tentative.

The reasons are many. Some are objective and reside principally in the job; some are subjective and reside principally in the man. The line between them, however, is not a clear one. Behind the man's refusal to take a job or his decision to quit one is not a simple impulse or value-choice but a complex combination of assessments of objective reality on the one hand, and values, attitudes and beliefs drawn from different levels of his experience on the other.

Objective economic considerations are frequently a controlling factor in a man's refusal to take a job. How much the job pays is a crucial question but seldom asked. He knows how much it pays. Working as a stockclerk, a delivery boy, or even behind the counter of liquor stores, drug stores and other retail businesses pays one dollar an hour. So, too, do most busboys, car-wash, janitorial and other jobs available to him. Some jobs, such as dishwasher, may dip as low as eighty cents an hour and others, such as elevator operator or work in a junk yard may offer $1.15 or $1.25. Take-home pay for jobs such as these range from $35 to $50 a week, but a take-home pay of over $45 for a 5-day week is the exception rather than the rule.

One of the principal advantages of these kinds of jobs is that they offer fairly regular work. Most of them involve essential services and are therefore somewhat less responsive to business conditions than are some higher paying, less menial jobs. Most of them are also inside jobs not dependent on the weather, as are constructions jobs and other higher-paying outside work.

Another seemingly important advantage of working in hotels, restaurants, office and apartment buildings and retail establishments is that they frequently offer an opportunity for stealing on the job. But stealing can be a two-edged sword. Apart from increasing the cost of the goods or services to the general public, a less obvious result is that the practice usually acts as a depressant on the employee's own wage level. Owners of small retail establishments and other employers frequently anticipate employee stealing and adjust the wage-rate accordingly. Tonk's employer explained why he was paying Tonk $35 for a 55-60 hour workweek. These men will all steal, he said. Although he keeps close watch on Tonk, he estimates that Tonk steals from $35 to $40 a week.[3] What he steals, when added to his regular earnings, brings his take-home pay to $70 or $75 per week. The employer said he did not mind this because Tonk is worth that much to the business. But if he were to pay Tonk outright the full value of his labor, Tonk would still be stealing $35-$40 per week and this, he said, the business simply would not support.

This wage arrangement, with stealing built-in, was satisfactory to both parties, with each one independently expressing his satisfaction. Such a wage-theft system, however, is not as balanced and equitable as it appears. Since the wage level rests on the premise that the employee will steal the unpaid value of his labor, the man who does not steal on the job is penalized. And furthermore, even if he does not steal, no one would believe him; the employer and others believe he steals because the system presumes it.

Nor is the man who steals, as he is expected to, as well off as he believes himself to be. The employer may occasionally close his eyes to the worker's stealing but not often and not for long. He is, after all, a business man and cannot always find it within himself to let a man

[3]Exactly the same estimate as the one made by Tonk himself. On the basis of personal knowledge of the stealing routine employed by Tonk, however, I suspect the actual amount is considerably smaller.

steal from him, even if the man is stealing his own wages. Moreover, it is only by keeping close watch on the worker that the employer can control how much is stolen and thereby protect himself against the employee's stealing more than he is worth. From this viewpoint, then, the employer is not in wage-theft collusion with the employee. In the case of Tonk, for instance, the employer was not actively abetting the theft. His estimate of how much Tonk was stealing was based on what he thought Tonk was able to steal despite his own best efforts to prevent him from stealing anything at all. Were he to have caught Tonk in the act of stealing, he would, of course, have fired him from the job and perhaps called the police as well. Thus, in an actual if not in a legal sense, all the elements of entrapment are present. The employer knowingly provides the conditions which entice (force) the employee to steal the unpaid value of his labor, but at the same time he punishes him for theft if he catches him doing so.

Other consequences of the wage-theft system are even more damaging to the employee. Let us, for argument's sake, say that Tonk is in no danger of entrapment; that his employer is willing to wink at the stealing and that Tonk, for his part, is perfectly willing to earn a little, steal a little. Let us say, too, that he is paid $35 a week and allowed to steal $35. His money income—as measured by the goods and services he can purchase with it—is, of course, $70. But not all of his income is available to him for all purposes. He cannot draw on what he steals to build his self-respect or to measure his self-worth. For this, he can draw only on his earnings—the amount given him publicly and voluntarily in exchange for his labor. His "respect" and "self-worth" income remains at $35—only half that of the man who also receives $70 but all of it in the form of wages. His earnings publicly measure the worth of his labor to his employer, and they are important to others and to himself in taking the measure of his worth as a man.[4]

With or without stealing, and quite apart from any interior processes going on in the man who refuses such a job or quits it casually and without apparent reason, the objective fact is that menial jobs in retailing or in the service trades simply do not pay enough to support a man and his family. This is not to say that the worker is underpaid; this may or may not be true. Whether he is or not, the plain fact is that, in such a job, he cannot make a living. Nor can he take much comfort in the fact that these jobs tend to offer more regular, steadier work. If he cannot live on the $45 or $50 he makes in one week, the longer he works, the longer he cannot live on what he makes.

[4]Some public credit may accrue to the clever thief but not respect.

Construction work, even for unskilled laborers, usually pays better, with the hourly rate ranging from $1.50 to $2.60 an hour.[5] Importantly, too, good references, a good driving record, a tenth grade (or even high school) education, previous experience or ability to "bring police clearance with you" are not normally required of laborers as they frequently are for some of the jobs in retailing or in the service trades.

Construction work, however, has its own objective disadvantages. It is, first of all, seasonal work for the great bulk of the laborers, beginning early in the spring and tapering off as winter weather sets in.[6] And even during the season the work is frequently irregular. Early or late in the season, snow or temperatures too low for concrete frequently sends the laborers back home, and during late spring or summer, a heavy rain on Tuesday or Wednesday, leaving a lot of water and mud behind it, can mean a two or three day work-week for the pick and shovel men and other unskilled laborers.[7]

The elements are not the only hazard. As the project moves from one construction stage to another, laborers—usually without warning—are laid off, sometimes permanently or sometimes for weeks at a time. The more fortunate or the better workers are told periodically to "take a walk for two, three days."

Both getting the construction job and getting to it are also rela-

[5]The higher amount is 1962 union scale for building laborers. According to the Wage Agreement Contract for Heavy Construction Laborers (Washington, D.C. and vicinity), covering the period from May 1, 1963 to April 30, 1966, minimum hourly wage for heavy construction laborers was to go from $2.75 (May, 1963) by annual increments to $2.92½ effective November 1, 1965.

[6]"Open-sky" work, such as building over-passes, highways, etc., in which the workers and materials are directly exposed to the elements, traditionally begins in March and ends around Thanksgiving. The same is true for much of the street repair work and the laying of sewer, electric, gas, and telephone lines by the city and public utilities, all important employers of laborers. Between Thanksgiving and March, they retain only skeleton crews selected from their best, most reliable men.

[7]In a recent year, the crime rate in Washington for the month of August jumped 18 percent over the preceding month. A veteran police officer explained the increase to David L. Bazelon, Chief Judge, U. S. Court of Appeals for the District of Columbia. "It's quite simple. . . . You see, August is a very wet month. . . . These people wait on the street corner each morning around 6:00 or 6:30 for a truck to pick them up and take them to a construction site. If it's raining, that truck doesn't come, and the men are going to be idle that day. If the bad weather keeps up for three days . . . we know we are going to have trouble on our hands—and sure enough, there invariably follows a rash of purse-snatchings, house-breakings and the like. . . . These people have to eat like the rest of us, you know." David L. Bazelon, Address to the Federal Bar Association, National Press Club, Washington, D.C., April 30, 1963, mimeo, p. 3.

tively more difficult than is the case for the menial jobs in retailing and the service trades. Job competition is always fierce. In the city, the large construction projects are unionized. One has to have ready cash to get into the union to become eligible to work on these projects and, being eligible, one has to find an opening. Unless one "knows somebody," say a foreman or a laborer who knows the day before that they are going to take on new men in the morning, this can be a difficult and disheartening search.

Many of the nonunion jobs are in suburban Maryland or Virginia. The newspaper ads say, "Report ready to work to the trailer at the intersection of Rte. 11 and Old Bridge Rd., Bunston, Virginia (or Maryland)," but this location may be 10, 15, or even 25 miles from the Carry-out. Public transportation would require two or more hours to get there, if it services the area at all. Without access to a car or to a car-pool arrangement, it is not worthwhile reading the ad. So the men do not. Jobs such as these are usually filled by word of mouth informaton, beginning with someone who knows someone or who is himself working there and looking for a paying rider. Furthermore, nonunion jobs in outlying areas tend to be smaller projects of relatively short duration and to pay somewhat less than scale.

Still another objective factor is the work itself. For some men, whether the job be digging, mixing mortar, pushing a wheelbarrow, unloading materials, carrying and placing steel rods for reinforcing concrete, or building or laying concrete forms, the work is simply too hard. Men such as Tally and Wee Tom can make such work look like child's play; some of the older work-hardened men, such as Lovely and Stanton, can do it too, although not without showing unmistakeable signs of strain and weariness at the end of the workday. But those who lack the robustness of a Tally or the time-inured immunity of a Lovely must either forego jobs such as these or pay a heavy toll to keep them. For Leroy, in his early twenties, almost six feet tall but weighing under 140 lbs., it would be as difficult to push a loaded wheelbarrow, or to unload and stack 96-pound bags of cement all day long, as it would be for Stoopy with his withered leg.

Heavy, back-breaking labor of the kind that used to be regularly associated with bull-gangs or concrete gangs is no longer characteristic of laboring jobs, especially those with the larger well-equipped construction companies. Brute strength is still required from time to time, as on smaller jobs where it is not economical to bring in heavy equipment or where the small, undercapitalized contractor has none to bring in. In many cases, however, the conveyor belt has replaced the wheelbarrow or the Georgia buggy, mechanized forklifts have eliminated heavy, manual lifting, and a variety of digging machines have replaced the pick and shovel. The result is fewer jobs for unskilled laborers and, in many cases, a work speed-up for those who do have jobs. Machines now set the pace formerly set by men. Formerly, a laborer pushed a wheelbarrow of wet cement to a particular spot, dumped it, and returned for another load. Another laborer, in hip boots, pushed the wet concrete around with a shovel or a hoe, getting it roughly level in preparation for the skilled finishers. He had relatively small loads to contend with and had only to keep up with the men pushing the wheelbarrows. Now, the job for the man pushing the wheelbarrow is gone and the wet concrete comes rushing down a chute at the man in the hip boots who must "spread it quick or drown."

Men who have been running an elevator, washing dishes, or "pulling trash" cannot easily move into laboring jobs. They lack the basic skills for "unskilled" construction labor, familiarity with tools and materials, and tricks of the trades without which hard jobs are made harder. Previously unused or untrained muscles rebel in pain against the new and insistent demands made upon them, seriously compromising the man's performance and testing his willingness to see the job through.

A healthy, sturdy, active man of good intelligence requires from two to four weeks to break in on a construction job.[8] Even if he is willing somehow to bull his way through the first few weeks, it frequently happens that his foreman or the craftsman he services with materials and general assistance is not willing to wait that long for him to get into condition or to learn at a glance the difference in size between a rough 2″x8″ and a finished 2″x10″. The foreman and the craftsman are themselves "under the gun" and cannot "carry" the man when other men, who are already used to the work and who know the tools and materials, are lined up to take the job.

Sea Cat was "healthy, sturdy, active, and of good intelligence." When a judge gave him six weeks in which to pay his wife $200 in back child-support payments, he left his grocery-store job in order to take a higher-paying job as a laborer, arranged for him by a foreman friend. During the first week, the weather was bad and he worked only Wednesday and Friday, cursing the elements all the while for cheating him out of the money he could have made. The second week, the weather was fair but he quit at the end of the fourth day,

[8]Estimate of Mr. Francis Greenfield, President of the International Hod Carriers, Building and Common Laborers' District Council of Washington, D. C. and Vicinity. I am indebted to Mr. Greenfield for several points in these paragraphs dealing with construction laborers.

saying frankly that the work was too hard for him. He went back to his job at the grocery store and took a second job working nights as a dishwasher in a restaurant,[9] earning little if any more at the two jobs than he would have earned as a laborer, and keeping at both of them until he had paid off his debts.

Tonk did not last as long as Sea Cat. No one made any predictions when he got a job in a parking lot, but when the men on the corner learned he was to start on a road construction job, estimates of how long he would last ranged from one to three weeks. Wednesday was his first day. Sunday afternoon, Tonk explained that after working three days, he knew enough about the job to know that it was too hard for him. He knew he wouldn't be able to keep it up and he'd just as soon quit now as get fired later.

Logan was a tall, two-hundred-pound man in his late twenties. His back used to hurt him only on the job, he said, but now he can't straighten up for increasingly longer periods of time. He said he had traced this to the awkward walk he was forced to adopt by the loaded wheelbarrows which pull him down into a half-stoop. He's going to quit, he said, as soon as he can find another job. If he can't find one real soon, he guesses he'll quit anyway. It's not worth it, having to walk bent over and leaning to one side.

Sometimes, the strain and effort is greater than the man is willing to admit, even to himself. In the early summer of 1963, Richard was rooming at Nancy's place. His wife and children were "in the country" (his grandmother's home in Carolina), waiting for him to save up enough money so that he could bring them back to Washington and start over again after a disastrous attempt to "make it" in Philadelphia. Richard had gotten a job with a fence company in Virginia. It paid $1.60 an hour. The first few evenings, when he came home from work, he looked ill from exhaustion and the heat. Stanton said Richard would have to quit, "he's too small [thin] for that kind of work." Richard said he was doing O.K. and would stick with the job.

At Nancy's one night, when Richard had been working about two weeks, Nancy and three or four others were sitting around talking, drinking, and listening to music. Someone asked Nancy when was Richard going to bring his wife and children up from the country. Nancy said she didn't know, but it probably depended on how long it would take him to save up enough money. She said she didn't think he could stay with the fence job much longer. This morning, she said the man Richard rode to work with knocked on the door and Richard didn't answer. She looked in his room. Richard was still asleep. Nancy

[9]Not a sinecure, even by streetcorner standards.

tried to shake him awake. "No more digging!" Richard cried out, "No more digging! I can't do no more God-damn digging!" When Nancy finally managed to wake him, he dressed quickly and went to work.

Richard stayed on the job two more weeks, then suddenly quit, ostensibly because his pay-check was three dollars less than what he thought it should have been.

In summary of objective job considerations, then, the most important fact is that a man who is able and willing to work cannot earn enough money to support himself, his wife, and one or more children. A man's chances for working regularly are good only if he is willing to work for less than he can live on, and sometimes not even then. On some jobs, the wage rate is deceptively higher than on others, but the higher the wage rate, the more difficult it is to get the job, and the less the job security. Higher-paying construction work tends to be seasonal and, during the season, the amount of work available is highly sensitive to business and weather conditions and to the changing requirements of individual projects.[10] Moreover, high paying construction jobs are frequently beyond the physical capacity of some of the men, and some of the low-paying jobs are scaled down even lower in accordance with the self-fulfilling assumption that the man will steal part of his wages on the job.[11]

Bernard assesses the objective job situation dispassionately over a cup of coffee, sometimes poking at the coffee with his spoon, sometimes staring at it as if, like a crystal ball, it holds tomorrow's secrets. He is twenty-seven years old. He and the woman with whom he lives have a baby son, and she has another child by another man. Bernard does odd jobs—mostly painting—but here it is the end of January, and his last job was with the Post Office during the Christmas mail rush. He would like postal work as a steady job, he says. It pays well

[10]The overall result is that, in the long run, a Negro laborer's earnings are not substantially greater—and may be less—than those of the busboy, janitor, or stock clerk. Herman P. Miller, for example, reports that in 1960, 40 percent of all jobs held by Negro men were as laborers or in the service trades. The average annual wage for nonwhite nonfarm laborers was $2400. The average earnings of nonwhite service workers was $2500. *Rich Man, Poor Man,* New York: Thos. P. Crowell Co., 1964, p. 90. Francis Greenfield estimates that in the Washington vicinity, the 1965 earnings of the union laborer who works whenever work is available will be about $3200. Even this figure is high for the man on the streetcorner. Union men in heavy construction are the aristocrats of the laborers. Casual day labor, and jobs with small firms in the building and construction trades, or with firms in other industries, pay considerably less.

[11]For an excellent discussion of the self-fulfilling assumption (or prophecy) as a social force, see "The Self-Fulfilling Prophecy," Ch. XI in Robert K. Merton, *Social Theory and Social Structure,* 2d. ed. rev., Glencoe: The Free Press, 1957, pp. 421-436.

(about $2.00 an hour) but he has twice failed the Post Office examination (he graduated from a Washington high school) and has given up the idea as an impractical one. He is supposed to see a man tonight about a job as a parking attendant for a large apartment house. The man told him to bring his birth certificate and driver's license, but his license was suspended because of a backlog of unpaid traffic fines. A friend promised to lend him some money this evening. If he gets it, he will pay the fines tomorrow morning and have his license reinstated. He hopes the man with the job will wait 'til tomorrow night.

A "security job" is what he really wants, he said. He would like to save up money for a taxicab. But having twice failed the postal examination and having a bad driving record as well, it is highly doubtful that he could meet the qualifications or pass the written test. That would be "a good life." He can always get a job in a restaurant or as a clerk in a drug-store but they don't pay enough, he said. He needs to take home at least $50 to $55 a week. He thinks he can get that much driving a truck somewhere . . . Sometimes he wishes he had stayed in the army . . . A security job, that's what he wants most of all, a real security job . . .

When we look at what the men bring to the job rather than at what the job offers the men, it is essential to keep in mind that we are not looking at men who came to the job fresh, just out of school, perhaps, and newly prepared to undertake the task of making a living, or from another job where they earned a living and are prepared to do the same on this job. Each man comes to the job with a long job history characterized by his not being able to support himself and his family. Each man carries this knowledge, born of his experience, with him. He comes to the job flat and stale, wearied by the sameness of it all, convinced of his own incompetence, terrified of responsibility—of being tested still again and found wanting. Possible exceptions are the younger men not yet, or just, married. They suspect all this but have yet to have it confirmed by repeated personal experience over time. But those who are or have been married know it well. It is the experience of the individual and the group; of their fathers and probably their sons. Convinced of their inadequacies, not only do they not seek out those few better-paying jobs which test their resources, but they actively avoid them, gravitating in a mass to the menial, routine jobs which offer no challenge—and therefore pose no threat—to the already diminished images they have of themselves.

Thus Richard does not follow through on the real estate agent's offer. He is afraid to do on his own—minor plastering, replacing broken windows, other minor repairs and painting—exactly what he had been doing for months on a piece-work basis under someone else (and which provided him with a solid base from which to derive a cost estimate).

Richard once offered an important clue to what may have gone on in his mind when the job offer was made. We were in the Carry-out, at a time when he was looking for work. He was talking about the kind of jobs available to him.

> I graduated from high school [Baltimore] but I don't know anything. I'm dumb. Most of the time I don't even say I graduated, 'cause then somebody asks me a question and I can't answer it, and they think I was lying about graduating. . . . They graduated me but I didn't know anything. I had lousy grades but I guess they wanted to get rid of me.
>
> I was at Margaret's house the other night and her little sister asked me to help her with her homework. She showed me some fractions and I knew right away I couldn't do them. I was ashamed so I told her I had to go to the bathroom.

Thus, the man's low self-esteem generates a fear of being tested and prevents him from accepting a job with responsibilities or, once on a job, from staying with it if responsibilities are thrust on him, even if the wages are commensurately higher. Richards refuses such a job, Leroy leaves one, and another man, given more responsibility and more pay, knows he will fail and proceeds to do so, proving he was right about himself all along.

Lethargy, disinterest and general apathy on the job, so often reported by employers, has its streetcorner counterpart. The men do not ordinarily talk about their jobs or ask one another about them.[12] Although most of the men know who is or is not working at any given time, they may or may not know what particular job an individual man has. There is no overt interest in job specifics as they relate to this or that person, in large part perhaps because the specifics are not especially relevant. To know that a man is working is to know approximately how much he makes and to know as much as one needs or wants to know about how he makes it.

A crucial factor in the streetcorner man's lack of job commitment is the overall value he places on the job. *For his part, the streetcorner*

[12]This stands in dramatic contrast to the leisure-time conversation of stable, working-class men. For the coal miners (of Ashton, England), for example, "the topic [of conversation] which surpasses all others in frequency is work—the difficulties which have been encountered in the day's shift, the way in which a particular task was accomplished, and so on." Josephine Klein, *Samples from English Cultures*, London: Routledge & Kegan Paul, 1965, Vol. I, p. 88.

man puts no lower value on the job than does the larger society around him. He knows the social value of the job by the amount of money the employer is willing to pay him for doing it. In a real sense, every pay day he counts in dollars and cents the value placed on the job by society at large. He is no more (and frequently less) ready to quit and look for another job than his employer is ready to fire him and look for another man. Neither the streetcorner man who performs these jobs nor the society which requires him to perform them assesses the job as one "worth doing and worth doing well." Both employee and employer are contemptuous of the job. The employee shows his contempt by his reluctance to accept it or keep it, the employer by paying less than is required to support a family.[13] Nor does the low-wage job offer prestige, respect, interesting work, opportunity for learning or advancement, or any other compensation. With few exceptions, jobs filled by the streetcorner men are at the bottom of the employment ladder in every respect, from wage level to prestige. Typically, they are hard, dirty, uninteresting and underpaid. The rest of society (whatever its ideal values regarding the dignity of labor) holds the job of the dishwasher or janitor or unskilled laborer in low esteem if not outright contempt.[14] So does the streetcorner man. He cannot do otherwise. He cannot draw from a job those social values which other people do not put into it.[15]

Only occasionally does spontaneous conversation touch on these matters directly. Talk about jobs is usually limited to isolated statements of intention, such as "I think I'll get me another gig [job]," "I'm

[13]It is important to remember that the employer is not entirely a free agent. Subject to the constraints of the larger society, he acts for the larger society as well as for himself. Child labor laws, safety and sanitation regulations, minimum wage scales in some employment areas, and other constraints, are already on the books; other control mechanisms, such as a guaranteed annual wage, are to be had for the voting.

[14]See, for example, the U. S. Bureau of the Census, *Methodology and Scores of Socioeconomic Status,* Working Paper No. 15, Washington, D.C., 1963. The assignment of the lowest SES ratings to men who hold such jobs is not peculiar to our own society. A low SES rating for "the shoe-shine boy or garbage man . . . seems to be true for all [industrial] countries." Alex Inkeles, "Industrial Man," *American Journal of Sociology,* LXVI, No. 1 (July, 1960), p. 8.

[15]That the streetcorner man downgrades manual labor should occasion no surprise. Merton points out that "the American stigmatization of manual labor . . . *has been found to hold rather uniformly in all social classes.*" (Emphasis in original.) *Social Theory and Social Structure,* p. 145. That he finds no satisfaction in such work should also occasion no surprise: "[There is] a clear positive correlation between the over-all status of occupations and the experience of satisfaction in them." Inkeles, *American Journal of Sociology,* LXVI, No. 1, p. 12.

going to look for a construction job when the weather breaks," or "I'm going to quit. I can't take no more of his shit." Job assessments typically consist of nothing more than a noncommittal shrug and "It's O.K." or "It's a job."

One reason for the relative absence of talk about one's job is, as suggested earlier, that the sameness of job experiences does not bear reiteration. Another and more important reason is the emptiness of the job experience itself. The man sees middle-class occupations as a primary source of prestige, pride and self-respect; his own job affords him none of these. To think about his job is to see himself as others see him, to remind him of just where he stands in this society.[16] And because society's criteria for placement are generally the same as his own, to talk about his job can trigger a flush of shame and a deep, almost physical ache to change places with someone, almost anyone, else.[17] The desire to be a person in his own right, to be noticed by the world he lives in, is shared by each of the men on the streetcorner.

Whether they articulate this desire (as Tally does below) or not, one can see them position themselves to catch the attention of their fellows in much the same way as plants bend or stretch to catch the sunlight.[18]

Tally and I were in the Carry-out. It was summer, Tally's peak earning season as a cement finisher, a semiskilled job a cut or so above that of the unskilled laborer. His take-home pay during these weeks was well over a hundred dollars—"a lot of bread." But for Tally, who no longer had a family to support, bread was not enough.

> "You know that boy came in last night? That Black Moozlem? That's what I ought to be doing. I ought to be in his place."

[16][In our society] a man's work is one of the things by which he is judged, and certainly one of the more significant things by which he judges himself. . . . A man's work is one of the more important parts of his social identity, of his self; indeed, of his fate in the one life he has to live." Everett C. Hughes, *Men and Their Work,* Glencoe: The Free Press, 1958, pp. 42-43.

[17]Noting that lower class persons "are constantly exposed to evidence of their own irrelevance," Lee Rainwater spells out still another way in which the poor are poor: "The identity problems of lower class persons make the soul-searching of middle class adolescents and adults seem rather like a kind of conspicuous consumption of psychic riches." "Work and Identity in the Lower Class," paper prepared for Washington University Conference on Planning for the Quality of Urban Life, April, 1965, p. 3. (Mimeographed.)

[18]Sea Cat cuts his pants leg off at the calf and puts a fringe on the raggedy edges. Tonk breaks his "shades" and continues to wear the horn-rimmed frames minus the lenses. Richard cultivates a distinctive manner of speech. Lonny gives himself a birthday party. And so on.

"What do you mean?"

"Dressed nice, going to [night] school, got a good job."

"He's no better off than you, Tally. You make more than he does."

"It's not the money. [Pause.] It's position, I guess. He's got position. When he finish school he gonna be a supervisor. People respect him. . . . . Thinking about people with position and education gives me a feeling right here [pressing his fingers into the pit of his stomach]."

"You're educated, too. You have a skill, a trade. You're a cement finisher. You can make a building, pour a sidewalk."

"That's different. Look, can anybody do what you're doing? Can anybody just come up and do your job? Well, in one week I can teach you cement finishing. You won't be as good as me 'cause you won't have the experience but you'll be a cement finisher. That's what I mean. Anybody can do what I'm doing and that's what gives me this feeling. [Long pause.] Suppose I like this girl. I go over to her house and I meet her father. He starts talking about what he done today. He talks about operating on somebody and sewing them up and about surgery. I know he's a doctor 'cause of the way he talks. Then she starts talking about what she did. Maybe she's a boss or a supervisor. Maybe she's a lawyer and her father says to me, 'And what do you do, Mr. Jackson?'
[Pause.] You remember at the court house, Lonny's trial? You and the lawyer was talking in the hall? You remember? I just stood there listening. I didn't say a word. You know why? 'Cause I didn't even know what you was talking about. That's happened to me a lot."

"Hell, you're nothing special. That happens to everybody. Nobody knows everything. One man is a doctor, so he talks about surgery. Another man is a teacher, so he talks about books. But doctors and teachers don't know anything about concrete. You're a cement finisher and that's your specialty."

"Maybe so, but when was the last time you saw anybody standing around talking about concrete?"

Furthermore, menial jobs are not, by and large, the starting point of a track system which leads to even better jobs for those who are able and willing to do them. The busboy or dishwasher who works hard becomes, simply, a hard working busboy or dishwasher. Neither hard work nor perserverance can conceivably carry the janitor to a sit-down job in the office building he cleans up. And it is the apprentice who becomes the journeyman electrician, plumber, steam fitter or bricklayer, not the common unskilled Negro laborer.

Thus, the job is a dead end. It promises to deliver no more tomorrow, next month or next year than it does today.

Delivering little, and promising no more, the job is "no big thing." The man appears to treat the job in a cavalier fashion, working and not working as the spirit moves him, as if all that matters is the immediate satisfaction of his present appetites, the surrender to present moods and the indulgence of whims with no thought for the cost, the consequences, the future. To the middle-class observer, this behavior reflects a "present-time orientation"—"an "inability to defer gratification." It is this "present time" orientation—as against the "future orientation" of the middle-class-person— that "explains" to the outsider why Leroy chooses to spend the day at the Carry-out rather than report to work; why Richard, who was paid Friday, was drunk Saturday and Sunday and penniless Monday; why Sweets quit his job today because the boss looked at him "funny" yesterday.

But from the inside looking out, what appears as a "present-time" orientation to the outside observer is, to the man experiencing it, as much a future orientation as that of his middle-class counterpart.[19] The difference between the two men lies not so much in their different orientations to time as in their different orientations to future time or, more specifically, to their different futures.[20]

The future orientation of the middle-class person presumes, among other things, a surplus of resources to be invested in the future and a belief that the future will be sufficiently stable both to justify his investment (money in a bank, time and effort in a job, investment of himself in marriage and family, etc.) and to permit the consumption of his investment at a time, place and manner of his own choosing and to his greater satisfaction. But the streetcorner man lives in a sea of want. He does not, as a rule, have a surplus of resources, either economic or psychological. Gratification of hunger and the desire for simple creature comforts cannot be long deferred. Neither can support for one's flagging self-esteem. Living on the edge of both

[19]Taking a somewhat different point of view, S. M. Miller and Frank Riessman suggest that "the entire concept of deferred gratification may be inappropriate to understanding the essence of workers' lives." "The Working Class Subculture: A New View," *Social Problems,* IX, No. 1 (Summer, 1961), p. 87.

[20]This sentence is a paraphrase of a statement made by Marvin Cline at a 1965 colloquium at the Mental Health Study Center, National Institute of Mental Health.

economic and psychological subsistence, the streetcorner man is obliged to expend all his resources on maintaining himself from moment to moment.[21]

As for the future, the young streetcorner man has a fairly good picture of it. In Richard or Sea Cat or Arthur he can see himself in his middle twenties; he can look at Tally to see himself at thirty, at Wee Tom to see himself in his middle thirties, and at Lovely and Stanton to see himself in his forties. It is a future in which everything is uncertain except the ultimate destruction of his hopes and the eventual realization of his fears. The most he can reasonably look forward to is that these things do not come too soon.

Sometimes this kind of response appears as a conscious, explicit choice. Richard had had a violent argument with his wife. He said he was going to leave her and the children, that he had had enough of everything and could not take any more, and he chased her out of the house. His chest still heaving, he leaned back against the wall in the hallway of his basement apartent.

> "I've been scuffling for five years," he said. "I've been scuffling for five years from morning 'til night. And my kids still don't have anything, my wife don't have anything, and I don't have anything.
>
> "There," he said, gesturing down the hall to a bed, a sofa, a couple of chairs and a television set, all shabby, some broken, "there's everything I have and I'm having trouble holding on to that."
>
> Leroy came in, presumably to petition Richard on behalf of Richard's wife, who was sitting outside on the steps, afraid to come in. Leroy started to say something but Richard cut him short.

[21]And if, for the moment, he does sometimes have more money than he chooses to spend or more food than he wants to eat, he is pressed to spend the money and eat the food anyway since his friends, neighbors, kinsmen, or acquaintances will beg or borrow whatever surplus he has or, failing this, they may steal it. In one extreme case, one of the men admitted taking the last of a woman's surplus food allotment after she had explained that, with four children, she could not spare any food. The prospect that consumer soft goods not consumed by oneself will be consumed by someone else may be related to the way in which portable consumer durable goods, such as watches, radios, television sets or phonographs, are sometimes looked at as a form of savings. When Shirley was on welfare, she regularly took her television set out of pawn when she got her monthly check. Not so much to watch it, she explained, as to have something to fall back on when her money runs out toward the end of the month. For her and others, the television set or the phonograph is her savings, the pawnshop is where she banks her savings, and the pawn ticket is her bankbook.

"Look, Leroy, don't give me any of that action. You and me are entirely different people. Maybe I look like a boy and maybe I act like a boy sometimes but I got a man's mind. You and me don't want the same things out of life. Maybe some of the same, but you don't care how long you have to wait for yours and *I—want—mine—right—now.*"[22]

Thus, apparent present time concerns with consumption and indulgences—material and emotional—reflect a future-time orientation. "I want mine right now" is ultimately a cry of despair, a direct response to the future as he sees it.[23]

In many instances, it is precisely the streetcorner man's orientation to the future—but to a future loaded with "trouble"—which not only leads to a greater emphasis on present concerns ("I want mine right now,") but also contributes importantly to the instability of employment, family and friend relationships, and to the general transient quality of daily life.

The constant awareness of a future loaded with "trouble" re-

[22]This was no simple rationalization for irresponsibility. Richard had indeed "been scuffling for five years" trying to keep his family going. Until shortly after this episode, Richard was known and respected as one of the hardest-working men on the street. Richard had said, only a couple of months earlier, "I figure you got to get out there and try. You got to try before you can get anything." His wife Shirley confirmed that he had always tried. "If things get tough, with me I'll get all worried. But Richard get worried, he don't want me to see him worried. . . . He *will* get out there. He's shoveled snow, picked beans, and he's done some of everything. . . . He's not ashamed to get out there and get us something to eat." At the time of the episode reported above, Leroy was just starting marriage and raising a family. He and Richard were not, as Richard thought, "entirely different people." Leroy had just not learned, by personal experience over time, what Richard had learned. But within two years Leroy's marriage had broken up and he was talking and acting like Richard. "He just let go completely," said one of the men on the street.

[23]There is no mystically intrinsic connection between "present-time" orientation and lower-class persons. Whenever people of whatever class have been uncertain, skeptical or downright pessimistic about the future, "I want mine right now" has been one of the characteristic responses, although it is usually couched in more delicate terms: e.g., Omar Khayyam's "Take the cash and let the credit go," or Horace's "Carpe diem". In wartime, especially, all classes tend to slough off conventional restraints on sexual and other behavior (i.e., become less able or less willing to defer gratification). And when inflation threatens, darkening the fiscal future, persons who formerly husbanded their resources with commendable restraint almost stampede one another rushing to spend their money. Similarly, it seems that future time orientation tends to collapse toward the present when persons are in pain or under stress. The point here is that, the label notwithstanding, (what passes for) present time orientation appears to be a situation-specific phenomenon rather than a part of the standard psychic equipment of Cognitive Lower Class Man.

sults in a constant readiness to leave, to "make it," to "get out of town," and discourages the man from sinking roots into the world he lives in.[24]

It discourages him from committing himself to a job, especially one whose pay-off lies in the promise of future rewards rather than in the present. In the same way, it discourages him from deep and lasting commitments to family and friends or to any other persons, places or things, since such commitments could hold him hostage, limiting his freedom of movement and thereby compromising his security which lies in that freedom.

What lies behind the response to the driver of the pick-up truck, then, is a complex combination of attitudes and assessments. The streetcorner man is under continuous assault by his job experiences and job fears. His experiences and fears feed on one another. The kind of job he can get— and frequently only after fighting for it, if then—steadily confirms his fears, depresses his self-confidence and self-esteem until finally, terrified of an opportunity even if one presents itself, he stands defeated by his experiences, his belief in his own self-worth destroyed and his fears a confirmed reality.

Racial Integration in the Armed Forces

Charles C. Moskos, Jr.[1]

[*From* The American Journal of Sociology, *September, 1966, by permission.*]

On July 28, 1948, President Truman issued an executive order abolishing racial segregation in the armed forces of the United States. By

[24]For a discussion of "trouble" as a "focal concern of lower class culture," see Walter Miller, "Lower Class Culture as a Generating Milieu of Gang Delinquency," *Journal of Social Issues*, XIV, No. 3, pp. 7, 8.

[1]Many persons have given the writer invaluable assistance during his collection and analysis of the materials for this paper. I would especially like to thank Lieutenant Colonel Roger W. Little, U.S. Military Academy, John B. Spore, editor of *Army* magazine, Philip M. Timpane, staff assistant for civil rights, Department of Defense, and Morris Janowitz, University of Chicago. Also, the writer's access to military personnel at all levels was made possible by the more than perfunctory co-operation of numerous military information officers, men who perform a difficult task with both efficiency and good humor. Financial support was given by the Inter-University Seminar on Armed Forces and Society sponsored by the Russell Sage Foundation. Additional funds for travel were made available by the University of Michigan, and the Council for Intersocietal Studies of Northwestern University. It must be stressed, however, that the usual caveat that the author alone accepts responsibility for the interpretations and conclusions is especially relevant here.

the middle 1950's this policy was an accomplished fact. The lessons of the racial integration of the military are many. Within a remarkably short period the makeup of a major American institution underwent a far-reaching transformation. At the same time, the desegregation of the military can be used to trace some of the mutual permeations between the internal organization of the military establishment and the racial and social cleavages found in the larger setting of American society. Further, because of the favorable contrast in the military performance of integrated Negro servicemen with that of all-Negro units, the integration of the armed services is a demonstration of how changes in social organization can bring about a marked and rapid improvement in individual and group achievement. The desegregated military, moreover, offers itself as a graphic example of the abilities of both whites and Negroes to adjust to egalitarian racial relations with surprisingly little strain. Also, an examination of the racial situation in the contemporary military establishment can serve as a partial guideline as to what one might expect in a racially integrated America. It is to these and related issues that this paper is addressed.[2]

[2]The information on which the observations presented in this paper are based is of a varied sort. A primary source are Department of Defense statistics and those United States government reports dealing with racial relations in the armed forces: President's Committee on Equality of Treatment and Opportunity in the Armed Forces ("Fahy Committee"), *Freedom to Serve: Equality of Treatment and Opportunity in the Armed Forces* (Washington, D.C.: Government Printing Office, 1950); U.S. Commission on Civil Rights, "The Negro in the Armed Forces," *Civil Rights '63* (Washington, D.C.: Government Printing Office, 1963), pp. 169–224; President's Committee on Equal Opportunity in the Armed Forces ("Gesell Committee"), "Initial Report: Equality of Treatment and Opportunity for Negro Personnel Stationed within the United States" (mimeographed; June, 1963), and "Final Report: Military Personnel Stationed Overseas and Membership and Participation in the National Guard" (mimeographed; November, 1964). Also, participant observations were made by the writer while on active duty in the Army and during field trips to military installations in Germany, Viet Nam, and Korea in the summer of 1965 and in the Dominican Republic in the spring of 1966. Additionally, during the field trip in Germany, sixty-seven formal interviews were conducted with soldiers who made up nearly all of the total Negro enlisted personnel in two Army companies. Another source of data is found in Operations Research Office ("ORO"), *Project Clear: The Utilization of Negro Manpower in the Army* (Chevy Chase, Md.: Operations Research Office, Johns Hopkins University, April, 1955). The ORO surveys queried several thousand servicemen during the Korean War on a variety of items relating to attitudes toward racial integration in the Army. The findings of Project Clear, heretofore classified, have now been made available for professional scrutiny. Some comparable data were obtained from the section dealing with Negro soldiers in Samuel A. Stouffer *et al., The American Soldier: Adjustment during Army Life,* Vol. I (Princeton, N.J.: Princeton University Press, 1949), pp. 486–599.

Desegregating the Military[3]

Negroes have taken part in all of this country's wars. An estimated 5,000 Negroes, some scattered as individuals and others in segregated units, fought on the American side in the War of Independence. Several thousand Negroes saw service in the War of 1812. During the Civil War 180,000 Negroes were recruited into the Union army and served in segregated regiments.[4] Following the Civil War four Negro regiments were established and were active in the Indian wars on the Western frontier and later fought with distinction in Cuba during the Spanish-American War. In the early twentieth century, however, owing to a general rise in American racial tensions and specific outbreaks of vio-

[3]This background of the Negro's role in the American military is derived, in addition to the sources cited above, from Seymour J. Schoenfeld, *The Negro in the Armed Forces* (Washington, D.C.: Associated Publishers, 1945); Paul C. Davis, "The Negro in the Armed Services," *Virginia Quarterly,* XXIV (Autumn, 1948), 499–520; Herbert Aptheker, *Essays in the History of the American Negro* (New York: International Publishers, 1945); Arnold M. Rose, "Army Policies toward Negro Soldiers," *Annals of the American Academy of Political and Social Science,* CCXLIV (March, 1946), 90–94; Eli Ginzberg, "The Negro Soldier," in his *The Negro Potential* (New York: Columbia University Press, 1956), pp. 61–91; David G. Mandelbaum, *Soldiers Groups and Negro Soldiers* (Berkeley: University of California Press, 1952); and Benjamin Quarles, *The Negro in the Making of America* (New York: Collier Books, 1964), *passim.* A good account of the early days of military desegregation is Lee Nichols, *Breakthrough on the Color Front* (New York: Random House, 1954).

Though the last several years have seen little social science research on racial relations in the armed forces, there has recently been a spate of novels dealing with this theme. See, e.g., John Oliver Killens, *And Then We Heard the Thunder* (New York: Alfred A. Knopf, Inc., 1963); James Drought, *Mover* (New York: Avon Books, 1963); Webb Beech, *Article* 92 (Greenwich, Conn.: Gold Medal Books, 1964); Gene L. Coon, *The Short End* (New York: Dell Publishing Co., 1964); Hari Rhodes, *A Chosen Few* (New York: Bantam Books, 1965); and Jack Pearl, *Stockade* (New York: Pocket Books, 1965).

It should be noted that Negroes have not been the only ethnic or racial group to occupy a unique position in the American military. Indians served in separate battalions in the Civil War and were used as scouts in the frontier wars. Filipinos have long been a major source of recruitment for stewards in the Navy. The much decorated 442nd ("Go For Broke") Infantry Regiment of World War II was composed entirely of Japanese-Americans. Also in World War II, a separate battalion of Norwegian-Americans was drawn up for intended service in Scandinavia. The participation of Puerto Ricans in the American military deserves special attention. A recent case of large-scale use of non-American soldiers are the Korean fillers or "Katusas" (from Korean Augmentation to the U.S. Army) who make up roughly one-sixth of the current personnel of the Eighth Army.

[4] A particularly insightful contemporary report on Negro soldiers in the Civil War is Thomas Wentworth Higgins, *Army Life in a Black Regiment* (New York: Collier Books, 1962).

lence between Negro troops and white, opinion began to turn against the use of Negro soldiers. Evaluation of Negro soldiers was further lowered by events in World War I. The combat performance of the all-Negro 92nd Infantry, one of its regiments having fled in the German offensive at Meuse-Argonne, came under heavy criticism. Yet it was also observed that Negro units operating under French command, in a more racially tolerant situation, performed well.

In the interval between the two world wars, the Army not only remained segregated but also adopted a policy of a Negro quota that was to keep the number of Negroes in the Army proportionate to the total population. Never in the pre-World War II period, however, did the number of Negroes approach this quota. On the eve of Pearl Harbor, Negroes constituted 5.9 per cent of the Army; and there were only five Negro officers, three of whom were chaplains. During World War II Negroes entered the Army in larger numbers, but at no time did they exceed 10 per cent of total personnel. Negro soldiers remained in segregated units, and approximately three-quarters served in the quartermaster, engineer, and transportation corps. To make matters worse from the viewpoint of "the right to fight," a slogan loudly echoed by Negro organizations in the United States, even Negro combat units were frequently used for heavy-duty labor. This was highlighted when the 2nd Cavalry was broken up into service units owing to command apprehension over the combat qualities, even though untested, of this all-Negro division. The record of those Negro units that did see combat in World War II was mixed. The performance of the 92nd Infantry Division again came under heavy criticism, this time for alleged unreliability in the Italian campaign.

An important exception to the general pattern of utilization of Negro troops in World War II occurred in the winter months of 1944–45 in the Ardennes battle. Desperate shortages of combat personnel resulted in the Army asking for Negro volunteers. The plan was to have platoons (approximately 40 men) of Negroes serve in companies (approximately 200 men) previously all-white. Some 2,500 Negroes volunteered for this assignment. Both in terms of Negro combat performance and white soldiers' reactions, the Ardennes experiment was an unqualified success. This incident would later be used to support arguments for integration.

After World War II, pressure from Negro and liberal groups coupled with an acknowledgment that Negro soldiers were being poorly utilized led the Army to reexamine its racial policies. A report by an Army board in 1945, while holding racial integration to be a desirable goal and while making recommendations to improve Negro opportunity in the Army, concluded that practical considerations required a maintenance of segregation and the quota system. In light of World War II experiences, the report further recommended that Negro personnel be exclusively assigned to support rather than combat units. Another Army board report came out in 1950 with essentially the same conclusions.[5] Both reports placed heavy stress on the supervisory and disciplinary problems resulting from the disproportionate number of Negroes, as established by Army examinations, found in the lower mental and aptitude classification levels. In 1950, for example, 60 per cent of the Negro personnel fell into the Army's lowest categories compared with 29 per cent of the white soldiers. From the standpoint of the performance requirements of the military, such facts could not be lightly dismissed.

After the Truman desegregation order of 1948, however, the die was cast. The President followed his edict by setting up a committee, chaired by Charles Fahy, to pursue the implementation of equal treatment and opportunity for armed forces personnel. Under the impetus of the Fahy committee, the Army abolished the quota system in 1950, and was beginning to integrate some training camps when the conflict in Korea broke out. The Korean War was the coup de grâce for segregation in the Army. Manpower requirements in the field for combat soldiers resulted in many instances of *ad hoc* integration. As was true in the Ardennes experience, Negro soldiers in previously all-white units performed well in combat. As integration in Korea became more standard, observers consistently noted that the fighting abilities of Negroes differed little from those of whites.[6] This contrasted with the blemished record of the all-Negro 24th Infantry Regiment.[7] Its performance in the Korean War was judged to be so poor that its divisional commander recommended the unit be dissolved as quickly as possible. Concurrent with events in Korea, integration was introduced in the United States. By 1956, three years after the end of the Korean War, the remnants of Army Jim Crow disappeared at home and in overseas installations. At the time of the Truman order, Negroes constituted 8.8 per cent of Army personnel. In 1964 the figure was 12.3 per cent.

In each of the other services, the history of desegregation varied

[5] The 1945 and 1950 Army board reports are commonly referred to by the names of the officers who headed these boards: respectively, Lieutenant General Alvan C. Gillem, Jr., and Lieutenant General S. J. Chamberlin.

[6] These evaluations are summarized in ORO, *op.cit.*, pp. 16–19, 47–105, and 582–83.

[7] The notoriety of the 24th Infantry Regiment was aggravated by a song—"The Bug-Out Boogie"—attributed to it: "When them Chinese mortars begin to thud/ The old Deuce-Four begin to bug/ When they started falling 'round the CP [command post] tent/ Everybody wonder where the high brass went/ They were buggin' out/ Just movin' on."

from the Army pattern. The Army Air Force, like its parent body, generally assigned Negroes to segregated support units. (However, a unique military venture taken during the war was the formation of three all-Negro, including officers, air combat units.) At the end of World War II the proportion of Negroes in the Army Air Force was only 4 per cent, less than half what it was in the Army. Upon its establishment as an independent service in 1947, the Air Force began to take steps toward integration even before the Truman order. By the time of the Fahy committee report in 1950, the Air Force was already largely integrated. Since integration there has been a substantial increase in the proportion of Negroes serving in the Air Force, from less than 5 per cent in 1949 to 8.6 per cent in 1964.

Although large numbers of Negroes had served in the Navy during the Civil War and for some period afterward, restrictive policies were introduced in the early 1900's, and by the end of World War I only about 1 per cent of Navy personnel were Negroes. In 1920 the Navy adopted a policy of total racial exclusion and barred all Negro enlistments. This policy was changed in 1932 when Negroes, along with Filipinos, were again allowed to join the Navy but only as stewards in the messman's branch. Further modifications were made in Navy policy in 1942 when some openings in general service for Negroes were created. Negro sailors in these positions, however, were limited to segregated harbor and shore assignments.[8] In 1944, in the first effort toward desegregation in any of the armed services, a small number of Negro sailors in general service were integrated on ocean-going vessels. After the end of World War II the Navy, again ahead of the other services, began to take major steps toward elimination of racial barriers. Even in the integrated Navy of today, however, approximately a quarter of Negro personnel still serve as stewards. Also, despite the early steps toward integration taken by the Navy, the proportion of Negro sailors has remained fairly constant over the past two decades, averaging around 5 per cent.

The Marine Corps has gone from a policy of exclusion to segregation to integration. Before World War II there were no Negro marines. In 1942 Negroes were accepted into the Marine Corps but assigned to segregated units where they were heavy-duty laborers, ammunition handlers, and anti-aircraft gunners. After the war small-scale integration of Negro marines into white units was begun. In

[8]A lesson in the rewriting of history is gained from the movie *PT-109*, a dramatization of John Kennedy's war exploits. In this film, released in the early 1960's, the Navy is portrayed as racially integrated in World War II.

TABLE 1

NEGROES IN THE ARMED FORCES AND EACH SERVICE AS A PERCENTAGE OF TOTAL PERSONNEL, 1962, AND 1964

Service	1962	1964
Army	11.1	12.3
Air Force	7.8	8.6
Navy	4.7	5.1
Marine Corps	7.0	8.2
Total armed forces	8.2	9.0

Source: U.S. Commission on Civil Rights, op. cit., p. 218; Department of Defense statistics.

1949 and 1950 Marine Corps training units were integrated, and by 1954 the color line was largely erased throughout the Corps. Since integration began, the proportion of Negroes has increased markedly. In 1949 less than 2 per cent of all marines were Negroes compared with 8.2 per cent in 1964.

Although the various military services are all similar in being integrated today, they differ in their proportion of Negroes. As shown in Table 1, the Negro distribution in the total armed forces in 1962 and 1964, respectively, was 8.2 per cent and 9.0 per cent, lower than the 11–12 per cent constituting the Negro proportion in the total population. It is virtually certain, however, that among those *eligible,* a higher proportion of Negroes than whites enter the armed forces. That is, a much larger number of Negroes do not meet the entrance standards required by the military services. In 1962, for example, 56.1 per cent of Negroes did not pass the preinduction mental examinations given to draftees, almost four times the 15.4 per cent of whites who failed these same tests.[9] Because of the relatively low number of Negroes obtaining student or occupational deferments, however, it is the Army drawing upon the draft that is the only military service where the percentage of Negroes approximates the national proportion. Thus, despite the high number of Negroes who fail to meet induction standards, Army statistics for 1960–65 show Negroes constituted about 15 per cent of those drafted.

[9]Department of Labor ("Moynihan Report"), *The Negro Family: The Case for National Action* (Washington, D.C.: Government Printing Office, 1965), p. 75.

Even if one takes acount of the Army's reliance on the selective service for much of its personnel, the most recent figures still show important differences in the number of Negroes in those services meeting their manpower requirements solely through voluntary enlistments; the 5.1 per cent Negro in the Navy is lower than the 8.2 per cent for the Marine Corps or the 8.6 per cent for the Air Force. Moreover, the Army, besides its drawing upon the draft, also has the highest Negro initial enlistment rate of any of the services. As reported in Table 2, we find in 1964 that the Army drew 14.1 per cent of its volunteer incoming personnel from Negroes as compared with 13.1 per cent for the Air Force, 8.4 per cent for the Marine Corps, and 5.8 per cent for the Navy. As also shown in Table 2, there has been a very sizable increase in Negro enlistments from 1961 to 1965 in all four of the armed forces.

There are also diverse patterns between the individual services as to the rank or grade distribution of Negroes. Looking at Table 3, we find the ratio of Negro to white officers is roughly 1 to 30 in the Army, 1 to 70 in the Air Force, 1 to 250 in the Marine Corps, and 1 to 300 in the Navy. Among enlisted men, Negroes are underrepresented in the top three enlisted ranks in the Army and the top four ranks in the other three services. We also find a disproportionate concentration of Negroes in the lower non-commissioned officer ranks in all of the armed forces, but especially so in the Army. An assessment of these data reveals that the Army, followed by the Air Force, has not only the largest proportion of Negroes in its total personnel, but also the most equitable distribution of Negroes throughout its ranks. Although the Navy was the first service to integrate and the Army the last, in a

TABLE 2

NEGROES IN EACH OF THE ARMED SERVICES AS A PERCENTAGE OF INITIAL ENLISTMENTS 1961, 1963, AND 1965

Year	Army	Air Force	Navy	Marine Corps
1961	8.2	9.5	2.9	5.9
1963	11.2	10.5	4.3	5.5
1965	14.1	13.1	5.8	8.4

Source: Department of Defense statistics.

TABLE 3

NEGROES AS A PERCENTAGE OF TOTAL PERSONNEL IN EACH GRADE FOR EACH SERVICE, 1964

Grade	Army	Air Force	Navy	Marine Corps
Officers:				
Generals/admirals	—	0.2	—	—
Colonels/captains	0.2	0.2	—	—
Lt. cols./commanders	1.1	0.5	0.6	—
Majors/lt. commanders	3.6	0.8	0.3	0.3
Captains/lieutenants	5.4	2.0	0.5	0.4
1st lieutenants/lts. (j.g.)	3.8	1.8	0.2	0.4
2d lieutenants/ensigns	2.7	2.5	0.7	0.3
Total officers	3.4	1.5	0.3	0.4
Enlisted:*				
E-9 (sgt. major)	3.5	1.2	1.5	0.8
E-8 (master sgt.)	6.1	2.2	1.9	1.2
E-7 (sgt. 1st class)	8.5	3.2	2.9	2.3
E-6 (staff sgt.)	13.9	5.3	4.7	5.0
E-5 (sgt.)	17.4	10.8	6.6	11.2
E-4 (corp.)	14.2	12.7	5.9	10.4
E-3 (pvt. 1st class)	13.6	9.7	6.6	7.8
E-2 (private)	13.1	11.7	5.7	9.5
E-1 (recruit)	6.8	14.4	7.1	9.1
Total enlisted men	13.4	10.0	5.8	8.7

*Army and Marine Corps enlisted titles indicated in parentheses have equivalent pay grades in Navy and Air Force.

Source: Department of Defense statistics.

kind of tortoise and hare fashion, it is the Army that has become the most representative service for Negroes.

Changing Military Requirements and Negro Opportunities

A pervasive trend within the military establishment singled out by students of this institution is the long-term direction toward greater technical complexity and narrowing of civilian-military occupational

TABLE 4

TOTAL NEGRO ARMY ENLISTED PERSONNEL AND WHITE AND NEGRO ENLISTED PERSONNEL IN COMBAT ARMS, 1945 AND 1962

Category	1945*	1962
Negroes as percentage of total personnel	10.5	12.2
Percentage of total personnel in combat arms	44.5	26.0
Percentage of total white personnel in combat arms	48.2	24.9
Percentage of total negro personnel in combat arms	12.1	33.4

*Excludes Army Air Force.

Source: ORO, op. cit., pp. 563-64; U.S. Civil Rights Commission op. cit., pp. 219-22.

skills.[10] An indicator, albeit a crude one, of this trend toward "professionalization" of military roles is the changing proportion of men assigned to combat arms. Given in Table 4, along with concomitant white-Negro distributions, are figures comparing the percentage of Army enlisted personnel in combat arms (e.g., infantry, armor, artillery) for the years 1945 and 1962. We find that the proportion of men in combat arms—that is, traditional military specialties—dropped from 44.5 per cent in 1945 to 26.0 per cent in 1962. Also, the percentage of white personnel in traditional military specialties approximates the total proportional decrease in the combat arms over the seventeen-year period.

For Negro soldiers, however, a different picture emerges. While the percentage of Negro enlisted men in the Army increased only slightly between 1945 and 1962, the likelihood of a Negro serving in a combat arm is almost three times greater in 1962 than it was at the end of World War II. Further, when comparisons are made between military specialties *within* the combat arms, the Negro proportion is

[10] Morris Janowitz with Roger Little, *Sociology and the Military Establishment* (New York: Russell Sage Foundation, 1965), pp. 17–49; and Kurt Lang, "Technology and Career Management in the Military Establishment," in Morris Janowitz (ed.), *The New Military: Changing Patterns of Organization* (New York: Russell Sage Foundation, 1964), pp. 39–81.

noticeably higher in line rather than staff assignments. This is especially the case in airborne and marine units. Put in another way, the direction in assignment of Negro soldiers in the desegregated military is testimony to the continuing consequences of differential Negro opportunity originating in the larger society. That is, even though integration of the military has led to great improvement in the performance of Negro servicemen, the social and particularly educational deprivations suffered by the Negro in American society can be mitigated but not entirely eliminated by the racial egalitarianism existing within the armed forces.[11] These findings need not be interpreted as a decline in the "status" of the Negro in the integrated military. Actually there is evidence that higher prestige—but not envy—is accorded combat personnel by those in non-combat activities within the military.[12] And taken within the historical context of "the right to fight," the Negro's overrepresentation in the combat arms is a kind of ironic step forward.[13]

Moreover, the military at the enlisted ranks has become a major avenue of career mobility for many Negro men.[14] As shown earlier in Table 3, in all four services, and especially in the Army, there is some overrepresentation of Negroes at the junior NCO levels (pay grades E-4–E-6). The disproportionate concentration of Negroes at these levels implies a higher than average reenlistment as these grades are not normally attained until after a second enlistment. This assumption is supported by the data given in Table 5. We find that in 1965 for all four services the Negro reenlistment rate is approximately twice that

[11]World War II evidence shows much of the incidence of psychoneurotic breakdown among Negro soldiers, compared to whites, was associated with psychological handicaps originating before entrance into military service (Arnold M. Rose, "Psychoneurotic Breakdown among Negro Soldiers," *Phylon*, XVII, No. 1 [1956], pp. 66–73).

[12]Stouffer *et al., op. cit.*, II, 242–89; Raymond W. Mack, "The Prestige System of an Air Base: Squadron Rankings and Morale," *American Sociological Review*, XIX (June, 1954), 281–87; Morris Janowitz, *The Professional Soldier* (Glencoe, Ill.: Free Press, 1960), pp. 31–36.

[13]There are, as should be expected, differences among Negro soldiers as to their desire to see combat. From data not shown here, interviews with Negro soldiers stationed in Germany revealed reluctance to go to Viet Nam was greatest among those with high-school or better education, and northern home residence. This is in direct contrast with the findings reported in *The American Soldier*. In the segregated Army of World War II, northern and more highly educated Negro soldiers were most likely to want to get into combat, an outcome of the onus of inferiority felt to accompany service in support units (Stouffer, *op. cit.*, I, 523–24).

[14]The emphasis on academic education for officer careers effectively limits most Negro opportunity to the enlisted levels (Lang, *op. cit.*, p. 62).

of white servicemen. Indeed, about half of all first-term Negro servicemen chose to remain in the armed forces for at least a second term. The greater likelihood of Negroes to select a service career suggests that the military establishment is undergoing a significant change in its NCO core. Such an outcome would reflect not only the "pull" of the appeals offered by a racially egalitarian institution, but also the "push" generated by the plight of the Negro in the American economy.[15] At the minimum, it is very probable that as the present cohort of Negro junior NCO's attains seniority there will be a greater representation of Negroes in the advanced NCO grades. The expansion of the armed forces arising from the war in Viet Nam and the resulting opening up of "rank" will accelerate this development.

Attitudes of Soldiers

So far the discussion has sought to document the degree of penetration and the kind of distribution characterizing Negro servicemen in the integrated military establishment. We now introduce certain survey and interview data dealing more directly with the question of soldiers' attitudes toward military desegregation. Commenting on the difficulties of social analysis, the authors of *The American Soldier* wrote that few problems are "more formidable than that of obtaining dependable records of attitudes toward racial separation in the Army."[16] Without underestimating the continuing difficulty of this problem, an opportunity exists to compare attitudes toward racial integration held by American soldiers in two different periods. This is done by contrasting reponses to equivalent items given in World War II as reported in *The American Soldier* with those reported in Project Clear a study sponsored by the Defense Department during the Korean War.[17]

In both *The American Soldier* and Project Clear (the surveys

[15]Documentation shows the gap between Negro and white job opportunities has not diminished appreciably, if at all, in the past twenty years (Department of Labor, *op. cit.*, pp. 19–21; Thomas F. Pettigrew, *A Profile of the Negro American* [Princeton, N.J.: D. Van Nostrand Co., 1964], pp. 168–74).

[16]Stouffer *et al.*, *op. cit.*, p. 566.

[17]What methodological bias exists is that the Korean War question was a stronger description of racial integration than the item used in World War II. Compare "What is your feeling about serving in a platoon containing both whites and colored soldiers, all working and training together, sleeping in the same barracks and eating in the same mess hall?" with "Do you think white and Negro soldiers should be in separate outfits or should they be together in the same outfits?" (respectively, ORO, *op. cit.*, p. 453, and Stouffer *et al.*, *op. cit.*, p. 568).

TABLE 5

FIRST-TERM RE-ENLISTMENT RATES IN THE ARMED FORCES AND EACH SERVICE BY RACE, 1965
(Per Cent)

Race	Total Armed Forces	Army	Air Force	Navy	Marine Corps
White	21.6	18.5	27.4	21.6	12.9
Negro	46.6	49.3	50.3	41.3	50.3

Source: Department of Defense statistics.

under consideration were conducted in 1943 and 1951, respectively) large samples of Army personnel in segregated military settings were categorized as to whether they were favorable, indifferent, or opposed to racial integration in Army units. We find, as presented in Table 6, massive shifts in soldiers' attitudes over the eight-year period, shifts showing a much more positive disposition toward racial integration among both whites and Negroes in the later year. A look at the distribution of attitudes held by white soldiers reveals opposition to integration goes from 84 per cent in 1943 to less than half in 1951. That such a change could occur in less than a decade counters viewpoints that see basic social attitudes in large populations being prone to glacial-like changes. Yet, an even more remarkable change is found among the Negro soldiers. Where in 1945, favorable, indifferent, or opposing attitudes were roughly equally distributed among the Negro soldiers, by 1951 opposition or indifference to racial integration had become negligible. Such a finding is strongly indicative of a reformation in Negro public opinion from traditional acquiescence to Jim Crow to the ground swell that laid the basis for the subsequent civil rights movement.

While the data on Negro attitudes toward integration given in Table 6 were elicited during the segregated military of 1943 and 1951, we also have evidence on how Negro soldiers react to military integration in the contemporary setting. As reported in Table 7, the Army is overwhelmingly thought to be more racially egalitarian than civilian life. Only 16 per cent of sixty-seven Negro soldiers interviewed in 1965 said civilian life was more racially equal or no different than the Army. By region, as might be expected, we find southern

TABLE 6

ATTITUDES OF WHITE AND NEGRO SOLDIERS TOWARD RACIAL INTEGRATION IN THE SEGREGATED ARMY, 1943 AND 1951

Attitude Toward Integration	White Soldiers (Per Cent)		Negro Soldiers (Per Cent)	
	1943	1951	1943	1951
Favorable	12	25	37	90
Indifferent	4	31	27	6
Oppose	84	44	36	4
Total	100	100	100	100
(No. of cases)	(4,800)	(1,983)	(3,000)	(1,384)

Source: Stouffer et al., op. cit., p. 568; ORO, op. cit., pp. 322, 433.

Negroes more likely than northern Negroes to take a benign view of racial relations in the Army when these are compared to civilian life. The data in Table 7 support the proposition that, despite existing deviations from military policy at the level of informal discrimination, the military establishment stands in sharp and favorable contrast to the racial relations prevalent in the larger American society.

One of the most celebrated findings of *The American Soldier* was the discovery that the more contact white soldiers had with Negro troops, the more favorable was their reaction toward racial integration.[18] This conclusion is consistently supported in the surveys conducted by Project Clear. Again and again, comparisons of white soldiers in integrated units with those in segregated units show the former to be more supportive of desegregation. Illustrative of this pattern are the data shown in Table 8. Among combat infantrymen in Korea, 51 per cent in all-white units say outfits are better segregated as compared to 31 per cent in integrated units. For enlisted personnel stationed in the United States, strong objection to integration characterizes 44 per cent serving in segregated units while less than one-fifth of the men in integrated units feel the same way. Seventy-nine per cent of officers on segregated posts rate Negroes worse than white

[18] *Ibid.*, p. 594.

TABLE 7

ATTITUDES OF NEGRO SOLDIERS IN 1965 COMPARING RACIAL EQUALITY IN MILITARY AND CIVILIAN LIFE, TOTAL AND BY HOME REGION

Where More Racial Equality	Per Cent		
	Total	Home Region	
		North	South
Military life	84	75	93
Civilian life	3	6	0
No difference	13	19	7
Total	100	100	100
(No. of cases)	(67)	(36)	(31)

soldiers as compared with 28 per cent holding similar beliefs on integrated posts.

Official Policy and Actual Practice

For the man newly entering the armed forces, it is hard to conceive that the military was one of America's most segregated institutions less than two decades ago. For today color barriers at the formal level are absent throughout the military establishment. Equal treatment regardless of race is official policy in such non-duty facilities as swimming pools, chapels, barbershops, post exchanges, movie theaters, snack bars, and dependents' housing as well as in the more strictly military endeavors involved in the assignment, promotion, and living conditions of members of the armed services.[19] Moreover, white personnel are often commanded by Negro superiors, a situation rarely obtaining in civilian life. Recently the military has sought to implement its policy of equal opportunity by exerting pressure on local communities where segregated patterns affect military personnel. This policy deserves careful examination owing to its ramifications on the traditional separation of civilian and military spheres in American society. A measure of the extent and thoroughness of military desegre-

[19]The comprehensive scope of military integration is found in the official guidelines set forth under "Equal Opportunity and Treatment of Military Personnel," in *Army Regulation 600-21, Air Force Regulation 35-78,* and *Secretary of the Navy Instruction 5350.6.*

gation is found in comparing the 1950 President's committee report dealing with racial integration and the 1963 and 1964 reports of a second President's committee. Where the earlier report dealt entirely with internal military organization, the recent reports address themselves primarily to the National Guard and off-base discrimination.[20] Along this same line, Congressman Adam Clayton Powell has said that up to the middle 1950's he used to receive 5,000 letters a year from Negro servicemen complaining of discrimination in the military. In recent years, he receives less than 1,500 such letters annually and these largely pertain to off-base problems.[21] In brief, military life is characterized by an interracial equalitarianism of a quantity and of a kind that is seldom found in the other major institutions of American society.

In their performance of military duties, whites and Negroes work together with little display of racial tension. This is not to say racial animosity is absent in the military. Racial incidents do occur, but these are reduced by the severe sanctions imposed by the military for such acts. Such confrontations are almost always off-duty, if not off-base. In no sense, however, is the military sitting on top of a racial volcano, a state of affairs differing from the frequent clashes between the races that were a feature of the military in the segregated era. Additionally, it must be stressed that conflict situations stemming from non-racial causes characterize most sources of friction in the military establishment, for example, enlisted men versus officers, lower-ranking enlisted men versus non-commissioned officers, soldiers of middle-class background versus those of the working-class, conscriptees versus volunteers, line units versus staff units, rear echelon versus front echelon, combat units versus non-combat units, newly arrived units versus earlier stationed units, etc.

Yet the fact remains that the general pattern of day-to-day relationships *off the job* is usually one of mutual racial exclusivism. As one Negro soldier put it, "A man can be my best buddy in the Army, but he won't ask me to go to town with him." Closest friendships normally develop within races between individuals of similar educational back-

[20]Cf. the Fahy committee report (1950), with the Gesell committee reports (1963 and 1964). The Moynihan Report comments, "Service in the United States Armed Forces is the only experience open to the Negro American in which he is truly treated as an equal. . . . If this is a statement of the ideal rather than reality, it is an ideal that is close to realization" (Department of Labor, *op. cit.*, p. 42).

[21]In an interview with the *Overseas Weekly,* a newspaper published in Germany with a large readership among American servicemen. Personal communication with staff members.

TABLE 8

RACIAL ATTITUDES OF WHITE SOLDIERS IN SEGREGATED AND INTEGRATED SETTINGS, 1951

Racial Attitudes	All-White Units		Integrated Units	
	Per Cent	No.	Per Cent	No.
Combat infantrymen in Korea saying segregated outfits better	51	(195)	31	(1,024)
Enlisted personnel in the U.S. strongly objecting to racial integration	44	(1,983)	17	(1,683)
Officers rating Negroes worse than white soldiers	79	(233)	28	(385)

Source: ORO, op, cit., pp. 141, 322, 333, 356.

ground. Beyond one's hard core of friends there exists a level of friendly acquaintances. Here the pattern seems to be one of educational similarities overriding racial differences. On the whole, racial integration at informal as well as formal levels works best on duty, vis-à-vis off-duty, on-base vis-à-vis off-base, basic training and maneuvers vis-à-vis garrison, sea vis-à-vis shore duty, and combat vis-à-vis non-combat. In other words, the behavior of servicemen resembles the racial (and class) separatism of the larger American society, the more they are removed from the military environment.

For nearly all white soldiers the military is a first experience with close and equal contact with a large group of Negroes. There has developed what has become practically a military custom: the look over the shoulder, upon the telling of a racial joke, to see if there are any Negroes in hearing distance. Some racial animosity is reflected in accusations that Negro soldiers use the defense of racial discrimination to avoid disciplinary action. Many white soldiers claim they like Negroes as individuals but "can't stand them in bunches." In a few extreme cases, white married personnel may even live off the military base and pay higher rents rather than live in integrated military housing. On the whole, however, the segregationist-inclined white soldier regards racial integration as something to be accepted pragmatically, if not enthusiastically, as are so many situations in military life.

The most overt source of racial unrest in the military community centers in dancing situations. A commentary on American mores is a finding reported in Project Clear: three-quarters of a large sample of white soldiers said they would not mind Negro couples on the same dance floor, but approximately the same number disapproved of Negro soldiers dancing with white girls.[22] In many non-commissioned officer (NCO) clubs, the likelihood of interracial dancing partners is a constant producer of tension. In fact, the only major exception to integration within the military community is on a number of large posts where there are two or more NCO clubs. In such situations one of the clubs usually becomes tacitly designated as the Negro club.

Although there is almost universal support for racial integration by Negro soldiers, some strains are also evident among Negro personnel in the military. There seems to be a tendency among lower-ranking Negro enlisted men, especially conscriptees, to view Negro NCO's as "Uncle Toms" or "handkerchief heads." Negro NCO's are alleged to pick on Negroes when it comes time to assign men unpleasant duties. Negro officers are sometimes seen as being too strict or

[22]ORO, *op. cit.*, p. 388.

"chicken" when it comes to enforcing military discipline on Negro soldiers. As one Negro serviceman said, "I'm proud when I see a Negro officer, but not in my company."

One Negro writer, who served in the segregated Army and now has two sons in the integrated military, has proposed that what was thought by soldiers in all-Negro units to be racial discrimination was sometimes nothing more than harassment of lower-ranking enlisted personnel.[23] In fact, the analogy between enlisted men vis-à-vis officers in the military and Negroes vis-à-vis whites in the larger society has often been noted.[24] It has been less frequently observed, however, that enlisted men's behavior is often similar to many of the stereotypes associated with Negroes, for example, laziness, boisterousness, emphasis on sexual prowess, consciously acting stupid, obsequiousness in front of superiors combined with ridicule of absent superiors, etc. Placement of white adult males in a subordinate position within a rigidly stratified system, that is, appears to produce behavior not all that different from the so-called personality traits commonly held to be an outcome of cultural or psychological patterns unique to Negro life. Indeed, it might be argued that relatively little adjustment on the part of the command structure was required when the infusion of Negroes into the enlisted ranks occurred as the military establishment was desegregated. It is suggested, in other words, one factor contributing to the generally smooth racial integration of the military might be due to the standard treatment—"like Negroes" in a sense—accorded to all lower-ranking enlisted personnel.

Looking at changes in Negro behavior in the integrated military we find other indications of the immediate effects of social organization on individual behavior. Even though I am fully cognizant of the almost insurmountable difficulties involved in comparing crime statistics, the fact remains that students of the problem agree Negro crime is far higher than white crime.[25] There is no consensus, however, on what amount of the difference is due, on the one hand, to Negro cultural or psychological conditions or, on the other, to structural and class variables. Presented here, in a very preliminary fashion, is some

[23]James Anderson, "Fathers and Sons: An Evaluation of Military Racial Relations in Two Generations" (term paper, University of Michigan, December, 1965).

[24]Stouffer and his associates, for example, report enlisted men as compared to officers, as Negro soldiers to white soldiers, were more prone to have "low spirits," to be less desirous of entering combat, and to be more dissatisfied than perceived by others (Stouffer *et al.*, *op. cit.*, II, 345, and I, 392–94, 506, 521, and 538.

[25]Marvin E. Wolfgang, *Crime and Race* (New York: Institute of Human Relations Press, 1964); and Department of Labor, *op. cit.*, pp. 38–40.

evidence bearing on the consequences arising from changes in social organization on Negro crime. Reported by Project Clear are Negro-white crime differentials for three segregated posts in 1950. Proportionately, Negro soldiers committed four times more crime than white soldiers.[26] In 1964, in the integrated military, statistics of a major Army Command in Europe show Negroes accounting for 21 per cent of the crime while constituting 16 per cent of the total personnel. In a large combat unit in Viet Nam, for a three-month period in the summer of 1965, Negroes received 19 per cent of the disciplinary reports but made up 22 per cent of the troop assignment. These are the only Negro-white crime ratios in the integrated military that the writer has seen.[27] Although these findings, of course, are incomplete, they do point to a marked drop in Negro crime as compared with both the earlier segregated military as well as contemporary civilian life.[28]

Conclusion

Although the military was until recent times one of America's most segregated institutions, it has leaped into the forefront of racial equality in the past decade. What features of the military establishment can account for this about-face? There is a combination of mutually supporting factors that operate in the successful racial integration of the armed forces. For one thing, the military—an institution revolving around techniques of violence—is to an important degree discontinuous from other areas of social life. And this apartness served to allow, once the course had been decided, a rapid and complete racial integration. The path of desegregation was further made easier by characteristics peculiar or at least more pronounced in the military compared to other institutions. With its hierarchical power structure, predicated on stable and patterned relationships, decisions need take relatively little account of the personal desires of service personnel. Additionally, because roles and activities are more defined and specific in the military than in most other social arenas, conflicts that

[26]ORO, *op cit.*, p. 354.

[27]The data reported here are from offices of the Military Police, private communication.

[28]A caution to be introduced in assessing these findings is that the Army discharged many personnel of limited potential as determined by aptitude tests in 1957–58. Negroes were disproportionately represented in the released personnel (U.S. Commission on Civil Rights, *op. cit.*, pp. 176–77). Although Negroes are still overrepresented in the lower classification levels, there are probably proportionately fewer in these categories today than in 1950, and this most likely has some effect on the drop in Negro crime in the Army.

might have ensued within a more diffuse and ambiguous setting were largely absent. Likewise, desegregation was facilitated by the pervasiveness in the military of a bureaucratic ethos, with its concomitant formality and high social distance, that mitigated tensions arising from individual or personal feelings.

At the same time it must also be remembered that the military establishment has means of coercion not readily available in most civilian pursuits. Violations of norms are both more visible and subject to quicker sanctions. The military is premised, moreover, on the accountability of its members for effective performance. Owing to the aptly termed "chain of command," failures in policy implementation can be pinpointed. This in turn means that satisfactory carrying out of stated policy advances one's own position. In other words, it is to each individual's personal interest, if he anticipates receiving the rewards of a military career, to insure that decisions going through him are executed with minimum difficulty. Or put in another way, whatever the internal policy decided upon, racial integration being a paramount but only one example, the military establishment is uniquely suited to realize its implementation.

What implications does the military integration experience have for civilian society? Although it is certainly true that the means by which desegregation was accomplished in the military establishment are not easily translated to the civilian community, the end result of integration in the contemporary armed forces can suggest some qualities of what—if it came about—an integrated American society would be *within the context of the prevailing structural and value system.* Equality of treatment would be the rule in formal and task-specific relationships. Racial animosity would diminish but not disappear. We would expect a sharp improvement in Negro mobility and performance in the occupational sphere even taking into consideration on-going social and educational handicaps arising from existing inequities. Yet, because of these inequities, Negroes would still be overconcentrated in less skilled positons. We would also expect primary group ties and informal associations to remain largely within one's own racial group. But even at primary group levels, the integrated society would exhibit a much higher interracial intimacy than exists in the non-integrated society.

Such a description of the racially integrated society is, of course, what one finds in today's military establishment. Although the advent of the integrated society in this country is yet to occur, the desegregation of the armed forces has served to bring that day closer.

Suggested Additional Readings

1. Bloch, Herman D. "Some Effects of Discrimination in Employment," *American Journal of Economics and Sociology,* 25 (January 1966).
2. Blumer, Herbert. "Industrialisation and Race Relations," *Industrialisation and Race Relations.* Ed. Guy Hunter. New York: Oxford University Press, 1965.
3. Gilman, Harry J. "Economic Discrimination and Unemployment," *American Economic Review,* 54 (December 1965).
4. Hill, Herbert. "Planning the End of the American Ghetto: A Program of Economic Development for Equal Rights," *Poverty and Human Resources Abstracts,* 2 (March-April 1967).
5. Hill, Herbert. "Racial Discrimination in Employment: The Patterns of Discrimination," *Annals,* 357 (January 1965).
6. Strauss, George. "How Management Views Its Race Relations Responsibilities," *Employment, Race and Poverty.* Ed. Arthur M. Ross and Herbert Hill. New York: Harcourt, Brace and World, 1967.

Chapter 6

The Equalization of Negro-White Employment Opportunities

Introduction

Previous chapters have examined many facets of the Negro's employment situation in American society. The various materials have clearly demonstrated the economic and occupational inequalities which Negroes experience, and the causal roots and sustaining conditions of that disadvantagement. What emerges is the conclusion that the economic disadvantagement of the Negro is not a single problem but a composite of interrelated issues. Whatever policies are developed and programs effectuated to improve the Negro's employment potential and job opportunities must take this into account.

This chapter examines a number of issues and policy recommendations regarding the equalization of employment opportunities for Negroes. From the materials presented in previous chapters a number of general statements are suggested that have implications for policy and program development for reducing the job inequalities of Negroes.

First, it should be recognized that the Negro is not a recent arrival to American society and cannot be expected to repeat the cycle of assimilation and social mobility which many immigrant groups of the nineteenth and twentieth centuries experienced. Those who contend that Negroes are in a position basically similar to that of the earlier immigrants fail to recognize two essential features of the Negro's situation: (a) The Negro's exclusion is not a matter of cultural strangeness bred in a foreign land, rather it is a product of American society—the decades and centuries of political disfranchisement and *de jure* and *de facto* segregation. (b) Technological changes occurring over the last half-century have eliminated many unskilled and semiskilled jobs and have fostered a growing emphasis on formal education and technical skills as a means of job mobility, thus making sweeping changes in the whole structure of opportunities for occupational mobility.

Second, the passage of fair employment practices legislation has been a beneficial, though certainly not a sufficient, development in the field of equal employment opportunity. Such legislation has provided a statutory source of appeal for redress of discriminatory treatment, but unaided by parallel policy and program developments it is limited in its power to further the economic and occupational integration of Negroes into American society.

Third, substantial improvement of the Negro's employment position is best effected in a prosperous and full employment economy, but such conditions do not by themselves insure such progress. The availability of job openings is meaningful only when job seekers have the requisite educational and training backgrounds. In the case of many Negroes as well as poor whites, opportunities for increased educational attainment and skills development are a necessary accompaniment of changes on the broader economic front.

Fourth, the job problems of Negroes, particularly in regions outside the South, must be viewed within the context of the urban social milieu. In non-Southern regions of the United States, over 90 percent of the Negro population live in urban centers; even in the South, three out of five Negroes live in urban areas. The patterns of residential segregation that typify metropolitan and other urban areas create ecological barriers affecting the Negro's access to job opportunities within the community, and the deteriorated community and institutional facilities within the ghetto slums are detrimental to the Negro's preparation for the job market.

Fifth, although most employers and labor unions are now covered by municipal, state, or federal fair employment practices ordinances or statutes, formal and informal barriers to Negro employment and job advancement continue to persist. Some of these are products of traditions that have escaped reexamination, others of unrealistic or unevaluated hiring or membership standards. Whatever their source, they function to deny equal consideration to Negro job applicants.

Sixth, the job problems of Negroes are not simply reducible to the operation of prejudice on the part of those who control access to job opportunities. To view the employment inequalities which Negroes experience as products of prejudicial attitudes is to fail to recognize that patterns of exclusion are not merely psychological side issues in an otherwise sound social and economic order. Within the context of Negroes and jobs, attitudes are relevant only insofar as they give rise to and sustain inequities in the opportunity structure which affects employment. The strategy which places attitudinal changes as the antecedents of social change neglects the significance of structural barriers limiting the Negro's access to job opportunities.

Seventh, nothing is gained by attempting to deny the existence of educational and skill deficiencies on the part of many Negroes today. These are employment liabilities, regardless of color; at the same time, they offer an effective springboard for efforts to ameliorate the unequal condition of the Negro's participation in the American economy.

Eighth, there are many indications of a continuing need for special and experimental programs to secure employment for Negroes currently underemployed, unemployed, or working in jobs of marginal security. Such programs could simultaneously attempt three types of service: *job placement,* matching Negro applicants with available job openings; *job development,* placing Negroes in jobs for which they are not fully qualified at the time of entry and providing supportive services to bring performance up to standards; and *job creation,* segmentalizing existing jobs into simpler component tasks. A primary feature of this last is the rapidly developing body of sub-professional jobs, which require fewer skills and training than the original unit job of which they were part. The major issue in job development and job creation programs is the extent to which the undertrained individual must be brought up to the existing job standard or the existing job structure can be adapted to the existing training and ability level of the individual.

Finally, it seems profitable to view employment problems of Negroes against the backdrop of national manpower needs and issues. Today, many advocate a national civil rights manpower policy. This recommendation has merit, but it is questionable whether such a policy could or should be developed apart from a comprehensive manpower policy for the nation. Economic improvement of Negro workers cannot be separated from more general economic growth and development in society.

Programs and activities to improve and expand equal employment opportunities for Negroes and other minorities must be advanced on many fronts, utilizing the resources and talents of both public and private agencies and organizations. Corrective action may require the development of a massive public works program to meet the needs of unskilled and semiskilled workers whose employment is becoming less and less secure as technological change occurs. At the same time definite emphasis must be placed upon training and skills development that is adaptable to the expanding white collar and service sectors of the economy. Finally, the extent to which the socio-economic problems of Negroes are solved depends on how far society will accept them as full-fledged participants and close the gap between promise and performance in a functioning democracy.

Fair Employment Practices Legislation and Enforcement in the United States

John E. Means

[*From the* International Labour Review, *March 1966, by permission.*]

"In a government of laws, existence of the government will be imperilled if it fails to observe the law scrupulously. Our Government is the potent, the omnipresent teacher. For good or for ill, it teaches the whole people by its example."

The above statement by Mr. Justice Brandeis, U.S. Supreme Court, well describes the movement in the United States by the federal, state and local governments to eradicate discrimination in employment through fair employment practices legislation and administrative enforcement machinery. Concentrated efforts towards this end started as far back as 1941 and culminated in 1964 in the enactment by Congress of the Civil Rights Act, which provides a uniform fair employment practices law for the whole of the United States and reiterates that administrative enforcement of the laws against discrimination provides the best means of educating the community in the practical application of the values it seeks to preserve. An educated public demands compliance with the substantive law. "Legislation is the final and most impressive way of putting the community on record as supporting a particular principle or rule of conduct."[1]

In the following pages, after a brief review of early agitation for equal employment opportunity, this article will consider the action taken by the Federal Executive from 1941 to secure non-discrimination in industries working under government contracts, the evolution of fair employment practices legislation in the states and municipalities, the role of Congress culminating in enactment of the

[1]Arthur Earl Bonfield: "State civil rights studies: some proposals", in *Iowa Law Review,* 49 (Summer 1964), p. 1086.

Civil Rights Act of 1964, and the attitudes adopted by the Supreme Court and the National Labour Relations Board towards discrimination in employment.

Agitation for Equal Employment Opportunity

Although the progress made in the economic condition of Negroes during the First World War was very limited, it did represent the beginning of the great surge towards equal opportunity in employment for all minority groups. Soon after the war, the passage by Congress of the Immigration Acts of 1921 and 1924, severely curtailing new immigration, allowed the various minority groups to consolidate what gains they had made without the danger of losing them to newly arrived immigrants.[1] However, it was still true that "White America, with few exceptions, was little interested in ameliorating the lot of the Negro or in gaining a more sympathetic understanding of his needs."[2] Only through militant action was better economic opportunity for all minority groups to be gained: by demonstrations, protest meetings, mass marches.

Between the two world wars many groups organised to agitate and propagandise for equal opportunity; these groups were from all segments of American society: Negro, Jewish, inter-racial, church and civil libertarian. After the beginning of the Depression in 1929, when minority groups knew better the efficacy of pressure techniques and tactics, better organisation, and the importance of the ballot box for social gains, many changes in the social organisation and thought of "White America" took place. New and powerful allies came to the aid of the oppressed minorities. Of particular importance was the formation of the Congress of Industrial Organisations, which immediately and consistently took a forthright stand for equality for all Americans and advocated the abolition of inequality and discrimination against every minority group.

The misery and deprivation of the 1930s, which affected all Americans, and the vast unemployment which continued for almost a decade, helped to injec' into American political thought an egalitarian spirit which had been lacking since the Jacksonian era. Mass unemployment, destitution and stark economic depression produced a sense of public responsibility for all classes irrespective of race, colour or

[1]The Negro was no threat to the skilled immigrant, inasmuch as he was limited mostly to unskilled or, at best, semi-skilled occupations.

[2]Louis Ruchames; *Race, jobs and politics: the story of FEPC* (New York, Columbia University Press, 1953), p. 8.

national origin. There gradually dawned in American social thought a realisation that there was a direct relationship between unemployment and discrimination; for the effect of job discrimination was to concentrate the employment of minorities in certain industry categories, limit their income, reduce their opportunities for promotion, and contribute further to a feeling of inferiority.

This egalitarian spirit, although present in the executive branch of the Government throughout the decade of the 1930s, did not manifest itself until 1941. It must be pointed out, however, that the non-discrimination clauses in much of the Congressional relief legislation of that period was due mainly to the prodding of the executive branch.[1]

After the outbreak of the Second World War, the Government realised the necessity of utilising all available manpower resources for the war effort, and the National Defence Advisory Commission set forth a non-discriminatory employment policy for minority groups in defence industries. Since, however, there was no governmental machinery through which government officials could enforce this national policy, many pleas were received by the President for its enforcement.

In the absence of concrete action by the President, various leaders of the Negro community discussed the possibility of a mass march on Washington to exact their rights for equal job opportunity. The number of possible marchers was estimated to be approximately 100,000. At a time of national crisis, the Government could not be indifferent to mass marches and the reasons for them. After much negotiating, conferences with government leaders and the pledge that the President would take action to ensure equal access to employment, the march was called off and Executive Order 8802[2] was issued, asserting that national unity and the morale of minority groups were being affected by continued discrimination, and reaffirming the national policy of non-discrimination. It has been said that this order "constituted the most important effort in the history of this country to eliminate discrimination in employment by use of government authority."[3]

[1]See the section entitled "Congress and fair employment practices legislation" below.

[2]Executive orders in the United States are administrative decrees used by the President to implement certain policies without the necessity for full Congressional approval, whether in the domestic or foreign domain. However, should an executive order have financial implications, the Congress must give its acquiescence if the order is to be fully implemented.

[3]RUCHAMES, *op. cit.*, p. 22.

Equal Job Opportunity and Presidential Initiatives Through Executive Orders

1941–43 (Executive Order 8802)

The use of a Presidential executive order in 1941 to ensure equal employment opportunity was considered quite revolutionary: it was the first time in American history that administrative machinery had been established for the implementation of the national policy of equality. During the long period since the Civil War the country had relied on the Thirteenth, Fourteenth and Fifteenth Amendments to the Federal Constitution for the removal of barriers of equality. American society had deemed it sufficient that the substantive law had been enacted and there were few, if any, attempts to spell out for the minorities what was available to them under the law. Even the position taken by the Supreme Court led to charges that it, too, was acquiescing in discrimination against minorities.[1]

Executive Order 8802, in establishing a Fair Employment Practices Committee (F.E.P.C.), decreed that there should be no discrimination in employment based on race, colour, creed or national origin.

The order applied to the government establishment, employers and labour organisations, and stated that it was their duty to provide for the full and equitable participation of all workers in defence industries without discrimination.

The committee, in its hearings throughout the country, made the public aware of the threat to national unity created by racial discrimination. It succeeded, to a degree, in inducing employers to abandon discriminatory practices in employment and to adopt a policy of employment based on merit. Perhaps more important for the long-range future, it gave millions of citizens a glimmer of hope and uplifted their morale. For various reasons the committee lost its effectiveness when it was transformed from an autonomous entity into an "organisational entity". Powerful pressures from newspaper, Congress, and many government officials caused the committee to crumble from within.

1943–46 (Executive Order 9346)

Following strong requests by liberal, labour and minority groups, Presidential Executive Order 9346 was issued in 1943, creating a new

[1]See *Plessy* v. *Ferguson,* 163 U.S. 537 (1896). This case enunciated for Americans the doctrine of "equal but separate" facilities. It was not until 1954 that the Court reversed itself and declared in favour of equal treatment for all irrespective of race, colour or creed. *Brown* v. *D.C. Board of Education,* 347 U.S. 483 (1954).

Fair Employment Practice Committee, once more an independent agency specifically charged with recommending measures to eliminate discrimination and to promote the fullest utilisation of manpower.

The committee did not conceive of itself as an agent to punish contractors for non-compliance with the President's order. Although all government defence contracts contained provisions against discrimination, and the committee had power to recommend the cancellation of contracts, this power was never used. Like the first committee, its principal weapons were publicity and moral pressure. Many businesses opened their doors to Negro-American, Mexican-American and Japanese-American workers, admitting them to previously closed occupations.

The committee did not receive Congressional support and was continuously under attack from Congress. In July 1945 it was given appropriations solely for the purpose of liquidating its affairs, and its final report was issued on 28 June 1946. The dissolution of this committee ended another stage in co-ordinated government-wide efforts to promote the policy of equal opportunity until the issuance of Executive Order 10925 in March 1961, which established a single government committee with responsibility for effecting a policy of equal opportunity in employment.

Although forced to terminate its activities, the committee was not discouraged as to the effectiveness of fair employment practices legislation. In its final report it spoke convincingly of the gains during the five years of its existence in the employment opportunities of such minority groups as Negro-Americans, Mexican-Americans and Japanese-Americans in the industrial sphere. It pointed out too that "discrimination in New York and New Jersey cities, covered by fair employment practices laws, was far lower than in cities where no attempts were being made to control discrimination".[1] In its final report, it reached certain conclusions:

(1) The majority of all discrimination cases could be settled by informal procedures such as negotiation and persuasion.

(*a*) With local union help, the determined employer could effectively initiate a policy of equal employment opportunity.

(*b*) Non-discriminatory policies of national unions could succeed if local unions firmly asserted the same policy.

(2) Discrimination could be quickly ended by negotiation when the national Government had made unequivocal its authority and intent.

[1]*Final report of the Fair Employment Practice Committee*, 28 June 1946, p. xiv.

(3) When negotiations failed, public hearings were essential.

(4) Congressional enactment of federal fair employment practices legislation was mandatory.[1]

1946–53 (Executive Orders 9691, 9808, 9980)

Between 1946 and 1953 there were various efforts to tackle discrimination in employment. In 1946 when the Civil Service returned to its former career basis, Presidential Executive Order 9691 forbidding racial discrimination in temporary appointments was issued. Executive Order 9980, proclaimed in 1948, created the Fair Employment Board to enforce the policy of non-discrimination in the executive branch of the federal Government.

A further executive order (No. 9808 issued in 1946), although not specifically concerned with fair employment practices, was in effect a mandate from the President to take stock of the past and make recommendations for the future. It established a President's Committee on Civil Rights "to inquire into and to determine whether and in what respect current law-enforcement measures and the authority and means possessed by federal, state, and local governments may be strengthened and improved to safeguard the civil rights of the people".

This committee evaluated the extent of achievement in civil rights in many fields including the employment of minority groups and pointed out in its report: "The opportunity of each individual to obtain useful employment ... must be provided with complete disregard for race, colour, creed, and national origin. Without this equality of opportunity the individual is deprived of the chance to develop his potentialities and to share the fruits of society."[2] Among its recommendations for equality of opportunity, the committee recommended enactment of a federal Fair Employment Practice Act prohibiting all forms of discrimination in private employment, based on race, colour, creed, or national origin, and including provisions for complaint procedures, public hearings, issuance of "cease-and-desist" orders, and enforcement powers through the courts, as well as penalties for non-compliance. It recommended that the provisions of the Act should apply to labour unions and trade and professional associations as well as to employers. The Committee held that such legislation was within the competence of the Congress in virtue of its powers to regulate inter-state commerce. The executive branch was not, of course, to be

[1]*Ibid.*, p. xv.

[2]*To secure these rights,* report of the President's Committee on Civil Rights (Washington, U.S. Government Printing Office, 1947), p. 9.

exempted from continuing active policies of non-discrimination throughout the federal establishment. The committee recommended also the establishment of a government fair employment practices committee "with authority to implement and enforce the Presidential mandate".[1]

Examination of federal action from 1946 to 1964 in the civil rights field suggests that the exhaustive study made by the President's Committee on Civil Rights and the well-considered recommendations set forth in its report may have laid the foundation for Congressional action in 1964 on the Government's broad and far-reaching legislation to ensure equal opportunity.

1953–61 (Executive Orders 10479, 10557)

Executive Order 10479, promulgated in 1953, reiterated that the Government's policy was to ensure support for all qualified citizens on the basis of merit in the areas where public funds were used. To this end the order charged each government agency to take all necessary action, including the establishment of enforcement machinery, to counter discriminatory employment practices in firms doing business with the Government. To ensure a uniform policy and implementation, the order established the President's Committee on Government Contracts.

This committee attempted to intensify the fight against discrimination by (*a*) clarifying and strengthening the non-discrimination clause in government contracts[2]; and (*b*) further developing the complaint procedures and implementing the procedure for compliance.

The new anti-discrimination clause referred not only to employment itself, but also to upgrading, demotion, transfer, recruitment and recruitment advertising, lay-offs or termination, rates of pay and other forms of remuneration, and the apprenticeship programme.

Under the terms of the order, compliance with the clause was to be mandatory. However, the effectiveness of the committee in this field was weakened by the fact that it was authorised to grant exemptions in special cases of emergency or if special requirements warranted them; the committee's records show that exemptions proved to be the rule rather than the exception.

One major contribution of the Committee on Government Contracts to the eradication of discrimination lay in its intensive development of the complaint procedure, which it improved in all its aspects—

[1] *Ibid.*, pp. 167–168.
[2] See Executive Order 10557.

receipt, processing, analysis and disposition. When complaints were received and verified, the committee attempted by direct negotiation, conciliation and mediation with the contractor concerned to eliminate the discriminatory practices. This procedure brought some benefits but it proved slow and cumbersome; some complaints were not settled for months and some even for years.

The fact that the committee emphasised voluntary compliance and did not use its implied legal powers to enforce compliance resulted in few companies seeking out confirmatory evidence of their own progress towards compliance. Indeed, many companies preferred to refuse the government contract rather than accept the non-discrimination clause. In many cases, however, failure to comply did not necessarily indicate insincerity on the part of top management, but rather its failure to communicate its intent effectively and to initiate measures sufficient to overcome inaction and inertia.

Like that of the first Fair Employment Practices Committee (1941-43), perhaps the major contribution of the 1953-61 Committee on Government Contracts lay in its role as an educator. In fact, its reluctance to use its enforcement powers and its hesitancy to recommend positive action to enforce compliance left it with only that role. Its vigorous programme of explanations to management, labour, public and private organisations, state, local and federal contracting agencies, and its negotiations and policy of persuasion established the committee as a real force.

Although the committee did not completely eliminate discriminatory practices, it contributed enormously to laying the groundwork for advancement.[1]

1961–65 (Executive Order 10925)

The most far-reaching of all executive orders aimed at the elimination of discrimination in employment was Executive Order 10925, issued in 1961, which, *inter alia,* established the President's Committee on Equal Employment Opportunity. Although the aims and intentions of the order did not materially differ in substance from previous executive orders on the subject, it represented a milestone in executive administrative action, if for no other reason by providing for specified sanctions to be used in the event of non-compliance by a firm doing business with the Government. Further, the order charged the committee to use the tools available to its predecessors but never used by them.

[1] *Employment,* report of the United States Commission on Civil Rights, *op. cit.,* p. 59.

The new committee was authorised to cancel contracts with contracting firms refusing to comply with the Government's policy of equal opportunity and merit employment. It also had the power to block future contracts placed with non-complying firms. Although primary responsibility for enforcement was placed with the contracting government agency, the committee itself retained ultimate authority; it could assume jurisdiction over any complaint filed with any contracting agency as well as over any case pending before an agency, and process it to completion. A power lacking in former committees but possessed by the new one was that of initiating inquiries or directing any contracting agency to institute investigations. Labour union activities came within the committee's purview only indirectly: contractors were charged with the responsibility of supplying information on any union activities which might hamper their own compliance.

Under the committee's mandate, new emphasis was placed on government efforts to wipe out discrimination in firms using public funds. The committee required both the contracting agencies and the contracting firms within their jurisdiction to develop positive programmes for affirmative action. This meant the employers had to make clear in newspaper advertisements or requests to employment agencies, for example, that their jobs were open to all qualified applicants. The employing company had to make an effort to ensure that its whole personnel programme—hiring, job placement, promotion, upgrading, training, disciplinary action, and firing—was free from discrimination.

Unlike the previous committees, the new committee established in 1961 required a report on compliance to be made within 30 days of conclusion of a contract by all firms doing business with the Government.[1] Compliance reports also had to be made at specified regular intervals after the initial report.

In the first nine months the number of complaints received by the Committee on Equal Employment Opportunity was three-fourths of the previous total for the whole period from 1953 to 1960. Corrective action was taken in 29 per cent of the cases.[2] On the other hand, in 1964 the committee received fewer complaints against government contractors than it did in 1963. Towards the end of 1964 an

[1]The previous committees received reports only when a complaint had been made or a compliance survey conducted.

[2]See the statement of Arthur H. Goldberg, former Secretary of Labour, in *Hearings before the Special Subcommittee on Labor of the Committee on Education and Labor,* U.S. House of Representatives, 87th Congress, 1st Session, p. 1019.

average of 70 complaints were being received each month. In May 1965 the monthly average had dropped to approximately 44 complaints. In two-and-a-half years of operation 36,668 complaints had been received and 2,065 had been resolved; corrective action had been taken in six out of ten.[1]

Perhaps the most important of all the provisions of Executive Order 10925 were its provisions for sanctions that could be applied by either the contracting government agency or the committee. These ranged from publication of the names of violators (whether management or union) to actual debarment, i.e. complete ineligibility for federal contracts. Further, an ineligible contractor could only be restored after submission of a programme for future compliance, or verification that it had already complied with the non-discrimination provisions of the executive order.

The committee's experience demonstrated that persuasion can be effective when the legal duty has been defined in sufficient detail.

Fair Employment Practices Legislation in the Various States

State laws prohibiting discrimination in certain types of employment, particularly in the civil service and public employment, date back to the early 1900s. Before 1945, some 25 state constitutions contained specific provisions against discrimination in employment. In 1945, 16 western and northern states were considering legislation against discrimination; only New York and New Jersey succeeded in passing the statutes that year.

Between 1945 and the passage of the federal Civil Rights Act in 1964, more than 25 states and more than 50 major cities had adopted fair employment practices ordinances or an anti-discrimination policy authorising a city attorney to enforce the law in respect of employers, labour unions or employment agencies that did not comply with cease-and-desist orders issued under the statutory regulations. Many of the municipalities adopted the statutes prior to the enactment of legislation by the state legislatures. The statutes in some states (for example Pennsylvania) expressly recognise the municipal ordinances. In others, for example Minnesota, the prevailing interpretation is that the municipal laws are not invalidated by the state law. The Michigan statute specifically provides for the suspension of local ordinances, as does the California state law.

[1]The President's Committee on Equal Employment Opportunity: *Committee Reporter*, No. 111, May 1965, p. 6.

Main features of the laws

Although all the state laws have the purpose of ending discrimination, there is wide diversity as to method and enforcement procedures. All are modelled on the New York statute and cover hiring, discharge, upgrading and pay; all apply to employers, employment agencies and labour unions. The majority cover hiring by government employment agencies and ban discriminatory inquiries or advertising for workers. Jurisdiction over employers, labour organisations and employment services located within the state or doing business with it is taken irrespective of their engagement in inter-state commerce. The laws, including that of New York State, in general provide for enforcement by an administrative agency responsible for receiving complaints, investigation, conciliation and persuasion, the holding of public hearings, and the issuance of cease-and-desist orders enforceable in the courts.[1]

The agencies responsible for administration and enforcement of the laws vary from state to state. In most cases they are special commissions, though in some administration is entrusted to an existing state agency (e.g. a department of labour or education). In New Jersey the task is entrusted to the Division on Civil Rights of the state Department of Education, while in Oregon an elected Commissioner of Labour administers the law. In both Hawaii and Alaska, the Acts are administered by the state Departments of Labour. In many cases the commissions are called upon to administer other laws as well as the anti-discriminatory laws on employment.

Enforcement procedure

The administrative enforcement of fair employment practices or anti-discrimination legislation proceeds on the basis of a complaint by an "aggrieved person" or, in many states, by the administrative organ itself (it may be a commission or a state officer). Some states permit service organisations[2] to file a complaint.[3]

An idea of the methods of enforcement can be obtained from the following figures on the disposal of complaints taken from a report

[1]In appropriate cases an appeal against such orders also lies to the courts.

[2]"Service organisations" are any non-profit organisations dedicated to civil liberties.

[3]In some states, initiatory power is a statutory right while in others either the Attorney-General or an interested person may initiate the complaint. See *American Jewish Congress* v. *Arabian American Oil Co.*, Sup.Ct. New York County Sp.Term, Part I, No. 17182 (1962).

submitted by the state of New York to the House of Representatives Committee on Education and Labour.[1] During the period from 1 July 1945 to 31 December 1962, of a total of 7,725 complaints filed in the state 1,405 (18.8 per cent.) were settled "by conference and conciliation". Less than 1 per cent. were ordered for public hearing, and a substantial proportion of these, too, were settled before or during the hearings. Nearly three-quarters of all complaints were found to have no "probable cause", while 2.3 per cent were withdrawn by the complainants.

In the case of the state of Michigan, from 1955 to 1961, more than 1,400 cases on discrimination were filed. In 50 per cent. of the cases, there was sufficient evidence of discrimination, or difference in treatment, to warrant conciliation efforts. In all but seven of the cases, settlement was made by persuasion and conciliation. The ultimate weapon, that of public hearings, was used only in these seven cases. More than 90 per cent of the cases involved the question of race.

In the state of California the formal process of hearing and appeal became necessary in only four of the 1,216 cases docketed by the state commission in its first two years of operation. In all, 749 cases were found to involve discrimination; in 264 of these (35.2 per cent) discrimination was proved and satisfactory adjustments reached, the remaining 485 cases being dismissed for insufficient proof or no evidence of discrimination.

In all states conciliation and persuasion are compulsory after the finding of "probable cause". This procedure is the very core and essence of the administrative enforcement of fair employment practices legislation. Normally conciliation and persuasion are effected by staff members where the members of the commission are unsalaried, and the results are presented to the full commission for approval, as required by nearly all the laws. In cases where the commissioner is salaried, he may conduct his own investigation and in general he is given wide liberty in drawing up his conciliation procedures. In some states (for example New York) the commissioner may make his judgment without the consent of the commission.

The commissions are not coercive bodies. Their strength lies in public acceptance of their role as service agencies, and without exception they rely mainly on the procedure of conciliation and persuasion. Heavy use of coercion and public hearings, as well as court injunctions, would quickly destroy the efficacy of the commissions. It is for this

[1]*Hearings before the General Subcommittee on Labor of the Committee on Education and Labor,* U.S. House of Representatives, 88th Congress, 1st Session, 1963, p. 45.

reason that the process or procedure of public hearing is used most sparingly:

> Conciliation is a mixture of coercion and educative persuasion. In many cases, the prospect of public hearing followed by court enforcement is a strong inducement for the respondent to accept the commission's terms, but the effectiveness of a threat of publicity varies considerably with the type of respondent involved and the fields in which discrimination is being practised.[1]

In conciliation in employment cases, drastic remedies are seldom demanded, as they are in cases relating to "public accommodations". Obviously if an employer rehired an employee only under threat, the gains to the employee would be offset by the psychological effects of working for an employer who does not desire his services and may even bear hostility towards him.

Many states have follow-up procedures to determine whether an employer is obeying both the spirit and letter of the law. The state of New York, for example, makes it mandatory for the commission to have access to all records of a firm which has been cited before it for discriminatory practice.

As regards reconsideration of cases, a dissatisfied respondent may simply await the public hearing. A complainant is usually at the mercy of the commission, but may request reconsideration in some instances: for example in Michigan a case must be reconsidered if the complainant is dissatisfied; in Colorado, it may be at the discretion of the commission; in the state of Washington the dissatisfied complainant has the statutory right to appear before the full commission with legal counsel. When reconsideration brings no relief, the complainant may seek redress in the courts, irrespective of the provisions of the Act concerning reconsideration.

All the laws require that the decision for a public hearing must be reached by a quorum of the commission. Normally, respondents shun public hearings because of possible notoriety, which could hurt their business. Some, on the other hand, profit from such notoriety—particularly real estate agents.

Generally the commissions are represented in the public hearing by their attorney; they have the authority to amend, draft or redraft a complaint. Witnesses are called, sworn and cross-examined. Many commissions lack the right to subpoena either witnesses or records,

[1]Michael A. BAMBERGER and Nathan LEWIN: "The right to equal treatment: administrative enforcement of anti-discrimination legislation", in *Harvard Law Review,* Vol. 74, No. 3, Jan. 1961, pp. 540-541.

which often impairs the hearing and lessens the effectiveness of the commission.

Proving the existence of discrimination is often difficult. Some states (e.g. Ohio and Rhode Island) empower their commission to take into account "all evidence, statistical or otherwise, which may tend to prove the existence of a predetermined pattern of employment or membership".[1] Normally, commissions place the burden of proof of non-discrimination on the respondent. When discrimination has been found to exist, remedial action is required (compulsory employment or reemployment, upgrading, back pay, restoration of union membership and an order for the respondent to cease and desist discrimination). However, the judgment is not self-enforcing, and since none of the commissions has direct power to impose penalties for violations, they have to seek judicial enforcement.

Results achieved under state legislation

The policy of conciliation and persuasion has been largely successful. The respondent is in a difficult position, inasmuch as the burden of proof of non-discrimination is on him. In addition, staff investigators and those who must recommend public hearings are generally quite thorough and very selective; they seldom recommend cases that are not certain of decision in favour of the complainant. However, as indicated above, the procedure of public hearing is rarely used, conciliation and persuasion being much preferred.

Statistics reflecting the outcome of cases coming before the commissions cannot alone tell the entire story of changing patterns of employment. They do not reveal the extent and nature of job discrimination or how far the influence of the fair employment practices legislation is reaching. Nor do they reveal the pace of compliance. A single complaint, for example, sometimes even one which proves to be without merit, may lead to great improvement in the practice of a particular employer, and possibly of other firms in the same industry or area. Sometimes the hiring or working conditions of thousands of men and women are eventually affected. The progressive attitude towards minority employment that now exists in most of the industrial states is best illustrated by the findings concerning industries that have been investigated by commissions.

In 1952 the New York State Commission Against Discrimination investigated discrimination complaints brought against an aircraft factory in Long Island and noted that the large and diverse population

[1]Ohio Rev. Code Ann. Paras. 4112.05 (E) (p. Supp. 1960); Rhode Island General Laws Ann. para. 28-5-22 (1955).

of the surrounding community was not reflected by the firm's employment practices. Of the company's 11,032 workers only 247 were estimated to be Negroes; none of them, moreover, held a supervisory position and the majority were occupied as assemblers, sweepers and riveters. By 1959, in a follow-up review, it was noted that a substantial change had taken place: between 7 and 8 per cent. of the company's total working force of 14,500 were estimated to be Negroes and they were being hired at all levels and were working in all parts of the company's operations. A similar pattern of progress prevailed in another aviation firm at Deer Park, Long Island, when that company was observed in 1958.

As a result of the commission's investigations, the managements of several chain stores have made significant efforts, with observable results, to encourage more integrated patterns of employment and to increase the opportunities available to minority group employees. In 1957, after a successful complaint had been brought against the local branch of one of the largest chain stores in the United States, the company initiated an appraisal of its personnel policies, which had traditionally placed the Negro in the lower echelons of employment, especially in positions which did not involve direct contact with the public. As a result Negro sales persons are now regularly employed by the company, whereas they were excluded as recently as 1945. A study of 25 major department stores released by the commission in November 1958 indicated the extent of the change in employment. One large department store employing 5,600 persons had more than 200 Negroes working in sales as foremen, supervisors, cashiers, secretaries and clerks, although a report issued by the commission ten years earlier had revealed the presence of only six Negro sales persons in the store.[1]

In Detroit, Michigan, the policy of persuasion has been used with equal effectiveness. Two examples will illustrate the case: (1) It was discovered that in a particular taxicab company in Detroit no Negroes were employed. As a result of one or two cases brought against the company, it agreed to apply a policy of merit employment, and out of a total of 1,200 employees some 300 Negroes were hired. Other taxicab companies followed suit. (2) After conciliation efforts in another case involving an automobile supply company that employed

[1]Statement by Elmer A. Carter, Commissioner and Chairman, New York State Commission Against Discrimination, in *Hearings before the General Subcommittee on Labor of the Committee on Education and Labor*, U.S. House of Representatives, 88th Congress, 1st Session, 1963, pp. 491–494.

no Negroes, the company subsequently opened all its plants in the state of Michigan to Negroes.

The acceptance and workability of state fair employment practices legislation may perhaps be best illustrated by the fact that no such statute has ever been repealed or crippled by amendment. On the contrary, many states have broadened their laws to include such measures as initiatory and enforcement powers in order to strengthen the administrators' ability to eradicate discrimination in employment.

There has been relatively little litigation on the constitutionality of state fair employment practices laws.[1] Only in one instance has it been challenged in the courts since 1945 and that was in 1961 in the state of Michigan; but the state supreme court upheld the statute.[2] In the case of *Colorado Anti-Discrimination Commission v. Continental Airlines*[3], the Colorado court ruled that the Colorado Fair Employment Practices Commission could not regulate hiring practices in inter-state commerce. The United States Supreme Court reversed the decision.[4]

Most of the litigation on fair employment practices legislation has been on procedure, scope and coverage of legislation; that is to say concerning the powers of the administrative agency, sufficient evidence in judgments, conditions of appeal, right of state laws to pre-empt local ordinances, interpretation of "aggrieved person", rights of the courts vis-à-vis findings of the commission, delegation of state powers to the commissions, filing of complaints, parties to hearings, and forms of administrative orders. The experience of all the state and local commissions in administering the anti-discriminatory measures for equal access to employment shows that, in the vast majority of cases, discrimination by employers and unions can be either reduced or eliminated by negotiation and persuasion when there is sufficient backing by firm and explicit policy.

Criticism of State Fair Employment Practices Legislation

Much of the criticism of fair employment practices legislation has been directed at its reliance on the complaints procedure—which is, however, in accordance with a long tradition in the Anglo-American

[1]The main cases are *James* v. *Marinship Corporation* (25 Cal. 2c1721,-19c. para. 62, 475 (1944), and *Railway Mail Association* v. *Corsi*, 326 U.S. 88 (1945).

[2]*City of Highland Park* v. *F.E.P.C.* (1961) 364 Michigan 508, 111 N.W. (2nd) 797.

[3]149 Colorado 259,368 P (2nd) 970 (1962).

[4]372 U.S. 714 (1963).

legal system—and the failure of minority groups to utilise fully the existing legal processes dealing with discrimination, a failure that widens the gap in understanding between the minority community and the administrators and legislators who deal with their problems. In addition, the processing of complaints and the ineffectiveness of the legislation in certain fields have given cause for criticism. Some of the most frequently voiced criticisms are briefly discussed below.

Administration of the Legislation

The question whether the law has been effectively administered is intimately related to the procedure by which the law is enforced. The administrators of fair employment practices laws have chosen to rely on complaints by members of minority groups before they take action to remedy discrimination.

In the initial enactment of the laws most states deemed it sufficient to record the substantive law, which provided a forum where anyone aggrieved by violation could secure redress upon filing a complaint. It was assumed that this procedure would ensure an adequate level of conformity to the legal norms of the community. In many states failure to complain was taken to indicate at least minimal contentment with the existing situation.

Many states now have the power to act (initiatory power) without the formal filing of a complaint. But for various reasons these powers have never been used in some states and only sparingly in others.

Experience has shown that complainants rarely come forward. If a person suspects that he will be discriminated against he will often avoid the potentially embarrassing situation by staying away from where he is not wanted. In this way he permits the discriminatory practice to continue by avoiding the act of discrimination against himself. Often the complainant will not file a claim even when the case is quite blatant. On the other hand the nature of discriminatory practices in some fields is such that the victims are not aware of it; this is the case in the real estate market and in many labour unions.

Observing the prevalence and persistence of discrimination and yet desiring to protect himself from embarrassment, the member of a minority group may well come to believe that the law will not assist him in improving his situation. This belief leads the individual to the inevitable conclusion that equal treatment cannot be secured through legislation and that the demand for it must be pressed through extra-legal activities.

The thesis that minority groups are reluctant to file complaints and the states' hesitancy to use their initiatory powers are extremely significant for they imply that what is merely a procedural point (reliance on complaints) can have the effect of placing a serious limitation on enforcement of the law.

On the other hand, if commissions initiate investigation of discriminatory employment practices without an individual complainant, they face certain difficulties of proof because the substantive statutory provisions are drafted in terms of individual complaints, which require proof that a specific individual has been harmed. When a person complains of discrimination in hiring, for example, the evidence adduced must prove that he was qualified for the job but it was given to someone else, and that the apparent basis for the distinction was the race, religion or national origin of the complainant. But if an agency takes the initiative there is no individual complainant; the evidence adduced will therefore have to show, in some less direct way, that the respondent has engaged in discrimination.

It is also charged that fair employment practices legislation is not as effective as it should be because of the cautiousness of those who administer the laws. The question here is whether the agencies charged with enforcement have construed their powers as broadly as reason permits so as to encompass the full range of discriminatory conduct envisaged by the legislature. All too often, it is argued, the policy statements, state constitutions, statutes, and judicial decisions that condemn discrimination, although broad, are too narrowly interpreted by the administering bodies, with the result that the legislative will is frustrated.

Processing of Complaints

The most frequently voiced criticism of fair employment practices legislation is the length of time it takes for agencies to process complaints.[1] Some state commissions have considered the possibility of asking the legislatures for power to issue interim injunctions so as to preserve the *status quo* pending final solution of complaints. The New Jersey statute implicitly gives the administering agent (the Attorney-General) such authority on the grounds that the disposition of property subject to a proceeding before the Civil Rights Division could frustrate the statutory purpose for which the law was enacted.[2] The

[1]The federal 1964 Civil Rights Act sets a definite period of time for processing claims for voluntary compliance before instituting court action (section 706(*c*), (*d*), (*e*).

[2]See New Jersey Revised Statute 18: 25–26.

California Attorney-General now has the power to seek permanent as well as temporary injunctive relief through the courts.[1]

Ineffectiveness of the laws

There are several areas where state fair employment practices legislation has had no appreciable effect: apprenticeship training programmes, vocational training and state employment services.

Apprenticeship

In the United States there is a direct relationship between discrimination against minority groups and the limited number of skilled craftsmen from these groups in industry. Of all the barriers to training, those restricting entry into apprenticeship programmes seem to have been the most unyielding to minority groups. The resulting lack of apprenticeship opportunity has been the greatest tragedy facing them, for it has severely limited their access to lucrative jobs and opportunities that have long been accessible to the majority.

The hearings before the United States House of Representatives' Subcommittee on Labour in 1962 indicated that the volume of apprenticeship in the United States is insufficient to meet the needs of the economy.[2] Nevertheless, the report filed with the subcommittee by the Department of Labour states that apprenticeship openings are given little publicity, and too frequently Negroes and other minorities know nothing of them.[3]

Much of the ineffectiveness of federally stimulated apprenticeship programmes can be attributed to the absence of clear directives from the federal Government.

Participation in apprenticeship is voluntary and effective training cannot take place without the wholehearted co-operation of the employer, the apprentice and the craftsman who supervises and trains him. The selection of apprentices is the responsibility of the sponsor or sponsors of the programme. Some preference is usually given to

[1]The California legislature did not expressly give the Attorney-General any power with respect to the law against discrimination and it did not establish an administrative agency to implement the law. As a result there was not spelled out direct connection between the effectuation of statutory provisions and the actions of the Attorney-General. The power to seek permanent and interim injunctions had to be decided in the courts.

[2]*Hearings before the Special Subcommittee on Labor of the Committee on Education and Labor,* U.S. House of Representatives, 87th Congress, 2nd Session, Part 2, p. 1031. See, in particular, the report filed by the Assistant Secretary of Labour, Jerry R. Holleman.

[3]*Ibid.*, p. 1035.

persons who have already had the experience in industry, who have some knowledge of the trade or who have a close relative in it. This restricts apprenticeship opportunities.

The U.S. Bureau of Apprenticeship and Training is not a regulatory agency and does not subsidise apprenticeship in any way, but merely provides stimulation and technical assistance for programmes. Standards of apprenticeship programmes are established to meet local needs and registration with the Bureau is purely voluntary. Be this as it may, Presidential Executive Order 10925 took a different view and required the inclusion of a specific non-discrimination statement in all apprenticeship standards for firms handling government contracts. As a result of this action, many crafts included a so-called "equal opportunity clause" in their national standards.

Only two of the states with fair employment practices laws have tackled the question of discrimination in the apprenticeship programmes within their jurisdiction by legislative means. This neglect on the part of the states has been remedied by the adoption by the national legislature of the Civil Rights Act of 1964, which makes it illegal to deny access to "apprenticeship or other training" on "account of race, colour, religion, sex or national origin".[1]

The stand of the federal Government on merit employment and equal opportunity for all is summed up in a statement by President Johnson in his 1965 Manpower Report to the Congress:

> The Civil Rights Act, when fully implemented, should enable Negro workers to compete more effectively for the jobs they are qualified to hold. But no solution, either economic growth or legislative mandate, will be found until better preparation for work is ensured for all Negro workers. The education and the training from which Negroes have been barred for so long are in fact the very channels that have enabled other minorities to enter the main streams of American life.[2]

Vocational Training

The vocational training programme administered by the Department of Health, Education, and Welfare—unlike the apprenticeship programme, which is voluntary and enjoys no government subsidies—is wholly operated and subsidised by the federal Government.

Although a regulation was issued in 1948 stating that there should be no discrimination, the programme as construed and administered

[1]Section 703 (3) (*d*).

[2]*Manpower report of the President, 1965*, p. 23.

by the Department does not preclude the granting of funds to segregated schools. (This point is not dealt with by either state or federal legislation.)

Employment Services

Another area which has resisted the influence of fair employment practices legislation is that of the state employment services, which are a most important avenue of access to industrial jobs. These services were established by the Wagner-Peyser Act of 1933, the principal provisions of which are as follows: (*a*) the federal Government is required to promote and develop a national system of employment offices; (*b*) the Act sets standards and provides for reviews of state plans of operation and statistical research; (*c*) the Act makes provision for the institution and maintenance of an inter-state recruitment programme; (*d*) the Act provides for federal funds, but the services themselves are operated exclusively by the respective state employment agencies. Thus, the states do the actual placement work and provide services to employers and job seekers through approximately 1,900 local offices throughout the country. The agencies, however, are 100 per cent financed by the federal Government. About three-fourths of all hiring in the nation's job market takes place without the use of any employment agency, public or private.

The official policy of the United States Employment Service, as laid down in its policy statements and regulations, is one of non-discrimination and encouragement of employment solely on merit.[1] Further, employees of state employment agencies are prohibited from accepting and filling job offers from the federal Government that are discriminatory.

Notwithstanding this fact, there is no state in which a policy of discrimination in employment is not widespread.[2] This policy is laid down by the employers and acquiesced in, willingly, almost without exception, by the employment agencies, which therefore serve as the protective screen for discriminatory employers. In places like New York employment agencies have worked out elaborate codes to screen job applicants in violation of state fair employment practices laws. Of all the states that have enacted such laws none has *specifically* prohib-

[1] 20 C.F.R. Section 604.8 (1961).

[2] "Even if a federal regulation were to prohibit state employment offices from accepting and filling *all* discriminatory job orders, other extant U.S.E.S. regulations would still invite discrimination in recruitment services." (*Employment*, Report of the United States Commission on Civil Rights, *op cit.*, p. 117.)

ited the employment agencies from engaging in discriminatory practices.[1] However, since discrimination itself is illegal, it is implied that all discriminatory practices by state employment agencies are also illegal. Nevertheless, even in such communities as New York, Illinois, Michigan and California, efforts to break through the discriminatory practices of state employment agencies have not been altogether successful.

> In Michigan the Fair Employment Practice Commission (F.E.P.C.) has asked the state employment offices to refer to it discriminatory job placement orders which violate state law. They have refused to do so. In Baltimore there is an Equal Employment Opportunities Commission (E.E.O.C.), whose job is substantially similar to Michigan's F.E.P.C. As in the case of Michigan, E.E.O.C. has asked the employment service to inform it of discriminatory job orders and the employment service has refused.[2]

Under the new Civil Rights Act of 1964, such practices have been declared illegal. Section 703 (*f*) of the Act declares that—

> . . . it shall be an unlawful employment practice for any employment agency to fail or refuse to refer to employment, or otherwise to discriminate against, any individual because of his race, colour, religion, sex, or national origin.

However, it would seem that the provision is too general and does not fully cover state employment offices. Further, there is no machinery established whereby discriminatory practices by employment services are reported to the proper enforcement agency. It is the responsibility of the person discriminated against to file the complaint. Such a method is unrealistic, for the individual has no idea whether a discriminatory job order has in fact been filed.

Congress and Fair Employment Practices Legislation

Congressional enactment of such legislation is the direct result of manifestation against economic and social injustice; mass demonstrations and protests and an increasingly aroused public conscience forced the State to intervene to correct the worst of these injustices. The history of efforts to secure fair employment practices legislation has established the fact that it is "both a result of social forces and an

[1]Paul H. Norgren and Samuel E. Hill: *Toward fair employment* (New York and London, Columbia University Press, 1964), pp. 35–39 and 130–136.

[2]*Employment, op. cit.*, p. 117.

instrument of social control".[1] Congress, however, was slow to perceive its role despite the fact that as early as the first decade of the twentieth century two eminent American jurists, John Chipman Gray and Oliver Wendell Holmes, saw clearly that economics and business interests are both makers and products of the law. Legislation is a means of effecting social change, though society changes more rapidly than the law evolves.

> As modern social conditions demand more and more active control, the State extends its purpose. Consequently custom recedes before deliberately made law, mainly statute and decree. At the same time, law emanating from central authority as often moulds social habits as it is moulded itself.[2]

The first sign that Congress was slowly moving towards reflecting accurately the national mood was in its enunciation in the Unemployment Relief Act of 1933 of the principle that in the employment of citizens there should be no discrimination according to race, colour or creed. Subsequent provisions incorporating this principle were included in Relief Acts from 1937 to 1943. The enabling legislation for the Civilian Conservation Corps of 1937, as well as the various Acts providing appropriations for the National Youth Administration, contained similar provisions. However, the fact that minority rights are incorporated in legislative Acts and written constitutions does not mean that they are inviolable—a fact that the Congress was slow to heed.

The first *specific* legislation proposed in the Congress for the express purpose of eradicating discrimination in employment was introduced in 1942. Since that time and until the enactment of the Civil Rights Act in 1964, more than 100 Bills and resolutions were introduced; only one of these (a Bill) passed the House of Representatives, and none the Senate.

It had been apparent, and was explicitly stated, in 1946 that fair employment practices legislation was desperately needed if minority groups were to keep the gains they had made during the Second World War[3]; and in 1947 the President's Committee on Civil Rights recommended "the enactment of a federal Fair Employment Practice Act prohibiting all forms of discrimination in private employment, based on race, colour, creed, or national origin".[4] However, it was not

[1] W. FRIEDMANN: Legal theory (London, Stevens & Sons, 1944), p. 186.

[2] W. FRIEDMANN, *op. cit.*, p. 183.

[3] "The future status of minority group workers depends, the Committee believes, on the course of action to be taken by the Congress relative to the passage of federal fair employment legislation." (*Final report of the Fair Employment Practice Committee, op. cit.*, p. 5.)

[4] *To secure these rights, op. cit.*, p. 167.

until 1964 that the concept of employment based on merit alone without regard to race, colour, sex, religion or national origin finally found its way into the mainstream of the American legislative process.

The Civil Rights Act of 1964

The enactment of the Civil Rights Act of 1964[1], in general terms, was based on the realisation that continued discrimination in employment:
(*a*) is a violation of basic individual rights;
(*b*) interferes with the effective utilisation of a nation's manpower resources.
It was a recognition that discrimination in employment is one of the most pressing problems affecting the American social scene.[2] The Act provides, in a real sense, "both protection of existing rights and means for creating new rights or altering old ones when required by new circumstances".[3] The Congress, in its enactment, considered law as a desirable tool for eradicating discrimination, and that it could be effective once the community had reached the realisation of the depth of its discrimination policies.

In short, what the Act did was to note changes in the United States social institutions. "As a society grows and changes, its laws must grow and change."[4] It had become clear from a number of cases handed down by the Supreme Court on the illegality of unequal treatment that the national legislature could not remain indifferent indefinitely.[5] The organic nature of American law permitted such a change.

[1]Title VII.

[2]"Of those forms of discrimination which are the target of this Act, discrimination in employment is the most widespread and undoubtedly the most harmful to its victims and to the nation as a whole. Denial to Negroes and all members of other minority groups of the right to be gainfully employed shuts off to them nearly all prospects of economic advancement." (Richard K. BERG: "Equal employment opportunity under the Civil Rights Act of 1964", in *Brooklyn Law Review*, Dec. 1964, p. 62.)

[3]Whitney N. SEYMOUR and Norman S. MARSH: "The evolving concept of the rule of law—an American view", in *Journal of the International Commission of Jurists*, IV, Summer 1963, p. 273.

[4]*Ibid.*

[5]*United States* v. *Darby*, 312 U.S. 100 (1941); *National Labor Relations Board* v. *Jones and Laughlin Steel Corp.*, 301 U.S. 1 (1937); *Steele v. Louisville and Nashville R.Co.*, 323 U.S. 192 (1944); *Tunstall* v. *Brotherhood of Locomotive Firemen and Enginemen*, 323 U.S. 210 (1944); *Graham* v. *Brotherhood*, 338 U.S. 239 (1949); *Brotherhood of Railway Trainmen* v. *Howard*, 343 U.S. 763 (1952); *Syres* v. *Oil Workers International Union*, 350 U.S. 892 (1955), reversing *per curiam*, 223 F. 2d 739 (5 Cir.).

The legal justification of the Congress to consider freedom from racial discrimination in employment lay in the United States Constitution's provisions of "due process", and the commerce clause.

Due Process[1]

Concerning "due process", the United States Supreme Court had stated in *Railway Mail Association* v. *Corsi*[2] that fair employment legislation did not deprive the employer of his property without due process and did not deprive him of equal protection of the law. In this case, the Supreme Court entertained an argument by a labour union that admitted only Caucasians and native American Indians to its membership to the effect that the New York State legislation prohibiting discrimination according to race interfered with its right to select its members and abridged its property rights and freedom of contract. The Court was unanimous in its ruling that the New York statute was constitutional. It stated that it would be a distortion of policy manifested in the Fourteenth Amendment if the Court determined "that such legislation violated the Fourteenth Amendment". It further stated that the amendment "was adopted to prevent state legislation designed to perpetuate discrimination on the basis of race or colour".[3] Justice Frankfurter in a concurring opinion went further:

> The Railway Mail Association is a union of railway clerks. To operate as a union in New York it must obey the New York Civil Rights Law. That law prohibits such an organisation from denying membership in the union by reason of race, colour or creed, with all the economic consequences that such denial entails. Apart from other objections, which are too unsubstantial to require consideration, it is urged that the due process clause of the Fourteenth Amendment precludes the state of New York from prohibiting racial and religious discrimination against those seeking employment. Elaborately to argue against this contention is to dignify a claim devoid of constitutional substance. Of course a state may leave abstention from such discrimination to the conscience of individuals. On the other hand, a state may choose to put its authority behind one of the cherished aims of American feeling by forbidding indulgence in racial or religious prejudice to

[1]"Due Process" is a doctrine of justice explicitly set forth in the Fourteenth Amendment to the United States Constitution, which provides that no state shall "deprive any person of life, liberty, or property without due process of law; nor deny to any person within its jurisdiction the equal protection of the laws".

[2]326 U.S. 88 (1945).

[3]326 U.S. 88 (1945), pp. 93–94.

> another's hurt. To use the Fourteenth Amendment as a sword against such state power would stultify that amendment. Certainly the insistence by individuals on their private prejudices as to race, colour or creed, in relations like those now before us, ought not to have a higher constitutional sanction than the determination of a state to extend the area of non-discrimination beyond that which the Constitution itself exacts.[1]

What the Court ruled was that the "due process" clause in the Constitution was a doctrine of "basic justice and fairness"[2] irrespective of race, colour, creed or religion.

The Commerce Clause

Title VII of the 1964 Civil Rights Act is even more reliant upon the commerce clause—or the right of the Congress to regulate interstate commerce. The legislative history of this clause shows that the Congress has enacted many laws which affect, or interfere with, the freedom of an employer to contract with an employee.

In 1938 Congress enacted the Fair Labour Standards Act, which required employers to pay minimum wages for a maximum number of hours, with increased compensation for overtime, and to keep such records of wages and hours as were prescribed by administrative regulation or order. Violators of this law were to be punished by fine and imprisonment. A case[3] was brought before the Supreme Court that same year appealing from a judgment of a lower court which voided an employer's indictment under the Act. The Supreme Court reversed the judgment of the lower court, stating that the fixing of a minimum wage is within the competence and legislative power of the Congress; it was wholly within the power of the Congress to fix maximum hours of employment and a statute was not objectionable because the hours and wages it prescribed were applicable equally to men and women. Congress, declared the Court, may require an employer, as a means of enforcement of a valid statute, to keep records showing whether he has complied with it. This Act *was within the commerce power of the Congress,* the Court decreed.

Another celebrated case contesting the power of Congress to act under the commerce clause was *National Labour Relations Board* v. *Jones and Laughlin Steel Corporation.*[4] The National Labour Relations Act of 1935, *inter alia,* made it an unfair labour practice for an

[1] *Ibid.*, pp. 97–98.
[2] Seymour and Marsh, *loc. cit.*, p. 273.
[3] *United States* v. *Darby*, 312 U.S. 100 (1944).
[4] 301 U.S. 1 (1937).

employer to discriminate against an employee in hiring or terms of employment because of his membership in a union. The Court held that prohibition of this kind of discrimination in employment was within the power of Congress under the commerce clause.

The Supreme Court has consistently upheld national legislation forbidding discriminatory practices; the constitutionality of the Railway Labour Act was upheld in *Steele* v. *Louisville and Nashville Railway Co.*[1], *Tunstall* v. *Brotherhood of Locomotive Firemen and Enginemen*[2], *Graham* v. *Brotherhood*[3], *and Brotherhood of Railway Trainmen* v. *Howard.*[4]

The Court was not hesitant to declare that provisions of the National Labour Relations Act regarding the exercise of a union's bargaining power without discrimination according to race are mandatory.[5]

These cases leave no doubt that the Congress had the power to require non-discriminatory practices in employment through the commerce clause.

When the President's Committee on Civil Rights made its report in 1947, the authority of the Congress vis-à-vis the commerce clause was not neglected.

> Congress has exercised its broad power to regulate inter-state commerce, derived from article I, section 8 of the Constitution, to institute reforms in many fields. Outstanding examples are the Fair Labour Standards Act, which fixes maximum hours and minimum wages in work relating to inter-state commerce, the National Labour Relations Act, which regulates labour-management relations affecting interstate commerce, and the Federal Safety Appliance Act, which specifies safety standards for inter-state transportation. *The commerce power could be the basis for fair employment legislation relating to activities affecting inter-state commerce, and for laws prohibiting discriminatory practices by inter-state carriers.*[6]

An Analysis of Title VII of the Civil Rights Act

Title VII of the Civil Rights Act of 1964 concerns equal employment opportunity without respect to race, colour, religion, sex or

[1] 323 U.S. 192 (1944), discussed below.

[2] 323 U.S. 210 (1944).

[3] 338 U.S. 232 (1949).

[4] 343 U.S. 763 (1951). This case is quite similar to *Steele* v. *Louisville and Nashville Railway Co.*

[5] 350 U.S. 892 (1955) reversing *per curiam,* 223 F. 2d 739 (5 Cir.).

[6] *To secure these rights, op. cit.*, p. 108. Emphasis added.

national origin in matters of hiring, firing, wages, promotions, working conditions, etc. Its coverage is broad and is applicable to all the states, territories and possessions of the United States where business and labour unions are engaged in inter-state commerce.[1]

The only exemptions in the Act are those given: (1) to employers with respect to the employment of aliens in their offices abroad; (2) to religious institutions with respect to employment of persons of a particular religion for work connected with their religious activities; and (3) to educational institutions, which are exempt from all the provisions of the Act with respect to employment connected with their educational activities.

Among the important prohibitions of the Act are the following:

(1) It is an unlawful employment practice for an employment agency to classify an individual, or to fail or refuse to refer him for employment, or to refer him for employment, or otherwise to discriminate against him on the basis of race, colour, religion, sex, or national origin.

(2) It is an unlawful employment practice for a labour organisation to exclude a person from its membership, or to discriminate among its members in any way, or to attempt to persuade an employer to discriminate, on the basis of race, colour, religion, sex or national origin.

(3) Discrimination on the ground of race, colour, religion, sex or national origin in admission to or employment in any apprenticeship or other training programme, including on-the-job training, is prohibited.

(4) Recriminations for opposing unfair employment practices or for instigating or testifying in any proceeding brought under the title are prohibited.[2]

On the other hand the Act provides that it is *not* unlawful employment practice—

(*a*) to employ an individual on the basis of his religion, sex or national origin when one of those is a bona fide occupational

[1]The phrase used in the Act is "industry affecting commerce", which is defined as any activity, business or industry in commerce or in which a labour dispute would hinder or obstruct commerce or the free flow of commerce. "Commerce" means trade, traffic, transportation or communication between a state and any place outside thereof. Cf. National Labour Relations Act, 29 USC 152(7); Labour-Management Reporting and Disclosure Act of 1959, 29 USC 402(*c*); *National Labor Relations Board* v. *Reliance Fuel Corp.* 371 U.S. 224, 226 (1963); and *Polish National Alliance* v. *NLRB* 322 U.S. 643, 647 (1944).

[2]See *NLRB* v. *Fansteel Corp.,* 306 U.S. 240 (1939); and *NLRB* v. *Electrical Workers,* 346 U.S. 463 (1933).

qualification reasonably necessary to the normal operation of a particular establishment;

(*b*) for an educational institution owned, supported, controlled or managed by a religious organisation, or one whose curriculum is directed toward the propagation of a particular religion, to hire and employ persons of that religion in any of its activities;

(*c*) to apply different conditions of employment, including compensation, based on a bona fide seniority or merit system, a piece-work system, or job location system, so long as the differences do not result from an intention to discriminate because of race, colour, religion, sex or national origin;

(*d*) to act upon the results of a professionally developed ability test so long as the test is not designed to discriminate because of race, colour, religion, sex or national origin.

Moreover, no action taken against a member of the Communist Party of the United States or any other organisation required by a final order of the Subversive Activities Control Board to register as a Communist-action or Communist-front organisation shall be an unfair employment practice.

The Act permits preferential treatment to be given to Indians living on or near a reservation in businesses conducted on or near a reservation.

Finally it is provided that Title VII is not to be interpreted to require anyone to give preferential treatment to any individual or group because of race, colour, religion, sex or national origin, or to correct a racial, or religious, etc., imbalance between the number of persons of a particular race, etc., employed in a particular establishment and the total number of persons of that race, etc., living in the particular community, state or area.

Equal Employment Opportunity Commission

In the hearings of the House of Representatives Subcommittee on Labour much emphasis was given to the organisation, functions and effectiveness of the fair employment practices commissions of the various states having fair employment practices legislation. Not surprisingly the Congress in enacting the 1964 Civil Rights Act patterned the federal Equal Employment Opportunity Commission along the lines of the state commissions.

The federal Act establishes an Equal Employment Opportunity Commission composed of five members drawn from the two major political parties of the United States and appointed by the President, with the advice and consent of the Senate, for staggered five-year terms. The President designates the chairman and vice-chairman. The commission is given power to co-operate with public or private state and local agencies and, with their permission, to use their services; to pay witness fees; to furnish technical assistance to help those covered by the title to comply with it; at the request of an employer or labour organisation, to attempt to effectuate the provisions of the title by conciliation or other remedial action when employees or union members have refused to co-operate; to make and publish appropriate technical studies; and to refer matters to the Attorney-General with recommendations to bring suit or intervene (sections 706 and 707). The commission's attorneys (like those of the state commissions) may represent it in court cases.

As in the case of the state fair employment practices legislation, the law is enforced through administrative procedures; in other words, the federal Government will rely heavily upon the complaint procedure. Under the federal Act an aggrieved individual, or a member of the commission who has reason to believe there has been an unfair employment practice, may file a written complaint with the commission. If, upon investigation, the latter finds reason to believe the charge to be true, it must attempt to eliminate it by conference, conciliation and persuasion. No part of such efforts is to be made public without the consent of the parties, and any commission employee who violates this provision is subject to a fine of not more than $1,000 and imprisonment for not more than a year.

When a violation of the law occurs in a state which prohibits the practice, an aggrieved person must wait 60 days (120 days during the first year after enactment of a state law) after notifying the appropriate state or local agency, unless state proceedings are terminated earlier, before filing a charge with the Equal Employment Opportunity Commission. Sending a written statement of the facts by registered mail is sufficient notice, regardless of any other requirement of state law.

When a commissioner files a charge with respect to a violation occurring in a state which prohibits the practice, the commission, before taking further action, must notify the appropriate state or local agency and give it reasonable time (but not less than 120 days during the first year after enactment of the state law or 60 days thereafter unless the state requests less) to act under their law.

With respect to violations occurring in states which have no laws prohibiting the practices concerned, aggrieved persons must file charges with the commission no later than 90 days after the date of the violation. In states with laws prohibiting these practices, aggrieved persons must file charges with the commission not later than 210 days after the violation occurred or 30 days after receiving notice that state proceedings have been terminated, whichever is earlier. The commission must notify the appropriate state agency of the charge.

If the commission has failed to eliminate an unfair employment practice within 30 days after a charge is filed or within 30 days after expiration of any period of reference to a state agency (but the period may be extended to 60 days if the commission determines that further efforts to secure voluntary compliance are warranted), it must so notify the aggrieved party who may, within 30 days thereafter, file a civil action for appropriate relief. Upon application, the court may waive payment of costs, fees and security, and may appoint an attorney for the complainant. In its discretion, it may permit the Attorney-General to intervene upon timely application if he certifies that the case is of general public importance. Upon application, the court, in its discretion, may also stay further proceedings for not more than 60 days pending termination of state proceedings or efforts on the part of the commission to secure voluntary compliance.

If the court finds that a defendant has "intentionally engaged in an unlawful employment practice", it may not only enjoin such practice but may issue appropriate affirmative orders including reinstatement or hiring, with or without back pay; but no such order is to be issued if the adverse action against the complainant was taken with any intent other than discrimination on account of race, colour, religion, sex or national origin, or recrimination for having participated in efforts to enforce Title VII of the Act.

The commission may commence proceedings to compel compliance with any court order that an employer, labour organisation or employment agency has refused to obey.

Investigation and Records

The Attorney-General may bring a civil action if he has reasonable cause to believe that any person or group is engaged in a pattern or practice of resistance to the rights outlined in Title VII if the intent is to deny full exercise of those rights. He may also request that the action be heard by a three-judge court from which an appeal will lie directly to the Supreme Court. If the Attorney-General makes no such request, the Chief Judge of the District is to assign the case immediately to one of the District Judges who is to conduct the hearing and determination of the case.

The Congress, taking cognisance of the structure and intent of the existing legislation against discrimination in employment in the several states, made provision that nothing in the federal Act is to interfere with the operation of any state law. The Act does, however, permit interference should there be a state law which permits an unlawful employment practice (section 708).

If there is evidence of discrimination in connection with the filing of charges, the commission or its agents have the right to examine and copy any evidence relating thereto (section 709). Several of the states with fair employment practices legislation have enjoined their local fair employment practices agencies from engaging in discriminatory practices in matters of employment.

The Act requires employers, employment agencies and labour organisations to keep relevant records and make such reports from them as the commission may prescribe by appropriate regulation or order, after a public hearing. Those in control of covered apprenticeship or other training programmes are required to keep appropriate records, including a list of applicants and the order in which they applied, and to furnish a detailed description of the methods of selecting trainees or apprentices. Such records need not be kept by those who are covered by a state or local fair employment law unless the commission finds that certain records are necessary because of differences in coverage or methods of enforcement between the state or local and federal laws.

The commission has the authority to examine witnesses under oath and to require the production of documentary evidence relevant to investigation of any charge.

When a defendant or witness refuses to testify or comply with a demand for production of evidence, the commission may seek and the courts may issue appropriate orders requiring compliance, but the attendance of a witness may not be required outside the state in which he is found, resides or transacts business, and the production of documentary evidence may not be required outside the state where such evidence is kept.

Within 21 days of a demand by the commission to produce, or permit copying of, documentary evidence, a person may petition a court to modify or set aside the demand.

The Act further requires employers, employment agencies and labour organisations to post on employee and applicant bulletin boards notices approved or prepared by the commission containing excerpts from or summaries of pertinent provisions of the title. Wilful violations are punishable by a fine of not more than $100 for each separate offence (section 711).

It is to be pointed out that the Bill originally presented by the administration has no provisions regarding private employment or labour organisations. It simply gave the President's Committee on

Equal Employment Opportunity, established in 1961 under Executive Order 10925 with responsibility for carrying out the Government's programme of non-discrimination, statutory authority to deal with discrimination in federal employment and under federal and federally assisted contracts and subcontracts. It was the House Committee on the Judiciary which added provisions prohibiting discrimination by private employers, employment agencies and labour organisations, establishing the Equal Employment Opportunity Commission and permitting the commission itself to initiate court action to enforce the prohibitions of the title.

The Senate's amendments, on the other hand, had the main effect of emphasising local enforcement and voluntary compliance. Under the House Bill, an aggrieved individual could file a charge with the commission immediately. It was the Senate that added the provision requiring a person to wait 60 days after notifying the appropriate state or local agency, if the violation occurred in a state with a fair employment law, before filing a charge with the commission, and therafter at least 30 days for the commission to try to obtain voluntary compliance before bringing a court action. Even after an individual has filed an action, it will be remembered, the court may stay proceedings for as long as 60 days pending termination of state or local proceedings or efforts of the commission to obtain voluntary compliance.

Of increasing interest as the administration of the law develops will be the relations between the commission established under it and the President's Committee on Equal Employment Opportunity, which will continue to carry out the Government's programme of non-discrimination in government employment and in employment by government contractors. The powers of the President's committee to deal with discrimination (the power to cancel contracts) and its investigatory powers are far broader than those given to the commission. However, in some respects the commission possesses power superior to the President's committee. The latter has no direct authority over labour unions, for example, while the commission's jurisdiction extends to a very wide class of employers who in the main are untouched by any executive order. Not to be forgotten is that the President's committee has no statutory basis and has to rely on voluntary compliance.

The Supreme Court and Equal Job Opportunity

A major role of the Supreme Court in upholding anti-discriminatory legislation has already been cited above. Here a brief review will be made of the Court's role in ruling against discrimination designed to deprive citizens of economic livelihood, which has been consistent since the last century.[1]

As early as 1886, in *Yick Wo* v. *Hopkins*[2], the Court ruled that city ordinances (City of San Francisco) designed to prevent employment for arbitrary reasons were null and void.

> For the cases present the ordinances in actual operation, and the facts shown, establish an administration directed so exclusively against a particular class of persons [Chinese] as to warrant and require the conclusion that, whatever may have been the intent of the ordinances as adopted, they are applied by the public authorities charged with their administration, and thus representing the state itself, with a mind so unequal and oppressive as to amount to a practical denial by the state of that equal protection of the laws [secured] by the broad and benign provisions of the Fourteenth Amendment of the Constitution of the U.S.

This policy was re-enunciated in *New Negro Alliance* v. *Grocery Co.*[3] when the Court upheld paragraph 13 of the Norris-La Guardia Act providing for fair and equitable conditions of employment irrespective of race, colour, or persuasion. Perhaps the Court reached its zenith in a number of rulings handed down between 1944 and 1951[4] in which, whether against unions or management, it upheld equality of treatment.

In a concurring opinion in *Steele* v. *L and N.R. Company*, Mr. Justice Murphy stated:

> The Constitution voices its disapproval whenever economic discrimination is applied under authority of law against any race, creed or colour. . . . Racism is far too virulent today to permit the slightest refusal, in the light of a Constitution that abhors it, to expose and condemn it whenever it appears in the course of statutory interpretation.

The *Railway Mail Association* v. *Corsi,* as cited above, established the primacy of the Fourteenth Amendment in ensuring equality in employment as forcefully as the *Steele* case.

[1]This notwithstanding the fact that the Supreme Court declared null and void the Civil Rights Act of 1875 (18 Stat. 335); 109 U.S. 3 (1883).

[2]118 U.S. 356 (1886).

[3]303 U.S. 552 (1938).

[4]*Steele* v. *L and N.R. Company,* 323 U.S. 192 (1944), discussed above; *Railway Mail Association* v. *Corsi,* 326 U.S. 88 (1945), discussed above; *Takahashi* v. *Fish and Game Commission,* 334 U.S. 410 (1948); *Hughes* v. *Superior Court of California,* 339 U.S. 460 (1950); and *Railroad Trainmen* v. *Howard,* 343 U.S. 768 (1951).

A case of a different nature, but no less important, concerned the right of the state of California, under the federal Constitution and laws pursuant to it, to use racial ineligibility for citizenship as a basis for barring a person from earning his livelihood.[1] The Court was sweeping in its judgment:

> The Fourteenth Amendment and the laws adopted under its authority thus embody a general policy that all persons lawfully in this country shall abide in any state on an equality of legal privileges with all citizens under non-discriminatory laws.

Justices Murphy and Rutledge, concurring, stated: "Even the most cursory examination of the background of the statute demonstrates that it was designed solely to discrimination against such persons in a manner inconsistent with the concept of equal protection of the laws. Legislation of that type is not entitled to wear the cloak of constitutionality."

Of late in the United States, much has been said about "reverse discrimination". Such a concept is not new to the Court. In 1950[2] the Supreme Court affirmed that picketing was illegal when used to coerce employment on the basis of race. The Court declared: "We cannot construe the Due Process Clause as precluding California from securing respect for its policy against involuntary employment on racial lines by prohibiting systematic picketing that would subvert such policy." What was at stake was the petitioners' demand for proportional employment, i.e. a demand that a place of business should hire its employees in proportion to the racial origin of its customers. It was the judgment of the Court that an employer need adopt such a policy at his discretion only.

The National Labor Relations Board and Non-Discrimination

In conclusion a brief word must be said concerning the authority of the National Labour Relations Board and non-discrimination. Under the statutory powers given to the board, the specific authority to prevent racial discrimination was not made clear and unions are not specifically denied the right to discriminate in membership on racial grounds. The board does, however, have the power to revoke certification of a union for violating its duty of fair representation and to enforce the union security and unfair labour practices provisions of

[1] *Takahashi* v. *Fish and Game Commission,* 334 U.S. 410 (1948).
[2] *Hughes* v. *Superior Court of California,* 339 U.S. 460.

the National Labour Relations Act. This authority was only used once, in 1964.[1]

The result of the board's cautiousness is that it has been more reluctant than the Supreme Court to take specific action against discrimination on racial grounds. Nevertheless, it would be unfair to say that over the years it did not move steadily towards the inevitable action it eventually took in the *Hughes Tool* case. As far back as 1945 there were hints at its power to strike out against racial discrimination in union practices.[2]

Conclusion

Although the fair employment practice legislation of the several states, the Civil Rights Act of 1964, decisions of the Supreme Court and the rulings of the National Labour Relations Board form an impressive array of measures to combat discrimination in employment in the United States, such discrimination is nevertheless widespread and will continue to be for a long time to come. What is important is the emphatic resolve at all levels of society to eradicate economic discrimination as a source of unequal treatment leading to other forms of discrimination. An indication of the legislative resolve is that in the last four years the United States Congress has enacted more legislation aimed directly at inequities in employment than it did from 1919 to 1961.

The adoption of a public policy and the enactment of legislation to eliminate discrimination in employment is a relatively recent development—scarcely 25 years old—and the process of educating the public to accept the proposition that employment and promotion should be based exclusively on merit has been slow and often painful. The legislation has sometimes been weak and the administrators have not all been zealous in administering the policy. But irrespective of these shortcomings, fair employment practices legislation has been successful in breaking through the legal and social barriers with which minority groups had to cope, and has now been accepted as an important and necessary manifestation of the prevailing moral sentiment of the community.

The experience of the several states with fair employment prac-

[1]In the *Hughes Tool* case (104 N.L.R.B., No. 33).

[2]Cf. *Larus Brothers* (1945), 62 N.L.R.B., 1075; *Pioneer Bus Company, Inc.* (1962), 140 N.L.R.B., 54; *Independent Metal Workers Union, Local 1* (1964), 147 N.L.R.B., No. 166; *Boyce Machinery Corporation* (1963), 141 N.L.R.B., 756; *Sewell Manufacturing Co.* (1962), 140 N.L.R.B., 220; *Allen-Morgan Sign* (1962), 138 N.L.R.B., 73; *Associated Grocers of Port Arthur, Inc.* (1961), 134 N.L.R.B., 468.

tices legislation and the recent adoption by the Congress of the Civil Rights Act (Title VII) illustrates the heavy reliance placed in the United States on the tools of conciliation and persuasion backed up by the ultimate sanction of legal enforcement. Throughout the history of this legislation the means to this end was the maximum utilisation of administrative enforcement rather than the application of legal sanctions. The experiment has shown that the most substantial progress in combating organised discrimination was made in states with enforceable laws, and that discrimination is considerably less in those states now than it was before the passage of the laws. The inclusion in the federal legislation of the type of administrative machinery long existent in the states demonstrates conclusively that until some other method has been devised, administrative enforcement of the law by fair employment practices commissions is the most effective manner of ensuring the oppressed minorities equal treatment when discrimination in employment has occurred.

The method most consistently used by the administrators has been that of voluntary compliance with the non-discrimination policy. Although under many of the state laws recourse has been had to measures of compulsion in order to stimulate voluntary compliance, there is no evidence that a purely compulsory non-discrimination programme is more successful than a voluntary programme backed up by the ultimate threat of sanctions. On the contrary, the results of the use of education, persuasion and conciliation are impressive. Substantial gains in employment on an egalitarian basis have been made with firms holding government contracts, amounting to billions of dollars annually and affecting millions of employees either directly or indirectly; and although the various government committees on contracts have at times had to employ the threat of sanctions and of contract cancellation with recalcitrant contractors, the emphasis is on voluntary compliance. This has also had the effect of influencing areas that are beyond the reach of the law.

Of importance in employers' attitudes towards equal job opportunity has been the pressure from certain segments of the public, especially the vigilant civil rights organisations whose militancy relieved the employers from certain social pressures that perpetuated job discrimination. A particularly effective tool used by these organisations has been the economic boycott. Everything indicates that this instrument of pressure will continue to be applied to employers until job discrimination and inequities in employment have been completely eliminated from the public sphere. However, in spite of the vast array of legislation on the books, a determined employer may still find ways to refuse employment on merit. The legislation as now enacted is far too loose to prohibit every degree of discrimination and it is doubtful if any legislation can be devised that is absolutely foolproof. Nevertheless, the enactment of legislation, especially of the Civil Rights Act of 1964, is necessary if for no other reason than to create an affirmative environment for minorities. This should not mean either preferential treatment or the use of quota systems for the disadvantaged groups; such is prohibited by legislation in practically all the states. Nevertheless, the administration of the laws by the various fair employment practices commissions and by the President's Committee on Equal Employment Opportunity certainly implies adoption of quota systems and preferential treatment. Decisions by the National Labour Relations Board also lend themselves to such an interpretation. The 1964 Act is not clear as to the legality of these practices, but consistency would surely dictate that discrimination against the majority of the population would be quite illegal. Although preferential treatment for the minorities should not be practised to the detriment of others, this is not to say that special measures to ensure equal employment opportunity are not desirable. Such measures do not in any way imply discrimination against any segment of the population, whereas preferential treatment would mean employment of minorities irrespective of qualifications. They would include the improvement of the quality of education, an active manpower policy providing better job training, improved counselling and information as to the availability of jobs, co-ordination of anti-discrimination and manpower policies to assist minority groups to equip themselves better to compete in the open employment market.

The enactment of fair employment practices legislation has also had a salutary effect on the practices of labour unions in the United States. Throughout the history of the labour movement, discrimination has been widespread, especially in the craft unions. Legislation has assisted the more liberal union leaders to change formal discriminatory practices and open up job opportunities by removing the restrictions on union membership and apprenticeship training. Many unions have now given high priority to minority group demands as a result of these pressures. Effective administration of state and federal fair employment practices legislation will further erode the nepotic practices still existing in many trade unions.

Although the key is enforcement, much of the effectiveness of fair employment practices commissions has been due to their public image: that of service agencies dedicated to conciliation and persuasion and not that of police agencies. It is important for students of fair employment practices legislation to understand that, where there is a pattern of non-enforcement of the laws, this is intimately related to two intertwined concepts of American law. These concepts involve the difference between public interest and private rights, and the distinction between enforcement and education. A cardinal feature of the legislation is to prohibit employers and unions from discriminating in their commercial affairs as long as these ventures are in the public domain, and yet to preserve their constitutional prerogatives.

Twenty Years of State Fair Employment Practices Commissions: A Critical Analysis with Recommendations*

Herbert Hill

[From the Buffalo Law Review, *Fall 1964 by permission.]*

III. The Operational Approach of State Antidiscrimination Commissions

Twenty-five states now have fair employment practices commissions in operation. Their domain covers 41 per cent of the Negro population in the United States. Provisions in state fair employment practice laws make it unlawful to refuse to hire, employ, bar, discharge or promote individuals because of race, creed, color or national origin. The provisions cover labor unions and employment agencies as well as employers. The commissions have the power to receive, investigate and pass upon complaints which allege the existence of unlawful racial practices. They are empowered to hold hearings and compel attendance, secure enforcement of subpoena and production of records, and to gain and enforce such power through the state courts.

The enforceable state statutes have the following provisions in common according to Konvitz and Leskes:

> they declare discrimination in public and private employment on racial, religious, or ethnic grounds to be illegal; they authorize a state administrative agency to receive and investigate complaints; they empower the agency to eliminate, by persuasion and media-

*For an expansion of the material contained in this essay, see also: Herbert Hill, "The Role of Law in Securing Equal Employment Opportunity: Legal Powers and Social Change," *Boston College Industrial and Commercial Law Review*, 7 (Spring, 1966), pp. 625-652; and, Testimony of Herbert Hill, Labor Secretary NAACP, before the New York City Commission on Human Rights, Construction Trades Hearings, New York, September 26, 1966.

tion, any discrimination found to exist; if unsuccessful in such efforts, the agency is authorized to proceed by public hearings, findings of fact and law, and cease and desist orders, which are enforceable by court decree; judicial review is available to a person claiming to be aggrieved by an agency ruling; and finally, the state agency is responsible for an educational program intended to reduce and eliminate discrimination and prejudice."[1]

On the face of it, the powers enumerated above seem to indicate that FEPC is a worthwhile mechanism for eliminating job discrimination. Early studies of the state FEP commissions, however, reveal that from their very inception, they were ineffectual agents of social change. Berger's study of the New York State Commission Against Discrimination,[2] the first state FEP agency (it became effective on July 1, 1945) revealed that in its first 18 months the Commission found insufficient evidence to uphold 57 per cent of the complaints filed. In 1947, SCAD found no evidence of discriminatory practice in 62 per cent of cases filed, in 1948 in 72 per cent, in 1949 in 63 per cent and in 1950 in 68 per cent. "The Commission itself," Berger wrote, "does not present the data in precisely this way and has not commented on the large proportion of complaints (65 percent) in which it found insufficient evidence to support the specific charge of discrimination, and the small proportion of cases (25 percent) in which it did sustain the complainants's claim."[3]

Berger pointed out that SCAD's disposition of complaint cases was not likely to encourage other workers to file complaints. Regardless of whether or not SCAD was able to rule in any other way than against the 65 per cent of complainants who charged discrimination, "when two out of three complainants find their charges not sustained . . . it is probable that few workers come away from an experience with SCAD in a mood to recommend the same procedure to their friends among minority groups."[4]

Moreover, the length of time it takes to settle a case is a discouraging factor to potential complainants. To the end of 1947, the average time required to dispose of a case was three months. Berger states that, "This is obviously too long a period to be effective for a worker who has experienced discrimination, since it is not likely that he can afford to remain unemployed for more than a few weeks while his

[1]Konvitz and Leskes, A Century of Civil Rights 203 (1961).
[2]Hereinafter cited as SCAD.
[3]Berger, Equality by Statute 128–29 (1952).
[4]*Id.* at 135.

complaint is being handled. If many weeks go by and the Commission has not yet come to a decision, the worker [who has experienced discrimination] probably has to get another job. When he does, the chances are he is no longer interested in the one where he experienced the discrimination."[5] SCAD's first chairman told a United States Senate subcommittee that less than 243 persons had actually obtained jobs as a result of filing complaints with the Commission between 1945 and 1947.[6] "Such a record," Berger notes, "is not one to encourage the filing of complaints."[7]

Berger is critical of three months as being "too long a period" for the disposition of a complaint, but recently in New York state important cases have been filed which have taken a year or two or more to resolve.

On September 27, 1962, Harold Mitchell, a member of the NAACP branch in Spring Valley, New York, filed a complaint against Local 373 of the AFL-CIO Plumbers Union in Rockland county with the State Commission for Human Rights (previously SCAD). The union, he alleged, had forced him out of a job he had held for more than 10 years with the R&S Plumbers and Mechanical Systems Company, after the Plumbers Union had entered into a collective bargaining agreement with his employer, and they refused to admit him into membership. Mr. Mitchell also charged that the union was "lily white" in its membership and had never admitted a Negro into the Union-controlled apprenticeship program. On February 21, 1964, the New York State Commission handed down an order requiring re-employment of Mr. Mitchell, payment of some back wages and admittance into the union.[8] *Seventeen months after the filing of the complaint, the Commission issued its determination.* (The significance of this important decision will be discussed below.)

On April 4, 1961, a complaint was filed against Local 10 of the International Ladies Garment Workers Union with the New York State Commission for Human Rights. On May 18, 1963, 25 *months later in the case of Ernest Holmes, a Negro worker,*[9] the ILGWU entered into a stipulation upon which the complaint was finally withdrawn. In the agreement obtained by the Commission the union agreed to admit Holmes into the Cutter's local of the ILGWU, to assist

[5]*Ibid.*

[6]*Id.* at 136.

[7]*Ibid.*

[8]Mitchell v. R & S Plumbers & Mechanical Systems, Inc., C-9092-62 (N.Y. State Comm'n for Human Rights, 1964).

[9]Holmes v. Falikman, C-7580-61 (N.Y. State Comm'n for Human Rights, 1963).

him in seeking employment and in gaining training experience as an apprentice cutter.

This is precisely what the State Commission had ordered the ILGWU to do a year before when a finding of "probable cause" was issued by the investigating commissioner. I quote from *The New York Times,* July 2, 1962, in a report headlined "Union Told to Get Job For A Negro":

> A garment cutters' union has been ordered by the State Commission for Human Rights to arrange for employment of a Negro at union rates commensurate with his skill and to admit the Negro into union membership if his work is satisfactory.

The *Times* story also states "With regard to the union, the decision found that 'the evidence raises serious doubt as to its good faith to comply with the State Law Against Discrimination in the matter of this complaint; and that there was "probable cause" to credit the allegations of the complaint.'"

On September 14, 1962, Rupert Ruiz, Investigating Commissioner, New York State Commission for Human Rights, in a letter to Emil Schlesinger, Attorney for Local 10, stated that the Commission had "repeatedly requested and for a period of eight months tried to obtain data pertinent to a resolution of the charges of discrimination against Amalgamated Ladies Garment Cutters Union—Local 10. These efforts were unsuccessful. The failure of representatives of that local to cooperate in the investigation despite their promises to do so, left me no alternative but to find 'probable cause to credit the allegations of the complaint.'" However, eight more months were to elapse before the Commission finally acted to secure enforcement of the law.

It is of some significance to note that this was not the first encounter by the ILGWU with the New York state antidiscrimination agency. In 1946, an action was brought by a Negro member of Local 22 who was barred from higher paying jobs controlled by Local 89, an Italian local.[10] After the Commission called the Union's attention to relevant portions of the state antidiscrimination law and informed the ILGWU that the existence of nationality locals was a violation of the statute, a conference was held on January 22, 1947, at the offices of the State Commission Against Discrimination in New York City. Frederick Umhey, Executive Secretary of the ILGWU represented the union and Commissioner Caroline K. Simon, the State Commission. The ILGWU entered into an agreement with the Commission that it would not bar Negroes, Spanish-speaking or other persons from

[10]Hunter v. Sullivan Dress Shop, C-1439-46 (N.Y. State Comm'n Against Discrimination 1947).

membership in the all-Italian locals. Today, eighteen years later, not a single Negro or Spanish-speaking person holds membership in the two Italian locals which have control of some of the highest paying jobs in the industry and no action has been taken to comply with the state law forbidding such practices. These cases are important because the garment industry is the major manufacturing industry in New York City and of great importance in the economy of the entire state.[11]

In its early years, SCAD relied on the technique of conference, conciliation and education as the basic approach in ending employment discrimination. The Commission anticipated danger in utilizing the threat of punitive measures, and therefore sought only voluntary compliance. The Commission resisted the demands of those who sought pressure to enforce compliance and frequently claimed that the alternative to its timid approach was to administer the law in an atmosphere of hostility and conflict. It presented an either/or alternative of conciliation or conflict, disregarding that a possible middle path between conciliation and harshness could be achieved. The Commission was extremely reluctant to enter into public hearings or to issue cease and desist orders because of the fear that employer and labor union opposition would then increase resistance to SCAD's conciliatory efforts. By the end of 1950, SCAD had only twice invoked its powers beyond the conciliation stage.[12] In its early years, SCAD handled complaints which were very few in number compared to the established pattern of employment discrimination. This evidently suited the overly cautious administrators of the Commission, who were apparently concerned that frequent processing of many cases would produce hostility. Thus, Berger concluded, SCAD carried a very small caseload and took too long to settle complaints.[13]

Louis Ruchames of Smith College reached similar conclusions. Absence of the issuance of cease and desist orders was described by Ruchames as "symptomatic of a weakness in the commission's policy." SCAD gained the reputation of being willing to settle for less than full compliance with the law. Employers would be likely to continue discriminatory practices if they knew that doing so did not involve any penalty or other difficulty, but merely entailed a promise to obey the law in the future or at worse suffer the adjustment of an individu-

[11]For a documentation of the status of nonwhite workers in the ladies garment industry in New York City and in the ILGWU see Herbert Hill, Testimony Before the House Committee on Education and Labor, 88th Cong., 1st Sess. 1569-72 (1963); see also Hill, *The ILGWU, Fact and Fiction,* 2 New Politics 7-27 (1962).

[12]Berger, *op. cit. supra* note 43, at 117.

[13]*Id.* at 127, 133.

al compliant. "This has created in the minds of many of New York's citizens the impression that it is possible to evade the law and that the filing of a complaint with the Commission will not necessarily bring satisfaction to the complainant."[14]

In 1951, SCAD declared that settlement of cases involving discrimination in hiring did not entail compulsory hiring of the complainant at once or at the next available opportunity. SCAD felt even less impelled to demand partial or complete back pay from an employer who was found guilty of discriminatory practices. Its main function seemed to be the promotion of an "educational message" rather than the satisfactory settlement of complaints based upon enforcement of the law. That weakness was aggravated by the small number of complaints which the agency found to be valid. Either many complaints filed with the commission are weak—an assertion that can only be questioned because the existence of widespread discriminatory employment patterns is sustained by ample data—or the standards of adequate evidence required by the Commission are too severe and unrealistic. "In either case," commented Ruchames, "its rejection of two thirds or almost three fourths of all complaints is hardly calculated to increase its stature in the eyes of the average worker."[15]

SCAD's policies contributed to the impression that it accomplished little, that its scrutiny is easily evaded, and that individuals filing complaints are not likely to emerge with any gain. The result is that only a small number of complaints are filed each year, "far smaller than prevailing discriminatory practice would seem to call forth."[16] In 1949 there were 315 verified complaints, 257 in 1950 and 243 in 1951. It is the number of complaints filed and the extent and rapidity of enforcement that determines the law's effectiveness. "As a result of the current small number of complaints being received," Ruchames concluded, ". . . and the fact that they do not reflect existing discriminatory practices, the commission's efforts must ultimately prove inadequate."[17]

V. The Record of State Fair Employment Practice Commissions

By making a close examination of the records of various state fair employment practices commissions, it is possible to evaluate more

[14]Ruchames, Race, Jobs & Politics 173 (1953).

[15]*Id.* at 175.

[16]*Ibid.*

[17]*Ibid.* Significant changes in the operation of the N.Y. State Commission, together with important recent decisions, are noted below.

fully the consequences of their past operations and to indicate the need for new policies by federal and state agencies in the future.

California

In 1959, the California state legislature enacted a fair employment practice act. From September 18, 1959, the date the new law was put into effect through December 30, 1960, 565 complaints were received. Eighty-nine per cent of these cited alleged discrimination because of race. Out of these 511 cases, 502 or 87 per cent involved discrimination against Negroes. Fifty-seven per cent of the 502 involved refusal to hire, 24 per cent dismissal from employment, 8 per cent involved refusal to upgrade, 14 per cent the withholding of employment agency referral, and 35 per cent involved union discrimination. Sixty-seven per cent of the cases charged private employers, 24 per cent cited public employers, 18 per cent, agencies, and 26 per cent named labor unions.

In 287 of the cases, or 86 per cent, the Commission was able to make a determination as to whether or not discrimination had occurred. Forty-five cases, or 14 per cent, were dismissed because of lack of jurisdiction or failure of the complainant to proceed. Only 96 cases, or 33.5 per cent of complaints filed were found to be valid and were corrected by conference and conciliation. One hundred and ninety-one cases, or 67 per cent of those filed, were dismissed because of insufficient evidence.

Of the 96 cases in which the Commission found discriminatory practice, 29 cases or 30 per cent were settled by offers of immediate hiring of the complainant. But 64 per cent involved agreements that the respondent would comply with the state law and would issue a merit employment policy and also declare an intent to cease discriminatory practices. It is quite evident that the mere issuance of a nondiscriminatory statement does not assure equal opportunity for Negroes. Twelve cases in fact were adjusted by a commitment to consider hiring or promoting the complainant at the first opportunity. Why a firm commitment was not demanded in the specific case before the Commission is not explained.

Records of the Commission further reveal the limited nature of FEP settlements. In one case, a Negro salesman in an automobile agency was finally granted the opportunity to sell on the floor and thereby earn higher commissions. The Commission noted that the salesman was re-instated, given equal floor time, and his performance was evaluated after 90 days. It was found he had the third best sales record on the floor. The Commission concludes that equal opportunity led to rising sales and thereby showed the company that they too would profit by a nondiscriminatory policy. One asks whether the Negro salesman would have the right to make a low sales record on some weeks, and if he had, whether he then would have been dismissed. The Commission acknowledges that a city-wide check found that only six Negro salesmen were allowed to sell cars on the floor. No effort was made to provide the same right for other Negro salesmen in other automobile agencies. (During March 1964, 102 persons were arrested in the course of mass demonstrations organized by the local branch of the NAACP, at the General Motor Showrooms in San Francisco. On April 11, 226 persons again were arrested during demonstrations at auto showrooms.)

In another case, a young Negro was rejected after trying to file a job application with gas stations of a large oil company. The Commission learned that the company's standing policy was to accept applications from all potential employees. The firm's 36 stations in the area had 180 attendants, but not one was Negro. The FEP Commission persuaded the company to accept the complainant's application, evaluate it, and hire the respondent if he were qualified. "His qualifications were better than average," it noted, "and he got the job." This is what the Negro community today regards as token integration—the granting of one job to a highly qualified Negro, and is not acceptable as such, but is regarded by the California FEPC as proof of successful adjustment—although the Commission itself admits that the company has no other Negro employees. That such token standards are accepted as progress further indicates that the traditional approach of FEPC is obsolete and that the statute is not enforced in a manner that would make possible the fullest gains for nonwhite workers under the law. [18]

The rather anxious desire to appease business concerns that are guilty of discriminatory employment practices rather than to use all available powers to open new job opportunities for Negroes is attested to by the attitude of Commission executives. John Anson Ford, California FEP Commission Chairman, emphasized that its work is accomplished mainly by conference, conciliation, education and persuasion. "We have never yet had to invoke the enforcement power provided by the law," he commented. Ford, in a press release aimed at gathering support for FEP emphasized that "our sincere attempt to find the facts is shown by the number of cases—well over half—which have been closed on the basis of 'insufficient evidence' or 'no evi-

[18] 1959–1960 Cal. F.E.P.C. Ann. Rep. 9–10, 19–27, 31–34.

dence' of discrimination."[19] The fact that the Commission has ruled against defendants in only approximately half the cases filed is not a record of which to be proud, especially when it is admitted that the entire number of complaints filed does not adequately indicate the serious extent of racial discrimination. Even if one claims that the Commission could not have ruled in any other manner in these cases, the decisions are geared to gain the confidence of the business and trade union community and the scorn of the Negro workers.

The Commission has chosen to answer conservative critics by claiming that FEPC action will not really alter the status quo. This tactic succeeds in placating the business interests that originally opposed FEPC, but it also reveals the actual character of FEPC to the Negro worker and his community. Thus there should be no cause to wonder at increasing Negro disillusionment with antidiscrimination commissions and the frequent recourse to direct mass action.

By 1961-1962, in California, 1,321 employment cases had been completed and closed by the Commission. One hundred and eighteen cases were dismissed for being outside the Commission's jurisdiction, and 414 were corrected after discriminatory practices were found. Seven hundred and eighty-seven cases however were closed for insufficient evidence or no evidence of discrimination. Three public hearings were held for respondents who did not make what the Commission accepted as a satisfactory settlement. But the courts set aside Commission orders in two cases and the third was pending at the end of the year.[20]

The FEP Commission in California takes it as a strong point that public disclosure of the identity of a respondent is prohibited on the assumption that this protects the accused against implications of guilt and might impair settlement efforts during the conciliation process. I believe that disclosure would facilitate reaching the goal of eliminating discrimination if this were the sole purpose of the Commission. The public would be able to exert pressure upon discriminatory company and union practices and also to judge whether the FEP Commission was an effective agent of social change.

Events occurring in March and April of 1964 reveal that extralegal militant action for jobs has been more successful in attacking overt employment discrimination in some areas than the years of FEPC operations in California. On March 6 and 7, 1964, 1000 demonstrators picketed the Sheraton-Palace Hotel in San Francisco, and

[19]Cal. Dep't of Industrial Relations, Div. of Fair Employment Practices, *News from FEPC* (April 29, 1962).

[20]Cal. Dep't of Industrial Relations, 1961–1962 Employment Relations Agency Biennial Rep., *Fair Employment Practices* 15–16.

demanded that the hotel honor its avowed equal opportunity policy and hire 15 to 20 per cent of its total staff from the Negro and Mexican population in the area. At first representatives of the Hotel Employers' Association refused to negotiate with "irresponsible" groups and claimed that their hotels had always had an "equal opportunity" policy. But when 135 persons staged a sit-in during the midst of the evening hours and when the demonstrators let it be known that the mass demonstrations would continue, the Hotel Employers agreed to the demands of the civil rights organizations.

A two-year agreement was signed in which the civil rights groups pledged to halt demonstrations, and the hotels agreed to refrain from pressing charges againt those arrested, and further they agreed to hire the same percentage of Negroes as demanded before July 20th of the same year.[21]

The two-day demonstrations forced the hotels, which previously denied the existence of discriminatory employment practices to change the previous standard of judgment, by recognizing that the small percentage of Negroes they had hired in the past was not sufficient proof that they actually had a nondiscriminatory policy. The method used by the FEP Commission—that of judging intent and evaluating individual complaints—was also proven to be useless in changing the discriminatory practices of the Hotel Employers' Association. The standards used by the FEPC Commission in fact were virtually the same as those employed by the Hotel Association. Negroes in California will increasingly engage in mass action and participation in the militant Negro civil rights movement to effect significant change in the racial situation—with or without FEPC.

Massachusetts

The record of the Massachusetts Commission Against Discrimination is a dismal one especially since the Massachusetts Commission is one of the oldest in years of operation and is given extensive powers under the statute, powers which it uses only very rarely. Thus, like many other state FEP commissions, it can not be regarded as a law enforcement agency. The Massachusetts Commission has been in existence since 1946 and has the authority to initiate investigations and to invoke its compliance procedures without the filing of complaints by aggrieved persons in instances where "trouble is manifest and can be traced to race." Conciliation and conferences are used in these investigations, but in 15 years, only 5 cases were brought to the stage of public hearing from the Massachusetts FEP docket. From November

[21]The New York Times, March 8, 1964 1, p. 53.

10, 1946 to December 31, 1961, 2,149 complaints were initiated and received. Of these, 722 were dismissed for lack of probable cause, 76 for lack of jurisdiction, and 101 were withdrawn by complainants. The Commission found evidence of discriminatory practices in 1,186 cases, and closed them as satisfactorily adjusted. The Commission initiated 864 cases; 847 of these were closed after conciliation.[22]

Although the Commission found probable cause of discrimination in 1,186 cases, the reasons why Governor Peabody found that the Commission did not eliminate employment discrimination is quite clear after an examination of some typical cases which were "settled."

In an employment case, a Negro just recently discharged from the Air Force applied for a position as an IBM tabulator operator. Although he had been trained to operate the 407 tabulator and had successfully completed seven courses of study in IBM machine operation, he was not hired. The company claimed that it did not hire him because he did not have enough experience, but then decided that he would qualify for another lessor position and hired him.[23] No information was gathered as to how many Negroes are employed by the company, or what is the occupational distribution of nonwhites, nor is such information used as a basis of determining discriminatory intent. The employment of the individual Negro complainant by the company in a position lower than that for which he applied and had been trained, evidently provided enough justification for the state FEP Commission to close the case. In my opinion this is not adequate.

In another case, a complainant declared that she had not been hired because she was Negro. The Commission found that the company employed 75 people and that only one employee was colored. It was determined that three white women had been hired two days after the Negro complainant applied for the job. Hence the Commission asked the company to hire the Negro applicant, and "the complainant was given the next vacancy as a means of conciliating the matter."[24] By agreeing to hire the Negro complainant, after having been caught in a clear example of discriminatory racial practices, the company avoided the shame of exposure in a public hearing and the possibility of facing a court enforcement order. The Commission, however, made no effort to inquire how many other Negro applicants may have applied for a job and been refused. It made no recommendation that the company basically alter its racial employment practices

[22] 16 Mass. Comm'n Against Discrimination Ann. Rep. 35 (1961).
[23] 15 Mass. Comm'n Against Discrimination Ann. Rep. 4–5 (1959-1960).
[24] 17 Mass. Comm'n Against Discrimination Ann. Rep. 5 (1962).

nor did it determine that the hiring of two Negroes did not constitute compliance with the state anti-discrimination law. Because the data show that unemployment is much higher for the Negro than for the white workers in Massachusetts, the possibility exists that other Negroes might have applied and been turned down by the same company. It is also possible that many Negro applicants felt a sense of futility in filing a formal complaint with the Massachusetts Commission. Yet the Commission made no attempt to have the company publicly pledge to hire all qualified Negro applicants in the future—and to affirmatively seek and train Negroes in an effort to remedy and compensate for its previous record of discriminatory racial practices.

In yet another case, the Commission revealed that some investigations took longer than one year, a period quite long, so that a worker in need of employment is not able to wait for the verdict of the Commission. A Negro applicant had been interviewed by a company and was advised by the personnel department to try and find employment elsewhere. After applying two more times for a job, the Negro complainant charged the company with unlawful discrimination because of race. Investigation by the MCAD revealed that the company's employees were "numbered in the hundreds" and that although "there were colored persons living in the same community and surrounding areas, none was employed." The particular Negro applicant had applied for a production job, a category in which the yearly turnover amounted to 6 per cent. Two hundred applications for production positions were on file with the company, but the personnel director said that few Negroes applied for employment. Investigation of the company's files revealed that the Negro applicant's card was distinctly marked to separate it from the others, and was dated three months after the actual date of application.

Two months after the Negro applicant first applied, when the MCAD began investigation, 130 persons were hired. Ninety-two of these were new employees. The company adamantly denied that the Negro applicant had been discriminated against because of her race. Yet the MCAD noted that its file showed that "no Negroes were employed despite information" and that "a few had applied." MCAD had the company give another test and interview to the applicant, upon completion of which her application was put into the active file. In the meantime, the Negro complainant took another job and notified the MCAD that she was no longer interested in working for the respondent company. In this case, where the MCAD took into consideration the fact that many other Negroes were unemployed in the nearby area and that some *had* applied for jobs, the Commission evidently dropped the case upon receipt of the information that the particular complainant had taken another job. The fact that a most clear discriminatory pattern existed throughout this company's operations did not lead the MCAD to take the necessary action obviously indicated by all the available evidence.[25]

New Jersey

Other state commissions reveal a similar potential of unused powers. New Jersey's Division Against Discrimination reports that "monumental" tasks still have to be accomplished. In the period from July, 1957 to June 30, 1958, the New Jersey Commission investigated 123 employment cases. Out of this number only 53 cases were adjusted and declared to be based upon valid complaints. Fifty-nine per cent of cases registered were dismissed.[26–29]

In one case, Puerto Rican workers complained of discriminatory working conditions and charged their union with failing to give them proper protection and representation. Fifty-five per cent of the workers in the shop were Puerto Ricans. The union responded by accusing the Puerto Rican workers of holding anti-union attitudes. The Commission settled the grievance by arranging conferences between the Puerto Rican workers, the union leadership and employer representatives. The union agreed to promote better communication with the workers and to print material in both English and Spanish. The Puerto Rican production industries as a result of automation and other technological change state FEP commissions are impotent to deal with this very serious problem.

Minnesota

Another state commission which shows a poor record is the Minnesota Commission. This body has been in existence since 1955, but in seven years of operation it has handled only 205 cases through 1962. Of these, 136 dealt with employment discrimination. Out of the total of 205 cases, 81 were dismissed for no probable cause, 9 for lack of jurisdiction, 3 were withdrawn by the complainants, 4 were dismissed for insufficient evidence and only 32 were judged to be valid and then adjusted. If conciliation is found to be unsuccessful in Minnesota, the Commission may ask the Governor to appoint a three member hearing body from a 12 man Board of Review. This Board may then hold a public hearing, and determine whether an unfair discriminatory practice does exist. If it finds this is the case, the Board may then

[25] 11 Mass. Comm'n Against Discrimination Ann. Rep. 8–9 (1955–1956).

[26–29] 1957–1958 N.J. Dep't of Education, Div. Against Discrimination Ann. Rep. 12–13.

issue a cease and desist order. This absurd and unwieldy procedure is clearly unsuited to meaningful action against recalcitrant companies and labor unions and certainly explains the very small number of complaints filed with the Commission.[30]

However, even when cases are brought before the Minnesota agency, there is evidence to show a general reluctance on the part of the Commission to take affirmative action. In one case, a Negro woman had applied for the position of airline stewardess and had been rejected. The commission took four years to complete the investigation, at which time they recommended that the case be held over pending further investigation.

In another case, a Negro man was not hired as a salesman by a department store in a small Minnesota community. The local manager informed the Commission that he believed company policy forbade the hiring of Negroes. The company stated that this interpretation was not correct and proceeded to inform all local managers of the company's nondiscriminatory hiring policy. This affirmation of a nondiscriminatory policy was evidently enough to settle the case, although the firm had still not hired a Negro. No investigation was made to determine how many Negroes, if any, were employed in the future with this firm.[31]

The Minnesota Commission stated that it is aware that the pattern of complaints filed does not indicate the actual pattern of discrimination. Actually most people seek employment where they know that they have a chance to be hired. Firms which do not have Negro employees may seldom get an application from one. The FEP commission may be the least likely agency to receive complaints based upon attempts to gain jobs in these firms. "Thus, the Commission is least likely to receive complaints against the very firms, industries, unions and employment agencies which may be most discriminatory in their employment practices."[32] Minnesota proposes an "educational" program as an answer. But we already know that this approach has become quite meaningless and that much more than education is necessary.

Minnesota, in fact, seems to rely to such a great degree on so-called "education and persuasion" to resolve complaints that requests for Review Board hearings are seldom made. In 1956, one case was not "settled" during the process described as "education and persuasion" and a hearing was requested. But this action "was not taken until after the Commission had tried unsuccessfully for fourteen

[30] 7 Minn. Comm'n Against Discrimination Ann. Rep. 1–9 (1962).

[31] *Id.* at 4–5.

[32] 4 Minn. F.E.P.C. Ann Rep. 9 (1959).

months to secure a satisfactory adjustment of the complaint through the process of conference and conciliation."[33]

In another complaint, a Negro truck driver who weighed over 220 pounds was informed that he could not be employed because he was overweight. The management presented evidence to show that it was concerned about the over-all weight of men and produce on its trucks. However, the Commission was not persuaded that overweight was the real disqualifying factor, because white drivers working for the company in some cases also weighed over 200 pounds. The Commission asked that the applicant be given another test. The applicant, having obtained another job during the protracted negotiations between the Commission and the company, failed to appear. Because the company agreed to affirm a nondiscriminatory policy—although they had not hired a Negro for 6 or 7 years—the "Commission made a finding of no discrimination," and the company was asked to put the policy into practice by employing Negro drivers when the opportunity presented itself in the future. The Commission's standards, so vague and indefinite, point to the conclusion that much more is needed to clear a company, which does not hire Negroes, of the charge of discrimination than a mere promise to hire Negroes sometime in an indefinite future when and if there are job vacancies and if Negroes apply. The Commission's judgment in this case was really absurd as the Commission saw fit to accept a mere statement of alleged nondiscriminatory policy, although the company obviously employed no Negroes. Nor did the Commission take action to provide for compliance with the state law in the future.[34]

New York State—The Test of FEPC

The experience of the New York State Commission Against Discrimination, later re-named the State Commission for Human Rights, is most important to evaluate. New York was the first state to enact an FEPC law. Beginning in 1945, its Commission has had the largest staff and highest budget of all state FEP commissions. Unlike some other commissions, the New York agency does investigate discriminatory *employment patterns* and attempts to correct them.

The Commission is empowered to investigate discriminatory patterns even if no individual complaint is filed. If discriminatory patterns are found to exist and the accusation is accompanied by reasonable factual support, the Commission may authorize the start of an informal investigation and may seek to remedy the discriminatory

[33] 2 Minn. F.E.PC. Ann. Rep. 10 (1957).
[34] 3 Minn. F.E.P.C. Ann. Rep. 7–8 (1958).

pattern through education, conciliation and persuasion. Although the Commission may not call a formal hearing in these cases, the State Industrial Commissioner or the State Attorney General may file a formal complaint with the Commission against the respondent.

In 1962, the New York State Commission received 1,171 complaints; 740 verified complaints from the previous year had not been settled, making a total of 1,911 cases under consideration. This figure represented the greatest number of complaints filed with the Commission in its 17 year history. Of these, 611 or 52.2 per cent pertained to employment. This amounted to a drop from 660 filed in 1961, a drop of 7.4 per cent. Sixty-six and two-tenths per cent of the employment complaints were based on discrimination because of race. Refusal to hire was alleged in 235 complaints (38.5 per cent of the employment complaints.) One hundred and fifty-four concerned dismissal from employment, 113 conditions and privileges of employment and 48 concerned the withholding of employment agency referral. The remaining charged refusal of union membership and other forms of labor union discrimination and pre-employment inquiries.[35]

Of the 1392 complaints closed in 1962, probable cause was found to sustain charges of discrimination in 340, or 24.4 per cent of cases filed. Another 111 cases, or 8 per cent disclosed other unlawful practice which was adjusted. Thus, in 32.4 per cent of cases closed some discriminatory practices were found and adjusted. This means, however, that in nearly 70 per cent of cases filed by complainants, no evidence of discrimination was found. The percentage of cases rejected remains close to the amount which Berger studied in 1950. In that year, Berger noted that SCAD had ruled against 65 per cent of the cases filed. It is interesting to note that in 1962 the percentage of rejected cases is very close to what it was in 1950; thus the pattern of Commission rulings does not give the Negro worker confidence in the ability of FEPC to eradicate job discrimination, that is to help solve his employment problem. Probable cause was found to sustain the allegations in only 12.3 per cent of the employment complaints, 40 per cent of public accommodation complaints, and 45.1 per cent of housing complaints.

The Commission is authorized to make informal investigations of potential discriminatory situations. Since 1945, 1,463 of these were conducted. Three hundred and six were conducted in 1962 alone; 301 of these dealt with employment discrimination.[36]

New York's FEPC record reveals that more complaints were filed

[35]1962 N.Y. State Comm'n for Human Rights Ann. Rep. 2–4 (Mimeographed.)

[36]*Id.* at 4–5.

with the Commission as the years moved on. From 1945 through 1949, 1,583 employment complaints were filed. Two hundred and fifty-six were filed in 1950, 321 in 1955, 650 in 1957, 794 in 1959 and 611 in in 1962.[37] Of the 611 employment cases filed in 1962, 405 (or 66.2 per cent) alleged discrimination on grounds of race. For 1945 through 1962, a total of 5,244 employment complaints alleging racial discrimination were filed. Thus, discrimination based on color was charged in 67.9 per cent of the employment cases brought before the New York Commission during this seventeen year period.[38]

Out of the 611 filed in 1962, 235 cases concerned refusal to employ, 154 alleged dismissal from employment, 113 cited conditions of employment, 48 agency referral and 46 concerned trade unions. Out of the 7,725 employment complaints filed from 1945 through 1962, 3,365 concerned refusal to employ, 1,732 dismissal, 1,054 conditions of employment, 493 employment agencies and 743 involved labor union discrimination.[39]

What was the disposition of the employment cases for the year 1962 and for the period from 1945 to 1962? The record is clearly revealed in the statistics presented by the Commission itself:

Complaints Closed by Types of Closing[40]

Closing	Employment Cases 1962	Employment Cases 1945-1962
1. Probable cause—specific complaint sustained		
a. Adjusted after conference and conciliation	103	1,405
b. Ordered for hearing or consent order issued	1	64
2. No probable cause found as to specific complaint but other discriminatory practices or policies found and adjusted	96	1,620
3. No probable cause found—specific complaint dismissed and no other discriminatory practices or policies found	588	3,811
4. Withdrawn by complainant	19	171
5. Lack of jurisdiction—specific complaint dismissed	36	387
Total	843	7,458

[37] *Id.* at 10, Table 2.
[38] *Id.* at 12, Table 4.
[39] *Id.* at 13, Table 5.
[40] *Id.* at 14, Table 6.

Translated into percentage distribution figures, the Commission's analysis of closings shows that for category two above, no probable cause was found as to the discrimination charged by the complainant in 11.4 per cent of 1962 employment cases and in 21.7 per cent of 1945 to 1962 employment cases. No discrimination of *any kind* (category three above) was found in 69.7 per cent of 1962 cases and in 51.1 per cent of 1945 to 1962 employment cases. In generalized terms, therefore, the Commission found no probable cause to credit the specific discrimination alleged in the complaint of 81.1 per cent of employment cases in 1962 and in 72.8 per cent of employment cases from 1945 to 1962. The over-all record substantiates the fact that the same pattern exists as that studied by Morroe Berger five years after the New York Commission came into existence; the large percentages of cases invalidated still does not tend to create confidence in the Commission among Negro workers, and that given the enormity of the problems of the very large Negro community in New York state, the actual number of complaints received by the New York Commission is very small indeed.

New York's Commission—despite the fact that it rejects half of the complaints which are filed with it—is the only Commission with a substantial annual budget and a fairly adequate staff. Its 1960 budget was $950,000 and the Commission had a working staff of 80 people. California, a state that had two-thirds as large a Negro population, had a Commission budget of only $203,000 and a staff of 15. Pennsylvania, a state with a sixteenth as many Negroes had a budget of $100,000 for its FEPC commission and a staff of 3. Yet even the large budget and staff for New York's agency is not sufficient to cope with the very serious problems of racial and other forms of discrimination. Hence it is obvious that the other state commissions would be extremely understaffed and ill-equipped to function properly. The other commissions are forced to limit their activity to processing complaints. Only the New York Commission had a budget that is large enough to enable it to conduct activity on a patttern-centered compliance basis.

During its eighteen years of existence, New York's FEPC concluded agreements with over 2,000 separate firms. This is but a small fraction of companies which have six or more employees—but they do account for business operations in which the Commission found proof of discriminatory practices. If all the firms revised their previous discriminatory policy, the result would have to be some general improvement in employment opportunity. The Commission's post-settlement investigations reveal that many of the firms did hire an increased number of Negro employees after settlements took place, as a direct consequence of revised employment policies. Therefore New York's Commission did demand and secure some significant enforcement of the law, a step which other state FEP settlements did not entail. In 1951, for example, SCAD had studied 334 cases for follow-up review. In 85 per cent of cases investigated it found that there was "a definite improvement in the employment pattern as compared with the conditions which existed at the time the original complaints against them were filed. These changes were reflected in substantial increases in the number of members of different racial ... groups employed in professional, technical, skilled, semiskilled and unskilled job categories."[41]

But this very improvement delineates the actual inability of the Commission to make meaningful changes in the total pattern of employment discrimination. By the very nature of the process used by the Commission—investigation of the employment pattern of respondent firms—the Commission can influence only a small minority of business firms operating in the state. The change in employment patterns achieved by later investigation of agreements is certainly to be commended—but unfortunately it touches only a small minority of New York's manufacturing and other industries. Thus, as Herman Miller pointed out, the occupational status of Negroes in the 1960's in New York remains close to the levels reached in 1940.

In 1958, some relative progress in specific industries for Negro "white collar" employees can be noted. The Commission made an analysis of reviews of Negro employment in several important industries—banking, insurance companies and department stores. These institutions traditionally excluded Negroes from all but menial jobs. Comparison of the findings of their follow-up investigations with the original employment pattern revealed that originally Negroes held only menial jobs in these firms. In the middle 1950's, however, 7 banks which had been respondent firms had more than 100 Negroes in white collar positions, and 2 of the banks had 300 Negroes in each. The progress appears to be great, however, because for a Negro, any job above a menial position is regarded as a significant change in occupational status.

Of 20 insurance companies investigated by the Commission, 8 firms showed that they had no Negro employment; 1 showed that Negroes were employed but that no general increase in Negro employment had been registered. Ten firms had no Negro employees at the time of the analysis. The largest firm studied had no Negro employees in 1945, at the time of the original investigation. By 1956, it

[41] 1951 N.Y. State Comm'n Against Discrimination Ann. Rep. 7–8.

had employed 750 Negroes in many different positions, and 200 Puerto Ricans. Similarly, few retail stores had Negroes employed in any but menial jobs in 1945 and most had no Negro employees at all. By the 1950's, Negroes comprised approximately 10 per cent of the work force of New York department stores. However, these gains for Negro middle class white collar workers are more than offset by losses in employment opportunity for Negro industrial workers especially in mass production manufacturing. Although increases in Negro employment have taken place, they appear to be significant only in contrast to the complete exclusion which was the standard 20 years ago. In the communication industry in New York state, Negroes may now comprise 5 per cent of the total work force, compared to only 2 per cent in the 1940's, but the percentage of change does not signify a great increase in the actual number of Negroes whose occupational status has changed. A few Negroes have been employed, but the demand for jobs is much higher than the number of Negroes who are working at them or who are qualified for such positions. As automation begins to eliminate many of the jobs in these industries, the ability of Negroes to gain entrance becomes even more difficult. Racial bias in the allocation of jobs has changed slightly, and this change reflects the positive aspects of New York's FEPC. But it also reveals the inability of FEPC as an institution to cope with the over-all pattern of job discrimination. Even when FEPC has worked most effectively compared to other states—and it has worked most effectively in New York—it is simply unable to fundamentally alter the Negro employment pattern.

New York's FEPC commission has tried to avoid the defects inherent in the other state FEPC agencies. It has tried to do more than rectify the situation of an individual complainant. One Negro man charged that he had received no referrals for a job as a front elevator operator in an East Side luxury apartment. The Commission failed to find evidence to support the contention that he was not employed because of his color. Nevertheless, it investigated to determine whether a combination of geographic area factors and the specific category of employment acted to discriminate against Negroes. It found that no Negroes had ever been employed as front elevator operators in the expensive East Side apartment buildings. The Commission then had the specifications for jobs in the area changed. It would no longer be acceptable for employers to ask for "East Side apartment house experience" or "comparable experience" as a prerequisite for employment. Because Negroes never held the job, this type of qualification automatically excluded them. The Commission emphasized that such "localized prior experience is certainly not the only way to acquire the necessary training."[42] This ruling does not insure Negro employment as front elevator operators, but it certainly sets the basis for ending their absolute exclusion.

Nevertheless, the Commission's efforts to affect the employment pattern are not always successful. In 1953, 228 respondent firms were involved in complaints which were closed that year. One hundred and seventy-nine companies were first complaint cases; 49 had previously been investigated in connection with other complaints. Checking on the latter group is a method of examining whether changes had taken place in employment patterns and of testing how effective earlier conciliation agreements were. Of these 49 firms, 13 were found to be no longer practicing any discrimination. Fifteen were found to have nondiscriminatory employment policies currently, although in previous years they did not. Fourteen companies were found still to be engaged in discriminatory practices, indicating that "the earlier conciliation agreements had not been completely effective."[43] Adjustments made with these 14 companies were proved to have been based upon meaningless agreements, for the employers did not end their discriminatory pattern of employment. Promises are not always kept, and satisfactory adjustment does not mean that respondent firms will always act upon the agreements they sign. The remaining 7 firms were found to have a discriminatory policy which had not been disclosed during earlier investigations. This result shows that companies may often avoid scrutiny of their policies, despite an FEPC investigation.

New York's Commission tries to prevent lack of compliance by undertaking a review of complaints six months after they have been closed. In 1953, 103 reviews were made. Field representatives visited respondents, made inquiries about employment practices, policies and patterns as well as general compliance with the terms of the conciliation agreement. The Commission found that in one Long Island defense plant there was a steady increase in Negro employees. At the time of the original investigation the plant had 900 employees and no Negro workers. At the first review, it employed 1,600 persons and 19 Negroes. At the second review, it employed 1,800 employees and 32 Negroes. A large bakery employed 1,000 people, but used Negro sales people only in Negro neighborhoods. At the first review, the Commission found that Negroes sold goods in 9 shops where they had not been previously employed. A Fifth Avenue department store had 2,900 employees. Of the 135 Negroes employed, only 1 was in sales

[42] 1961 N.Y. State Comm'n Against Discrimination Ann. Rep. 60.
[43] 1953 N.Y. State Comm'n Against Discrimination Ann. Rep. 15.

work. At the first review, the store was using 18 Negro salespeople.[44] The Commission thus notes an increase in the use of Negro workers—but it cannot do anything about the small percentage which this increase comprises. This kind of limited increase against the background of Negro unemployment and underemployment does not effect a change in the Negro's occupational status, and is of benefit only to the few who are fortunate enough to have been chosen for the token advance. It is necessary to observe that this kind of progress might have been very important as symbolic achievement 20 years ago, but today given the reality of Negro life in the north, it can be regarded only as token compliance with the law at best.

New York's Commission has indicated a serious effort to attempt a review of its cases and to secure compliance. This has amounted to an increase in the number of Negroes employed by industries in which investigations have been made. But in all the categories cited, only a very small percentage of Negroes has benefited. There has been no general increase that would match the increased percentage of Negroes in the population and give them equality in employment on the same terms as that enjoyed by whites. Moreover, most Negro migrants are unskilled, having been accustomed to life and work in rural areas. No significant training programs involving large numbers of workers have been initiated to make them eligible for clerical, professional and skilled craft jobs in which employment opportunities are available.

In one case, the Commission received the complaint of a Negro welder that he had not been referred for employment by a local craft union because he was Negro. This local union controlled all hiring for welding operations on the St. Lawrence Seaway construction project. The local had 800 members, all of whom were white. Negroes were denied the opportunity to work because in practice the union was the exclusive hiring agent and refused to refer Negroes for work. After the Commission acted, the complainant and two other Negroes were sent out for work by the Union. "These men represented the first Negroes in this job category to be employed on the seaway."

In this case, SCAD made no effort to establish the permanent right of Negroes to belong to a union which rigidly controlled the hiring hall operation and to make certain that all qualified Negroes seeking jobs in the future would be referred for employment by the union. Thus they achieved the goal of getting a job for the complainant, but did not initiate action to change the over-all pattern of

[44] *Id.* at 16–17.

discrimination by craft unions which control the hiring process and which exclude Negroes from membership.[45]

In 1948, SCAD had ordered the New York Sheet Metal Workers Union to desist from "executing and/or maintaining constitution or by-law provisions which exclude Negroes." Yet seventeen years later no progress had been made in that area although the "Caucasian only" clause was removed from the union's constitution, apparently for public relations purposes only.

In December of 1963, the New York City Commission on Human Rights investigated the problem, and found "a pattern of exclusion in a substantial portion of the building and construction industry which effectively bars non-whites from participating in this area of the city's economic life."

A major factor in perpetuating Negro exclusion is the union's use of father-son clauses and preferences for relatives, plus the need to be recommended by a group of *union* members. When the right to become an apprentice is limited to sons and relatives of members, Negroes are automatically excluded since none have ever belonged to these unions. Union members may view this provision as a source of job security and claim that they are not discriminating against Negroes, but only against people who are not related to members. Yet the logic of the arrangement is to exclude, on a systematic basis, all Negroes as a class. The situation is analogous to the exclusion of Negroes from the all-white southern primaries in the 1920's. According to defenders of the "white primary," it was not anti-Negro, it merely allowed only those citizens whose grandfathers had voted to take part in primaries. But in effect the rule prevented all Negroes as a group from voting. Only when the courts ruled that the "white primaries" were unconstitutional and in fact were a device meant to bar Negroes, did the exclusion of Negroes from voting in primary elections come to an end in southern states.

The analogy suggests that what is needed is a new definition, a new standard by state FEP commissions. It is necessary to recognize that father-son clauses and preference to relatives is *prima facie* evidence of a discriminatory position; that, in effect, their use as a basis of admittance to apprentice programs is as anti-Negro as the more overt discriminatory clauses which used to be in many union constitutions until the law forced them to be removed. The same standard should be applied to the more common sponsorship clauses. When

[45]For a discussion of trade union racial practices see Hill, *Labor Unions and the Negro*, 28 Commentary 479–88 (Dec. 1959) and Hill, *Has Organized Labor Failed the Negro Worker*, 11 The Negro Digest 41 (May 1962).

union practice requires that a youth be sponsored by two members of five years good standing, a Negro almost never can obtain such sponsorship.

On March 4, 1964, the Commission ruled that Local 28 of the Sheet Metal Workers Union had "automatically excluded" Negroes over the entire 78 years of the unions' existence. This was held to be a violation of New York State Law Against Discrimination. The Commission announced that it would issue an order for the union to "cease and desist" from such discriminatory practices and would demand affirmative action to guarantee an end to job discrimination.[46]

The decision was called "revolutionary" by the Commission's chairman, George H. Fowler, because "it takes into account a historical pattern of exclusion and not merely a specific complaint." Thus the Commission ruled against the union as an institution functioning within a given racial situation and with a history, and not on the basis of the "validity" of an individual complaint. The decision was based on public hearings against the union conducted by three commissioners. They had been called to investigate charges against Local 28 of the Sheet Metal Workers Union filed by the Civil Rights Bureau of the State Attorney General's office. The Bureau, which has been quite effective in this area, charged that the union and a contractors committee responsible for selecting apprentices had systematically discriminated against Negroes. The contractors committee had refused apprenticeship to a qualified Negro applicant. The State Commission charged that Local 28's admission program bore "a remarkable resemblance to the medieval guilds" by maintaining a father-son admission standard. The Commission noted that in a provision of its International Union constitution, which was deleted in 1946, the union declared that "no Negro could ever become a full member."

Observers agree, as The New York Times put it, that the ruling by the Commission was "a key harvest of the seeds planted by the massive civil rights protests at construction sites here last year. Local 28 has been a prime target of the rights groups."[47] What the decision demonstrates is that despite years of a state FEPC law and a previous ruling against Local 28, discrimination in the building trades continued unabated. Voluntary union programs, investigations, exposure, education, interminable negotiations and conciliation brought no results to Negroes. The historic pattern was retained and the union leadership, supported by the Building Trades Council of the AFL-CIO bitterly defended its anti-Negro practices. The state antidiscrimi-

[46]Lefkowitz v. Farrell, C-9287-63 (N.Y. State Comm'n for Human Rights, 1964).

[47]The New York Times, March 5, 1961.

nation law was not enforced and for the Negro job seeker in the building trades, for all practical purposes, it just did not exist in New York City and state. Therefore, civil rights demonstrations took place in a state with the oldest and strongest FEP Commission in the nation. Another factor is the litigation initiated by the NAACP currently pending in the New York State Supreme Court against Local 28 and eight other building unions and against the city and state of New York.

What the ruling also indicates is that if FEPC is to work, it must change the entire basis of its function. No longer can FEPC serve merely as a complaint-taking agency or remain content to settle cases on an individual level, often agreeing to token settlements. It must be able to rule against respondents on the basis of a broad pattern of racial practices even when the respondent avows a nondiscriminatory policy in some vague future. It must take into account what Mr. Fowler called the "historical pattern of exclusion" and not only individual complaints. And then, it must take affirmative actions to assure that the pattern is really ended. Later, on March 23, the State Commission announced that it had given Local 28 sixty days to discard the old apprentice list of some 900 names of white persons and that it had ordered the Local to "cease and desist" from excluding Negroes from membership and to abandon the practice of requiring that an applicant be sponsored by a union member. The order is, in effect, a significant breakthrough for Negro workers and can have far reaching consequences. What is now necessary, as Roy Wilkins, Executive Secretary of the NAACP, requested, is that Governor Rockefeller and Mayor Wagner take immediate steps to order the cancellaton of any contracts for public construction in which the hiring of apprentices and journeymen is controlled by Local 28 and other AFL-CIO craft unions guilty of similar practices. The state and city governments must abide by the State Commission's ruling by cancelling all contracts, and refusing to enter into new ones, in which hiring is controlled by unions that engage in discriminatory racial practices. The State Commission's ruling, Mr. Wilkins stated, in his letters of March 6, 1964 to Governor Rockefeller and Mayor Wagner, has now "removed whatever justification existed, and we contend that there was none, for failure of city and state officials to cancel such contracts." Moreover, authorization of new contracts should be withheld until a realistic policy of nondiscrimination has been effected. Wilkins also called for "the institution of foolproof practices and procedures to insure the policing and affirmative enforcement by the city and state of their policies of nondiscrimination in employment." Unfortunately, in his reply to Roy Wilkins, Governor Rockefeller stated that it has been his "consistent policy . . . to encourage voluntary compliance with the laws against discrimination." In declining to act immediately, the Governor stated, the union would be given a "reasonable time within which to comply." The Governor also noted that ". . . Local 28 is still entitled to test the recent opinion of the Commission in the Courts." Mayor Wagner did not reply to the request of the NAACP Executive Secretary.

State FEP commissions could function more effectively if in addition to the development of new criteria, other law enforcement agencies worked in close conjunction with them. In New York, the state Attorney General, Louis J. Lefkowitz, has proposed an amendment to the state antidiscrimination law, making it illegal under an apprentice program, registered with the state, to select persons, "on any other basis than their qualifications as determined by objective criteria which permit review." The proposal was enacted into law in March 1964[48] over the vigorous opposition of the state AFL-CIO Council and the bitter objections of the Building Trades Unions. Now that new standards are established, and the FEP Commission performs the review, the means by which discriminatory practices can be legally ended is at hand.

The decision of the New York State Commission for Human Rights in the Sheet Metal Workers Union case holds great importance insofar as it influences FEPC operations throughout the nation. The decision, if its implications are carried to their logical conclusion, clearly indicates that state FEP commissions need not be obsolescent. State commissions however must qualitatively change their operational assumptions by using a new public standard based upon the realities of the social situation. Individual complaint settlements must now become a secondary function of the commission and for the first time, FEP commissions should demand that employers and labor unions change their entire institutional pattern in relation to Negroes and other nonwhite citizens.

Negro militancy in the north has created a new set of conditions for state FEP commissions. Now they must proceed boldly to the attack upon discriminatory patterns in entire industries and crafts, with new standards of evidence and new concepts of permanent affirmative compliance and above all, a far greater use of mandatory measures including the frequent issuance of cease and desist orders and court enforcement of commission rulings.

If state FEP commissions continue instead to operate with timidity and a general reluctance to broadly and rapidly enforce antidiscrim-

[48]L 1964, ch. 948. The New York Times, March 21, 1964.

ination statutes then they are obsolete, for the rising Negro mass movement will proceed to the attack in its own way. What state antidiscrimination commissions do within the next months and years and how rapidly they go about doing it will determine in large measure the nature of the racial confrontation in the northern states. This is now especially important as it becomes clearer each passing day that the next great crisis in American race relations will be in the north.

A Way Out of the Exploding Ghetto

Bayard Rustin

[Reprinted with permission from The New York Times Magazine, *August 13, 1967. Copyright 1967 The New York Times Company.]*

Not since the Great Depression have social policy, our national institutions, our political order been more severely tested than at present. The coming months will shape the character of America in the remainder of the 20th century—and I am trying to speak with the utmost sobriety, precision and restraint.

Why does the Republic find itself at a crossroads? What has actually happened?

The term "race riot" is unilluminating and anachronistic. It describes the Detroit disorders of 1943, when the Negro and white communities were locked in combat. White mobs invaded the ghetto. Negroes forayed downtown. Men were beaten and murdered for the color of their skins. In the upheavals of the last four summers, destruction has been confined to the ghetto; nor, discounting the police, were black and white citizens fighting. In fact, in Detroit whites joined in the looting and sniping. And I am told that whites were free to walk through the embattled ghetto without fear of violence from Negroes.

This is not to deny the importance of antiwhite hostility. One has only to hear the sick racial epithets "honkey" and "whitey" to recognize the deep and bitter hatred that is loose on the streets of the ghettos. But if white blood was what the rioters thirsted for, they didn't go very far to get it. What they assaulted were the symbols of white power—police and property, the latter embracing the entire ghetto. These are traditional targets of rebellions and in that sense the riots can be called rebellions.

That sense, however, must be sharply qualified. Is it correct to speak of "race rebellion," or "Negro rebellion"? Are America's Negroes on the verge of revolution? More than one newspaper and television commentator has already begun to draw comparisons between the ghetto uprisings and the French, Russian, Algerian, Irish and Black African independence revolutions. Some Black Power advocates have proclaimed the beginnings of guerrilla warfare and see the urban Negro as a counterpart to the Vietcong. And in Paris it has become fashionable to speak of the "*révolution des noires*" in the U.S.

The reality is that the revolutionary rhetoric now employed by some young Negro militants cannot create the preconditions for successful, or even authentic, revolution. The independence movements in colonial territories provide no model for the simple reason that American Negroes can have no geographical focus for nationalist sentiment.

Moreover, American Negroes do not constitute a popular majority struggling against a relatively small white colonial ruling group—the ideal condition for guerrilla warfare. Whatever separatist impulses exist among American Negroes cannot find appropriate models in the colonial world.

If independence revolutions are no model, what of social revolutions? This is a more interesting subject because the phrase "social revolution" has been widely used by the civil-rights and liberal movements generally. But in this sense—and the sense in which I have been using it for 30 years—the phrase designates fundamental changes in social and economic class relations resulting from mass political action. Such action would be democratic. That is, it would aim to create a new majority coalition capable of exercising political power in the interest of new social policies. By definition the coalition has to be interracial.

As a minority, Negroes by themselves cannot bring about such a social revolution. They can participate in it as a powerful and stimulating force; or they can provoke a counter-revolution. In either case the decisive factor will be the political direction in which the majority will move.

Numbers are not the only issue. Also important is the class content of revolt. At least in the French and Russian revolutions, revolutionary leaders and parties sought to mobilize fairly definable and cohesive socio-economic classes—workers, peasants, the middle class—which, though oppressed or aggrieved, were part of the society they sought to transform. Upon what classes do the advocates of rioting, the voices of the apocalypse, base their revolutionary perspective? This is another way of posing the question I left hanging earlier: Who is rioting?

Daniel Patrick Moynihan is correct in locating the riots in the "lower class" or in the words of another controversial man, Karl Marx, in the "*lumpenproletariat*" or "slum proletariat." Lower class does not mean working class; the distinction is often overlooked in a middle-class culture that tends to lump the two together.

The distinction is important. The working class is employed. It has a relation to the production of goods and services; much of it is organized in unions. It enjoys a measure of cohesion, discipline and stability lacking in the lower class. The latter is unemployed or marginally employed. It is relatively unorganized, incohesive, unstable. It contains the petty criminal and antisocial elements. Above all, unlike the working class, it lacks the sense of a stake in society. When the slum proletariat is black, its alienation is even greater.

From the revolutionist point of view, the question is not whether steps could be taken to strengthen organization among the *lumpen-proletariat* but whether that group could be a central agent of social transformation. Generally, the answer has been no.

The black slum proletariat has been growing in numbers and density. As agricultural mechanization and other factors continue pushing Negroes out of the South, the urban ghettos expand each year by half a million; only 40,000 Negroes annually find their way into the suburbs. This trend has not been affected at all by any antipoverty or Great Society programs.

When the migration of Negroes to Northern and Western cities was at its height during World War II, factory jobs were available at decent wages. With the advent of advanced technology eliminating many semiskilled and unskilled jobs, and with the movement of plants from the central cities to the suburbs (New York lost 200,000 factory jobs in a decade), urban Negroes suffered rising joblessness or employment in low-paying service jobs.

The depth of the unemployment problem in the slum ghettos is indicated in a recent U.S. Department of Labor report on "subemployment" in cities and slums. While the traditional unemployment rate counts only those "actively looking" but unable to find work, the subemployment index reflects in addition: (1) those who have dropped out of the labor market in despair, (2) those who are working part-time but want full-time jobs, (3) heads of households under 65 working full time but earning poverty wages (less than \$60 a week), (4) individuals under 65 who are not heads of households and earn less than \$56 a week in full-time jobs and (5) a conservatively estimated portion of males known to be living in the slums but who somehow do not show up in employment or unemployment counts.

The report states: "If the traditional statistical concept of 'unemployment' (which produced the nationwide average of 3.7 per cent unemployment rate for January, 1967) is applied to the urban slum situation, the *'unemployment rate' in these areas is about 10 per cent*

. . . *three times the average for the rest of the country.*" [Original italics.] The figure for Detroit"s Central Woodward area, incidentally, is 10.1 per cent.

The subemployment rate in the 10 cities surveyed yields an average figure of almost 35 per cent. Though possibly in need of further refining, the subemployment rate is the more meaningful figure. Not only does it include the categories listed above, but it also tends to reflect the number of people who experience unemployment over a period of time. By contrast, the official rate counts those unemployed at a point in time (i.e., the time the survey is taken).

High unemployment and low income are not the only problems afflicting the black slum proletariat, but they are the crucial ones. Without adequate income, there is no access to the decent housing market, educational opportunity, even proper health care.

The tendency of much current antipoverty rhetoric to create a multitude of disparate problems out of a central multifaceted one is a mistake. It is precisely in the expansion of public facilities and social services that new employment opportunities can be generated, at varying skill levels. High subemployment rates and the lack of decent housing in the slums are two sides of the same coin.

Meanwhile, within the slum proletariat, youth constitutes a subdivision of increasing economic and political importance. While according to the official unemployment rates the joblessness gap between Negro and white men over 20 has been narrowing since 1961, even this official rate records a widening of the gap between Negro and white teen-agers since 1957. Right now the national Negro unemployment rate is 25 per cent nationally but for 16-to-19-year-olds in the 10 slum areas surveyed, it is over 38 per cent! Moreover, this rate was unaffected by the downward trend of the nation's over-all unemployment rate late last year. For white teen-agers, on the other hand, unemployment since 1957 never went beyond 15 per cent and is now at 10 per cent.

Nor is there any evidence that Negro teen-agers do not want to work. Whenever job programs have been announced, they have turned out in large numbers, only to find that the jobs weren't there. In Oakland, a "Job Fair" attracted 15,000 people; only 250 were placed. In Philadelphia, 6,000 were on a waiting list for a training program.

What Negro teen-agers are not inclined to accept are dead-end jobs that pay little and promise no advancement or training. Many would prefer to live by their wits as hustlers or petty racketeers, their version of the self-employed businessman or salesman. That their pursuit of this distorted entrepreneurial ideal only mires them deeper in the slum proletariat is not the point. They want to be part of the white collar organization man's world that is America's future, not trapped behind brooms and pushcarts.

Nor can they fairly be blamed by a society which has itself produced these yearnings, reveled in its affluence, encouraged the consumption of trivia and proclaimed the coming of computerized utopias. The middle classes may nostalgically extol their immigrant parents' fortitude and perseverance in manual labor, but they do not steer their own children toward the construction gang or the garment district. They show them the push buttons, not the pushcart. Might they not then show some compassionate understanding of black youngsters who dream of better things even when crippled by poor education, broken families, and the disabilities bred by slum life. If it is true that a Negro boy is nobody unless he owns alligator shoes and an alpaca sweater, who created these symbols? Who whetted his appetite? Who profited from the sale of these commodities, and who advertised them? And who is victimized?

The ghetto youth who is out of school, unemployed, and rejected even by the draft (as 52 per cent are in Harlem) is the extreme embodiment of the bitter frustration in the slum proletariat. He is utterly propertyless, devoid of experience in the productive process, and without a stake in existing social arrangements. At the same time, because he is young and not beaten down, he is irreverent, filled with bravado, hostile to the alien authority of the police, and determined to "make it" in any way that he can. He is at the core of the rioting.

In Detroit, the riot begins when pimps and prostitutes taunt police who are raiding a "blind pig" at 5 A.M. In Minneapolis, two women fight over a wig, the police try to break it up and a riot erupts in an atmosphere already charged by delays in the mailing of Federal Youth Opportunity Program paychecks to youths in the ghetto area. In Cairo, Ill., a Negro soldier dies in the city jail; police say it was suicide but order the body embalmed without an autopsy, and fire bombing and shooting follow.

In these cases, the police figure prominently in the incidents that triggered the rioting. Sometimes they are not directly involved, but rumors of police brutality flood through the ghetto. Although it may be of some interest to search for a pattern, no very profound purpose is served by concentrating on who struck the match. There are always matches lying around. We must ask why there was also a fuse and why the fuse was connected to a powder keg.

To pursue this analogy: Whether the match is struck by police misconduct or by an "extremist" exhorting his listeners to violence, the fuse is the condition of life among the black slum proletariat—hostile, frustrated and with nothing to lose. The powder keg is the social background against which the riots break out and which extends their scope. They become more than riots pure and simple, yet less than politically coherent rebellions. They are *riotous manifestations of rebellion.*

The social background is defined by the fact that the black slum proletariat is part of a larger community of oppressed and segregated citizens—the overwhelming majority of the Negro population. Were it not for this the riots could be dismissed merely as wild, inchoate sprees of looting and violence, the expressions of criminal greed, a carnival of destruction to be suppressed by police force. Such actions, detached from political policies, programs and goals—and, make no mistake about it, the riots were not on behalf of the Black Power ideology; the latter is an after-the-fact justification employed by people in search of a constituency—do not properly constitute a rebellion. But because of the social background, the riots, while not *the rebellion* of the Negro people, are charged with manifestations of rebellion.

It is because of this background that the riots can set off a chain reaction, fan out from the slum proletariat and, as Detroit showed, involve people who ordinarily would not be found looting stores. It is because of this background that snipers and the most violent elements can feel that their actions are in some sense heroic. And it is because of this background that the riots have enormous implications for the future of all Negroes.

As Martin Luther King, A. Philip Randolph, Roy Wilkins and Whitney Young pointed out in their recent statement, the most severe and immediate damage has been to the Negro community itself. In addition to those who lost their lives, thousands lost their homes, food supplies, access to schools. There is danger of a counterreaction enlisting the most bigoted, vigilante-minded elements in the white community. Ammunition has been given to the reactionaries in an already backlash-dominated Congress. Many whites sincerely in favor of integration will be silenced out of fear and confusion. Riots do not strengthen the power of black people; they weaken it and encourage racist power.

But why, asks white America, do the Negroes riot now—not when conditions are at their worst but when they seem to be improving? Why now, after all of the civil-rights and antipoverty legislation? There are two answers.

First, "progress" has been considerably less than is generally supposed. While the Negro has won certain important legal and constitutional rights (voting, desegregation of public accommodations, etc.), his relative socioeconomic position has scarcely improved. There simply has not been significant, visible change in his life.

Second, if a society is interested in stability, it should either not make promises or it should keep them. Economic and social deprivation, if accepted by its victims as their lot in life, breeds passivity, even docility. The miserable yield to their fate as divinely ordained or as their own fault. And, indeed, many Negroes in earlier generations felt that way.

Today, young Negroes aren't having any. They don't share the feeling that something must be wrong with them, that they are responsible for their own exclusion from this affluent society. The civil-rights movement—in fact, the whole liberal trend beginning with John Kennedy's election—has told them otherwise.

Conservatives will undoubtedly seize the occasion for an attack on the Great Society, liberalism, the welfare state and Lyndon Johnson. But the young Negroes are right: the promises made to them were good and necessary and long, long overdue. The youth were right to believe in them. The only trouble is that they were not fulfilled. Prominent Republicans and Dixiecrats are demanding not that the promises be fulfilled, but that they be revoked.

What they and the American people absolutely must understand now is that the promises cannot be revoked. They were not made to a handful of leaders in a White House drawing room; they were made to an entire generation, one not likely to forget or to forgive. If Republican leaders Everett Dirksen and Gerald Ford, hand in glove with the die-hards of the Confederacy, continue their contemptible effort to exploit the nation's tragedy for partisan political advantage, they will sow the dangerous seeds of race hate and they will discredit themselves morally in the eyes of the coming generations and of history. This is not a wise policy for a party that only yesterday reduced itself to a shamble by catering to the most backward and reactionary elements in the country.

It is ironic that in a nation which has not undertaken a massive social and economic reform since the New Deal one now hears even liberal voices asking: "Don't the causes of the riots go deeper than economics, than jobs, housing, schools? Aren't there profound moral, cultural, psychological and other factors involved—powerlessness, an identity crisis?"

Of course, but in the present context such questions smack of a trend toward mystification which, if it gains ascendancy, will paralyze public policy. Then, too, I cannot help but suspect that they are rationalizations for the yearning of some white liberals to withdraw. "Obviously," they are saying, "there seems to be nothing we can do. We're not even wanted. Why not give the ghettos over to the Black Power people?"

I have no hesitation in saying that this recommendation simply aids and abets the Congressional reactionaries, who would have no objection to letting Negroes run their own slum tenements, dilapidated schools and tax-starved communities. Isn't this in the best tradition of rugged self-help, Horatio Alger and all that? Haven't Barry Goldwater and William F. Buckley endorsed this notion of Black Power? Just so long as white people are left alone. Just so long as the total society is not forced to examine its own inner contradictions. Just so long as the Federal Government isn't challenged to launch radical and massive programs to rebuild our cities, end poverty, guarantee full employment at decent wages, clear our poluted air and water and provide mass transportation.

This is just the challenge posed by A. Philip Randolph's $185-billion "Freedom Budget for all Americans"—a carefully designed, economically feasible program for the obliteration of poverty in 10 years. Unless the nation is prepared to move along these lines—to rearrange its priorities, to set a timetable for achieving them and to allocate its resources accordingly—it will not be taking its own commitments seriously. Surely it cannot then turn amazedly to responsible Negro leaders, whose pleas for large-scale programs it has failed to heed, for an explanation of the consequences.

The present Administration has a grave responsibility. It is very well for it to proclaim that we can have guns *and* butter, that we can pursue our course in Vietnam and still make progress at home. We do have the economic capacity for both, as the Freedom Budget itself shows. But we are not doing both. Let us stop proclaiming that we *can* do what we *don't* do and start *doing* it.

If Administration actions are not to mock its own rhetoric, the President must not take the lead in mobilizing public opinion behind a new resolve to meet the crisis in our cities. He should now put before Congress a National Emergency Public Works and Reconstruction bill aimed at building housing for homeless victims of the riot-torn ghettos, repairing damaged public facilities and in the process generating maximum employment opportunities for unskilled and semiskilled workers. Such a bill should be the first step in the reconstruction of all our decaying center cities.

Admittedly, the prospects for passage of such a bill in the present Congress are dismal. Congressmen will cry out that the rioters must not be rewarded, thereby further penalizing the very victims of the riots. This, after all, is a Congress capable of defeating a meager $40-million rat extermination program the same week it votes $10-million for an aquarium in the District of Columbia!

But the vindictive racial meanness that has descended upon this

Congress, already dominated by the revived coalition of Republicans and Dixiecrats, must be challenged—not accommodated. The President must go directly to the people, as Harry Truman did in 1948. He must go to them, not with slogans, but with a timetable for tearing down every slum in the country.

There can be no further delay. The daydreamers and utopians are not those of us who have prepared massive Freedom Budgets and similar programs. They are the smugly "practical" and myopic philistines in the Congress, the state legislatures and the city halls who thought they could sit it out. The very practical choice now before them and the American people is whether we shall have a conscious and authentic democratic social revolution or more tragic and futile riots that tear our nation to shreds.

On Improving the Economic Status of the Negro

James Tobin

[*From* Daedalus, *Fall 1965, by permission of The American Academy of Arts and Sciences.*]

I start from the presumption that the integration of Negroes into the American society and economy can be accomplished within existing political and economic institutions. I understand the impatience of those who think otherwise, but I see nothing incompatible between our peculiar mixture of private enterprise and government, on the one hand, and the liberation and integration of the Negro, on the other. Indeed the present position of the Negro is an aberation from the principles of our society, rather than a requirement of its functioning. Therefore, my suggestions are directed to the aim of mobilizing existing powers of government to bring Negroes into full participation in the main stream of American economic life.

The economic plight of individuals, Negroes and whites alike, can always be attributed to specific handicaps and circumstances: discrimination, immobility, lack of education and experience, ill health, weak motivation, poor neighborhood, large family size, burdensome family responsibilities. Such diagnoses suggest a host of specific remedies, some in the domain of civil rights, others in the war on poverty. Important as these remedies are, there is a danger that the diagnoses are myopic. They explain why certain individuals rather than others suffer from the economic maladies of the time. They do not explain why the over-all incidence of the maladies varies dramatically from time to time—for example, why personal attributes which seemed to doom a man to unemployment in 1932 or even in 1954 or 1961 did not so handicap him in 1944 or 1951 or 1956.

Public health measures to improve the environment are often more productive in conquering disease than a succession of individual treatments. Malaria was conquered by oiling and draining swamps, not by quinine. The analogy holds for economic maladies. Unless the global incidence of these misfortunes can be diminished, every individual problem successfully solved will be replaced by a similar problem somewhere else. That is why an economist is led to emphasize the importance of the over-all economic climate.

Over the decades, general economic progress has been the major factor in the gradual conquest of poverty. Recently some observers, J. K. Galbraith and Michael Harrington most eloquently, have contended that this process no longer operates. The economy may prosper and labor may become steadily more productive as in the past, but "the other America" will be stranded. Prosperity and progress have already eliminated almost all the easy cases of poverty, leaving a hard core beyond the reach of national economic trends. There may be something to the "backwash" thesis as far as whites are concerned.[1] But it definitely does not apply to Negroes. Too many of them are poor. It cannot be true that half of a race of twenty million human beings are victims of specific disabilities which insulate them from the national economic climate. It cannot be true, and it is not. Locke Anderson has shown that the pace of Negro economic progress is peculiarly sensitive to general economic growth. He estimates that if nationwide per capita personal income is stationary, nonwhite median family income falls by .5 per cent per year, while if national per capita income grows 5 per cent, nonwhite income grows nearly 7.5 per cent.[2]

National prosperity and economic growth are still powerful engines for improving the economic status of Negroes. They are not doing enough and they are not doing it fast enough. There is ample room for a focused attack on the specific sources of Negro poverty. But a favorable over-all economic climate is a necessary condition for the global success—as distinguished from success in individual cases—of specific efforts to remedy the handicaps associated with Negro poverty.

The Importance of a Tight Labor Market

But isn't the present over-all economic climate favorable? Isn't the economy enjoying an upswing of unprecedented length, setting new records almost every month in production, employment, profits, and income? Yes, but expansion and new records should be routine in an economy with growing population, capital equipment, and productivity. The fact is that the economy has not operated with reasonably full utilization of its manpower and plant capacity since 1957. Even now, after four and one-half years of uninterrupted expansion, the economy has not regained the ground lost in the recessions of 1958 and 1960. The current expansion has whittled away at unemployment, reducing it from 6.5 to 7 per cent to 4.5 to 5 per cent. It has diminished idle plant capacity correspondingly. The rest of the gains since 1960 in employment, production, and income have just offset the normal growth of population, capacity, and productivity.

The magnitude of America's poverty problem already reflects the failure of the economy in the second postwar decade to match its performance in the first.[3] Had the 1947-56 rate of growth of median family income been maintained since 1957, and had unemployment been steadily limited to 4 per cent, it is estimated that the fraction of the population with poverty incomes in 1963 would have been 16.6 per cent instead of 18.5 per cent.[4] The educational qualifications of the labor force have continued to improve. The principle of racial equality, in employment as in other activities, has gained ground both in law and in the national conscience. If, despite all this, dropouts, inequalities in educational attainment, and discrimination in employment seem more serious today rather than less, the reason is that the over-all economic climate has not been favorable after all.

The most important dimension of the overall economic climate is the tightness of the labor market. In a tight labor market unemployment is low and short in duration, and job vacancies are plentiful. People who stand at the end of the hiring line and the top of the layoff list have the most to gain from a tight labor market. It is not surprising that the position of Negroes relative to that of whites improves in a tight labor market and declines in a slack market. Unemployment itself is only one way in which a slack labor market hurts Negroes and other disadvantaged groups, and the gains from reduction in unemployment are by no means confined to the employment of persons counted as unemployed.[5] A tight labor market means not just jobs, but better jobs, longer hours, higher wages. Because of the heavy demands for labor during the second world war and its economic aftermath, Negroes made dramatic relative gains between 1940 and 1950. Unfortunately this momentum has not been maintained, and the blame falls largely on the weakness of labor markets since 1957.[6]

The shortage of jobs has hit Negro men particularly hard and thus has contributed mightily to the ordeal of the Negro family, which is in turn the cumulative source of so many other social disorders.[7] The unemployment rate of Negro men is more sensitive than that of Negro women to the national rate. Since 1949 Negro women have gained in median income relative to white women, but Negro men have lost ground to white males.[8] In a society which stresses breadwinning as the expected role of the mature male and occupational achievement as his proper goal, failure to find and to keep work is devastating to the man's self-respect and family status. Matriarchy is in any case a strong tradition in Negro society, and the man's role is further downgraded when the family must and can depend on the woman for its livelihood. It is very important to increase the proportion of Negro children who grow up in stable families with two parents. Without a strong labor market it will be extremely difficult to do so.

Unemployment. It is well known that Negro unemployment rates are multiples of the general unemployment rate. This fact reflects both the lesser skills, seniority, and experience of Negroes and employers' discrimination against Negroes. These conditions are a deplorable reflection on American society, but as long as they exist Negroes suffer much more than others from a general increase in unemployment and gain much more from a general reduction. A rule of thumb is that changes in the nonwhite unemployment rate are twice those in the white rate. The rule works both ways. Nonwhite unemployment went from 4.1 per cent in 1953, a tight labor market year, to 12.5 per cent in 1961, while the white rate rose from 2.3 per cent to 6 per cent. Since then, the Negro rate has declined by 2.4 per cent, the white rate by 1.2.

Even the Negro teenage unemployment rate shows some sensitivity to general economic conditions. Recession increased it from 15 per cent in 1955-56 to 25 per cent in 1958. It decreased to 22 per cent in 1960 but rose to 28 per cent in 1963; since then it has declined somewhat. Teenage unemployment is abnormally high now, relative to that of other age groups, because the wave of postwar babies is coming into the labor market. Most of them, especially the Negroes, are crowding the end of the hiring line. But their prospects for getting jobs are no less dependent on general labor market conditions.

Part-time work. Persons who are involuntarily forced to work part time instead of full time are not counted as unemployed, but their number goes up and down with the unemployment rate. Just as Negroes bear a disproportionate share of unemployment, they bear more than their share of involuntary part-time unemployment.[9] A tight labor market will not only employ more Negroes; it will also give more of those who are employed full-time jobs. In both respects, it will reduce disparities between whites and Negroes.

Labor-force participation. In a tight market, of which a low unemployment rate is a barometer, the labor force itself is larger. Job opportunities draw into the labor force individuals who, simply because the prospects were dim, did not previously regard themselves as seeking work and were therefore not enumerated as unemployed. For the economy as a whole, it appears that an expansion of job opportunities enough to reduce unemployment by one worker will bring another worker into the labor force.

This phenomenon is important for many Negro families. Statistically, their poverty now appears to be due more often to the lack of a breadwinner in the labor force than to unemployment.[10] But in a tight labor market many members of these families, including families now on public assistance, would be drawn into employment. Labor-force participation rates are roughly 2 per cent lower for nonwhite men than for white men, and the disparity increases in years of slack labor markets.[11] The story is different for women. Negro women have always been in the labor force to a much greater extent than white women. A real improvement in the economic status of Negro men and in the stability of Negro families would probably lead to a reduction in labor-force participation by Negro women. But for teenagers, participation rates for Negroes are not so high as for whites; and for women twenty to twenty-four they are about the same. These relatively low rates are undoubtedly due less to voluntary choice than to the same lack of job opportunities that produces phenomenally high unemployment rates for young Negro women.

Duration of unemployment. In a tight labor market, such unemployment as does exist is likely to be of short duration. Short term unemployment is less damaging to the economic welfare of the unemployed. More will have earned and fewer will have exhausted private and public unemployment benefits. In 1953 when the over-all unemployment rate was 2.9 per cent, only 4 per cent of the unemployed were out of work for longer than twenty-six weeks and only 11 per cent for longer than fifteen weeks. In contrast, the unemployment rate in 1961 was 6.7 per cent; and of the unemployed in that year, 17 per cent were out of work for longer than twenty-six weeks and 32 per cent for longer than fifteen weeks. Between the first quarter of 1964 and the first quarter of 1965, overall unemployment fell 11 per cent, while unemployment extending beyond half a year was lowered by 22 per cent.

As Rashi Fein points out,[12] one more dimension of society's inequity to the Negro is that an unemployed Negro is more likely to stay unemployed than an unemployed white. But his figures also show that Negroes share in the reduction of long-term unemployment accompanying economic expansion.

Migration from agriculture. A tight labor market draws the surplus rural population to higher paying non-agricultural jobs. Southern Negroes are a large part of this surplus rural population. Migration is the only hope for improving their lot, or their children's. In spite of the vast migration of past decades, there are still about 775,000 Negroes, 11 per cent of the Negro labor force of the country, who depend on the land for their living and that of their families.[13] Almost a half million live in the South, and almost all of them are poor.

Migration from agriculture and from the South is the Negroes' historic path toward economic improvement and equality. It is a smooth path for Negroes and for the urban communities to which they move only if there is a strong demand for labor in towns and cities North and South. In the 1940's the number of Negro farmers and farm laborers in the nation fell by 450,000 and one and a half million Negroes (net) left the South. This was the great decade of Negro economic advance. In the 1950's the same occupational and geographical migration continued undiminished. The movement to higher-income occupations and locations should have raised the relative economic status of Negroes. But in the 1950's Negroes were moving into increasingly weak job markets. Too often disguised unemployment in the countryside was simply transformed into enumerated unemployment, and rural poverty into urban poverty.[14]

Quality of jobs. In a slack labor market, employers can pick and choose, both in recruiting and in promoting. They exaggerate the skill, education, and experience requirements of their jobs. They use diplomas, or color, or personal histories as convenient screening devices. In a tight market, they are forced to be realistic, to tailor job specifications to the available supply, and to give on-the-job training. They recruit and train applicants whom they would otherwise screen out, and they upgrade employees whom they would in slack times consign to low-wage, low-skill, and part-time jobs.

Wartime and other experience shows that job requirements are adjustable and that men and women are trainable. It is only in slack times that people worry about a mismatch between supposedly rigid occupational requirements and supposedly unchangeable qualifications of the labor force. As already noted, the relative status of Negroes improves in a tight labor market not only in respect to unemployment, but also in respect to wages and occupations.

Cyclical fluctuation. Sustaining a high demand for labor is important. The in-and-out status of the Negro in the business cycle damages his long-term position because periodic unemployment robs him of experience and seniority.

Restrictive practices. A slack labor market probably accentuates the discriminatory and protectionist proclivities of certain crafts and unions. When jobs are scarce, opening the door to Negroes is a real threat. Of course prosperity will not automatically dissolve the barriers, but it will make it more difficult to oppose efforts to do so.

I conclude that the single most important step the nation could take to improve the economic position of the Negro is to operate the economy steadily at a low rate of unemployment. We cannot expect to restore the labor market conditions of the second world war, and we do not need to. In the years 1951-1953, unemployment was roughly 3 per cent, teenage unemployment around 7 per cent, Negro unemployment about 4.5 per cent, long-term unemployment negligible. In the years 1955-57, general unemployment was roughly 4 per cent, and the other measures correspondingly higher. Four per cent is the official target of the Kennedy-Johnson administration. It has not been achieved since 1957. Reaching and maintaining 4 per cent would be a tremendous improvement over the performance of the last eight years. But we should not stop there; the society and the Negro can benefit immensely from tightening the labor market still further, to 3.5 or 3 per cent unemployment. The administration itself has never defined 4 per cent as anything other than an "interim" target.

Why Don't We Have a Tight Labor Market?

We know how to operate the economy so that there is a tight labor market. By fiscal and monetary measures the federal government can control aggregate spending in the economy. The government could choose to control it so that unemployment *averaged* 3.5 or 3 per cent instead of remaining over 4.5 per cent except at occasional business cycle peaks. Moreover, recent experience here and abroad shows that we can probably narrow the amplitude of fluctuations around whatever average we select as a target.

Some observers have cynically concluded that a society like ours can achieve full employment only in wartime. But aside from conscription into the armed services, government action creates jobs in wartime by exactly the same mechanism as in peacetime—the government spends more money and stimulates private firms and citizens to spend more too. It is the *amount* of spending, not its purpose, that does the trick. Public or private spending to go to the moon, build schools, or conquer poverty can be just as effective in reducing unemployment as spending to build airplanes and submarines—if there is enough of it. There may be more political constraints and ideological inhibitions in peacetime, but the same techniques of economic policy are available if we want badly enough to use them. The two main reasons we do not take this relatively simple way out are two obsessive fears, inflation and balance of payments deficits.

Running the economy with a tight labor market would mean a somewhat faster upward creep in the price level. The disadvantages of this are, in my view, exaggerated and are scarcely commensurable with the real economic and social gains of higher output and employment. Moreover, there are ways of protecting "widows and orphans" against erosion in the purchasing power of their savings. But fear of inflation is strong both in the U.S. financial establishment and in the public at large. The vast comfortable white middle class who are never touched by unemployment prefer to safeguard the purchasing power of their life insurance and pension rights than to expand opportunities for the disadvantaged and unemployed.

The fear of inflation would operate anyway, but it is accentuated by U.S. difficulties with its international balance of payments. These difficulties have seriously constrained and hampered U.S. fiscal and monetary policy in recent years. Any rise in prices might enlarge the deficit. An aggressively expansionary monetary policy, lowering interest rates, might push money out of the country.

In the final analysis what we fear is that we might not be able to defend the parity of the dollar with gold, that is, to sell gold at thirty-five dollars an ounce to any government that wants to buy. So great is the gold mystique that this objective has come to occupy a niche in the hierarchy of U.S. goals second only to the military defense of the country, and not always to that. It is not fanciful to link the plight of Negro teenagers in Harlem to the monetary whims of General de Gaulle. But it is only our own attachment to "the dollar" as an abstraction which makes us cringe before the European appetite for gold.

This topic is too charged with technical complexities, real and imagined, and with confused emotions to be discussed adequately here. I will confine myself to three points. First, the United States is the last country in the world which needs to hold back its own economy to balance its international accounts. To let the tail wag the dog is not in the interests of the rest of the world, so much of which depends on us for trade and capital, any more than in our own.

Second, forces are at work to restore balance to American international acounts—the increased competitiveness of our exports and the income from the large investments our firms and citizens have made overseas since the war. Meanwhile we can finance deficits by gold reserves and lines of credit at the International Monetary Fund and at foreign central banks. Ultimately we have one foolproof line of defense—letting the dollar depreciate relative to foreign currencies. The world would not end. The sun would rise the next day. American products would be more competitive in world markets. Neither God nor the Constitution fixed the gold value of the dollar. The U.S. would not be the first country to let its currency depreciate. Nor would it be the first time for the U.S.—not until we stopped "saving" the dollar and the gold standard in 1933 did our recovery from the Great Depression begin.

Third, those who oppose taking such risks argue that the dollar today occupies a unique position as international money, that the world as a whole has an interest, which we cannot ignore, in the stability of the gold value of the dollar. If so, we can reasonably ask the rest of the world, especially our European friends, to share the burdens which guaranteeing this stability imposes upon us.

This has been an excursion into general economic policy. But the connection between gold and the plight of the Negro is no less real for being subtle. We are paying much too high a social price for avoiding creeping inflation and for protecting our gold stock and "the dollar." But it will not be easy to alter these national priorities. The interests of the unemployed, the poor, and the Negroes are under-represented in the comfortable consensus which supports and confines current policy.

Another approach, which can be pursued simultaneously, is to diminish the conflicts among these competing objectives, in particular to reduce the degree of inflation associated with low levels of unemployment. This can be done in two ways. One way is to improve the mobility of labor and other resources to occupations, locations, and industries where bottlenecks would otherwise lead to wage and price increases. This is where many specific programs, such as the training and retraining of manpower and policies to improve the technical functioning of labor markets, come into their own.

A second task is to break down the barriers to competition which now restrict the entry of labor and enterprise into certain occupations and industries. These lead to wage- and price-increasing bottlenecks even when resources are not really short. Many barriers are created by public policy itself, in response to the vested interests concerned. Many reflect concentration of economic power in unions and in industry. These barriers represent another way in which the advantaged and the employed purchase their standards of living and their security at the expense of unprivileged minorities.

In the best of circumstances, structural reforms of these kinds will be slow and gradual. They will encounter determined economic and political resistance from special interests which are powerful in Congress and state legislatures. Moreover, Congressmen and legislators represent places rather than people and are likely to oppose, not facilitate, the increased geographical mobility which is required. It is no accident that our manpower programs do not include relocation allowances.

Increasing the Earning Capacity of Negroes

Given the proper over-all economic climate, in particular a steadily tight labor market, the Negro's economic condition can be expected to improve, indeed to improve dramatically. But not fast enough. Not as fast as his aspirations or as the aspirations he has taught the rest of us to have for him. What else can be done? This question is being answered in detail by experts elsewhere in this volume. I shall confine myself to a few comments and suggestions that occur to a general economist.

Even in a tight labor market, the Negro's relative status will suffer both from current discrimination and from his lower earning capacity, the result of inferior acquired skill. In a real sense both factors reflect discrimination, since the Negro's handicaps in earning capacity are the residue of decades of discrimination in education and employment. Nevertheless for both analysis and policy it is useful to distinguish the two.

Discrimination means that the Negro is denied access to certain markets where he might sell his labor, and to certain markets where he might purchase goods and services. Elementary application of "supply and demand" makes it clear that these restrictions are bound to result in his selling his labor for less and buying his livelihood for more than if these barriers did not exist. If Negro women can be clerks only in certain stores, those storekeepers will not need to pay them so much as they pay whites. If Negroes can live only in certain houses, the prices and rents they have to pay will be high for the quality of accommodation provided.

Successful elimination of discrimination is not only important in itself but will also have substantial economic benefits. Since residential segregation is the key to so much else and so difficult to eliminate by legal fiat alone, the power of the purse should be unstintingly used. I see no reason that the expenditure of funds for this purpose should be confined to new construction. Why not establish private or semi-public revolving funds to purchase, for resale or rental on a desegregated basis, strategically located existing structures as they become available?

The effects of past discrimination will take much longer to eradicate. The sins against the fathers are visited on the children. They are deprived of the intellectual and social capital which in our society is supposed to be transmitted in the family and the home. We have only begun to realize how difficult it is to make up for this deprivation by formal schooling, even when we try. And we have only begun to try, after accepting all too long the notion that schools should acquiesce in, even re-enforce, inequalities in home backgrounds rather than overcome them.

Upgrading the earning capacity of Negroes will be difficult, but the economic effects are easy to analyze. Economists have long held that the way to reduce disparities in earned incomes is to eliminate disparities in earning capacities. If college-trained people earn more money than those who left school after eight years, the remedy is to send a larger proportion of young people to college. If machine operators earn more than ditchdiggers, the remedy is to give more people the capacity and opportunity to be machine operators. These changes in relative supplies reduce the disparity both by competing down the pay in the favored line of work and by raising the pay in the less remunerative line. When there are only a few people left in the population whose capacities are confined to garbage-collecting, it will be a high-paid calling. The same is true of domestic service and all kinds of menial work.

This classical economic strategy will be hampered if discrimination, union barriers, and the like stand in the way. It will not help to increase the supply of Negro plumbers if the local unions and contractors will not let them join. But experience also shows that barriers give way more easily when the pressures of unsatisfied demand and supply pile up.

It should therefore be the task of educational and manpower policy to engineer over the next two decades a massive change in the relative supplies of people of different educational and professional attainments and degrees of skill and training. It must be a more rapid change than has occurred in the past two decades, because that has not been fast enough to alter income differentials. We should try particularly to increase supplies in those fields where salaries and wages are already high and rising. In this process we should be very skeptical of self-serving arguments and calculations—that an increase in supply in this or that profession would be bound to reduce quality, or that there are some mechanical relations of "need" to population or to Gross National Product that cannot be exceeded.

Such a policy would be appropriate to the "war on poverty" even if there were no racial problem. Indeed, our objective is to raise the earning capacities of low-income whites as well as of Negroes. But Negroes have the most to gain, and even those who because of age or irreversible environmental handicaps must inevitably be left behind will benefit by reduction in the number of whites and other Negroes who are competing with them.

Assuring Living Standards in the Absence of Earning Capacity

The reduction of inequality in earning capacity is the fundamental solution, and in a sense anything else is stopgap. Some stopgaps are useless and even counter-productive. People who lack the capacity to earn a decent living need to be helped, but they will not be helped by minimum wage laws, trade union wage pressures, or other devices which seek to compel employers to pay them more than their work is worth. The more likely outcome of such regulations is that the intended beneficiaries are not employed at all.

A far better approach is to supplement earnings from the public fisc. But assistance can and should be given in a way that does not force the recipients out of the labor force or give them incentive to withdraw. Our present system of welfare payments does just that, causing needless waste and demoralization. This application of the means test is bad economics as well as bad sociology. It is almost as if our present programs of public assistance had been consciously contrived to perpetuate the conditions they are supposed to alleviate.

These programs apply a strict means test. The amount of assistance is an estimate of minimal needs, less the resources of the family from earnings. The purpose of the means test seems innocuous enough. It is to avoid wasting taxpayers' money on people who do not really need help. But another way to describe the means test is to note that it taxes earnings at a rate of 100 per cent. A person on public assistance cannot add to his family's standard of living by working. Of course, the means test provides a certain incentive to work in order to get off public assistance altogether. But in many cases, especially where there is only one adult to provide for and take care of several children, the adult simply does not have enough time and earning opportunities to get by without financial help. He, or more likely she, is essentially forced to be both idle and on a dole. The means test also involves limitations on property holdings which deprive anyone who is or expects to be on public assistance of incentive to save.

In a society which prizes incentives for work and thrift, these are surprising regulations. They deny the country useful productive services, but that economic loss is minor in the present context. They deprive individuals and families both of work experience which could teach them skills, habits, and self-discipline of future value and of the self-respect and satisfaction which comes from improving their own lot by their own efforts.

Public assistance encourages the disintegration of the family, the key to so many of the economic and social problems of the American Negro. The main assistance program, Aid for Dependent Children, is not available if there is an able-bodied employed male in the house. In most states it is not available if there is an able-bodied man in the house, even if he is not working. All too often it is necessary for the father to leave his children so that they can eat. It is bad enough to provide incentives for idleness but even worse to legislate incentives for desertion.[15]

The bureaucratic surveillance and guidance to which recipients of public assistance are subject undermine both their self-respect and their capacity to manage their own affairs. In the administration of assistance there is much concern to detect "cheating" against the means tests and to ensure approved prudent use of the public's money. Case loads are frequently too great and administrative regulations too confining to permit the talents of social workers to treat the roots rather than the symptoms of the social maladies of their clients. The time of the clients is considered a free good, and much of it must be spent in seeking or awaiting the attention of the officials on whom their livelihood depends.

The defects of present categorical assistance programs could be, in my opinion, greatly reduced by adopting a system of basic income allowances, integrated with and administered in conjunction with the federal income tax. In a sense the proposal is to make the income tax symmetrical. At present the federal government takes a share of family income in excess of a certain amount (for example, a married couple with three children pays no tax unless their income exceeds $3700). The proposal is that the Treasury pay any family who falls below a certain income a fraction of the shortfall. The idea has sometimes been called a negative income tax.

The payment would be a matter of right, like an income tax refund. Individuals expecting to be entitled to payments from the government during the year could receive them in periodic installments by making a declaration of expected income and expected tax withholdings. But there would be a final settlement between the individual and the government based on a "tax" return after the year was over, just as there is now for taxpayers on April 15.

A family with no other income at all would receive a basic allowance scaled to the number of persons in the family. For a concrete example, take the basic allowance to be $400 per year per person. It might be desirable and equitable, however, to reduce the additional basic allowance for children after, say, the fourth. Once sufficient effort is being made to disseminate birth control knowledge and technique, the scale of allowances by family size certainly should provide some disincentive to the creation of large families.

A family's allowance would be reduced by a certain fraction of every dollar of other income it received. For a concrete example, take this fraction to be one third. This means that the family has considerable incentive to earn income, because its total income including allowances will be increased by two-thirds of whatever it earns. In contrast, the means test connected with present public assistance is a 100 per cent "tax" on earnings. With a one-third "tax" a family will be on the receiving end of the allowance and income tax system until its regular income equals three times its basic allowance.[16]

Families above this "break-even" point would be taxpayers. But the less well-off among them would pay less taxes than they do now. The first dollars of income in excess of this break-even point would be taxed at the same rate as below, one-third in the example. At some income level, the tax liability so computed would be the same as the tax under the present income tax law. From that point up, the present law would take over; taxpayers with incomes above this point would not be affected by the plan.

The best way to summarize the proposal is to give a concrete graphical illustration. On the horizontal axis of Figure 1 is measured family income from wages and salaries, interest, dividends, rents, and so forth—"adjusted gross income" for the Internal Revenue Service. On the vertical axis is measured the corresponding "disposable income," that is, income after federal taxes and allowances. If the family neither paid taxes nor received allowance, disposable income would be equal to family income; in the diagram this equality would be shown by the 45° line from the origin. Disposable income above this 45° line means the family receives allowances; disposable income below this line means the family pays taxes. The broken line OAB describes the present income tax law for a married couple with three children, allowing the standard deductions. The line CD is the revision which the proposed allowance system would make for incomes below $7963. For incomes above $7963, the old tax schedule applies.

Beneficiaries under Federal Old Age Survivors and Disability

Insurance would not be eligible for the new allowances. Congress should make sure that minimum benefits under OASDI are at least as high as the allowances. Some government payments, especially those for categorical public assistance, would eventually be replaced by basic allowances. Others, like unemployment insurance and veterans' pensions, are intended to be rights earned by past services regardless of current need. It would therefore be wrong to withhold allowances from the beneficiaries of these payments, but it would be reasonable to count them as income in determining the size of allowances, even though they are not subject to tax.

Although the numbers used above are illustrative, they are indicative of what is needed for an effective program. It would be expensive for the federal budget, involving an expenditure of perhaps fifteen billion dollars a year. Partially offsetting this budgetary cost are the savings in public assistance, on which governments now spend five and six-tenths billion dollars a year, of which three and two-tenths billion are federal funds. In addition, savings are possible in a host of other income maintenance programs, notably in agriculture.

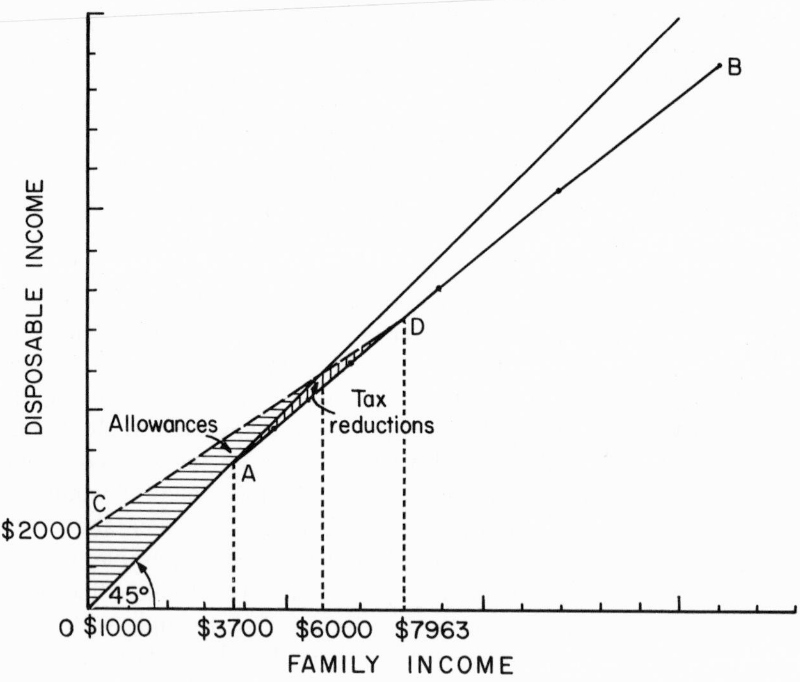

Figure 1: Illustration of Proposed Income Allowance Plan (Married couple with three children)

The program is expensive, but it need not be introduced all at once. The size of allowances can be gradually increased as room in the budget becomes available. This is likely to happen fairly rapidly. First of all, there is room right now. The budget, and the budget deficit, can and should be larger in order to create a tight labor market. Second, the normal growth of the economy increases federal revenues from existing tax rates by some six to seven billion dollars a year. This is a drag on the economy, threatening stagnation and rising unemployment unless it is matched by a similar rise in federal spending or avoided by cutting taxes. With defense spending stable or declining, there is room both for increases in civilian spending, as in the war on poverty, and for further tax cuts. Indeed, periodic tax reduction is official administration policy, and President Johnson agrees that the next turn belongs to low-income families. Gradually building an allowance system into the federal income tax would be the best way to lower the net yield of the tax—fairer and more far-reaching then further cuts in tax rates.

I referred to programs which make up for lack of earning capacity as stopgaps, but that is not entirely fair. Poverty itself saps earning capacity. The welfare way of life, on the edge of subsistence, does not provide motivation or useful work experience either to parents or to children. A better system, one which enables people to retain their self-respect and initiative, would in itself help to break the vicious circle.

The proposed allowance system is of course not the only thing which needs to be done. Without attempting to be exhaustive, I shall mention three other measures for the assistance of families without adequate earning capacity.

It hardly needs emphasizing that the large size of Negro families or non-families is one of the principal causes of Negro poverty. There are too many mouths to feed per breadwinner, and frequently the care of children keeps the mother, the only possible breadwinner, at home. A program of day care and pre-school education for children five and under could meet several objectives at once—enriching the experience of the children and freeing the mother for training or for work.

The quality of the medical care of Negroes is a disgrace in itself and contributes to their other economic handicaps.[16] Even so the financing of the care of "the medically indigent" is inadequate and chaotic. Sooner or later we will extend the principle of Medicare to citizens under sixty-five. Why not sooner?

As mentioned above, much Negro poverty in the South reflects the inability of Negroes to make a livelihood in agriculture. As far as the traditional cash crop, cotton, is concerned, mechanization and the competition of larger-scale units in the Southwest are undermining the plantation and share-cropping system of the Southeast. The Negro subsistence farmer has too little land, equipment, and know-how to make a decent income. Current government agricultural programs, expensive as they are to the taxpayer, do very little to help the sharecopper or subsistence farmer. Our whole agricultural policy needs to be recast, to give income support to people rather than price support to crops and to take people off the land rather than to take land out of cultivation. The effects on the social system of the South may be revolutionary, but they can only be salutary. Obviously there will be a tremendous burden on educational and training facilities to fit people for urban and industrial life. And I must emphasize again that substantial migration from agriculture is only possible, without disaster in the cities, in a booming economy with a tight labor market.

Conclusion

By far the most powerful factor determining the economic status of Negroes is the over-all state of the U.S. economy. A vigorously expanding economy with a steadily tight labor market will rapidly raise the position of the Negro, both absolutely and relatively. Favored by such a climate, the host of specific measures to eliminate discrimination, improve education and training, provide housing, and strengthen the family can yield substantial additional results. In a less beneficent economic climate, where jobs are short rather than men, the wars against racial inequality and poverty will be uphill battles, and some highly touted weapons may turn out to be dangerously futile.

The forces of the market place, the incentives of private self-interest, the pressures of supply and demand—these can be powerful allies or stubborn opponents. Properly harnesed, they quietly and impersonally accomplish objectives which may elude detailed legislation and administration. To harness them to the cause of the American Negro is entirely possible. It requires simply that the federal government dedicate its fiscal and monetary policies more wholeheartedly and singlemindedly to achieving and maintaining genuinely full employment. The obstacles are not technical or economic. One obstacle is a general lack of understanding that unemployment and related evils are remediable by national fiscal and monetary measures. The other is the high priority now given to competing financial objectives.

In this area, as in others, the administration has disarmed its conservative opposition by meeting it halfway, and no influential political voices challenge the tacit compromise from the "left." Negro rights movements have so far taken no interest in national fiscal and monetary policy. No doubt gold, the federal budget, and the actions of the Federal Reserve System seem remote from the day-to-day firing line of the movements. Direct local actions to redress specific grievances and to battle visible enemies are absorbing and dramatic. They have concrete observable results. But the use of national political influence on behalf of the goals of the Employment Act of 1946 is equally important. It would fill a political vacuum, and its potential long-run pay-off is very high.

The goal of racial equality suggests that the federal government should provide more stimulus to the economy. Fortunately, it also suggests constructive ways to give the stimulus. We can kill two birds with one stone. The economy needs additional spending in general; the wars on poverty and racial inequality need additional spending of particular kinds. The needed spending falls into two categories: government programs to diminish economic inequalities by building up the earning capacities of the poor and their children, and human public assistance to citizens who temporarily or permanently lack the capacity to earn a decent living for themselves and their families. In both categories the nation, its conscience aroused by the plight of the Negro, has the chance to make reforms which will benefit the whole society.

References

1. As Locke Anderson shows, one would expect advances in median income to run into diminishing returns in reducing the number of people below some fixed poverty-level income. W. H. Locke Anderson, "Trickling Down: The Relationship between Economic Growth and the Extent of Poverty Among American Families," *Quarterly Journal of Economics,* Vol. 78 (November 1964), pp. 511-524. However, for the economy as a whole, estimates by Lowell Galloway suggest that advances in median income still result in a substantial reduction in the fraction of the population below poverty-level incomes. "The Foundation of the War on Poverty," *American Economic Review,* Vol. 55 (March 1965), pp. 122-131.
2. Anderson, *op. cit.,* Table IV, p. 522.
3. This point, and others made in this section, have been eloquently argued by Harry G. Johnson, "Unemployment and Poverty," unpublished paper presented at West Virginia University Conference on Poverty Amidst Affluence, May 5, 1965.
4. Galloway, *op. cit.* Galloway used the definitions of poverty originally suggested by the Council of Economic Advisers in its 1964 Economic

Report, that is: incomes below $3000 a year for families and below $1500 a year for single individuals. The Social Security Administration has refined these measures to take better account of family size and of income in kind available to farmers. Mollie Orshansky, "Counting the Poor: Another Look at the Poverty Profile," *Social Security Bulletin,* Vol. 28 (January 1965), pp. 3-29. These refinements change the composition of the "poor" but affect very little their total number; it is doubtful they would alter Galloway's results.

5. Galloway, *op. cit.,* shows that postwar experience suggests that, other things equal, every point by which unemployment is diminished lowers the national incidence of poverty by .5 per cent of itself. And this does not include the effects of the accompanying increase in median family income, which would be of the order of 3 per cent and reduce the poverty fraction another 1.8 per cent.

6. For lack of comparable nationwide income data, the only way to gauge the progress of Negroes relative to whites over long periods of time is to compare their distributions among occupations. A measure of the occupational position of a group can be constructed from decennial Census data by weighting the proportions of the group in each occupation by the average income of the occupation. The ratio of this measure for Negroes to the same measure for whites is an index of the relative occupational position of Negroes. Such calculations were originally made by Gary Becker, *The Economics of Discrimination* (Chicago, 1957). They have recently been refined and brought up to date by Dale Hiestand, *Economic Growth and Employment Opportunities for Minorities,* (New York, 1964), p. 53. Hiestand's results are as follows:

Occupational position of Negroes relative to whites:

	1910	*1920*	*1930*	*1940*	*1950*	*1960*
Male	78.0	78.1	78.2	77.5	81.4	82.1
Female	78.0	71.3	74.8	76.8	81.6	84.3

The figures show that Negro men lost ground in the Great Depression, that they gained sharply in the nineteen forties, and that their progress almost ceased in the nineteen fifties. Negro women show a rising secular trend since the nineteen twenties, but their gains too were greater in the tight labor markets of the nineteen forties than in the nineteen thirties or nineteen fifties.

Several cautions should be borne in mind in interpreting these figures: (1) Much of the relative occupational progress of Negroes is due to massive migration from agriculture to occupations of much higher average income. When the over-all relative index nevertheless does not move, as in the nineteen fifties, the position of Negroes in non-agricultural occupations has declined. (2) Since the figures include unemployed as well as employed persons and Negroes are more sensitive to unemployment, the occupational index understates their progress when unemployment declined (1940-50) and overstates it when unemployment rose (1930-40 and 1950-60). (3) Within any Census occupational category, Negroes earn less than whites. So the absolute level of the index overstates the Negro's relative position. Moreover, this overstatement is probably greater in Census years of relatively slack labor markets, like 1940 and 1960, than in other years.

The finding that labor market conditions arrested the progress of Negro men is confirmed by income and unemployment data analyzed by Alan B. Batchelder, "Decline in the Relative Income of Negro Men," *Quarterly Journal of Economics,* Vol. 78 (November 1964), pp. 525-548.

7. This is emphasized by Daniel Patrick Moynihan in his contribution to *Daedalus,* Fall 1965.

8. Differences between Negro men and women with respect to unemployment and income progress are reported and analyzed by Alan Batchelder, *op. cit.*

9. Figures are given in other papers in *Daedalus,* Fall 1965: see, for example, the essays by Rashi Fein and Daniel Patrick Moynihan.

10. In 34 per cent of poor Negro families, the head is not in the labor force; in 6 per cent, the head is unemployed. These figures relate to the Social Security Administration's "economy-level" poverty index. Mollie Orshansky, *op. cit.*

11. See *Manpower Report of the President,* March 1964, Table A-3, p. 197.

12. Rashi Fein, "An Economic and Social Profile of the Negro American," *Daedalus* (Fall 1965), pp. 815-846.

13. Hiestand, *op. cit.,* Table I, pp. 7-9.

14. Batchelder, *op. cit.,* shows that the incomes of Negro men declined relative to those of white men in every region of the country. For the country as a whole, nevertheless, the median income of Negro men stayed close to half that of white men. The reason is that migration from the South, where the Negro-white income ratio is particularly low, just offset the declines in the regional ratios.

15. The official Advisory Council on Public Assistance recommended in 1960 that children be aided even if there are two parents or relatives *in loco parentis* in their household, but Congress has ignored this proposal. *Public Assistance: A Report of the Findings and Recommendations of the Advisory Council on Public Assistance,* Department of Health, Education, and Welfare, January 1960. The Advisory Council also wrestled somewhat inconclusively with the problem of the means test and suggested that states be allowed to experiment with dropping or modifying it for five years. This suggestion has been ignored.

16. Adjusting the size of a government benefit to the amount of other income is not without precedent. Recipients of Old Age Surviviors and Disability Insurance benefits under the age of seventy-two lose one dollar of benefits and only one dollar for every two dollars of earned income above $1200 but below $1700 a year.

A Freedom Budget for All Americans

A. Philip Randolph Institute

[*From* A "Freedom Budget" For All Americans, *by permission of the A. Philip Randolph Institute.*]

Introduction

The "Freedom Budget" contends that this nation has the resources to abolish poverty, for the first time in human history, and to do so within a decade. Indeed, the very process of abolishing poverty will add enormously to our resources, raising the living standard of Americans at all income levels. By serving our unmet social needs—in slum clearance and housing, education and training, health, agriculture, natural resources and regional development, social insurance and welfare programs—we can achieve and sustain a full employment economy (itself the greatest single force against poverty) and a higher rate of economic growth, while simultaneously tearing down the environment of poverty. All of these problems interact, whether viewed as causes or results, and they are in truth both.

Only such a massive and sustained program—which sees poverty in terms of the national economy, and not only in terms of the personal characteristics of the poor—can bring success. Goals must be set, along with timetables for achieving them. We must plan the allocation of our resources in accord with our priorities as a nation and people.

I. The "Freedom Budget" in Brief

Basic objectives

The seven basic objectives of the "Freedom Budget" are these:

(1) *To restore full employment as rapidly as possible,* and to maintain it thereafter, for all able and willing to work, and for all whom adequate training and education would make able and willing.

(2) *To assure adequate incomes for those employed.*

(3) *To guarantee a minimum adequacy level of income to all those who cannot or should not be gainfully employed.*

(4) *To wipe out the slum ghettos, and provide a decent home for every American family, within a decade.*

(5) *To provide, for all Americans, modern medical care and educational opportunity up to the limits of their abilities and ambitions, at costs within their means.*

(6) *To overcome other manifestations of neglect in the public sector, by purifying our airs and waters, and bringing our transportation systems and natural resource development into line with the needs of a growing population and an expanding economy.*

(7) *To unite sustained full employment with sustained full production and high economic growth.*

The key role of our Federal Government

The "Freedom Budget" is a call to action. But the response to this call must take the form of national programs and policies, with the Federal Government exercising that leadership role which is consistent with our history, our institutions, and our needs. The six prime elements in this Federal responsibility are now set forth.

(1) *Beginning with 1967, the President's Economic Reports should embody the equivalent of a "Freedom Budget."* These Reports should quantify ten-year goals for full employment and full production, for the practical liquidation of U.S. poverty of 1975, for wiping out the slum ghettos, and indeed for each of the seven basic objectives set forth in the "Freedom Budget."

(2) *The bedrock civilized responsibility rests with our Federal Government to guarantee sustained full employment.*

(3) *The Federal Government should exert the full weight of its authority toward immediate enactment of a Federal minimum wage of $2.00 an hour, with coverage extended to the uppermost constitutional limits of Federal power.*

(4) *A new farm program, with accent upon incomes rather than prices, should focus upon parity of income for farmers and liquidation of farm poverty by 1975.*

(5) *To lift out of poverty and also above deprivation those who cannot or should not be employed, there should be a Federally-initiated and supported guaranteed annual income, to supplement rather than to supplant a sustained full-employment policy at decent pay.*

(6) *Fiscal and monetary policies should be readjusted to place far more weight upon distributive justice.*

The "economic growth dividend"

We cannot enjoy what we do not produce. The "Freedom Budget" recognizes that all of the goals which it sets must be supported by the output of the U.S. economy. This output should grow greatly from year to year, under policies designed to assure sustained maximum employment, production, and purchasing power in accord with the objectives of the Employment Act of 1946.

The "Freedom Budget" does not contemplate that this "economic growth dividend" be achieved by revolutionary nor even drastic changes in the division of responsibility between private enterprise and government under our free institutions. To illustrate, in 1965, 63.7 percent of our total national production was in the form of private consumer outlays, 16.5 percent in the form of private investment, and 19.8 percent in the form of public outlays at all levels for goods and services. Under the "higher" goals in the "Freedom Budget," these relationships in 1975 would be 63.5 percent, 16.9 percent, and 19.6 percent.

But while the "Freedom Budget" will not be regarded as socialistic, it is indeed socially-minded. It insists that we must make deliberate efforts to assure that, through combined private and public efforts, a large enough proportion of this "economic growth dividend" shall be directed toward the great priorities of our national needs: liquidation of private poverty, restoration of our cities, abolition of the slum ghettos, improvement of rural life, and removal of the glaring deficiencies in facilities and services in "the public sector" of our economy. The "Freedom Budget" thus has moral as well as materialistic purposes.

Responsibilities of the Federal Budget

The following table reveals the "Freedom Budget" proposals for the Federal Budget (measured in 1964 dollars).

These proposals for the Federal Budget will seem excessive only to those who do not appreciate the growing productive powers of the U.S. economy, under conditions of sustained full employment and full production.

Looked at even more broadly, the whole program set forth in the "Freedom Budget" would not subtract from the income of anyone. It would facilitate progress for practically all, but with accent upon the dictates of the social conscience that those at the bottom of the heap should make relatively the most progress.

	1967 (Actual)		1970		1975	
	Total Bil. $	$ Per Capita	Total Bil. $	$ Per Capita	Total Bil. $	$ Per Capita
All Federal Outlays	104.1	521.79	135.0	645.93	155.0	685.84
National Defense, Space Technology, All International	64.6	323.77	77.5	370.82	87.5	387.17
All Domestic Programs	39.5	198.04	57.5	275.12	67.5	298.67
Economic Opportunity Program	1.5	7.39	3.0	14.36	4.0	17.70
Housing and Community Development	0.1	0.57	3.4	16.03	3.8	16.81
Agriculture and Natural Resources	5.9	29.75	10.5	50.24	12.0	53.10
Education	2.6	13.10	7.0	33.49	9.5	42.04
Health Services and Research	3.3	16.74	4.8	22.97	7.0	30.97
Public Assistance; Labor, Manpower, and Other Welfare Services	4.4	21.92	6.6	31.58	7.5	33.18

II. The Role of The American Negro In The "Freedom Budget"

The "Freedom Budget" will benefit all

In one sense the American Negro, relative to his numbers, has an unusually large stake in a "Freedom Budget." When unemployment is excessive, the rate tends to be more than twice as high among Negroes as others. Viewing U.S. multiple-person families in 1964, 37.3 percent of the nonwhites lived in poverty with annual incomes under $3,000, contrasted with only 15.4 percent of the whites. About 14 percent of the nonwhite families had incomes between $1,000 and $2,000, contrasted with 5.4 percent of the whites. And 7.7 percent of the nonwhite families had incomes below $1,000, contrasted with only 2.7 percent of the whites. Among unattached individuals, 52.3 percent of the nonwhites lived in poverty with annual incomes under $1,500, contrasted with 40.5 percent of the whites; and 35.8 percent of the nonwhites were below $1,000, contrasted with 24.4 percent of the whites.

Thus, the only reason why the Negro will benefit relatively more than others from the liquidation of excess unemployment and poverty is not because he is a Negro, but rather because he is at the bottom of the heap.

Aside from this dismal phenomenon, which is a liability rather than an asset to the Negro, others will benefit far more in absolute numbers through achievement of the goals of the "Freedom Budget." There are far more unemployed among whites than among non-whites. In 1964, 6.6 million white families and 4.2 million white unattached individuals lived in poverty, contrasted with 1.8 million nonwhite families and 0.9 million nonwhite unattached individuals.

The "Freedom Budget" in relation to civil rights

There is an absolute analogy between the crusade for civil rights and liberties and the crusade which the "Freedom Budget" represents. This is because the "Freedom Budget" would achieve the freedom from economic want and oppression which is the necessary complement to freedom from political and civil oppression. And just as the progress thus far made on the front of civil rights and liberties has immeasurably strengthened the entire American political democracy, so will the "Freedom Budget" strengthen immeasurably our entire economic and social fabric.

The Negro's greatest role on both of these fronts is not as a beneficiary, but rather as a galvanizing force. Out of his unique suffering, he has gone a long way toward awakening the American conscience with respect to civil rights and liberties. The debt which the whole nation owes him will be increased many times, as he helps to win the battle against unemployment and poverty and deprivation.

White House Conference Recommendations

[*From "To Fulfill These Rights," Report and Recommendations to the White House Conference, June 1-2, 1966.*]

There is no single, simple, or quick solution for the economic problems of Negroes but nothing less than a broadly based "crash" program can significantly improve the life-chances of hundreds of thousands of Negro Americans now trapped in joblessness and poverty. The range of action needed to achieve an adequate level of employment and income security must cover the multifaceted problems of many different subgroups. Assistance to jobless Negro youths would not be adequate to meet the needs of underemployed Negro adults. Action to help farmers and farm workers would not necessarily improve the lot of people seeking work in metropolitan areas. Lowering bars against Negro women in professional employment must be paralleled by upgrading pay and status of the nearly one million Negro women in household employment. Programs to aid the unemployed mother who depends on public assistance for a livelihood are not likely to enhance opportunities for the Negro professional or businessman. Lasting solutions must be tailored, therefore, to the particular needs of specific components of the Negro population.

Moreover, it must be re-emphasized that the economic problems Negroes share with other disadvantaged workers are compounded for Negroes by the continuing widespread presence of racial segregation and racial discrimination. Because of the effects of discrimination and ghetto life, solutions must go beyond strictly economic measures and be related to social, political, and psychological needs.

Recommendations to improve the economic security and welfare of the Negro people must take into account the magnitude of the Negro's disadvantages in the job market, the wide gap between the income and employment status of whites and nonwhites, and the changing characteristics and geographic distribution of the Negro population and labor force. They must take into account sharp and decisive advances in technology and other such forces which generate abundant benefits to some and disproportionate burdens to others.

Attention is called to one fundamental point which underlies the various specific proposals in this report. This point, which must be stressed, is that measures to improve the economic security and welfare of Negroes take effect most rapidly in a healthy, growing, full employment economy. The availability of jobs at fair wages to all who need them eases the task of eliminating discrimination, upgrading the Negro work force, raising labor standards, and providing income security. Consequently, the attainment and maintenance of *a full employment economy is an item of continuing high priority.*

Action recommended in this report involves all sectors of the American community—business enterprises and organized labor; Federal as well as state and local governments; educational bodies; private foundations; community organizations such as churches and health and welfare groups; and the spectrum of national associations as well as Negro organizations and groups themselves. The intention is to mobilize the nation's brainpower and material resources for a systematic and many-sided effort to eliminate the barriers that prevent the full participation of Negro men and women in the economic and social process.

I. Establish Metropolitan Jobs Councils In All Major Urban Areas to Plan, Coordinate, and Implement Local Programs to Increase Jobs.

No longer can access to a job or the acquisition of a job by Negroes be left to chance. Large scale and systematic efforts by employers, labor unions, and other community groups to provide and sustain a climate within which Negroes can get more and better jobs are necessary. To make these efforts effective, and to coordinate them with training, welfare, and other services, it is necessary to develop a new approach whereby local leadership can be mobilized for planning and action.

What Should Be Done.

Metropolitan Jobs Councils should be established in each major urban area with a substantial Negro population.

The Councils should be concerned with developing accurate information on the Negro labor force and its job opportunities in the area, helping to coordinate and improve existing government and private programs to meet the economic needs of the community's Negro population, and planning programs and resources to provide additional services. The Councils should complement and assist the efforts of the Employment Service and private groups such as the Urban League, while its assumption of key functions should make it possible to reduce the number of overlapping local agencies.

The Councils should *develop and keep up-to-date a Metropolitan Human Resources Action Program for the community.*

The following illustrate the urgent and important activities that should be included in the Program.

1. The Councils should *take positive steps to ensure that the business community, labor organizations, and government agencies assume maximum responsibility for expanding job opportunities for Negro workers.*

This should involve the acceptance by each employer of definite targets for employing and upgrading Negro workers. Technical assistance should be provided by the Councils to help employers make positive efforts to recruit Negro workers, review the potentials for promotion of Negro workers who are already employed, *restructure vacant jobs* to help Negro workers meet job requirements, expand employer training activities, and *eliminate unnecessarily rigid hiring specifications* such as artificial test criteria, ...

3. The Councils should *assume leadership in the local implementation of national year-round youth job placement programs.*

4. The Councils should develop a system of periodic reports from local employers to identify jobs and occupations in which unemployed Negroes may find employment, to provide data on hiring, employ-

ment levels, and occupational status of Negro workers, and assist in developing occupational training programs to help Negro applicants qualify for employment or upgrading.

5. The Councils should provide leadership in efforts to improve the processes and institutions of the job market, including:

a. Analyzing transportation facilities and fares to identify improvements needed to make all jobs in the community accessible to Negro residential areas;
b. Analyzing the kind of information on employment opportunities which is available to Negro workers, and developing improved means of communication in this area, adapted to the special needs of disadvantaged ghetto residents;
c. Working with local educational authorities to improve the quality and availability of vocational education in the area's public schools.

6. The Councils should *conduct an extensive program of public education to combat prejudice and discrimination affecting the economic status of the Negro.*

II. Create a Rural Jobs Task Force to Develop and Coordinate a Comprehensive Program of Economic Assistance for Rural Negroes

For several decades the economic position of the southern Negro farmer and other rural residents has grown steadily worse. A substantial proportion of the more than four million Negroes still living in southern rural areas are impoverished.

What Should Be Done

The Conference urgently recommends the *appointment of an emergency Rural Jobs Task Force*

The Task Force should focus on developing programs to provide jobs and other economic assistance for rural Negroes, to eliminate job handicaps caused by discriminatory denials of opportunity, to increase the effectiveness of existing government agricultural programs in meeting the needs of disadvantaged rural people, and to facilitate the economic and social adjustment of rural families moving to urban areas.

Specifically, the Task Force should recommend prompt and practical steps by which private and public resources can be used to:

1. Provide Negroes who are engaged in or who wish to engage in the operation of commercial or subsistence farms with means and

incentives for achieving successful farm ownership and management.

2. Improve and accelerate action to remove all racially discriminatory practices in the administering of Federal programs and other publicly and privately supported programs affecting the lives of rural residents.

3. Provide intensive job training programs, directly tied to the new job opportunities stimulated by local and regional economic planning—such training to be accompanied by provision of adequate living income for trainees and their families.

4. Ensure that jobs created by local economic development programs are open to Negroes on an equal opportunity basis.

5. Provide part-time or off-season work opportunities in rural areas for farmers and hired farm workers, to supplement their incomes from agriculture. Such jobs financed mainly by Federal, state, or local government funds, should provide socially useful work in such fields as area beautification, conservation, and public services.

6. Sharply upgrade the substandard conditions under which migratory workers and their families are employed, housed and educated by (a) improving government education, vocational training, health, and housing programs for migrants, such as those conducted under the Economic Opportunity Act; (b) strengthening labor standards legislation; (c) developing new institutions and practices to rationalize the job market and to provide year-round employment opportunities for seasonal farm workers; and (d) continuing the progress made in reducing the use of foreign farm workers on U.S. farms.

7. *Facilitate the Economic and Social Adjustment of Rural Negroes Migrating to the City by* (a) establishment of centers in rural surplus labor areas, with technical and financial assistance provided by the Federal Government and private institutions, to help potential migrants make advance arrangements for jobs and housing and to provide vocational and personal counseling for would-be migrants; (b) expanded county agent and home demonstration agent programs, in both rural and city areas, designed to help rural Negroes secure employment in cities and to cope with the transition from rural to urban life; and (c) development of reception facilities by local governments and community organizations in urban labor demand areas. These facilities should be equipped to help the rural in-migrant solve employment and housing problems; to make available to them the range of health, welfare and other urban services; and to provide temporary quarters (Halfway Houses, Youth Hostels) for youthful and adult migrants during the initial adjustment period.

8. For *the aged or physically disabled low-income farmer who* cannot take steps to improve his economic security, provide a system of *supplemental income payments* which, combined with farm earnings, will yield a decent standard of family living.

III. Develop a Comprehensive Human Resource Program to Set Goals, to Measure Progress, and to Structure the Action Undertaken "To Fulfill These Rights"

The need for a Comprehensive Human Resource Program is pointed up by recent experience in the Watts section of Los Angeles. After the riots, private and public groups went to Watts for the purpose of determining what programs were needed to eliminate Negro social and economic problems which, it was generally assumed, were causal factors underlying the riots. One of the immediate problems which confronted the groups was the absence of basic information on the Watts population, on factors influencing its labor status, on its access to jobs and training, and on the impact of private, local and state government, and Federal manpower and economic programs in the area.

What Should Be Done

1. The U.S. Department of Labor should assume leadership in *developing and conducting an effective program for collecting and analyzing information on the number, characteristics, employment, unemployment, and job opportunities of Negro workers.* Data should be obtained for *both urban and rural areas,* and on a *neighborhood basis* in areas of heavy unemployment and underemployment. The current gap in employment and unemployment statistics by race on an area basis should be promptly filled, and this information made available to help local agencies plan to meet their manpower needs.

2. The Department of Labor should develop and keep up-to-date a *Human Resources Budget:*

a. Identifying the number, types and problems of Negro youths, unskilled workers, older workers, women, and other specific groups of the working age population in need of intensive manpower services;
b. Establishing specific goals and timetables for providing these services;
c. Determining the extent to which existing government and non-government programs can help meet the goals;

3. The Human Resources Budget should include short and long

run estimates of expected employment and unemployment by race, major industry, area, and occupation; estimates of the need for government action to supplement expected employment opportunities; and definite program plans for Federally financed public works or service employment opportunities in advance of serious manpower dislocations at the local or national level.

4. The Department of Labor should prepare periodic reports systematically evaluating the progress of Negroes in the job market and the effectiveness of government and non-government services in meeting the needs of the Negro working age population.

IV. Develop Government Financed Employment Programs on Public Works and Services to Guarantee the Availability of Jobs to Able Workers Who Cannot be Placed In, or Promptly Trained for, Regular Employment

Jobs must be provided without delay to solve the Negro unemployment crisis. *And these jobs must be made available for Negroes at their existing level of skill attainment.*

What Should Be Done

1. The Federal Government should develop and finance a program of *guaranteed employment* for able workers who cannot be placed in, or promptly trained for, regular employment. The work experience provided should help upgrade the worker's job skills and prepare him for regular employment.

To guide this program, an *annual job budget* should be developed in which short-run and long-run estimates of labor force, employment, and underemployment should be considered in relation to the whole range of the nation's economic and social resources and needs, in order to develop goals and priorities on the numbers and location of workers and projects to be served. This job budget should be tied closely to the Comprehensive Human Resources Program (See Recommendation III).

2. A large-scale Federally financed *public works program* to provide jobs through the private sector should be undertaken at once. Immediate targets should be the major urban centers where Negro unemployment is most severe and the Southern States where most of the rural farm and nonfarm Negro population live. In addition, long-range blue prints for public works and services should be developed for emergency use to prevent national or local manpower dislocations such as sharp dips in employment. Priority should be given to public

works which produce the greatest manpower requirements for the industries, types of workers, and areas most in need of jobs.

V. Mount Comprehensive Year-Round Employment, Training, and Counseling Programs for Negro Youth

Because of their disadvantages in the job market, young Negroes need especially intensive vocational counseling to determine their best occupational prospects, and to plan the most effective educational and training programs tailored to their individual needs. Large numbers of them have yet to be convinced that employment opportunities are increasing and job restrictions are diminishing, particularly in skilled, technical, and white collar work.

What Should Be Done

1. A *year-round youth job placement program* should be developed. Jobs must be generated for male and female Negro teenagers which utilize their present skills while preparing them with new and better skills for occupational advancement.

2. *Counseling services for in-school youths should be vastly improved and expanded,* making available skilled vocational advisers who are acquainted with the requirements of industry. A target of at least one counselor for every 100 youths should be set for schools in poverty areas. Public employment offices should expand their vocational counseling services in the schools.

3. *Community organizations should supplement the counseling services* of government with emphasis on the needs of disadvantaged youth with especially severe employment and training problems.

4. High school vocational education programs should be expanded and strengthened in both urban and rural areas to train youths effectively for occupations in which employment opportunities are available. School systems should work closely with industry and labor unions to gear the training realistically to job requirements.

VI. Affirmative Actions by Private Employers, Labor Organizations, and Government to Provide More and Better Jobs

Affirmative Action by Private Employers

There is no single affirmative action plan which will apply to all companies in all situations. Overcoming past traditions of discrimination and insuring the acceptance of equal employment opportunity will require great initiative and creative thinking. Management must devote as much thought and effort to this as it does to other major functions of administration.

Affirmative Action by Labor Unions

Organized labor, especially at the national level, has made significant contributions to the furthering of equal job opportunities. However, there are many localities in which some labor organizations have failed to take affirmative action commensurate with the problems faced by Negro job seekers. It is recommended, therefore, that national, regional, and local unions *review and revise union regulations, programs, and practices* which have the effect of . . . hampering the access of Negroes to jobs and job training.

Affirmative Action by Community Organizations

Churches, educational institutions, health and welfare groups, and associations can undertake affirmative action through technical assistance and through the example of their own practices.

Action Required by the Federal Government

Title VII of the *Civil Rights Act of 1964* should be strengthened by amending it to:

a. *Expand coverage* to employees of state and local governments, private membership clubs, educational institutions, and employers and unions with eight or more employees or members;
b. Authorize the Equal Employment Opportunity Commission to issue "cease and desist" orders;
c. Authorize the Equal Employment Opportunity Commission *to order back pay to persons suffering financial loss through denial of equal employment opportunity.*

Technical assistance and educational programs should be greatly expanded to help employers, labor unions, and others develop capabilities for providing equal employment opportunities and to reduce employment prejudice and discrimination.

VII. Initiate and Reinforce Supportive Services to Facilitate Movement of Negroes Into Jobs

There is a crucial need to make available occupational training and related basic and remedial education to help prepare jobless Negroes for employment. There is also a need for training to upgrade employed Negroes who are working below their skill potentials. In many cases, existing training or educational programs are of inadequate size, inconveniently located, and not geared to the needs of disadvantaged groups. On-the-job training by employers has also been relatively limited for Negroes.

Formal training is not enough to assist Negroes at the lower end of the economic scale. A variety of supportive services to ease their adjustment to the demands of the job market is a necessity. They need supportive community services such as child care centers for working mothers and specialized help involving health, family, housing, and welfare problems which interfere with their success at seeking and holding jobs. Those who migrate from the countryside to the city often need help in adjusting to their new environment. Many disadvantaged people require counseling and related services to develop effective work, job seeking, and human relations attitudes and behavior patterns. It is very important, also, to facilitate access to jobs by Negroes, introducing new concepts of urban transportation for this purpose.

What Should Be Done

1. There is a need to *federalize the public employment service,* which currently is operated by state agencies, although financed entirely by Federal funds.

a. A national system to bring together jobs and job applicants without regard to local boundaries is needed to keep pace with today's complex job market. This system must be available to handle rapid shifts in manpower requirements, such as those caused by technological change and changes in defense needs. It is needed to give maximum mobility to the work force, to utilize unemployed workers in depressed areas, and to meet manpower shortages which are currently on the increase. A federalized employment service is in a position to effectively deal with the continuing large-scale movement of rural people to urban areas and other inter-regional migration patterns which have received little or no government services in the past. Furthermore, for an increasing number of occupations, such as engineering and other professional and technical jobs, the labor market is actually a national one.

b. Federalization is needed to strengthen program standards, to eliminate discrimination in referral of applicants to jobs, and to raise the quality of services, such as intensive counseling, furnished to applicants.

2. *Access of Negro workers to all available jobs in the community must be improved.* The location of most Negro workers in segregated ghettos sharply reduces not only their physical access to jobs in the community but often prevents them from knowing of the range of existing jobs. Transportation difficulties discourage job seekers and impose unfair costs on workers least able to meet them. Lack of child care services impedes the employment of women at a distance from their homes. The problem is aggravated by the growing trend of locating new business and government establishments in distant suburban areas. It is recommended that:

a. The Federal Government should locate new Federal facilities in places readily accessible to residential areas where Negroes live.
b. In awarding government contracts, the Federal Government should require, to the maximum practicable extent, that the work be performed in establishments accessible to areas with substantial Negro unemployment problems.
c. Unless there are compelling business reasons to the contrary, new business establishments should be located by private employers in areas accessible to places where Negroes live, such as downtown areas, rather than in distant suburban or or other out-of-the-way sites.
d. *Local and state governments should evaluate and modify local transportation routes, fares, and facilities* to improve the access of Negroes to available jobs.

Suggested Additional Readings

1. A. Philip Randolph Institute. *A 'Freedom Budget' for All Americans.* New York: A. Philip Randolph Institute, 1966.

2. Blumrosen, Alfred W. "Antidiscrimination Laws in Action in New Jersey: A Law-Sociology Study," *Rutgers Law Review,* 19 (Winter, 1965).

3. Broom, Leonard and Glenn, Norval D. *Transformation of the Negro American.* New York: Harper and Row, 1965.

4. Chalmers, W. Ellison. "A More Productive Role for the Negro in the South's Economy," Institute of Labor and Industrial Relations, The University of Illinois, 1965. unpublished manuscript.

5. Hill, Herbert. "The Role of Law in Securing Equal Employment Opportunity: Legal Powers and Social Change," *Boston College Industrial and Commercial Law Review,* 7 (Spring, 1966).

6. Meier, August. "Civil Rights Strategies for Negro Employment," *Em-*

ployment, Race, and Poverty, ed. Arthur M. Ross and Herbert Hill. New York: Harcourt, Brace and World, Inc., 1967.

7. Norgren, Paul H. and Hill, Samuel E. *Toward Fair Employment.* New York: Columbia University Press, 1964.
8. Rustin, Bayard. "The Watts 'Manifesto' and the McCone Report," *Commentary* (March, 1966).
9. Sovern, Michael. *Legal Restraints on Racial Discrimination in Employment.* New York: Twentieth Century Fund, 1966.
10. Young, Whitney M., Jr. *To Be Equal.* New York: McGraw-Hill Book Co., 1964.

Advice to the Urban Coalition

Eli Ginzberg

The Urban Coalition, a voluntary group of leaders from American business, labor, religion, the civil-rights movement, and local government, called on the nation to mount new programs to cope with the riots that have wracked our cities this summer and to enable "the disadvantaged minorities to share in all of the benefits of our society." The group mobilized citizen participation in a convocation of eight hundred delegates in Washington on August 24, and has put forward two major proposals: an Emergency Work and Reconstruction Program under Federal auspices, and Earn and Learn Centers as the joint venture of business, labor, and local government.

To set these in perspective, we must first go back to the Employment Act of 1946 in which Congress, by a large bipartisan majority, affirmed that "It is the continuing policy and responsibility of the Federal government" to bring about "conditions under which there will be afforded useful employment opportunities . . . for those able, willing, and seeking work." As with so many commitments of the American people, particularly those affecting Negroes and the poor, this one has been fulfilled only in part.

Fifteen years elapsed after the passage of the Employment Act before Congress passed the first legislation to include provisions for training the unemployed and underemployed (Area Redevelopment Act). It took the country eighteen years—from 1946 until the tax-reduction program was passed in 1964—to make proper use of fiscal and monetary measures to establish and maintain a high level of output and employment. And it was not until 1965-1966, two decades after the passage of the Employment Act, that Congress took the first halting steps toward a job-creation plan of the most modest proportions—the Nelson-Scheuer and the Kennedy-Javits programs. These have provided jobs for the unemployed in public agencies concerned with beautifying rural America and in providing basic services to urban America.

The Coalition's proposal that the Federal government launch an Emergency Work and Reconstruction Program recalls the large-scale public works undertaken by the government during the great depression of the 1930's. The WPA provided jobs and income for the unemployed and helped to construct roads, parks, schools, and airports. But the men who were on WPA in the 1930's were a broader cross-section of the labor force in terms of age, skill, and color than are the unemployed of the slums today. Moreover, today the economy is operating at a high level and many jobs are unfilled. This much is clear: a simple replication of WPA would not be fully responsive to today's problems.

A Matter of Self-Respect

What would an effective job program entail? Apart from being adequate in scale and scope, providing a job for every man and woman able and willing to work, it would have to supply incentives to break the habits of prolonged idleness. For one thing, the jobs would have to carry a living wage. If a man is to gain a sense of accomplishment and self-respect from working, then he must be able to support himself and his family through his work. Today in New York City alone there are twenty thousand heads of household who are unable to earn enough through their work and must receive supplemental welfare allowances or food stamps. Futhermore, the jobs would have to be real jobs, not make-work assignments. The alienation of the slum population is deep enough: we must not isolate them further from the rest of society by offering them pseudo-jobs.

To this end, the jobs that are provided should be part of an employment structure that has built-in progression through supervision, on-the-job training, and promotion based on experience and seniority. If work is to be meaningful, it must provide opportunities for growth and self-improvement. This is of critical importance.

Can the Federal government design a job program that will fulfill these requirements? To understand the magnitude of this task, it is necessary merely to recall that WPA did not provide work for all; it did not offer a living wage; at least some of its jobs were make-work; and there was little or no opportunity for a man to advance up the job ladder. The Urban Coalition's proposal for a Federal job program, in short, has no model ready at hand.

The Federal government should certainly be able to mount a considerable number of useful projects in urban areas that would provide employment for many who are currently without work. But these alone would do little to meet the other important requirements —a living wage and career opportunities. Indeed, once the Federal government begins to pay a living wage to men and women on a work program, many now employed in the profit and non-profit sectors of the economy who earn less than a living wage may choose to join the ranks of the unemployed in order to qualify for the new program. According to the recent *Manpower Report of the President* the number of slum dwellers with subminimum wages exceeds by far the numbers who are unemployed.

Nor is this the only untoward eventuality that must be anticipated. What of the very substantial numbers of poor whites and poor Negroes who, despite the massive cityward migration of the last two decades, still live on farms or in rural non-farm locations? We must expect them, too, to drift into the cities and attempt to get jobs on the Federal work program. A very substantial number of poor people, especially Negroes, did just that in the 1930's, once they realized that in the city they would have a better opportunity for employment, and that if they failed they would be eligible for one or another type of relief. Indeed, most of the population in today's slums are migrants from the South.

The truth is that it will not be possible to design a work program satisfactory to the disadvantaged of the slums without also creating a magnetic pull on many other poorly paid workers in the urban and rural economy, a pull so powerful that the Federal government would not be able to cope with the numbers seeking jobs on the new program.

What then can the Federal government possibly do to help in the critically important area of employment?

Let us first consider the other end of the spectrum, the profit and non-profit sectors, where good jobs are going begging, and where, even if they are eventually filled, few go to the unemployed of the slums. Many of these jobs, especially in manufacturing, are on the periphery of the metropolitan regions, two hours of travel time and three dollars of carfare away from the inner city. While fundamental improvements in inter-urban transportation will require years, the Federal government should be able to improvise.

Many of these unemployed are women with responsibilities for young children. But many of them would prefer to work if they could, and there are jobs awaiting them in hospitals, department stores, offices, and households. To take them, however, they must be able to leave their children in day care centers. The Federal government could do much more to speed the establishment, expansion, and improvement of such services.

The Federal government is the single largest employer in the country and through its contract compliance system can exercise a potent influence over hiring in the private sector. Many of the hard-core unemployed or underemployed are unable to apply for good jobs that pay well and have a future because of union restrictions or employers' hiring standards. A man without a high-school diploma or one with a police record is often automatically disqualified. The U.S. Civil Service Commission might take the lead to open job opportunities to those now excluded; the Federal government's contract mechanism could also be used effectively to the same end.

Some days ago, the newspapers carried a report of the special effort that Mayor James H. J. Tate made to elicit the co-operation of Philadelphia businessmen in providing jobs for unemployed persons "in an effort to relieve racial tensions." He received pledges of 1,500 jobs from 250 employers. Among the jobs offered were those of waiters, dishwashers, maintenance men, painters, clerks, hospital aides, chauffeurs, and busboys. If the Federal government were persuaded that good jobs, not just any jobs, were an essential ingredient of a solution to our rising racial tension, it might well consider the advisability of devising a system of quotas—Britain has long had such a system for the physically disabled—in which every large and medium-sized employer must absorb a limited number of disadvantaged workers. It might also be willing to venture into another untested arena and provide subsidies for employers willing to absorb—and who demonstrate that they are able to retain and eventually promote—persons certified as handicapped for employment. The subsidy would be a method of underwriting the indoctrination and training costs involved in upgrading a man's qualifications.

Another approach open to Congress is to expand substantially the small number of workshops now subsidized by the Vocational Rehabilitation Administration in which disadvantaged people, especially older persons, are able to earn money and to make some useful contribution in a protected environment. Some of these, as their work habits, self-confidence, and skill improve, will eventually be able to move out into the general labor market.

We have identified several ways in which the Federal government can make a significant contribution to speeding the employment of the hard-core unemployed other than by seeking to do the whole job through a work program. It can and should move along the following axes: subsidize interurban transportation fares, expand day-care centers, adjust its own employment criteria and persuade its contractors to do likewise, explore the use of a quota system for placing the disadvantaged in jobs, consider the use of subsidies to the same end, and expand sheltered workshops to meet the needs of those who cannot be employed, initially or ever, in the competitive market.

These several recommendations are not easy to put into practice, but they have the merit that the unemployed of the slums would not only get jobs, but jobs that pay a living wage and have a future. These are the only jobs that many will accept. But unless angry, frustrated young Negroes see how these jobs will lead them to a better life, they may still reject them. Unless Negroes who earn a living wage can escape from the slums, many young people will see little point in trying to become self-supporting.

What about the Urban Coalition's proposal that business, labor, and local government co-operate to promote "Earn and Learn Centers in the cities of the country to provide job training and jobs"? What lessons can be extracted from our sizable experience with the different forms of training the hard-to-employ which the country entered upon five years ago under the Manpower Development and Training Act and to which it has directed ever increasing money and effort?

The Lessons of Experience

Several generalizations can be safely ventured. First, many of the hard-to-employ cannot be trained until they have been persuaded to come to a center for counseling and appraisal, have had pressing health defects remedied and have received instruction to meet basic literacy standards—all before entering the first training class. Many of the unemployed who need help most have neither the know-how nor the incentive to leave the "security" of their isolated but familiar corner of society for the uncertain gains that might follow upon fitting themselves into society at large. Therefore, the first major task is to make contact with them and to encourage them while they make the effort to acquire a skill.

We have also learned that the poor, adolescents and adults alike, must be paid while in training or they will not enter or complete a program. We know, too, that by far the most successful training takes place on the job. The process is usually easier where others are engaged in operating machines similar to those on which they are being taught.

Finally, many who complete training and who start on a job don't last. The reason usually is not that they have been poorly trained in skills but that their work habits are not satisfactory. They come late;

they don't report at all on Mondays; they balk if asked to go on the night shift; they become belligerent if their work is criticized. Or they just feel unhappy in their new environment and drift back to their old haunts and companions. It may be necessary to counsel a man when he is first processed. But we have learned that many who have never held steady jobs must be supported as they make the difficult transition to the world of work. Without understanding employers, foremen, and fellow workers, many newly trained workers will not be able to make it.

For this reason, centers in which to evaluate the unemployed and to provide various services for them are essential. They can provide some orientation and some supplementary instruction, but should not do the actual training.

Making the Earn and Learn Centers a joint responsibility of the principal groups in the community rather than a Federal government program is sound. Federal funds will be needed to help underwrite training allowances, but the bulk of the task requires the serious commitment of local entities. Business must take the lead in pinpointing its hiring needs and in helping to structure and staff the training programs. Labor must be much more co-operative than it has been under MDTA in supporting pre-apprenticeship training programs and it must abolish the restrictive requirements for apprenticeship to allow more minority youth to qualify. Finally, local government must make available its multiple services in education, health, and welfare. All these are inseparable, major efforts without which the training and retraining of the unemployed of the slums cannot succeed.

Contributors

DAVID P. AUSUBEL is a professor of psychology, education, and educational theory at the University of Toronto. He is also a research associate in medical education at the same university.

ALAN B. BATCHELDER is an associate professor of economics at Kenyon College.

BERT ROBERT BROWN is a research associate in the Institute for Developmental Studies at the New York Medical College.

MARTIN DEUTSCH is the director of the Institute for Developmental Studies at New York University and a professor in the Department of Psychiatry at New York College of Medicine.

JAN E. DIZARD is an assistant professor of sociology at the University of California, Berkeley.

ST. CLAIR DRAKE is a professor of sociology at Roosevelt University.

DANIEL R. FUSFELD is a professor of economics at the University of Michigan.

ELI GINZBERG is professor of economics and director of the Conservation of Human Resources Project at Columbia University.

ROBERT M. GUION is chairman of the Department of Psychology at Bowling Green State University.

MARION HAYES is an economist with the Bureau of Labor Statistics of the United States Department of Labor.

HERBERT HILL is national labor secretary of the National Association for the Advancement of Colored People.

JOSEPH S. HIMES is a professor of sociology at North Carolina College. During the 1966-1967 academic year he served as Fulbright lecturer in sociology at Madras University in India.

SIDNEY INGERMAN is an assistant professor of economics at McGill University.

TOM KAHN is the executive secretary of the League for Industrial Democracy.

JOHN F. KAIN is an assistant professor of economics at Harvard University.

ROBERT F. KENNEDY is United States Senator from the state of New York.

WILLIAM LADD is associate director of the Center for Urban Studies at the University of Michigan, Dearborn.

ELLIOT LIEBOW is a staff member of the National Institute of Mental Health of the United States Department of Health, Education, and Welfare.

MELVIN LURIE is a professor of economics at the University of Wisconsin at Milwaukee.

RAY MARSHALL is a professor of economics at the University of Kentucky.

JOHN E. MEANS is a staff member of the International Labour Office in Geneva, Switzerland.

CHARLES C. MOSKOS, JR. is an associate professor of sociology at Northwestern University.

EVA MUELLER is a professor of economics and program director in the Institute for Social Research at the University of Michigan.

MAHLON T. PURYEAR is associate director of the National Urban League.

A. PHILIP RANDOLPH is a vice-president and member of the Executive Council of the AFL–CIO.

ELTON RAYACK is a professor of economics at the University of Rhode Island.

JOE L. RUSSELL is acting chief of the Branch of Skilled Manpower and Industrial Employment Studies in the Bureau of Labor Statistics of the United States Department of Labor.

BAYARD RUSTIN is executive director of the A. Philip Randolph Institute.

PATRICIA CAYO SEXTON is a professor of educational sociology at New York University.

HAROLD L. SHEPPARD is a staff social scientist at the W. E. Upjohn Institute for Employment Research.

GEORGE STRAUSS is a professor of business administration and associate director of the Institute of Industrial Relations at the University of California at Berkeley.

HERBERT E. STRINER is program director at the W. E. Upjohn Institute for Employment Research.

JAMES TOBIN is a professor in the department of economics at Yale University.

Index